Select Material from

Social Ethics
Morality and Social Policy
Seventh Edition

Thomas A. Mappes
Frostburg State University

Jane S. Zembaty
University of Dayton

W9-CUQ-264

With Additional Readings from

Classic Cases in Medical Ethics
Accounts of the Cases and Issues that Define Medical Ethics
Fifth Edition

Gregory E. Pence
Professor of Philosophy
School of Medicine and Department of Philosophy
University of Alabama at Birmingham

Barbara Tucker

Boston   Burr Ridge, IL   Dubuque, IA   New York   San Francisco   St. Louis
Bangkok   Bogotá   Caracas   Lisbon   London   Madrid
Mexico City   Milan   New Delhi   Seoul   Singapore   Sydney   Taipei   Toronto

Select Material from
Social Ethics: Morality and Social Policy, Seventh Edition
With Additional Readings

This book is a McGraw-Hill Learning Solutions textbook and contains select material
from the following sources:
Social Ethics: Morality and Social Policy, Seventh Edition by Thomas A. Mappes and
Jane S. Zembaty. Copyright © 2007, 2002, 1997, 1992, 1987, 1987, 1977 by The
McGraw-Hill Companies, Inc.
*Classic Cases in Medical Ethics: Accounts of the Cases and Issues that Define Medical
Ethics*, Fifth Edition by Gregory E. Pence. Copyright © 2008, 2004, 2000, 1995,
1990, by The McGraw-Hill Companies, Inc.
Both reprinted with permission of the publisher. Many custom published texts are
modified versions or adaptations of our best-selling textbooks. Some adaptations are
printed in black and white to keep prices at a minimum, while others are in color.

4 5 6 7 8 9 0 QDB QDB 14 13 12

ISBN-13: 978-0-07-746992-4
ISBN-10: 0-07-746992-5

Learning Solutions Manager: Judson Harper
Production Editor: Nina Meyer
Printer/Binder: Quad/Graphics
Cover Design: Felicia Cornish

Contents

UNIT THREE

UNIT FOUR

CHAPTER 6   EUTHANASIA AND PHYSICIAN-ASSISTED SUICIDE   269

CHAPTER 7   TERRORISM, HUMAN RIGHTS, AND CIVIL LIBERTIES   321

UNIT FIVE

Unit One

Introduction Notes

In this course, we will be examining ethics—how to make decisions that are just and fair. There are many reasons why we might want to ensure that our decisions are just and fair. Reasons may include the fact that we live in a social structure, a society, and a society functions better when its members believe they have value and are being treated fairly by the majority. However, this leads us to another reason for wanting to make ethical decisions. We want to feel good about ourselves. At the end of the day, we want to know that we have done the best that we could. It is a matter of honor and "doing the right thing." We want to know that we deserve respect from ourselves. Why does this matter? Most philosophers would say that thinking critically and responding ethically is what identifies us a human. It is also true that self-respect is important. We may lose our job or our home or our friends and recover, but a loss of self-respect is catastrophic. It is part of our identity.

So how do we do this? That is where philosophy steps in. If we want to measure the room to see if it is seventeen feet long, all we need is a measuring tape. Either it is seventeen feet or it isn't. But what about questions that are not so easily resolved? Those are the questions dealt with by philosophy. Philosophy looks at the questions for which there may be few clear answers and tries to determine which answer may have the best support or reason. This means having to have the facts and doing some critical thinking to make a decision. It does not mean that everyone is going to agree on the conclusion. There may be several different conclusions that all have good reasons. That is what makes philosophy both frustrating and fascinating. It is frustrating because sometimes there are no absolute answers (except on your tests...). It is fascinating because, by hearing the reasoning of others, our own minds are opened to new possibilities.

But shouldn't this be a simple process? After all, everyone knows what is right and what is wrong. Don't they? Based on what? Is the fact that Mom said so enough? Well, Mom may be right (aren't all moms right?), but that doesn't tell us anything about why it is right. All it tells us is the source of the decision, not the reason it is right. In philosophy, the source does not matter. It is the reason for the conclusion that matters. We will look at some of the things involved with critical thinking and cautions about what not to say a bit later, but for now, you may be wondering why any of this matters. In the end, isn't philosophy just opinion? Well, yes and no. The important distinction between opinion and philosophy is that philosophy uses supported opinion. In other words, you have to be able to back up your conclusion with facts and logical argument.

To see how this works, you don't have to go far. Just turn on your TV and look for a campaign add for an election. Let's say the candidate is running on the promise that he will end generational welfare. He is running for governor. The logical fallacy in this promise is that a governor does not have the power to end welfare or increase welfare, or do much of anything with welfare. That is in the hands of the legislative body, not the governor's office. So, that's an easy one to dismiss.

How about a candidate who talks about the how he (or she) stands for democracy. Okay, but what does this mean? It could mean just about anything. When the terminology is so unspecified, it becomes meaningless. Political campaigns, no matter what party, are full of promises that can't be fulfilled, statements that are unclear, and arguments meant to persuade through appeal to our emotions rather than our reason. That is why they are so interesting to observe. Listen critically and you will see what I mean.

It is easy to hear something that appears to make sense, but really doesn't give us enough information to make a decision. Here is an example: "Mary had a little lamb." Okay, I know, we have all heard this story. But, do we really know what is being said? Let's start with "Mary." Does the meaning of the sentence change it we discover that Mary is a sheep rather than a human? What about "had"? Does this mean Mary no longer has the lamb? Is the lamb lost? Is there a poster out saying "lost lamb—reward for its return"? How about the word "little"? Well, it depends on what is going on. If Mary is eating lamb at the Ritz dinning room, is she eating just a small portion of lamb, or is she pigging out on a whole small lamb? For that matter, could this be meant as an analogy? What if it is meant to be interpreted as: "Mary (Virgin Mary) had a little lamb (Christ)? Do you see the problem? Until we determine some facts, we can't even begin to know what we are talking about. And, by the way, congratulations, you have just been exposed to your first exercise in philosophy. Fun? Frustrating?

To begin sorting this out, we are going to look at five different approaches to "doing the right thing." Come now, you didn't really think all philosophers were going to agree, did you? That would be too simple. The five philosophies are Virtue Ethics by Aristotle, Deontological Ethics by Emmanuel Kant, Teleological Ethics by John Stuart Mill, Existentialism by Jean-Paul Sartre, and Care Ethics by Carol Gilligan. These will be brief reviews, but they will give us an idea of how ethics have been determined. Also note that each ethical theory has its strong points and it weak points. Let's get started.

ARISTOTLE AND VIRTUE ETHICS

Aristotle (384–333 BC) is the son of the physician to the King of Macedonia, where Aristotle learns about biology and medicine. He attends Plato's Academy in Athens and becomes Plato's primary student. Later, Aristotle will establish a second university in Athens, the Lyceum. He establishes one of the first great library collections and serves as the tutor to Alexander the Great. When Alexander dies, Aristotle, like Plato's teacher, Socrates, is accused of impiety. Rather than stay and risk possible execution (as happened to Socrates), Aristotle chooses to flee Athens. He formulates ideas about the classification of the sciences, fashions the new science of Logic, and is known for his studies in ethics, metaphysics, biology, psychology, and aesthetics. He believes that ethics, found in his book, the *Nichomachean*

Ethics (named after his son), should help people to live happily. Happiness is a "final end." What he means is that living a virtuous life leads to the happiness that is life's ultimate goal. Happiness is a "final end" because it is (1) always chosen for its own sake, (2) never chosen for the sake of something else, and (3) self-sufficient. For example, why are you in college? You might answer that it is to get an education. Aristotle would then ask, "Why do you want an education?" You might answer that an education will get you a job that is more satisfying and allow a better life-style than a less interesting job with less pay. Aristotle would then ask, "Why do you want more pay?" You might answer that it will afford you the goods that make you comfortable. We could keep going on and on, but at the end, the reason, the "final reason" for all of this is to make you happy. Aristotle just believes you can't really be happy unless you achieve happiness through virtuous means.

Aristotle believes that the key to acting in a virtuous (ethical) manner is to establish a virtuous character. In other words, if someone is raised to always tell the truth, then he or she will automatically tell the truth. Telling the truth will become second nature. This system of ethics becomes known as **Virtue Ethics**. You might consider if this applies to your own behavior. Have you ever been tempted to lie, but decided against it? Was it because your conscience made you feel uncomfortable? If so, then you were reacting as predicted by Aristotle.

The next question is how do we define a virtue for telling the truth? After all, we cannot very well follow the right action nor have the right character, if we do not understand what it means to lie vs. telling the truth. To determine what is appropriate, Aristotle says we should look for the "mean" between extremes. For example, to determine truth from lie, we should take the concept we are trying to define, such as truth, and then draw a line between it and its extreme on either side. The extreme of not telling the truth will define "lying," and the extreme of telling the truth too much will define someone who tells the truth even when it will bring great harm, someone who goes overboard, who tells the truth without caring for the consequences. Telling too little of the truth, or too much of the truth, can be equally detrimental. There is a comfortable middle ground, and that is what Aristotle would consider a virtue.

You can try this method with any characteristic that might be considered a virtue. For example, if you want to determine the definition of "courage," just look at the extremes on either side. Too little courage would be cowardice. Too much courage would be foolhardy (the general who urges his men on into battle when he knows they are outnumbered 1000 to 1). We do not want to be cowards or fools. What lies between them is "courage."

The advantage of this system is that it allows for some flexibility. The line between the definition of too much and too little and a middle ground is not an absolute. This flexibility allows for exceptions and extenuating circumstances.

The weakness of this system is that, while it assumes a virtuous person/character will lead someone to find a balanced approach to ethics, it does not help tell us what to do in cases where we do not have an established category. For example, how does being brave or being truthful help us to determine if computer chips should be implanted into everyone at birth so that their entire medical and life record can be instantly available?

IMMANUEL KANT AND DEONTOLOGICAL THEORIES OF ETHICS

Deontology is a Greek word that means that the action itself has inherent value—that the virtue is in the action rather than its consequence. Deontological theories are absolutist theories. They do not allow for exceptions. We will just look at one such theory, that by Emmanuel Kant.

Emmanuel Kant (1724–1804) is a Prussian philosopher who taught a wide range of subjects at the University of Koningsberg. Kant believes that logic and mind and a scientific view of the universe are essential to ethics. He asks us to question: "what would happen if everyone did this action?" This formula is known as a **Categorical Imperative**. It is also known as Kant's Golden Rule. It asks us to assess actions on a universal basis. In other words, if we want to know if it alright to lie we need to first ask ourselves what would happen if everyone lied? The answer would be that no one would trust anyone. Since that would lead to chaos, we can conclude that lying is bad and telling the truth is a better option. Once we determine that lying is bad and telling the truth is good, it becomes a "universal" law, that is, a law without exception.

Deontological systems focus on the action itself rather than its consequences, and they do not allow for exceptions. Once exceptions are made, the whole system collapses. A way to remember this formula is to think that the "means justify the ends." Kant believes human will is designed by nature to give (come up with) universal laws. Only rational beings have the capacity to act according to the concepts of law. He believes we can all use the Categorical Imperative to figure out what is the right thing to do by using logic. He believes feelings are unreliable guides, because feelings change from one moment to another. Instead, he wants us to treat everyone the same. He believes the basis of human dignity is autonomy, the ability to think logically and independently. He wants us to always treat persons as ends, never as means. In other words, everyone has inherent value; value that is apart from any usefulness that person may have for us or others. So, we do not have the right to adopt a person as a pet. That would violate both inherent value and the rule to treat people as ends—not means. On the other hand, because animals do not have rational capacity (according to Kant), we can treat them as pets. We can treat them as means (to our happiness) rather than ends.

A deontological theory, and Kant's Categorical Imperative in particular, works very well for Institutions. For example, in the legal system (institution) we want everyone to be treated under the same rules. We don't want there to be exceptions because someone is wealthy or well-connected. The same holds true for the educational system. You want to be graded according to merit and you want that merit to be assigned equitably, not according to favoritism or some other subjective value.

However, there is also a drawback to the Categorical Imperative. The same factor, that it is absolute and without exception, does not work well when it comes to personal relationships. For example, have you ever had your significant other ask you "Honey, does this make me look fat?" There are times when we want to make exceptions to telling the truth.

Another problem with the Categorical Imperative is that, because it is absolute, there is no way to resolve a hierarchy between two Categorical Imperatives. For example, what if the choice is between a lie, such as "Honey, you look just fine," and a lie such as "Sure, go ahead and eat that arsenic. It won't hurt you." Surely, the second lie is much worse than the first, but under a Categorical Imperative absolute there is no way to assign a greater or lesser value. Nor is there a way to resolve a conflict between two categorical imperatives.

JOHN STUART MILL AND TELEOLOGICAL THEORIES

For Mill, the way to determine the right thing is to use the **Principle of Utility** (also know as **Utilitarianism**). The formula goes as follows: after giving equal consideration to all concerned, determine the best outcome or consequences that will result in the greatest good/pleasure/happiness for the greatest number. Because it looks at the outcome or consequences of an action, rather than the action itself (as does, for example, Kant), Mill's theory is often referred to as a **"Consequentialist" theory**. For Mill, the Principle of Utility is the fundamental principle that underlies all of morality.

Teleology is a word coming from the Ancient Greek meaning "end" or "goal-oriented." Teleological theories are the exact opposite of deontological theories. Deontological theories consider that the action makes something right or wrong ("the means justify the ends"). Teleological theories look at the consequences of actions ("the ends justify the means").

John Stuart Mill (1806–1873), is an English philosopher who helps develop the philosophy of Utilitarianism. John Stuart Mill worked for the East India Company, and also served in Parliament. He is known as a strong supporter of the underrepresented in society, and he is a strong advocate for women's rights during a time when women did not have the vote and had great difficulty getting published.

Utilitarianism has the following formula: The right thing to do is what will bring about the greatest good/happiness/pleasure for the greatest number of people who will be affected by the action. By focusing on the consequences of actions, Mill allows for the exceptions we found missing in Kant's theory.

However, it is important to realize that when Mill says the "greatest pleasure for the greatest number," he is not talking about just any pleasure. For Mill, pleasures should be "higher" pleasures—pleasures achieved from the pursuit of goals that will help us develop our human capacity, not those that give us immediate (and usually, physical) satisfaction.

One other component of Mill's theory is essential—**the Harm Principle**. The Harm Principle says that you may do anything you like so long as it does not harm another person, their property, or their liberty. You will find that many of the arguments found in your textbook are based on the Harm Principle. For example, anyone who argues that drugs should be legalized, will usually do so based on the Harm Principle. The Harm Principle believes we have the right to harm ourselves, but not others. We do all sorts of things that are potentially harmful—from roller skating to racing cars to hang gliding. The question is when does a society have the right to legislate against individual actions. Mill believes the answer is when those actions may interfere with the rights of others to pursue their own lives and lifestyles.

If we put together the Principle of Utility (Utilitarianism) with the Harm Principle, we get something like this: Do the action that will bring about the greatest good/pleasure/happiness (Mill uses these terms interchangeably) for the greatest number affected by the action, so long as no one is harmed in the process. This principle says that I may drink myself into oblivion, but I may not drink and drive. To drink and drive endangers others. Drinking alone only endangers myself.

The obvious benefit of using Utilitarianism as a guide to ethics is that it allows us to adjust our ethics to the needs of the situation. For example, we do not have to tell the truth to that question of "Honey does this make me look fat?" On the other hand, we do have to tell the truth and admit that arsenic is not safe to eat.

However, like all ethical theories, there are drawbacks. One of the worst is that it can lead to the tyranny of the majority. Another problem is that there are times when something is simply the right thing to do, regardless of whether anyone is happy with the situation. For example, you may have a relative who is always complaining and is never satisfied with anything or anyone. This relative has just broken a leg and needs someone to help out with household chores. Being around this person is the last thing anyone in the family wants to do. It will just make everyone miserable, but helping out is the right thing to do.

JEAN-PAUL SARTRE AND EXISTENTIALISM

Sartre defines existentialism as "Existence precedes essence." Existence precedes essence simply means that we are born with no predetermined human nature. First we exist, we are born into the world, then we establish who we are by the choices we make—and there are always choices.

At any given moment, we are the sum total of all our choices. Potential and what we might have done just don't count. We are the product of our choices and have no one to blame or praise but ourselves. This is what Sartre means when he says that "man is nothing else but what he makes of himself." If we don't like who we are or what we are doing, then it is up to us to change it.

Sartre also says that in "making his choice he also chooses for all man." By this, he means that when we make a choice of action, that action either confirms that the action is part of human character, or expands the meaning of character. If we do something that is beneficial to humankind then that confirms that humans can be generous and sharing. If we do something terrible, then that also defines what it means to be human. Every choice we make not only impacts us, but every human being, because it defines or confirms or expands what it means to be human and stands as an example that others may use in making their own decisions. In this sense, existentialism is both a very freeing philosophy while at the same time it asks us for ultimate responsibility. It gives us unlimited opportunity to change, but our way of doing so will forever provide a model for others, so we have to make our choices with care and responsibility.

Even asking for advice does not free us from responsibility, because who we choose to ask demonstrates that we have already made up our mind. We tend to look for confirmation, not real advice.

The strength of this system is that it leaves us with wide open options. It allows us to establish our own identity through our cumulative actions over a lifetime. It allows us to become the person we wish to be. But that is also its weakness. It assumes that, in carrying the weight of responsibility as models for "all men," we will strive to do the right thing. Not all people are going to have a conscience that urges them in this direction. There is a lot more the Existentialism than what has been suggested here, and you are encouraged to examine it in more depth.

CAROL GILLIGAN AND CARE ETHICS

Carol Gilligan is an American Psychology professor, who is best know for her 1982 book, *In a Different Voice*. Gilligan is one of the first to center ethics around relationships. Her **Ethics of Care** centers around families and how men and women tend to use different criteria for evaluating "doing the right thing."

For example, if your child needs a heart transplant, would any of the above ethical systems really help you decide the "right thing to do"? Perhaps, Virtue Ethics might give you some parameters, and Existentialism might say "go for it—it will just help define how to be human," but none are very comforting. Kant wants you to do the right thing by thinking about what if everyone acted the same. Mill wants to hold you to "higher goods" and act on what best suits the majority. But this is your child. He or she is not just a part of the herd. Theories of justice and equality don't fit very well when it comes to those we love.

We don't want to treat our loved ones the same as everyone else. Gilligan suggests that treating family first, so long as no one else is directly harmed, is an ethical option.

The strength of this system is that it allows for feelings and love-based relationships. Most other theories are grounded in universals. The weakness to this theory is that it only works within the context of relationships. It does not work for guiding institutions or groups.

****

Please note that I have given you some of the strengths and weaknesses of each of five systems (by Aristotle, Kant, Mill, Sartre, and Gilligan). Hold them in mind because no system is perfect. There are strengths and weaknesses to every ethical system—even your own.

In addition to needing some framework for your ethical decisions, you also need to support your conclusions. In doing so, here are a few things to avoid. They are known as fallacies, argument that are not legitimate. Here are just a few.

ETHICAL FALLACIES

Ad Hominem – an Ad Hominem is when you steer the argument away from the relevant facts and, instead turn it into an attack on the person you disagree with. For example:

Husband: Jane, I can't believe you ran that red light. Now we have a $400 fine, and we were going to use the money for a new lawn mower.

Wife: There you go again! Always thinking of yourself and what you want! And, it's not like you never had a ticket!

Notice how any discussion about why she went through the red light disappeared in a flash. Instead of talking about it, or taking responsibility, or determining any-thing useful—like what to do in the future to avoid the problem (not talking on the cell phone, texting, or whatever caused the inattention), or how they are going to afford the lawn mower—the discussion is now about the husband's selfishness and how he has had tickets in the past. Do you think this couple can have a good rela-tionship?

Appeal to Ignorance – and Appeal to ignorance is when the fact can't be proven, and the lack of proof is then used as an argument that it exists. For example:

Husband: Did you know that the pyramids were built by Ancient Alien from another planet?

Wife: I don't believe it.

Husband: Well it has never been disproven!

Wife: Oh, well, then I guess it might be true.

Lack of proof does not provide proof.

Slippery Slope – a Slippery Slope is when you start with a simple fact, but then "slide down that slope" into an extreme conclusion. For example:

Father in a letter to his daughter: "Do not go to the dance with Tom. I know college is a new and scary experience and you want to go to the dance, and Tom is some-one from our town. But when Tom was in the tenth grade, he was caught smoking pot. If you go to the dance with Tom, you will begin dating and the next thing you know you will drop out of college and end up selling drugs on some street corner to support a pimp."

Wow, Dad! Notice how he slid down that slippery slope?

Appeal to Authority – Appeal to Authority is when you base your justification on the authority who pronounced a statement rather than giving any actual argument to support the correctness of the statement. For example, "My father says we must always wipe our feet before coming into the house, so that is that!" In other words, the reason given does not explain why it is a good thing (or a bad thing) to wipe feet before entry. Instead, it just tells us who makes the statement. Dad is probably right, but how do we know WHY he is right unless there is some explanation. The reason is probably because that prevents dirt from being tracked into the house.

The same thing happens when someone says we should do something one way or the other because "The Bible says we should." Well, okay, now we know the authority, but that does not explain WHY it is a good thing to do. Surely, there is some reason behind it. Otherwise, it just becomes arbitrary. No matter who is the "authority" the action still needs to be justified if we are to understand why it makes sense. Philosophy always wants to know, to understand. And conclusions always have to be explained.

****

During this semester, as you read the various articles, keep in mind the ethical theories and the fallacies. See if you spot any during the readings. We are going to start off with a chapter from *Classic Cases in Medical Ethics: Accounts of Cases That Have Shaped Medical Ethics, with Philosophical, Legal, ad Historical Backgrounds* by Gregory E. Pence. Note how carefully the author analyzes the situation. In the end he points out that the Tuskegee experiment was unethical because there was a "likelihood" of harm to the subjects. You may wish to refresh your memory of the Harm Principle found in the section on John Stuart Mill and the Principle of Utility.

Pence says, "since harm was possible, their motivations should have included an intention not to do harm. Instead, through systematic deceit and non-treatment, these researchers put their subjects at risk of harm, depriving them of their rights." Note that Pence has just brought one of the rights that every person has a right to: not to be harmed. We will revisit this right in other chapters.

CHAPTER 1

Research on Human Subjects

This chapter describes the Tuskegee study of untreated syphilis in Alabama between 1929 and 1972. It also discusses medical experimentation by Nazi physicians, secret American medical research, studies in Africa to prevent transmission of HIV from mother to child, the death of Jesse Gelsinger in 2000, and the growing problem of financial conflicts in medical research.

INFAMOUS MEDICAL EXPERIMENTS

In 1822 in a famous case of abuse of an experimental subject, physician William Beaumont, "the father of gastric physiology," treated Alexis St. Martin for a bullet wound in the stomach; St. Martin survived, but the wound healed strangely, leaving a hole. To observe the hole, Beaumont employed St. Martin as a servant, and proved the previously unknown fact that stomach juices digest food. St. Martin soon ran away and Beaumont had him caught to continue to exhibit him. Hospitals today in Texas and Michigan bear his name.

Nazi Medical Research

Besides participating in the Holocaust, physicians during the Nazi regime conducted heinous experiments on human subjects. The physicians reasoned that the people in the concentration camps were going to die anyway, so why not use them to benefit medical science?

Across the globe during the same war, Japanese physicians carried out deadly experiments on Chinese prisoners at unit 731 in Harbin, killing 3,000. To study the natural course of diseases, physicians injected prisoners with anthrax, syphilis, plague, and cholera.[1]

---

[1]S. Gomer, H. Powell, and G. Rolino, "Japan's Biological Weapons"; H. Powell, "A Hidden Chapter in History," *Bulletin of Atomic Scientists*, October 1981, pp. 43, 44.

From 1943 to 1945, gay men, convicted criminals, Russian officers, Polish dissidents, Jews, and Gypsies on Ward 46 at Buchenwald in Germany got experimental vaccines against typhus. Physicians injected blood infected with typhus into 40 involuntary subjects, who served as a treatment group. Overall, they infected a thousand prisoners, 158 of whom died. They established no thresholds of infection.[2]

In experiments at Buchenwald, physicians tried to cure gay men with hormone shots, had inmates shot to study gunshot wounds, starved inmates to study the physiology of nutrition, and amputated women's bones and limbs to study regeneration. To study malaria, physicians used anopheles mosquitoes to infect subjects. Physician Ernst Grawitz infected legs of women with staphylococci, gas, and tetanus bacilli. In testing sulfa drugs, he rubbed particles of glass and stone into wounds.

In experiments at Ravensbrück, physician Sigmund Rascher devised his "sky ride wagon" to simulate rapid changes in altitude. Victims were locked inside an enclosed box on wheels with monitoring equipment inside.[3] Rascher also froze a hundred nude Jewish and Russian prisoners in icy waters to study techniques to revive downed pilots in similar waters. In one study, he forced nude Jewish women to revive the subjects sexually. Since such women would be unavailable to revive pilots downed in icy seas, this exercise simply degraded the women.

Josef Mengele

The most infamous Nazi physician, Josef Mengele, known as the Angel of Death, participated in the death of 400,000 victims in concentration camps.

Ambitious, the young Mengele sought fame. To get it, he studied medicine and anthropological genetics in Munich between 1930 and 1936, when eugenics movements swept Germany and America. The Nazi party and its ideology of racial purity were then centered in Munich.

Contrary to some accounts, German medical schools did not resist Nazi eugenics and killing undesirables, but led these movements. To advance, Mengele joined the Brownshirts, a fanatical Nazi movement.

Mengele needed groundbreaking research to reach his goal of appointment as a Professor. In 1943 at the Auschwitz concentration camp, he began experiments to overcome the effects of genetics by modifying environments. He wanted to produce blue eyes, blonde hair, and healthy bodies free of genetic disease. As subjects, he needed identical twins, natural controls for environmental differences.

Mengele greeted incoming trains of boxcars filled with Jews destined for execution. He examined them, looking for twins and other usable subjects, signaling his choices with a flick of his wrist.

[2]Eugene Kogon, *The Theory and Practice of Hell*, Farrar, Straus, and Cudahy, New York, 1950; Berkeley reprint, 1980, p. 166.
[3]Eugene Kogon, *The Theory and Practice of Hell*.

Describing Mengele's experiments is painful. He injected blue dye into children's eyes to see if he could create blue eyes. He forced female twins to engage in coitus with male twins to see if twins could be produced. He interchanged blood of identical twins to observe results; he interchanged blood between pairs of twins.

One pair of fraternal twins consisted of a hunchback and a normal child; Mengele surgically grafted the hunchback to the normal child's back, creating the effect of conjoined twins; he accentuated this effect by sewing their wrists back to back. A witness reported that when these conjoined children returned to the barracks: "There was a terrible smell of gangrene. The cuts were dirty and the children cried every night."[4]

Mengele obtained between 150 and 200 twins, most of whom died. As one participant observer related:

> After that, the first twin was brought in, a fourteen-year-old girl. Dr. Mengele ordered me to undress the girl and put her head on the dissecting table. Then he injected the Epival into her right arm intravenously. After the child had fallen asleep, he felt for the left ventricle of the heart and injected 10 cc of chloroform. After one little twitch the child was dead, whereupon Dr. Mengele had her taken to the corpse chamber. In this manner, all fourteen twins were killed during the night.[5]

Mengele also tested endurance by subjecting 75 prisoners to electric shock; 25 of them died immediately. To study sterility, he severely burned Polish nuns by giving them high dosages of radiation.

He once found a hunchback and the hunchback's son; he had both of them killed, their bodies boiled, their flesh stripped, and their skeletons dipped in gasoline for preservation for his anthropological studies of body types. When he came upon seven dwarfs from a Rumanian circus family, he kept them alive to exhibit them to visiting physicians.

Cool, impersonal, and detached, when 300 Jewish children escaped a gas chamber and fled to a nearby field, Mengele had them recaptured, lit a gasoline fire set in a large pit, and had the children thrown in. Some children, on fire and screaming for their lives, clawed their way over dead bodies to the top, where Mengele and his men kicked them back in.

When the Russian army approached Auschwitz in 1945, Mengele escaped to Paraguay. He lived there for 40 years, eluding Israelis who tried to capture him as a war criminal. In later conversations with his grown son Rolf, he expressed no regret for his actions: it was not his fault that Jews had to die at Auschwitz, he said, so why not use them to advance medical knowledge and his own chances for a professorship? Never captured or tried as a war criminal, Mengele died in Brazil in the summer of 1985.[6]

---

[4]Vera Alexander, *The Search for Mengele*, HBO movie, October 1985; interviewed by Central Television (London) and quoted in Posner and Hare, op. cit., p. 37.

[5]Miklos Nyiszli, quoted in R. Lifton, "What Made This Man Mengele?" *New York Times Magazine*, July 21, 1985, p. 22, See also Gerald Posner and Jerome Ware, *Mengele: The Complete Story*, McGraw-Hill, New York, 1986, p. 39.

[6]William Curran, "The Forensic Investigation of the Death of Joseph Mengele," *New England Journal of Medicine* 315, no. 17, Ocober 23, 1985, pp. 1071–1073.

American Military Research during World War II

In 1941, American researchers experimented on orphans at the Ohio Soldiers and Sailors Orphanage, on retarded inmates at New Jersey State Colony for the Feeble-Minded, and on patients at a mental institution in Dixon, Illinois.[7] To develop a vaccine against shigella, they injected deadened forms into subjects. None died, but many got sick.

Some questionable research used military personnel as subjects. Cornelius Rhoads, Director of Memorial Sloan Kettering Cancer Hospital in New York City, became head of the military's secret chemical warfare service. Rhoads

> supervised the long secret and now infamous tests where thousands of American troops were intentionally exposed to mustard and other poisonous gases. Rhoads discovered that the mustard gas killed white blood cells and other cells that divided rapidly. After the war he and others began to experiment with mustard gas as a cancer treatment and also to search for other systemic poisons that kill dividing cells.[8]

In research conducted by the armed forces on poisonous agents, 60,000 subjects did not know what they were undergoing.[9] Between 4,000 to 5,000 subjects inhaled mustard gas in gas chambers.

During the war, Franklin Roosevelt established the Committee on Medical Research, which approached its work with a wartime mentality that carried over into researchers' attitudes after the war: disease was the enemy, researchers were the soldiers, and victory could be won—with enough resources and enough will. During the war, ethical concerns about experiments carried little weight:

> A wartime environment also undercut the protection of human subjects, because of the power of the example of the draft. Every day thousands of men were compelled to risk death, however limited their understanding of the aims of the war or the immediate campaign might be. By extension, researchers doing laboratory work were also engaged in a military activity, and they did not need to seek the permission of their subjects any more than the selective service or field commanders did of draftees.... In a society mobilized for war, these arguments carried great weight. Some people were ordered to face bullets and storm a hill; others were told to take an injection and test a vaccine. In philosophical terms, wartime inevitably promoted utilitarian over absolutistic positions.

When subjects of secret chemical research later applied for treatment at veterans' hospitals, the Veterans Administration (VA) denied that they had been exposed to these agents. This scenario recurred after the war in Vietnam and after Operation Desert Storm.

World War II institutionalized some doubtful attitudes in medical experimentation. When the war ceased, the fight against diseases did not: "The prospect of winning the war against contagious and degenerative illness gave researchers in the

---

[7]David Rothman, "Ethics and Human Experimentation," *New England Journal of Medicine* 317, no. 19 (November 5, 1987), p. 1198.

[8]Robert Bazell, "Growth Industry," *New Republic*, March 15, 1993, p. 14.

[9]Constance Pechura, "From the Institute of Medicine," *Journal of the American Medical Association* 269, no. 4 (January 27, 1993), p. 453.

1950s and 1960s a sense of both mission and urgency that kept the spirit of the wartime laboratories alive."[10]

The Nuremberg Code

After World War II at the Nuremberg trials in 1946, German physicians defended themselves against charges of war crimes by saying that they had merely been following orders, that their experiments had been properly related to solving medical problems of war, and that what they had done did not differ from similar research done on captives by American physicians.

The judges at Nuremberg lacked a code of ethics for experimentation on captive populations, so they created 10 principles for ethical experimentation, known as the *Nuremberg Code*. Its most important principle was that people should freely consent to participation in any experiment.

Postwar Criticisms

By the 1970s, faith waned in scientific and medical progress. Rachel Carson's *Silent Spring* described the ravages of pesticides; the Cuban missile crisis brought America close to nuclear war; and drugs such as thalidomide (an antinausea drug during pregnancy), once hailed as miraculous, were found to cause children to be born lacking arms and legs.

In 1966, Harvard medical professor Henry Beecher criticized 22 specific medical experiments published in medical journals that had not obtained consent of subjects, asserting that this was the norm.[11] About the same time, physician Henry Pappworth similarly criticized 500 medical experiments.[12] That year, the United States Public Health Service began to require informed consent of subjects.

THE TUSKEGEE STUDY (OR "THE STUDY")

Nature and History of Syphilis

In the past, victims who suffered from untreated syphilis included Cleopatra, King Herod of Judea, Charlemagne, Henry VIII, Napoleon Bonaparte, Frederick the Great, Pope Sixtus IV, Pope Alexander VI, Pope Julius II, Catherine the Great, Christopher Columbus, Paul Gauguin, Franz Schubert, Albrecht Dürer, Johann Wolfgang von Goethe, Friedrich Nietzsche, John Keats, and James Joyce.[13]

For hundreds of years, syphilis was attributed to sin and associated with prostitutes, though attempts to check its spread by expelling prostitutes failed because their customers were disregarded. Efforts to eradicate it by quarantine also failed.

[10]David Rothman, "Ethics and Human Experimentation," p. 1198.

[11]H. Beecher, "Ethics and Clinical Research," *New England Journal of Medicine* 274, 1966, pp. 1354–1360.

[12]H. Pappworth, *Human Guinea Pigs*, Beacon, Boston, Mass., 1968.

[13]Molly Selvin, "Changing Medical and Societal Attitudes toward Sexually Transmitted Diseases: A Historical Overview," in King K. Holmes et al., eds., *Sexually Transmitted Diseases*, McGraw-Hill, New York, 1984, pp. 3–19.

Between 1900 and 1948, and especially during the two world wars, American reformers mounted the *Syphilophobia Campaign*. Reformers emphasized that prostitutes spread syphilis, and that syphilis rapidly killed. As an alternative to visiting prostitutes, they advocated clean, active sports, a view known as "Muscular Christianity."

Antisyphilis crusaders split twice over methods to prevent spread of syphilis: once during World War I over giving out condoms, and again during World War II over giving out penicillin. In each conflict, reformers who wanted to reduce the harm of syphilis battled those who wanted to reduce illicit behavior.[14]

This conflict repeated over the next century in battles about venereal diseases, prostitution, alcoholism, drug addiction, gambling, and sex education. *The Harm Reduction Movement (HRM)* focuses on reducing the associated harms of these behaviors, not on moral censure or eliminating the behaviors. Popular in public health, moralists who oppose HRM attack the illicit behavior and view HRM as enabling it, for example, by teaching men how to use condoms.

The armed services during the world wars were pragmatic. Commanders who needed healthy troops overruled moralists and ordered the release of condoms in the first war and penicillin in the second. After the wars, returning troops continued to use condoms and to get penicillin, normalizing these practices among Americans.

Schaudinn discovered in 1906 the spirochete that causes syphilis. It is a chronic, contagious bacterial disease, often venereal and sometimes congenital.

Syphilis has three stages. In the first, *primary syphilis*, spirochetes mass and produce a primary lesion, a chancre (pronounced "SHANK-er"). During this stage, syphilis is highly infectious. After the chancre subsides, the disease spreads silently for a time, but then produces an outbreak of secondary symptoms such as fever, rash, and swollen lymph glands.

In the second state of *latent syphilis*, spirochetes disseminate from the primary lesion throughout the body, producing systemic and widespread lesions, usually in internal organs. Syphilis then spreads silently from one to 30 years. During this stage, symptoms vary so widely that syphilis was once known as the Great Pretender.

In the last stage of *tertiary syphilis*, chronic destructive lesions damage the cardiac and neurological systems. Syphilis then may produce paresis (slight or incomplete paralysis), gummas (gummy or rubbery tumors), altered gait, blindness, or lethal narrowing of the aorta.

Today syphilis is treated with penicillin. Such treatment has been possible only since 1948, when penicillin became available to everyone.

Beginning in the 16th century, to treat syphilis, physicians applied the heavy metal mercury as a paste on the back. During the 19th century, they administered another heavy metal, bismuth, the same way. Neither mercury nor bismuth killed the spirochetes, though they ameliorated symptoms.

In 1909, after the spirochete of syphilis had been identified, two researchers—a German, Paul Erlich, and a Japanese, S. Hata—tried 605 forms of arsenic and discovered a "magic bullet" against it in combination 606 of heavy metals (which

---

[14]Alan Brandt, "Racism and Research: The Case of the Tuskegee Syphilis Study," *Hastings Center Report* 8, no. 6 (December 1978), pp. 21–29.

included arsenic). Erlich humbly called this Salvarsan (implying salvation from syphilis) and patented it; its generic name is arsphenamine.[15] After finding that it cured syphilis in rabbits, Erlich injected it intramuscularly into men with syphilis.

At first, Salvarsan seemed to work wonders, and during 1910, physicians greeted Erlich with standing ovations. Later, however, syphilis recurred in some patients treated with Salvarsan, and some of them died, both from syphilis and worse, from Salvarsan. Erlich maintained that the drug had not been given correctly, but he also developed another, less toxic form, Neosalvarsan.

Physicians injected Neosalvarsan intramuscularly in 20 to 40 dosages over a year, charging patients a dollar a visit. To get full treatment, patients needed both the time and money for these visits. As most did not, it was no one-shot, magic bullet for syphilis.

Between 1890 and 1910, Norwegian Caesar Boeck studied the natural course of untreated syphilis in 1,978 subjects. He believed that heavy metals removed only the symptoms of syphilis. Because heavy metals killed some syphilitics, he studied whether they might do better untreated.

In 1929, Boeck's successor, J. E. Bruusgaard, selected 473 of Boeck's subjects for further evaluation.[16] Bruusgaard learned that of subjects who had had syphilis for more than 20 years, 73 percent were asymptomatic. This discovery dramatically contradicted the Syphilophobia Campaign, so people resisted the fact that syphilis did not universally kill, much less did not do so rapidly. Even more disturbing to the Syphilophobia Campaign, Bruusgaard confirmed that some latent syphilitics might never develop symptoms at all.

So when the Tuskegee study began in 1932, Boeck's and Bruusgaard's studies had caused physicians to question the received views about the natural course of untreated syphilis, as well as the medical view that all syphilitics should be treated with heavy metals.

The Racial Environment

In the 1930s, American medicine was racist. Most physicians condescended to African-American patients and held stereotypes about them, as in this example from a 1914 *Journal of the American Medical Association*:

> The negro springs from a southern race, and as such his sexual appetite is strong; all of his environments stimulate this appetite, and as a general rule his emotional type of religion certainly does not decrease it.[17]

Physicians saw African-Americans as dirty, shiftless, promiscuous, and incapable of personal hygiene. In 1900, a Georgia physician wrote, "Virtue in the negro race is like 'angels' visits'—few and far between. In a practice of 16 years in the

---

[15]Paul de Kruif, *The Microbe Hunters*, Harcourt Brace, New York, 1926, p. 323.

[16]J. E. Bruusgaard, "ber das Schicksal der nicht spezifisch behandelten Luetiker" ("Fate of Syphilitics Who Are Not Given Specific Treatment"), *Archives of Dermatology of Syphilis* 157, April 1929, pp. 309–332.

[17]H. H. Hazen, "Syphilis in the American Negro," *Journal of the American Medical Association* 63, August 8, 1914, p. 463.

South, I have never examined a virgin over 14 years of age."[18] In 1919, a medical professor in Chicago wrote that African-American men were like bulls in *furor sexualis*, unable to resist copulation around females.[19]

Given such racism, white physicians around 1929 saw syphilis as a natural consequence of low character in African-Americans, described by one white physician as a "notoriously syphilis-soaked race."[20] Such physicians also assumed that African-American men would not seek treatment for venereal disease.

Historian Alan Brandt argues that in the early 1900s, almost all white American physicians were racists and most remained so throughout the decades of the Tuskegee study. Brandt writes, "There can be little doubt that the Tuskegee researchers regarded their subjects as less than human."[21]

DEVELOPMENT OF THE TUSKEGEE STUDY

A Study in Nature Begins

Physiologist Claude Bernard in 1865 distinguished *studies in nature* from normal *experiments* by saying that in experiments, some factor is manipulated, whereas studies in nature merely observe what would have happened anyway. In centuries before the Tuskegee study, physicians sough to understand the natural history of diseases and in doing so, they relied on studies in nature.

The great physician William Osler once said, "Know syphilis in all its manifestations and relations, and all other things clinical will be added unto you."[22] Yet as late as 1932, syphilis's natural history had not been documented, and because of Boeck's and Brussgaard's results, physicians doubted the inexorability of its course.

This explains why the United States Public Health Service (USPHS) in 1929 believed that a study in the nature of syphilis was needed. A second factor was that USPHS discovered an opportunity for such a study. Around 1929, several counties in America had extraordinary rates of syphilis and a philanthropical organization— the Julius Rosenwald Foundation in Philadelphia—started a project to eradicate it. With help from USPHS, the foundation intended to treat with Neosalvarsan all syphilitics in six counties with rates of syphilis above 20 percent. In 1930, the Rosenwald foundation surveyed African-American men in Macon County, Alabama, which was 82 percent black, and found the highest rate of syphilis in the nation, 36 percent. The Rosenwald Foundation planned to treat these African-American syphilitics with Neosalvarsan, and it did treat or partially treat some of these 3,694 syphilitics. Tuskegee is the chief town in Macon County.

Then something unforeseen happened: in 1929 the great Depression began. As it ground on, funds for philanthropy plummeted, and the Rosenwald Foundation pulled out of Tuskegee, hoping that USPHS would continue the treatment program.

---

[18]James Jones, *Bad Blood*, Free Press, New York, 1981.p. 74.

[19]James Jones, *Bad Blood*, p. 74.

[20]James Jones, *Bad Blood*, p. 74.

[21]Alan Brandt, "Racism and Research."

[22]Quoted in E. Ramont, "Syphilis in the AIDS Era," *New England Journal of Medicine* 316, no. 25 (June 18, 1987), pp. 600–601.

Funds available for public health also plummeted, and the USPHS saw its budget drop from $1 million to less than $60,000 in 1935.

In 1931, USPHS repeated the Rosenwald foundation's survey of syphilis in Macon County, testing 4,400 African-American residents, and then found a 22 percent rate of syphilis in men, as well as a dangerous 62 percent rate of congenital syphilis. Of great importance for the Tuskegee Study, this survey identified 399 African-American men who had had syphilis of several years' duration but who had never been treated.

It was the identification of these 399 untreated men in 1931 by the USPHS that created the opportunity for a study in nature of syphilis. The Surgeon General himself, Raymond Vonderlehr, suggested that these 399 men should be merely observed rather than treated. In 1936, he wrote in the *Journal of the American Medical Association* that the Tuskegee Study was "an unusual opportunity to study the untreated syphilitic patient from the beginning of the disease to the death of the infected person."[23] His decision was the key one that began the study.

Three points deserve emphasis here. First, the 399 subjects had *latent* syphilis, not infectious syphilis. During this stage, syphilis is largely noninfectious during sexual intercourse. Second, the 399 subjects were not divided into the typical experimental and control groups: they were all simply observed. There was, however, another group of natural controls, 200 age-matched African-American men living in Macon County who never had syphilis. Third, these men were perfect for a study in nature because they were *so vulnerable*; they were poor, illiterate, and tied to the land as tenant farmers. As such, unlike other people with syphilis over the next four decades, *they were unlikely to ever leave Macon County.* Partly because of this vulnerability, Vonderlehr implied, they presented an "unusual opportunity."

Vonderlehr had no sense that it might be wrong to use such vulnerable subjects in a life-long experiment. Perhaps he assumed, like many of his time, that people with syphilis got what they deserved, as some also assumed later about the first victims of AIDS.

The Middle Phase: Poor Design

No one physician oversaw this study. It lacked written protocols, and the subjects in the no-treatment group of 399 syphilitics were often mixed up with the 200 controls without syphilis. Record keeping in the Tuskegee Study was poor, records were often lost, and the names of the syphilitic subjects were often confused with the controls.

Researchers assumed that controls would remain uninfected, but in a county where one in three people had syphilis, many controls eventually contracted syphilis. So they were switched to the no-treatment group of syphilitics.

The study had gaps. Federal doctors visited in 1939 and then not again until 1948; seven years passed between visits in 1963 and 1970. Only Eunice Rivers, an African-American nurse permanently assigned to Macon County, held the shaky study together.

[23]R. A. Vonderlehr, T. Clark, and J. R. Heller, "Untreated Syphilis in the Male Negro," *Journal of the American Medical Association* 107, no. 11 (September 12, 1936), pp. 856–860.

During the course of the research, many of the 399 syphilitic subjects, who were supposed to remain untreated, did get Neosalvarsan or penicillin outside Macon County. James Lucas, a CDC physician, said that "effective and undocumented treatment had been given to the vast majority of patients in the syphilitic group."[24] As a result, researchers could not know whether a subject observed really represented the consequences of untreated syphilis.

Even as a study in nature, the study proved nothing. Before it began, physicians knew that syphilitics had greater morbidity and mortality than nonsyphilitics, and from Bruusgaard's discovery, that not all men in the latent phase died of syphilis. The Tuskegee Study added nothing to that knowledge.

Spinal Taps

When physicians returned, they wanted to know, first, if they had a subject in the study group; and second, if so, how far his syphilis had progressed. To determine progression, they did spinal punctures on 271 of the 399 syphilitic subjects.

In doing spinal taps, they inserted a 10-inch needle between two vertebrae into the cerebrospinal fluid to withdraw a small amount of fluid. Because this is a delicate and uncomfortable process, subjects were warned to stay still, lest the needle swerve and puncture the fluid sac, causing infection and possible paralysis.

Some physicians then and now regard spinal taps as insignificant, justified by the need to prove a diagnosis. On the other hand, professionals who describe a spinal tap this way may be thinking about administering it rather than receiving it.

A spinal tap is not a minor procedure, like taking blood. Some patients experience side effects, such as being unable to stand for a week without a severe headache. One person in a million will become paralyzed or permanently comatose.[25]

Tapping someone involuntarily, without obtaining informed consent, is legally a battery. Researchers who need healthy volunteers for spinal taps offer as much as $1,000 for them. Even then, some people will not undergo a nontherapeutic tap for $5,000 or for any amount. That should tell us something.

Deception

To induce subjects to travel to town and undergo these painful taps, physicians offered a series of freebies: free transportation, free hot lunches, free medicine for any disease other than syphilis, and free burials. In return for these benefits, physicians did spinal taps and later, autopsies, to inspect for damage from syphilis.

But these freebies and the persuasion of Nurse Rivers failed to get all men to come to town for the "round-ups," so researchers resorted to deception. *Infamously,*

[24]Jean Heller, "Syphilis Victims in U.S. Study Went Untreated for 40 Years," *New York Times*, July 26, 1972, pp. 1, 8.

[25]Or worse: in 1988, a malpractice suit brought against a hospital in Vermont was settled out of court for $2.7 million on behalf of a 28-year-old woman who had gone into a coma after being incompetently tapped by a resident. "Malpractice Suit Settled for $2.7 Million," *Burlington Free Press*, December 21, 1988.

they told the black men that they had "bad blood" and that the spinal taps were treatment for their bad blood. Researchers sent the subjects the following letter, under the imposing letterhead "Macon County Health Department," with the sub-heading "Alabama State Board of Health and U.S. Public Health Service Cooperating with Tuskegee Institute":

> Dear Sir:
>
> Some time ago you were given a thorough examination and since that time we hope you have gotten a great deal of treatment for bad blood. You will now be given your last chance to get a second examination. This examination is a very special one and after it is finished you will be given a special treatment if it is believed you are in a condition to stand it.[26]

The "special treatment" mentioned was the spinal tap to culture for neu-rosyphilis. The subjects were instructed to meet Nurse Rivers for transportation to "Tuskegee Institute Hospital for this free treatment." The letter closed, in capitals:

> REMEMBER THIS IS YOUR LAST CHANCE FOR SPECIAL FREE TREATMENT. BE SURE TO MEET THE NURSE.

To repeat, the researchers never treated the subjects for syphilis. *Although penicillin was developed around 1941–1943 and was widely available by 1948, the subjects in the Tuskegee study never received it, even during the 1960s or up to 1972.* In fact, during World War II, the researchers contacted the local draft board and prevented any eligible subject from being drafted, and hence from being treated for syphilis with penicillin by the armed services.

The First Investigations

In 1966, Peter Buxtun, a USPHS venereal disease investigator in San Francisco learned about the Tuskegee Study and criticized it. By this time, supervision of the study (and Buxtun) had moved to the newly created Centers for Disease Control (CDC) in Atlanta, but CDC stonewalled Buxtun and threatened to fire him.

By 1969, Buxtun's protests led to a meeting of a small group of physicians at CDC to consider stopping the Tuskegee Study or revealing it. At the end, the com-mittee voted to continue the study and to keep it secret.

In 1970, a monograph on syphilis was published by the American Public Health Association. It stated that treatment for late benign syphilis should consist of "6.0 to 9.0 million units of benzathine penicillin G given 3.0 million units at sessions seven days apart."[27] The first author was William J. Brown, head of CDC's Tuskegee section from 1957 to 1971. Brown had been on the CDC committee in

---

[26]Archives of the National Library of Medicine; quoted in James Jones, *Bad Blood*, p. 127.
[27]W. J. Brown et al., *Syphilis and Other Venereal Diseases*, Harvard University Press, Cambridge, Mass., 1970, p. 34.

1969 and had argued for continuing the study in which, of course, subjects with late benign syphilis received no penicillin.

The Story Breaks

In 1972, Peter Buxtun told his story to Jean Heller, a medical reporter for the Associated Press. Six months later, on July 26, 1972, her story began to appear on front pages of newspapers nationwide.[28] Her series of stories described a medical study run by the federal government in Tuskegee, Alabama, in which poor, uneducated African-American men had been used as guinea pigs. After noting the terrible effects of tertiary syphilis, the story said that in 1969 a CDC study of 276 of the untreated subjects had proved that at least seven subjects died "as a direct result of syphilis."

Heller's story had an immediate effect. Congressmen were amazed to learn of the study. Senator William Proxmire called it a "moral and ethical nightmare." J. D. Millar, chief of Venereal Disease Control at CDC, said that the study "was never clandestine," correctly pointing to 15 published articles in medical and scientific journals over a 30-year span.

The Aftermath

After Heller's story appeared, the Secretary of Health, Education, and Welfare terminated the Tuskegee Study. At that time, CDC estimated that during the study, 28 syphilitics had died of syphilis. The remaining syphilitic subjects then received penicillin.

In 1973, lawyer Fred Gray filed a class-action suit against the federal government on behalf of the Tuskegee subjects. In 1974, the U.S. Government settled out of court. According to the settlement, living syphilitics received $37,500 each; heirs of deceased syphilitics, $15,000 (since children might have had congenital syphilis); heirs of living controls, $16,000; heirs of deceased controls, $5,000. Controls and their descendants received compensation because they and their families had been deprived of antibiotics during the decades of the study. The government also provided free lifetime medical care for Tuskegee subjects, their wives, and their children.

In 1972, and as a direct revelation of the study, the federal government required all institutions that conduct human medical experimentation and receive federal funds to have Institutional Review Boards (IRBs). Today, IRBs must scrutinize written proposals and are the first line of defense against abuses in medical research.

In 1988, 21 of the original 399 syphilitic subjects were still alive, each of whom had had syphilis for at least 62 years.[29] In addition, 41 wives and 19 children had evidence of syphilis and were receiving free medical care.

In 1997, President Clinton met four of the eight living survivors to apologize for the Tuskegee Study, "What the United States did was shameful, and I am sorry."[30]

---

[28]Jean Heller, "Syphilis Victims in U.S."
[29]Jean Heller, "Syphilis Victims in U.S."
[30]Allison Mitchell, "Survivors of Tuskegee Study Get Apology from Clinton," *New York Times*, May 17, 1997, p. A1.

The youngest survivor then was 87, the oldest between 100 and 109.[31] By then, the government had paid $10 million to the study's original 600 members or to their families or heirs, who by then numbered more than 6,000. Because of lack of treatment for syphilis of men in the study, any of these other people might have contracted syphilis.[32]

Perhaps the most pervasive effect of revelation of the study was that African-Americans came to distrust medical experiments, a legacy that medical researchers today must struggle to overcome.

ETHICAL ISSUES

Informed Consent and Deception

In the Tuskegee Study, the subjects did not know they were part of a government study lasting throughout their lives, did not even know what syphilis was, and did not know that they weren't being treated with available drugs. In other words, they had no informed consent, which many critics considered to be ethically outrageous.

R. H. Kampmeier, an emeritus professor of medicine at Vanderbilt Medical School, worked as a syphilologist during the decades of the Study.[33] He argued that a study undertaken in the 1930s could not be faulted for lack of informed consent, which began only after 1966. Would it make sense, he argued, to judge Pasteur unethical because he, too, did not get consent?

Kampmeier cites another landmark study by USPHS in 1943 that examined giving penicillin to 35,000 syphilitics; it did not get consent from subjects. He claims that during the 1930s and 1940s, it was accepted practice for physicians to walk into a patient's room and simply announce they were taking out the patient's gallbladder.

Medical historian and physician Thomas Benedek dismisses the issue of informed consent in the Tuskegee Study as "anachronistic." He agrees that USPHS did not require informed consent until 1966.[34]

While it is true that informed consent in medical experiments was not mandated by court decisions until 1966, the presumption had always been that physicians would "First, do no harm" to their patients. Not obtaining consent for procedures that might benefit subjects differs from procedures that might *harm* subjects.

Finally, and granted that telling patients the truth was not *legally* required before 1966, was it *ethical* for the Tuskegee researchers to lie to their subjects for all those decades? Isn't the truth what one person owes another, especially as doctor and patient?

---

[31]Carol Yoon, "Families Emerge as Silent Victims of Tuskegee Syphilis Experiments, *New York Times*, May 9, 1998, p. A1.

[32]Marcia Angell, "The Ethics of Clinical Research in the Third World," *New England Journal of Medicine* 337, no. 12 (September 18, 1997), pp. 847–49.

[33]R. H. Kampmeier, "The 'Tuskegee Study' of Untreated Syphilis" (editorial), *Southern Medical Journal* 65, no. 10, (October 1972), pp. 1247–1251.

[34]Thomas Benedek, "The 'Tuskegee Study' of Untreated Syphilis: Analysis of Moral Aspects versus Methodological Aspects," *Journal of Chronic Diseases* 31, 1978, pp. 35–50. I have drawn considerably on this excellent article.

Racism

The Tuskegee Study took place in Alabama in the deep South and all its subjects were African-American. Under such circumstances, was it only a coincidence that no subjects were white? Would white subjects have been deceived and left untreated the same way?

In his classic work, *Bad Blood*, medical historian James Jones saw the Tuskegee study as a result of pervasive racism in American medicine during the 1930s. How bad was that? To take one example, black students at Tuskegee Institute in the 1930s lived in fear of rural white toughs just outside their campus.

Although studies in nature were important in medicine during the early 1930s, there was no reason why a study in nature of syphilis should use only African-American subjects. On the contrary: some physicians believed then that syphilis ran a different course in different races, and this implied the need for a parallel study of untreated white syphilitics. That no parallel study of white subjects occurred shows that poor black subjects were regarded as expendable.

Media Coverage

In defending the Tuskegee study, Kampmeier objected to the "great hue and cry" in the media in 1972, and to journalists' claim that "treatment was purposefully withheld to evaluate the course of untreated disease." He said about *Time* and *American Medical News*: "In complete disregard of their abysmal ignorance, members of the fourth estate bang out anything on their typewriters that will make headlines."[35]

To begin with the second objection, Kampmeier attacked the media for reporting the damaging aspects of the study, such as the withholding of treatment; but withholding treatment was precisely the intention of the study. The media reported the study accurately.

With regard to the first objection, Kampmeier's description of a "hue and cry" was exaggerated. Indeed, the media botched the story. Coverage shrank within days, and the story moved to the back pages of newspapers, where only short paragraphs followed it.

Yet the Tuskegee Study deserved more attention. True, its issues were complicated and they involved racism at a time when racial turmoil upset Americans. Yet today such a story would receive weeks of nationwide scrutiny, and probably get a Congressional hearing on television.

The relation then between medicine and the media can also be questioned. Before Heller's story broke, the Tuskegee Study had been reported repeatedly in medical journals in at least 17 articles between 1936 and 1972. Researchers did not conceal the study within medicine. Despite this, no professional publication, physician, or editor alerted the nation to the story.

Between 1966 and 1971, one African-American professional at CDC did mail boxes of documents about the study to several national newspapers and magazines.[36] Nothing happened. Why is that?

[35]R. H. Kampmeier, "The Tuskegee Study of Untreated Syphilis."
[36]"The Deadly Deception" (with George Strait), *Nova*, January 28, 1992.

The answer is important to understanding many issues in medical ethics and to whistle-blowing about corruption. Print and television reporters need an expert to help them understand such complex stories and, equally important, to take responsibility for claims about wrongdoing. Virtually no reporters then or now have the medical background to understand such complicated stories and, without that, cannot risk charging physicians with possible crimes.

A natural tendency also exists to want *someone* else to be the whistle-blower and to bear the brunt of the kind of retaliation that CDC threatened against Peter Buxtun. As a result, merely mailing information or passing it along conversationally is usually not enough for reporters to publicize wrongdoing.

Harm to Subjects

Kampmeier argued that if the Tuskegee Study had never occurred, its subjects would have received no treatment and would have been no worse off. Such a claim can never be proved. If the Tuskegee Study had not occurred, many things might have happened. Another charity might have provided Neosalvarsan. A writer like John Steinbeck might have soon written a novel about syphilis in Macon County, arousing national concern and getting penicillin to people there infected with syphilis.

Withholding Treatment

What harm, if any, resulted to subjects with syphilis from nontreatment? This question might seem even absurd: if subjects were left untreated, of course they must have been harmed! However, the issue is not that simple.

In 1931, penicillin was unavailable, so physicians withheld Neosalvarsan from subjects. Because Neosalvarsan was expensive and cumbersome to administer, even if this study had not occurred, subjects might not have received it. Boeck and Bruusgaard had also undermined claims about the benefits of heavy metals, so harm is difficult to prove. In a review of medical evidence available in 1940, medical historian Benedek concluded that in 1937, untreated syphilitics actually lived longer and better than those partially treated with heavy metals.[37]

Not everyone agrees. UAB professor of internal medicine, Benjamin Friedman, whose career spanned the decades of this study, countered that:

> In the 1940s it was known that patients receiving as few as 20 injections of arsenicals rarely developed symptomatic aortic disease. Since we could not determine in advance which of the latent syphilitics would, after 20 or 30 years, develop symptomatic aortic disease, it was necessary to treat all of them. One cannot maintain that some small number of syphilitics deprived of treatment did not therefore suffer injury.[38]

By 1934 the major professional organization of physicians treating syphilis, the Cooperating Clinical Group, had demonstrated that use of heavy metals improved

[37]Thomas Benedek, "The 'Tuskegee Study' of Untreated Syphilis," p. 44.
[38]Personal correspondence, April 25, 1985. Benjamin Friedman is Professor Emeritus of Medicine, UAB.

Bruusgaard's statistics and had recommended that all syphilitics get Neosalvarsan, mercury, and bismuth.[39] Even if many patients could not afford such therapy or complete it, they should have been told about it.

Later during the study, penicillin became available. Although Alexander Fleming discovered penicillin in 1929, his discovery was not appreciated until 1941. Penicillin became available only around 1946, as a result of wartime production and to treat soldiers with syphilis. By 1948, any American could get it.[40]

Kampmeier argued, first, that withholding penicillin in 1946 did not harm subjects. Latent syphilis, he said, is a "chronic, granulomatous, self-limiting disease" and not fatal. Second, proof of penicillin's effectiveness did not come until 1948 and then only for primary syphilis. So third, the Tuskegee subjects by 1948 could no longer have been helped by penicillin; the damage to them from syphilis had already been done.[41]

Benedek disagreed somewhat with Kampmeier. He concluded that giving penicillin to latent syphilitics in 1948 "might have exerted a definitely beneficial effect on the prognosis of only 12.5 percent of the subjects."[42] Still, that would have been 50 subjects who could have been helped.

Effects on Subjects' Families

Virtually all subjects were or had been married and had an average of 5.2 children.[43] Recall that Macon County had a rate of congenital syphilis of 62 percent.

When we consider the subjects' families, wouldn't the men in the study want to know they had syphilis? Even in the latent stage, wouldn't they want to know they could become infectious again? Did the researchers withhold the truth because they thought these men couldn't refrain from sex?

These researchers subjected women and children in Macon County to harm. Either the researchers discounted this harm, or thought it didn't matter compared to their study in nature.

Kant and Motives of Researchers

When physicians at CDC and USPHS debated the Tuskegee Study in 1969, many assumed that if no harm could be proved, nothing unethical had been done. This is

---

[39]Thomas Benedek, "The 'Tuskegee Study' of Untreated Syphilis."

[40]G. W. Hayes et al., "The Golden Anniversary of the Silver Bullet," *Journal of the American Medical Association* 270, no. 13 (October 6, 1993), p. 1610.

[41]R. H. Kampmeier, "Final Report of the 'Tuskegee Study' of Syphilis," *Southern Medical Journal* 67, no. 11, 1974, pp. 1349–1353. Kampmeier advances a fourth argument which is somewhat more technical. Penicillin achieves seroreversal in latent syphilis, but Kampmeier insists that such seroreversal has never been proved to be associated with decreased morbidity or mortality. A related point is possible uncertainty over diagnosis and thus over therapeutic effects. (S. Edberg and S. Berger, *Antibiotics and Infection,* Churchill Livingstone, New York, 1983, pp. 141–142; K. Holmes et al., *Sexually Transmitted Diseases,* McGraw-Hill, New York, 1984, p. 1352; John Hotson, "Modern Neurosyphilis: A Partially Treated Chronic Meningitis, *Western Journal of Medicine* 135, September 1981, pp. 191–200; Sarah Polt, Professor of Pathology, UAB, personal correspondence.)

[42]Thomas Benedek, "The 'Tuskegee Study' of Untreated Syphilis."

[43]Thomas Benedek, "The 'Tuskegee Study' of Untreated Syphilis."

also Kampmeier's unstated assumption. Focusing on consequences, however, is only one way to judge morality. We can also adopt, not a consequentialism or utilitarianism, but a Kantian ethics focused on motives and the character of researchers.

Although we cannot prove that Tuskegee subjects were harmed by being left untreated, it may have been only good luck that the study caused no more harm than it did. Why is that?

Because the historical evidence cuts both ways. We cannot use differing historical standards at differing times to excuse lack of informed consent, but not pay attention to what else was believed at the time. Let us put ourselves in the minds of researchers in the late 1940s, *and the crucial fact is, that when penicillin became available, most physicians then believed that penicillin would help latent syphilitics.*

So they believed that subjects would be harmed by not getting penicillin. For all anyone knew in 1948, penicillin could have helped patients with aortic heart disease or would have prevented it.

So in terms of Kantian ethics, the researchers deliberately willed harm on these subjects. They used them as "mere means," as guinea pigs, and could not universalize such behavior as a maxim for all physicians or all people to act on. Not only did they lack what Kant calls a "good will," they had an ill will toward their vulnerable subjects.

It is no good appealing to sophisticated knowledge that came later that the damage from syphilis had already occurred. That was not known then. At the time, researchers must have known they were depriving syphilitics of something likely to help them, or depriving them of something that could help them not pass syphilis on to their female partners. But out of a desire to see the final ravages of syphilis, subjects were not told, and harm was intentionally allowed to occur.

Tuskegee and HIV Prevention in Africa

In 1994, the federally sponsored 076 study proved that giving AZT (zidovudine) during pregnancy cut by two-thirds the risk of transmission of HIV from mother to child.[44] CDC, NIH, and WHO then set out to prevent the 1,600 babies born with HIV every day to HIV-infected mothers in developing countries.

In 1997, Marcia Angell, executive editor of the *New England Journal of Medicine*, claimed that American research in Africa to study AZT resembled the Tuskegee Study because half of pregnant, HIV-infected black women were given placebos. Researchers permitted many babies in their care to be born with preventable HIV infection.[45]

So this study had subjects who were (1) black, (2) female, (3) poor, (4) illiterate, (5) victims of sexually transmitted diseases, and (6) without other available treatment. Like the Tuskegee Study, research was conducted by magisterial but distant governmental agencies. Like the Tuskegee Study, subjects were about as

---

[44]Sheryl Gay Stolberg, "U. S. Ends Overseas HIV Studies Involving Placebos," *New York Times*, February 19, 1998.
[45]Marcia Angell, "Tuskegee Revisited," *Wall Street Journal*, October 28, 1997.

vulnerable as subjects can get, and hence, powerless to reject the study or to go elsewhere. Columnist Ellen Goodman noted that the Tuskegee Study had not ended, but had been merely exported.[46] Public Citizen, a consumer rights organization founded by Ralph Nader and its physicians Sidney Wolfe and Peter Lurie, echoed her charges.[47]

Dr. Angell's comparison of these studies to the Tuskegee Study sparked a firestorm of rebuttals. Researchers retorted that, if the research had not been done, these infected mothers would never have gotten AZT. So the women were no worse off than they had been before.

Angell replied that it had long been established that placebo-controlled studies could not be done on American women. Once AZT had been proven effective in preventing transmission of HIV, it became *the standard of care* for all pregnant, HIV+ women. Angell argued, "If it is unethical to do placebo-controlled trials in America, it should also be unethical to do them in third-world countries."[48]

Apologists for the study, including officials in developing countries, replied that it was ethical imperialism to impose American ethical standards on African countries.[49] Moreover, many local officials were black and had lost children to HIV, so they were not like the white USPHS physicians of the Tuskegee Study.[50]

The sponsoring agencies replied that 300,000 children were infected every year with HIV by perinatal transmission, and that if they could prove—via a placebo-controlled trial—that a shorter regimen could reduce transmission by half—they could save 150,000 thousand children a year. If skeptics such as Angell caused delays of proof, they would cost many children their lives.

Central to the defense of these studies by public health agencies were two more claims: a placebo-controlled trial of HIV-transmission could be done faster and with fewer subjects than an AZT-controlled study, and that once good results were obtained, African and Asian governments would give all pregnant, HIV+ women the new, smaller dosage of AZT.

Researchers also defended themselves procedurally, arguing that review committees in both countries had approved the studies and that, unlike the Alabama men, the women themselves had consented. Subsequent interviews by the *New York Times* cast doubt on how much the women understood, a claim disputed by local health officials in Africa, who said the women had understood.

Angell argued that placebo-controlled studies were not necessary to prove such results, that comparing dosages of AZT to other treatments could prove the same thing. She denied that, given the poverty of such countries, a proven, reduced dosage would later be given to all pregnant women. Even a cheap AZT regimen of $80 exceeded by 11 times the amount spent per year on average on medical care for such African women.

[46]Ellen Goodman, "Is Tuskegee Study OK Abroad?" *The Boston Globe.*
[47]Public Citizen News Release, April 22, 1997.
[48]Ruth Macklin, "Ethics and International Collaborative Research, Part I," *American Society for Bioethics and Humanities Exchange* 1, no. 2, p.1
[49]Ellen Goodman, "Is Tuskegee OK Abroad?"
[50]D. Bagenda and P. Musoke-Mudido, "We're Trying to Help Our Sickest People, Not Exploit Them," *Washington Post*, September 28, 1997, p. C3.

Both sides invoked justice.[51] Here, philosophical medical ethics collided, not factual medicine. Philosophically, on one side resided Jeremy Bentham, utilitarianism, and public health ethics. On the other side resided Immanuel Kant, his axiom that people can never be used as a "mere means," and his belief that ethical principles are not local but universal.

For researchers, the risk-benefit ratio had to be different for poor, illiterate women in backward countries who otherwise would not have gotten treatment. For critics, the same reasoning had led to the Tuskegee Study and to Nazi experiments: "they're going to get it anyway, so we might as well study them to learn something."[52] As Angell retorted, "People can't be used as a means to a noble end.[53]

In 1998, CDC suspended the studies, announcing that the experimental, reduced-dosage treatment had been proven effective in reducing mother-to-child HIV transmission: $80 worth of AZT in the last four weeks of pregnancy cut transmission in half.[54] At this early cessation of the American-sponsored studies, both sides claimed victory.

Meanwhile many thousands of subjects in third-world countries continued to be subjects of HIV-vaccination studies, many of which were placebo-controlled.

Secret Governmental Medical Experiments

During the 1940s, radiation enthralled some physicians. Joseph Hamilton of the University of California at Berkeley injected plutonium into 18 unsuspecting patients diagnosed with cancer. According to Kenneth Scott, a scientist who later investigated these abuses, two patients were mistakenly diagnosed with cancer but nevertheless given "many times the lethal dose of plutonium."[55]

Physicians also studied radioactive isotopes used in diagnosis and research. In the late 1940s at Vanderbilt University, physicians injected 819 pregnant women with radioactive iron in a nutritional study. A study in 1960 found that three of their children died of rare forms of cancer.[56] In 1945, Eda Charlton entered Strong Memorial Hospital in Rochester, New York, with a mild case of hepatitis, and was secretly injected with plutonium-239 to study how her body eliminates radiation. Physicians there secretly followed her for years to observe the effects (she died of a heart attack in 1983).

From World War II to the mid-1970s, physician-researchers subjected over 16,000 American patients to radiation experiments.[57] At least 435 experiments were

[51]Ruth Macklin, "Ethics and International Collaborative Research."
[52]Marcia Angell, "Tuskegee Revisited," *Wall Street Journal*, October 28, 1997.
[53]Ellen Goodman, "Is Tuskegee OK Abroad?"
[54]Sheryl Gay Stolberg, "U. S. Ends Overseas HIV Studies."
[55]Dan Stober, Knight-Ridder Newspapers, "Dr. Hamilton Was Enthusiastic Experimenter in Radiation," *Birmingham News*, February 20, 1994, p. 10A; "America's Nuclear Secrets," *Newsweek* December 27, 1993, p. 15.
[56]Keith Schneider, "Scientists Are Sharing the Anguish over Nuclear Experiments on People," *New York Times*, March 2, 1994, p. A9.
[57]Robert Burns, "Radiation Experiments Were Far-Reaching," Associate Press, August 18, 1995, *Birmingham Post-Herald*, p. E6.

conducted by the Department of Energy or its predecessors in 21 states. From the 1940s to the 1960s, physicians exposed 1,500 military aviators and submarine crewmen to encapsulated radium on the end of wires inserted high into their nostrils for several minutes.[58] In another experiment, 130 male prisoners were paid $200 to undergo x-ray radiation of their testicles; afterwards, these men got vasectomies. In another, an indigent 36-year-old Texan was given a shot of plutonium in an injured leg, which was then amputated.

In 1995, the President's Committee on Human Radiation Experiments investigated these experiments and concluded that the government should apologize to those who were involuntary subjects of the tests and should compensate people who had been injured.[59]

In 1991 in Operation Dessert Storm, military personnel were forced to take antibiological warfare, experimental vaccines. Federal law stated that soldiers could not refuse such vaccinations under operational conditions. Subsequently, many soldiers became sick. For years afterwards, the Pentagon and Department of Defense denied that their sickness was service-related. Yet the military's own records showed many causes of such sickness, especially all acting in combination: such as sand storms, biological weapons, oil fires, contaminated water, rare microorganisms, the above vaccines, chemical vapors from bombed Iraqi storage ages, unspent rocket fuel, and high levels of stress.[60]

The above cases show a pattern where physicians in the armed services subjected people to experimental risks. In such cases, service men and women can be ordered to take such risks by superiors who are both physicians and higher-ranking officers.

The Krieger Lead Paint Study

In 2001, the federal Office of Protection from Research Risks (OPRR) halted all federally funded research at Johns Hopkins Medical School after Ellen Roche died in a study of a drug to prevent asthma. When she volunteered for the study, Ellen was healthy; soon, she was dead.

After its research was halted, a physician from Hopkins on television denounced suspension of Hopkins' research monies, claiming Hopkins had only killed one person in many decades of medical research and that lives would be lost from such a suspension because of delayed cures.

Normally, when a hospital kills someone, its spokesperson should go on television to say it's sorry, not to complain about being disciplined. So in this case, lack of remorse motivated reporters to dig further, and they uncovered interesting details about the workings of Hopkins' IRB and the Krieger case.

[58]Dennis Domerzalski, Scripps-Howard News Service, "Radiation 'Guinea Pigs' Tell Stories," *Birmingham Post-Herald*, February 3, 1994, p. A8.

[59]Philip J. Hilts, "U.S. Is Urged to Repay Some in Radiation Tests," *New York Times*, July 17, 1995, p. A9. See also *Final Report*, Advisory Committee on Human Radiation Experiments, Washington, D.C.: US Government Printing Office.

[60]Arthur Caplan, "Rethinking the Cost of War," *Due Consideration*, New York: N.Y.: 1998, pp. 123–124.

The Krieger case was a study by a branch of Johns Hopkins Medical School that examined retardation in children from lead paint, and which six of seven judges on Maryland's highest court likened to the Tuskegee Study.[61] The study, conducted in the mid-1990s by Hopkins's Kennedy Krieger Institute, recruited 108 poor, black families to live in East Baltimore in houses with lead paint.

Ingesting lead-based paint is a known cause of mental retardation in small children. According to the Krieger Institute, the study sought cheaper ways to reduce lead contamination in houses, so landlords in East Baltimore would not abandon them.

Did the parents understand the nature of the study? Did they understand the risk to their children by living in these houses? "It can be argued that the researchers intended that the children be the canaries in the mines but never clearly told the parents," one critic said.[62] Moreover,

> Maryland Court of Appeals Judge Dale R. Cathell, who wrote last week's scathing opinion, said the board [had] instructed Kennedy Krieger researchers to write consent forms for study participants that skirted federal regulations requiring disclosure about risks.
>
> The Court of Appeals ruling ordered trials to be held in lawsuits filed against Kennedy Krieger by two women, Viola Hughes and Catina Higgins, whose children were involved in the study. Hughes's daughter now suffers from learning disabilities and cognitive impairments, both of which are often associated with lead poisoning. . . . Higgins says researchers withheld tests results from her that showed high levels of lead contamination.
>
> Kennedy Krieger is a major institution in the study of lead paint abatement. Marc Farfel, who conducted the study, said today that it identified more effective ways to remove lead hazards and prompted legislation forcing landlords to remove those hazards.[63]

Amazingly, an investigation by OPRR revealed that the IRB at Johns Hopkins, which supposedly had reviewed and discussed the ethics of the Krieger Study and all other research at the medical school, had rarely met face-to-face.

The Krieger Study resembled the Tuskegee Study in that poor black people were deliberately recruited to a study where physicians foresaw harm to subjects. Researchers rationalized the harm by saying that if the study had not occurred, the subjects would have lived in such housing. Revelation of the Krieger Study further damaged already bad relations between Baltimore African-Americans and Hopkins.

The Death of Jesse Gelsinger

In 1999, the death of teenager Jesse Gelsinger from gene therapy, like revelations of the Tuskegee Study or Gennarelli's head-injuries on baboons, changed regulation of American medical research.

In 1999 in Tucson, Arizona, 17-year-old Jesse Gelsinger worked as clerk and rode a motorcycle on weekends. He heard about experimental gene therapy at the University of Pennsylvania for his inherited disorder, ornithine transcarbamylase deficiency (OTC).

---

[61]Manuel Roig-Franzia, "Probe Opens on Study Tied to Johns Hopkins," *Washington Post*, August 23, 2001; p. B1.

[62]Tamar Levin, "U.S. Investigating Johns Hopkins Study of Lead Paint Hazard," *New York Times*, August 24, 2001.

[63]Tamar Levin, "U.S. Investigating."

In the genetic disease OTC, the liver doesn't properly cleanse blood of ammonia (produced in normal metabolism) resulting in toxic levels. Many OTC newborns die around birth; half don't live to age five. A new regimen of drugs and diet enabled Jesse to live to be a teenager, but without a cure, he would eventually die.

Jesse entered the study as a healthy research volunteer. A friend said he "wanted to prove he was a man."[64] Penn researchers claim Jesse was informed that the experiment wouldn't help him, and told him that it might help OTC babies. His father said Jesse wanted "to help save lives."

But why weren't studies done on dying OTC patients? Answer: Because OTC babies are born dying, their parents are so desperate they will consent to anything, no matter how dangerous the experiment.

So Penn researcher James Wilson sought adults with OTC whose livers were still functioning. He wanted to inject into them an adenovirus that contained copies of the gene lacking in OTC patients. Adenoviruses are quite common and can transmit genes to patients with genetic diseases.

What actually happened when Dr. Wilson injected his adenovirus into Jesse is quite grim:

> Four days after scientists infused trillions of genetically engineered viruses into Jesse Gelsinger's liver . . . the 18-year-old lay dying in a hospital bed at the University of Pennsylvania. His liver had failed, and the teenager's blood was thickening like jelly and clogging key vessels while his kidneys, brain, and other organs shut down.[65]

The wrongful death lawsuit claimed that Wilson knew the virus had injured other OTC adults and that Wilson failed to use simple, direct language to explain this dangerous study to the Gelsingers. As Penn bioethicist Arthur Caplan said,

> Not only is it sad that Jesse Gelsinger died, there was never a chance that anybody would benefit from these treatments. They are safety studies. They are not therapeutic in goal. If I gave it to you, we would try to see if you died, too, and if you did, OK.
> If you cured anybody, you'd publish it in a religious journal. It would be a miracle. All you're doing is you're saying, I've got this vector. I want to see if it can deliver the gene where I want it to go without killing or hurting or having any side effects.[66]

Doctor Wilson also had a financial conflict of interest from his biotech company, Genovo, which owned a patent on the adenovirus, should it prove therapeutic. Biogen, Inc. had paid Genovo $37 million for rights to market its genetic therapies.

Wilson denies that money influenced his decisions. He claims his main desire was to be the first to cure a genetic disease.[67]

Wilson reported to the FDA only 39 of 700 problems about the virus, although the law required reporting all of them. In 2000, researchers concluded that

[64]Richard Jerome, "Death by Research," *People*, February 21, 2000, 123.
[65]Deborah Nelson and Rick Weiss, "Hasty Decisions in the Race to a Cure? Gene Therapy Proceeded Despite Safety, Ethics Concerns," *Washington Post*, November 21, 1999, A1.
[66]Arthur Caplan is quoted extensively in Complaint for Civil Action filed by John Gelsinger for estate of Jesse Gelsinger against Trustees of University of Pennsylvania et al., www.sskrplaw.com/links/healthcare2.html.
[67]Deborah Nelson and Rick Weiss, "Hasty Decisions."

adenoviruses should only be used as a last resort, not on healthy volunteers. They curtailed gene therapy until it could be proved safe.

After an investigation of Wilson's research, the NIH in 2000 suspended medical research at Penn. After a Congressional hearing into Jesse's death, the NIH vowed to better monitor medical research. As a result, it suspended medical research at the University of Colorado Medical Center, the University of North Carolina, Johns Hopkins Hospitals, and the University of Alabama at Birmingham. The Gelsinger family settled out of court with Penn for undisclosed monies. After improving their regulation of medical research and conflicts of interest, these medical centers regained their grants, although Wilson's protocols were stopped.

Financial Conflicts and 21st Century Research

The Bayh-Dole Act of 1980 erased an ethical bright line between academic and corporate medicine and allowed universities and their researchers to patent and reap royalties together. Since then, scandals keep recurring in medical research about money.

Twenty-five years later, pharmaceutical companies fund most research into drugs and devices at universities; they do not fund independent peer review of their new drugs and do not publicize bad results. By indirectly paying physicians to test new drugs and by financially encouraging physicians to recruit patients for experiments, drug companies cause physicians to choose their drug and not the best drug for their patients.

In 1998, a study by the Department of Health and Human Services concluded that IRBs could no longer handle the job of protecting subjects from abuses in medical experimentation.[68] It found that IRBs were underfunded, overworked, and that the volume of work expected of volunteers could not be accurately and conscientiously performed. Another study in 2002 by the Institute of Medicine reached similar conclusions.[69] Since then, several medical research centers improved their structures for reviewing research, although financial conflicts continue.

Several scandals erupted in the 1990s wherein a few physicians appeared to have taken millions of dollars from drug companies for dubious research.[70] Some doctors in Georgia allegedly made $4 million over seven years from aggressively soliciting people with schizophrenia for drug trials; they made another $6 million over the same period from testing other drugs.[71]

Some physicians who worked for drug companies made an extra $100,000 a year flying around the country to give talks to physicians to promote a drug for a pharmaceutical company.

[68]Rick Weiss, "Research Volunteers Unwittingly at Risk," *Washington Post*, August 1, 1998, A1. See also this article from the online journal *Target Health*, June 14, 1998. http://www.targethealth.com/
[69]Institute of Medicine, *Responsible Research: A Systems Approach to Protecting Research Participants*, National Academy Press, Washington, D.C., 2002.
[70]For psychiatrists who abused patients in psychiatric research on schizophrenia, see Robert Whitaker, "Lure of Riches Fuels Testing," *Boston Globe*, November 17, 1998, p. A1; for the UAB story about abuse of subjects and fraud in medical research, see Douglas M. Birch and Gary Cohn, "Howa Cancer Drug Trial Ended in Betrayal," *Baltimore Sun*, June 24, 2001.
[71]Steve Stecklow and Laura Johannes, "Drug Makers Relied on Clinical Researchers who Now Await Trial," *Wall Street Journal*, A1, August 15, 1997.

Today, all medical journals continue to take expensive ads from drug companies and almost all medical practices allow drug representatives to buy them and their staffs expensive daily lunches or dinners. Drug companies give these gifts because they work. In many states, drug companies can monitor how much of their drugs are prescribed each month by a particular physician and adjust their gifts accordingly. Learning to take free stuff from drug companies begins in medical school, when students learn to expect free food at lunch paid for by drug companies. Everyone ignores the corrupting influence of taking these gifts on their later decisions about prescribing drugs to patients.

FURTHER READING AND RESOURCES

Thomas Benedek, "The 'Tuskegee Study' of Untreated Syphilis: Analysis of Moral Aspects versus Methodological Aspects," *Journal of Chronic Diseases*, vol. 31, 1978.

Alexee Deep, "Placebo-Controlled Zidovine Trials in the Developing World," *Princeton Journal of Bioethics*, vol. 1, no. 2, Fall, 1998, pp. 21–39.

James Jones, *Bad Blood*, Free Press, New York, 1981.

Unit Two

World Hunger
and Poverty Notes

Peter Singer: Singer argues that suffering and death from poverty is not necessary if only everyone would feel an obligation to give. Individuals can make a difference. The problem is that individuals think of giving as charity rather than duty. When we use the concept of charity, we don't think someone is negligent for not giving. All giving is voluntary. We are praised if we do give, but there are no negative criticisms if we do not give. Singer would like to change all that by changing our concept to one of obligation. Further, he would like to see that obligation extent to the point where giving to others might jeopardize our own lifestyles.

Singer says that "if it is in our power to prevent something bad from happening, without thereby sacrificing anything of comparable moral importance, we ought, morally to do it." It should make no difference whether someone is next door or far away. If everyone gave what they really could give, on an individual, local, national, and international basis, there would be no hunger. When he says "comparable moral importance," he means giving to the point where we might need to be given charity. He doesn't want us to become poor ourselves, but think about the number of things we purchase merely to be in fashion, or because our neighbor has one, or to use as a prestige symbol. For Singer, the money spent on those purchases could have meant the difference between life or starvation for another human being.

Singer believes the money to prevent hunger is there. The problem is that we spend our money on the wrong things and end up wasting money on ill-conceived projects. For example, he points out the millions used to support the development of the Concord plane, a plane that was too large to land at most airport runways, and so costly that its use was ended after a few years.

Garrett Hardin: Hardin gives us a brief history of what metaphors we have used to describe Earth. We began (in the United States) with the metaphor of Earth as running on a "cowboy economy." This was the view that resources where unlimited, so their use and destruction didn't matter. There would always be more—more forests, more minerals, more animals, more land.

When the "cowboy" metaphor no longer served, when we ran out of land, when we realized that resources would not be unlimited, we went to a "spaceship economy." This was the idea that "spaceship earth" needed some stewardship, that all nations were interrelated and what happened in one area of world could affect other or all parts of the world.

Today, Hardin believes we are beyond the spaceship metaphor to one of being in a lifeboat. We are in a crisis of resources. We are in a lifeboat that holds 60 people, with a safety margin that could allow room for a few more. But, swimming all around us are a hundred people who will drown if we don't rescue them. We have three choices. We can bring in everyone and all die together, we can take in no one and keep our safety margin for our own optimal survival, or we can take in those few within our safety margin so that some are rescued while not jeopardizing our own survival.

Hardin favors the last. But, how do we choose? Who do we take into the lifeboat? Hardin suggest a system of triage. Similar to the medical triage used on the site of a disaster, some will be too injured to help, some will be able to heal themselves, and some have a chance of recovery with assistance. This last is the group that should be helped. Our "lifeboat" should only help out those nations that show that our help can actually do some good in getting them on their feet and independence. Countries whose own behavior makes it obvious that they lack responsibility and will not change, should not be helped. To help them would only waste more scarce resources and would not be helpful.

Hardin believes uncontrolled birth rates are the single greatest contributor to the scarcity of resources. By "rescuing" a population that does not believe in birth control, you set up a means of saving people who will grow up to reproduce, without an increase of food resources, so they will have to also be "rescued," and the problem will become worse and worse with each generation. Too many mouths to feed is the cause of poverty. The belief that poverty is caused by overpopulation is called "**Neo-Malthusian**."

When Hardin talks about responsibility, he means that we must recognize that we are a part of a world of shared resources. He uses the "**tragedy of the commons**" to illustrate his point. The term comes from the British history of sharing a field or plot of land used by all the villagers. If every villager had one cow, then the system worked. The field could support that number of cows. But, let's say that one villager becomes greedy and adds a second cow to the mix. Now the entire village suffers because none of the cows have enough to eat. Hardin uses this analogy when he talks about the **World Food Bank**. The bank distributes food to countries in need, but Hardin has already given his objection to doing this unless it is coupled with responsibility in reproduction.

Amartya Sen: Sen points out that, sometimes, what should be a "right" depends on the resulting good that it can bring about. For example, we think of the right to property to be an absolute right. However, Sen asks us to consider what would happen if property rights led to starvation. At that point, the right to have food should take precedence over the right to hold property. Sen suggests that rights should not be seen as absolute, but should be judged by how they affect the most basic rights to life and wellbeing.

Thomas Pogge: Pogge begins his article with some dramatic statistics on poverty worldwide. His argument is that wealthy nations bear some responsibility for the conditions of poor nations. Wealthy nations have often contributed, through colonialism, to the poverty of conquered nations, and when those nations gain self-rule, they are left so far behind in the world economic market that it is extremely difficult to ever catch up—and most don't. Adding to the difficulty of economic viability are the trade protectionist quotas, tariffs, etc. imposed on the import goods from poor nations. In addition, the governments of poor countries are often riddled with corruption—corruption enabled by the richer nations who support a corrupt elite in order to facilitate trade. However, Pogge does not suggest how this can be remedied.

Max Borders: Borders asks us to consider working conditions from the perspective of the people in developing nations rather than by current U.S. expectations. He suggests that we are creating more problems than solutions when we insist that other countries follow our working standards.

United Trauma Relief: This document refutes several common arguments for the legitimacy of sweatshops. They include the argument that "any job is better than no job," companies will relocate if forced to pay higher wages, most companies contract out the sweatshop jobs and have no say in the conditions of workers, a demand for a living wage will just end up in the use of fewer workers and more automation, and that sweatshops are the only way to "raise people out of poverty."
    The document argues that none of these reasons justify the conditions found in sweatshops, where workers have been subjected to everything from physical abuse, health burdens, severe safety violations, and wages that do not allow even a minimum standard of living. It points out that protection for workers, and respect for human rights, have "never been mutually exclusive."

Matt Zwolinski: Zwolinski represents the same viewpoint as Borders.' He starts out by saying the sweatshop conditions are horrific, but quickly cautions us not to impose our western standards of rights and expectations and seems to suggest that sweatshops are not really that bad. He addresses the same arguments found in the article by United Trauma Relief, but comes to the conclusion that any change in policy needs to carefully assess whether it would leave worker worse off rather than with improved conditions.

CHAPTER 2

World Hunger
and Poverty

Widespread hunger and poverty are undeniable facts in the world today. Famines are commonplace in Africa and Southeast Asia, and, for many people in very diverse places on the globe, malnutrition is an everyday fact of life. According to the United Nation's *Human Development Report 2005,* over a billion people in the world survive on less than one dollar a day while another 1.5 billion people live on between one and two dollars a day. There is a close link between poverty and hunger. "More than 850 million people, including one in three preschool children, are trapped in a vicious cycle of malnutrition and its effects."[1] Very few of the victims of famine and malnutrition actually "die of hunger." More commonly, they die of illnesses, such as flu and intestinal problems, which they could have survived if they had not been weakened by hunger. The victims are often very old or very young. Aftereffects for those who survive are often tragic and long-lasting. A large number of children are stunted in growth and suffer incapacitating brain damage as a result of malnutrition. Whole populations are permanently weakened, listless, and lethargic, lacking the energy for any economic advances that might help prevent future famines. At the same time, globalization, with its massive flow of money and technology across territorial boundaries, is changing economic conditions in many developing nations, benefiting some members of these nations but impoverishing others. One of the results of globalization is the proliferation in developing countries of so-called sweatshops that produce goods sold primarily in affluent countries. These places are called sweatshops because the workers are very poorly paid and work under conditions that are considered inhumane by Western ethical standards.

The moral issues raised by ongoing world hunger and poverty are many and complex. In this chapter we focus on only three questions regarding the responsibilities of affluent countries and of individuals who live in those countries. First, what should affluent nations do to prevent and alleviate devastating hunger,

---

[1]"The State of Human Development" in *Human Development Report 2005,* http://hdr.undp.org/reports/global/2005, chap. 1, p. 24.

malnutrition, and poverty in developing countries? Second, what are the moral obligations of individuals in affluent nations with respect to world hunger and poverty? Third, what ethical standards should individuals in affluent nations use when deciding whether to buy goods produced in international sweatshops?

THE MORAL OBLIGATIONS OF AFFLUENT NATIONS AND THE CAUSES OF WORLD HUNGER AND POVERTY

As many of the readings in this chapter show, answers to questions concerning the moral obligations of more affluent nations with regard to world hunger and poverty are intertwined with answers to questions concerning the *causes* of world hunger and poverty. Four major approaches to answering these questions are discussed below.

The Neo-Malthusian Approach

The first approach taken regarding the causes of world hunger and poverty is offered by people labeled "neo-Malthusians." Following Thomas Robert Malthus (1766–1834), they identify the cause as *overpopulation*. According to Malthus, unrestricted population growth necessarily outstrips economic growth, especially the growth in food supplies. This, in turn, *necessarily* results in famines. Uncontrolled fertility is the cause of poverty, and poverty is the cause of the miseries of the poor, including starvation. It has been shown that Malthus was wrong in certain respects, since in many countries the economic growth rate, including the growth in food supplies, has far outstripped the population growth rate. But contemporary neo-Malthusians hold that, in the long run, economic growth rate cannot be sustained. Having identified overpopulation as *the cause* of scarcity, neo-Malthusians locate the solution to problems of world hunger in population control. Optimistic neo-Malthusians hold that birth-control measures can eventually succeed in curbing population growth sufficiently to avert future famines. Pessimistic neo-Malthusians hold that serious political and psychological obstacles to planned population-control measures make famine inevitable in some countries. They predict that these famines will in turn effectively curb unsustainable population growth unless those in more affluent countries intervene.

Some pessimistic neo-Malthusians, including Garrett Hardin in this chapter, use their Malthusian analyses of world hunger to support claims about what more affluent individuals and nations *ought* to do regarding the needs of potential famine victims. Using a lifeboat metaphor, Hardin compares nations to boats and maintains that many countries have outstripped their "carrying capacity." He advances a consequentialist argument to support his claim that the affluent *ought not* help those in the overpopulating countries. In Hardin's view, the long-range effects of food aid will be not only harmful but disastrous for everyone. These effects will be disastrous for countries whose fertility rates remain uncontrolled by either human planning or nature because, sooner or later, future generations in these countries will suffer massive starvation and profound misery. They will also be disastrous for affluent countries that will use up their resources to help overpopulating countries. Hardin even suggests that the very survival of human beings is at risk. He maintains that if giving food to *any* overpopulated country does more harm than good, that food should not be given.

A Contra Neo-Malthusian Approach

The second approach taken regarding the causes of world hunger and poverty focuses on identifying the causes of high fertility rates among the poor in developing countries. Only if we understand *why* the poor have high rates of reproduction can we help instigate and support social practices that will tend to end the cycle of poverty, high birth rates, and starvation. Against the pessimistic neo-Malthusians, proponents of this approach argue that famines and malnutrition are not inevitable. Against the optimistic neo-Malthusians, they argue that planned birth-control practices backed by government policies are not the solution. Ironically, the major factors influencing high fertility rates are identified as hunger and poverty. On this analysis, eradicating famine and malnutrition requires social and economic changes in the developing countries themselves, changes that would eliminate some of the gross inequalities of wealth and property in these countries. Without the recommended changes, it is argued, economic growth, including growth in the food supply, will not take place, population growth will not be slowed, and the tragic cycle will be repeated indefinitely. Amartya Sen, for example, argues in this chapter that the primary cause of famine, hunger, and high population growth is a system of entitlements, which leaves some people without the entitlements to obtain the necessities of life. In his view, eradicating hunger and famine would require the development of policies that would give entitlements to those who are deprived, perhaps by reducing the entitlements of the more prosperous groups.

The Interconnectedness or Interaction Approach

The third approach taken to the causes of world hunger and poverty focuses on the interconnections and interactions among nations—interconnections and interactions that are especially significant given the rapid increase in globalization. These interconnections and interactions can be seen as seriously undermining Hardin's lifeboat metaphor. Those who take this approach frequently argue that affluent nations are often causally responsible for the hunger and poverty in poorer countries since, for example, they adopt practices that prevent some of the poorest countries from increasing their own food supply. The identified culprits include multinational agribusinesses based in Western societies. It is charged that these multinationals have shifted the production of luxury items for the Western market from the highly industrialized countries to underdeveloped ones, where cheap land and labor are available. As a result, the land in needy, underdeveloped countries is used to produce cash crops—crops that can be sold to members of the more affluent countries—while the food that is needed for the home market remains unproduced.

In addition, it is argued that the international economic order favors the affluent, industrialized nations and is shaped by their needs. It is the affluent, industrialized societies that largely determine the prices for both the manufactured goods developing nations must import and the agricultural products the needy countries export. To the extent that the practices of those in affluent societies work against the potential self-sufficiency and real economic growth of developing countries, they help create and perpetuate the cycle of poverty, high fertility rates, and hunger. Thomas Pogge, in this chapter, argues in this vein and uses the WTO (World Trade Organization) to exemplify the ways that affluent nations disadvantage impoverished developing ones.

The WTO, created in 1995, is an international organization with 148 member countries that serves as a forum for negotiating international trade agreements.It is also the monitoring and regulating body for enforcing these agreements.[2] Supporters of the WTO argue that by expanding world trade, the WTO helps to raise living standards around the world. Critics, like Pogge, point out that developing countries are at a disadvantage in the WTO decision-making processes because they lack the expertise and staffing capabilities of affluent countries. They are also adversely affected by many of the decisions made. Affluent nations, for example, are especially protectionist in sectors where developing countries are in a good position to compete—agriculture, textiles, and clothing—leading to tariff decisions that adversely affect developing nations. In Pogge's view, one of the reasons why affluent nations have a moral obligation to alleviate poverty in the world is that, through the WTO, they continue to support a world order that disadvantages poorer countries and makes it more difficult for them to eliminate poverty and hunger.

The United Nations' member states have made a commitment to alleviate extreme poverty in the world. In the *United Nations Millennium Declaration (2000)*, the UN's 191 member states agreed on a set of goals to be met by 2015. The first and primary goal is "to halve, by the year 2015, the proportion of the world's people whose income is less than one dollar a day and the proportion of people who suffer from hunger."[3] Pogge, in a longer version of the article reprinted in this chapter,[4] analyzes the UN's interpretation of this goal and finds the resulting actual commitment to be inadequate.

Pogge reasons as follows. In 2000, the total human population was 6,070.6 million; 1,094 million were reported to be living below one dollar per day (considered extreme poverty). Thus, in 2000, 18.02 percent of the people in the world were living in extreme poverty. If the goal is to halve that proportion, then it would seem that the goal is that by 2015 no more than 9.01 percent of people would be living in extreme poverty. Given an expected human population of 7,197 million in 2015, the implied goal would seem to be to reduce the number of extremely poor people to 648.5 million by 2015.[5] However, Pogge argues, in reality the planned poverty

---

[2]http://www.wto.org.
[3]*United Nations Millennium Declaration (2000)*, http://www.undp.org.in.
[4]Thomas Pogge, "The First United Nations Millennium Development Goal: A Cause for Celebration?" *Journal of Human Development,* vol. 5, November 2004, pp. 377–397.
[5]Ibid., p. 378.

reduction is much less than that, largely because the UN's interpretation of the goal uses 1990 rather than 2000 as the baseline, understanding its goal to be that the proportion of extremely poor people in 2015 should be no more than one-half of what it was in 1990.[6] In 1990, the number of people reported to be living in extreme poverty was 1,218.5 million or 23.15 percent of the total human population at that time. Halving this percentage would commit world governments to a goal of no more than 11.575 percent of the human population living in extreme poverty in 2015. Given a projected world population of 7,197 million in 2015, this would still leave 833 million living on less than one dollar per day. Pogge goes on to point out other aspects of the UN's interpretation that result in an even less ambitious goal—to cut the number of people living in extreme poverty in 2015 to 883.5 million, or 12.276 percent of the projected 2015 population. This is only 19 percent less than the 1,094 million living on less than one dollar per day in 2000. For Pogge, this is morally reprehensible. (Pogge also rejects the view that any more ambitious goal would be too costly.)

Yet, according to the *Human Development Report 2005*, it is doubtful that even this goal will be met. One of the problems has already been noted above—international trade policies. As the 2005 report states,

> Rich country trade policies continue to deny poor countries and poor people a fair share of global prosperity—and they fly in the face of the Millennium Declaration. More than aid, trade has the potential to increase the share of the world's poorest countries and people in global prosperity. Limiting that potential through unfair trade policies is inconsistent with a commitment to the MDGs [millennium development goals]. More than that, it is unjust and hypocritical.[7]

The Socialist Approach

The fourth approach, taken by Marxists and other socialists, incorporates some of the elements already discussed above. (Socialism is discussed in the introduction to Chapter 3 and in a reading by Kai Nielsen in that chapter.) Socialists reject both the contention that overpopulation is the cause of scarcity in the world and the contention that the requisite economic growth is impossible. They identify capitalism as the major cause of worldwide scarcity. Agreeing with the kinds of claims just discussed concerning the negative impact of multinational corporations on the economic growth of developing countries, they see a socialist economic system as the only solution to the problem of world hunger and poverty.[8]

---

[6]The problem is that the UN's formulation of the goal specifies the year 2015 as the end of the plan period but does not specify a baseline year. One might naturally assume that the missing baseline year is the year 2000 in which the MDGs (millennium development goals) were adopted. But the UN actually uses 1990, which makes a significant difference in determining just what the actual goal is (pp. 378–379).

[7]"Overview," *Human Development Report 2005*, p. 3.

[8]See, for example, Kai Nielsen, "Global Justice, Capitalism and the Third World," in Robin Attfield and Barry Wilins, eds., *International Justice and the Third World* (New York: Routledge, 1992), pp. 17–34.

THE MORAL OBLIGATIONS OF INDIVIDUALS

What moral obligations do individuals who live in affluent nations have toward those in impoverished developing nations? With respect to famine and poverty, as the above discussion shows, answers to this question may depend on what we take to be a correct analysis of the causes of famine and poverty in the world. But, if we set aside the kind of factual questions discussed earlier, we can still ask questions about the basis of a possible *moral obligation* that we as individuals might have to prevent starvation and malnutrition among the needy. In this chapter, Peter Singer, a utilitarian, argues for such a moral obligation. Utilitarianism holds that an action or a practice is morally correct only if it is likely to produce the greatest balance of good over evil, everyone considered. Proceeding in a utilitarian spirit, Singer argues for an obligation to famine victims on the basis of the following principle: Persons are morally required to prevent something bad from happening if they can do so "without sacrificing anything of comparable moral importance." In Singer's view, even a weaker version of this principle is sufficient to establish a moral obligation to aid the victims of severe famines.

But famines are not the only events in developing countries calling for a moral response. International sweatshops have also caused a great deal of moral concern. The term *sweatshops* may be understood in various ways. However, as Matt Zwolinski points out in this chapter, in the historical and social context in which the term arose, sweatshops were seen as places where the basic rights of employees were violated, or simple standards of decency were not observed. On this understanding of the term, reference to a place of employment as a "sweatshop" entails a moral judgment of condemnation.

Sweatshops in the developing world have been both defended and criticized. Defenders, such as Max Borders in this chapter, see these places as providing employment not otherwise available and as a first step toward economic prosperity. Critics have a different view, claiming that Western corporations can afford to pay "living wages," even when that is not the norm in a society, and that anything else is exploitation. They also point to various abuses and abysmal working conditions in these places. These critics include student activists on university campuses who have raised questions about where goods sold in university shops have been produced. One student group, United Trauma Relief, which was founded at the Massachusetts Institute of Technology (MIT), formulated the consensus statement reprinted in this chapter that first identifies and then rebuts claims made by defenders of sweatshops. Zwolinski takes an intermediate approach. After defining sweatshops, Zwolinski addresses two moral questions with respect to them. The first focuses on whether Western companies that use sweatshop manufacturers are acting in a morally reprehensible manner. The second deals with our individual responsibilities regarding the purchase of items produced in sweatshops. In both cases, Zwolinski's responses are cautious. His concern is that we make informed decisions and act in ways that will actually benefit those employed in sweatshops and not cause them further harm.

Jane S. Zembaty

Famine, Affluence, and Morality

Peter Singer

Singer expresses concern over the fact that, whereas members of the more affluent nations spend money on trivia, people in the needier nations are starving. He argues that it is morally wrong not to prevent suffering whenever one can do so without sacrificing anything of comparable moral importance. Giving aid to the victims of famine can prevent such suffering. Even if giving requires a drastic reduction in the standard of living of the members of the more affluent societies, the latter are morally required to meet at least the basic need for food of people who will otherwise starve to death.

As I write this, in November 1971, people are dying in East Bengal from lack of food, shelter, and medical care. The suffering and death that are occurring there now are not inevitable, not unavoidable in any fatalistic sense of the term. Constant poverty, a cyclone, and a civil war have turned at least nine million people into destitute refugees; nevertheless, it is not beyond the capacity of the richer nations to give enough assistance to reduce any further suffering to very small proportions. The decisions and actions of human beings can prevent this kind of suffering. Unfortunately, human beings have not made the necessary decisions. At the individual level, people have, with very few exceptions, not responded to the situation in any significant way. Generally speaking, people have not given large sums to relief funds; they have not written to their parliamentary representatives demanding increased government assistance; they have not demonstrated in the streets, held symbolic fasts, or done anything else directed toward providing the refugees with the means to satisfy their essential needs. At the government level, no government has given the sort of massive aid that would enable the refugees to survive for more than a few days. Britain, for instance, has given rather more than most countries. It has, to date, given £14,750,000. For comparative purposes, Britain's share of the nonrecoverable development costs of the Anglo-French Concorde project is already in excess of £275,000,000, and on present estimates will reach £440,000,000. The implication is that the British government values a supersonic transport more than thirty times as highly as it values the lives of the nine million refugees. Australia is another country which, on a per capita basis, is well up in the "aid to Bengal" table. Australia's aid, however, amounts to less than one-twelfth of the cost of Sydney's new opera house. The total amount given, from all sources, now stands at about £65,000,000. The estimated cost of keeping the refugees alive for one year is £464,000,000. Most of the refugees have now been in the camps for more than six months. The World Bank has said that India needs a minimum of £300,000,000 in assistance from other countries before the end of the year. It seems obvious that assistance on this scale will not be forthcoming. India will be forced to choose

Peter singer, "Famine, Affluence, and Morality," *Philosophy & Public Affairs,* 1, no. 3 (Spring 1972).

between letting the refugees starve or diverting funds from her own development program, which will mean that more of her own people will starve in the future.[1]

These are the essential facts about the present situation in Bengal. So far as it concerns us here, there is nothing unique about this situation except its magnitude. The Bengal emergency is just the latest and most acute of a series of major emergencies in various parts of the world, arising both from natural and from man-made causes. There are also many parts of the world in which people die from malnutrition and lack of food independent of any special emergency. I take Bengal as my example only because it is the present concern, and because the size of the problem has ensured that it has been given adequate publicity. Neither individuals nor governments can claim to be unaware of what is happening there.

What are the moral implications of a situation like this? In what follows, I shall argue that the way people in relatively affluent countries react to a situation like that in Bengal cannot be justified; indeed, the whole way we look at moral issues—our moral conceptual scheme—needs to be altered, and with it, the way of life that has come to be taken for granted in our society.

In arguing for this conclusion I will not, of course, claim to be morally neutral. I shall, however, try to argue for the moral position that I take, so that anyone who accepts certain assumptions, to be made explicit, will, I hope, accept my conclusion.

I begin with the assumption that suffering and death from lack of food, shelter, and medical care are bad. I think most people will agree about this, although one may reach the same view by different routes. I shall not argue for this view. People can hold all sorts of eccentric positions, and perhaps from some of them it would not follow that death by starvation is in itself bad. It is difficult, perhaps impossible, to refute such positions, and so for brevity I will henceforth take this assumption as accepted. Those who disagree need read no further.

My next point is this: if it is in our power to prevent something bad from happening, without thereby sacrificing anything of comparable moral importance, we ought, morally, to do it. By "without sacrificing anything of comparable moral importance" I mean without causing anything else comparably bad to happen, or doing something that is wrong in itself, or failing to promote some moral good, comparable in significance to the bad thing that we can prevent. This principle seems almost as uncontroversial as the last one. It requires us only to prevent what is bad, and not to promote what is good, and it requires this of us only when we can do it without sacrificing anything that is, from the moral point of view, comparably important. I could even, as far as the application of my argument to the Bengal emergency is concerned, qualify the point so as to make it: if it is in our power to prevent something very bad from happening, without thereby sacrificing anything morally significant, we ought, morally, to do it. An application of this principle would be as follows: if I am walking past a shallow pond and see a child drowning in it, I ought to wade in and pull the child out. This will mean getting my clothes muddy, but this is insignificant, while the death of the child would presumably be a very bad thing.

The uncontroversial appearance of the principle just stated is deceptive. If it were acted upon, even in its qualified form, our lives, our society, and our world would be fundamentally changed. For the principle takes, firstly, no account of proximity or distance. It makes no moral difference whether the person I can help is a neighbor's child ten yards from me or a Bengali whose name I shall never know, ten thousand miles away. Secondly, the principle makes no distinction between cases in which I am the only person who could possibly do anything and cases in which I am just one among millions in the same position.

I do not think I need to say much in defense of the refusal to take proximity and distance into account. The fact that a person is physically near to us, so that we have personal contact with him, may make it more likely that we *shall* assist him, but this does not show that we *ought* to help him rather than another who happens to be further away. If we accept any principle of impartiality, universalizability, equality, or whatever, we cannot discriminate against someone merely because he is far away from us (or we are far away from him). Admittedly, it is possible that we are in a better position to judge what needs to be done to help a person near to us than one far away, and perhaps also to provide the assistance we judge to be necessary. If this were the case, it would be a reason for helping those near to us first. This may once have been a justification for being more concerned with the poor in one's own town than with famine victims in India. Unfortunately for those who like to keep their moral responsibilities limited, instant communication and swift transportation have changed the situation. From the moral point of view, the development of the world into a "global village" has made an important, though still unrecognized, difference to our moral situation. Expert observers and supervisors, sent out by famine relief organizations or permanently stationed in famine-prone areas, can direct our aid to a refugee in Bengal almost as effectively as we could get it to someone in our own block. There would seem, therefore, to be no possible justification for discriminating on geographical grounds.

There may be a greater need to defend the second implication of my principle—that the fact that there are millions of other people in the same position, in respect to the Bengali refugees, as I am, does not make the situation significantly different from a situation in which I am the only person who can prevent something very bad from occurring. Again, of course, I admit that there is a psychological difference between the cases; one feels less guilty about doing nothing if one can point to others, similarly placed, who have also done nothing. Yet this can make no real difference to our moral obligations. Should I consider that I am less obliged to pull the drowning child out of the pond if on looking around I see other people, no further away than I am, who have also noticed the child but are doing nothing? One has only to ask this question to see the absurdity of the view that numbers lessen obligation. It is a view that is an ideal excuse for inactivity; unfortunately most of the major evils—poverty, overpopulation, pollution—are problems in which everyone is almost equally involved.

The view that numbers do make a difference can be made plausible if stated in this way: if everyone in circumstances like mine gave £5 to the Bengal Relief Fund, there would be enough to provide food, shelter, and medical care for the refugees; there is no reason why I should give more than anyone else in the same circumstances as I am; therefore I have no obligation to give more than £5. Each premise in this argument is true, and the argument looks sound. It may convince us, unless we notice that it is based on a hypothetical premise, although the conclusion is not stated hypothetically. The argument would be sound if the conclusion were: if everyone in circumstances like mine were to give £5, I would have no obligation to give more than £5. If the conclusion were so stated, however, it would be obvious that the argument has no bearing on a situation in which it is not the case that every-one else gives £5. This, of course, is the actual situation. It is more or less certain that not everyone in circumstances like mine will give £5. So there will not be enough to provide the needed food, shelter, and medical care. Therefore by giving more than £5 I will prevent more suffering than I would if I gave just £5.

It might be thought that this argument has an absurd consequence. Since the situation appears to be that very few people are likely to give substantial amounts, it follows that I and everyone else in similar circumstances ought to give as much as possible, that is, at least up to the point at which by giving more one would begin to cause serious suffering for oneself and one's dependents—perhaps even beyond this point to the point of marginal utility, at which by giving more one would cause oneself and one's dependents as much suffering as one would prevent in Bengal. If everyone does this, however, there will be more than can be used for the benefit of the refugees, and some of the sacrifice will have been unnecessary. Thus, if everyone does what he ought to do, the result will not be as good as it would be if everyone did a little less than he ought to do, or if only some do all that they ought to do.

The paradox here arises only if we assume that the actions in question—sending money to the relief funds—are performed more or less simultaneously, and are also unexpected. For if it is to be expected that everyone is going to contribute some-thing, then clearly each is not obliged to give as much as he would have been obliged to had others not been giving too. And if everyone is not acting more or less simultaneously, then those giving later will know how much more is needed, and will have no obligation to give more than is necessary to reach this amount. To say this is not to deny the principle that people in the same circumstances have the same obligations, but to point out that the fact that others have given, or may be expected to give, is a relevant circumstance: those giving after it has become known that many others are giving and those giving before are not in the same circumstances. So the seemingly absurd consequence of the principle I have put forward can occur only if people are in error about the actual circumstances—that is, if they think they are giving when others are not, but in fact they are giving when others are. The result of everyone doing what he really ought to do cannot be worse than the result of everyone doing less than he ought to do, although the result of everyone doing what he reasonably believes he ought to do could be.

If my argument so far has been sound, neither our distance from a preventable evil nor the number of other people who, in respect to that evil, are in the same sit-uation as we are, lessens our obligation to mitigate or prevent that evil. I shall there-fore take as established the principle I asserted earlier. As I have already said, I need to assert it only in its qualified form: if it is in our power to prevent something very bad from happening, without thereby sacrificing anything else morally significant, we ought, morally, to do it.

The outcome of this argument is that our traditional moral categories are upset. The traditional distinction between duty and charity cannot be drawn, or at least, not in the place we normally draw it. Giving money to the Bengal Relief Fund is regarded as an act of charity in our society. The bodies which collect money are known as "charities." These organizations see themselves in this way—if you send them a check, you will be thanked for your "generosity." Because giving money is regarded as an act of charity, it is not thought that there is anything wrong with not giving. The charitable man may be praised, but the man who is not charitable is not condemned. People do not feel in any way ashamed or guilty about spending money on new clothes or a new car instead of giving it to famine relief. (Indeed, the alternative does not occur to them.) This way of looking at the matter cannot be justified. When we buy new clothes not to keep ourselves warm but to look "well-dressed" we are not providing for any important need. We would not be sacrificing anything significant if we were to continue to wear our old clothes, and give the money to famine relief. By doing so, we would be preventing another person from starving. It follows from what I have said earlier that we ought to give money away, rather than spend it on clothes which we do not need to keep us warm. To do so is not charitable, or generous. Nor is it the kind of act which philosophers and theologians have called "supererogatory"—an act which it would be good to do, but not wrong not to do. On the contrary, we ought to give the money away, and it is wrong not to do so.

I am not maintaining that there are no acts which are charitable, or that there are no acts which it would be good to do but not wrong not to do. It may be possible to redraw the distinction between duty and charity in some other place. All I am arguing here is that the present way of drawing the distinction, which makes it an act of charity for a man living at the level of affluence which most people in the "developed nations" enjoy to give money to save someone else from starvation, cannot be supported. It is beyond the scope of my argument to consider whether the distinction should be redrawn or abolished altogether. There would be many other possible ways of drawing the distinction—for instance, one might decide that it is good to make other people as happy as possible, but not wrong not to do so.

Despite the limited nature of the revision in our moral conceptual scheme which I am proposing, the revision would, given the extent of both affluence and famine in the world today, have radical implications. These implications may lead to further objections, distinct from those I have already considered. I shall discuss two of these.

One objection to the position I have taken might be simply that it is too drastic a revision of our moral scheme. People do not ordinarily judge in the way I have suggested they should. Most people reserve their moral condemnation for those who violate some moral norm, such as the norm against taking another person's property. They do not condemn those who indulge in luxury instead of giving to famine relief. But given that I did not set out to present a morally neutral description of the way people make moral judgments, the way people do in fact judge has nothing to do with the validity of my conclusion. My conclusion follows from the principle which I advanced earlier, and unless that principle is rejected, or the arguments shown to be unsound, I think the conclusion must stand, however strange it appears. . . .

The second objection to my attack on the present distinction between duty and charity is one which has from time to time been made against utilitarianism. It follows from some forms of utilitarian theory that we all ought, morally, to be working full time to increase the balance of happiness over misery. The position I have taken here would not lead to this conclusion in all circumstances, for if there were no bad occurrences that we could prevent without sacrificing something of comparable moral importance, my argument would have no application. Given the present conditions in many parts of the world, however, it does follow from my argument that we ought, morally, to be working full time to relieve great suffering of the sort that occurs as a result of famine or other disasters. Of course, mitigating circumstances can be adduced—for instance, that if we wear ourselves out through overwork, we shall be less effective than we would otherwise have been. Nevertheless, when all considerations of this sort have been taken into account, the conclusion remains: we ought to be preventing as much suffering as we can without sacrificing something else of comparable moral importance. This conclusion is one which we may be reluctant to face. I cannot see, though, why it should be regarded as a criticism of the position for which I have argued, rather than a criticism of our ordinary standards of behavior. Since most people are self-interested to some degree, very few of us are likely to do everything that we ought to do. It would, however, hardly be honest to take this as evidence that it is not the case that we ought to do it. . . .

The conclusion reached earlier [raises] the question of just how much we all ought to be giving away. One possibility, which has already been mentioned, is that we ought to give until we reach the level of marginal utility—that is, the level at which, by giving more, I would cause as much suffering to myself or my dependents as I would relieve by my gift. This would mean, of course, that one would reduce oneself to very near the material circumstances of a Bengali refugee. It will be recalled that earlier I put forward both a strong and a moderate version of the principle of preventing bad occurrences. The strong version, which required us to prevent bad things from happening unless in doing so we would be sacrificing something of a comparable moral significance, does seem to require reducing ourselves to the level of marginal utility. I should also say that the strong version seems to me to be the correct one. I proposed the more moderate version—that we should prevent bad occurrences unless, to do so, we had to sacrifice something morally significant—only in order to show that even on this surely undeniable principle, a great change in our way of life is required. On the more moderate principle, it may not follow that we ought to reduce ourselves to the level of marginal utility, for one might hold that to reduce oneself and one's family to this level is to cause something significantly bad to happen. Whether this is so I shall not discuss, since, as I have said, I can see no good reason for holding the moderate version of the principle rather than the strong version. Even if we accepted the principle only in its moderate form, however, it should be clear that we would have to give away enough to ensure that the consumer society, dependent as it is on people spending on trivia rather than giving to famine relief, would slow down and perhaps disappear entirely. There are several reasons why this would be desirable in itself. The value and necessity of economic growth are now being questioned not only by conservationists, but by economists as well.[2] There is no doubt, too, that the consumer society has had a distorting effect on the goals and purposes of its members. Yet looking at the matter purely from the point of view of overseas aid, there must be a limit to the extent to which we should deliberately slow down our economy; for it might be the case that if we gave away, say, forty percent of our Gross National Product, we would slow down the economy so much that in absolute terms we would be giving less than if we gave twenty-five percent of the much larger GNP that we would have if we limited our contribution to this smaller percentage.

I mention this only as an indication of the sort of factor that one would have to take into account in working out an ideal. Since Western societies generally consider one percent of the GNP an acceptable level for overseas aid, the matter is entirely academic. Nor does it affect the question of how much an individual should give in a society in which very few are giving substantial amounts.

It is sometimes said, though less often now than it used to be, that philosophers have no special role to play in public affairs, since most public issues depend primarily on an assessment of facts. On questions of fact, it is said, philosophers as such have no special expertise, and so it has been possible to engage in philosophy without committing oneself to any position on major public issues. No doubt there are some issues of social policy and foreign policy about which it can truly be said that a really expert assessment of the facts is required before taking sides or acting, but the issue of famine is surely not one of these. The facts about the existence of suffering are beyond dispute. Nor, I think, is it disputed that we can do something about it, either through orthodox methods of famine relief or through population control or both. This is therefore an issue on which philosophers are competent to take a position. The issue is one which faces everyone who has more money than he needs to support himself and his dependents, or who is in a position to take some sort of political action. These categories must include practically every teacher and student of philosophy in the universities of the Western world. If philosophy is to deal with matters that are relevant to both teachers and students, this is an issue that philosophers should discuss.

Discussion, though, is not enough. What is the point of relating philosophy to public (and personal) affairs if we do not take our conclusions seriously? In this instance, taking our conclusion seriously means acting upon it. The philosopher will not find it any easier than anyone else to alter his attitudes and way of life to the extent that, if I am right, is involved in doing everything that we ought to be doing. At the very least, though, one can make a start. The philosopher who does so will have to sacrifice some of the benefits of the consumer society, but he can find compensation in the satisfaction of a way of life in which theory and practice, if not yet in harmony, are at least coming together.

NOTES

1 There was also a third possibility: that India would go to war to enable the refugees to return to their lands. Since I wrote this paper, India has taken this way out. The situation is no longer that described above, but this does not affect my argument, as the next paragraph indicates.
2 See, for instance, John Kenneth Galbraith, *The New Industrial State* (Boston, 1967); and E. J. Mishan, *The Costs of Economic Growth* (London, 1967).

QUESTIONS

1 Think about the following claim: Contributing to famine relief is not a moral obligation that we must perform if we are to act in a morally correct way, but an act of charity that we may or may not perform. Can you offer any arguments to defend it?
2 Singer says, "We ought to be preventing as much suffering as we can without sacrificing something else of comparable moral importance." What moral considerations would outweigh the obligation Singer claims we have to aid famine victims?

Living on a Lifeboat

Garrett Hardin

Using the metaphor of a lifeboat, Hardin argues that the time may have come to refuse to give aid in the form of food to needy countries that do not accept the responsibility for limiting their population growth. He maintains that adherence to the principle "from each according to his ability; to each according to his need" will have strong adverse effects. Bolstered by our aid, needy countries will continue their irresponsible policies in regard to food production and population growth. Furthermore, the food we supply will enable these populations to continue to increase. This, in the long run, jeopardizes human survival.

No generation has viewed the problem of the survival of the human species as seriously as we have. Inevitably, we have entered this world of concern through the door of metaphor. Environmentalists have emphasized the image of the earth as a spaceship—Spaceship Earth. Kenneth Boulding (1966) is the principal architect of this metaphor. It is time, he says, that we replace the wasteful "cowboy economy" of the past with the frugal "spaceship economy" required for continued survival in the limited world we now see ours to be. The metaphor is notably useful in justifying pollution control measures.

Unfortunately, the image of a spaceship is also used to promote measures that are suicidal. One of these is a generous immigration policy, which is only a particular instance of a class of policies that are in error because they lead to the tragedy of the commons (Hardin 1968). These suicidal policies are attractive because they mesh with what we unthinkingly take to be the ideals of "the best people." What is missing in the idealistic view is an insistence that rights and responsibilities must go together. The "generous" attitude of all too many people results in asserting inalienable rights while ignoring or denying matching responsibilities.

For the metaphor of a spaceship to be correct the aggregate of people on board would have to be under unitary sovereign control (Ophuls 1974). A true ship always has a captain. It is conceivable that a ship could be run by a committee. But it could not possibly survive if its course were determined by bickering tribes that claimed rights without responsibilities.

What about Spaceship Earth? It certainly has no captain, and no executive committee. The United Nations is a toothless tiger, because the signatories of its charter wanted it that way. The spaceship metaphor is used only to justify spaceship demands on common resources without acknowledging corresponding spaceship responsibilities.

An understandable fear of decisive action leads people to embrace "incrementalism"—moving toward reform in tiny stages. As we shall see, this strategy is

Reprinted, with permission, from the October 1974 issue of *BioScience,* © American Institute of Biological Sciences.

counterproductive in the area discussed here if it means accepting rights before responsibilities. Where human survival is at stake, the acceptance of responsibilities is a pre-
condition to the acceptance of rights, if the two cannot be introduced simultaneously.

LIFEBOAT ETHICS

Before taking up certain substantive issues let us look at an alternative metaphor,
that of a lifeboat. In developing some relevant examples the following numerical
values are assumed. Approximately two-thirds of the world is desperately poor, and
only one-third is comparatively rich. The people in poor countries have an average
per capita GNP (Gross National Product) of about $200 per year; the rich, of about
$3,000. (For the United States it is nearly $5,000 per year.) Metaphorically, each
rich nation amounts to a lifeboat full of comparatively rich people. The poor of the
world are in other, much more crowded lifeboats. Continuously, so to speak, the
poor fall out of their lifeboats and swim for a while in the water outside, hoping to
be admitted to a rich lifeboat, or in some other way to benefit from the "goodies"
on board. What should the passengers on a rich lifeboat do? This is the central
problem of "the ethics of a lifeboat."

First we must acknowledge that each lifeboat is effectively limited in capacity.
The land of every nation has a limited carrying capacity. The exact limit is a matter
for argument, but the energy crunch is convincing more people every day that we
have already exceeded the carrying capacity of the land. We have been living on
"capital"—stored petroleum and coal—and soon we must live on income alone.

Let us look at only one lifeboat—ours. The ethical problem is the same for all,
and is as follows. Here we sit, say 50 people in a lifeboat. To be generous, let us
assume our boat has a capacity of 10 more, making 60. (This, however, is to violate
the engineering principle of the "safety factor." A new plant disease or a bad change
in the weather may decimate our population if we don't preserve some excess
capacity as a safety factor.)

The 50 of us in the lifeboat see 100 others swimming in the water outside, asking for admission to the boat, or for handouts. How shall we respond to their calls?
There are several possibilities.

One. We may be tempted to try to live by the Christian ideal of being "our
brother's keeper," or by the Marxian ideal (Marx 1875) of "from each according
to his abilities, to each according to his needs." Since the needs of all are the
same, we take all the needy into our boat, making a total of 150 in a boat with a
capacity of 60. The boat is swamped, and everyone drowns. Complete justice,
complete catastrophe.

Two. Since the boat has an unused excess capacity of 10, we admit just 10 more
to it. This has the disadvantage of getting rid of the safety factor, for which action
we will sooner or later pay dearly. Moreover, *which* 10 do we let in? "First come,
first served?" The best 10? The neediest 10? How do we *discriminate*? And what
do we say to the 90 who are excluded?

Three. Admit no more to the boat and preserve the small safety factor. Survival
of the people in the lifeboat is then possible (though we shall have to be on our
guard against boarding parties).

The last solution is abhorrent to many people. It is unjust, they say. Let us grant that it is.

"I feel guilty about my good luck," say some. The reply to this is simple: *Get out and yield your place to others.* Such a selfless action might satisfy the conscience of those who are addicted to guilt but it would not change the ethics of the lifeboat. The needy person to whom a guilt-addict yields his place will not himself feel guilty about his sudden good luck. (If he did he would not climb aboard.) The net result of conscience-stricken people relinquishing their unjustly held positions is the elimination of their kind of conscience from the lifeboat. The lifeboat, as it were, purifies itself of guilt. The ethics of the lifeboat persist, unchanged by such momentary aberrations.

This then is the basic metaphor within which we must work out our solutions. Let us enrich the image step by step with substantive additions from the real world.

REPRODUCTION

The harsh characteristics of lifeboat ethics are heightened by reproduction, particularly by reproductive differences. The people inside the lifeboats of the wealthy nations are doubling in numbers every 87 years; those outside are doubling every 35 years, on the average. And the relative difference in prosperity is becoming greater.

Let us, for a while, think primarily of the U.S. lifeboat. As of 1973 the United States had a population of 210 million people, who were increasing by 0.8% per year, that is, doubling in number every 87 years.

Although the citizens of rich nations are outnumbered two to one by the poor, let us imagine an equal number of poor people outside our lifeboat—a mere 210 million poor people reproducing at a quite different rate. If we imagine these to be the combined populations of Colombia, Venezuela, Ecuador, Morocco, Thailand, Pakistan, and the Philippines, the average rate of increase of the people "outside" is 3.3% per year. The doubling time of this population is 21 years.

Suppose that all these countries, and the United States, agreed to live by the Marxian ideal, "to each according to his needs," the ideal of most Christians as well. Needs, of course, are determined by population size, which is affected by reproduction. Every nation regards its rate of reproduction as a sovereign right. If our lifeboat were big enough in the beginning it might be possible to live *for a while* by Christian-Marxian ideals. *Might.*

Initially, in the model given, the ratio of non-Americans to Americans would be one to one. But consider what the ratio would be 87 years later. By this time Americans would have doubled to a population of 420 million. The other group (doubling every 21 years) would now have swollen to 3,540 million. Each American would have more than eight people to share with. How could the lifeboat possibly keep afloat?

All this involves extrapolation of current trends into the future, and is consequently suspect. Trends may change. Granted: but the change will not necessarily be favorable. If—as seems likely—the rate of population increase falls faster in the ethnic group presently inside the lifeboat than it does among those now outside, the future will turn out to be even worse than mathematics predicts, and sharing will be even more suicidal.

RUIN IN THE COMMONS

The fundamental error of the sharing ethics is that it leads to the tragedy of the commons. Under a system of private property the man (or group of men) who own property recognize their responsibility to care for it, for if they don't they will eventually suffer. A farmer, for instance, if he is intelligent, will allow no more cattle in a pasture than its carrying capacity justifies. If he overloads the pasture, weeds take over, erosion sets in, and the owner loses in the long run.

But if a pasture is run as a commons open to all, the right of each to use it is not matched by an operational responsibility to take care of it. It is no use asking independent herdsmen in a commons to act responsibly, for they dare not. The considerate herdsman who refrains from overloading the commons suffers more than a selfish one who says his needs are greater. (As Leo Durocher says, "Nice guys finish last.") Christian-Marxian idealism is counterproductive. That it *sounds* nice is no excuse. With distribution systems, as with individual morality, good intentions are no substitute for good performance.

A social system is stable only if it is insensitive to errors. To the Christian-Marxian idealist a selfish person is a sort of "error." Prosperity in the system of the commons cannot survive errors. If *everyone* would only restrain himself, all would be well; but it takes *only one less than everyone* to ruin a system of voluntary restraint. In a crowded world of less than perfect human beings—and we will never know any other—mutual ruin is inevitable in the commons. This is the core of the tragedy of the commons. . . .

WORLD FOOD BANKS

In the international arena we have recently heard a proposal to create a new commons, namely an international depository of food reserves to which nations will contribute according to their abilities, and from which nations may draw according to their needs. Nobel laureate Norman Borlaug has lent the prestige of his name to this proposal.

A world food bank appeals powerfully to our humanitarian impulses. We remember John Donne's celebrated line, "Any man's death diminishes me." But before we rush out to see for whom the bell tolls let us recognize where the greatest political push for international granaries comes from, lest we be disillusioned later. Our experience with Public Law 480 clearly reveals the answer. This was the law that moved billions of dollars worth of U.S. grain to food-short, population-long countries during the past two decades. When P.L. 480 first came into being, a headline in the business magazine *Forbes* (Paddock 1970) revealed the power behind it: "Feeding the World's Hungry Millions: How it will mean billions for U.S. business."

And indeed it did. In the years 1960 to 1970 a total of $7.9 billion was spent on the "Food for Peace" program, as P.L. 480 was called. During the years of 1948 to 1970 an additional $49.9 billion were extracted from American taxpayers to pay for other economic aid programs, some of which went for food and food-producing machinery. (This figure does *not* include military aid.) That P.L. 480 was a giveaway program was concealed. Recipient countries went through the motions of paying for P.L. 480 food—with IOU's. In December 1973 the charade was brought to an end as far as India was concerned when the United States "forgave" India's $3.2 billion debt (Anonymous 1974). Public announcement of the cancellation of the debt was delayed for two months: one wonders why. . . .

What happens if some organizations budget for emergencies and others do not? If each organization is solely responsible for its own well-being, poorly managed ones will suffer. But they should be able to learn from experience. They have a chance to mend their ways and learn to budget for infrequent but certain emergencies. The weather, for instance, always varies and periodic crop failures are certain. A wise and competent government saves out of the production of the good years in anticipation of bad years that are sure to come. This is not a new idea. The Bible tells us that Joseph taught this policy to Pharaoh in Egypt more than 2,000 years ago. Yet it is literally true that the vast majority of the governments of the world today have no such policy. They lack either the wisdom or the competence, or both. Far more difficult than the transfer of wealth from one country to another is the transfer of wisdom between sovereign powers or between generations.

"But it isn't their fault! How can we blame the poor people who are caught in an emergency? Why must we punish them?" The concepts of blame and punishment are irrelevant. The question is, what are the operational consequences of establishing a world food bank? If it is open to every country every time a need develops, slovenly rulers will not be motivated to take Joseph's advice. Why should they? Others will bail them out whenever they are in trouble.

Some countries will make deposits in the world food bank and others will withdraw from it: there will be almost no overlap. Calling such a depository-transfer unit a "bank" is stretching the metaphor of *bank* beyond its elastic limits. The proposers, of course, never call attention to the metaphorical nature of the word they use.

THE RATCHET EFFECT

An "international food bank" is really, then, not a true bank but a disguised one-way transfer device for moving wealth from rich countries to poor. In the absence of such a bank, in a world inhabited by individually responsible sovereign nations, the population of each nation would repeatedly go through a cycle of the sort shown in Figure 1. P_2 is greater than P_1, either in absolute numbers or because a

Fig. 1

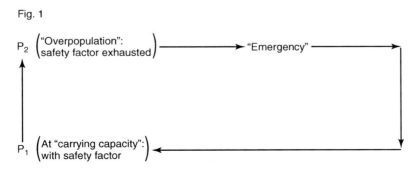

deterioration of the food supply has removed the safety factor and produced a dangerously low ratio of resources to population. P_2 may be said to represent a state of overpopulation, which becomes obvious upon the appearance of an "accident," e.g., a crop failure. If the "emergency" is not met by outside help, the population drops back to the "normal" level—the "carrying capacity" of the environment—or even below. In the absence of population control by a sovereign, sooner or later the population grows to P_2 again and the cycle repeats. The long-term population curve (Hardin 1966) is an irregularly fluctuating one, equilibrating more or less about the carrying capacity.

A demographic cycle of this sort obviously involves great suffering in the restrictive phase, but such a cycle is normal to any independent country with inadequate population control. The third century theologian Tertullian (Hardin 1969) expressed what must have been the recognition of many wise men when he wrote: "The scourges of pestilence, famine, wars, and earthquakes have come to be regarded as a blessing to overcrowded nations, since they serve to prune away the luxuriant growth of the human race."

Only under a strong and farsighted sovereign—which theoretically could be the people themselves, democratically organized—can a population equilibrate at some set point below the carrying capacity, thus avoiding the pains normally caused by periodic and unavoidable disasters. For this happy state to be achieved it is necessary that those in power be able to contemplate with equanimity the "waste" of surplus food in times of bountiful harvests. It is essential that those in power resist the temptation to convert extra food into extra babies. On the public relations level it is necessary that the phrase "surplus food" be replaced by "safety factor."

But wise sovereigns seem not to exist in the poor world today. The most anguishing problems are created by poor countries that are governed by rulers insufficiently wise and powerful. If such countries can draw on a world food bank in times of "emergency," the population *cycle* of Figure 1 will be replaced by the population *escalator* of Figure 2. The input of food from a food bank acts as the pawl of a ratchet, preventing the population from retracing its steps to a lower level. Reproduction pushes the population upward, inputs from the world bank prevent its moving downward. Population size escalates, as does the absolute magnitude of "accidents" and "emergencies." The process is brought to an end only by the total collapse of the whole system, producing a catastrophe of scarcely imaginable proportions.

Such are the implications of the well-meant sharing of food in a world of irresponsible reproduction. . . .

To be generous with one's own possessions is one thing; to be generous with posterity's is quite another. This, I think, is the point that must be gotten across to those who would, from a commendable love of distributive justice, institute a ruinous system of the commons. . . .

If the argument of this essay is correct, so long as there is no true world government to control reproduction everywhere it is impossible to survive in dignity if we are to be guided by Spaceship ethics. Without a world government that is sovereign in reproductive matters mankind lives, in fact, on a number of sovereign lifeboats.

Fig. 2

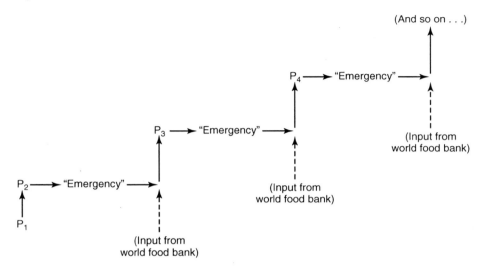

For the foreseeable future survival demands that we govern our actions by the ethics of a lifeboat. Posterity will be ill served if we do not.

REFERENCES

Anonymous. 1974. *Wall Street Journal,* 19 Feb.

Boulding, K. 1966. The economics of the coming spaceship earth. In H. Jarrett, ed. *Environmental Quality in a Growing Economy.* Johns Hopkins Press, Baltimore.

Hardin, G. 1966. Chap. 9 in *Biology: Its Principles and Implications,* 2nd ed. Freeman, San Francisco.

————. 1968. The tragedy of the commons. *Science* 162: 1243–1248.

————. 1969. Page 18 in *Population, Evolution, and Birth Control,* 2nd ed. Freeman, San Francisco.

Marx, K. 1875. *Critique of the Gotha program.* Page 388 in R. C. Tucker, ed. *The Marx-Engels Reader,* Norton, N.Y., 1972.

Ophuls, W. 1974. The scarcity society. *Harpers* 248 (1487): 47–52.

Paddock, W. C. 1970. How green is the green revolution? *Bioscience* 20: 897–902.

QUESTIONS

1 What evidence is available to support the claim that the resources of the world will not be able to save all the poor countries? If it cannot be conclusively proved that all the poor countries cannot be saved, can a moral justification be given for refusing to aid famine victims in all those countries?

2 Suppose that it is highly unlikely that all the nations in the world can be saved. Which would be the better moral choice: (1) to deliberately cut off aid to those least likely to survive in order to ensure the survival of the others or (2) to continue our aid, despite our awareness of the consequences that will probably follow?

Property and Hunger

Amartya Sen

Sen's article falls into three parts. First, he discusses property rights. He argues for the importance of incorporating empirical realities, especially economic ones, into the moral analyses of property rights. Property rights may have consequences that call for moral assessment. If a set of property rights leads to hunger and starvation, for example, then the moral approval of these property rights is severely compromised. Second, in Sen's view, famines are best understood in terms of the entitlement systems that leave many people without the entitlements that would give them the resources to acquire necessities, such as food. Public policies, such as a guaranteed minimum moral entitlement, could be designed to increase the entitlements of the deprived groups in order to prevent famine and starvation. But, as long as property rights are seen as inviolate, such public policies will be seen as morally unacceptable to the extent that they require that the property rights and related entitlements of those who are better off are violated. Third, Sen argues for the institutionalization of a moral right not to be hungry.

. . . [T]he claims of property rights, which some would defend and some . . . would dispute, are not just matters of basic moral belief that could not possibly be influenced one way or the other by any empirical arguments. They call for sensitive moral analysis responsive to empirical realities, including economic ones.

Moral claims based on intrinsically valuable rights are often used in political and social arguments. Rights related to ownership have been invoked for ages. But there are also other types of rights which have been seen as "inherent and inalienable," and the American Declaration of Independence refers to "certain unalienable rights," among which are "life, liberty and the pursuit of happiness." The Indian constitution talks even of "the right to an adequate means of livelihood."[1] The "right not to be hungry" has often been invoked in recent discussions on the obligation to help the famished.

RIGHTS: INSTRUMENTS, CONSTRAINTS, OR GOALS?

Rights can be taken to be morally important in three different ways. First, they can be considered to be valuable *instruments* to achieve other goals. This is the "instrumental view," and is well illustrated by the utilitarian approach to rights. Rights are, in that view, of no intrinsic importance. Violation of rights is not in itself a bad thing, nor fulfillment intrinsically good. But the acceptance of rights promotes, in this view, things that are ultimately important, to wit, utility. Jeremy Bentham rejected "natural rights" as "simple nonsense," and "natural and imprescriptible rights" as

From *Economics and Philosophy,* vol. 4, no. 1 (1988), pp. 57–68. Copyright © Cambridge University Press. Reprinted with the permission of Cambridge University Press.

"rhetorical nonsense, nonsense upon stilts." But he attached great importance to rights as instruments valuable to the promotion of a good society, and devoted much energy to the attempt to reform appropriately the actual system of rights.

The second view may be called the "constraint view," and it takes the form of seeing rights as *constraints* on what others can or cannot do. In this view rights *are* intrinsically important. However, they don't figure in moral accounting as goals to be generally promoted, but only as constraints that others must obey. As Robert Nozick has put it in a powerful exposition of this "constraint view": "Individuals have rights, and there are things no person or group may do to them (without violating their rights)." Rights "set the constraints within which a social choice is to be made, by excluding certain alternatives, fixing others, and so on."[2]

The third approach is to see fulfillments of rights as goals to be pursued. This "goal view" differs from the instrumental view in regarding rights to be intrinsically important, and it differs from the constraint view in seeing the fulfillment of rights as goals to be generally promoted, rather than taking them as demanding only (and exactly) that we refrain from violating the rights of others. In the "constraint view" there is no duty to help anyone with his or her rights (merely not to hinder), and also in the "instrumental view" there is no duty, in fact, to help unless the right fulfillment will also promote some other goal such as utility. The "goal view" integrates the valuation of rights—their fulfillment and violation—in overall moral accounting, and yields a wider sphere of influence of rights in morality.

I have argued elsewhere that the goal view has advantages that the other two approaches do not share, in particular, the ability to accommodate integrated moral accounting including inter alia the intrinsic importance of a class of fundamental rights. I shall not repeat that argument here. But there is an interesting question of dual roles of rights in the sense that some rights may be *both* intrinsically important and instrumentally valuable. For example, the right to be free from hunger could—not implausibly—be regarded as being valuable in itself as well as serving as a good instrument to promote other goals such as security, longevity or utility. If so, both the goal view and the instrumental view would have to be simultaneously deployed to get a comprehensive assessment of such a right. . . .

The instrumental aspect is an inescapable feature of every right, since irrespective of whether a certain right is intrinsically valuable or not, its acceptance will certainly have other consequences as well, and these, too, have to be assessed along with the intrinsic value of rights (if any). A right that is regarded as quite valuable in itself may nevertheless be judged to be morally rejectable if it leads to disastrous consequences. This is a case of the rights playing a *negative* instrumental role. It is, of course, also possible that the instrumental argument will *bolster* the intrinsic claims of a right to be taken seriously. . . .

There are two general conclusions to draw, at this stage, from this very preliminary discussion. First, we must distinguish between (1) the intrinsic value of a right, and (2) the overall value of a right taking note inter alia of its intrinsic importance (if any). The acceptance of the intrinsic importance of any right is no guarantee that its overall moral valuation must be favorable. Second, no moral assessment of a right can be independent of its likely consequences. The need for empirical assessment of the effects of accepting any right cannot be escaped. Empirical arguments are quite central to moral philosophy.

PROPERTY AND DEPRIVATION

The right to hold, use and bequeath property that one has legitimately acquired is often taken to be inherently valuable. In fact, however, many of its defenses seem to be actually of the instrumental type, e.g., arguing that property rights make people more free to choose one kind of a life rather than another. But even if we do accept that property rights may have some intrinsic value, this does not in any way amount to an overall justification of property rights, since property rights may have consequences which themselves will require assessment. Indeed, the causation of hunger as well as its prevention may materially depend on how property rights are structured. If a set of property rights leads, say, to starvation, as it well might, then the moral approval of these rights would certainly be compromised severely. In general, the need for consequential analysis of property rights is inescapable whether or not such rights are seen as having any intrinsic value. . . .

. . . I have tried to argue elsewhere . . . that famines are, in fact, best explained in terms of failures of entitlement systems. The entitlements here refer, of course, to legal rights and to practical possibilities, rather than to moral status, but the laws and actual operation of private ownership economies have many features in common with the moral system of entitlements analyzed by Nozick and others.

The entitlement approach to famines need not, of course, be confined to private ownership economies, and entitlement failures of other systems can also be fruitfully studied to examine famines and hunger. In the specific context of private ownership economies, the entitlements are substantially analyzable in terms, respectively, of what may be called "endowments" and "exchange entitlements." A person's endowment refers to what he or she initially owns (including the person's own labor power), and the exchange entitlement mapping tells us what the person can obtain through exchanging what he or she owns, either by production (exchange with nature), or by trade (exchange with others), or a mixture of the two. A person has to starve if neither the endowments, nor what can be obtained through exchange, yields an adequate amount of food.

If starvation and hunger are seen in terms of failures of entitlements, then it becomes immediately clear that the total availability of food in a country is only one of several variables that are relevant. Many famines occur without any decline in the availability of food. For example, in the Great Bengal famine of 1943, the total food availability in Bengal was not particularly bad (considerably higher than two years earlier when there was no famine), and yet three million people died, in a famine mainly affecting the rural areas, through rather violent shifts in the relative purchasing powers of different groups, hitting the rural laborers the hardest. The Ethiopian famine of 1973 took place in a year of average per capita food availability, but the cultivators and other occupation groups in the province of Wollo had lost their means of subsistence (through loss of crops and a decline of economic activity, related to a local drought) and had no means of commanding food from elsewhere in the country. Indeed, some food moved *out* of Wollo to more prosperous people in other parts of Ethiopia, repeating a pattern of contrary movement of food that was widely observed during the Irish famines of the 1840s (with food moving out of famine-stricken Ireland to prosperous England which had greater power in the battle for entitlements). The Bangladesh famine of 1974 took place in a year of *peak* food availability, but several occupation groups had lost their entitlement to food through loss of employment and other economic changes (including inflationary pressures causing prices to outrun wages). Other examples of famines without significant (or any) decline in food availability can be found, and there is nothing particularly surprising about this fact once it is recognized that the availability of food is only one influence among many on the entitlement of each occupation group. Even when a famine *is* associated with a decline of food availability, the entitlement changes have to be studied to understand the particular nature of the famine, e.g., why one occupation group is hit but not another. The causation of starvation can be sensibly sought in failures of entitlements of the respective groups.

The causal analysis of famines in terms of entitlements also points to possible public policies of prevention. The main economic strategy would have to take the form of increasing the entitlements of the deprived groups, and in general, of guaranteeing minimum entitlements for everyone, paying particular attention to the vulnerable groups. This can, in the long run, be done in many different ways, involving both economic growth (including growth of food output) and distributional adjustments. Some of these policies may, however, require that the property rights and the corresponding entitlements of the more prosperous groups be violated. The problem, in fact, is particularly acute in the short run, since it may not be possible to engineer rapid economic growth instantly. Then the burden of raising entitlements of the groups in distress would largely have to fall on reducing the entitlements of others more favorably placed. Transfers of income or commodities through various public policies may well be effective in quashing a famine (as the experience of famine relief in different countries has shown), but it may require substantial government intervention in the entitlements of the more prosperous groups.

There is, however, no great moral dilemma in this if property rights are treated as purely *instrumental*. If the goals of relief of hunger and poverty are sufficiently powerful, then it would be just right to violate whatever property rights come in the way, since—in this view—property rights have no intrinsic status. On the other hand, if property rights are taken to be morally inviolable irrespective of their consequences, then it will follow that these policies cannot be morally acceptable even though they might save thousands, or even millions, from dying. The inflexible moral "constraint" of respecting people's legitimately acquired entitlements would rule out such policies.

In fact this type of problem presents a reductio ad absurdum of the moral validity of constraint-based entitlement systems. However, while the conclusions to be derived from that approach might well be "absurd," the situation postulated is not an imaginary one at all. It is based on studies of actual famines and the role of entitlement failures in the causation of mass starvation. If there is an embarrassment here, it belongs solidly to the consequence-independent way of seeing rights.

I should add that this dilemma does not arise from regarding property rights to be of intrinsic value, which can be criticized on other grounds, but not this one. Even if property rights *are* of intrinsic value, their violation may be justified on grounds of the favorable consequences of that violation. A right, as was mentioned earlier, may be intrinsically valuable and still be justly violated taking everything into account. The "absurdum" does not belong to attaching intrinsic value to property rights, but to regarding these rights as simply acceptable, regardless of their consequences. A moral system that values both property rights and other goals— such as avoiding famines and starvation, or fulfilling people's right not to be hungry—can, on the one hand, give property rights intrinsic importance, and on the other, recommend the violation of property rights when that leads to better overall consequences (*including* the disvalue of rights violation).

The issue here is not the valuing of property rights, but their alleged inviolability. There is no dilemma here either for the purely instrumental view of property rights or for treating the fulfillment of property rights as one goal among many, but specifically for consequence-independent assertions of property rights and for the corresponding constraint-based approaches to moral entitlement of ownership.

That property and hunger are closely related cannot possibly come as a great surprise. Hunger is primarily associated with not owning enough food and thus property rights over food are immediately and directly involved. Fights over that property right can be a major part of the reality of a poor country, and any system of moral assessment has to take note of that phenomenon. The tendency to see hunger in purely technocratic terms of food output and availability may help to hide the crucial role of entitlements in the genesis of hunger, but a fuller economic analysis cannot overlook that crucial role. Since property rights over food are derived from property rights over other goods and resources (through production and trade), the entire system of rights of acquisition and transfer is implicated in the emergence and survival of hunger and starvation.

THE RIGHT NOT TO BE HUNGRY

Property rights have been championed for a long time. In contrast, the assertion of "the right not to be hungry" is a comparatively recent phenomenon. While this right is much invoked in political debates, there is a good deal of skepticism about treating this as truly a right in any substantial way. It is often asserted that this concept of "right not to be hungry" stands essentially for nothing at all ("simple nonsense," as Bentham called "natural rights" in general). That piece of sophisticated cynicism reveals not so much a penetrating insight into the practical affairs of the world, but a refusal to investigate what people mean when they assert the existence of rights that, for the bulk of humanity, are not in fact guaranteed by the existing institutional arrangements.

The right not to be hungry is not asserted as a recognition of an institutional right that already exists, as the right to property typically is. The assertion is primarily a moral claim as to what should be valued, and what institutional structure we should aim for, and try to guarantee if feasible. It can also be seen in terms of Ronald Dworkin's category of "background rights—rights that provide a justification for political decisions by society in abstract."[3] This interpretation serves as the basis for a reason to change the existing institutional structure and state policy.

It is broadly in this form that the right to "an adequate means of livelihood" is referred to in the Constitution of India: "The state shall, in particular, direct its policy towards securing . . . that the citizens, men and women equally, have the right to an adequate means of livelihood." This does not, of course, offer to each citizen a guaranteed right to an adequate livelihood, but the state is asked to take steps such that this right could become realizable for all.

In fact, this right has often been invoked in political debates in India. The electoral politics of India does indeed give particular scope for such use of what are seen as background rights. It is, of course, not altogether clear whether the reference to this right in the Indian constitution has in fact materially influenced the political debates. The constitutional statement is often cited, but very likely this issue would have figured in any case in these debates, given the nature of the moral and political concern. But whatever the constitutional contribution, it is interesting to ask whether the implicit acceptance of the value of the right to freedom from hunger makes any difference to actual policy.

It can be argued that the general acceptance of the right of freedom from acute hunger as a major goal has played quite a substantial role in preventing famines in India. The last real famine in India was in 1943, and while food availability per head in India has risen only rather slowly (even now the food availability per head is no higher than in many sub-Saharan countries stricken by recurrent famines), the country has not experienced any famine since independence in 1947. The main cause of that success is a policy of public intervention. Whenever a famine has threatened, a public policy of intervention and relief has offered minimum entitlements to the potential famine victims, and thus have the threatening famines been averted. It can be argued that the quickness of the response of the respective governments (both state and central) reflects a political necessity, given the Indian electoral system and the importance attached by the public to the prevention of starvation. Political pressures from opposition groups and the news media have kept the respective governments on their toes, and the right to be free from acute hunger and starvation has been achieved largely because it has been seen as a valuable right. Thus the recognition of the intrinsic moral importance of this right, which has been widely invoked in public discussions, has served as a powerful political instrument as well.

On the other hand, this process has been far from effective in tackling pervasive and persistent undernourishment in India. There has been no famine in post-independence India, but perhaps a third of India's rural population is perennially undernourished. So long as hunger remains non-acute and starvation deaths are avoided (even though morbidity and mortality rates are enhanced by undernourishment), the need for a policy response is neither much discussed by the news media, nor forcefully demanded even by opposition parties. The elimination of famines coexists with the survival of widespread "regular hunger." The right to "adequate means" of *nourishment* does not at all seem to arouse political concern in a way that the right to "adequate means" to *avoid starvation* does.

The contrast can be due to one of several different reasons. It could, of course, simply be that the ability to avoid undernourishment is not socially accepted as very important. This could be so, though what is socially accepted and what is not is also partly a matter of how clearly the questions are posed. It is, in fact, quite possible that the freedom in question would be regarded as a morally important right if the question were posed in a transparent way, but this does not happen because of the nature of Indian electoral politics and that of news coverage. The issue is certainly not "dramatic" in the way in which starvation deaths and threatening famines are.

Continued low-key misery may be too familiar a phenomenon to make it worthwhile for political leaders to get some mileage out of it in practical politics. The news media may also find little profit in emphasizing a non-spectacular phenomenon—the quiet survival of disciplined, non-acute hunger.

If this is indeed the case, then the implications for action of the goal of eliminating hunger, or guaranteeing to all the means for achieving this, may be quite complex. The political case for making the quiet hunger less quiet and more troublesome for governments in power is certainly relevant. Aggressive political journalism might prove to have an instrumental moral value if it were able to go beyond reporting the horrors of visible starvation and to portray the pervasive, non-acute hunger in a more dramatic and telling way. This is obviously not the place to discuss the instrumentalities of practical politics, but the endorsement of the moral right to be free from hunger—both acute and non-acute—would in fact raise pointed questions about the means which might be used to pursue such a goal. . . .

NOTES

1 This is presented as a "Directive Principle of State Policy." It does not have a direct operational role in the working of the Indian legal system, but it has considerable political force.
2 Robert Nozick, *Anarchy, State, and Utopia* (New York: Basic, 1974), pp. ix, 166.
3 Ronald Dworkin, *Taking Rights Seriously* (Cambridge, Mass.: Harvard University Press, 1977), p. 93.

QUESTIONS

1 Sen maintains that property rights may be overriden in order to prevent hunger, malnutrition, and poverty. Does he provide adequate supporting reasons for his claim?
2 Should the right not to be hungry be institutionalized in any society that purports to be a just society?

Two Reflections on the First United Nations Millennium Development Goal

Thomas Pogge

The first and most prominent development goal stated in the *United Nations* (UN) *Millennium Development Declaration* (2000) was "to halve, by the year 2015, the proportion of the world's people whose income is less than one dollar a day and

Reprinted with permission of the author and Taylor & Francis Ltd. from *Journal of Human Development* (www.tandf.co.uk/journals), vol. 5, no. 3 (November 2004), pp. 385–392.

the proportion of people who suffer from hunger." On Pogge's analysis of this goal, as discussed in the introduction to this chapter, the actual goal is to reduce the number of those living in extreme poverty (below one dollar per day) by 19 percent by 2015, from 1,094 million in 2000 to 883.5 million. Pogge sees this goal as grossly inadequate and morally reprehensible, given the magnitude of the problem and the resources possessed by affluent countries. In his first reflection, Pogge presents information about the catastrophic extent of world poverty before addressing and rebutting the claims of those who maintain that the cost of any more ambitious program would be too high. In his second reflection, Pogge makes two claims regarding affluent nations' responsibility for world poverty: (1) Both the great privileges of those in affluent nations and the extreme poverty of others arose through a historical process that was pervaded by unimaginable crimes. (2) Affluent nations use their economic, technological, and military advantages to impose a global institutional order that is manifestly and grievously unjust. In conclusion, Pogge responds to two objections raised by those who reject these two claims.

REFLECTION [ONE]—ON THE SPEED
AND COST OF ALLEVIATING POVERTY

However little may be known about income poverty trends, we certainly know that the problem of world poverty is catastrophic. According to the official statistics, about:

- 799 million are undernourished (UNDP, 2003, p. 87);
- 1000 million lack access to safe drinking water *(ibid., p. 9)*;
- 2400 million lack basic sanitation *(ibid.)*;
- 880 million have no access to basic medical care (UNDP, 1999, p. 22);
- 1000 million lack adequate shelter (UNDP, 1998, p. 49);
- 2000 million have no electricity *(ibid.)*;
- 876 million adults are illiterate (UNDP, 2003, p. 6);
- 250 million children (aged 5–14 years) do wage work outside their family, at least 8.4 million of them in the "unconditionally worst" forms of child labor, which involve slavery, forced or bonded labor, forced recruitment for use in armed conflict, forced prostitution or pornography, or the production or trafficking of illegal drugs (International Labour Organisation, 2002, pp. 9, 11, 17, 18); and
- "Worldwide 34,000 children under age five die daily from hunger and preventable diseases" (USDA, 1999a, iii). Nearly one-third of all human deaths— some 18 million per year or 50,000 daily—are due to poverty-related causes (such as starvation, diarrhea, pneumonia, tuberculosis, measles, malaria, perinatal and maternal conditions) that could be prevented or cured cheaply through food, safe drinking water, vaccinations, rehydration packs, medicines, or better sanitation and hygiene (World Health Organisation, 2004, Annex Table 2). Women and girls are substantially over-represented among those suffering these deprivations (UNDP, 2003, pp. 310–330).

At 18 million per year, the global poverty death toll over the 15 years since the end of the Cold War was around 270 million, roughly the population of the United States. If the magnitude of the world poverty problem remains constant, the poverty death toll for the period from the *Millennium Declaration* [2000] to 2015 will likewise be about 270 million. Of course, this UN *Declaration* is a commitment to reduce the number of extremely poor, and hence presumably also the number of poverty deaths, by 19%. If all goes according to plan, we may then gradually reach an annual poverty death toll of 14 million in 2015, with 'only' 240 million deaths from poverty-related causes in the 2000–2015 period. Is this really a morally acceptable plan? A plan to be celebrated?

Consider some of the other catastrophes of the past century. The genocide in Rwanda, for example, when the UN and the rest of the world stood idly by while some 800,000 people were hacked to death. . . . Suppose some US politician had said, in April 1994, that the genocide in Rwanda is really terrible and that the world's governments should commit themselves to reducing the slaughter by 19% by the year 2009. How would this have been received? Or suppose a US politician had said, in 1942, that the German concentration camps are morally intolerable and that the world's governments should aim to achieve a 19% reduction in the population of these camps by the year 1957. . . . People would have been absolutely horrified by such a proposal.

So why were we not similarly horrified when the world's politicians proposed, in 2000, to reduce extreme poverty so that, 15 years later, the number it affects will have declined from 1094 million to 883.5 million and the annual death toll from 18 million to 14 million? Why do we greet such a proposal with celebration and self-congratulations?

Some would respond that the reason is cost. We simply cannot solve the problem any faster without huge costs to the cultures and economies of the advanced industrialized countries. They will admit that fighting the Nazis was quite costly too, and that decent people, even ones not themselves under threat, were nonetheless convinced that the Nazis simply had to be stopped, with all deliberate speed. But the cost of fighting world poverty, they may say, is much greater still. As Richard Rorty puts it, "the rich parts of the world may be in the position of somebody proposing to share her one loaf of bread with a hundred starving people. Even if she does share, everybody, including herself, will starve anyway" (1996, p. 10). How could it be wrong to refuse such a pointless course of self-sacrifice?

This response rests on a misconception. However immense the world poverty problem is in human terms, it is amazingly tiny in economic terms. Using the World Bank's poverty estimates, we can get a very rough sense of what the aggregate income is of all the people the Bank considers extremely poor. Assessed at market exchange rates, these 1092.7 million people together live on about $100 billion annually and would need some $40 billion more per year to reach the Bank's $ 1/day benchmark.[1]

To be sure, the Bank's IPL [the WTO's international poverty line of one dollar per day] is too low. So let us look at the Bank's statistics about those living on less than twice its IPL. Assessed at market exchange rates, these 2735.6 million people (nearly one-half of humankind) together live on about $406 billion annually and would need some $294 billion more per year to reach the $2/day benchmark.[2] How large are these amounts?

Start with the former: the collective income of the $2/day-poor. These $406 billion constitute about 1.3% of the annual global social product of ca. $31,500 billion. With only one-third as many people, the rich countries, by contrast, have over 60 times as much income: 81% of the global social product (World Bank, 2003, p. 235).

Consider the second amount, the additional annual income of $294 billion that the presently poor would need in order to reach the $2/day benchmark. This is 1.15% (1/87th) of the $25,506 billion annual aggregate national incomes of the rich countries *(ibid.)*.

This $294 billion also is only about 40% of what the world is spending this year just on crude oil. It is well below the military budget of the United States alone. And it is far less also than the so-called peace dividend, which the rich countries reaped when they reduced their military spending after the end of the Cold War. Rorty's idea that universal starvation would result from an all-out effort to eradicate world poverty completely is simply preposterous.

While the $294 billion is quite small relative to our means, it is also four times larger than what the rich countries are actually spending on official development assistance (ODA). Initially meant to reach 1%, later 0.7%, of the rich countries' Gross National Product, actual ODA has steadily fallen throughout the prosperous 1990s, from 0.33% to 0.22% of the rich countries' aggregate Gross National Product—mainly through a drop from 0.21% to 0.10% in the United States, which has nearly one-third of the entire global social product (UNDP, 2002, p. 202). Moreover, most ODA is spent for the benefit of agents capable of reciprocation: only 23% goes to the 49 least developed countries. While India receives about $1.50 annually per citizen, high-income countries like the Czech Republic, Malta, Cyprus, Bahrain, and Israel receive between $40 and $132 per citizen annually (UNDP, 2002, pp. 203–205). A large part of ODA is allocated to support exporters at home or small affluent elites abroad, and only a tiny fraction, $4.31 billion, goes for 'basic social services' targeted on the poor. . . .

To be sure, some affluent countries do much better than the average, and five small ones—Norway, Sweden, Denmark, Luxembourg, and the Netherlands— come close to fulfilling their obligations (UNDP, 2003, p. 290). If the other affluent countries spent as much on ODA as these five and focused their ODA sharply on poverty eradication (notably including basic health care and education), then severe poverty worldwide could be essentially eliminated by 2015, if not before.

Many human beings live in severe poverty, lacking secure access to basic necessities. This is nothing new. What is new is that global inequality has increased to such an extent that such poverty is now completely avoidable at a cost that would barely be felt in the affluent countries.

REFLECTION [TWO]—ON POSITIVE AND NEGATIVE
RESPONSIBILITY, BENEFITING VERSUS NOT HARMING

The hypothetical of US politicians proposing a planned 19% reduction over 15 years in response to the mass deaths in Germany or Rwanda suggested that the go-slow approach adopted and celebrated by the world's privileged today is morally no better than such a hypothetical go-slow approach would have been in 1942 or 1994.

The fact that a real effort toward eradicating severe poverty worldwide would be much less costly than the defeat of Nazi Germany suggests that the present go-slow approach against world poverty may actually be morally worse than the hypothetical go-slow approach against the Nazi concentration camps: it is for the sake of *small* gains that the world's affluent elites are refusing to undertake a much more substantial push against world poverty.

My [second] . . . reflection will highlight an additional asymmetry. The US bore no significant responsibility for the existence of the Nazi death camps; and the (hypothetical) commitment to reduce them by 19% over 15 years was then responsive to a merely positive duty to assist innocent persons at risk. The governments and citizens of today's affluent countries conceive of their relation to world poverty analogously: we tend to believe that we bear no significant responsibility for the existence of this problem and that our only moral reason to help alleviate it is our merely positive duty to assist innocent persons caught in a life-threatening emergency. This belief, however, is highly questionable.

Our world is marked by enormous inequalities in economic starting places. Some are born into abject poverty with a 30% chance of dying before their fifth birthday. Others are born into the civilized luxury of the Western middle class. These huge inequalities have evolved in the course of *one* historical process that was pervaded by monumental crimes of slavery, colonialism, and genocide—crimes that have devastated the populations, cultures, and social institutions of four continents.

The privileged of today are quick to point out that they had nothing to do with these crimes and that they should not be held to account for the sins of their forefathers. And right they are! But if they cannot inherit their ancestors' sins, then why can they inherit the *fruits* of those sins, the huge economic superiority prevailing at the end of the colonial period? In 1960, when most former colonies gained their independence, the inequality in per-capita income between Europe and Africa, for example, was 30:1. Foreign rule was removed. But the great inequality built up in the colonial period was left intact, making for a very unequal start into the post-colonial era.

One may think that the situation in 1960 is too long ago to contribute much to the explanation of severe poverty today. But consider what a 30:1 inequality means. Even if Africa had consistently achieved growth in per-capita income one full percentage point higher than Europe, this inequality ratio would still be nearly 20:1 today. At that rate, Africa would be catching up with Europe at the beginning of the twenty-fourth century.

Consider also the impact such huge inequalities have in negotiations about the terms of trade. With the exception of a few giants, such as China and India, poor countries have little bargaining power in international negotiations and also cannot afford the expertise needed to represent their interests effectively. (Such expertise can be quite costly. . . . [T]he initial World Trade Organisation [WTO] Treaty weighed in at 400 lbs or 26,000 pages.) As a result, they typically end up with a lousy deal. They opened their markets widely to foreign companies, paid royalties to foreign firms for films, music, drugs, and even seeds—and still found their own exports severely hampered by rich-country quotas, tariffs, anti-dumping duties as well as subsidies and export credits to domestic producers, all of which were somehow exempted from the supposed Big Move to free and open markets. Such asymmetries in the terms of trade surely play a role in explaining why the inequality in per-capita income between Europe and Africa has not declined, but has rather increased considerably since the end of the colonial period, standing today at roughly 40:1.

When they influence the design of common rules, pre-existing inequalities tend to be preserved and often aggravated. This phenomenon is evident within national societies, in which economic inequality tends to be quite stable over time. High inequality in Latin America and the United States persists over time, just as low inequality does in Scandinavia and Japan. Such stable diversity suggests that inequality is path dependent—that high inequality tends to reproduce itself because it gives the rich much greater power and also much stronger incentives to shape the common rules in their favor. Within national societies, one-person–one-vote democracy may mitigate the tendency for large inequalities to expand more and more. But there are no democratic practices the global poor might use to affect the economic rules beyond their own society. Even 85% of humankind, united, could not amend the WTO system.

The affluent countries and their citizens are then implicated in world poverty in two ways. We are implicated, first, because *our* great privileges and advantage as well as *their* extreme poverty and disadvantage have emerged through *one* historical process that was pervaded by unimaginable crimes. To be sure, we bear absolutely no moral responsibility for these crimes, even if we are direct descendants of people who do. Still, we are at fault for continuing to enforce the extreme inequalities that emerged in the course of that deeply unjust historical process.

Second, and independently, we are implicated because we are using our economic, technological, and military advantages to impose a global institutional order that is manifestly and grievously unjust. How do I know this order is unjust? Simply by the fact that an alternative global order would avoid most of the suffering that foreseeably persists under the present order: one-half of humankind living in abject poverty and 18 million dying annually from poverty-related causes. By imposing this grievously unjust global order upon the rest of the world, the affluent countries, in collaboration with the so-called elites of the developing countries, are harming the global poor—to put it mildly. To put it less mildly, the imposition of this global order constitutes the largest (although not the gravest) crime against humanity ever committed.

Most of those who reject this view are misled by either of two thoughts, which I will briefly address in conclusion. One thought is that our global institutional order cannot possibly be harming the global poor when severe poverty worldwide is in decline. This thought is powerfully reinforced by the lively debate about globalization in which statements about the global poverty trend, about being 'on track' toward the first UN MDG, have come to play a pivotal role.

. . . [I]t is by no means clear that severe poverty is in decline globally. But assume that it is. It does not follow that the existing global order is not harming the poor. After all, severe poverty may be going down not *because of*, but *despite* this order. Just as a boat may make progress even against a strong current or headwind, so the global poor may be making progress even against global rule-making processes that are slanted against them.

Moreover, even if the global institutional order were having a poverty-reducing effect, it might still be harming the global poor severely. Think of a slave-holding society, like the United States in its first 90 years. Suppose its institutional order, by raising overall prosperity, was gradually improving the slaves' condition. Does it follow that this order was not harmful to those whose enslavement it authorized and enforced? Or does a gradual improvement in the condition of those condemned to serfdom or corvée labor in feudal Russia or France really show that they were not harmed by this imposition? Obviously not! Obviously, whether an institutional order is harming people in the morally relevant sense depends not on a diachronic comparison with an earlier time, but on a counterfactual comparison with its feasible institutional alternatives. Most citizens of the affluent countries take comfort in the asserted decline of global poverty, thinking of themselves as benefactors of the global poor in the belief that the global institutional order they impose kills and scars fewer people each year. They should instead take intense discomfort in the fact that a feasible alternative global order could have avoided most life-threatening poverty and its associated evils.

The other misleading thought is that severe poverty today must be traced back to causal factors that are domestic to the countries in which it persists. This seems self-evident from the fact that severe poverty has evolved very differently in different countries—rapidly melting away in Japan, the Asian Tigers, and more recently China, while greatly worsening in Africa. Since all these countries were developing under the same global institutional order, this order cannot be at fault for the persistence of massive severe poverty in some of them.

Now it is true that there are great international variations in the evolution of severe poverty. And it is true that these variations must be caused by local (typically country-specific) factors. But it does not follow that these must be the only causally relevant factors, that global factors are irrelevant.

To see the fallacy, consider this parallel: there are great variations in the performance of my students. These variations must be caused by local (student-specific) factors. These factors, together, fully explain the overall performance of my class. Clearly, this parallel reasoning results in a falsehood: the overall performance of my class also crucially depends on the quality of my teaching and on various other 'global' factors besides. This shows that the inference is invalid.

To see this more precisely, one must distinguish two questions about the evolution of severe poverty. One concerns the observed variation in national trajectories. In the answer to this question, local factors must play a central role. Yet, however full and correct, this answer may not suffice to answer the other question, which concerns the overall evolution of poverty worldwide: even if student-specific factors explain observed variations in the performance of my students, the quality of my teaching may still play a major role in explaining why they did not on the whole do much better or worse than they actually did. Likewise, even if country-specific factors fully explain the observed variations in the economic performance of developing countries, global factors may still play a major role in explaining why they did not on the whole do much better or worse than they in fact did.

Many aspects of the global institutional order have such causal relevance. I have already mentioned the protectionist quotas, tariffs, anti-dumping duties, subsidies and export credits that the rich countries allowed themselves under WTO rules. Likewise, the absence of a global minimum wage and minimal global constraints on working hours and working conditions fosters a 'race to the bottom' where the ruling elites of poor countries, competing for foreign investment, are outbidding one another by offering ever more exploitable and mistreatable workforces.

Another important example is the global pharmaceutical regime, which rewards the inventors of new drugs by allowing them to charge monopoly prices for 20 years. These rules price most existing drugs out of the reach of the global poor. And they also skew medical research toward the affluent: medical conditions accounting for 90% of the global disease burden receive only 10% of all medical research world-wide. Of the 1393 new drugs approved between 1975 and 1999, only 13 were specifically indicated for tropical diseases (Médecins Sans Frontières, 2001, pp. 10–11). Millions of annual deaths could be avoided if rewards for medical research were based instead on its impact on the global disease burden. Such incentives could be funded, for instance, through a global 'Polluter Pays' regime that raises funds from countries in proportion to their citizens' and corporations' contributions to transnational environmental pollution. This would replace the current rules under which the more industrialized countries can pollute the oceans and atmosphere at will, thereby imposing much of the cost of their prosperity on the rest of the world, with the global poor generally benefiting least and being least able to protect themselves from the effects of pollution.

Global institutional factors also play an important role in sustaining many of the country-specific factors commonly adduced to explain the persistence of poverty. Thus, Rawls is quite right that when societies fail to thrive, "the problem is commonly the nature of the public political culture and the religious and philosophical traditions that underlie its institutions. The great social evils in poorer societies are likely to be oppressive government and corrupt elites" (1993, p. 77). But Rawls completely fails to note that such oppression and corruption are very substantially encouraged and sustained by global factors such as the international resource and borrowing privileges (Pogge, 2002, chapter 4), the still poorly policed bribe-paying practices of multinational corporations and the international arms trade.

This point also puts into perspective the popular cliché that membership in the WTO (and other international organizations) is voluntary. Yes, voluntary for a country's rulers. But not for the ruled. Nigeria's accession to the WTO was effected by its brutal dictator Sani Abacha, Myanmar's by the notorious SLORC (State Law and Order Restoration Council) junta, Indonesia's by kleptocrat Suharto, Zimbabwe's by Robert Mugabe, the Congo's (then named Zaire) by Mobutu Sese Seko, and so on.

Reflection two . . . supports the conclusion that the affluent countries, partly through the global institutional order they impose, bear a great causal and moral responsibility for the massive global persistence of severe poverty. Citizens of these countries thus have not merely a positive duty to assist innocent persons mired in life-threatening poverty, but also a more stringent negative duty to work politically and personally toward ceasing, or compensating for, their contribution to this ongoing catastrophe. . . .

NOTES

1 These figures are rough estimates derived as follows. If all people with incomes below $1/day were exactly at this benchmark, then the purchasing power of their collective annual income would be that of $430 billion in the US in 1993 ($32.74 × 12 months × 1092.7 million), which corresponds to the purchasing power of $560 billion in 2004 (www.bls.gov/cpi/home.htm). Yet, those who are extremely poor in this sense live, on average 28.4% below the $1/day benchmark (Chen and Ravallion, 2004, Tables 3 and 6; dividing the poverty gap index by the headcount index). So they have collective annual income with aggregate purchasing power of about $400 billion and would need additional annual income with aggregate purchasing power of about $160 billion annually for all of them to reach the Bank's $1/day benchmark. I divide these two figures by 4 to adjust for the fact that the purchasing power the Bank ascribes to the incomes of very poor people is, on average, at least four times greater than their value at market exchange rates. Thus the World Bank equates India's per-capita gross national income of $460 to $2450 PPP, China's $890 to $4260 PPP, Nigeria's $290 to $830 PPP, Pakistan's $420 to $1920 PPP, Bangladesh's $370 to $1680 PPP, Ethiopia's $100 to $710 PPP, Vietnam's $410 to $2130 PPP, and so on (World Bank, 2003, pp. 234–235).

2 These estimates are derived analogously. If all people with incomes below '2/day' were exactly at this benchmark, then the purchasing power of their collective annual income would be that of $2150 billion in the United States in 1993 ($65.48 × 12 months × 2735.6 million), which corresponds to the purchasing power of $2800 billion in 2004 (www.bls.gov/cpi/home.htm). Those who are poor in this sense live, on average, 42% below the $2/day benchmark (Chen and Ravallion, 2004, Tables 3 and 6; again dividing the poverty gap index by the headcount index). So they have collective annual income with aggregate purchasing power of about $1624 billion and would need additional annual income with aggregate purchasing power of about $1176 billion annually for all of them to reach the Bank's $2/day benchmark. I again divide both figures by 4 to estimate what these amounts come to at market exchange rates.

REFERENCES

International Labour Organisation (2002) *A Future without Child Labour,* International Labour Office, Geneva (also available through www.ilo.org).

Médecins Sans Frontiéres (2001) *Fatal Imbalance: The Crisis in Research and Development for Drugs for Neglected Diseases,* Médecins Sans Frontiéres, Geneva.

Pogge, T. (2002) *World Poverty and Human Rights,* Polity Press, Cambridge.

Rawls, J. (1993) 'The law of peoples', in S. Shute and S. Hurley (Eds.), *On Human Rights,* Basic Books, New York.

Rorty, R. (1996) 'Who are we? Moral universalism and economic triage', *Diogenes,* 173, pp. 5–15.

United Nations Development Programme (UNDP) (1998) *Human Development Report 1998,* Oxford University Press, New York.

UNDP (1999) *Human Development Report 1999,* Oxford University Press, New York.

UNDP (2002) *Human Development Report 2002,* Oxford University Press, New York.

UNDP (2003) *Human Development Report 2003,* Oxford University Press, New York.

United States Department of Agriculture (USDA)(1999a) *U.S. Action Plan on Food Security,* USDA, Washington, DC (www.fas.usda.gov/icd/summit/usactplan.pdf).

World Health Organisation (2004) *The World Health Report 2004,* WHO Publications, Geneva (www.who.int/whr/2004).

World Bank (2003) *World Development Report 2003,* Oxford University Press, New York.

QUESTIONS

1 Mindful of Pogge's analysis, what criticisms can you develop of Hardin's arguments in general and his lifeboat metaphor in particular?

2 What should be the UN's goal regarding the alleviation of extreme poverty by the year 2015?

Western Ethical Imperialism?

Max Borders

Borders raises a number of questions about first-world criticisms of the working conditions in foreign-owned factories in developing countries. He argues that we need to look at the situation from the perspective of people in the developing nations rather than simply applying first-world standards.

Almost daily, we are treated to stories about ghastly working conditions in the developing world. No minimum wage. No labor laws. No safety regulations. It's hot. It's cramped. Days are long. Breaks are short. It must be awful.

Some say globalization is the problem because it spreads without regard for the plight of those laborers who enable it to spread. In the parlance of the Marxist, people are being exploited by corporations in search of profit—and third world governments either can't keep up or are receiving kickbacks from the companies doing the exploiting.

It's true. Many of these conditions may truly be horrible by our western lights. Those of us who have benefited from air conditioning and indoor plumbing our entire lives can't imagine working more than twelve hours in a place where literally everyone is sweating. But have you talked to your grandparents about what life was like for them? Maybe your great grandparents? They may have a different story to tell about sweat and toil in a time when America and Europe were still developing.

In any case, we are seldom treated to the other side of the globalization story, especially the story about the indigenous people who actually want to work in these places. For example, consider:

- A 2004 story from a Hong Kong newspaper *Ming Pao*,[1] (via this Asian Labor blog,[2]) tells of riots by laborers in a Nike factory demanding more working hours. (Nike, due to pressure by western labor groups seeking "social justice," had begun limiting working hours.) Were these Taiwanese workers having their livelihoods undermined by a Western activist ethos? Sadly, it appears this story never made the English-speaking press.

Reprinted with permission of the author from the website of AWorldConnected, Institute for Humane Studies, George Mason University (www.aworldconnected.org), 2005.

- A story from Tomas Larrson's *A Race to the Top*,[3] demonstrates how child labor laws resulted in terrible unintended consequences: "The celebrated French ban on soccer balls sewn in Pakistan for the World Cup in 1998 resulted in significant dislocation of children from employment. Those who tracked them found that a large proportion ended up begging and/or in prostitution."[4] Begging? Prostitution? Surely factory work is better for families in countries struggling to achieve universal secondary education.
- Glenn Garvin's work for the *Miami Herald* detailed conditions in a Nicaraguan free trade zone, where Nicaraguans insisted "we need these jobs" after activists tried to pressure companies to close down due to "deplorable" conditions. "These may not be very good jobs in the United States," said Nicaraguan trade official Gilberto Wong, "but they're great jobs for Nicaragua. If we lose them, it will be a terrible blow." Working conditions are deplorable everywhere in Nicaragua, not just in the foreign-owned factories.[5]

People want to belong to noble causes. . . . But many college students, for example, believe they are doing good when they insist that their university sweatshirts and memorabilia come from non-sweatshop labor. Consider this excerpt from the USAS:

> United Students Against Sweatshops is an international student movement of campuses and individual students fighting for sweatshop free labor conditions and workers' rights. We define "sweatshop" broadly and recognize that it is not limited to the apparel industry, but everywhere among us. We believe that university standards should be brought in line with those of its students who demand that their school's logo is emblazoned on clothing made in decent working conditions.[6]

Might one reasonably ask: what are "decent" working conditions to an American college student who has not likely had to work much beyond a summer at Chili's? Do such students realize what sorts of alternatives are available to the poorest people of the world?

The problem lies in what we may think of as "ethical" here in the comfortable West. But people in the developing world live very different lives, and we have to try and look at things from their perspective. If Jose works for $0.45 per hour, that sounds terrible to us. But what are his peers earning on average? In the Glenn Garvin series cited above, factory workers made as much or more than the police. $0.45 per hour has a lot more purchasing power in Nicaragua than in Nantucket, so figures like that don't really make much sense until we understand the context. In other words, we have to consider the costs of living relative to a country—along with a number of other factors.[7]

Suppose more "socially responsible" companies were to offer more money and US-style working standards to their employees. Would the companies be able to give as many people the opportunity to work? After all, the labor (not to mention the regulatory costs) would be more expensive, so it would be more difficult for the company to grow. Furthermore, might local people wonder why factory employees now get, say, $0.50 per hour instead of $0.45—(which is already five cents more per hour than the police make!)

As the developing world continues to grow, laborers will have more bargaining power—both in terms of hours, pay, and working conditions. But they will not be able to get such power until they develop further economically. If we expect them to go from nothing to Western working conditions and pay immediately, we are only hurting them with our naïveté. (We may also be hurting poor people here at home who benefit from cheaper goods.)

These are difficult issues. When we think about the lives of people in poor countries, it can be disturbing. Maybe the best thing we can do in the rich, developed world is to try and understand the realities of our developing world counterparts. Maybe we should believe them when they tell us "we want these jobs." And while we might bristle at the idea of having to work in sweatshop conditions ourselves, we might also consider what an opportunity looks like for someone with very limited options living in one of the poorest parts of the world.

NOTES

1 http://www.mingpaonews.com.
2 Stephen Frost, "China Workers Riot for the Right to Work Overtime." http://www. asianlabour.org).
3 Tomas Larrson, *A Race to the Top* (Washington, D.C.: Cato Institute, 2001), p. 48.
4. Thomas DeGregori, "Child Labor or Prostitution?" (http://www.aworldconnected.com), October 8, 2002.
5 Glenn Garvin, "We Need These Jobs, *The Miami Herald,* November 30, 1997.
6 http://www.studentsagainstsweatshops.org.
7 Richard M. Ebeling, "Titled Real Estate" (http://www.aworldconnected.org).

QUESTIONS

1 What moral standards should be applied in our evaluations of working conditions in third-world countries?
2 Should we refuse to purchase goods made by workers who are subjected to inhumane working conditions?

A Consensus Statement on Sweatshop Abuse
United Trauma Relief

This document focuses on an assumption made by those who object to antisweatshop actions: International sweatshops are currently an economic necessity that, given economic development, will cease to exist. Several arguments defending international sweatshops are examined and rebutted.

http://web.mit.edu/utr/www/consensus.doc, August 2001. Reprinted with permission of the principal author, Sanjay Basu.

The term "sweatshop" refers to those factories relying on the exploitation and abuse of workers. Often (although not always) located in developing countries, these factories have been frequented by independent university researchers, who have published numerous accounts of worker imprisonment and physical abuse, as well as economic evidence revealing that many of these factories pay wages so small that their workers cannot live outside poverty. Several factories use horrific labor practices, and many factory workers have also been severely burned or mutilated in the workplace, while women among the labor population have often been forced to take birth control or abort their pregnancies (Given, 1997; Fernandez, 1997). The health burdens placed upon sweatshop workers have been extensively documented, and include exposure to noxious fumes, organophosphate compounds, and silica dust, resulting in record high cancer, asthma, bronchitis, pneumoconiosis, and leukemia rates in many regions because workers aren't provided with masks and gloves (Kim *et al.*, 2000).

These abuses are neither just nor irremediable, but many people believe that sweatshops are an economic necessity and will come to pass on their own with economic development. Closer examination of both the social and economic dimensions of sweatshop labor, however, reveals this presumption to be far from the truth.

Most objections to anti-sweatshop action stem from the idea that sweatshop jobs are the best opportunities available to people living in poor conditions. "They keep coming back day after day, so they must want these jobs." Trying to make the jobs better will simply mean that fewer jobs will be available, and people dependent on them will suffer. But those who have advanced this "economic" syllogism have ignored much of the evidence to the contrary. Although this idea may appear "intuitive," the reality surrounding the improvement of sweatshop conditions is quite contrary to intuition. Nevertheless, these "intuitive" arguments in support of sweatshops proliferate. Among them:

- "Any job is better than no job. These people would rather work in a sweatshop than starve."

Slavery might also be better than starvation, yet nobody advocates a return to slavery. Just because a bad job may be better than starvation doesn't justify labor abuses such as the beating and raping of workers or the threatening of worker's families—all abuses that have been regularly documented by independent researchers visiting sweatshop factories (Breslow, 1995; Foek, 1997). While accepting that a bad job might be better than nothing, we should continue to fight the abuse of human lives, and even a basic study of history reveals that most human progress as a society has occurred through such struggles for progress, not through maintenance of the status quo. If we justify abuse under the premise that is better than the worst alternative, we create a slippery slope leading down to the complete devaluation of human life. As *New York Times* columnist Bob Herbert, a vocal critic of sweatshop abuse, writes, "What's next, employees who'll work for a bowl of gruel?" (Herbert, 1996).

- "If companies are forced to increase wages or improve conditions, they won't simply pay the same number of workers more. They will relocate to somewhere with fewer restrictions."

The idea that companies will "not like" the improvement of conditions is indeed correct. But, obviously, if corporations were allowed to do whatever they wanted, our world would go to hell. That's precisely the reason we have regulations to mandate what is permissible and what isn't—it's the very reason we have seatbelts in our cars and arsenic limits for our water. The idea that corporations "won't simply pay" is ignorant of the basic idea of a corporate charter. Corporations, in becoming incorporated, are granted a charter by the state under the edict that they are responsible to the state, just like any citizen. The state sets a minimum wage, but one could say that corporations wouldn't "simply pay" that either. Because every corporation is ultimately required to be responsive to the state according to its charter, every corporation is required to pay a minimum wage anyway. Common sense and history argue against the idea that it would be best for corporations to act without any guidelines and have free reign over society. Therefore it's society's responsibility to determine what we allow and what we require of corporations, and corporations, because of the charter they have received, are just as responsible as regular citizens in having to follow law.

Can corporations afford to pay? The statistics speak for themselves: in 1965 the average CEO made 44 times the average factory worker; today, the average CEO makes 212 times the factory worker salary. Michael Eisner of Disney could pay every worker in his Haitian toy factories enough to feed and clothe themselves and their families annually if he would devote just 1% of his advertising budget to worker's salaries (Given, 1997).

As members of society, we should also ask ourselves: should corporations really be allowed to shop around the world for the most easily abused workforce, or should measures be put into place to prevent this abuse altogether? Indeed, such measures are starting to be put in place, and rather than engaging in a "race to the bottom"—a race for corporations to find the most abused workforce to manipulate—international response to the problem is calling for the construction of rules to put the rights of persons before the rights of exploiters (Cholewinski, 1997; Human Rights Watch, 1997; Rosen, Maurren, & Perez-Lopez, 1997). Such is the very nature of human progress through history, and only those who favor exploitation over human well-being are arguing that these rules should not be put into place.

- "Most companies that use sweatshops are actually just contracting through local producers, so they don't have a say in the conditions of factories."

This idea rests on a fundamental fallacy: that large multinational companies (e.g., NIKE, adidas, Jansport) contracting with local producers are helpless entities unable to have an effect on conditions in local factories. Modern evidence, however, disproves such a contention (Ross, 1997). Independent academics have learned that corporations often "squeeze their contractors into paying sub-minimum wages. Large retailers and retail chains pressure contract manufacturers by refusing to pay more than a rock-bottom price for manufacturing orders" (Given, 1997).

Public pressure, history shows, causes many multinationals to pressure local owners to improve working conditions in order to improve their reputations. As Iowa Senator Tom Harkin suggested, in rallying to produce a list of abusers and generate American consumer pressure against them, "Just as human rights organizations such as Amnesty International are able to document cases of human rights abuses and torture around the world, so can the identities of those industries and their host countries that are violating international labor standards . . . be identified" (Harkin, 1996). In fact, agencies have been created to monitor the conditions of such factories, and monitoring combined with public pressure can result in the improvement of such facilities. For example, reacting to public outrage in 1996, Liz Claiborne, NIKE, Phillips-Van Heusen, and L.L. Bean joined into an "Apparel Industry Partnership" to take steps to end sweatshop abuses (Salomon, 1996). Continued pressure will force the compliance of other companies as well.

- "Demands for a living wage will result in fewer workers as tasks will become automated. While those who remain employed will probably be better off, those who lose their jobs will not."

The cost of paying a fair, living wage in many countries is still far lower than the cost of automation. If automation did provide such an advantage, companies would have simply automated American plants, and reaped the many advantages of manufacturing close to home. Instead, they chose not to automate any further, and took advantage of lower wages and a more willing work force abroad. For the most part, the clothing industry is about as automated as is effective, and further automation is not very likely to occur. As a result, paying a living wage is highly unlikely to result in the "economic elite" scenario presented above. As evidenced by interviews with sweatshop workers, laborers are not seeking U.S. or European-level wages; workers in poorer countries want decent workplaces, ones in which they are not constantly threatened by torture or death (Mort, 1996).

- "You are trying to restrict global free trade. This type of trade is the only way to raise people out of poverty, and cause economies to develop. Once economies do develop, sweatshops will cease to exist. In a developed economy, companies will stop abusing their workers and will treat them well."

Those opposed to sweatshops are not trying to prevent trade, but are trying to prevent the abuse that has been justified under the premise of global trade. Protection for workers, and indeed respect for human rights, has never been mutually exclusive with trade (Richburg & Swardson, 1996). Companies should not be permitted to benefit by violating the rights of human beings, and "free trade" has never implied the blacklisting and killing of workers by death squads in Central America, the prevention of union building in Mexico, or the raping and beating of women in Sri Lanka (Human Rights Watch/Asia, 1995). As New York Times columnist Karl Meyer wrote, "We can no longer believe that anything goes in the global marketplace, regardless of social consequences. It is precisely this conviction that underlies efforts to attach human rights conditions to trading relations—to temper the amorality of the market" (Meyer, 1997).

Indeed, evidence against the idea that development necessarily results in improved conditions is abundant in American history. Not only do sweatshops continue to exist (mostly in Los Angeles and New York), but even places of employment that are not considered sweatshops are often far from optimal (Lee & Mitchell, 1998). Many employers, including even Harvard University, still fail to pay a living wage. Workers will continue to be exploited on a global scale until adequate protections are put into place through public pressure. Public pressure resulted in the improvement of sweatshop labor conditions within the American northeast after the industrial revolution; those sweatshops of the late 19th and early 20th centuries virtually disappeared after World War II because of increased public pressure (through programs like the National Consumers League's "White Label" inspections) resulting in government regulation of monopolies and the rise of trade unions (Golodner, 1997). Public pressure is the only insurance that conditions will improve elsewhere. Conditions do not simply improve as a result of economic growth. In El Salvador, for example, 50,000 new sweatshop jobs have been created in the last 10 years, with the country's exports jumping 4,000 percent. But real wages have been halved. "Its women can't afford to buy the clothes they make," says Neil Kearney, president of the International Textile, Garment and Leather Workers Union. "And people who protest are subject to rape and murder" (Clark, 1996).

As Lance Compa, an international labor law professor at Cornell University's School of Industrial and Labor Relations, recently wrote in *The Washington Post:* "After wealth has been created, respecting workers' rights and paying them fairly is still a choice, one that doesn't always depend on economics. Instead, choosing justice for workers is driven by organizing, bargaining and political action, increasingly on an international scale. . . . With a human rights dimension, more trade and investment are a potential source of great good for working people. Genuine comparative advantage for lower-wage countries is something the international community can accept, if it helps poorer nations develop, if wages and conditions can rise and if workers have a voice in society. But artificial advantage based on human rights violations is something else that the international community should stop" (Compa, 2001).

REFERENCES

Breslow, Marc. (1995, November/December). Crimes of Fashion: Those Who Suffer to Bring You Gap T-Shirts. *Dollars and Sense.*

Cholewinski, Ryszard. (1997). *Migrant Workers in International Human Rights Law: Their Protection in Countries of Employment.* New York: Oxford University Press.

Clark, Charles S. (1996). Child Labor and Sweatshops: The Issues. *Congressional Quarterly Researcher.*

Compa, Lance. (2001 July 31). Ensuring a Decent Global Workplace. *The Washington Post.*

Fernandez, Mary Rose. (1997, September). Commodified Women. *Peace Review.*

Foek, Anton. (1997, January/February). Sweatshop Barbie: Exploitation of Third World Labor. *Humanist.*

Given, Olivia. (1997). An Indictment of Sweatshops. In M. E. Williams (Ed.), *Child Labor and Sweatshops* (pp. 21–25). San Diego: Greenhaven.

Golodner, Linda. (1997, October 6). [Lecture] Apparel Industry Code of Conduct: A Consumer Perspective on Responsibility. *Notre Dame Center for Ethics and Religious Values in Business.*

Harkin, Tom. (1996, January). Put an End to the Exploitation of Child Labor. *USA Today Magazine.*

Herbert, Bob. (1996, June 10). Nike's Pyramid Scheme. *The New York Times.*

Human Rights Watch. (1997). *Corporations and Human Rights: Freedom of Association in a Maquila in Guatemala*. New York: Human Rights Watch.

Human Rights Watch/Asia. (1995). *Rape for Profit: Trafficking of Nepali Girls and Women to India's Brothels*. New York: Human Rights Watch, 1995.

Kim, Jim Yong *et al*. (2000). *Dying for Growth: Global Inequality and the Health of the Poor*. Cambridge: Common Courage Press.

Lee, Siu Hin & Mitchell, Celeste. (1998, February). Sweat Shop Workers Struggle in New York's Chinatown. *Z Magazine*.

Meyer, Karl. (1997, June 28). Editorial Notebook. *The New York Times*.

Mort, Jo-Ann. (1996, Fall). Immigrant Dreams: Sweatshop Workers Speak. *Dissent*.

Richburg, Keith B. & Swardson, Anne. (1996, August 5–11). Sweatshops or Economic Development? *Washington Post National Weekly Edition*.

Rosen, Sonia A., Jaffe, Maurren, & Perez-Lopez, Jorge. (1997). *The Apparel Industry and Codes of Conduct: A Solution to the International Child Labor Problems*. Upland, PA: Diane.

Ross, Andrew. (1997). *No Sweat: Fashion, Free Trade, and the Rights of Garment Workers*. New York: Verso.

Salomon, Larry. (1996, September/October). Sweatshops in the Spotlight. *Third Force*.

QUESTIONS

1 Do university students have an obligation to determine whether clothing sold in that university's shops is produced by workers in international sweatshops?
2 Does this consensus statement succeed in countering the various arguments that are often advanced in defense of international sweatshops?

Sweatshops

Matt Zwolinski

Zwolinski first looks at definitions of sweatshops. He holds that in the context of social criticism in which the term arose, the description of a place of employment as a "sweatshop" is best understood as reflecting a judgment regarding the producer's morally unacceptable treatment of employees. Zwolinski next examines the moral questions raised by international sweatshops. Like Borders, he asks whether it is appropriate to apply first-world standards to industries in third-world countries. Zwolinski's discussion focuses on two questions: (1) Are companies who contract with sweatshop manufacturers doing anything wrong? (2) Regardless of whether these companies are acting wrongly, what should we do about the situation of sweatshops? Zwolinski's response to each question is a cautious one. With respect to the first question, he discusses some of the prosweatshop arguments and holds that they are not decisive. With respect to the second question, Zwolinski stresses the need to do careful empirical research before engaging in specific antisweatshop actions to ensure that we adopt the best measures available to help those employed in sweatshops.

INTRODUCTION

The term 'sweatshop' is heavy with emotional, historical, and moral significance. It calls to mind images of women and children working long days in cramped, rat-infested quarters, abused by their supervisors and paid barely enough to survive and work another day. To others it will suggest the horrors of Mexican *maquiladoras,* where young female apparel workers are often subject to sexual harassment from the local supervisors, and punished severely for any attempt to organize.

Perhaps most frighteningly of all, the term suggests that the *responsibility* for these situations falls squarely on the shoulders of the average consumer. By as simple an act as buying a dress for oneself or running shoes for one's children, the story goes, one is providing economic support to the system which leads to the sorts of oppression described above. The only difference between the consumer who buys sweatshop-made products and the supervisor who runs the sweatshop his or her self is physical proximity to the offense. Morally speaking, we are all guilty.

But guilty of what, exactly? The term 'sweatshop' undoubtedly connotes something objectionable. But what precisely are the conditions which have to be met by a business before this term is appropriately applied? What makes a sweatshop a sweatshop?

DEFINITIONS

Unfortunately, the issues surrounding sweatshops and their economic context are so contentious that not even the definition of the term is free from controversy. . . . [T]he term has a historical reference, which picks out a particular method of production in the apparel industry in the early part of the 1900s. But we do not want our definition to rule out the possibility that sweatshops might exist *today,* in *other* industrial contexts. To tie the term 'sweatshop' to a particular industry in a particular historical era is to put too strict a limit on the broader social criticism that term was intended to invoke.

The term also has a legal meaning. The U.S. General Accounting Office defines a sweatshop as "an employer that violates more than one federal or state law governing minimum wage and overtime, child labor, industrial homework, occupational safety and health, workers compensation, or industry regulation." The advantage of this definition is that it provides a clear, quantifiable standard with which to assess the status of sweatshops within the United States, and a basis for pursuing legal action against them. In certain contexts, this definition may be entirely appropriate. Its disadvantage is much the same as that found in the historical definition discussed above—it seems too narrow to serve as a *general* definition. In the history of the United States, many sweatshops existed *prior* to the enactment of many of the worker-protection laws referenced in the GAO's definition.

Does this mean they were not really sweatshops? Similarly, many of today's sweat-shops exist outside of the United States, in countries where legal protection for labor is minimal at best. Often, these companies operate without breaking any of the laws of their home country at all. If we wish to condemn these operations as 'sweatshops,' the legal definition will be inadequate.

Ultimately, then, the precise meaning of the term 'sweatshop' will vary depending on context. Historical and legal definitions have their place, but usually our description of a certain producer as a sweatshop will reflect a *moral* judgment. In other words, it will reflect our judgment that the producer is treating its employees inhumanely, or that it is violating their basic human rights or simple standards of decency. This definition, too, is not without its problems, for it raises a whole host of complicated moral questions such as what moral obligations employers have toward their employees, or what constitutes a fair wage for a day's work. Furthermore, by building moral wrongness into the definition, this approach rules out from the start the question of whether sweatshops might ever be morally permissible. Nevertheless, understanding 'sweatshop' as a moral term seems to best fit the way in which the term has been used in the context of social criticism in which it arose.

MORAL QUESTIONS

For all the controversy that surrounds the issue of sweatshops, one thing is perfectly clear: conditions in sweatshops are usually horrible. There may be debate about *how* horrible conditions are: whether wages are enough to maintain an adequate diet, whether physical abuse takes place in a particular factory, whether manufacturers are living up to their contractual and legal agreements, and so on. But no matter how significant these details may be, they are dwarfed by the broader conclusion: by any first-world standard of decency, sweatshop conditions are atrocious.

But are first-world standards of decency the appropriate standard to apply to industries in third-world countries? Even if we agree that conditions in sweatshops are horrible, we still must answer two important questions in order to reach any settled moral conclusion. First, are companies who contract with sweatshop manufacturers doing anything *wrong*? And second, whether they are wrong or not, what should we *do* about the situation of sweatshops?

Let us begin by considering the first question. Certain individuals, especially economists, have defended sweatshops on the grounds that they currently constitute the best available alternative for people living in developing countries. The wages paid by Nike's firm in Jakarta, they point out, might seem low by U.S. standards, but they are actually fairly high by the standards of the local economy. People freely choose to work at these factories because they can make more money there than they can anywhere else. If Nike were to close down the factory and begin producing exclusively in the United States, the situation of the workers it would have to lay off would not be improved—it would be worsened. They would either need to seek lower-paying employment elsewhere in the legitimate economy, or try to make money by illicit means, often by prostitution or theft.

This argument draws its support from the claim that individuals *choose* to work at sweatshops. If those individuals had a better alternative, they would have taken it.

Of course, this argument only holds where workers are not physically coerced into working at a particular plant. Cases of sweatshops hiring armed guards to ensure that their workforce does not leave exist but they are rare. For the rest, the argument runs, the fact that employees chose to work at sweatshops shows that they view sweatshops as the best employment available. Taking that option away by forcing sweatshops to shut down would end up harming precisely the people the anti-sweatshop activists are trying to help.

Not only would shutting down factories harm the individuals who would lose their jobs as a result, the argument continues, it would also slow down the development of the economy as a whole, and thus prevent the development of better options for future generations. Sweatshops, economists are quick to point out, tend not to dominate an economy for very long. Often, they are the first step in a long path of economic development, injecting capital and management training into an economy where it can serve as the basis for the creation of new domestic industries. In Korea and Taiwan, for instance, Nike is no longer able to maintain manufacturing operations because, as one source reports, "workers in these quickly developing economies are no longer interested in working in low-paying shoe and textile factories." Sweatshops, according to this argument, are a *symptom* of poverty, not a *cause* of poverty. But moreover, they are a *hopeful* symptom: for they signal the beginning of an economic development which will eventually bring that poverty to an end.

These arguments are powerful, and caution those opposed to sweatshops to think carefully about the results of the policy they advocate. But it is not clear that they are decisive. We began this section with two questions, and the sorts of arguments described above might give us reason to suppose that we have arrived at an answer to the first. If companies who contract with sweatshops thereby provide individuals in developing countries with better opportunities than they would otherwise have had, then maybe they are not acting wrongly, or at least, not as wrongly as some have supposed them to be.

But this still leaves us without an answer to the second question: what should we *do* about sweatshops? The arguments given above seem to leave this question largely unaddressed. After all, by and large, anti-sweatshop activists are not calling for U.S. companies to pull out of third-world countries altogether. They do not want sweatshops to be shut down, they want them to be *improved.* Students who agitate for code of conduct programs want U.S. companies to ensure that their subcontractors pay a living wage, that they provide safe and sanitary working conditions for employees, and that they respect workers' basic human rights. Sophisticated anti-sweatshop activists recognize that companies are making employees better off by their providing individuals with jobs. They simply demand that companies ensure that those jobs be provided in a way which meets some basic ethical guidelines.

Still, the issue of what guidelines companies, consumers, or international organizations should impose on sweatshops is a complicated matter. Many of the proposals to regulate sweatshops suffer from the same sort of problem as proposals to abolish them. In 1992, for instance, the U.S. Congress considered a bill known as the Child Labor Deterrence Act, which sought to prohibit the importation of any product made in whole or in part by individuals under the age of

15 who are employed in industry or mining. Proposals such as this seem not to recognize that in a developing economy, child labor can play a vital role. For families living in such conditions, almost all income is directed toward the basic necessities of life: food, medicine, shelter, clothing. When parents grow too old or sick to work, children often become the main breadwinners of the family. An effective ban on products made by child labor would mean that these children would lose their jobs. Because developing countries generally have little in the way of social welfare programs for families to fall back on, the effect of this loss can be devastating.

In dealing with sweatshops, then, good intentions are simply not enough. Well-intentioned proposals to provide workers with a living wage, or health or maternity benefits, can raise [the] amount of money companies are forced to spend on each worker, and in so doing create a pressure to lay off all but the most essential.

But these considerations do not settle the matter in favor of sweatshops; they simply caution that close empirical research is necessary before drawing any conclusion. Sweatshop critics Edna Bonacich and Richard Appelbaum are quick to respond to the above arguments, for instance, by pointing out that in the case of a typical $100 dress sold and made in the United States, only 6% of the purchase price goes to the individual who actually made the garment. 25% goes to profit and overhead for the manufacturer, 50% goes to the retailer, and the remaining is spent on raw materials. Using similar reasoning, the National Labor Committee pointed out to Disney Chairman Michael Eisner in 1996 that the effect of raising the pay of workers at the Classic Apparel facility in Haiti from their then-current 35 cents per hour wage to 58 cents an hour would be a mere 3 cent raise in price for an $11.99 garment. And if certain economists are right, raising wages in many circumstances might actually *lower* costs, or at least have no negative effect. Workers who are not paid enough to provide for their nutritional needs might not be as productive as those who are able to afford a steady and reliable diet.

It is difficult, then, to come to any generally applicable conclusions about the wrongness of sweatshops or the desirability of any sort of regulatory or consumer-driven alternative. By way of general principle, we can only say that any reasonable policy will need to pay careful attention to the way in which alternative stances towards sweatshops actually affect the persons they are intended to help. Discovering what helps and what doesn't is less a matter of applying a pre-packaged ideology (free-market or anti-sweatshop) than it is of doing careful research into the unique local conditions of particular sweatshops and their political and economic contexts. . . .

QUESTIONS

1 Corporations in the United States frequently move jobs from the United States to third-world countries, paying much lower wages and benefits. Are their actions morally defensible?

2 Should there be some international body charged with the responsibility of setting working standards and minimum wages globally?

SUGGESTED ADDITIONAL READINGS FOR CHAPTER 2

AIKEN, WILLIAM and HUGH LAFOLLETTE. eds.: *World Hunger and Morality,* 2d ed. Englewood Cliffs, N.J.: Prentice-Hall, 1995. Many of the essays in this book were written especially for this volume. The anthology is divided into five parts: (1) Lifeboat Ethics; (2) A Responsibility to Aid; (3) Rights and Justice; (4) Justice and Development; and (5) Hunger and the Environment.

BELSEY, ANDREW: "World Poverty, Justice and Equality." In Robin Attfield, ed., *International Justice and the Third World.* New York: Routledge, 1992. Belsey argues against the claim that the special obligations that inhabitants of affluent countries have to people who are geographically or genetically closer to them override the interests of people in the third world.

CHATTERJEE, DEEN K., ed.: *The Ethics of Assistance and the Distant Needy.* New York: Cambridge University Press, 2004. Several of the articles in this volume deal with the question of the moral significance of distance in determining our duties to those in need. The articles by Thomas Pogge, Henry Shue, Onora O'Neill, and Charles R. Beitz are especially useful in illustrating how philosopohical discussions of the justification of international actions with respect to world poverty should be informed by the reality of international politics.

MAITLAND, IAN: "The Great Non-Debate Over International Sweatshops." In Thomas L. Beauchamp and Norman E. Bowie, eds., *Ethical Theory and Business.* Upper Saddle River, N.J.: Prentice-Hall, 2001. Maitland, a defender of international sweatshops, advances arguments, based on both factual and ethical grounds, against the critics of sweatshops.

MURDOCH, WILLIAM W., and ALLAN OATEN: "Population and Food: Metaphors and the Reality." *Bioscience,* September 9, 1975, pp. 561–567. Murdoch and Oaten criticize Garrett Hardin's lifeboat, commons, and ratchet metaphors and bring out various factors, other than food supply, that affect population growth.

NUSSBAUM, MARTHA: *Women and Human Development: The Capabilities Approach.* New York: Cambridge University Press, 2000. Nussbaum wants to alter the theoretical grounds on which international development policy is based. She argues that international political and economic thought should be feminist in orientation and grounded in a cross-cultural normative account of central human capabilities.

O'NEILL, ONORA: "Justice, Gender, and International Boundaries." In Martha Nussbaum, ed., *The Quality of Life.* New York: Oxford University Press, 1993. O'Neill argues that an account of justice can combine abstract principles with a consideration of differences in their application. She illustrates her claim by an account of the case of poor women in impoverished economies.

RACHELS, JAMES: "Killing and Starving to Death." *Philosophy,* vol. 54, April 1979, pp. 159–171. Rachels, attacking the view that killing is worse than letting die, argues that letting die is just as bad as killing. For Rachels our duty not to let people die from starvation is as strong as our duty not to kill them.

VISVANATHAN, NALINI, LYNN DUGGAN, LAURIE NISONOFF, and NAN WIEGERSMA, eds.: *The Women, Gender and Development Reader.* London: Zed, 1997. This reader features landmark articles and essays on the impact of development on women's lives. The book is divided into five parts: (1) Theories of Women, Gender and Development; (2) Households and Families; (3) Women in the Global Economy; (4) International Women in Social Transformations; and (5) Women Organizing Themselves for Change.

Welfare and Social
Justice Notes

Although the following are not necessarily in our readings, it is helpful to know the following in order to understand the issue:

TANF: TANF stands for Temporary Assistance for Needy Families. Over the years, TANF has done nothing to help the poverty rates decline across racial groups.

Transfer Payments: Transfer payments involve the transfer of wealth from one segment of the population to another through taxation and dispersal.

Socialism: Also sometimes called "Radical Egalitarianism" by Kai Nielsen, Socialism tries to maximize equality and justice through economic "public means of production." In other words, Socialism eliminates private ownership in favor of public ownership. The bailout of American car companies, such as the bailout for GM, is an example of socialist principle. The American taxpayer now owns part of GM. If this were true socialism, then the taxpayer would also have some say in the oversight of the company and would have a right to determine how its profits should be used. Socialism believes everyone has the right to share in the benefits of a country, be it medical care, housing, education, etc. In a Socialist system the concept of human rights is probably the most expansive as they include the right to medical care, shelter, and other basic life needs, that are not considered rights under some other forms of government.

Libertarianism: Libertarians try to maximize individual freedom of life, liberty, and property. Libertarianism concentrates on what is owed to the individual through that individual's labor and efforts. The less government interference the better. In fact, the only legitimate role of the government is to protect life, liberty, and property. There should be no taxes or other infringements on the individual's earnings. If an individual wishes to contribute to charity, that is fine, but the government has no right to take the earnings of one person in order to support another through "transfer payments." Property is private, as is business and the means of production. If GM fails, that is GM's problem. Wealth and poverty, economic success or failures are the responsibility of the individual. Individuals do not have a right to healthcare, shelter, or anything else, except that they earn it and pay for it out of their own labor.

Capitalism: There are several types of Capitalism. Laissez-faire Capitalism is closest to Libertarianism. It advocates a free market economy uncontrolled and unregulated by any government policy or action. It is assumed that individuals own their own business or work for a wage and that the success or failure of business rests on the supply and demand of the market place. Sometimes, we hear of "trickle-down economics." This is consistent with Laissez-faire Capitalism in that is assumes that the wealthy and successful will benefit the economy by stimulating constant growth—growth that will allow jobs to flourish and the economy to hum along. Welfare State Capitalism is closest to what the American economy does today. Welfare State Capitalism uses the private means of production (as in Laissez-faire Capitalism and Libertarianism), but the government may regulate business and use taxes for the common good.

Your authors in this chapter include the following:

John Hospers: John Hospers is a Libertarian. He makes two main arguments for a form of laissez-faire capitalism and a free market economy.

His first argument is that (1) no one is anyone else's master, and no one is anyone else's slave; (2) other men's lives are not yours to dispose of; and (3) no human being should be a non-voluntary mortgage on the life of another. What Hospers is arguing in the first part is that your labor provides wages and no one has the right to take your money and use it for programs that you do not support. Hospers argues that you have worked hard for what you have. Why should someone who has not worked as hard be given some of your wages just because he now has lost a job or can't find one? This seems unfair to Hospers. By the same thinking, why should you pay to support a public school system if you don't have children or you choose to send you children to a private school? The same goes for health care, welfare, etc. In other words, let me keep what I make. Don't tax me to support others. Every man for himself.

In his second argument, Hospers says that government is the most dangerous institution known to man because it is the most powerful. Therefore, government needs to be limited. Hospers argues that the only role of government should be to protect (1) the right to life, (2) the right to liberty, and (3) the right to property. Hospers believes the only valid argument to limiting an individual's freedom is the Harm Principle.

The **Harm Principle** states that you have the right to do whatever you wish as long as it does not interfere with the rights of another (harm another). For example, you may drink yourself under the carpet every night if that is what you wish, but you may not drink and drive. As soon as you pick up your car keys, while drunk, the state may have an interest in what you are doing. If you actually get into your car with the intent to drive it, the state has the right to stop you because you are now a danger to others. The harm principle is the one rule that almost any philosophical system can agree to. Please note that the harm principle protects others, but does not protect you from yourself and your own stupidity. You will find that many other authors in this textbook use the harm principle as part of their arguments.

Keeping you from harming yourself is called "Legal Paternalism." Legal paternalism is the basis for laws insisting that we wear seat belts when driving cars or wearing helmets when driving motorcycles. Hospers does not advocate legal paternalism.

Kai Nielsen: Kai Nielsen argues that Radical Egalitarianism (Democratic Socialism) can provide people with greater autonomy, democracy and equality, and, therefore, **justice**, than the best forms of Capitalism. The easiest way to understand his argument is to compare it with Capitalism: Capitalism uses private means of production, and results in a greater disparity between wealth and poverty. This disparity leads to fewer opportunities for those at the lower end of the socio-economic group. Capitalism affords political democracy, but not workplace democracy. Capitalism is concerned with the economy and rewards the top earners. Capitalism believes that if business flourishes then the society as a whole will flourish. Socialism uses a public means of production, and this results in greater economic equality. Ensuring the basic needs of everyone in society leads to more opportunities to excel. Socialism affords both political democracy and workplace democracy. Socialism is concerned with the social welfare of all.

If placing Nielsen's argument in chart form, this is what it would look like:

Capitalism	Socialism
Private ownership	Public ownership
Class society	Classless society
Less autonomy: Owners determine market, which is central to being able to live in a "self-directed" manner.	More autonomy: Workers have a voice in labor conditions.
Less democracy: Political democracy is possible, but no workplace democracy.	More democracy: both political and workplace democracy.
Less moral equality (life opportunity): Differentials of wealth give rise to differentials in power and control in politics, media, social life, and education.	More moral equality (life opportunity): More equal access to the goods of society, including power, politics, media, social life, and education.

Conclusion: By making equality difficult to achieve, Capitalism is a less just social structure than that made possible by democratic socialism.

Iris M. Young: Iris M. Young argues that oppression, in the form of exploitation, marginalization, powerlessness, cultural imperialism, and violence, prevents many Americans from being able to fully access the opportunities offered by the liberal individualism with which the United States is usually identified.

Argument: Exploitation

Definition: Young follows a theory similar to Nielsen's on the exploitation of the average person under Capitalism. She says, "Oppression occurs through a steady process of transfer of the results of the labor of one social group to benefit another."

Example: women's labor. "...in most systems of agricultural production in the world, men take to market the goods women have produced, and more often than not men receive the status and often the entire income from their labor."

Argument: Marginalization

Definition: "...people the system of labor cannot or will not use." Dependent people are excluded from equal citizenship rights.

Example: This includes not only minorities, but the elderly, single mothers and their children, many mentally and physically disabled people, and other involuntarily unemployed people.

Argument: Powerlessness

Definition: The labor of many augments the power of relatively few.

Example: Most workplaces are not organized democratically. The inequality begins with unequal access to education, limits autonomy, and extends beyond the workplace.

Argument: Cultural Imperialism

Definition: To "experience how the dominant meanings of a society render the particular perspective of one's own group invisible at the same time as they stereotype one's group and mark it out as the Other."

Example: "...the difference of women from men, American Indians or Africans from Europeans, Jews from Christians, homosexuals from heterosexuals, workers from professionals, becomes reconstructed largely as deviance and inferiority."

Argument: Violence

Definition: "Members of some groups live with the knowledge that they must fear random, unprovoked attacks on their person or property, which have no motive but to damage, humiliate, or destroy the person."

Example: "Rape Crisis Center networks estimate that more than one-third of all American women experience an attempted or successful sexual assault in their lifetimes."

Conclusion: "The presence of any of these five conditions is sufficient for calling a group oppressed."

Howard McGary: McGary asks the question of why members of the underclass in society seem to be locked into their status. In other words, why are the people who end up poor, have such a hard time breaking the cycle of poverty, and, sometimes, generational welfare. McGary examines the problem from the perspective of the African-American community, but while reading his argument, you might want to ask yourself if the same argument might apply to the poor of our society—regardless of race or gender.

McGary's argument is that the very structure of our society creates impediments to getting out of poverty. He bases his argument on the concept of "full citizenship." People with full citizenship believe they will be treated with "equal concern and respect." He points out that this psychological perspective has a great impact on a person's self-concept.

The effects are not only psychological. "Full citizens," according to McGary, have the "right to participate in the political process. They have the right to earn a living without being forced to engage in activities that are degrading or exploitative. Citizens are not denied opportunities simply because of their race, sex, or religious affiliations. Citizens also have legal due process." When we take a look at the death penalty chapter, we will see that race and class are heavy factors in terms of whether an accused person receives a just trial. McGary is arguing that being poor means starting off life with disadvantages.

Poor women may not get good prenatal care, or any prenatal care. They may live in older housing where they and their children are exposed to lead paint, mold, violence, etc. The child who grows up in a poor neighborhood may have an inferior education and little preparation for finding or keeping a job. There may be no transportation available to reach most jobs. There will probably be a lack of healthcare. The jobs the candidate can qualify for are probably minimum wage—which means an inability to get out of the cycle of poverty.

McGary touches briefly on the issue of welfare. He points out that welfare might well provide more than a minimum wage job, thereby, providing little assistance or incentive to work. For example, under welfare, medical care is provided. Childcare costs are covered. Subsidized housing is available (eventually). Food stamps are issued. College tuition is covered (Pell Grants). However, if someone is working and makes one dollar over the limit, none of this help is available. It is an all or nothing situation. The thought of struggling at a boring, minimum wage job without any benefits, knowing that this is your future is discouraging.

Nancy Fraser: Fraser points out that the nuclear family, long the "normative picture of the proper family," (male head of household earning enough to support children and a stay at home wife) no longer exists as the majority model. She divides her analysis of the "postindustrial phase of capitalism" into seven points. The first is simply a statement. The rest explain why poverty today is more likely to be experienced by women than by men:

  1 The Antipoverty Principle: This is the idea that we should prevent poverty.

  2 The Anti-exploitation Principle: People who are needy are also vulnerable to exploitation. For example, women "with no other way to feed themselves and their children" are ready made victims for abusive husbands/boyfriends, bosses, etc. Dependency leads to exploitation.

  3 The Income-Equality Principle: Currently, women's labor still earns far less than men's when it comes to equal or comparable jobs, and when a divorce occurs, a woman's income is usually reduced by half.

  4 The Leisure-Time-Equality Principle: Fraser is talking about the time available after work, where women (and some men) go from paid labor to unpaid labor (cleaning, cooking, driving the children to activities, etc.) or to a second job. She points out that women are more likely to suffer from a "double-shift" syndrome.

5 The Equality-of-Respect Principle: Fraser points out that women are still represented as "sexual objects for the pleasure of male subjects" (just look at the many computer games that are based on the degradation and violence against women). The problem is that this affects the view of women as equals, including in the workforce.

6 The Antimarginalization Principle: Here, Fraser is pointing out that women, who are still the main caregivers, and often the ones who take time out from work to give birth, raise children, take care of elderly parents, etc. do not get economic or retirement credit for this work. To equalize the workforce would mean providing for day care and elder care—the activities usually assumed, without pay, by women.

7 The Antiandrocentrism Principle: Fraser says that the workplace is currently designed for men. For example, it assumes an uninterrupted career and extra work time whenever needed. It ignores the fact that women may need to take time out of a career for caregiving and, instead, asks that women "become like men" in order to maintain or succeed in a job.

Fraser's conclusion is that neither a "universal breadwinner" (male centered) nor "caregiver" (female centered) model fully work. What she would like to see happen, in order to meet the problems of the seven principles above, is a postindustrial society that does not make distinctions between breadwinners and caregivers. She suggests that this model—"Universal Caregiver" model—can only happen if we deconstruct gender. By this, she means that we should not divide roles into gender categories, but, instead, assign value to all roles as human roles. Whether breadwinner or caregiver, public or private, that all roles be given respect for their important contribution to society, without gender stereotypes. It shouldn't matter whether a man or a women brings home the bacon or which one cooks it up in a pan (sorry, I couldn't resist that one).

CHAPTER 3

Social and
Economic Justice

Some people maintain that governmental domestic welfare programs are unjust because the government has no right to tax those who are relatively well off in order to provide funds for those in need. Others argue that it is unjust not to provide government aid to those who lack adequate food, clothing, and shelter. Some people argue that it is the government's role to promote gender equity; others disagree. Disagreements about issues such as these stem in large measure from different conceptions of justice and divergent views on a closely related issue—the morally correct role of government in economic activity. Thus, one of the concerns in this chapter is with the nature of justice and the closely related issue of the role that the government should play in a just society. In addition, some theorists argue that we cannot completely understand injustice without understanding the concept of oppression and the ways that oppressive social structures are inimical to justice. Hence, another concern in this chapter is the nature of oppression.

LIBERTY, EQUALITY, AND CONCEPTIONS OF JUSTICE

Two moral ideals, liberty and equality, are of key importance in conceptions of justice in general and economic justice in particular. A *libertarian* or *individualist* conception of justice holds liberty to be the ultimate moral ideal. A *socialist* conception of justice takes social equality to be the ultimate ideal; and a *liberal* conception of justice tries to combine both equality and liberty into one ultimate moral ideal.

The Libertarian Conception of Justice

For the libertarian, a society is just when individual liberty is maximized. To understand the libertarian position on liberty, it is necessary to see that liberty is not synonymous with freedom. Freedom is the broader category; liberty is one aspect of freedom. If freedom is understood as the overall absence of constraint, liberty can be understood as the absence of a specific kind of constraint—*coercion,* the forceful and deliberate interference by human beings in the affairs of other human beings. Coercion can take two forms—either the direct use of physical force or the threat of harm, backed up by enforcement power. An example will illustrate why liberty is not synonymous with freedom. In some countries, citizens need a government permit to live and work in certain cities. Thus, their freedom, more specifically their liberty to live and work in those cities, is restricted by coercion, the threat of harm should they disobey the rules. In the United States, citizens do not need such permits. There are no laws that threaten them with harm should they choose to move to New York City or Los Angeles. But not everyone who wants to do so is free to go to live and work in either city. All kinds of constraints may prevent it. Individuals may not have the money for transportation, for example, and this lack may limit their freedom to do what they wish to do. The jobs they are capable of doing may not be available, and this lack, too, may prevent them from moving to the city of their choice. Thus, individual freedom may be limited in many ways. It is important to see that when libertarians advocate the maximization of liberty, they are not concerned with maximizing freedom in general. Their focus is on minimizing coercion, especially on minimizing the coercive interferences of governments.

In a libertarian view, individuals have certain moral rights to life, liberty, and property, which any just society must recognize and respect. These rights are sometimes described as warnings against interference: If A has a right to X, no one should prevent A from pursuing X or deprive A of X, since A is entitled to it. According to a libertarian, the sole function of the government is to protect the individual's life, liberty, and property against force and fraud. Everything else in society is a matter of individual responsibility, decision, and action. Providing for the welfare of those who cannot or will not provide for themselves is not a morally justifiable function of government. To make such provisions, the government would have to take from some against their will in order to give to others. This is perceived as an unjustifiable coercive limitation on individual liberty. Individuals own their own bodies (or lives) and, therefore, the labor they exert. It follows, for the libertarian, that individuals have the right to whatever income or wealth their labor can earn in a free marketplace. Taxing some to give to others is analogous to robbery. John Hospers, who defends a libertarian position in this chapter, argues that laws requiring people to help one another (e.g., via welfare payments) rob Peter to pay Paul.

Libertarians consider *laissez-faire capitalism* to be the only just economic system, because it is based on individual rights. Capitalism is an economic system based on the private ownership of the means of production, the means whereby consumer goods and services are produced (for example, land used to produce food crops, as well as factories and equipment used to manufacture goods). Under *laissez-faire* capitalism, all the means of production are privately owned, and there is a totally *free market.* In a free market system, the economy is uncontrolled and unregulated by any governmental actions or policies. Income is distributed and production is guided through the operation of markets. The government's only role in the economic sphere is to protect individuals against force and fraud.

The Socialist Conception of Justice

A direct challenge to libertarians comes from those who defend a socialist conception of justice. There are many varieties of socialism. However, there are two common elements in socialist thought: (1) a commitment to the public ownership of the means of production and (2) a commitment to the ideal of equality. Equality is a complex ideal, including both the conception of moral equality and the conception of equality of condition. Moral equality is the belief that everyone's life matters equally. Equality of condition includes such ideals as equality of opportunity, the equal satisfaction of needs, and other factors that foster greater social equality. Since equality of condition is a central ideal, limitations on individual liberty, specifically on certain economic liberties, are seen as justified when they are necessary to promote equality.

Socialists attack libertarian views on the primacy of liberty, in at least three ways. *First,* they offer defenses of their ideal of social equality. These take various forms and will not concern us here. *Second,* they point out the meaninglessness of libertarian rights to those who lack adequate food, shelter, health care, and so on. For those who lack the money to buy the food and health care needed to sustain life, the libertarian right to life is an empty sham. The rights of liberty, such as the right to freedom of speech, are a joke to those who cannot exercise them because of economic considerations. *Third,* some defenders of socialism, such as Kai Nielsen in this chapter, argue that most people will have much more freedom in a socialist system than in a libertarian one because they will have more control over their economic lives. The freedom that the socialist wants to maximize, however, requires a society in which individuals have the greatest possible range of choices and not simply one in which government interference is minimal. It is important to recognize the difference between the socialist's conception of freedom and the libertarian's conception of liberty. Whereas libertarians stress liberty—understood as freedom from coercion, especially from government interference—socialists stress freedom from want. Whereas libertarians stress negative rights (rights not to be interfered with), socialists stress positive rights—rights *to* food, health care, productive work, and so on. Whereas libertarians criticize socialism for the limitations it imposes on liberty, socialists criticize libertarianism for allowing gross inequalities among those who are *moral equals.*

The Liberal Conception of Justice

Like the socialist, the liberal[1] rejects the libertarian conception of justice. Socialists and liberals agree in recognizing the extent to which economic constraints in industrial and technologically advanced societies effectively limit the exercise of libertarian rights by those lacking economic power. Unlike the socialist, however, the liberal considers some of the libertarian's negative rights extremely important and advocates social institutions that do two important things: (1) ensure certain basic liberties for all (e.g., freedom of speech), not allowing these liberties to be set aside

---

[1] There is a great deal of disagreement about the correct characterization of liberalism. The presentation here encapsulates one prominent way of understanding the term. For a different approach see Ronald Dworkin, "Liberalism," in *A Matter of Principle* (Cambridge, Mass.: Harvard University Press, 1985), pp. 181–204.

to promote other goals, such as social or economic equality, and (2) provide for the economic needs of the disadvantaged members of society. Like the socialists, liberals see equality as an important value, but they do not oppose all social and economic inequalities. Rather, they are committed to a principle of *basic worth*—all individuals are entitled to equal concern for their interests in the design of the basic institutions of their society. Moreover, all individuals also have the right to be equally respected in their desire to lead their lives on their own terms.

Liberals disagree among themselves, however, concerning the morally acceptable extent of social and economic inequalities and their correct justification. A utilitarian liberal might hold that inequalities are justified to the extent that allowing them maximizes the total amount of good in a society. If, for example, increased productivity depends on giving workers a significantly higher income than that given to welfare recipients, and if such incentive-stimulated productivity increases the total amount of good in a society, then the inequalities between the assembly-line workers and the welfare recipient would be justified for the utilitarian. A different approach is taken by John Rawls, who is considered a liberal egalitarian. He maintains that social and economic inequalities are justified only if they are compatible with fair equality of opportunity and contribute to raising the position of the least advantaged in society. Rawls's view is expressed in *the difference principle,* which asserts that social and economic inequalities are to be arranged so that they are both (a) reasonably expected to be to everyone's advantage, especially to the advantage of the least advantaged, and (b) attached to positions and offices open to all.[2]

In one of this chapter's readings, Howard McGary, arguing from a liberal perspective, maintains that some of our society's basic institutions are unjust with respect to a group of people who could be considered among the least advantaged in our society—the African-American underclass. He points, for example, to the inadequacies of the current health-care system and to an economic system that effectively denies members of the underclass any real equality of opportunity to obtain work that is satisfying and that draws on their abilities and talents.

The socioeconomic system that best coheres with the liberal conception of justice is *welfare-state capitalism.* In welfare-state capitalism, as in any form of capitalism, the means of production are, for the most part, privately owned. However, under welfare-state capitalism, the state plays an important role in protecting and promoting the economic and social well-being of its citizens. Under welfare-state capitalism, for example, the state bears the responsibility for protecting workers against the power of the capitalists. Laws that mandate a minimum wage are an example of this sort of protection, as are laws that require humane and safe working conditions. The government also bears the responsibility for structuring social reality in such a way that those who are unable to provide themselves with the necessities of life have their needs met. Thus, in accordance with the liberal conception of justice, raising money through taxation in order to provide funds for programs designed to help the needy attain food, clothing, shelter, and medical care is considered a morally legitimate (in fact, a morally required) state activity. Lessening social and economic inequalities is also seen as a legitimate goal in welfare-state capitalism.

[2]John Rawls, *A Theory of Justice* (Cambridge, Mass.: Harvard University Press), pp. 60, 302.

In one of this chapter's readings, Nancy Fraser argues that we need a new vision of the welfare state for the postindustrial age. In her view, the ideal underlying welfare programs during the industrial age was the now-outdated family-wage model premised on a nuclear family headed by a male breadwinner who would be paid a "family wage"—one sufficient to meet the needs of all the family members. Welfare programs that were geared to this model provided various forms of social insurance to cover the loss of the breadwinner's earnings, such as disability and unemployment insurance. They also provided aid to families without such breadwinners through welfare programs such as the now discarded Aid to Families with Dependent Children (AFDC). Fraser, writing from a feminist perspective, presents and evaluates three different visions of the postindustrial welfare state, each of which includes a commitment to gender equity.

OPPRESSION AND INJUSTICE

Much of the discussion of injustice in the United States is formulated in the language and within the framework of liberalism. However, some would argue that the categories of liberalism are inadequate tools for analyzing and evaluating the failure of our current social structures and practices to accord with justice. According to this line of reasoning, one of the categories that must be used when attempting to identify systematic injustices in our society is the category of oppression.

As normally understood, *oppression* is not a value-neutral term. To say that one person oppresses another or that an institution systematically oppresses some people is to express a criticism of the oppressor or institutional practice. Of course, not every constraint or limitation can correctly be described as oppressive. When laws are passed threatening individuals with harm if they harm others, those laws can be seen as constraining. But it would be a mistake to claim that the very existence of such laws is a form of oppression. Parents limit their children's freedom in all sorts of ways for their own good, but requiring their children to do a reasonable amount of schoolwork instead of playing video games all the time can hardly be seen as a form of oppression. Thus, whatever oppression is, it cannot be identified simply with constraints or limitations imposed on individuals by either other individuals or social structures.

Traditionally, oppression has been understood as the abuse of power by a ruling group and, hence, has been treated as synonymous with tyranny or despotism. On this understanding of oppression, a powerful group deliberately adopts policies intended to subjugate another group. The now disbanded system of apartheid in South Africa provides one example of this kind of oppression. But oppression, as it is understood by many writers today, need not involve the conscious and intentional subjugation of one group by another. The focus of these writers is on the way that economic, political, and cultural institutions systematically function to disadvantage certain groups even in well-intentioned societies. According to this view of oppression, all oppression involves two characteristics. First, a person is not oppressed as *a particular individual* but as *a member of a specific group*. Thus, one's oppressive treatment is due not to one's personal characteristics but to the characteristics attributed to one's group. Second, oppression is systematic. As Kenneth Clatterbaugh explains,

> Oppression of a group is systematic; that is, it exists throughout a society, usually over a substantial period of time, and the institutions of society interlock and reinforce each other in ways that create and maintain the oppression. For example, oppressed groups may be denied access to valuable resources of the society and in turn their lack of such resources may be used as evidence that they should continue to be denied access. Thus, the practice feeds the justification and the justification supports the practice.[3]

Iris M. Young maintains in this chapter that it is not possible to give a general definition of oppression. She grants that all oppressed people have something in common: They all suffer some inhibition of their ability to develop and exercise their capacities and express their needs, thoughts, and feelings. Beyond this, however, we cannot identify an attribute or a set of attributes that all oppressed people have in common. Rather, there are different forms of oppression: exploitation, marginalization, powerlessness, cultural imperialism, and systematic violence. The first three involve relations of power and oppression that result from the social division of labor. (Young's discussion of exploitation is particularly relevant to Nielsen's criticisms of capitalism in this chapter.) Cultural imperialism involves the acceptance of one group's experiences, values, goals, and achievements as universal. These norms are then used in judging members of other groups as deviant and inferior. Finally, systematic violence against individuals because of their group membership is seen as a form of oppression. Members of such groups share the knowledge that they may be victims of violence solely on the basis of their group identity. Young brings out the ways that these forms of oppression intersect, so that some groups can be judged to be more oppressed than others even though no one definition of oppression is possible.

Jane S. Zembaty

[3]Kenneth Clatterbaugh, "The Oppression Debate in Sexual Politics," in Larry May and Robert A. Strikwerda, eds., *Rethinking Masculinity* (Lanham, Md.: Rowman and Littlefield, 1992), p. 171.

What Libertarianism Is

John Hospers

Hospers defends two ideas central to libertarianism: (1) Individuals own their own lives. They, therefore, have the right to act as they choose unless their actions interfere with the liberty of others to act as they choose. (2) The only appropriate function of government is to protect human rights, understood as negative rights (i.e., rights of noninterference).

Reprinted with permission of Nelson-Hall Inc., Publishers, from Tibor R. Machan, ed., *The Libertarian Alternative* (1974).

The political philosophy that is called libertarianism (from the Latin *libertas,* liberty) is the doctrine that every person is the owner of his own life, and that no one is the owner of anyone else's life; and that consequently every human being has the right to act in accordance with his own choices, unless those actions infringe on the equal liberty of other human beings to act in accordance with *their* choices.

There are several other ways of stating the same libertarian thesis:

1 *No one is anyone else's master, and no one is anyone else's slave.* Since I am the one to decide how my life is to be conducted, just as you decide about yours, I have no right (even if I had the power) to make you my slave and be your master, nor have you the right to become the master by enslaving me. Slavery is *forced* servitude, and since no one owns the life of anyone else, no one has the right to enslave another. Political theories past and present have traditionally been concerned with who should be the master (usually the king, the dictator, or government bureaucracy) and who should be the slaves, and what the extent of the slavery should be. Libertarianism holds that no one has the right to use force to enslave the life of another, or any portion or aspect of that life.

2 *Other men's lives are not yours to dispose of.* I enjoy seeing operas; but operas are expensive to produce. Opera-lovers often say, "The state (or the city, etc.) should subsidize opera, so that we can all see it. Also it would be for people's betterment, cultural benefit, etc." But what they are advocating is nothing more or less than legalized plunder. They can't pay for the productions themselves, and yet they want to see opera, which involves a large number of people and their labor; so what they are saying in effect is, "Get the money through legalized force. Take a little bit more out of every worker's paycheck every week to pay for the operas we want to see." But I have no right to take by force from the workers' pockets to pay for what I want.

Perhaps it would be better if he *did* go to see opera—then I should try to convince him to go voluntarily. But to take the money from him forcibly, because in my opinion it would be good for *him,* is still seizure of his earnings, which is plunder.

Besides, if I have the right to force him to help pay for my pet projects, hasn't he equally the right to force me to help pay for his? Perhaps he in turn wants the government to subsidize rock-and-roll, or his new car, or a house in the country? If I have the right to milk him, why hasn't he the right to milk me? If I can be a moral cannibal, why can't he too?

We should beware of the inventors of utopias. They would remake the world according to their vision—with the lives and fruits of the labor of *other* human beings. Is it someone's utopian vision that others should build pyramids to beautify the landscape? Very well, then other men should provide the labor; and if he is in a position of political power, and he can't get men to do it voluntarily, then he must *compel* them to "cooperate"—i.e. he must enslave them.

A hundred men might gain great pleasure from beating up or killing just one insignificant human being; but other men's lives are not theirs to dispose of. "In order to achieve the worthy goals of the next five-year-plan, we must forcibly collectivize the peasants . . ."; but other men's lives are not theirs to dispose of. Do you want to occupy, rent-free, the mansion that another man has worked for twenty years to buy? But other men's lives are not yours to dispose of. Do you want operas so badly that everyone is forced to work harder to pay for their subsidization through taxes? But other men's lives are not yours to dispose of. Do you want to have free medical care at the expense of other people, whether they wish to provide it or not? But this would require them to work longer for you whether they want to or not, and other men's lives are not yours to dispose of.

> The freedom to engage in any type of enterprise, to produce, to own and control property, to buy and sell on the free market, is derived from the rights to life, liberty, and property . . . which are stated in the Declaration of Independence . . . [but] when a government guarantees a "right" to an education or parity on farm products or a guaranteed annual income, it is staking a claim on the property of one group of citizens for the sake of another group. In short, it is violating one of the fundamental rights it was instituted to protect.[1]

3 *No human being should be a nonvoluntary mortgage on the life of another.* I cannot claim your life, your work, or the products of your effort as mine. The fruit of one man's labor should not be fair game for every freeloader who comes along and demands it as his own. The orchard that has been carefully grown, nurtured, and harvested by its owner should not be ripe for the plucking for any bypasser who has a yen for the ripe fruit. The wealth that some men have produced should not be fair game for looting by government, to be used for whatever purposes its representatives determine, no matter what their motives in so doing may be. The theft of your money by a robber is not justified by the fact that he used it to help his injured mother.

It will already be evident that libertarian doctrine is embedded in a view of the rights of man. Each human being has the right to live his life as he chooses, compatibly with the equal right of all other human beings to live their lives as they choose.

All man's rights are implicit in the above statement. Each man has the right to life; any attempt by others to take it away from him, or even to injure him, violates this right, through the use of coercion against him. Each man has the right to liberty: to conduct his life in accordance with the alternatives open to him without coercive action by others. And every man has the right to property: to work to sustain his life (and the lives of whichever others he chooses to sustain, such as his family) and to retain the fruits of his labor.

People often defend the rights of life and liberty but denigrate property rights, and yet the right to property is as basic as the other two; indeed, without property rights no other rights are possible. Depriving you of property is depriving you of the means by which you live.

> . . . All that which an individual possesses by right (including his life and property) are morally his to use, dispose of and even destroy, as he sees fit. If I own my life, then it follows that I am free to associate with whom I please and not to associate with whom I please. If I own my knowledge and services, it follows that I may ask any compensation I wish for providing them for another, or I may abstain from providing them at all, if I so choose. If I own my house, it follows that I may decorate it as I please and live in it with whom I please. If I control my own business, it follows that I may charge what I please

for my products or services, hire whom I please and not hire whom I please. All that which I own in fact, I may dispose of as I choose to in reality. For anyone to attempt to limit my freedom to do so is to violate my rights.

Where do my rights end? Where yours begin. I may do anything I wish with my own life, liberty and property without your consent; but I may do nothing with your life, liberty and property without your consent. If we recognize the principle of man's rights, it follows that the individual is sovereign of the domain of his own life and property, and is sovereign of no other domain. To attempt to interfere forcibly with another's use, disposal or destruction of his own property is to initiate force against him and to violate his rights.

I have no right to decide how *you* should spend your time or your money. I can make that decision for myself, but not for you, my neighbor. I may deplore your choice of life-style, and I may talk with you about it provided you are willing to listen to me. But I have no right to use force to change it. Nor have I the right to decide how you should spend the money you have earned. I may appeal to you to give it to the Red Cross, and you may prefer to go to prizefights. But that is your decision, and however much I may chafe about it I do not have the right to interfere forcibly with it, for example by robbing you in order to use the money in accordance with *my* choices. (If I have the right to rob you, have you also the right to rob me?)

When I claim a right, I carve out a niche, as it were, in my life, saying in effect, "This activity I must be able to perform without interference from others. For you and everyone else, this is off limits." And so I put up a "no trespassing" sign, which marks off the area of my right. Each individual's right is his "no trespassing" sign in relation to me and others. I may not encroach upon his domain any more than he upon mine, without my consent. Every right entails a duty, true—but the duty is only that of *forbearance*—that is, of *refraining* from violating the other person's right. If you have a right to life, I have no right to take your life; if you have a right to the products of your labor (property), I have no right to take it from you without your consent. The non-violation of these rights will not guarantee you protection against natural catastrophes such as floods and earthquakes, but it will protect you against the aggressive activities *of other men*. And rights, after all, have to do with one's relations to other human beings, not with one's relations to physical nature.

Nor were these rights created by government; governments—some governments, obviously not all—*recognize* and *protect* the rights that individuals already have. Governments regularly forbid homicide and theft; and, at a more advanced stage, protect individuals against such things as libel and breach of contract. . . .

Government is the most dangerous institution known to man. Throughout history it has violated the rights of men more than any individual or group of individuals could do: it has killed people, enslaved them, sent them to forced labor and concentration camps, and regularly robbed and pillaged them of the fruits of their expended labor. Unlike individual criminals, government has the power to arrest and try; unlike individual criminals, it can surround and encompass a person totally, dominating every aspect of one's life, so that one has no recourse from it but to leave the country (and in totalitarian nations even that is prohibited). Government throughout history has a much sorrier record than any individual, even that of a ruthless mass murderer. The signs we see on bumper stickers are chillingly accurate: "Beware: the Government is Armed and Dangerous."

The only proper role of government, according to libertarians, is that of the protector of the citizen against aggression by other individuals. The government, of course, should never initiate aggression; its proper role is as the embodiment of the *retaliatory* use of force against anyone who initiates its use.

If each individual had constantly to defend himself against possible aggressors, he would have to spend a considerable portion of his life in target practice, karate exercises, and other means of self-defenses, and even so he would probably be helpless against groups of individuals who might try to kill, maim, or rob him. He would have little time for cultivating those qualities which are essential to civilized life, nor would improvements in science, medicine, and the arts be likely to occur. The function of government is to take this responsibility off his shoulders: the government undertakes to defend him against aggressors and to punish them if they attack him. When the government is effective in doing this, it enables the citizen to go about his business unmolested and without constant fear for his life. To do this, of course, government must have physical power—the police, to protect the citizen from aggression within its borders, and the armed forces, to protect him from aggressors outside. Beyond that, the government should not intrude upon his life, either to run his business, or adjust his daily activities, or prescribe his personal moral code.

Government, then, undertakes to be the individual's protector; but historically governments have gone far beyond this function. Since they already have the physical power, they have not hesitated to use it for purposes far beyond that which was entrusted to them in the first place. Undertaking initially to protect its citizens against aggression, it has often itself become an aggressor—a far greater aggressor, indeed, than the criminals against whom it was supposed to protect its citizens. Governments have done what no private citizen can do: arrest and imprison individuals without a trial and send them to slave labor camps. Government must have power in order to be effective—and yet the very means by which alone it can be effective make it vulnerable to the abuse of power, leading to managing the lives of individuals and even inflicting terror upon them.

What then should be the function of government? In a word, the *protection of human rights.*

1 *The right to life:* libertarians support all such legislation as will protect human beings against the use of force by others, for example, laws against killing, attempted killing, maiming, beating, and all kinds of physical violence.

2 *The right to liberty:* there should be no laws compromising in any way freedom of speech, of the press, and of peaceable assembly. There should be no censorship of ideas, books, films, or of anything else by government.

3 *The right to property:* libertarians support legislation that protects the property rights of individuals against confiscation, nationalization, eminent domain, robbery, trespass, fraud and misrepresentation, patent and copyright, libel and slander.

Someone has violently assaulted you. Should he be legally liable? Of course. He has violated one of your rights. He has knowingly injured you, and since he has initiated aggression against you he should be made to expiate.

Someone has negligently left his bicycle on the sidewalk where you trip over it in the dark and injure yourself. He didn't do it intentionally; he didn't mean you any harm. Should he be legally liable? Of course; he has, however unwittingly, injured you, and since the injury is caused by him and you are the victim, he should pay.

Someone across the street is unemployed. Should you be taxed extra to pay for his expenses? Not at all. You have not injured him, you are not responsible for the fact that he is unemployed (unless you are a senator or bureaucrat who agitated for further curtailing of business, which legislation passed, with the result that your neighbor was laid off by the curtailed business). You may voluntarily wish to help him out, or better still, try to get him a job to put him on his feet again; but since you have initiated no aggressive act against him, and neither purposely nor accidentally injured him in any way, you should not be legally penalized for the fact of his unemployment. (Actually, it is just such penalties that increase unemployment.)

One man, A, works hard for years and finally earns a high salary as a professional man. A second man, B, prefers not to work at all, and to spend wastefully what money he has (through inheritance), so that after a year or two he has nothing left. At the end of this time he has a long siege of illness and lots of medical bills to pay. He demands that the bills be paid by the government—that is, by the taxpayers of the land, including Mr. A.

But of course B has no such right. He chose to lead his life in a certain way— that was his voluntary decision. One consequence of that choice is that he must depend on charity in case of later need. Mr. A chose not to live that way. (And if everyone lived like Mr. B, on whom would he depend in case of later need?) Each has a right to live in the way he pleases, but each must live with the consequences of his own decision (which, as always, fall primarily on himself). He cannot, in time of need, claim A's beneficence as his right. . . .

Laws may be classified into three types: (1) laws protecting individuals against themselves, such as laws against fornication and other sexual behavior, alcohol, and drugs; (2) laws protecting individuals against aggressions by other individuals, such as laws against murder, robbery, and fraud; (3) laws requiring people to help one another; for example, all laws which rob Peter to pay Paul, such as welfare.

Libertarians reject the first class of laws totally. Behavior which harms no one else is strictly the individual's own affair. Thus, there should be no laws against becoming intoxicated, since whether or not to become intoxicated is the individual's own decision; but there should be laws against driving while intoxicated, since the drunken driver is a threat to every other motorist on the highway (drunken driving falls into type 2). Similarly, there should be no laws against drugs (except the prohibition of sale of drugs to minors) as long as the taking of these drugs poses no threat to anyone else. Drug addiction is a psychological problem to which no present solution exists. Most of the social harm caused by addicts, other than to themselves, is the result of thefts which they perform in order to continue their habit—and then the *legal* crime is the theft, not the addiction. The actual cost of heroin is about ten cents a shot; if it were legalized, the enormous traffic in illegal sale and purchase of it would stop, as well as the accompanying proselytization to get new addicts (to make more money for the pusher) and the thefts performed by addicts who often require eighty dollars a day just to keep up the habit. Addiction would not stop, but the crimes would: it is estimated that 75 percent of the burglaries in New York City today are performed by addicts, and all these crimes would be wiped out at one stroke through the legalization of drugs. (Only when the taking of drugs could be shown to constitute a threat to *others,* should it be prohibited by law. It is only laws protecting people against *themselves* that libertarians oppose.)

Laws should be limited to the second class only: aggression by individuals against other individuals. These are laws whose function is to protect human beings against encroachment by others; and this, as we have seen, is (according to libertarianism) the sole function of government.

Libertarians also reject the third class of laws totally: no one should be forced by law to help others, not even to tell them the time of day if requested, and certainly not to give them a portion of one's weekly paycheck. Governments, in the guise of humanitarianism, have given to some by taking from others (charging a "handling fee" in the process, which, because of the government's waste and inefficiency, sometimes is several hundred percent). And in so doing they have decreased incentive, violated the rights of individuals, and lowered the standard of living of almost everyone.

All such laws constitute what libertarians call *moral cannibalism.* A cannibal in the physical sense is a person who lives off the flesh of other human beings. A *moral* cannibal is one who believes he has a right to live off the "spirit" of other human beings—who believes that he has a moral claim on the productive capacity, time, and effort expended by others.

It has become fashionable to claim virtually everything that one needs or desires as one's *right.* Thus, many people claim that they have a right to a job, the right to free medical care, to free food and clothing, to a decent home, and so on. Now if one asks, apart from any specific context, whether it would be desirable if everyone had these things, one might well say yes. But there is a gimmick attached to each of them: *At whose expense?* Jobs, medical care, education, and so on, don't grow on trees. These are goods and services *produced only by men.* Who, then, is to provide them, and under what conditions?

If you have a right to a job, who is to supply it? Must an employer supply it even if he doesn't want to hire you? What if you are unemployable, or incurably lazy? (If you say "the government must supply it," does that mean that a job must be created for you which no employer needs done, and that you must be kept in it regardless of how much or little you work?) If the employer is forced to supply it at his expense even if he doesn't need you, then isn't *he* being enslaved to that extent? What ever happened to *his* right to conduct his life and his affairs in accordance with his choices?

If you have a right to free medical care, then, since medical care doesn't exist in nature as wild apples do, some people will have to supply it to you for free: that is, they will have to spend their time and money and energy taking care of you whether they want to or not. What ever happened to *their* right to conduct their lives as they see fit? Or do you have a right to violate theirs? Can there be a right to violate rights?

All those who demand this or that as a "free service" are consciously or unconsciously evading the fact that there is in reality no such thing as free services. All man-made goods and services are the result of human expenditure of time and effort. There is no such thing as "something for nothing" in this world. If you demand something free, you are demanding that other men give their time and effort to you without compensation. If they voluntarily choose to do this, there is no problem; but if you demand that they be *forced* to do it, you are interfering with their right not to do it if they so choose. "Swimming in this pool ought to be free!" says the indignant passerby. What he means is that others should build a pool, others should provide the materials, and still others should run it and keep it in functioning order, so that *he* can use it without fee. But what right has he to the expenditure of *their* time and effort? To expect something "for free" is to expect it *to be paid for by others* whether they choose to or not.

Many questions, particularly about economic matters, will be generated by the libertarian account of human rights and the role of government. Should government have no role in assisting the needy, in providing social security, in legislating minimum wages, in fixing prices and putting a ceiling on rents, in curbing monopolies, in erecting tariffs, in guaranteeing jobs, in managing the money supply? To these and all similar questions the libertarian answers with an unequivocal no.

"But then you'd let people go hungry!" comes the rejoinder. This, the libertarian insists, is precisely what would not happen; with the restrictions removed, the economy would flourish as never before. With the controls taken off business, existing enterprises would expand and new ones would spring into existence satisfying more and more consumer needs; millions more people would be gainfully employed instead of subsisting on welfare, and all kinds of research and production, released from the stranglehold of government, would proliferate, fulfilling man's needs and desires as never before. It has always been so whenever government has permitted men to be free traders on a free market. But *why* this is so, and how the free market is the best solution to all problems relating to the material aspect of man's life, is another and far longer story. . . .

NOTE

1 William W. Bayes, "What Is Property?" *The Freeman,* July 1970, p. 348.

QUESTIONS

1 Some libertarians argue that, from a moral standpoint, there is no difference between the actions of an ordinary thief and those of a government when it seizes money from some in order to support others. They assume that, if the former are wrong, then so are the latter. Are they correct?
2 Do you agree that the government should have no role in assisting the needy? What reasons can you advance to defend your answer?

A Moral Case for Socialism

Kai Nielsen

Nielsen puts forth a moral case for socialism. He identifies and explicates a cluster of values that are basic to our culture—freedom and autonomy, equality, justice, rights, and democracy—and then compares "pure socialism" and "pure capitalism" in respect to these values. Nielsen concludes that a socialist system is much more likely to exemplify our basic values than is a capitalist system.

I

In North America socialism gets a bad press. It is under criticism for its alleged economic inefficiency and for its moral and human inadequacy. I want here to address the latter issue. Looking at capitalism and socialism, I want to consider, against the grain of our culture, what kind of moral case can be made for socialism.

The first thing to do, given the extensive, and, I would add, inexcusably extensive, confusions about this, is to say what socialism and capitalism are. That done I will then, appealing to a cluster of values which are basic in our culture, concerning which there is a considerable and indeed a reflective consensus, examine how capitalism and socialism fare with respect to these values. Given that people generally, at least in Western societies, would want it to be the case that these values have a stable exemplification in our social lives, it is appropriate to ask the question: which of these social systems is more likely stably to exemplify them? I shall argue, facing the gamut of a careful comparison in the light of these values, that, everything considered, socialism comes out better than capitalism. And this, if right, would give us good reason for believing that socialism is preferable—indeed morally preferable—to capitalism if it also turns out to be a feasible socio-economic system.

What, then, are socialism and capitalism? Put most succinctly, capitalism requires the existence of private *productive* property (private ownership of the means of production) while socialism works toward its abolition. What is essential for socialism is public ownership and control of the means of production and public ownership means just what it says: *ownership by the public*. Under capitalism there is a domain of private property rights in the means of production which are not subject to political determination. That is, even where the political domain is a democratic one, they are not subject to determination by the public; only an individual or a set of individuals who own that property can make the final determination of what is to be done with that property. These individuals make the determination and not citizens at large, as under socialism. In fully developed socialism, by contrast, there is, with respect to productive property, no domain which is not subject to political determination by the public, namely by the citizenry at large. Thus, where this public ownership and control is genuine, and not a mask for control by an elite of state bureaucrats, it will mean genuine popular and democratic control over productive

Reprinted with permission from *Critical Review*, vol. 3, Summer/Fall 1989, pp. 542–552.

property. What socialism is *not* is *state* ownership in the absence of, at the very least, popular sovereignty, i.e., genuine popular control over the state apparatus including any economic functions it might have.

The property that is owned in common under socialism is the means of existence—the productive property in the society. Socialism does not proscribe the ownership of private personal property, such as houses, cars, television sets and the like. It only proscribes the private ownership of the means of production.

The above characterizations catch the minimal core of socialism and capitalism, what used to be called the essence of those concepts. But beyond these core features, it is well, in helping us to make our comparison, to see some other important features which characteristically go with capitalism and socialism. Minimally, capitalism is private ownership of the means of production but it is also, at least characteristically, a social system in which a class of capitalists owns and controls the means of production and hires workers who, owning little or no means of production, sell their labor-power to some capitalist or other for a wage. This means that a capitalist society will be a class society in which there will be two principal classes: capitalists and workers. Socialism by contrast is a social system in which every able-bodied person is, was or will be a worker. These workers commonly own and control the means of production (this is the characteristic form of public ownership). Thus in socialism we have, in a perfectly literal sense, a classless society for there is no division between human beings along class lines.

There are both pure and impure forms of capitalism and socialism. The pure form of capitalism is competitive capitalism, the capitalism that Milton Friedman would tell us is the real capitalism while, he would add, the impure form is monopoly or corporate capitalism. Similarly the pure form of socialism is democratic socialism, with firm workers' control of the means of production and an industrial as well as a political democracy, while the impure form is state bureaucratic socialism.

Now it is a noteworthy fact that, to understate it, actually existing capitalisms and actually existing socialisms tend to be the impure forms. Many partisans of capitalism lament the fact that the actually existing capitalisms overwhelmingly tend to be forms of corporate capitalism where the state massively intervenes in the running of the economy. It is unclear whether anything like a fully competitive capitalism actually exists—perhaps Hong Kong approximates it—and it is also unclear whether many of the actual players in the major capitalist societies (the existing capitalists and their managers) want or even expect that it is possible to have laissez-faire capitalism again (if indeed we ever had it). Some capitalist societies are further down the corporate road than other societies, but they are all forms of corporate, perhaps in some instances even monopoly, capitalism. Competitive capitalism seems to be more of a libertarian dream than a sociological reality or even something desired by many informed and tough-minded members of the capitalist class. Socialism has had a similar fate. Its historical exemplifications tend to be of the impure forms, namely the bureaucratic state socialisms. Yugoslavia is perhaps to socialism what Hong Kong is to capitalism. It is a candidate for what might count as an exemplification, or at least a near approximation, of the pure form.

This paucity of exemplifications of pure forms of either capitalism or socialism raises the question of whether the pure forms are at best unstable social systems and at worst merely utopian ideals. I shall not try directly to settle that issue here. What I shall do instead is to compare *models* with *models*. In asking about the moral case for socialism, I shall compare forms that a not inconsiderable number of the theoretical protagonists of each take to be pure forms but which are still, they believe, historically feasible. But I will also be concerned to ask whether these models—these pure forms—can reasonably be expected to come to have a home. If they are not historically feasible models, then, even if we can make a good theoretical moral case for them, we will have hardly provided a good moral case for socialism or capitalism. To avoid bad utopianism we must be talking about forms which could be on the historical agenda. (I plainly here do not take "bad utopianism" to be pleonastic.)

II

Setting aside for the time being the feasibility question, let us compare the pure forms of capitalism and socialism—that is to say, competitive capitalism and democratic socialism—as to how they stand with respect to sustaining and furthering the values of freedom and autonomy, equality, justice, rights and democracy. My argument shall be that socialism comes out better with respect to those values.

Let us first look at freedom and autonomy. An autonomous person is a person who is able to set her ends for herself and in optimal circumstances is able to pursue those ends. But freedom does not only mean being autonomous; it also means the absence of unjustified political and social interference in the pursuit of one's ends. Some might even say that it is just the absence of interference with one's ends. Still it is self-direction—autonomy—not non-interference which is *intrinsically* desirable. Non-interference is only valuable where it is an aid to our being able to do what we want and where we are sufficiently autonomous to have some control over our wants.

How do capitalism and socialism fare in providing the social conditions which will help or impede the flourishing of autonomy? Which model society would make for the greater flourishing of autonomy? My argument is (a) that democratic socialism makes it possible for more people to be more fully autonomous than would be autonomous under capitalism; and (b) that democratic socialism also interferes less in people's exercise of their autonomy than any form of capitalism. All societies limit liberty by interfering with people doing what they want to do in some ways, but the restrictions are more extensive, deeper and more undermining of autonomy in capitalism than in democratic socialism. Where there is private ownership of productive property, which, remember, is private ownership of the means of life, it cannot help but be the case that a few (the owning and controlling capitalist class) will have, along with the managers beholden to them, except in periods of revolutionary turmoil, a firm control, indeed a domination, over the vast majority of people in the society. The capitalist class with the help of their managers determines whether workers (taken now as individuals) can work, how they work, on what they work, the conditions under which they work and what is done with what they produce (where they are producers) and what use is made of their skills and the like. As we move to welfare state capitalism—a compromise still favoring capital which emerged out of long and bitter class struggles—the state places some restrictions on some of these powers of capital. Hours, working conditions and the like are controlled in certain ways. Yet whether workers work and continue to work, how they work and on what, what is done with what they produce, and the rationale for their work are not determined by the workers themselves but by the owners of capital and their managers; this means a very considerable limitation on the autonomy and freedom of workers. Since workers are the great majority, such socio-economic relations place a very considerable limitation on human freedom and indeed on the very most important freedom that people have, namely their being able to live in a self-directed manner, when compared with the industrial democracy of democratic socialism. Under capitalist arrangements it simply cannot fail to be the case that a very large number of people will lose control over a very central set of facets of their lives, namely central aspects of their work and indeed in many instances, over their very chance to be able to work.

Socialism would indeed prohibit capitalist acts between consenting adults; the capitalist class would lose its freedom to buy and sell and to control the labor market. There should be no blinking at the fact that socialist social relations would impose some limitations on freedom, for there is, and indeed can be, no society without norms and some sanctions. In any society you like there will be some things you are at liberty to do and some things that you may not do. However, democratic socialism must bring with it an industrial democracy where workers by various democratic procedures would determine how they are to work, on what they are to work, the hours of their work, under what conditions they are to work (insofar as this is alterable by human effort at all), what they will produce and how much, and what is to be done with what they produce. Since, instead of there being "private ownership of the means of production," there is in a genuinely socialist society "public ownership of the means of production," the means of life are owned by everyone and thus each person has a *right* to work: she has, that is, a right to the means of life. It is no longer the private preserve of an individual owner of capital but it is owned in common by us all. This means that each of us has an equal right to the means of life. Members of the capitalist class would have a few of their liberties restricted, but these are linked with owning and controlling capital and are not the important civil and political liberties that we all rightly cherish. Moreover, the limitation of the capitalist liberties to buy and sell and the like would make for a more extensive liberty for many, many more people.

One cannot respond to the above by saying that workers are free to leave the working class and become capitalists or at least petty bourgeoisie. They may indeed all in theory, taken *individually,* be free to leave the working class, but if many in fact try to leave, the exits will very quickly become blocked. Individuals are only free on the condition that the great mass of people, taken collectively, are not. We could not have capitalism without a working class and the working class is not free within the capitalist system to cease being wage laborers. We cannot all be capitalists. A people's capitalism is nonsense. Though a petty commodity production system (the family farm writ large) is a logical possibility, it is hardly a stable empirical possibility and, what is most important for the present discussion, such a system would not be a capitalist system. Under capitalism, most of us, if we are to find any work at all, will just have to sell (or *perhaps* "rent" is the better word) our labor-power as a commodity. Whether you sell or rent your labor power or, where it is provided, you go on welfare, you will not have much control over areas very crucial to your life. If these are the only feasible alternatives facing the working class, working class autonomy is very limited indeed. But these are the only alternatives under capitalism.

Capitalist acts between consenting adults, if they become sufficiently widespread, lead to severe imbalances in power. These imbalances in power tend to undermine autonomy by creating differentials in wealth and control between workers and capitalists. Such imbalances are the name of the game for capitalism. Even if we (perversely I believe) call a system of petty commodity production capitalism, we still must say that such a socio-economic system is inherently unstable. Certain individuals would win out in this exchanging of commodities and in fairly quick order it would lead to a class system and the imbalances of power—the domination of the many by the few—that I take to be definitive of capitalism. By abolishing capitalist acts between consenting adults, then (but leaving personal property and civil and political liberties untouched), socialism protects more extensive freedoms for more people and in far more important areas of their lives.

III

So democratic socialism does better regarding the value that epitomizes capitalist pride (*hubris,* would, I think, be a better term), namely autonomy. It also does better, I shall now argue, than capitalism with respect to another of our basic values, namely democracy. Since this is almost a corollary of what I have said about autonomy I can afford to be briefer. In capitalist societies, democracy must simply be *political* democracy. There can in the nature of the case be no genuine or thorough workplace democracy. When we enter the sphere of production, capitalists and not workers own, and therefore at least ultimately control, the means of production. While capitalism, as in some workplaces in West Germany and Sweden, sometimes can be pressured into allowing an ameliorative measure of worker control, once ownership rights are given up, we no longer have private productive property but public productive property (and in that way social ownership): capitalism is given up and we have socialism. However, where worker control is restricted to a few firms, we do not yet have socialism. What makes a system socialist or capitalist depends on what happens across the whole society, not just in isolated firms. Moreover, managers can become very important within capitalist firms, but as long as ownership, including the ability to close the place down and liquidate the business, rests in the hands of capitalists we can have no genuine workplace democracy. Socialism, in its pure form, carries with it, in a way capitalism in any form cannot, workplace democracy. (That some of the existing socialisms are anything but pure does not belie this.)

Similarly, whatever may be said of existing socialisms or at least of some existing socialisms, it is not the case that there is anything in the very idea of socialism that militates against political as well as industrial democracy. Socialists are indeed justly suspicious of some of the tricks played by parliamentary democracy in bourgeois countries, aware of its not infrequent hypocrisy and the limitations of its stress on purely legal and formal political rights and liberties. Socialists are also, without at all wishing to throw the baby out with the bath water, rightly suspicious of any simple reliance on majority rule, unsupplemented by other democratic procedures and safeguards. But there is nothing in socialist theory that would set it against political democracy and the protection of political and civil rights; indeed there is much in socialism that favors them, namely its stress on both autonomy and equality.

The fact that political democracy came into being and achieved stability within capitalist societies may prove something about conditions necessary for its coming into being, but it says nothing about capitalism being necessary for sustaining it. In Chile, South Africa and Nazi Germany, indeed, capitalism has flourished without the protection of civil and political rights or anything like a respect for the democratic tradition. There is nothing structural in socialism that would prevent it from continuing those democratic traditions or cherishing those political and civil rights. That something came about under certain conditions does not establish that these conditions are necessary for its continued existence. That men initially took an interest in chess does not establish that women cannot quite naturally take an interest in it as well. When capitalist societies with long-flourishing democratic traditions move to socialism there is no reason at all to believe that they will not continue to be democratic. (Where societies previously had no democratic tradition or only a very weak one, matters are more problematic.)

IV

I now want to turn to a third basic value, equality. In societies across the political spectrum, *moral* equality (the belief that everyone's life matters equally) is an accepted value. Or, to be somewhat cynical about the matter, at least lip service is paid to it. But even this lip service is the compliment that vice pays to virtue. That is to say, such a belief is a deeply held considered conviction in modernized societies, though it has not been at all times and is not today a value held in all societies. This is most evident concerning moral equality.

While this value is genuinely held by the vast majority of people in capitalist societies, it can hardly be an effective or functional working norm where there is such a diminishment of autonomy as we have seen obtains unavoidably in such societies. Self-respect is deeply threatened where so many people lack effective control over their own lives, where there are structures of domination, where there is alienated labor, where great power differentials and differences in wealth make for very different (and often very bleak) life chances. For not inconsiderable numbers, in fact, it is difficult to maintain self-respect under such conditions unless they are actively struggling against the system. And, given present conditions, fighting the system, particularly in societies such as the United States, may well be felt to be a hopeless task. Under such conditions any real equality of opportunity is out of the question. And the circumstances are such, in spite of what is often said about these states, that equality of condition is an even more remote possibility. But without at least some of these things moral equality cannot even be approximated. Indeed, even to speak of it sounds like an obscene joke given the social realities of our lives.

Although under welfare-state capitalism some of the worst inequalities of capitalism are ameliorated, workers still lack effective control over their work, with repercussions in political and public life as well. Differentials of wealth cannot but give rise to differentials in power and control in politics, in the media, in education, in the direction of social life and in what options get seriously debated. The life chances of workers and those not even lucky enough to be workers (whose ranks are growing and will continue to grow under capitalism) are impoverished compared to the life chances of members of the capitalist class and its docile professional support stratum.

None of these equality-undermining features would obtain under democratic socialism. Such societies would, for starters, be classless, eliminating the power and control differentials that go with the class system of capitalism. In addition to political democracy, industrial democracy and all the egalitarian and participatory control that goes with that would, in turn, reinforce moral equality. Indeed it would make it possible where before it was impossible. There would be a commitment under democratic socialism to attaining or at least approximating, as far as it is feasible, equality of condition; and this, where approximated, would help make for real equality of opportunity, making equal life chances something less utopian than it must be under capitalism.

In fine, the very things, as we have seen, that make for greater autonomy under socialism than under capitalism, would, in being more equally distributed, make for greater equality of condition, greater equality of opportunity and greater moral equality in a democratic socialist society than in a capitalist one. These values are values commonly shared by both capitalistically inclined people and those who are socialistically inclined. What the former do not see is that in modern industrial societies, democratic socialism can better deliver these goods than even progressive capitalism.

There is, without doubt, legitimate worry about bureaucratic control under socialism. But that is a worry under any historically feasible capitalism as well, and it is anything but clear that state bureaucracies are worse than great corporate bureaucracies. Indeed, if socialist bureaucrats were, as the socialist system requires, really committed to production for needs and to achieving equality of condition, they might, bad as they are, be the lesser of two evils. But in any event democratic socialism is not bureaucratic state socialism, and there is no structural reason to believe that it must—if it arises in a society with skilled workers committed to democracy—give rise to bureaucratic state socialism. There will, inescapably, be some bureaucracy, but in a democratic socialist society it must and indeed will be controlled. This is not merely a matter of optimism about the will of socialists, for there are more mechanisms for democratic control of bureaucracy within a democratic socialism that is both a political and an industrial democracy, than there can be under even the most benign capitalist democracies—democracies which for structural reasons can never be industrial democracies. If, all that notwithstanding, bureaucratic creepage is inescapable in modern societies, then that is just as much a problem for capitalism as for socialism.

The underlying rationale for production under capitalism is profit and capital accumulation. Capitalism is indeed a marvelous engine for building up the productive forces (though clearly at the expense of considerations of equality and autonomy). We might look on it, going back to earlier historical times, as something like a forced march to develop the productive forces. But now that the productive forces in advanced capitalist societies are wondrously developed, we are in a position to direct them to far more humane and more equitable uses under a socio-economic system whose rationale for production is to meet human needs (the needs of every-one as far as this is possible). This egalitarian thrust, together with the socialists' commitment to attaining, as far as that is possible, equality of condition, makes it clear that socialism will produce more equality than capitalism.

V

In talking about autonomy, democracy and equality, we have, in effect, already been talking about justice. A society or set of institutions that does better in these respects than another society will be a more just society than the other society.

Fairness is a less fancy name for justice. If we compare two societies and the first is more democratic than the second; there is more autonomy in the first society than in the second; there are more nearly equal life chances in the first society than in the second and thus greater equality of opportunity; if, without sacrifice of auton-omy, there is more equality of condition in the first society than in the second; and if there is more moral equality in the first society than in the second, then we can-not but conclude that the first society is a society with more fairness than the sec-ond and, thus, that it is the more just society. But this is exactly how socialism comes out vis-á-vis even the best form of capitalism.

A society which undermines autonomy, heels in democracy (where democracy is not violating rights), makes equality impossible to achieve and violates rights cannot be a just society. If, as I contend, that is what capitalism does, and cannot help doing, then a capitalist society cannot be a just society. Democratic socialism, by contrast, does not need to do any of those things, and we can predict that it would not, for there are no structural imperatives in democratic socialism to do so and there are deep sentiments in that tradition urging us not to do so. I do not for a moment deny that there are similar sentiments for autonomy and democracy in cap-italist societies, but the logic of capitalism, the underlying structures of capitalist societies—even the best of capitalist societies—frustrate the realization of the states of affairs at which those sympathies aim. A radical democrat with a commit-ment to human rights, to human autonomy and moral equality and fair equality of opportunity ought to be a democratic socialist and a firm opponent of capitalism—even a capitalism with a human face.

QUESTIONS

1 Does Nielsen provide good arguments in support of his claim that a socialist system makes it possible for more people to be more fully autonomous than does a capitalist sys-tem?

2 What arguments, if any, could Hospers offer to refute Nielsen's claim that a socialist system is more democratic than a capitalist system?

Five Faces of Oppression

Iris M. Young

In Young's view, all oppressed people have something in common: They all suffer some inhibition of their ability to develop and exercise their capacities and express their needs, thoughts, and feelings. However, no one set of criteria can be used to describe the condition of all those who are oppressed. Rather, oppression takes multiple forms: exploitation, marginalization, powerlessness, cultural imperialism, and systematic violence. In Young's view, the presence of even one of these five conditions is sufficient for calling a group oppressed.

Many people in the United States would not choose the term "oppression" to name injustice in our society. For contemporary emancipatory social movements, on the other hand—socialists, radical feminists, American Indian activists, Black activists, gay and lesbian activists—oppression is a central category of political discourse. Entering the political discourse in which oppression is a central category involves adopting a general mode of analyzing and evaluating social structures and practices which is incommensurate with the language of liberal individualism that dominates political discourse in the United States.

A major political project for those of us who identify with at least one of these movements must thus be to persuade people that the discourse of oppression makes sense of much of our social experience. We are ill prepared for this task, however, because we have no clear account of the meaning of oppression. While we find the term used often in the diverse philosophical and theoretical literature spawned by radical social movements in the United States, we find little direct discussion of the meaning of the concept as used by these movements.

In this [essay] I offer some explication of the concept of oppression as I understand its use by new social movements in the United States since the 1960s. My starting point is reflection on the conditions of the groups said by these movements to be oppressed: among others women, Blacks, Chicanos, Puerto Ricans and other Spanish-speaking Americans, American Indians, Jews, lesbians, gay men, Arabs, Asians, old people, working-class people, and the physically and mentally disabled. I aim to systematize the meaning of the concept of oppression as used by these diverse political movements, and to provide normative argument to clarify the wrongs the term names.

Obviously the above-named groups are not oppressed to the same extent or in the same ways. In the most general sense, all oppressed people suffer some inhibition of their ability to develop and exercise their capacities and express their needs, thoughts, and feelings. In that abstract sense all oppressed people face a common condition. Beyond that, in any more specific sense, it is not possible to define a single set of criteria that describe the condition of oppression of the above groups.

Consequently, attempts by theorists and activists to discover a common description or the essential causes of the oppression of all these groups have frequently led to fruitless disputes about whose oppression is more fundamental or more grave. The contexts in which members of these groups use the term oppression to describe the injustices of their situation suggest that oppression names in fact a family of concepts and conditions, which I divide into five categories: exploitation, marginalization, powerlessness, cultural imperialism, and violence. . . .

THE FACES OF OPPRESSION

Exploitation

The central function of Marx's theory of exploitation is to explain how class structure can exist in the absence of legally and normatively sanctioned class distinctions. In precapitalist societies domination is overt and accomplished through directly political means. In both slave society and feudal society the right to appropriate the product of the labor of others partly defines class privilege, and these societies legitimate class distinctions with ideologies of natural superiority and inferiority.

Capitalist society, on the other hand, removes traditional juridically enforced class distinctions and promotes a belief in the legal freedom of persons. Workers freely contract with employers and receive a wage; no formal mechanisms of law or custom force them to work for that employer or any employer. Thus the mystery of capitalism arises: when everyone is formally free, how can there be class domination? Why do class distinctions persist between the wealthy, who own the means of production, and the mass of people, who work for them? The theory of exploitation answers this question.

Profit, the basis of capitalist power and wealth, is a mystery if we assume that in the market goods exchange at their values. The labor theory of value dispels this mystery. Every commodity's value is a function of the labor time necessary for its production. Labor power is the one commodity which in the process of being consumed produces new value. Profit comes from the difference between the value of the labor performed and the value of the capacity to labor which the capitalist purchases. Profit is possible only because the owner of capital appropriates any realized surplus value. . . .

Marx's theory of exploitation lacks an explicitly normative meaning, even though the judgment that workers are exploited clearly has normative as well as descriptive power in that theory. C. B. Macpherson (1973, chap. 3) reconstructs this theory of exploitation in a more explicitly normative form. The injustice of capitalist society consists in the fact that some people exercise their capacities under the control, according to the purposes, and for the benefit of other people. Through private ownership of the means of production, and through markets that allocate labor and the ability to buy goods, capitalism systematically transfers the powers of some persons to others, thereby augmenting the power of the latter. In this process of the transfer of powers, according to Macpherson, the capitalist class acquires and maintains an ability to extract benefits from workers. Not only are powers transferred from workers to capitalists, but also the powers of workers diminish by more than the amount of transfer, because workers suffer material deprivation and a loss of control, and hence are deprived of important elements of self-respect. Justice, then, requires eliminating the institutional forms that enable and enforce this process of transference and replacing them with institutional forms that enable all to develop and use their capacities in a way that does not inhibit, but rather can enhance, similar development and use in others.

The central insight expressed in the concept of exploitation, then, is that this oppression occurs through a steady process of the transfer of the results of the labor of one social group to benefit another. The injustice of class division does not consist only in the distributive fact that some people have great wealth while most people have little. Exploitation enacts a structural relation between social groups. Social rules about what work is, who does what for whom, how work is compensated, and the social process by which the results of work are appropriated operate to enact relations of power and inequality. These relations are produced and reproduced through a systematic process in which the energies of the have-nots are continuously expended to maintain and augment the power, status, and wealth of the haves. . . .

Feminists have had little difficulty showing that women's oppression consists partly in a systematic and unreciprocated transfer of powers from women to men. Women's oppression consists not merely in an inequality of status, power, and wealth resulting from men's excluding them from privileged activities. The freedom, power, status, and self-realization of men is possible precisely because women work for them. Gender exploitation has two aspects, transfer of the fruits of material labor to men and transfer of nurturing and sexual energies to men.

Christine Delphy (1984), for example, describes marriage as a class relation in which women's labor benefits men without comparable remuneration. She makes it clear that the exploitation consists not in the sort of work that women do in the home, for this might include various kinds of tasks, but in the fact that they perform tasks for someone on whom they are dependent. Thus, for example, in most systems of agricultural production in the world, men take to market the goods women have produced, and more often than not men receive the status and often the entire income from this labor.

With the concept of sex-affective production, Ann Ferguson (1984; 1989, chap. 4) identifies another form of the transference of women's energies to men. Women provide men and children with emotional care and provide men with sexual satisfaction, and as a group receive relatively little of either from men. The gender socialization of women makes us tend to be more attentive to interactive dynamics than men, and makes women good at providing empathy and support for people's feelings and at smoothing over interactive tensions. Both men and women look to women as nurturers of their personal lives, and women frequently complain that when they look to men for emotional support they do not receive it. The norms of heterosexuality, moreover, are oriented around male pleasure, and consequently many women receive little satisfaction from their sexual interaction with men.

Most feminist theories of gender exploitation have concentrated on the institutional structure of the patriarchal family. Recently, however, feminists have begun to explore relations of gender exploitation enacted in the contemporary workplace and through the state. Carol Brown argues that as men have removed themselves from responsibility for children, many women have become dependent on the state for subsistence as they continue to bear nearly total responsibility for childrearing (Brown, 1981). This creates a new system of the exploitation of women's domestic labor mediated by state institutions, which she calls public patriarchy.

In twentieth-century capitalist economies the workplaces that women have been entering in increasing numbers serve as another important site of gender exploitation. David Alexander (1987) argues that typically feminine jobs involve gender-based tasks requiring sexual labor, nurturing, caring for others' bodies, or smoothing over workplace tensions. In these ways women's energies are expended in jobs that enhance the status of, please, or comfort others, usually men; and these gender-based labors of waitresses, clerical workers, nurses, and other caretakers often go unnoticed and undercompensated.

To summarize, women are exploited in the Marxist sense to the degree that they are wage workers. Some have argued that women's domestic labor also represents a form of capitalist class exploitation insofar as it is labor covered by the wages a family receives. As a group, however, women undergo specific forms of gender exploitation in which their energies and power are expended, often unnoticed and unacknowledged, usually to benefit men by releasing them for more important and creative work, enhancing their status or the environment around them, or providing them with sexual or emotional service.

Race is a structure of oppression at least as basic as class or gender. Are there, then, racially specific forms of exploitation? There is no doubt that racialized groups in the United States, especially Blacks and Latinos, are oppressed through capitalist superexploitation resulting from a segmented labor market that tends to reserve skilled, high-paying, unionized jobs for whites. There is wide disagreement about whether such superexploitation benefits whites as a group or only benefits the capitalist class and I do not intend to enter into that dispute here.

However one answers the question about capitalist superexploitation of racialized groups, is it possible to conceptualize a form of exploitation that is racially specific on analogy with the gender-specific forms just discussed? I suggest that the category of *menial* labor might supply a means for such conceptualization. In its derivation "menial" designates the labor of servants. Wherever there is racism, there is the assumption, more or less enforced, that members of the oppressed racial groups are or ought to be servants of those, or some of those, in the privileged group. In most white racist societies this means that many white people have dark- or yellow-skinned domestic servants, and in the United States today there remains significant racial structuring of private household service. But in the United States today much service labor has gone public: anyone who goes to a good hotel or a good restaurant can have servants. Servants often attend the daily—and nightly—activities of business executives, government officials, and other high-status professionals. In our society there remains strong cultural pressure to fill servant jobs—bellhop, porter, chambermaid, busboy, and so on—with Black and Latino workers. These jobs entail a transfer of energies whereby the servers enhance the status of the served.

Menial labor usually refers not only to service, however, but also to any servile, unskilled, low-paying work lacking in autonomy, in which a person is subject to taking orders from many people. Menial work tends to be auxiliary work, instrumental to the work of others, where those others receive primary recognition for doing the job. Laborers on a construction site, for example, are at the beck and call of welders, electricians, carpenters, and other skilled workers, who receive recognition for the job done. In the United States explicit racial discrimination once reserved menial work for Blacks, Chicanos, American Indians, and Chinese, and menial work still tends to be linked to Black and Latino workers. I offer this category of menial labor as a form of racially specific exploitation, as a provisional category in need of exploration. . . .

Marginalization

Increasingly in the United States racial oppression occurs in the form of marginalization rather than exploitation. Marginals are people the system of labor cannot or will not use. Not only in Third World capitalist countries, but also in most Western capitalist societies, there is a growing underclass of people permanently confined to lives of social marginality, most of whom are racially marked—Blacks or Indians in Latin America, and Blacks, East Indians, Eastern Europeans, or North Africans in Europe.

Marginalization is by no means the fate only of racially marked groups, however. In the United States a shamefully large proportion of the population is marginal: old people, and increasingly people who are not very old but get laid off from their jobs and cannot find new work; young people, especially Black or Latino, who cannot find first or second jobs; many single mothers and their children; other people involuntarily unemployed; many mentally and physically disabled people; American Indians, especially those on reservations.

Marginalization is perhaps the most dangerous form of oppression. A whole category of people is expelled from useful participation in social life and thus potentially subjected to severe material deprivation and even extermination. The material deprivation marginalization often causes is certainly unjust, especially in a society where others have plenty. Contemporary advanced capitalist societies have in principle acknowledged the injustice of material deprivation caused by marginalization, and have taken some steps to address it by providing welfare payments and services. The continuance of this welfare state is by no means assured, and in most welfare state societies, especially the United States, welfare redistributions do not eliminate large-scale suffering and deprivation.

Material deprivation, which can be addressed by redistributive social policies, is not, however, the extent of the harm caused by marginalization. Two categories of injustice beyond distribution are associated with marginality in advanced capitalist societies. First, the provision of welfare itself produces new injustice by depriving those dependent on it of rights and freedoms that others have. Second, even when material deprivation is somewhat mitigated by the welfare state, marginalization is unjust because it blocks the opportunity to exercise capacities in socially defined and recognized ways. I shall explicate each of these in turn.

Liberalism has traditionally asserted the right of all rational autonomous agents to equal citizenship. Early bourgeois liberalism explicitly excluded from citizenship all those whose reason was questionable or not fully developed, and all those not independent. Thus poor people, women, the mad and the feebleminded, and children were explicitly excluded from citizenship, and many of these were housed in institutions modeled on the modern prison: poorhouses, insane asylums, schools.

Today the exclusion of dependent persons from equal citizenship rights is only barely hidden beneath the surface. Because they depend on bureaucratic institutions for support or services, the old, the poor, and the mentally or physically disabled are subject to patronizing, punitive, demeaning, and arbitrary treatment by the policies and people associated with welfare bureaucracies. Being a dependent in our society implies being legitimately subject to the often arbitrary and invasive authority of social service providers and other public and private administrators, who enforce rules with which the marginal must comply, and otherwise exercise power over the conditions of their lives. In meeting needs of the marginalized, often with the aid of social scientific disciplines, welfare agencies also construct the needs themselves. Medical and social service professionals know what is good for those they serve, and the marginals and dependents themselves do not have the right to claim to know what is good for them. Dependency in our society thus implies, as it has in all liberal societies, a sufficient warrant to suspend basic rights to privacy, respect, and individual choice.

Although dependency produces conditions of injustice in our society, dependency in itself need not be oppressive. One cannot imagine a society in which some people would not need to be dependent on others at least some of the time: children, sick people, women recovering from childbirth, old people who have become frail, depressed or otherwise emotionally needy persons, have the moral right to depend on others for subsistence and support.

An important contribution of feminist moral theory has been to question the deeply held assumption that moral agency and full citizenship require that a person be autonomous and independent. Feminists have exposed this assumption as inappropriately individualistic and derived from a specifically male experience of social relations, which values competition and solitary achievement. Female experience of social relations, arising both from women's typical domestic care responsibilities and from the kinds of paid work that many women do, tends to recognize dependence as a basic human condition. Whereas on the autonomy model a just society would as much as possible give people the opportunity to be independent, the feminist model envisions justice as according respect and participation in decisionmaking to those who are dependent as well as to those who are independent. Dependency should not be a reason to be deprived of choice and respect, and much of the oppression many marginals experience would be lessened if a less individualistic model of rights prevailed.

Marginalization does not cease to be oppressive when one has shelter and food. Many old people, for example, have sufficient means to live comfortably but remain oppressed in their marginal status. Even if marginals were provided a comfortable material life within institutions that respected their freedom and dignity, injustices of marginality would remain in the form of uselessness, boredom, and lack of self-respect. Most of our society's productive and recognized activities take place in contexts of organized social cooperation, and social structures and processes that close persons out of participation in such social cooperation are unjust. Thus while marginalization definitely entails serious issues of distributive justice, it also involves the deprivation of cultural, practical, and institutionalized conditions for exercising capacities in a context of recognition and interaction. . . .

Powerlessness

As I have indicated, the Marxist idea of class is important because it helps reveal the structure of exploitation: that some people have their power and wealth because they profit from the labor of others. For this reason I reject the claim some make that a traditional class exploitation model fails to capture the structure of contemporary society. It remains the case that the labor of most people in the society augments the power of relatively few. Despite their differences from nonprofessional workers, most professional workers are still not members of the capitalist class. Professional labor either involves exploitative transfers to capitalists or supplies important conditions for such transfers. Professional workers are in an ambiguous class position, it is true, because . . . they also benefit from the exploitation of nonprofessional workers.

While it is false to claim that a division between capitalist and working classes no longer describes our society, it is also false to say that class relations have remained unaltered since the nineteenth century. An adequate conception of oppression cannot ignore the experience of social division reflected in the colloquial distinction between the "middle class" and the "working class," a division structured by the social division of labor between professionals and nonprofessionals. Professionals are privileged in relation to nonprofessionals, by virtue of their position in the division of labor and the status it carries. Nonprofessionals suffer a form of oppression in addition to exploitation, which I call powerlessness.

In the United States, as in other advanced capitalist countries, most workplaces are not organized democratically, direct participation in public policy decisions is rare, and policy implementation is for the most part hierarchical, imposing rules on bureaucrats and citizens. Thus most people in these societies do not regularly participate in making decisions that affect the conditions of their lives and actions, and in this sense most people lack significant power. At the same time, domination in modern society is enacted through the widely dispersed powers of many agents mediating the decisions of others. To that extent many people have some power in relation to others, even though they lack the power to decide policies or results. The powerless are those who lack authority or power even in this mediated sense, those over whom power is exercised without their exercising it; the powerless are situated so that they must take orders and rarely have the right to give them. Powerlessness also designates a position in the division of labor and the concomitant social position that allows persons little opportunity to develop and exercise skills. The powerless have little or no work autonomy, exercise little creativity or judgment in their work, have no technical expertise or authority, express themselves awkwardly, especially in public or bureaucratic settings, and do not command respect. Powerlessness names the oppressive situations Sennett and Cobb (1972) describe in their famous study of working-class men.

This powerless status is perhaps best described negatively: the powerless lack the authority, status, and sense of self that professionals tend to have. The status privilege of professionals has three aspects, the lack of which produces oppression for nonprofessionals.

First, acquiring and practicing a profession has an expansive, progressive character. Being professional usually requires a college education and the acquisition of a specialized knowledge that entails working with symbols and concepts. Professionals experience progress first in acquiring the expertise, and then in the course of professional advancement and rise in status. The life of the nonprofessional by comparison is powerless in the sense that it lacks this orientation toward the progressive development of capacities and avenues for recognition.

Second, while many professionals have supervisors and cannot directly influence many decisions or the actions of many people, most nevertheless have considerable day-to-day work autonomy. Professionals usually have some authority over others, moreover—either over workers they supervise, or over auxiliaries, or over clients. Nonprofessionals, on the other hand, lack autonomy, and in both their working and their consumer-client lives often stand under the authority of professionals.

Though based on a division of labor between "mental" and "manual" work, the distinction between "middle class" and "working class" designates a division not only in working life, but also in nearly all aspects of social life. Professionals and nonprofessionals belong to different cultures in the United States. The two groups tend to live in segregated neighborhoods or even different towns, a process itself mediated by planners, zoning officials, and real estate people. The groups tend to have different tastes in food, decor, clothes, music, and vacations, and often different health and educational needs. Members of each group socialize for the most part with others in the same status group. While there is some intergroup mobility between generations, for the most part the children of professionals become professionals and the children of nonprofessionals do not.

Thus, third, the privileges of the professional extend beyond the workplace to a whole way of life. I call this way of life "respectability." To treat people with respect is to be prepared to listen to what they have to say or to do what they request because they have some authority, expertise, or influence. The norms of respectability in our society are associated specifically with professional culture. Professional dress, speech, tastes, demeanor, all connote respectability. Generally professionals expect and receive respect from others. In restaurants, banks, hotels, real estate offices, and many other such public places, as well as in the media, professionals typically receive more respectful treatment than nonprofessionals. For this reason nonprofessionals seeking a loan or a job, or to buy a house or a car, will often try to look "professional" and "respectable" in those settings.

The privilege of this professional respectability appears starkly in the dynamics of racism and sexism. In daily interchange women and men of color must prove their respectability. At first they are often not treated by strangers with respectful distance or deference. Once people discover that this woman or that Puerto Rican man is a college teacher or a business executive, however, they often behave more respectfully toward her or him. Working-class white men, on the other hand, are often treated with respect until their working-class status is revealed. . . .

Cultural Imperialism

Exploitation, marginalization, and powerlessness all refer to relations of power and oppression that occur by virtue of the social division of labor—who works for whom, who does not work, and how the content of work defines one institutional position relative to others. These three categories refer to structural and institutional relations that delimit people's material lives, including but not restricted to the resources they have access to and the concrete opportunities they have or do not have to develop and exercise their capacities. These kinds of oppression are a matter of concrete power in relation to others—of who benefits from whom, and who is dispensable.

Recent theorists of movements of group liberation, notably feminist and Black liberation theorists, have also given prominence to a rather different form of oppression, which following Lugones and Spelman (1983) I shall call cultural imperialism. To experience cultural imperialism means to experience how the dominant meanings of a society render the particular perspective of one's own group invisible at the same time as they stereotype one's group and mark it out as the Other.

Cultural imperialism involves the universalization of a dominant group's experience and culture, and its establishment as the norm. Some groups have exclusive or primary access to what Nancy Fraser (1987) calls the means of interpretation and communication in a society. As a consequence, the dominant cultural products of the society, that is, those most widely disseminated, express the experience, values, goals, and achievements of these groups. Often without noticing they do so, the dominant groups project their own experience as representative of humanity as such. Cultural products also express the dominant group's perspective on and interpretation of events and elements in the society, including other groups in the society, insofar as they attain cultural status at all.

An encounter with other groups, however, can challenge the dominant group's claim to universality. The dominant group reinforces its position by bringing the other groups under the measure of its dominant norms. Consequently, the difference of women from men, American Indians or Africans from Europeans, Jews from Christians, homosexuals from heterosexuals, workers from professionals, becomes reconstructed largely as deviance and inferiority. Since only the dominant group's cultural expressions receive wide dissemination, their cultural expressions become the normal, or the universal, and thereby the unremarkable. Given the normality of its own cultural expressions and identity, the dominant group constructs the differences which some groups exhibit as lack and negation. These groups become marked as Other.

The culturally dominated undergo a paradoxical oppression, in that they are both marked out by stereotypes and at the same time rendered invisible. As remarkable, deviant beings, the culturally imperialized are stamped with an essence. The stereotypes confine them to a nature which is often attached in some way to their bodies, and which thus cannot easily be denied. These stereotypes so permeate the society that they are not noticed as contestable. Just as everyone knows that the earth goes around the sun, so everyone knows that gay people are promiscuous, that Indians are alcoholics, and that women are good with children. White males, on the other hand, insofar as they escape group marking, can be individuals.

Those living under cultural imperialism find themselves defined from the outside, positioned, placed, by a network of dominant meanings they experience as arising from elsewhere, from those with whom they do not identify and who do not identify with them. Consequently, the dominant culture's stereotyped and inferiorized images of the group must be internalized by group members at least to the extent that they are forced to react to behavior of others influenced by those images. This creates for the culturally oppressed the experience that W.E.B. Du Bois called "double consciousness"—"this sense of always looking at one's self through the eyes of others, of measuring one's soul by the tape of a world that looks on in amused contempt and pity" (Du Bois, 1969 [1903], p. 45). Double consciousness arises when the oppressed subject refuses to coincide with these devalued, objectified, stereotyped visions of herself or himself. While the subject desires recognition as human, capable of activity, full of hope and possibility, she receives from the dominant culture only the judgment that she is different, marked, or inferior.

The group defined by the dominant culture as deviant, as a stereotyped Other, *is* culturally different from the dominant group, because the status of Otherness creates specific experiences not shared by the dominant group, and because culturally oppressed groups also are often socially segregated and occupy specific positions in the social division of labor. Members of such groups express their specific group experiences and interpretations of the world to one another, developing and perpetuating their own culture. Double consciousness, then, occurs because one finds one's being defined by two cultures: a dominant and a subordinate culture. Because they can affirm and recognize one another as sharing similar experiences and perspectives on social life, people in culturally imperialized groups can often maintain a sense of positive subjectivity.

Cultural imperialism involves the paradox of experiencing oneself as invisible at the same time that one is marked out as different. The invisibility comes about when dominant groups fail to recognize the perspective embodied in their cultural expressions as a perspective. These dominant cultural expressions often simply have little place for the experience of other groups, at most only mentioning or referring to them in stereotyped or marginalized ways. This, then, is the injustice of cultural imperialism: that the oppressed group's own experience and interpretation of social life finds little expression that touches the dominant culture, while that same culture imposes on the oppressed group its experience and interpretation of social life. . . .

Violence

Finally, many groups suffer the oppression of systematic violence. Members of some groups live with the knowledge that they must fear random, unprovoked attacks on their persons or property, which have no motive but to damage, humiliate, or destroy the person. In American society women, Blacks, Asians, Arabs, gay men, and lesbians live under such threats of violence, and in at least some regions Jews, Puerto Ricans, Chicanos, and other Spanish-speaking Americans must fear such violence as well. Physical violence against these groups is shockingly frequent. Rape Crisis Center networks estimate that more than one-third of all American women experience an attempted or successful sexual assault in their lifetimes. Manning Marable (1984, pp. 238–41) catalogues a large number of incidents of racist violence and terror against Blacks in the United States between 1980 and 1982. He cites dozens of incidents of the severe beating, killing, or rape of Blacks by police officers on duty, in which the police involved were acquitted of any wrongdoing. In 1981, moreover, there were at least five hundred documented cases of random white teenage violence against Blacks. Violence against gay men and lesbians is not only common, but has been increasing in the last five years. While the frequency of physical attack on members of these and other racially or sexually marked groups is very disturbing, I also include in this category less severe incidents of harrassment, intimidation, or ridicule simply for the purpose of degrading, humiliating, or stigmatizing group members.

Given the frequency of such violence in our society, why are theories of justice usually silent about it? I think the reason is that theorists do not typically take such incidents of violence and harrassment as matters of social injustice. No moral theorist would deny that such acts are very wrong. But unless all immoralities are injustices, they might wonder, why should such acts be interpreted as symptoms of social injustice? Acts of violence or petty harrassment are committed by particular individuals, often extremists, deviants, or the mentally unsound. How then can they be said to involve the sorts of institutional issues I have said are properly the subject of justice?

What makes violence a face of oppression is less the particular acts themselves, though these are often utterly horrible, than the social context surrounding them, which makes them possible and even acceptable. What makes violence a phenomenon of social injustice, and not merely an individual moral wrong, is its systemic character, its existence as a social practice.

Violence is systemic because it is directed at members of a group simply because they are members of that group. Any woman, for example, has a reason to fear rape. Regardless of what a Black man has done to escape the oppressions of marginality or powerlessness, he lives knowing he is subject to attack or harrassment. The oppression of violence consists not only in direct victimization, but in the daily knowledge shared by all members of oppressed groups that they are *liable* to violation, solely on account of their group identity. Just living under such a threat of attack on oneself or family or friends deprives the oppressed of freedom and dignity, and needlessly expends their energy.

Violence is a social practice. It is a social given that everyone knows happens and will happen again. It is always at the horizon of social imagination, even for those who do not perpetrate it. According to the prevailing social logic, some circumstances make such violence more "called for" than others. The idea of rape will occur to many men who pick up a hitchhiking woman; the idea of hounding or teasing a gay man on their dorm floor will occur to many straight male college students. Often several persons inflict the violence together, especially in all-male groupings. Sometimes violators set out looking for people to beat up, rape, or taunt. This rule-bound, social, and often premeditated character makes violence against groups a social practice.

Group violence approaches legitimacy, moreover, in the sense that it is tolerated. Often third parties find it unsurprising because it happens frequently and lies as a constant possibility at the horizon of the social imagination. Even when they are caught, those who perpetrate acts of group-directed violence or harrassment often receive light or no punishment. To that extent society renders their acts acceptable.

An important aspect of random, systemic violence is its irrationality. Xenophobic violence differs from the violence of states or ruling-class repression. Repressive violence has a rational, albeit evil, motive: rulers use it as a coercive tool to maintain their power. Many accounts of racist, sexist, or homophobic violence attempt to explain its motivation as a desire to maintain group privilege or domination. I do not doubt that fear of violence often functions to keep oppressed groups subordinate, but I do not think xenophobic violence is rationally motivated in the way that, for example, violence against strikers is.

On the contrary, the violation of rape, beating, killing, and harrassment of women, people of color, gays, and other marked groups is motivated by fear or hatred of those groups. Sometimes the motive may be a simple will to power, to victimize those marked as vulnerable by the very social fact that they are subject to violence. If so, this motive is secondary in the sense that it depends on a social practice of group violence. Violence-causing fear or hatred of the other at least partly involves insecurities on the part of the violators; its irrationality suggests that unconscious processes are at work. . . .

Cultural imperialism, moreover, itself intersects with violence. The culturally imperialized may reject the dominant meanings and attempt to assert their own subjectivity, or the fact of their cultural difference may put the lie to the dominant culture's implicit claim to universality. The dissonance generated by such a challenge to the hegemonic cultural meanings can also be a source of irrational violence. . . .

APPLYING THE CRITERIA

Social theories that construct oppression as a unified phenomenon usually either leave out groups that even the theorists think are oppressed, or leave out important ways in which groups are oppressed. Black liberation theorists and feminist theorists have argued persuasively, for example, that Marxism's reduction of all oppressions to class oppression leaves out much about the specific oppression of Blacks and women. By pluralizing the category of oppression in the way explained in this [essay,] social theory can avoid the exclusive and oversimplifying effects of such reductionism.

I have avoided pluralizing the category in the way some others have done, by constructing an account of separate systems of oppression for each oppressed group: racism, sexism, classism, heterosexism, ageism, and so on. There is a double problem with considering each group's oppression a unified and distinct structure or system. On the one hand, this way of conceiving oppression fails to accommodate the similarities and overlaps in the oppressions of different groups. On the other hand, it falsely represents the situation of all group members as the same.

I have arrived at the five faces of oppression—exploitation, marginalization, powerlessness, cultural imperialism, and violence—as the best way to avoid such exclusions and reductions. They function as criteria for determining whether individuals and groups are oppressed, rather than as a full theory of oppression. I believe that these criteria are objective. They provide a means of refuting some people's belief that their group is oppressed when it is not, as well as a means of persuading others that a group is oppressed when they doubt it. Each criterion can be operationalized; each can be applied through the assessment of observable behavior, status relationships, distributions, texts and other cultural artifacts. I have no illusions that such assessments can be value-neutral. But these criteria can nevertheless serve as means of evaluating claims that a group is oppressed, or adjudicating disputes about whether or how a group is oppressed.

The presence of any of these five conditions is sufficient for calling a group oppressed. But different group oppressions exhibit different combinations of these forms, as do different individuals in the groups. Nearly all, if not all, groups said by contemporary social movements to be oppressed suffer cultural imperialism. The other oppressions they experience vary. Working-class people are exploited and powerless, for example, but if employed and white do not experience marginalization and violence. Gay men, on the other hand, are not qua gay exploited or powerless, but they experience severe cultural imperialism and violence. Similarly, Jews and Arabs as groups are victims of cultural imperialism and violence, though many members of these groups also suffer exploitation or powerlessness. Old people are oppressed by marginalization and cultural imperialism, and this is also true of physically and mentally disabled people. As a group women are subject to gender-based exploitation, powerlessness, cultural imperialism, and violence. Racism in the United States condemns many Blacks and Latinos to marginalization, and puts many more at risk, even though many members of these groups escape that condition; members of these groups often suffer all five forms of oppression.

Applying these five criteria to the situation of groups makes it possible to compare oppressions without reducing them to a common essence or claiming that one is more fundamental than another. One can compare the ways in which a particular form of oppression appears in different groups. For example, while the operations of cultural imperialism are often experienced in similar fashion by different groups, there are also important differences. One can compare the combinations of oppressions groups experience, or the intensity of those oppressions. Thus with these criteria one can plausibly claim that one group is more oppressed than another without reducing all oppressions to a single scale. . . .

REFERENCES

Alexander, David. 1987. "Gendered Job Traits and Women's Occupations." Ph.D. dissertation, Economics, University of Massachusetts.

Brown, Carol. 1981. "Mothers, Fathers and Children: From Private to Public Patriarchy." In Lydia Sargent, ed., *Women and Revolution*. Boston: South End.

Delphy, Christine. 1984. *Close to Home: A Materialist Analysis of Women's Oppression*. Amherst: University of Massachusetts Press.

Du Bois, W.E.B. 1969 [1903]. *The Souls of Black Folk*. New York: New American Library.

Ferguson, Ann. 1984. "On Conceiving Motherhood and Sexuality: A Feminist Materialist Approach." In Joyce Trebilcot, ed., *Mothering: Essays in Feminist Theory*. Totowa, N.J.: Rowman and Allanheld.

———. 1989. *Blood at the Root*. London: Pandora.

Fraser, Nancy. 1987. "Social Movements vs. Disciplinary Bureaucracies: The Discourse of Social Needs." CHS Occasional Paper No. 8. Center for Humanistic Studies, University of Minnesota.

Lugones, Maria C., and Elizabeth V. Spelman. 1983. "Have We Got a Theory for You! Feminist Theory, Cultural Imperialism and the Demand for 'the Woman's Voice.'" *Women's Studies International Forum* 6:573–81.

Macpherson, C. B. 1973. *Democratic Theory: Essays in Retrieval*. Oxford: Oxford University Press.

Marable, Manning. 1984. *Race, Reform and Rebellion: The Second Reconstruction in Black America, 1945–82*. Jackson: University Press of Mississippi.

Sennett, Richard, and Jonathan Cobb. 1972. *The Hidden Injuries of Class*. New York: Vintage.

QUESTIONS

1 How do stereotypes reinforce oppression?
2 Is marginalization the most dangerous form of oppression?
3 Can social institutions that systematically oppress members of some groups be considered just?

The African-American Underclass and the Question of Values

Howard McGary

McGary addresses the question: Why are members of the underclass locked into their underclass status? In his view, a correct response requires understanding both (1) the mindset of members of the underclass and (2) the effect that the unjust design of the basic structure of society has on their mindset. McGary begins by discussing the views of liberal theorists, such as John Rawls, on the meaning of *full citizenship* and explains the kinds of things that can count as evidence that one has full citizenship. He then advances arguments to support the claim that members of the underclass have good reason to doubt that they have full citizenship and explains how having reasonable doubts about their political status can affect the mindset, and hence the motivation, of members of the underclass.

The African-American underclass is said to be poor, badly educated, directly related to crime either as perpetrators or victims, and typically young. Data indicate that, unlike the African-American urban poor in the recent past, the underclass also appears to be locked into a cycle of poverty. If these data are accurate, then the crucial question is "Why are members of the underclass locked into their underclass status?" A debate rages between conservatives and liberals about how to answer this question. Conservatives maintain that the key to solving the problem is altering the values of the African-American underclass so that it might better participate in the capitalist market economy. Conservatives also typically add that the state should eliminate many of the burdensome regulations that they believe work to the detriment of people at the bottom rungs of the socioeconomic ladder, for example, minimum wage laws. Liberals, on the other hand, assert that the state must play an active role in solving the problems of the African-American underclass. The state, in their view, should create laws and programs that provide state funds to educate and house those who are said to be locked into the African-American underclass.

The dispute between conservatives and liberals over the African-American underclass often occurs in the political arena, but it occurs in academic circles as well. William Julius Wilson in his book *The Truly Disadvantaged*[1] argues that liberals have failed to keep up their side of the debate in the dispute over the African-American underclass. He attributes this to a reluctance by liberals to examine some of the controversial data about members of the African-American underclass. Wilson believes that the sensitive nature of these data causes liberals to believe that if they examine the data they will be accused of "blaming the victims." They also fear that focusing on the inadequacies of this class will allow some to intensify the racism that exists in American society. Refusing to focus on the personal shortcomings of the members of the underclass, the liberals find fault instead with the design of social institutions.

In my view, both the conservative and liberal solutions involve doctrinaire commitments that blind each approach to the virtues of the other's solution. Conservatives are right to focus on the mindset of members of the underclass, and liberals are correct when they maintain that we must focus on the social structure, but what they both fail to appreciate is just how much the design of social institutions influences the way people think. I argue that members of the underclass do suffer from an understandable but crippling resentment that is fostered by the unjust design of the basic structure of society.

My aim in this discussion is modest. I wish to suggest a possible reason why both conservatives and liberals miss the point. In doing so, I take it as a postulate that it is possible to solve the problems of the African-American underclass without rejecting the capitalist mode of production. This is a big assumption, but one that conservatives and liberals usually accept. First, I describe what prominent liberal theorists have meant by full citizenship, especially in modern democratic societies. Second, I explain the kinds of things that can count as evidence that one has full citizenship. Third, I argue that members of the African-American underclass have good reason to doubt that they have full citizenship. I conclude by showing what effects having reasonable doubts about one's political status can have on people considered to be in the "underclass." . . .

THE NATURE OF FULL CITIZENSHIP

Individuals join together to form civil society for a variety of reasons, many of which have been discussed by political theorists. Some say that the only valid ground for state authority is the protection of the individual. Others maintain that it is for the promotion of the interests of those who form the social union. Those of a more collectivist sort claim that the promotion of the common good is the basis for civil society. I do not want to enter into this debate. My point is that in the liberal tradition a person who is said to be a citizen has the same basic rights as any other citizen. Of course, this does not mean everyone within the liberal tradition has defined the consequences of equal citizenship in the same way. For instance, some have been strong supporters of individual rights, while others have focused on the common good and have supported the rights of individuals only when doing so promotes the common good. However, the US Constitution vests rights in individuals, and modern theorists—be they contractarians, human rights theorists, or utilitarians—have been leery of any proposal that denies equal protection under the law to any citizen.

As Ronald Dworkin has said, equal citizenship requires each citizen to be treated with "equal concern and respect."[2] The belief that one is treated with equal concern and respect has an important impact on one's self-concept and plays a vital role in the formula for flourishing in a social context. By flourishing, I have in mind being able to construct one's life plan consistent with one's abilities and talents. Citizenship, in the liberal tradition, is thought to provide one with the opportunity to flourish by arranging society, such that its basic structure does not unfairly inhibit or prohibit one's pursuit of a chosen plan of life. The belief that one has a full citizenship also allows one to feel comfortable in supporting and defending what John Rawls has called the "basic structure of society." By basic structure Rawls means "the way in which the major social institutions distribute fundamental rights and duties and determine the division of advantages from social cooperation." Rawls goes on to define major social institutions as "the political constitution and the principal economic and social arrangements." The major institutions "define people's rights and duties and influence their life prospects."[3] Full citizenship certainly does not entail that one will get whatever one wants, but it does say that one will have the opportunity to satisfy one's needs and desires. When these things cannot be satisfied, it cannot be blamed on the basic structure of society.

According to this view, citizens are competitors in a game of life in which rules are not rigged in favor of any of the competitors. However, this view does not assume that people cannot be treated unfairly because of the unjust actions of individuals; it is clearly understood that the unfairness is not the result of the design of the basic structure of society. Persons who feel that they are full citizens believe that their rights are recognized and protected and that their failings can be traced to some personal shortcoming, individual act of injustice, or poor fate, but not to the design of the basic structure of society.

EVIDENCE OF FULL CITIZENSHIP

What things count as evidence in modern liberal democratic societies that one has full citizenship? The following list is not all-inclusive, but it does include many important indicators of full citizenship. Citizens have the right to participate in the political process. They have the right to earn a living without being forced to engage in activities that are degrading or exploitative. Citizens are not denied opportunities simply because of their race, sex, or religious affiliations. Citizens also have legal due process. Notice that I have not included in this list a right to a certain income. Liberals have disagreed over whether citizens' basic rights include welfare rights. However, citizens who languish in a permanent condition of poverty in a society that has plenty have to wonder about their equal citizenship status.

Having the secure conviction that one has the aforementioned rights and opportunities helps to foster the belief that one can succeed, but just as important, it allows one to believe that one is a legitimate member of a social community, and that the community interprets the common good in a manner that is consistent with one's own good. Of course, this does not mean that everything always goes one's way. Nor does it mean that some individuals cannot have more of societal good than others. However, to use Rawlsian terminology, it does mean that even the least-advantaged members of society will have a secure conviction that the basic structure of society is just.

LAZINESS AND THE AFRICAN-AMERICAN UNDERCLASS

Wilson and others have defined the African-American underclass as young, poorly educated, intimately connected to crime either as perpetrators or as victims, and locked into a cycle of poverty. The important question is "Why is a certain segment of society plagued by these problems?" I said that both conservatives and liberals have their fingers on part of the answer. The liberals are correct in maintaining that there is still work to be done to guarantee equal opportunity to certain groups, particularly African-Americans. They are also correct in contending that the state must play some active role in this process. For example, because of their race African-Americans are still severely restricted when it comes to finding decent, inexpensive housing. This is true even for African-Americans who have been able to acquire middle-class status, but it is an especially acute problem for African-Americans who are members of the lower classes. A persistent worry for these people is finding and keeping a place to live. As psychological studies have shown, this type of insecurity is very debilitating, especially for the young.

Conservatives, of course, argue that we have equal housing legislation on the books, so adding additional legislation will not solve the problem. Conservatives may be right that equal housing laws are on the books, but they are wrong if they mean that these laws are being enforced. In fact, during the Reagan years in which we have seen the emergence of the African-American underclass, the enforcement of equal housing laws has been virtually nonexistent. Therefore, I think the liberals are right that there is more work for the state to do, even if it is primarily the enforcement of civil rights laws already on the books.

But liberals may be wrong if they believe that at this point in the process enforcement of civil rights laws will solve the problems facing the underclass. Of course, few liberals have said that legislation alone will solve the problems. This is just a caricature of the liberal view advanced by some conservatives. However, I think it is fair to say that liberals have been reluctant publicly to declare that something about the people who make up the underclass may contribute to their underclass status.

Here we can learn from the conservatives, but they are not the only people who have asked African-Americans to examine themselves for a solution to their predicament. Black Muslims, for example, have consistently urged African-Americans to examine their commitments, habits, and values and to fashion their own remedy to their problems rather than waiting for whites to solve them. But, unlike the conservatives, the Muslims are quick to warn that the initial cause of African-American problems is white people. Black Muslims have attempted to provide an economic and social structure for African-Americans to enhance their self-esteem while providing them with the necessary resources for putting their life plans into action. Booker T. Washington also asked African-Americans to do some critical self-evaluation before fashioning their own programs for economic and social improvement.[4]

Clearly there has been progress over the years when it comes to race relations, and it is probably true that the significance of race is declining; nonetheless, race is still an important defining characteristic of people in our society. It is my contention that African-Americans in the underclass have been placed in an untenable position that makes it extremely difficult for them to evaluate their personal successes and failures. They have been told that racism no longer exists, and wealthy and middle-class African-Americans are pointed to as support for this claim. So, when poor African-Americans fail, people are quick to say that it is because of personal shortcomings and not systemic failings. Some African-American scholars have recently claimed that the values of the African-American underclass are the source of its predicament. In other words, opportunities exist for these poor African-Americans, but the members of the underclass fail to take advantage of these opportunities because they are lazy, undisciplined, and too prone to satisfying their immediate desires. This view has become quite popular in some quarters.

Let us now examine this harsh critique of members of the African-American underclass. Being lazy means being resistant to work or disposed to idleness. Are all or most members of the African-American underclass lazy? I think not. First, it is not at all clear that African-Americans in the underclass are resistant to work. In order for someone to be properly described as being lazy, there must be a genuine opportunity for that person to engage in meaningful and nonexploitative work. For example, it would be wrong to call slaves lazy because they refused to work in the slavemaster's cotton fields. And it would be wrong to label as lazy someone who refused to prostitute his or her body for a wage. One thing is certainly clear. African-Americans in the underclass are not turning down good-paying, safe, and non-dead-end jobs. It is questionable whether enough gainful employment exists to successfully integrate members of the underclass into the broader economy. In fact, some economists have argued that integration of the underclass would require a rapid growth of the economy. There is no guarantee that such growth will occur. Another question is whether it is rational for mothers heading single-family households to accept jobs that do not have health plans and child care services. Given the tremendous costs of health care and child care, the welfare system may be the only viable alternative for many underclass families. But what about those women who do work their way off the welfare rolls? Typically, these are people who have families to draw upon. Of course, a few women manage to secure low-paying entry-level jobs that do provide some modest health coverage; however, such jobs are the exception rather than the rule.

Those who criticize the members of the African-American underclass for lacking in values will sometimes admit that members of the African-American underclass face harsh conditions, but they quickly add that these persons have to be tough and do those things that will allow them to flourish. But is it fair to expect members of the African-American underclass to fight through these adversities? I do not deny that some do, but should this be expected of all members of this group? For example, suppose a person loses both legs because of some unjust act, and that the injustice goes uncompensated. Suppose further that this person goes on to accomplish a great deal in spite of her handicap. Should anyone in her circumstances be expected to act as she does? I think not. This person receives high praise because she stands apart from the norm. If her accomplishments were what the average person could be expected to do, then we would not hold her in such high regard. So, it would seem to be wrong or at least insensitive to condemn people for not being exceptional at overcoming serious adversities. However, I think this is just what is being expected of members of the African-American underclass.

I have attempted thus far to cast doubt on the claim that most members of the African-American underclass are lazy. Now I would like to buttress my rejection of this claim by looking carefully at the claim that members of this class are poorly motivated due to laziness. Such a view overlooks the relationship between being motivated and having the secure conviction that the rules or structure of society are not stacked against one. Living in a society in which one has good reason to believe that the basic structure is just does a lot for enhancing or at least sustaining one's motivational level. Members of the underclass lack good evidence that they live in such a society. When they look around their community, they see that its members lack the material things and opportunities that many other communities take for granted. This is especially devastating when we note that a large segment of the underclass are children. It is extremely difficult for children to understand that they must use modest opportunities and resources to fight against awful odds if they are to succeed, especially when they know that children in other communities do not face such an uphill struggle. They often see this as too much to ask of them, and this belief works against their being highly motivated. Is this a reasonable conclusion? I think so.

Rawls has persuasively argued that people do not deserve the benefits that result from the luck of the natural lottery. Therefore, children in the African-American underclass do not deserve to be poor, nor do children born into affluent families deserve to be rich. The large number of children in the African-American underclass have a good reason for thinking that their situation is not something that they deserve. They are born into poor families and must work harder than people from more affluent families if they are to succeed. These beliefs have a negative impact on their motivational levels.

If what I have argued for so far is sound, then we have several reasons for doubting that members of the African-American underclass are lazy. Similar arguments would also seem to apply to the criticism that members of the African-American underclass are undisciplined and unable to defer gratification. Being disciplined and deferring gratification both depend upon having good evidence that the cards are not stacked against one. Exit studies for female and African-American students who have dropped out of graduate programs point to the difficulty of being disciplined when the environment in which one must operate is tainted by racism or sexism. Students in these studies report that it is difficult to separate their inadequacies from biased or unfair expectations. This uncertainty serves to impact negatively on their ability to gain strength through training. While in the process of growing and acquiring new skills, a time that is generally filled with self-doubt, they find it extremely taxing to separate the anguish and paranoia associated with a rigorous graduate program from the subtle forms of racism and sexism that still exist in institutions of higher learning. The underclass faces the same problem, but in more drastic circumstances. So, one should be cautious in such circumstances in condemning those who must deal with covert racism as suffering from a lack of discipline.

Of course, one could object that my argument is unsound because African-Americans in the past had to deal with racism and its effects, but nonetheless they were motivated to succeed and clearly did not suffer from "poor" values. However, such a response does not succeed when examined closely. First, the claim that African-Americans suffer because of poor values has existed since slavery. In fact, it was even offered as a justification for slavery. So, the idea that the downtrodden position of underclass African-Americans can be attributed to their poor values or lack of values is not new. What is new, though, is that we now have a chorus of African-American voices singing this tune. Unlike in the past, the increase in violent crime and the drug problem have caused many, including African-Americans, to search frantically for answers that may help to eliminate social problems that touch all of our lives. However, many critics might agree that the appeal to poor values was once a smoke screen, but that now this position has credibility.

Another explanation exists for why the effects of racism severely hamper members of the African-American underclass to a degree not experienced by blacks up until the 1960s. Several commentators, discussing the impact of integration on African-American communities in the United States, have pointed out that middle-class African-Americans have left these communities and taken with them the tax base and many of the things associated with stable communities. Large, urban African-American communities are now pretty much populated by people from the bottom rung of the economic ladder. Major institutions in these communities have been either destroyed or severely weakened by the flight of the black middle class. One consequence of this flight is that people do not have the resources at their disposal to address many day-to-day problems. This may seem like a small point, but I assure you that it is not. It is one thing for a person from the outside to say that you can make it and another for someone who is struggling with the inadequate resources to do so. At one time, "making it" meant rising to the top in one's community; and as individuals progressed, so did the community. However, since the integration movement, "making it" has meant escaping from one's community. This has the consequence of intensifying any antagonisms that exist between poor African-Americans and those who are better-off. Members of the so-called African-American underclass now face a society in which the basic structure is not just, intense competition for scarce resources, and abandonment by those best able to help ward off the effects of living in a society that is still plagued by racism.

Some may find my conclusion about laziness and the African-American underclass disturbing because they believe that it provides a convenient rationale for underclass African-Americans to acquiesce in their downtrodden position. Others may conclude that it supports the more disturbing position that African-Americans (especially healthy black males) should be excused for failing to do what is necessary in order to provide for their families. However, neither of these things follow from anything that I have said. It is not my contention that African-Americans should not go beyond what is expected of whites if they are to overcome the adversities that are so much a part of their daily lives. What I do say, however, is that those who cannot muster this strength should not be described as lazy. Many people in the African-American underclass are putting forth a gallant effort against bad odds to secure a living for their families. We must draw a line between what people are required to do as a matter of moral duty and supererogatory acts. People should not have to sacrifice their sense of self completely, even if doing so would serve some noble end, such as providing for the well-being of one's family. Of course, the morally good person is willing to make some sacrifice; however, at some point we must draw the line. When we fail to do so, then we are too willing to accept false accusations, such as that all the members of the African-American underclass are lazy, because such accusations wrongly shift the focus from institutional design and social structure to the individual.

The line of argument advanced here does not deny that some members of the underclass are lazy. However, all classes within our society have some lazy members. But for the argument, that attributes underclass status to laziness, to succeed it must be the case that all, many, or most of the African-American underclass is lazy. There is no evidence available to support this strong evaluative claim. . . .

. . . When African-American conservatives talk about opportunities, they typically mean that there are jobs available. They claim that certain jobs are crying out to be filled, particularly jobs requiring highly specialized skills or those in the service industries that require minimal skills. This may be true, but a further question has to be asked: If employers are in such desperate need of these employees, why are they not doing more to train and recruit these people? Their lack of effort in these areas may cast some doubt on how desperate they are to fill these jobs.

However, putting this issue aside, there is a more fundamental problem with the contention by African-American conservatives that ample opportunities exist for those who are willing to work. As we know, being positioned to take advantage of opportunities is conditioned by a number of things, for example, being properly educated or trained and having a work ethic. But several other things impinge on these two factors, for example, health care. All too often members of the underclass lack proper health care—not just health care in the narrow sense of being able to go to a doctor when one is very sick, but health care to the extent that pregnant women in this class can receive the proper prenatal care that is so crucial in preventing infants from experiencing physical and mental problems that will hamper their ability to learn. We also have to focus on environmental impediments such as the disproportionate number of persons from the underclass who are exposed to lead contamination, which can have disastrous effects on a developing child's ability to learn.

What these conservatives fail to see is that legitimate opportunities must be understood as more than whether or not there are jobs available. For example, in a number of large cities, such as Milwaukee, a number of jobs that underclass residents are qualified to fill have moved out of the inner cities to the suburbs, making transportation a major obstacle for people who would like to fill these positions. Furthermore, the cost of housing in the suburbs and housing discrimination prevent them from moving to where the jobs are. Once we see the obstacles that stand in the way of people who have few resources at their disposal, people who appear to lack motivation in the face of opportunity might really require motivational levels that would far exceed those of persons who we think are our most productive and successful citizens.

In light of this, is "lazy" or some other derogatory term the proper way to characterize members of the underclass? I think not. A number of people, including some liberals, are uneasy with my answer. They worry that such a response is a way of coddling people, of encouraging people to acquiesce in their misery. Very often these people will respond, "Surely you are not encouraging members of the underclass to prefer public assistance to earning their own living?" Nothing that I have said so far commits me to the view that members of the underclass should not attempt to help themselves. What I have tried to point out are some of the difficulties they encounter in trying to do so. However, if this question is posed to a member of the underclass who has had her motivational level damaged by racial discrimination and injustice, it is not clear that it would be unreasonable or immoral for such a person to prefer public assistance (which includes medical benefits) to a menial, low-paying, dead-end job without medical benefits. At first, this seems ridiculous because the model job we tend to use when analyzing such cases is one that draws on our abilities and talents in ways that we consider to be interesting or, if not, at least compensates such that the job is desirable even if it is uninteresting. If the job is low-paying and uninteresting, we might see it as a viable opportunity if it leads to a job that pays well or does draw on our abilities and talents in interesting ways. However, the question we must ask is, "Are members of the underclass being offered jobs that satisfy these conditions?" If the answer is yes, then clearly they should prefer working to public assistance. If the answer is no, I do not think that it is clearly rational to prefer a low-paying, uninteresting, dead-end job without medical benefits to public assistance that would provide one with the same income plus medical care.

Of course my critics would argue that I have excluded an important consideration, namely, the joy and satisfaction that a person receives from being self-reliant. In fact, Booker T. Washington, who some see as the father of the African-American conservative position, stressed the value of self-help in his famous "Atlanta Exposition Address." In this speech, Washington urged African-Americans to "Cast down your buckets where you are."[5] By this he meant that African-Americans should take any job, no matter how menial, as a first step on the road toward advancement. Clearly, self-reliance in most cases is a good thing, but even good things can be taken too far. It is clear that in some cases self-reliance can clash with rationality. Are the members of the underclass asked to be self-reliant at the expense of rationality?

Unfortunately, I think that in a large number of cases it is irrational for members of the underclass to choose self-reliance over public assistance. As I said earlier, adequate health care is an important component of any realistic appraisal of the opportunities available to members of the underclass. The United States is one of very few countries that do not provide some form of national health care. Health care in the United States is tied to certain jobs in the form of employee medical benefits. Given the high costs of medical care and the medical problems that correlate highly with poor people, adequate health care has to be a weighty consideration in the deliberations of members of the African-American underclass. Surely self-reliance ought to be given some weight by members of this class, but even if it is, it will lose out in their deliberations because being self-reliant would have the undesirable consequence of denying them adequate health care. In order to make self-reliance a rational choice for members of this group, there would have to be structural changes in the current welfare and health care systems.

To think that we can eliminate the problems faced by members of the underclass without altering some of our basic institutions and social policies is to look at the problem through rose-colored glasses.

NOTES

1 William Julius Wilson, *The Truly Disadvantaged* (Chicago: University of Chicago Press, 1987).
2 Ronald Dworkin, *Taking Rights Seriously* (Cambridge, MA: Harvard University Press, 1977), 180–3.
3 John Rawls, *A Theory of Justice* (Cambridge, MA: Harvard University Press, 1971), sec. 2, 7–11.
4 Booker T. Washington, "The Intellectuals and the Boston Mob," in *Negro Social and Political Thought, 1850–1920*, ed. Howard Brotz (New York: Basic Books, 1966).
5 Booker T. Washington, "Atlanta Exposition Address," in *Negro Social and Political Thought, 1850–1920*, 357.

QUESTIONS

1 According to McGary, those who are full citizens have a right to earn a living without being forced to engage in activities that are degrading or exploitative. Does a capitalist system necessarily involve exploitation? If so, does it follow that many (most) workers in our society are denied the rights of full citizens?
2 Do any of Young's five forms of oppression apply to the African-American underclass as it is described by McGary? Is there another form of oppression that would better describe the experiences of this underclass?

After the Family Wage: A Postindustrial Thought Experiment

Nancy Fraser

Fraser maintains that we are in a postindustrial age that calls for a new vision of the welfare state, a vision that will incorporate gender equity as one of its goals. Fraser first presents seven normative principles, each of which she sees as an essential element in gender equity: (1) the antipoverty principle, (2) the antiexploitation principle, (3) the income-equality principle, (4) the leisure-time-equality principle, (5) the equality-of-respect principle, (6) the antimarginalization principle, and (7) the antiandrocentrism principle. Fraser then evaluates two feminist visions of a postindustrial state—the Universal Breadwinner model and the Caregiver Parity model—before presenting, evaluating, and ultimately recommending a third feminist vision—the Universal Caregiver model.

The current crisis of the welfare state has many roots—global economic trends, massive movements of refugees and immigrants, popular hostility to taxes, the weakening of trade unions and labor parties, the rise of national and "racial"-ethnic antagonisms, the decline of solidaristic ideologies, and the collapse of state socialism. One absolutely crucial factor, however, is the crumbling of the old gender order. Existing welfare states are premised on assumptions about gender that are increasingly out of phase with many people's lives and self-understandings. They therefore do not provide adequate social protections, especially for women and children.

The gender order that is now disappearing descends from the industrial era of capitalism and reflects the social world of its origin. It was centered on the ideal of *the family wage*. In this world people were supposed to be organized into heterosexual, male-headed nuclear families, which lived principally from the man's labor-market earnings. The male head of the household would be paid a family wage, sufficient to support children and a full-time wife-and-mother, who performed domestic labor without pay. Of course, countless lives never fit this pattern. Still, it provided the normative picture of a proper family.

The family-wage ideal was inscribed in the structure of most industrial-era welfare states. That structure had three tiers, with social-insurance programs occupying the first rank. Designed to protect people from the vagaries of the labor market (and to protect the economy from shortages of demand), these programs replaced the breadwinner's wage in case of sickness, disability, unemployment, or old age. Many countries also featured a second tier of programs, providing direct support for full-time female homemaking and mothering. A third tier served the "residuum." Largely a holdover from traditional poor relief, public assistance programs provided paltry,

From Nancy Fraser, *Justice Interruptus: Critical Reflection on the "Postsocialist" Condition*, Chapter 2. Copyright © 1997. Reproduced by permission of the author and Routledge/Taylor & Francis Group, LLC.

stigmatized, means-tested aid to needy people who had no claim to honorable support because they did not fit the family-wage scenario.

Today, however, the family-wage assumption is no longer tenable—either empirically or normatively. We are currently experiencing the death throes of the old, industrial gender order with the transition to a new, *postindustrial* phase of capitalism. The crisis of the welfare state is bound up with these epochal changes. It is rooted in part in the collapse of the world of the family wage, and of its central assumptions about labor markets and families. . . .

What, then, should a postindustrial welfare state look like? Conservatives have lately had a lot to say about "restructuring the welfare state," but their vision is counterhistorical and contradictory; they seek to reinstate the male breadwinner/female homemaker family for the middle class, while demanding that poor single mothers "work." Neoliberal policies have recently been instituted in the United States but they, too, are inadequate in the current context. Punitive, androcentric, and obsessed with employment despite the absence of good jobs, they are unable to provide security in a postindustrial world. Both these approaches ignore one crucial thing: a postindustrial welfare state, like its industrial predecessor, must support a gender order. But the only kind of gender order that can be acceptable today is one premised on *gender equity*.

Feminists, therefore, are in a good position to generate an emancipatory vision for the coming period. They, more than anyone, appreciate the importance of gender relations to the current crisis of the industrial welfare state and the centrality of gender equity to any satisfactory resolution. Feminists also appreciate the importance of carework for human well-being and the effects of its social organization on women's standing. They are attuned, finally, to potential conflicts of interest within families and to the inadequacy of androcentric definitions of work.

To date, however, feminists have tended to shy away from systematic reconstructive thinking about the welfare state. Nor have we yet developed a satisfactory account of gender equity that can inform an emancipatory vision. We need now to undertake such thinking. We should ask: What new, postindustrial gender order should replace the family wage? And what sort of welfare state can best support such a new gender order? What account of gender equity best captures our highest aspirations? And what vision of social welfare comes closest to embodying it?

Two different sorts of answers are currently conceivable, I think, both of which qualify as feminist. The first I call the Universal Breadwinner model. It is the vision implicit in the current political practice of most U.S. feminists and liberals. It aims to foster gender equity by promoting women's employment; the centerpiece of this model is state provision of employment-enabling services such as day care. The second possible answer I call the Caregiver Parity model. It is the vision implicit in the current political practice of most Western European feminists and social democrats. It aims to promote gender equity chiefly by supporting informal carework; the centerpiece of this model is state provision of caregiver allowances.

Which of these two approaches should command our loyalties in the coming period? Which expresses the most attractive vision of a postindustrial gender order? Which best embodies the ideal of gender equity?

In this chapter, I outline a framework for thinking systematically about these questions. I analyze highly idealized versions of Universal Breadwinner and

Caregiver Parity in the manner of a thought experiment. I postulate, contrary to fact, a world in which both these models are feasible in that their economic and political preconditions are in place. Assuming very favorable conditions, then, I assess the respective strengths and weaknesses of each. . . .

GENDER EQUITY: A COMPLEX CONCEPTION

To evaluate alternative visions of a postindustrial welfare state, we need some normative criteria. Gender equity, I have said, is one indispensable standard. But of what precisely does it consist? . . .

I propose we reconceptualize gender equity as a complex, not a simple, idea. This means breaking with the assumption that gender equity can be identified with any single value or norm, whether it be equality, difference, or something else. Instead, we should treat it as a complex notion comprising a plurality of distinct normative principles. . . .

In what follows, I assume that gender equity is complex in this way. And I propose an account of it that is designed for the specific purpose of evaluating alternative pictures of a postindustrial welfare state. For issues other than welfare, a somewhat different package of norms might be called for. Nevertheless, I believe that the general idea of treating gender equity as a complex conception is widely applicable. The analysis here may serve as a paradigm case demonstrating the usefulness of this approach.

For this particular thought experiment, in any case, I unpack the idea of gender equity as a compound of seven distinct normative principles. Let me enumerate them one by one.

1 *The Antipoverty Principle.* The first and most obvious objective of social-welfare provision is to prevent poverty. Preventing poverty is crucial to achieving gender equity now, after the family wage, given the high rates of poverty in solo-mother families and the vastly increased likelihood that U.S. women and children will live in such families. If it accomplishes nothing else, a welfare state should at least relieve suffering by meeting otherwise unmet basic needs. Arrangements, such as those in the United States, that leave women, children, and men in poverty, are unacceptable according to this criterion. Any postindustrial welfare state that prevented such poverty would constitute a major advance. So far, however, this does not say enough. The antipoverty principle might be satisfied in a variety of different ways, not all of which are acceptable. Some ways, such as the provision of targeted, isolating, and stigmatized poor relief for solo-mother families, fail to respect several of the following normative principles, which are also essential to gender equity in social welfare.

2 *The Antiexploitation Principle.* Antipoverty measures are important not only in themselves but also as a means to another basic objective: preventing exploitation of vulnerable people. This principle, too, is central to achieving gender equity after the family wage. Needy women with no other way to feed themselves and their children, for example, are liable to exploitation—by abusive husbands, by sweatshop foremen, and by pimps. In guaranteeing relief of poverty, then, welfare provision should also aim to mitigate exploitable dependency. The availability of an alternative source of income enhances the bargaining position of subordinates in unequal relationships. The nonemployed wife who knows she can support herself and her children outside her marriage has more leverage within it; her "voice" is enhanced as her possibilities of "exit" increase. The same holds for the low-paid nursing-home attendant in relation to her boss. For welfare measures to have this effect, however, support must be provided as a matter of right. When receipt of aid is highly stigmatized or discretionary, the anti-exploitation principle is not satisfied. At best the claimant would trade exploitable dependence on a husband or a boss for exploitable dependence on a caseworker's whim. The goal should be to prevent at least three kinds of exploitable dependencies: exploitable dependence on an individual family member, such as a husband or an adult child; exploitable dependence on employers and supervisors; and exploitable dependence on the personal whims of state officials. Rather than shuttle people back and forth among these exploitable dependencies, an adequate approach must prevent all three simultaneously. This principle rules out arrangements that channel a homemaker's benefits through her husband. It is likewise incompatible with arrangements that provide essential goods, such as health insurance, only in forms linked conditionally to scarce employment. . . .

3 *The Income-Equality Principle.* One form of equality that is crucial to gender equity concerns the distribution of real per capita income. This sort of equality is highly pressing now, after the family wage, when U.S. women's earnings are approximately 70 percent of men's, when much of women's labor is not compensated at all, and when many women suffer from "hidden poverty" due to unequal distribution within families. As I interpret it, the principle of income equality does not require absolute leveling, but it does rule out arrangements that reduce women's incomes after divorce by nearly half, while men's incomes nearly double. It likewise rules out unequal pay for equal work and the wholesale undervaluation of women's labor and skills. The income-equality principle requires a substantial reduction in the vast discrepancy between men's and women's incomes. In so doing, it tends, as well, to help equalize the life-chances of children in that a majority of U.S. children are currently likely to live at some point in solo-mother families.

4 *The Leisure-Time-Equality Principle.* Another kind of equality that is crucial to gender equity concerns the distribution of leisure time. This sort of equality is highly pressing now, after the family wage, when many women, but only a few men, do both paid work and unpaid primary carework and when women suffer disproportionately from "time poverty." . . . The leisure-time-equality principle rules out welfare arrangements that would equalize incomes while requiring a double shift of work from women but only a single shift from men. It likewise rules out arrangements that would require women, but not men, to do either the "work of claiming" or the time-consuming "patchwork" of piecing together income from several sources and of coordinating services from different agencies and associations.

5 *The Equality-of-Respect Principle.* Equality of respect is also crucial to gender equity. This kind of equality is especially pressing now, after the family wage, when postindustrial culture routinely represents women as sexual objects for the pleasure of male subjects. The principle of equal respect rules out social arrangements that objectify and deprecate women—even if those arrangements prevent poverty and exploitation, and even if in addition they equalize income and leisure time. It is incompatible with welfare programs that trivialize women's activities and ignore women's contributions—hence with "welfare reforms" in the United States that assume AFDC claimants do not "work." Equality of respect requires recognition of women's personhood and recognition of women's work. . . .

6 *The Antimarginalization Principle.* A welfare state could satisfy all the preceding principles and still function to marginalize women. By limiting support to generous mothers' pensions, for example, it could render women independent, well provided for, well rested, and respected but enclaved in a separate domestic sphere, removed from the life of the larger society. Such a welfare state would be unacceptable. Social policy should promote women's full participation on a par with men in all areas of social life—in employment, in politics, in the associational life of civil society. The antimarginalization principle requires provision of the necessary conditions for women's participation, including day care, elder care, and provision for breast-feeding in public. It also requires the dismantling of masculinist work cultures and woman-hostile political environments. . . .

7 *The Antiandrocentrism Principle.* A welfare state that satisfied many of the foregoing principles could still entrench some obnoxious gender norms. It could assume the androcentric view that men's current life patterns represent the human norm and that women ought to assimilate to them. (This is the real issue behind the previously noted worry about equality.) Such a welfare state is unacceptable. Social policy should not require women to become like men nor to fit into institutions designed for men, in order to enjoy comparable levels of well-being. Policy should aim instead to restructure androcentric institutions so as to welcome human beings who can give birth and who often care for relatives and friends, treating them not as exceptions but as ideal-typical participants. The antiandrocentrism principle requires decentering masculinist norms—in part by revaluing practices and traits that are currently undervalued because they are associated with women. It entails changing men as well as changing women.

Here, then, is an account of gender equity in social welfare. On this account, gender equity is a complex idea comprising seven distinct normative principles, each of which is necessary and essential. No postindustrial welfare state can realize gender equity unless it satisfies them all. . . .

THE UNIVERSAL BREADWINNER MODEL

In one vision of postindustrial society, the age of the family wage would give way to the age of the Universal Breadwinner. This is the vision implicit in the current political practice of most U.S. feminists and liberals. (It was also assumed in the former communist countries!) It aims to achieve gender equity principally by promoting women's employment. The point is to enable women to support themselves and their families through their own wage-earning. The breadwinner role is to be universalized, in sum, so that women, too, can be citizen-workers.

Universal Breadwinner is a very ambitious postindustrial scenario, requiring major new programs and policies. One crucial element is a set of employment-enabling services, such as day care and elder care, aimed at freeing women from unpaid responsibilities so they could take full-time employment on terms comparable to men. Another essential element is a set of workplace reforms aimed at removing equal-opportunity obstacles, such as sex discrimination and sexual harassment. Reforming the workplace requires reforming the culture, however—eliminating sexist stereotypes and breaking the cultural association of breadwinning with masculinity. Also required are policies to help change socialization, so as, first, to reorient women's aspirations toward employment and away from domesticity, and second, to reorient men's expectations toward acceptance of women's new role. None of this would work, however, without one additional ingredient: macroeconomic policies to create full-time, high-paying, permanent jobs for women. These would have to be true breadwinner jobs in the primary labor force, carrying full, first-class social-insurance entitlements. Social insurance, finally, is central to Universal Breadwinner. The aim here is to bring women up to parity with men in an institution that has traditionally disadvantaged them.

How would this model organize carework? The bulk of such work would be shifted from the family to the market and the state, where it would be performed by employees for pay. Who, then, are these employees likely to be? In many countries today, including the United States, paid institutional carework is poorly remunerated, feminized, and largely racialized and/or performed by immigrants. But such arrangements are precluded in this model. If the model is to succeed in enabling *all* women to be breadwinners, it must upgrade the status and pay attached to carework employment, making it, too, into primary-labor-force work. Universal Breadwinner, then, is necessarily committed to a policy of "comparable worth"; it must redress the widespread undervaluation of skills and jobs currently coded as feminine and/or "nonwhite," and it must remunerate such jobs with breadwinner-level pay.

Universal Breadwinner would link many benefits to employment and distribute them through social insurance, with levels varying according to earnings. In this respect, the model resembles the industrial-era welfare state. The difference is that many more women would be covered on the basis of their own employment records. And many more women's employment records would look considerably more like men's.

Not all adults can be employed, however. Some will be unable to work for medical reasons, including some adults not previously employed. Others will be unable to get jobs. Some, finally, will have carework responsibilities that they are unable or unwilling to shift elsewhere. Most of these last will be women. To provide for these people, Universal Breadwinner must include a residual tier of social welfare that provides need-based, means-tested wage replacements.

Universal Breadwinner is far removed from present realities. It requires massive creation of primary-labor-force jobs—jobs sufficient to support a family single-handedly. That, of course, is wildly askew of current postindustrial trends, which generate jobs not for breadwinners but for "disposable workers." Let us assume for the sake of the thought experiment, however, that its conditions of possibility could be met. And let us consider whether the resulting postindustrial welfare state could claim title to gender equity.

1 *Antipoverty.* We can acknowledge straight off that Universal Breadwinner would do a good job of preventing poverty. A policy that created secure breadwinner-quality jobs for all employable women and men—while providing the services that would enable women to take such jobs—would keep most families out of poverty. And generous levels of residual support would keep the rest out of poverty through transfers.

2 *Antiexploitation.* The model should also succeed in preventing exploitable dependency for most women. Women with secure breadwinner jobs are able to exit unsatisfactory relations with men. And those who do not have such jobs but know they can get them will also be less vulnerable to exploitation. Failing that, the residual system of income support provides backup protection against exploitable dependency—assuming that it is generous, nondiscretionary, and honorable.

3 *Income equality.* Universal Breadwinner is only fair, however, at achieving income equality. Granted, secure breadwinner jobs for women—plus the services that would enable women to take them—would narrow the gender wage gap. Reduced inequality in earnings, moreover, translates into reduced inequality in social-insurance benefits. And the availability of exit options from marriage should encourage a more equitable distribution of resources within it. But the model is not otherwise egalitarian. It contains a basic social fault line dividing breadwinners from others, to the considerable disadvantage of the others—most of whom would be women. Apart from comparable worth, moreover, it does not reduce pay inequality among breadwinner jobs. To be sure, the model reduces the weight of gender in assigning individuals to unequally compensated breadwinner jobs, but it thereby increases the weight of other variables, presumably class, education, "race"-ethnicity, and age. Women—and men—who are disadvantaged in relation to those axes of social differentiation will earn less than those who are not.

4 *Leisure-time equality.* The model is quite poor, moreover, with respect to equality of leisure time, as we know from the communist experience. It assumes that all of women's current domestic and carework responsibilities can be shifted to the market and/or the state. But that assumption is patently unrealistic. Some things, such as childbearing, attending to family emergencies, and much parenting work, cannot be shifted—short of universal surrogacy and other presumably undesirable arrangements. Other things, such as cooking and (some) housekeeping, could—provided we were prepared to accept collective living arrangements or high levels of commodification. Even those tasks that are shifted, finally, do not disappear without a trace but give rise to burdensome new tasks of coordination. Women's chances for equal leisure, then, depend on whether men can be induced to do their fair share of this work. On this, the model does not inspire confidence. Not only does it offer no disincentives to free-riding, but in valorizing paid work, it implicitly devalues unpaid work, thereby fueling the motivation to shirk. Women without partners would in any case be on their own. And those in lower-income households would be less able to purchase replacement services. Employed women would have a second shift on this model, then, albeit a less burdensome one than some have now; and there would be many more women employed full-time. Universal Breadwinner, in sum, is not likely to deliver equal leisure. Anyone who does not free-ride in this possible postindustrial world is likely to be harried and tired.

5 *Equality of respect.* The model is only fair, moreover, at delivering equality of respect. Because it holds men and women to the single standard of the citizen-worker, its only chance of eliminating the gender respect gap is to admit women to that status on the same terms as men. This, however, is unlikely to occur. A more likely outcome is that women would retain more connection to reproduction and domesticity than men, thus appearing as breadwinners manqué. In addition, the model is likely to generate another kind of respect gap. By putting a high premium on breadwinner status, it invites disrespect for others. Participants in the means-tested residual system will be liable to stigmatization, and most of these will be women. Any employment-centered model, even a feminist one, has a hard time constructing an honorable status for those it defines as "nonworkers."

6 *Antimarginalization.* This model is also only fair at combating women's marginalization. Granted, it promotes women's participation in employment, but its definition of participation is narrow. Expecting full-time employment of all who are able, the model may actually impede participation in politics and civil society. Certainly, it does nothing to promote women's participation in those arenas. It fights women's marginalization, then, in a one-sided, "workerist" way.

7 *Antiandrocentrism.* Last, the model performs poorly in overcoming androcentrism. It valorizes men's traditional sphere—employment—and simply tries to help women fit in. Traditionally female carework, in contrast, is treated instrumentally; it is what must be sloughed off in order to become a breadwinner. It is not itself accorded social value. The ideal-typical citizen here is the breadwinner, now nominally gender-neutral. But the content of the status is implicitly masculine; it is the male half of the old breadwinner/homemaker couple, now universalized and required of everyone. The female half of the couple has simply disappeared. None of her distinctive virtues and capacities has been preserved for women, let alone universalized to men. The model is androcentric.

We can summarize the merits of Universal Breadwinner in Figure 2.1. Not surprisingly, Universal Breadwinner delivers the best outcomes to women whose lives most closely resemble the male half of the old family-wage ideal couple. It is especially good to childless women and to women without other major domestic

Fig. 2.1

Principle	Universal Breadwinner
Antipoverty	good
Antiexploitation	good
Income equality	fair
Leisure-time equality	poor
Equality of respect	fair
Antimarginalization	fair
Antiandrocentrism	poor

responsibilities that cannot easily be shifted to social services. But for those women, as well as for others, it falls short of full gender equity.

THE CAREGIVER PARITY MODEL

In a second vision of postindustrial society, the era of the family wage would give way to the era of Caregiver Parity. This is the picture implicit in the political practice of most Western European feminists and social democrats. It aims to promote gender equity principally by supporting informal carework. The point is to enable women with significant domestic responsibilities to support themselves and their families either through carework alone or through carework plus part-time employment. (Women without significant domestic responsibilities would presumably support themselves through employment.) The aim is not to make women's lives the same as men's but, rather, to "make difference costless." Thus, childbearing, child rearing, and informal domestic labor are to be elevated to parity with formal paid labor. The caregiver role is to be put on a par with the breadwinner role—so that women and men can enjoy equivalent levels of dignity and well-being.

Caregiver Parity is also extremely ambitious. On this model, many (though not all) women will follow the current U.S. female practice of alternating spells of full-time employment, spells of full-time carework, and spells that combine part-time carework with part-time employment. The aim is to make such a life-pattern costless. To this end, several major new programs are necessary. One is a program of caregiver allowances to compensate childbearing, child rearing, housework, and other forms of socially necessary domestic labor; the allowances must be sufficiently generous at the full-time rate to support a family—hence equivalent to a breadwinner wage. Also required is a program of workplace reforms. These must facilitate the possibility of combining supported carework with part-time employment and of making transitions between different life-states. The key here is flexibility. One obvious necessity is a generous program of mandated pregnancy and family leaves so that caregivers can exit and enter employment without losing security or seniority. Another is a program of retraining and job search for those not returning to old jobs. Also essential is mandated flextime so that caregivers can shift their hours to accommodate their carework responsibilities, including shifts between full- and part-time employment. Finally, in the wake of all this flexibility, there must be programs to ensure continuity of all the basic social-welfare benefits, including health, unemployment, disability, and retirement insurance.

This model organizes carework very differently from Universal Breadwinner. Whereas that approach shifted carework to the market and the state, this one keeps the bulk of such work in the household and supports it with public funds. Caregiver Parity's social-insurance system also differs sharply. To assure continuous coverage for people alternating between carework and employment, benefits attached to both must be integrated in a single system. In this system, part-time jobs and supported carework must be covered on the same basis as full-time jobs. Thus, a woman finishing a spell of supported carework would be eligible for unemployment insurance benefits on the same basis as a recently laid off employee in the event she could not find a suitable job. And a supported careworker who became disabled would receive disability payments on the same basis as a disabled employee. Years of supported carework would count on a par with years of employment toward eligibility for retirement pensions. Benefit levels would be fixed in ways that treat carework and employment equivalently.

Caregiver Parity also requires another, residual tier of social welfare. Some adults will be unable to do either carework or waged work, including some adults without prior work records of either type. Most of these people will probably be men. To provide for them, the model must offer means-tested wage-and-allowance replacements. Caregiver Parity's residual tier should be smaller than Universal Breadwinner's, however; nearly all adults should be covered in the integrated breadwinner-caregiver system of social insurance.

Caregiver Parity, too, is far removed from current U.S. arrangements. It requires large outlays of public funds to pay caregiver allowances, hence major structural tax reform and a sea change in political culture. Let us assume for the sake of the thought experiment, however, that its conditions of possibility could be met. And let us consider whether the resulting postindustrial welfare state could claim title to gender equity.

1 *Antipoverty.* Caregiver Parity would do a good job of preventing poverty— including for those women and children who are currently most vulnerable. Sufficiently generous allowances would keep solo-mother families out of poverty during spells of full-time carework. And a combination of allowances and wages would do the same during spells of part-time supported carework and part-time employment. Since each of these options would carry the basic social-insurance package, moreover, women with "feminine" work patterns would have considerable security.

2 *Antiexploitation.* Caregiver Parity should also succeed in preventing exploitation for most women, including for those who are most vulnerable today. By providing income directly to nonemployed wives, it reduces their economic dependence on husbands. It also provides economic security to single women with children, reducing their liability to exploitation by employers. Insofar as caregiver allowances are honorable and nondiscretionary, finally, recipients are not subject to caseworkers' whims.

3 *Income equality.* Caregiver Parity performs quite poorly, however, with respect to income equality, as we know from the Nordic experience. Although the system of allowances-plus-wages provides the equivalent of a basic minimum breadwinner wage, it also institutes a "mommy track" in employment—a market in flexible, noncontinuous full- and/or part-time jobs. Most of these jobs will pay considerably less even at the full-time rate than comparable breadwinner-track jobs. Two-partner families will have an economic incentive to keep one partner on the breadwinner track rather than to share spells of carework between them, and given current labor markets, making the breadwinner the man will be most advantageous for heterosexual couples. Given current culture and socialization, moreover, men are generally unlikely to choose the mommy track in the same proportions as women. So the two employment tracks will carry traditional gender associations. Those associations are likely in turn to produce discrimination against women in the breadwinner track. Caregiver Parity may make difference cost less, then, but it will not make difference costless.

4 *Leisure-time equality.* Caregiver Parity does somewhat better, however, with respect to equality of leisure time. It makes it possible for all women to avoid the double shift, if they choose, by opting for full- or part-time supported carework at various stages in their lives. (Currently, this choice is available only to a small percentage of privileged U.S. women.) We just saw, however, that this choice is not truly costless. Some women with families will not want to forego the benefits of breadwinner-track employment and will try to combine it with carework. Those not partnered with someone on the caregiver track will be significantly disadvantaged with respect to leisure time, and probably in their employment as well. Men, in contrast, will largely be insulated from this dilemma. On leisure time, then, the model is only fair.

    5 *Equality of respect.* Caregiver Parity is also only fair at promoting equality of respect. Unlike Universal Breadwinner, it offers two different routes to that end. Theoretically, citizen-workers and citizen-caregivers are statuses of equivalent dignity. But are they really on a par with each other? Caregiving is certainly treated more respectfully in this model than in current U.S. society, but it remains associated with femininity. Breadwinning likewise remains associated with masculinity. Given those traditional gender associations, plus the economic differential between the two lifestyles, caregiving is unlikely to attain true parity with breadwinning. In general, it is hard to imagine how "separate but equal" gender roles could provide genuine equality of respect today.

    6 *Antimarginalization.* Caregiver Parity performs poorly, moreover, in preventing women's marginalization. By supporting women's informal carework, it reinforces the view of such work as women's work and consolidates the gender division of domestic labor. By consolidating dual labor markets for breadwinners and caregivers, moreover, the model marginalizes women within the employment sector. By reinforcing the association of caregiving with femininity, finally, it may also impede women's participation in other spheres of life, such as politics and civil society.

    7 *Antiandrocentrism.* Yet Caregiver Parity is better than Universal Breadwinner at combating androcentrism. It treats caregiving as intrinsically valuable, not as a mere obstacle to employment, thus challenging the view that only men's traditional activities are fully human. It also accommodates "feminine" life-patterns, thereby rejecting the demand that women assimilate to "masculine" patterns. But the model still leaves something to be desired. Caregiver Parity stops short of affirming the universal value of activities and life-patterns associated with women. It does not value caregiving enough to demand that men do it, too; it does not ask men to change. Thus, Caregiver Parity represents only one-half of a full-scale challenge to androcentrism. Here, too, its performance is only fair.

    Caregiver Parity's strengths and weaknesses are summarized in Figure 2.2. In general, Caregiver Parity improves the lot of women with significant carework responsibilities, but for those women, as well as for others, it fails to deliver full gender equity.

TOWARD A UNIVERSAL CAREGIVER MODEL

Both Universal Breadwinner and Caregiver Parity are highly utopian visions of a postindustrial welfare state. Either would represent a major improvement over current U.S. arrangements, yet neither is likely to be realized soon. Both models assume background preconditions that are strikingly absent today. Both presuppose major political-economic restructuring, including significant public control over

Fig. 2.2

Principle	Caregiver Parity
Antipoverty	good
Antiexploitation	good
Income equality	poor
Leisure-time equality	fair
Equality of respect	fair
Antimarginalization	poor
Antiandrocentrism	fair

corporations, the capacity to direct investment to create high-quality permanent jobs, and the ability to tax profits *and wealth* at rates sufficient to fund expanded high-quality social programs. Both models also assume broad popular support for a postindustrial welfare state that is committed to gender equity.

If both models are utopian in this sense, neither is utopian enough. Neither Universal Breadwinner nor Caregiver Parity can actually make good on its promise of gender equity—even under very favorable conditions. Although both are good at preventing women's poverty and exploitation, both are only fair at redressing inequality of respect: Universal Breadwinner holds women to the same standard as men, while constructing arrangements that prevent them from meeting it fully; Caregiver Parity, in contrast, sets up a double standard to accommodate gender difference, while institutionalizing policies that fail to assure equivalent respect for "feminine" activities and life-patterns. When we turn to the remaining principles, moreover, the two models' strengths and weaknesses diverge. Universal Breadwinner fails especially to promote equality of leisure time and to combat androcentrism, while Caregiver Parity fails especially to promote income equality and to prevent women's marginalization. Neither model, in addition, promotes women's full participation on a par with men in politics and civil society. And neither values female-associated practices enough to ask men to do them too; neither asks men to change. (The relative merits of Universal Breadwinner and Caregiver Parity are summarized in Figure 2.3.) Neither model, in sum, provides everything feminists want. Even in a highly idealized form neither delivers full gender equity.

If these were the only possibilities, we would face a very difficult set of trade-offs. Suppose, however, we reject this Hobson's choice and try to develop a third alternative. The trick is to envision a postindustrial welfare state that combines the best of Universal Breadwinner with the best of Caregiver Parity, while jettisoning the worst features of each. What third alternative is possible?

So far we have examined—and found wanting—two initially plausible approaches: one aiming to make women more like men are now; the other leaving men and women pretty much unchanged, while aiming to make women's difference costless. A third possibility is to *induce men to become more like most women are now,* namely, people who do primary carework.

Fig. 2.3

Principle	Universal Breadwinner	Caregiver Parity
Antipoverty	good	good
Antiexploitation	good	good
Income equality	fair	poor
Leisure-time equality	poor	fair
Equality of respect	fair	fair
Antimarginalization	fair	poor
Antiandrocentrism	poor	fair

Consider the effects of this one change on the models we have just examined. If men were to do their fair share of carework, Universal Breadwinner would come much closer to equalizing leisure time and eliminating androcentrism, and Caregiver Parity would do a much better job of equalizing income and reducing women's marginalization. Both models, in addition, would tend to promote equality of respect. If men were to become more like women are now, in sum, both models would begin to approach gender equity.

The key to achieving gender equity in a postindustrial welfare state, then, is to make women's current life-patterns the norm for everyone. Women today often combine breadwinning and caregiving, albeit with great difficulty and strain. A postindustrial welfare state must ensure that men do the same, while redesigning institutions so as to eliminate the difficulty and strain. We might call this vision *Universal Caregiver*.

What, then, might such a welfare state look like? Unlike Caregiver Parity, its employment sector would not be divided into two different tracks; all jobs would be designed for workers who are caregivers, too; all would have a shorter work-week than full-time jobs have now; and all would have the support of employment-enabling services. Unlike Universal Breadwinner, however, employees would not be assumed to shift all carework to social services. Some informal carework would be publicly supported and integrated on a par with paid work in a single social-insurance system. Some would be performed in households by relatives and friends, but such households would not necessarily be heterosexual nuclear families. Other supported carework would be located outside households altogether—in civil society. In state-funded but locally organized institutions, childless adults, older people, and others without kin-based responsibilities would join parents and others in democratic, self-managed carework activities.

A Universal Caregiver welfare state would promote gender equity by effectively dismantling the gendered opposition between breadwinning and caregiving. It would integrate activities that are currently separated from one another, eliminate their gender-coding, and encourage men to perform them too. This, however, is tantamount to a wholesale restructuring of the institution of gender. The construction of breadwinning and caregiving as separate roles, coded masculine and feminine respectively, is a principal undergirding of the current gender order. To dismantle those roles and their cultural coding is in effect to overturn that order. It means subverting the existing gender division of labor and reducing the salience of gender as a structural principle of social organization. At the limit, it suggests deconstructing gender. By deconstructing the opposition between breadwinning and caregiving, moreover, Universal Caregiver would simultaneously deconstruct the associated opposition between bureaucratized public institutional settings and intimate private domestic settings. Treating civil society as an additional site for carework, it would overcome both the "workerism" of Universal Breadwinner and the domestic privatism of Caregiver Parity. Thus, Universal Caregiver promises expansive new possibilities for enriching the substance of social life and for promoting equal participation.

Only by embracing the Universal Caregiver vision, moreover, can we mitigate potential conflicts among our seven component principles of gender equity and minimize the need for trade-offs. Rejecting this approach, in contrast, makes such conflicts, and hence trade-offs, more likely. *Achieving gender equity in a postindustrial welfare state, then, requires deconstructing gender.*

Much more work needs to be done to develop this third—Universal Caregiver—vision of a postindustrial welfare state. A key is to develop policies that discourage free-riding. *Contra* conservatives, the real free-riders in the current system are not poor solo mothers who shirk employment. Instead, they are men of all classes who shirk carework and domestic labor, as well as corporations who free-ride on the labor of working people, both underpaid and unpaid.

A good statement of the Universal Caregiver vision comes from the Swedish Ministry of Labor: "To make it possible for both men and women to combine parenthood and gainful employment, a new view of the male role and a radical change in the organization of working life are required."[1] The trick is to imagine a social world in which citizens' lives integrate wage earning, caregiving, community activism, political participation, and involvement in the associational life of civil society—while also leaving time for some fun. This world is not likely to come into being in the immediate future, but it is the only imaginable postindustrial world that promises true gender equity. And unless we are guided by this vision now, we will never get any closer to achieving it.

NOTE

1 Quoted in Ruth Lister, "Women, Economic Dependency, and Citizenship," *Journal of Social Policy* 19, no. 4 (1990), p. 463.

QUESTIONS

1 In a just society, should the government play a significant role in promoting gender equity?
2 Should any of the three visions presented by Fraser be a guiding ideal in formulating policy decisions in a just society?

SUGGESTED ADDITIONAL READINGS FOR CHAPTER 3

CHRISTMAN, JOHN: "Autonomy, Independence, and Poverty-Related Welfare Programs." *Public Affairs Quarterly,* vol. 12, 1998, pp. 383–405. Christman argues that, insofar as autonomy is the justifying goal of welfare programs for the poor, these programs will fail unless provisions are made to guarantee the material conditions necessary for autonomous choice *prior to,* and independent of, labor force participation. He then advances a critical examination of recent U.S. programs whose aim is to reduce welfare dependency.

FRIEDMAN, MILTON: *Capitalism and Freedom.* Chicago: University of Chicago Press, 1962. For Friedman, an economist and libertarian, the ethical principle governing the distribution of income in a free society is "to each according to what he or the instruments he owns produces." He sees economic freedom as a necessary condition for political freedom.

GINSBERG, LEON: *Conservative Social Welfare Policy: A Description and Analysis.* Chicago: Nelson-Hall, 1998. Ginsberg analyzes conservative and neoconservative perspectives on social welfare. His account includes a description of the history of social welfare, as well as an examination of the role that American business and economics have played in shaping social policy.

GOVIER, TRUDY: "The Right to Eat and the Duty to Work." *Philosophy of the Social Sciences,* vol. 5, 1975, pp. 125–143. Govier identifies three possible positions on welfare: individualist, puritan, and permissive. Evaluating each from both a utilitarian and justice standpoint, she argues that the permissive position is morally superior to the others.

HARRINGTON, MICHAEL: *Socialism.* New York: Saturday Review Press, 1970, 1972. Harrington explores various "socialisms"—positions that he considers antisocialist. He presents his account of socialism as a possible alternative to both communism and the welfare state.

HASLETT, D. W.: "Is Inheritance Justified?" *Philosophy and Public Affairs,* vol. 15, Spring 1986, pp. 122–155. Haslett addresses the following question: Should property rights incorporate the practice of inheritance as it exists in the United States today? Giving a negative response, be argues that the inheritance of wealth is inconsistent with the fundamental values that underlie capitalism.

KYMLICKA, WILL: *Contemporary Political Philosophy.* Oxford: Oxford University Press, 1990. Kymlicka discusses the competing views of justice and community advanced by the major schools in contemporary political theory.

LAWSON, BILL E., ed.: *The Underclass Question.* Philadelphia: Temple University Press, 1992. This set of articles explores various philosophical questions raised by the recent growth of an economically and politically disadvantaged black group at a time when the black middle class is expanding.

NIELSEN, KAI: *Equality and Liberty: A Defense of Radical Egalitarianism.* Totowa, N.J.: Rowman & Littlefield, 1984. Nielsen defends the egalitarian ideal that is at the basis of socialist thinking.

NOZICK, ROBERT: *Anarchy, State, and Utopia.* New York: Basic, 1974. This book has engendered a great deal of discussion among philosophers concerned with distributive justice. Nozick, who endorses the libertarian conception of justice, holds the libertarian ideal to be exemplified by the principle "from each as he chooses, to each as he is chosen."

OKIN, SUSAN MOLLER: *Justice. Gender, and the Family.* New York: Basic, 1989. Okin argues that, without a just family structure, there will not be a just society. She criticizes various contemporary Anglo-American theories of justice, such as those of Robert Nozick and John Rawls, for their androcentrism. However, Okin finds Rawls's veil of ignorance useful in developing a theory of justice within the family.

RAWLS, JOHN: *A Theory of Justice,* rev. ed. Cambridge, Mass.: Harvard University Press, 1999. In his seminal work, *A Theory of Justice,* published in 1971, Rawls presents his theory of justice *as* fairness. In this revised edition, Rawls attempts to clear up a number of difficulties he and others have found in the original book.

Unit Three

Drug Control
and Addiction Notes

To begin this chapter, it is helpful to know the following terms:

Drug abuse can involve both addictive and non-addictive, legal and illegal drugs.

Legalization means providing a free market on all drugs, but it can also involve government controls over those drugs.

Decriminalization means the drug may still be illegal, but possession of small amounts will not be prosecuted.

Medicalization means a drug can be legally prescribed, but this does NOT mean that it can be made available to anyone who asks. It must be considered medically necessary.

Some background: Legal drugs (alcohol and smoking) cause half of the fatal car accidents, and contribute to child and spousal abuse, as well as illness and death.

Justice Jacob J. Spiegel: Justice Jacob J. Spiegel discusses the case of *Commonwealth v. Joseph D. Leis*. Justice Spiegel admits that there is no evidence that smoking marihuana does or does not cause problems such as motor vehicle accidents or lead to the use of more toxic drugs. However, he uses this lack of evidence to justify keeping the marihuana illegal. At this point, you may wish to go back to our "fallacies" from the first Unit see if Justice Spiegel's conclusion falls under the definition of a fallacy. However, he also points out that the use of marihuana may exacerbate any already underlying mental conditions a user might have, and there may be more evidence for this statement. The critical thinking problem with this position is whether it is good policy to base a rule on its exception.

In Spiegel's defense, please note that the case was brought to court in 1969. The use of drugs during this era brought out extreme reactions (for and against), seldom based on any evidence. The campaign against drugs resulted in some propaganda that has since been proven false, and some of it is so absurd as to be funny. Many of the claims fit under the category of "slippery slope." For example, it was claimed that after smoking pot once, a user would end up on Heroin. Justice Spiegel acknowledges that this causal connection had, by then, been disproven, but in the next breath he states that a causal relationship need not exist, and then contradicts the evidence he has just submitted by saying that there is (considerable) evidence that the "progression from marihuana to heroin or LSD is a frequent sequence."

As his judgment continues, he argues that one reason there is a need to prohibit the use of marihuana is that it can't be detected. In other words, if a driver is weaving across the road, there are ways to measure if alcohol (and how much) has been used. At that time, there were no comparable ways to measure whether marihuana had been used. This seems to be the main support in Spiegel's judgment on why alcohol can remain a legal drug (because abuse can be measured), while marihuana needs to remain illegal (because it cannot be measured).

The article is interesting to read from a philosophical perspective, because it violates so many of the rules for valid arguments. This does not mean that Justice Spiegel's decision on this case is necessarily wrong, but the support in getting to the conclusion would never be accepted in a philosophy class.

Thomas S. Szasz: Thomas S. Szasz argues that self-destructive behavior is no business of the state. He argues that it is not the use of drugs that make a person irresponsible. Rather, it is the irresponsible person who uses drugs as an excuse for his behavior. Szasz argues that just because a drug may be dangerous is no reason to make it illegal. We have many drugs (penicillin, insulin, etc.) that are not addictive or dangerous, but are prohibited for general use, and we have lots of things (like guns) that are very dangerous but we allow. So, danger in itself is no justification for criminalization. The justification used by Szasz follows the Harm Principle— that we should be permitted to do whatever we wish so long as it does not directly harm another.

Just for the fun of it, can you imagine a conversation between Justice Spiegel and Thomas Szasz? Wouldn't it be interesting to be a fly on the wall for that one?

Robert E. Goodin: Robert E. Goodin brings in the issue of smoking. However, he centers the issue around the use of Legal Paternalism. Legal Paternalism is the idea that the state, the "laws," may prevent you from engaging in activities that are detrimental to your health or safety. The issue of paternalism is important because it is also the basis for a restriction on the use of drugs. If paternalism is a legitimate justification for passing a law, a way to protect people from their own folly, then it applies equally to issue of smoking or any other addictive substance. Goodin argues that paternalism is a legitimate support for laws against the use of any substance that could prove harmful.

If you have trouble reading this article, just skip to the last page. He doesn't get to the point of his article until the last two paragraphs.

Ethan A. Nadelmann: Ethan A. Nadelmann's argument is that we are not consistent in our drug policies. He points out that far more deaths are caused each year by alcohol and tobacco than by illicit drugs. It is inconsistent to make marihuana and cocaine illegal, while legalizing the use of alcohol and tobacco. The harm done by our drug policies is greater than the harm would be if we legalized drugs. Adults should have the right to choose what substances they consume and the risks they take. The state has no right to control individuals, unless they are in danger of harming others. Legalizing drugs would create new tax revenues, police could concentrate on other crimes, there would be less incentive for people to go into criminal careers, and the homicide rates would decline.

James Q. Wilson: James Q. Wilson was appointed to the National Advisory Council on Drug Abuse Prevention by President Nixon (1972). Wilson disagrees with famous economist, Milton Freeman, who called for legalization of heroin and other drugs. Freeman, a highly respected economist, argued that the "war on drugs" caused more grief than would be caused by legalizing drugs. He suggested that legalizing drugs would take drugs out of the hands of criminals and allow all the money used to fight drugs, instead, used to educate people not to use drugs, or at least use them responsibly. Wilson disagreed. Wilson's greatest concern is that drugs dehumanize the user. He believes drugs keep us from developing and fulfilling our potential as human beings. And, he is particularly concerned with pregnant women who use drugs because of the damage to the fetus.

Daniel Shapiro: Daniel Shapiro argues that pharmacological dependence can't be the major factor in continued drug addiction. He points out that withdrawal symptoms are like having a week of a very bad flu, miserable, but something we can live through. Instead, he blames the setting and set in which drugs are used. In other words, he points out that when drugs are used in a setting where the use is expected to be responsible and temporary, that is usually what happens. Like Nadelmann and Szasz, Shapiro believes it is the individual who makes the difference. Responsible people will use drugs responsibly. Shapiro points out that when it comes to pharmacology, cigarettes are a better example of addiction than cocaine. He argues that smoking is such an example of dependence because the milder, easier to purchase, more easily integrated into life-styles, and the slower (less visible) and cumulative the effects of a drug, the more addictive they are likely to become.

CHAPTER 4

Drug Control and Addiction

Millions of Americans smoke marijuana, imbibe various forms of alcohol, smoke tobacco cigarettes, and use other substances that can be widely classified as drugs. The personal, economic, and social costs of these activities are extremely high. Alcohol, for example, is involved in about half of all fatal car collisions and in a large number of cases of child and spousal abuse. Deaths and illnesses caused by smoking tobacco, as well as the related medical costs, are now a matter of public knowledge. However, both alcohol and tobacco are legal substances, whereas drugs such as marijuana, cocaine, crack, and heroin are illegal, and users of them can face many years in prison if caught. The costs of enforcing prohibitory laws and conducting the drug war are constantly escalating, thus adding to the exhorbitant costs associated with drug abuse.

In this chapter, we focus on the question of the morally legitimate role of government in respect to drug use. Is a government justified in adopting measures designed to prevent or discourage adults from using drugs?

SOME PRELIMINARY CLARIFICATIONS

Drugs, for the purposes of this chapter, can be broadly defined as psychoactive chemicals—chemicals that are transported to the brain via the bloodstream, influencing consciousness directly and significantly. By this definition, alcohol, nicotine, and caffeine—as well as currently illegal substances, such as heroin—are all drugs. Drugs can serve many purposes besides medical ones. They can be used for recreation—that is, to achieve or enhance pleasure. They also can be used instrumentally, as the caffeine in coffee is sometimes used to enhance work performance. Drugs might also be used in religious practices or to stimulate creativity.

Drug abuse is sometimes defined as any nonmedical use of a drug that carries a serious risk of significant harm to oneself or others. *Drug abuse,* in its ordinary usage, is a pejorative expression and is often applied to any use of drugs that is seen as objectionable. Thus, any use of illegal drugs, such as marijuana, is frequently considered drug abuse because it involves breaking the law, even though mild marijuana use may not be harmful. In contrast, alcohol consumption is typically considered a form of drug abuse only if it is excessive.

Drug abuse can take various forms. Misuse may be occasional. Think of someone who drinks too much at a party and causes an embarrassing scene. If a drug is used more and more frequently, however, the user may become drug dependent. The dependency may be physical, psychological, or both. Someone with a severe dependency who attempts to stop using the drug may experience physiological withdrawal symptoms. *Drug addiction,* the most serious form of drug abuse, is frequently understood as involving a high degree of physical and psychological dependency and severe withdrawal symptoms, as well as a strong tendency to relapse after withdrawal. However, the precise nature of drug addiction remains a controversial issue. In this chapter, Daniel Shapiro rejects what he labels the standard model of addiction and develops an alternative model.

Arguments against current drug laws often use the word *legalization* as a blanket term to cover very different suggestions for policy changes. In its strictest sense, *legalization* means having a free market in all drugs. This is the position espoused by Thomas Szasz in this chapter, although he would allow some restrictions on the sale of drugs to minors. Other legalization proposals are less sweeping. Some would allow the government, but only the government, to produce and sell drugs. Others would allow a private market in drugs but incorporate restrictions on advertising, dosage, and place of consumption.

Often those who argue for legalization, however, advocate less sweeping proposals. As Ethan Nadelmann, a proponent of legalization, points out in a related article in this chapter,

> Drugs are here to stay. The time has come to abandon the concept of a "drug-free society." We need to focus on learning to live with drugs in such a way that they do the least possible harm. . . .
>
> There is a wide range of choice in drug-policy options between the free-market approach favored by Milton Friedman and Thomas Szasz and the zero-tolerance approach of William Bennett. These options fall under the concept of harm reduction. That concept holds that drug policies need to focus on *reducing harm,* whether engendered by drugs or by the prohibition of drugs. And it holds that disease and death can be diminished even among people who can't, or won't, stop taking drugs.[1]

Harm-reduction policies may involve decriminalization and/or medicalization. Decriminalization policies, for example, might eliminate criminal sanctions for the possession of small amounts of drugs for personal use while still forbidding the manufacture, importation, and sale of currently illegal drugs. Medicalization policies might allow physicians to prescribe drugs that are currently illegal to addicts who are already drug dependent.

Harm-reduction policies may take other forms as well—such as developing needle exchange programs to prevent the spread of HIV infections, advocating responsible drug use rather than no drug use, and providing "low threshold" methadone maintenance without requiring counseling or regular attendance.

---

[1]Ethan Nadelmann, "The War on Drugs Is Lost," *National Review,* February 12, 1996, pp. 38–39.

THE LEGALIZATION ISSUE

The major arguments for prohibitory drug laws can be best understood by reference to one or more of the following three liberty-limiting principles—the harm principle, the principle of legal paternalism, and the principle of legal moralism. Thus, the main arguments for some form of legalization can also be understood by reference to these principles.

Drug Laws, Legalization, and the Harm Principle

The harm principle allows interference with individual liberty in order to prevent harm to others, but only in those cases in which coercive legislation causes less harm than the harms that would occur in the absence of such legislation. The harm principle is a relatively uncontroversial liberty-limiting principle. Thus, much of the current debate regarding drug laws involves disputes about the harms caused by drug abuse and addiction, the harms *prevented* by current drug laws, and the harms *caused* by current policies. Many of those who argue for some form of legalization, like Nadelmann in this chapter, maintain that the majority of the harms related to drug abuse are caused by current drug policies. Among these harms, Nadelmann identifies the following: the enormous financial costs of the drug war, the crimes caused by addicts who need money to support their habits, the overloaded judicial system, the costs of maintaining the ever increasing number of jail inmates who are incarcerated on drug-related charges, police corruption, and the costs paid by innocent inner-city dwellers whose neighborhoods are dominated by those engaged in illegal drug trading. In addition, he cites the costs incurred by illegal drug users whose lives and health are at risk because there is no quality control over the drugs they use, because shared needles can transmit HIV infections, and because the possibility of arrest under drug laws is a threat to their livelihoods.

Many of those who argue in support of current drug policies, such as Justice Jacob J. Spiegel, who defends the constitutionality of Massachusetts's marijuana restrictions in this chapter, focus on the prevention of harms perpetrated by drug abusers. Justice Spiegel, for example, argues that antimarijuana laws are necessary to prevent harms that some experts associate with marijuana use, such as psychotic breaks and automobile accidents caused by marijuana-smoking drivers. James Q. Wilson, also in this chapter, focuses on users of crack cocaine. He maintains that crack users regularly neglect their children, fail to provide for their spouses, and short-change their employers as well as their coworkers because of their drug-induced lethargy. In Wilson's view, the harms resulting from drug legalization would far outweigh the harms caused by their prohibition. Without current drug laws, he maintains, drug addiction would rise exponentially, as would the harms caused by addicts. Both Nadelmann and Shapiro challenge that conclusion in this chapter.

Drug Laws, Legalization, and the Principle of Legal Paternalism

Those who want to retain current drug laws in order to prevent a possible rise in addiction may be motivated by paternalistic reasons. If harm to others is the concern, then the harm principle is the basis of the argument. If, however, the concern is with preventing potential addicts from engaging in risk-running, self-harming behavior, then the grounds are paternalistic, and the underlying idea is that interference with individual liberty is justified to prevent self-harm. When Justice Spiegel argues, for example, that current antimarijuana laws are justified insofar as they prevent psychotic breaks, he may simply be concerned with the harm to others that might be caused by a psychotic individual. In that case, his reasoning is related to the harm principle. If, however, he is concerned with preventing harm to the individual undergoing a psychotic break, then his reasoning is paternalistic. Thomas S. Szasz, in this chapter, rejects all paternalistically motivated laws, including drug laws, as unacceptable infringements on individual freedom.

The reasoning underlying antipaternalistic arguments for legalization can be summarized as follows. Adults have a right to self-determination (sometimes called a right of autonomy)—a right to live and act in accordance with their own aims and values, unless doing so violates others' rights. Some people value the pleasure they achieve by using recreational drugs and are willing to run the associated risks. Using these drugs does not, generally, dispose people to violate the rights of others—by committing crimes, for example. Heavily dependent and addicted drug users do sometimes fail to meet their obligations to others, but most drug users are neither heavily dependent nor addicted. Since adults do have a right to self-determination, they have a right to use drugs for recreation. However, individuals who commit crimes while under the influence of drugs should be held responsible for their actions and punished accordingly.

Philosophers who base their arguments for drug laws on paternalistic considerations often relate their reasoning to John Stuart Mill's argument against voluntary slavery. Despite his opposition to legal paternalism, Mill maintains that individuals cannot be allowed to sell themselves into voluntary slavery and argues as follows:

> . . . by selling himself for a slave, he abdicates his liberty; he foregoes any future use of it beyond that single act. He therefore defeats, in his own case, the very purpose which is the justification of allowing him to dispose of himself. . . . The principle of freedom cannot require that he should be free not to be free. It is not freedom, to be allowed to alienate his freedom. These reasons, the force of which is so conspicuous in this peculiar case, are evidently of far wider applications. . . .[2]

According to this line of reasoning, individuals must be protected against making and acting on a choice that will result in their forfeiting their freedom to make future choices. So, too, it can be argued, individuals must be protected from freely and voluntarily choosing to take drugs that will eventually result in addiction, and the concominant loss of autonomy (capacity for self-determination). In this chapter, Shapiro rejects this line of reasoning and challenges the underlying conception of addiction.

Somewhat implicit in the article by Robert E. Goodin included in this chapter, but explicitly developed by him in another article,[3] is his overall approach to the problem of the voluntariness of the choices made by addicted cigarette smokers.

---

[2]John Stuart Mill, *On Liberty* (New York: E. P. Dutton & Co., 1951), p. 213.
[3]Robert E. Goodin, "The Ethics of Smoking," *Ethics,* vol. 99, April 1989, pp. 579–587, 596–597.

In Goodin's view, addicted smokers lack free will with respect to the substance to which they are addicted and, hence, are not capable of giving their voluntary and informed consent to the continuation of the addictive behavior. Goodin's reasoning is based on his understanding of addiction (a conception challenged by Shapiro), as well as on a conception of autonomy and free will advanced by various philosophers who adopt a multitier approach to an agent's desires—an approach that distinguishes between first- and second-order desires and preferences.[4] First-order desires and preferences are those directed toward actions. Sally might have a desire to attend the Olympic Games in another country, for example. If she is able to act on this desire because nothing external prevents her from doing so— for example, tickets for the games are available, and there are no visa requirements that would prevent her traveling to the country where the games are taking place—she can accurately be described as performing free actions when she attends the games. Sally is doing what she wants to do. But a free action is not necessarily an autonomous one. Her action is autonomous only if her first-order desires are controlled by her second-order desires. For example, Sally might deplore the fact that her first-order desire to attend the Olympic Games is so strong that she has spent funds needed to pay overdue debts and has caused anguish to family members as a result, but she is still unable to resist the desire to attend. If Sally strongly desires not to be the kind of person who would give preference to attendance at athletic competitions over serious family considerations but cannot control her desire to attend the games, she is acting nonautonomously. Sally does not want to want what she wants to do. According to this view, whether an action is autonomous is a function of the relation between one's first- and second-order desires. Some philosophers identify second-order desires with a person's fundamental or settled aims and values—the aims and values with which the person identifies. Thus, Gerald Dworkin writes as follows:

> It is the attitude a person takes towards the influences motivating him which determines whether or not they are to be considered "his." Does he identify with them, assimilate them to himself, view himself as the kind of person who wishes to be motivated in these particular ways? If, on the contrary, a man resents his being motivated in certain ways, is alienated from those influences, resents acting in accordance with them, would prefer to be the kind of person who is motivated in different ways, then those influences, even though they may be causally effective, are not viewed as "his."[5]

According to this line of reasoning, addicted smokers are not acting autonomously when they act on their first-order desires to smoke if these desires are at odds with their settled aims and values. In that case, laws intended to prevent or discourage them from smoking need not factor out as violations of their right to self-determination. Goodin construes such laws as a very weak form of paternalism, since they do not

---

[4]See the following, for example: Gerald Dworkin, "Autonomy and Behavior Control," *Hastings Center Report,* vol. 6, February 1976, pp. 23–28 and Harry G. Frankfurt, "Freedom of the Will and the Concept of a Person," *Journal of Philosophy,* vol. 68, 1971, pp. 5–20.
[5]Dworkin, "Autonomy and Behavior Control," p. 25.

involve the imposition of others' values on the addict but, rather, help individuals to live in accordance with those values with which they themselves identify. Goodin's reasoning would support laws that prevent addicts from having access to drugs, whereas the earlier analogy between drug addiction and slavery would support laws prohibiting access to addictive drugs even to those who are not yet addicted. However, the cogency of both these arguments depends on an acceptance of the underlying conception of addiction.

Drug Laws, Legalization, and the Principle of Legal Moralism

A moral distinction is sometimes made between some psychoactive substances, such as cocaine and marijuana, on the one hand, and other psychoactive substances, such as tobacco and alcohol, on the other. The very use of the former for recreational purposes, or other nonmedicinal ends, is seen as immoral, whereas the same is not true of tobacco or alcohol use. Sometimes those who make this distinction believe that laws prohibiting the sale and use of drugs such as marijuana, crack, and heroin are justified because the very use of these drugs is immoral. The underlying reasoning here is based on the principle of legal moralism, which allows interferences with individual liberty in order to keep individuals from acting immorally. Aside from the problematic nature of the principle of legal moralism, such reasoning raises questions of consistency. Nadelmann denies, for example, that there are any morally significant differences between these two classes of psychoactive substances. It follows, for Nadelmann, that laws governing the sale and use of drugs that are currently illegal, on the one hand, and those governing the sale and use of tobacco and alcohol, on the other, are morally inconsistent. In contrast to Nadelmann, Wilson argues, specifically with respect to the difference between *nicotine* and cocaine, that there is a morally significant difference between these two substances. In his view, cocaine is debasing—that is, it destroys the user's essential humanity—whereas nicotine, even though it is harmful in other ways, does not. Although Wilson does not explicitly state that cocaine's power to effect such degradation makes its very use immoral, this seems to be the underlying idea. Thus, the reasoning Wilson advances to support the differential legal treatment of nicotine and cocaine seems to rely on the principle of legal moralism. But another thread in his reasoning seems to rely on the harm principle, since he expresses concern about the consequences for society if the degradation caused by cocaine becomes more commonplace. With respect to the differences between how the laws treat *alcohol* and cocaine, however, Wilson simply focuses on the harms that might result from the legalization of the latter. He grants that the harms resulting from alcohol are manifold. Nonetheless he does not want the laws to change. In his view, addiction to drugs such as cocaine would rise dramatically on legalization and would cause even greater harm than does current alcohol use.

Jane S. Zembaty

Opinion in *Commonwealth v. Joseph D. Leis*

Justice Jacob J. Spiegel

Six defendants, including Joseph D. Leis, were convicted for the unlawful possession of marijuana and for conspiracy to violate the Narcotic Drugs Law of Massachusetts. They were also indicted for illegal possession of marijuana with intent to sell it unlawfully. The defendants filed a motion with the Supreme Court of Massachusetts to dismiss the charges, on the grounds that the Commonwealth's statutory provisions regarding the possession, use, and sale of marijuana are unconstitutional. Ruling against the defendants, the Supreme Court of Massachusetts upheld the constitutionality of the Massachusetts laws.

In challenging the constitutionality of Massachusetts's marijuana laws, the defendants advanced two lines of argument in support of their claim that the laws are arbitrary, unreasonable, and irrational. First, they argued that the laws serve no legitimate state purpose because there is no evidence that the use of marijuana is a threat to the public health, safety, welfare, or morals. Second, they contended that the inclusion of marijuana among those substances defined as narcotic drugs is arbitrary for various reasons, including the exclusion from this classification of substances that are far more harmful. In rejecting their claims, Justice Spiegel maintains that, since the effects of marijuana and other illicit drugs are not known and subject to a great deal of dispute, it is legitimate for the state to treat these drugs differently than it treats alcohol and tobacco in its attempt to prevent some of the possible harms resulting from drug use.

1. The defendants allege that the Narcotic Drugs Law of the Commonwealth is "arbitrary and irrational and not suited to achieve any valid legislative end in that . . . it imposes harsh penalties upon mere possession of marihuana, or possession with intent to sell, or being present where marihuana is kept, without a showing that use of this substance poses a threat to the public health, safety, welfare or morals." They conclude that it therefore violates Part II, c. 1, § 1, art. 4, of the Constitution of the Commonwealth[1] and the Due Process Clause of the Fourteenth Amendment of the Constitution of the United States.[2] The defendants contend that the law, "as applied to marihuana, goes beyond the police power of the Commonwealth in that it is not and cannot be aimed at achieving any valid legislative end, namely protection of the health, safety, welfare and morals." They assert that it therefore violates, in addition to Part II, c. 1, § 1, art. 4, of the Constitution of the Commonwealth and the Due Process Clause of the Fourteenth Amendment of the Constitution of the United States, art. 7[3] and art. 1[4] of the Declaration of Rights of the Constitution of the Commonwealth.

The defendants first argue that the law is "irrational and unreasonable" because the Legislature did not thoroughly investigate the available scientific and medical evidence concerning marihuana when enacting and revising the law.

Supreme Judicial Court of Massachusetts (1969). 355 Mass. 189; 243 N.E.2d 898. Reprinted with permission of West Group.

We know of nothing that *compels* the Legislature to thoroughly investigate the available scientific and medical evidence when enacting a law. The test of whether an act of the Legislature is rational and reasonable is not whether the records of the Legislature contain a sufficient basis of fact to sustain that act. The Legislature is presumed to have acted rationally and reasonably. "Unless the act of the Legislature cannot be supported upon any rational basis of fact that reasonably can be conceived to sustain it, the court has no power to strike it down as violative of the Constitution."

The defendants then argue that the law is irrational and unreasonable and that it serves no legitimate State interest because there is no evidence that marihuana endangers the health, safety, welfare or morals of the community. They assert, inter alia, that there is no evidence to support the "allegations" that the smoking of marihuana causes psychotic reactions or "psychotic breaks" and that the use of marihuana leads to the use of more dangerous drugs. They summarily dispose of "[t]he charge that marihuana causes disorientation, psychomotor discoordination, excitement and confusion" as merely a statement that marihuana causes a state of intoxication if used to excess, and of the "charge" that marihuana causes automobile accidents as pure "speculation."

The testimony of the experts fully justifies the conclusion that marihuana is a "mind-altering" drug. There was evidence that the effect of such a drug is "a complex interaction between the physical or pharmacological properties of that drug . . . and most importantly the personality or character structure of the person consuming that drug, and . . . the social setting or context in which the drug is taken, including expectations, attitudes, et cetera." The smoking of marihuana may cause a state of euphoria and hallucinations or mental confusion and acute panic. It tends to exacerbate an underlying mental condition and to accentuate the smoker's basic personality makeup. When used by persons who have personality disorders or who are predisposed to "psychotic breaks," it may contribute to the onset of a "psychotic break."[5] The problem is magnified by the fact that persons having personality disorders and predispositions to "psychotic breaks" are more likely to experiment with marihuana and to become psychologically dependent upon it. Although the smoking of marihuana triggers only "acute [short-term] psychotic breaks" and does not apparently cause permanent psychotic injury or mental deterioration, an acute psychotic break, while it lasts, is as serious as a chronic mental disorder.

Essentially the experts do not point to any evidence of a direct, causal relationship between the smoking of marihuana and the use of more dangerous drugs. The studies that do exist discount the once prevalent belief that the smoking of marihuana inevitably leads to the use of more dangerous drugs. However, it is not necessary to show such a direct, causal relationship. There is considerable evidence that marihuana does lead some people to the use of more dangerous drugs. The progression from marihuana to heroin or LSD is a frequent sequence.

In an attempt to disprove the claim that the use of marihuana may cause automobile accidents, the defendants say that "no evidence [was] produced linking marihuana use with . . . [such] accidents." The evidence, however, showed there is no accurate, reliable scientific means of determining whether the operator of a motor vehicle has recently smoked marihuana. A person "high" on marihuana is unlikely to stagger or weave when he walks. While the smoking of marihuana may cause dilatation of the conjunctival blood vessels, there is recent evidence that it does not cause pupillary dilatation. The burning of marihuana does produce a recognizable odor, but that odor could be easily disguised. These properties of the drug undoubtedly account for the unavailability of statistical data. However, there is agreement among the experts that marihuana causes an alteration of sensory perception, a degree of psychomotor discoordination and an inability to concentrate. All of these effects of marihuana would interfere with the operation of a motor vehicle.

We do not think that the present unavailability of or inability to collect absolute, statistical and scientific proof that the smoking of marihuana (1) triggers "psychotic breaks," (2) leads to the use of more dangerous drugs and (3) causes automobile accidents prevents the Legislature from acting to prohibit its use. Surely the defendants would not contend, for example, that unless experiments absolutely establish that thalidomide causes birth defects the Legislature could not prevent the distribution of that drug. To prevent "psychotic breaks," to guard against the use of more dangerous drugs and to eliminate a cause of automobile accidents are valid State interests.

The defendants insist that the right to smoke marihuana is guaranteed by the Constitutions of the Commonwealth and of the United States and must be balanced against the interests of the State in prohibiting its use. No such right exists. It is not specifically preserved by either Constitution. The right to smoke marihuana is not "fundamental to the American scheme of justice . . . necessary to an Anglo-American regime of ordered liberty." It is not within a "zone of privacy" formed by "penumbras" of the First, Third, Fourth and Fifth Amendments and the Ninth Amendment of the Constitution of the United States. The defendants have no right, fundamental or otherwise, to become intoxicated by means of the smoking of marihuana.

We do not agree with the defendants that the Legislature is bound to adopt the "least restrictive alternative" that would fulfill its purpose of protecting the health, safety and welfare of the community. The least restrictive alternative doctrine does not apply to the instant case. It has been limited to regulations affecting interstate commerce. The Narcotic Drugs Law is not an economic regulation. It affects neither interstate commerce nor constitutionally sheltered activity.

In any event, there is ample justification for the Legislature to conclude that the total prohibition of marihuana is the "least restrictive alternative." The evidence indicates that the effects of smoking marihuana are unpredictable. No one can predict how a given person will react, or how such a person will react to the drug at any given time. There is no known means of determining whether a person has smoked marihuana, how much he has smoked or even how much causes intoxication. The difficulty of establishing the intoxication of the driver who is under the influence of marihuana renders G.L. c. 90, § 24(1) (a),[6] as amended through St.1963, c. 369, § 2, an insufficient safeguard with regard to the danger of automobile accidents.

2. The defendants maintain that the Narcotic Drugs Law "has singled out for prohibition and punishment possessors of and possessors of with intent to sell,

marihuana, while the laws permit the regulated use, sale and possession of substances far more harmful than marihuana . . . punish less harshly possession and sale of substances far more harmful than marihuana . . . and punish equally harshly substances far more harmful than marihuana." Therefore, they say that it violates art. 1 of the Declaration of Rights of the Constitution of the Commonwealth and the Equal Protection Clause of the Fourteenth Amendment of the Constitution of the United States.

The defendants argue that the inclusion of marihuana in the class of drugs defined by G.L. c. 94, § 197, to be "narcotic drugs" is arbitrary. This argument ignores "the rules by which this contention must be tested. . . . 1. The equal protection clause of the 14th Amendment does not take from the state the power to classify in the adoption of police laws, but admits of the exercise of a wide scope of discretion in that regard, and voids what is done only when it is without any reasonable basis, and therefore is purely arbitrary. 2. A classification having some reasonable basis does not offend against that clause merely because it is not made with mathematical nicety, or because in practice it results in some inequality. 3. When the classification in such a law is called in question, if any state of facts reasonably can be conceived that would sustain it, the existence of that state of facts at the time the law was enacted must be assumed. 4. One who assails the classification in such a law must carry the burden of showing that it does not rest upon any reasonable basis, but is essentially arbitrary."

"Narcotic drug" as defined in G.L. c. 94, § 197, as amended through St.1966, c. 71, §§ 1 and 2, includes "coca leaves, cocaine, alpha or beta eucaine . . . opium, morphine, heroin, codeine, apomorphine, isonipecaine, amidone, isoamidone, ketobemidone, peyote, LSD, psilocybin, D.M.T. . . . and cannabis (sometimes called marihuana . . .)." All of these substances are "mind-altering" drugs. The fact that some are more potent or more dangerous than others does not render the classification arbitrary. To some degree they are all capable of producing psychotic disorders, states of intoxication and psychological dependency, and consequently present some danger to the health and safety of the community. We do not think that the classification of marihuana with the others is arbitrary or irrational.

The defendants also contend that the noninclusion of other "mind-altering" drugs in G.L. c. 94, § 197, as amended through St.1966, c. 71, §§ 1 and 2, which are "acknowledged to be . . . more harmful" than marihuana, causes the law to "run afoul of the requirements of equal protection." They concede that the Legislature may select the kinds of behavior that it wishes to proscribe. They claim, however, that this "does not mean that a Legislature may actually proscribe behavior of one class of people (e. g., those who choose to obtain a mild state of intoxication with marihuana) and allow another class of people to freely indulge in behavior of an exactly similar nature (e. g., those who choose to obtain a mild state of intoxication with alcohol)."

We do not think that a statute which proscribes generally certain conduct can be said to be discriminatory simply because a certain group of persons tend to engage more often in that conduct than others. Such "de facto" discrimination does not violate the Equal Protection Clause. There are at least two distinctions between alcohol and the "mind-altering" intoxicants that are defined by the law to be narcotic drugs. First, alcohol is susceptible to a less restrictive alternative means of control. There are recognized, accurate means of determining its use and its abuse. Second, the effects of alcohol upon the user are known. We think that the Legislature is warranted in treating this known intoxicant differently from marihuana, LSD or heroin, the effects of which are largely still unknown and subject to extensive dispute. The Legislature is free to recognize degrees of harm and may confine its restrictions to instances where it determines the need for them is clearest. . . .

NOTES

1 "[F]ull power and authority are hereby given and granted to the said general court, from time to time, to make, ordain, and establish, all manner of wholesome and reasonable orders, laws, statutes, and ordinances, directions and instructions, either with penalties or without . . . as they shall judge to be for the good and welfare of this commonwealth, and for the government and ordering thereof, and of the subjects of the same."

2 "No state shall . . . deprive any person of life, liberty, or property, without due process of law."

3 "Government is instituted for the common good; for the protection, safety, prosperity and happiness of the people."

4 "All men are born free and equal, and have certain natural, essential, and unalienable rights; among which may be reckoned the right of enjoying and defending their lives and liberties; that of acquiring, possessing, and protecting property; in fine, that of seeking and obtaining their safety and happiness."

5 The defendants point to one witness at the hearing who denied that psychotic breaks triggered by marihuana exist and to another who considered the "so-called psychotic break" to be so rare as to be "non-existent." They overlook however other witnesses who testified that between one and ten percent of the population of the United States are susceptible to them. The credibility or reliability of these witnesses is not lessened by the fact they had not personally observed a substantial number of marihuana-induced "psychotic breaks." They were not testifying only with regard to their personal experiences and experiments but also with regard to information gathered from the vast amount of literature concerning marihuana. In addition, we note that the psychotic breaks triggered by marihuana are acute, and that it is unlikely that persons suffering from them would seek medical attention during the effects of the drug.

6 "Whoever . . . operates a motor vehicle while under the influence of . . . narcotic drugs, as defined in section one hundred and ninety-seven of chapter ninety-four . . . shall be punished by a fine of not less than thirty-five nor more than one thousand dollars, or by imprisonment for not less than two weeks nor more than two years, or both."

QUESTIONS

1 Is Justice Spiegel correct in concluding that the potential for harm stemming from marijuana use is sufficient to justify laws prohibiting its sale and use?

2 Is Justice Spiegel correct in concluding that the differences between marijuana and alcohol are sufficient to justify their different legal treatment?

3 Is the development of saliva-based drug tests that could be used on motorists to check for marijuana use, just as drunk-driving tests are currently used to determine alcohol use, relevant to Justice Spiegel's reasoning?

The Ethics of Addiction

Thomas S. Szasz

Szasz asserts a fundamental right to self-medication. He maintains that the harm principle is the only legitimate liberty-limiting principle and argues for free trade in all drugs, regardless of their possible dangerousness. In his view, currently illicit drugs should be treated as alcohol is treated. First, adults should be free to use and possess drugs, although their sale to minors should be prohibited. Second, those who break the law while under the influence of drugs should be held legally responsible for their actions.

PROPAGANDA TO JUSTIFY PROHIBITION

Like any social policy, our drug laws may be examined from two entirely different points of view: technical and moral. Our present inclination is either to ignore the moral perspective or to mistake the technical for the moral.

Since most of the propagandists against drug abuse seek to justify certain repressive policies because of the alleged dangerousness of various drugs, they often falsify the facts about the true pharmacological properties of the drugs they seek to prohibit. They do so for two reasons: first, because many substances in daily use are just as harmful as the substances they want to prohibit; second, because they realize that dangerousness alone is never a sufficiently persuasive argument to justify the prohibition of any drug, substance, or artifact. Accordingly, the more they ignore the moral dimensions of the problem, the more they must escalate their fraudulent claims about the dangers of drugs.

To be sure, some drugs are more dangerous than others. It is easier to kill oneself with heroin than with aspirin. But it is also easier to kill oneself by jumping off a high building than a low one. In the case of drugs, we regard their potentiality for self-injury as justification for their prohibition; in the case of buildings, we do not.

Furthermore, we systematically blur and confuse the two quite different ways in which narcotics may cause death: by a deliberate act of suicide or by accidental overdosage.

Every individual is capable of injuring or killing himself. This potentiality is a fundamental expression of human freedom. Self-destructive behavior may be regarded as sinful and penalized by means of informal sanctions. But it should not be regarded as a crime or (mental) disease, justifying or warranting the use of the police powers of the state for its control.

Therefore, it is absurd to deprive an adult of a drug (or of anything else) because he might use it to kill himself. To do so is to treat everyone the way institutional psychiatrists treat the so-called suicidal mental patient: they not only imprison such a person but take everything away from him—shoelaces, belts, razor blades, eating utensils, and so forth—until the "patient" lies naked on a mattress in a padded cell—lest he kill himself. The result is degrading tyrannization.

Death by accidental overdose is an altogether different matter. But can anyone doubt that this danger now looms so large precisely because the sale of narcotics and many other drugs is illegal? Those who buy illicit drugs cannot be sure what drug they are getting or how much of it. Free trade in drugs, with governmental action limited to safeguarding the purity of the product and the veracity of the labeling, would reduce the risk of accidental overdose with "dangerous drugs" to the same levels that prevail, and that we find acceptable, with respect to other chemical agents and physical artifacts that abound in our complex technological society.

This essay is not intended as an exposition on the pharmacological properties of narcotics and other mind-affecting drugs. However, I want to make it clear that in my view, *regardless* of their danger, all drugs should be "legalized" (a misleading term I employ reluctantly as a concession to common usage). Although I recognize that some drugs—notably heroin, the amphetamines, and LSD, among those now in vogue—may have undesirable or dangerous consequences, I favor free trade in drugs for the same reason the Founding Fathers favored free trade in ideas. In an open society, it is none of the government's business what idea a man puts into his mind; likewise, it should be none of the government's business what drug he puts into his body.

WITHDRAWAL PAINS FROM TRADITION

It is a fundamental characteristic of human beings that they get used to things: one becomes habituated, or "addicted," not only to narcotics, but to cigarettes, cocktails before dinner, orange juice for breakfast, comic strips, and so forth. It is similarly a fundamental characteristic of living organisms that they acquire increasing tolerance to various chemical agents and physical stimuli: the first cigarette may cause nothing but nausea and headache; a year later, smoking three packs a day may be pure joy. Both alcohol and opiates are "addictive" in the sense that the more regularly they are used, the more the user craves them and the greater his tolerance for them becomes. Yet none of this involves any mysterious process of "getting hooked." It is simply an aspect of the universal biological propensity for *learning,* which is especially well developed in man. The opiate habit, like the cigarette habit or food habit, can be broken—and without any medical assistance—provided the person wants to break it. Often he doesn't. And why, indeed, should he, if he has nothing better to do with his life? Or, as happens to be the case with morphine, if he can live an essentially normal life while under its influence?

Actually, opium is much less toxic than alcohol. Just as it is possible to be an "alcoholic" and work and be productive, so it is (or, rather, it used to be) possible to be an opium addict and work and be productive. According to a definitive study published by the American Medical Association in 1929, ". . . morphine addiction is not characterized by physical deterioration or impairment of physical fitness. . . . There is no evidence of change in the circulatory, hepatic, renal, or endocrine functions. When it is considered that these subjects had been addicted for at least five years, some of them for as long as twenty years, these negative observations are highly significant." In a 1928 study, Lawrence Kolb, an Assistant Surgeon General of the United States Public Health Service, found that of 119 persons addicted to opiates through medical practice, "90 had good industrial records and only 29 had poor ones. . . . Judged by the output of labor and their own statements, none of the normal persons had [his] efficiency reduced by opium. Twenty-two of them worked regularly while taking opium for twenty-five years or more; one of them, a woman aged 81 and still alert mentally, had taken 3 grains of morphine daily for 65 years. [The usual therapeutic dose is one-quarter grain, three to four grains being fatal for the nonaddict.] She gave birth to and raised six children, and managed her household affairs with more than average efficiency. A widow, aged 66, had taken 17 grains of morphine daily for most of 37 years. She is alert mentally . . . does physical labor every day, and makes her own living."

I am not citing this evidence to recommend the opium habit. The point is that we must, in plain honesty, distinguish between pharmacological effects and personal inclinations. Some people take drugs to help them function and conform to social expectations; others take them for the very opposite reason, to ritualize their refusal to function and conform to social expectations. Much of the "drug abuse" we now witness—perhaps nearly all of it—is of the second type. But instead of acknowledging that "addicts" are unfit or unwilling to work and be "normal," we prefer to believe that they act as they do because certain drugs—especially heroin, LSD, and the amphetamines—make them "sick." If only we could get them "well," so runs this comforting view, they would become "productive" and "useful" citizens. To believe this is like believing that if an illiterate cigarette smoker would only stop smoking, he would become an Einstein. With a falsehood like this, one can go far. No wonder that politicians and psychiatrists love it. . . .

The fear that free trade in narcotics would result in vast masses of our population spending their days and nights smoking opium or mainlining heroin, rather than working and taking care of their responsibilities, is a bugaboo that does not deserve to be taken seriously. Habits of work and idleness are deep-seated cultural patterns. Free trade in abortions has not made an industrious people like the Japanese give up work for fornication. Nor would free trade in drugs convert such a people from hustlers to hippies. Indeed, I think the opposite might be the case: it is questionable whether, or for how long, a responsible people can tolerate being treated as totally irresponsible with respect to drugs and drug-taking. In other words, how long can we live with the inconsistency of being expected to be responsible for operating cars and computers, but not for operating our own bodies? . . .

THE RIGHT OF SELF-MEDICATION

Clearly, the argument that marijuana—or heroin, methadone, or morphine—is prohibited because it is addictive or dangerous cannot be supported by facts. For one thing, there are many drugs, from insulin to penicillin, that are neither addictive nor dangerous but are nevertheless also prohibited; they can be obtained only through a physician's prescription. For another, there are many things, from dynamite to guns, that are much more dangerous than narcotics (especially to others) but are not prohibited. As everyone knows, it is still possible in the United States to walk into a store and walk out with a shotgun. We enjoy this right not because we believe that guns are safe but because we believe even more strongly that civil liberties are precious. At the same time, it is not possible in the United States to walk into a store and walk out with a bottle of barbiturates, codeine, or other drugs.

I believe that just as we regard freedom of speech and religion as fundamental rights, so we should also regard freedom of self-medication as a fundamental right. Like most rights, the right of self-medication should apply only to adults; and it should not be an unqualified right. Since these are important qualifications, it is necessary to specify their precise range.

John Stuart Mill said (approximately) that a person's right to swing his arm ends where his neighbor's nose begins. And Oliver Wendell Holmes said that no one has a right to shout "Fire!" in a crowded theater. Similarly, the limiting condition with respect to self-medication should be the inflicting of actual (as against symbolic) harm on others.

Our present practices with respect to alcohol embody and reflect this individualistic ethic. We have the right to buy, possess, and consume alcoholic beverages. Regardless of how offensive drunkenness might be to a person, he cannot interfere with another person's "right" to become inebriated so long as that person drinks in the privacy of his own home or at some other appropriate location, and so long as he conducts himself in an otherwise law-abiding manner. In short, we have a right to be intoxicated—in private. Public intoxication is considered an offense to others and is therefore a violation of the criminal law. It makes sense that what is a "right" in one place may become, by virtue of its disruptive or disturbing effect on others, an offense somewhere else.

The right to self-medication should be hedged in by similar limits. Public intoxication, not only with alcohol but with any drug, should be an offense punishable by the criminal law. Furthermore, acts that may injure others—such as driving a car—should, when carried out in a drug-intoxicated state, be punished especially strictly and severely. The right to self-medication must thus entail unqualified responsibility for the effects of one's drug-intoxicated behavior on others. For unless we are willing to hold ourselves responsible for our own behavior, and hold others responsible for theirs, the liberty to use drugs (or to engage in other acts) degenerates into a license to hurt others.

Such, then, would be the situation of adults, if we regarded the freedom to take drugs as a fundamental right similar to the freedom to read and worship. What would be the situation of children? Since many people who are now said to be drug addicts or drug abusers are minors, it is especially important that we think clearly about this aspect of the problem.

I do not believe, and I do not advocate, that children should have a right to ingest, inject, or otherwise use any drug or substance they want. Children do not have the right to drive, drink, vote, marry, or make binding contracts. They acquire these rights at various ages, coming into their full possession at maturity, usually between the ages of eighteen and twenty-one. The right to self-medication should similarly be withheld until maturity.

In short, I suggest that "dangerous" drugs be treated, more or less, as alcohol is treated now. Neither the use of narcotics, nor their possession, should be prohibited, but only their sale to minors. Of course, this would result in the ready availability of all kinds of drugs among minors—though perhaps their availability would be no greater than it is now, but would only be more visible and hence more easily subject to proper controls. This arrangement would place responsibility for the use of all drugs by children where it belongs: on parents and their children. This is where the major responsibility rests for the use of alcohol. It is a tragic symptom of our refusal to take personal liberty and responsibility seriously that there appears to be no public desire to assume a similar stance toward other "dangerous" drugs.

Consider what would happen should a child bring a bottle of gin to school and get drunk there. Would the school authorities blame the local liquor stores as pushers? Or would they blame the parents and the child himself? There is liquor in practically every home in America and yet children rarely bring liquor to school. Whereas marijuana, Dexedrine, and heroin—substances children usually do not find at home and whose very possession is a criminal offense—frequently find their way into the school.

Our attitude toward sexual activity provides another model for our attitude toward drugs. Although we generally discourage children below a certain age from engaging in sexual activities with others, we do not prohibit such activities by law. What we do prohibit by law is the sexual seduction of children by adults. The "pharmacological seduction" of children by adults should be similarly punishable. In other words, adults who give or sell drugs to children should be regarded as offenders. Such a specific and limited prohibition—as against the kinds of generalized prohibitions that we had under the Volstead Act or have now with respect to countless drugs—would be relatively easy to enforce. Moreover, it would probably be rarely violated, for there would be little psychological interest and no economic profit in doing so. . . .

LIFE, LIBERTY, AND THE PURSUIT OF HIGHS

Sooner or later we shall have to confront the basic moral dilemma underlying this problem: does a person have the right to take a drug, any drug—not because he needs it to cure an illness, but because he wants to take it?

The Declaration of Independence speaks of our inalienable right to "life, liberty, and the pursuit of happiness." How are we to interpret this? By asserting that we ought to be free to pursue happiness by playing golf or watching television, but not by drinking alcohol, or smoking marijuana, or ingesting pep pills?

The Constitution and the Bill of Rights are silent on the subject of drugs. This would seem to imply that the adult citizen has, or ought to have, the right to medicate his own body as he sees fit. Were this not the case, why should there have been a need for a Constitutional Amendment to outlaw drinking? But if ingesting alcohol was, and is now again, a Constitutional right, is ingesting opium, or heroin, or barbiturates, or anything else, not also such a right? If it is, then the Harrison Narcotic Act is not only a bad law but is unconstitutional as well, because it prescribes in a legislative act what ought to be promulgated in a Constitutional Amendment.

The questions remain: as American citizens, should we have the right to take narcotics or other drugs? If we take drugs and conduct ourselves as responsible and law-abiding citizens, should we have a right to remain unmolested by the government? Lastly, if we take drugs and break the law, should we have a right to be treated as persons accused of crime, rather than as patients accused of mental illness?

These are fundamental questions that are conspicuous by their absence from all contemporary discussions of problems of drug addiction and drug abuse. The result is that instead of debating the use of drugs in moral and political terms, we define our task as the ostensibly narrow technical problem of protecting people from poisoning themselves with substances for whose use they cannot possibly assume responsibility. This, I think, best explains the frightening national consensus against personal responsibility for taking drugs and for one's conduct while under their influence. In 1965, for example, when President Johnson sought a bill imposing tight federal controls over pep pills and goof balls, the bill cleared the House by a unanimous vote, 402 to 0.

The failure of such measures to curb the "drug menace" has only served to inflame our legislators' enthusiasm for them. In October 1970 the Senate passed, again by a unanimous vote (54 to 0), "a major narcotics crackdown bill."

To me, unanimity on an issue as basic and complex as this means a complete evasion of the actual problem and an attempt to master it by attacking and overpowering a scapegoat—"dangerous drugs" and "drug abusers." There is an ominous resemblance between the unanimity with which all "reasonable" men—and especially politicians, physicians, and priests—formerly supported the protective measures of society against witches and Jews, and that with which they now support them against drug addicts and drug abusers.

After all is said and done, the issue comes down to whether we accept or reject the ethical principle John Stuart Mill so clearly enunciated: "The only purpose [he wrote in *On Liberty*] for which power can be rightfully exercised over any member of a civilized community, against his will, is to prevent harm to others. His own good, either physical or moral, is not a sufficient warrant. He cannot rightfully be compelled to do or forbear because it will make him happier, because in the opinions of others, to do so would be wise, or even right . . . In the part [of his conduct] which merely concerns himself, his independence is, of right, absolute. Over himself, over his own body and mind, the individual is sovereign."

By recognizing the problem of drug abuse for what it is—a moral and political question rather than a medical or therapeutic one—we can choose to maximize the sphere of action of the state at the expense of the individual, or of the individual at the expense of the state. In other words, we could commit ourselves to the view that the state, the representative of many, is more important than the individual; that it therefore has the right, indeed the duty, to regulate the life of the individual in the best interests of the group. Or we could commit ourselves to the view that individual dignity and liberty are the supreme values of life, and that the foremost duty of the state is to protect and promote these values.

In short, we must choose between the ethic of collectivism and individualism, and pay the price of either—or of both.

QUESTIONS

1 Do we have a moral right to decide for ourselves what drugs we will and will not use?
2 Does society have a right—contra Szasz—to protect individuals from engaging in seriously risky behavior that might have irrevocable consequences on their ability to make future decisions rationally?

Permissible Paternalism:
Saving Smokers from Themselves

Robert E. Goodin

Goodin argues in favor of some paternalistic public policies. Using smoking, which he considers an addiction, as an example, Goodin maintains that public paternalism is justified when its intent is to prevent decisions that involve high stakes, have far-reaching consequences, and are substantially irreversible. Arguing for what he identifies as a very weak form of paternalism, Goodin holds that public policies designed to deter individuals from acting on their preferences are justifiable only if they are grounded in their own deeper preferences. He sees smokers, for example, as paradigms of individuals who apparently "choose" to smoke while at the same time wishing to refrain from smoking.

Paternalism is desperately out of fashion. Nowadays notions of "children's rights" severely limit what even parents may do to their own offspring, in their children's interests but against their will. What public officials may properly do to adult citizens, in their interests but against their will, is presumably even more tightly circumscribed. So the project I have set for myself—carving out a substantial sphere of morally permissible paternalism—might seem simply preposterous in present political and philosophical circumstances.

Here I shall say no more about the paternalism of parents toward their own children. My focus will instead be upon ways in which certain public policies designed to promote people's interests might be morally justifiable even if those people were themselves opposed to such policies.

Neither shall I say much more about notions of rights. But in focusing upon people's interests rather than their rights, I shall arguably be sticking closely to the sorts of concerns that motivate rights theorists. Of course, what it is to have a right is itself philosophically disputed; and on at least one account (the so-called "interest theory") to have a right is nothing more than to have a legally protected interest. But on the rival account (the so-called "choice theory") the whole point of rights is

Originally published as "Permissible Paternalism: In Defense of the Nanny State," *The Responsive Community*, vol. 1 (Summer 1991), pp. 42–51. Reprinted here, as slightly revised by the author.

to have a legally protected choice. There, the point of having a right is that your choice in the matter will be respected, even if that choice actually runs contrary to your own best interests.

It is that understanding of rights which leads us to suppose that paternalism and rights are necessarily at odds, and there are strict limits in the extent to which we might reconcile the two positions. Still, there is some substantial scope for compromise between the two positions.

Those theorists who see rights as protecting people's choices rather than promoting their interests would be most at odds with paternalists who were proposing to impose upon people what is judged to be *objectively* good for them. That is to say, they would be most at odds if paternalists were proposing to impose upon people outcomes which are judged to be good for those people, whether or not there were any grounds for that conclusion in those people's own subjective judgments of their own good.

Rights theorists and paternalists would still be at odds, but less at odds, if paternalists refrained from talking about interests in so starkly objective a way. Then, just as rights command respect for people's choices, so too would paternalists be insisting that we respect choices that people themselves have or would have made. The two are not quite the same, to be sure, but they are much more nearly the same than the ordinary contrast between paternalists and rights theorists would seem to suggest.

That is precisely the sort of conciliatory gesture that I shall here be proposing. In paternalistically justifying some course of action on the grounds that it is in someone's interests, I shall always be searching for some warrant in that person's own value judgments for saying that it is in that person's interests.

"Some warrant" is a loose constraint, to be sure. Occasionally will we find genuine cases of what philosophers call "weakness of will": people being possessed of a powerful, conscious present desire to do something that they nonetheless just cannot bring themselves to do. Then public policy forcing them to realize their own desire, though arguably paternalistic, is transparently justifiable even in terms of people's own subjective values. More often, though, the subjective value to which we are appealing is one which is present only in an inchoate form, or will only arise later, or can be appreciated only in retrospect.

Paternalism is clearly paternalistic in imposing those more weakly-held subjective values upon people in preference to their more strongly held ones. But, equally clearly, it is less offensively paternalistic thanks to this crucial fact: at least it deals strictly in terms of values that are or will be subjectively present, at some point or another and to some extent or another, in the person concerned.

I. THE SCOPE OF PATERNALISM

When we are talking about public policies (and maybe even when we are talking of private, familial relations), paternalism surely can only be justified for the "big decisions" in people's lives. No one, except possibly parents and perhaps not even they, would propose to stop you from buying candy bars on a whim, under the influence of seductive advertising and at some marginal cost to your dental health.

So far as public policy is concerned, certainly, to be a fitting subject for public paternalism a decision must first of all involve high stakes. Life-and-death issues most conspicuously qualify. But so do those that substantially shape your subsequent life prospects. Decisions to drop out of school or to begin taking drugs involve high stakes of roughly that sort. If the decision is also substantially irreversible—returning to school is unlikely, the drug is addictive—then that further bolsters the case for paternalistic intervention.

The point in both cases is that people would not have a chance to benefit by learning from their mistakes. If the stakes are so high that losing the gamble once will kill you, then there is no opportunity for subsequent learning. Similarly, if the decision is irreversible, you might know better next time but be unable to benefit from your new wisdom.

II. EVALUATING PREFERENCES

The case for paternalism, as I have cast it, is that the public officials might better respect your own preferences than you would have done through your own actions. That is to say that public officials are engaged in evaluating your (surface) preferences, judging them according to some standard of your own (deeper) preferences. Public officials should refrain from paternalistic interference, and allow you to act without state interference, only if they are convinced that you are acting on:

- *relevant* preferences;
- *settled* preferences;
- *preferred* preferences; and, perhaps,
- *your own* preferences.

In what follows, I shall consider each of those requirements in turn. My running example will be the problem of smoking and policies to control it. Nothing turns on the peculiarities of that example, though. There are many others like it in relevant respects.

It often helps, in arguments like this, to apply generalities to particular cases. So, in what follows, I shall further focus in on the case of one particular smoker, Rose Cipollone. Her situation is nowise unique—in all the respects that matter here, she might be considered the prototypical smoker. All that makes her case special is that she (or more precisely her heir) was the first to win a court case against the tobacco companies whose products killed her.

In summarizing the evidence presented at that trial, the judge described the facts of the case as follows.

> Rose . . . Cipollone . . . began to smoke at age 16 . . . while she was still in high school. She testified that she began to smoke because she saw people smoking in the movies, in advertisements, and looked upon it as something "cool, glamorous and grown-up" to do. She began smoking Chesterfields . . . primarily because of advertising of "pretty girls and movie stars," and because Chesterfields were described . . . as "mild." . . .
>
> Mrs. Cipollone attempted to quit smoking while pregnant with her first child . . . , but even then she would sneak cigarettes. While she was in labor she smoked an entire pack of cigarettes, provided to her at her request by her doctor, and after the birth. . . .

she resumed smoking. She smoked a minimum of a pack a day and as much as two packs a day.

In 1955, she switched . . . to L&M cigarettes . . . because . . . she believed that the filter would trap whatever was "bad" for her in cigarette smoking. She relied upon advertisements which supported that contention. She . . . switched to Virginia Slims . . . because the cigarettes were glamorous and long, and were associated with beautiful women—and the liberated woman. . . .

Because she developed a smoker's cough and heard reports that smoking caused cancer, she tried to cut down her smoking. These attempts were unsuccessful. . . .

Mrs. Cipollone switched to lower tar and nicotine cigarettes based upon advertising from which she concluded that those cigarettes were safe or safer . . . [and] upon the recommendation of her family physician. In 1981 her cancer was diagnosed, and even though her doctors advised her to stop she was unable to do so. She even told her doctors and her husband that she had quit when she had not, and she continued to smoke until June of 1982 when her lung was removed. Even thereafter she smoked occasionally—in hiding. She stopped smoking in 1983 when her cancer had metastasized and she was diagnosed as fatally ill.

This sad history contains many of the features that I shall be arguing make paternalism most permissible.

Relevant Preferences

The case against paternalism consists in the simple proposition that, morally, we ought to respect people's own choices in matters that affect themselves and by-and-large only themselves. But there are many questions we first might legitimately ask about those preferences, without in any way questioning this fundamental principle of respecting people's autonomy.

One is simply whether the preferences in play are genuinely *relevant* to the decision at hand. Often they are not. Laymen often make purely factual mistakes in their means-ends reasoning. They think—or indeed, as in the case of Rose Cipollone, are led by false advertising to suppose—that an activity is safe when it is not. They think that an activity like smoking is glamorous, when the true facts of the matter are that smoking may well cause circulatory problems requiring the distinctly unglamorous amputation of an arm or leg.

When people make purely factual mistakes like that, we might legitimately override their surface preferences (the preference to smoke) in the name of their own deeper preferences (to stay alive and bodily intact). Public policies designed to prevent youngsters from taking up smoking when they want to, or to make it harder (more expensive or inconvenient) for existing smokers to continue smoking when they want to, may be paternalistic in the sense of running contrary to people's own manifest choices in the matter. But this overriding of their choices is grounded in their own deeper preferences, so such paternalism would be minimally offensive from a moral point of view.

Settled Preferences

We might ask, further, whether the preferences being manifested are "settled" preferences or whether they are merely transitory phases people are going through.

It may be morally permissible to let people commit euthanasia voluntarily, if we are sure they really want to die. But if we think that they may subsequently change their minds, then we have good grounds for supposing that we should stop them.

The same may well be true with smoking policy. While Rose Cipollone herself thought smoking was both glamorous and safe, youngsters beginning to smoke today typically know better. But many of them still say that they would prefer a shorter but more glamorous life, and that they are therefore more than happy to accept the risks that smoking entails. Say what they may at age sixteen, though, we cannot help supposing that they will think differently when pigeons eventually come home to roost. The risk-courting preferences of youth are a characteristic product of a peculiarly dare-devil phase that virtually all of them will, like their predecessors, certainly grow out of.

Insofar as people's preferences are not settled—insofar as they choose one option now, yet at some later time may wish that they had chosen another—we have another ground for permissible paternalism. Policy-makers dedicated to respecting people's own choices have, in effect, two of the person's own choices to choose between. How such conflicts should be settled is hard to say. We might weigh the strength or duration of the preferences, how well they fit with the person's other preferences, and so on.

Whatever else we do, though, we clearly ought not privilege one preference over another just because it got there first. Morally, it is permissible for policy-makers to ignore one of a person's present preferences (to smoke, for example) in defer-ence to another that is virtually certain later to emerge (as was Rose Cipollone's wish to live, once she had cancer).

Preferred Preferences

A third case for permissible paternalism turns on the observation that people have not only multiple and conflicting preferences but also preferences for preferences. Rose Cipollone wanted to smoke. But, judging from her frequent (albeit failed) attempts to quit, she also wanted *not to want* to smoke.

In this respect, it might be said, Rose Cipollone's history is representative of smokers more generally. The US Surgeon General reports that some 90 percent of regular smokers have tried and failed to quit. That recidivism rate has led the World Health Organization to rank nicotine as an addictive substance on a par with heroin itself.

That classification is richly confirmed by the stories that smokers themselves tell about their failed attempts to quit. Rose Cipollone tried to quit while pregnant, only to end up smoking an entire pack in the delivery room. She tried to quit once her cancer was diagnosed, and once again after her lung was taken out, even then only to end up sneaking an occasional smoke.

In cases like this—where people want to stop some activity, try to stop it but find that they cannot stop—public policy that helps them do so can hardly be said to be paternalistic in any morally offensive respect. It overrides people's preferences, to be sure. But the preferences which it overrides are ones which people themselves wish they did not have.

The preferences which it respects—the preferences to stop smoking (like preferences of reformed alcoholics to stay off drink, or of the obese to lose weight)—are, in contrast, preferences that the people concerned themselves prefer. They would themselves rank those preferences above their own occasional inclinations to backslide. In helping them to implement their own preferred preferences, we are only respecting people's own priorities.

Finally, before automatically respecting people's choices, we ought to make sure that they are really their *own* choices. We respect people's choices because in that way we manifest respect for them as persons. But if the choices in question were literally someone else's—the results of a post-hypnotic suggestion, for example—then clearly there that logic would provide no reason for our respecting those preferences.

Some people say that the effects of advertising are rather like that. No doubt there is a certain informational content to advertising. But that is not all there is in it. When Rose Cipollone read the tar and nicotine content in advertisements, what she was getting was information. What she was getting when looking at the accompanying pictures of movie stars and glamorous, liberated women was something else altogether.

Using the power of subliminal suggestion, advertising implants preferences in people in a way that largely or wholly by-passes their judgment. Insofar as it does so, the resulting preferences are not authentically that person's own. And those implanted preferences are not entitled to the respect that is rightly reserved for a person's authentic preferences, in consequence.

Such thoughts might lead some to say that we should therefore ignore altogether advertising-induced preferences in framing our public policy. I demur. There is just too much force in the rejoinder that, "Wherever those preferences came from in the first instance, they are mine now." If we want our policies to respect people by (among other things) respecting their preferences, then we will have to respect all of those preferences with which people now associate themselves.

Even admitting the force of that rejoinder, though, there is much that still might be done to curb the preference-shaping activities of, for example, the tobacco industry. Even those who say "they're my preferences now" would presumably have preferred, ahead of time, to make up their own minds in the matter. So there we have a case, couched in terms of people's own (past) preferences, for severely restricting the advertising and promotion of products—especially ones which people will later regret having grown to like, but which they will later be unable to resist.

III.   CONCLUSIONS

What, in practical policy terms, follows from all that? Well, in the case of smoking, which has served as my running example, we might ban the sale of tobacco altogether or turn it into a drug available only on prescription to registered users. Or, less dramatically, we might make cigarettes difficult and expensive to obtain—especially for youngsters, whose purchases are particularly price-sensitive. We might ban all promotional advertising of tobacco products, designed as it is to attract new users.

We might prohibit smoking in all offices, restaurants, and other public places, thus making it harder for smokers to find a place to partake and providing a further inducement for them to quit.

All of those policies would be good for smokers themselves. They would enjoy a longer life expectancy and a higher quality of life if they stopped smoking. But that is to talk the language of interests rather than of rights and choices. In those latter terms, all those policies clearly go against smokers' manifest preferences, in one sense or another. Smokers want to keep smoking. They do not want to pay more or drive further to get their cigarettes. They want to be able to take comfort in advertisements constantly telling them how glamorous their smoking is.

In other more important senses, though, such policies can be justified even in terms of the preferences of smokers themselves. They do not want to die, as a quarter of them eventually will (and ten to fifteen years before their time) of smoking-related diseases; it is only false beliefs or wishful thinking that make smokers think that continued smoking is consistent with that desire not to avoid a premature death. At the moment they may think that the benefits of smoking outweigh the costs, but they will almost certainly revise that view once those costs are eventually sheeted home. The vast majority of smokers would like to stop smoking but, being addicted, find it very hard now to do so.

Like Rose Cipollone, certainly in her dying days and intermittently even from her early adulthood, most smokers themselves would say that they would have been better off never starting. Many even agree that they would welcome anything (like a workplace ban on smoking) that might now make them stop. Given the internally conflicting preferences here in play, smokers also harbor at one and the same time preferences pointing in the opposite direction; that is what might make helping them to stop seem unacceptably paternalistic. But in terms of other of their preferences—and ones that deserve clear precedence, at that— doing so is perfectly well warranted.

Smoking is unusual, perhaps, in presenting a case for permissible paternalism on all four of the fronts here canvassed. Most activities might qualify under only one or two of the headings. However, that may well be enough. My point here is not that paternalism is always permissible but merely that it may always be.

In the discourse of liberal democracies, the charge of paternalism is typically taken to be a knock-down objection to any policy. If I am right, that knee-jerk response is wrong. When confronted with the charge of paternalism, it should always be open to us to say, "Sure, this proposal is paternalistic—but is the paternalism in view permissible or impermissible, good or bad?" More often than not, I think we will find, paternalism might prove perfectly defensible along the lines sketched here.

QUESTIONS

1 Are the long-term deleterious effects of cigarette smoking sufficient to justify laws prohibiting the sale and use of cigarettes? If yes, are the laws justified on the basis of paternalistic reasoning or on the basis of some other liberty-limiting principle?

2 Can a case be made for the claim that those who smoke marijuana are not acting on preferences that are relevant, settled, preferred, and their own?

The Case for Legalization
Ethan A. Nadelmann

Nadelmann, a proponent of the harm-reduction approach to legalization, maintains that current drug laws are responsible for much of what Americans identify as the drug problem. He first discusses some of the costs of prohibition, such as expensive drug-enforcement measures, drug-related crimes, and the harms done to millions of illicit drug users who run the risk of imprisonment and job loss. Many of these users also suffer physical harms from the drugs they use—harms that could be prevented if the production and sale of drugs were subject to government regulation. Second, Nadelmann criticizes our inconsistent moral attitudes regarding alcohol and tobacco, on the one hand, and drugs such as marijuana and cocaine, on the other. Nadelmann advances arguments against those whose support of the current drug laws is implicitly based on the principle of legal moralism. Believing wrongly that there is a morally significant difference between alcohol and tobacco use, on the one hand, and the use of substances such as cocaine and heroin, on the other, they support public policies that are morally inconsistent. He grants that the strongest moral justification for treating the currently illicit drugs differently is a paternalistic one—to prevent those who lack sufficient self-restraint from harming themselves if drugs were easily available. Noting, however, that any such harms prevented by current laws are far outweighed by the harms resulting from the laws themselves, he concludes that we must rethink our moral position when laws intended to serve a moral end inflict tremendous damage on innocent parties. Finally, Nadelmann discusses the benefits of legalization. While acknowledging that legalization is a risky policy, he notes the failure of current policies and advocates exploring other options.

What can be done about the "drug problem"? Despite frequent proclamations of war and dramatic increases in government funding and resources in recent years, there are many indications that the problem is not going away and may even be growing worse. . . .

THE COSTS OF PROHIBITION

The fact that drug-prohibition laws and policies cannot eradicate or even significantly reduce drug abuse is not necessarily a reason to repeal them. They do, after all, succeed in deterring many people from trying drugs, and they clearly reduce the availability and significantly increase the price of illegal drugs. These accomplishments alone might warrant retaining the drug laws, were it not for the fact that these same laws are also responsible for much of what Americans identify as the "drug problem." Here the analogies to alcohol and tobacco are worth noting. There is little question that we could reduce the health costs associated with use and abuse of alcohol and tobacco if we were to criminalize their production, sale, and possession.

Reprinted with permission of the author from *The Public Interest*, no. 92 (Summer 1988), pp. 3, 11–14, 20–25, 30–31. © 1988 by National Affairs, Inc.

But no one believes that we could eliminate their use and abuse, that we could create an "alcohol-free" or "tobacco-free" country. Nor do most Americans believe that criminalizing the alcohol and tobacco markets would be a good idea. Their opposition stems largely from two beliefs: that adult Americans have the right to choose what substances they will consume and what risks they will take; and that the costs of trying to coerce so many Americans to abstain from those substances would be enormous. It was the strength of these two beliefs that ultimately led to the repeal of Prohibition, and it is partly due to memories of that experience that criminalizing either alcohol or tobacco has little support today.

Consider the potential consequences of criminalizing the production, sale, and possession of all tobacco products. On the positive side, the number of people smoking tobacco would almost certainly decline, as would the health costs associated with tobacco consumption. Although the "forbidden fruit" syndrome would attract some people to cigarette smoking who would not otherwise have smoked, many more would likely be deterred by the criminal sanction, the moral standing of the law, the higher cost and unreliable quality of the illicit tobacco, and the difficulties involved in acquiring it. Nonsmokers would rarely if ever be bothered by the irritating habits of their fellow citizens. The anti-tobacco laws would discourage some people from ever starting to smoke, and would induce others to quit.

On the negative side, however, millions of Americans, including both tobacco addicts and recreational users, would no doubt defy the law, generating a massive underground market and billions in profits for organized criminals. Although some tobacco farmers would find other work, thousands more would become outlaws and continue to produce their crops covertly. Throughout Latin America, farmers and gangsters would rejoice at the opportunity to earn untold sums of gringo greenbacks, even as U.S. diplomats pressured foreign governments to cooperate with U.S. laws. Within the United States, government helicopters would spray herbicides on illicit tobacco fields; people would be rewarded by the government for informing on their tobacco-growing, -selling, and -smoking neighbors; urine tests would be employed to identify violators of the anti-tobacco laws; and a Tobacco Enforcement Administration (the T.E.A.) would employ undercover agents, informants, and wire-taps to uncover tobacco-law violators. Municipal, state, and federal judicial systems would be clogged with tobacco traffickers and "abusers." "Tobacco-related murders" would increase dramatically as criminal organizations competed with one another for turf and markets. Smoking would become an act of youthful rebellion, and no doubt some users would begin to experiment with more concentrated, potent, and dangerous forms of tobacco. Tobacco-related corruption would infect all levels of government, and respect for the law would decline noticeably. Government expenditures on tobacco-law enforcement would climb rapidly into the billions of dollars, even as budget balancers longingly recalled the almost ten billion dollars per year in tobacco taxes earned by the federal and state governments prior to prohibition. Finally, the State of North Carolina might even secede again from the Union.

This seemingly far-fetched tobacco-prohibition scenario is little more than an extrapolation based on the current situation with respect to marijuana, cocaine, and heroin. In many ways, our predicament resembles what actually happened during Prohibition. Prior to Prohibition, most Americans hoped that alcohol could be effectively banned by passing laws against its production and supply. During the early years of Prohibition, when drinking declined but millions of Americans nonetheless continued to drink, Prohibition's supporters placed their faith in tougher laws and more police and jails. After a few more years, however, increasing numbers of Americans began to realize that laws and policemen were unable to eliminate the smugglers, bootleggers, and illicit producers, as long as tens of millions of Americans continued to want to buy alcohol. At the same time, they saw that more laws and policemen seemed to generate more violence and corruption, more crowded courts and jails, wider disrespect for government and the law, and more power and profits for the gangsters. Repeal of Prohibition came to be seen not as a capitulation to Al Capone and his ilk, but as a means of both putting the bootleggers out of business and eliminating most of the costs associated with the prohibition laws.

Today, Americans are faced with a dilemma similar to that confronted by our forebears sixty years ago. Demand for illicit drugs shows some signs of abating, but no signs of declining significantly. Moreover, there are substantial reasons to doubt that tougher laws and policing have played an important role in reducing consumption. Supply, meanwhile, has not abated at all. Availability of illicit drugs, except for marijuana in some locales, remains high. Prices are dropping, even as potency increases. And the number of drug producers, smugglers, and dealers remains sizable, even as jails and prisons fill to overflowing. As was the case during Prohibition, the principal beneficiaries of current drug policies are the new and old organized-crime gangs. The principal victims, on the other hand, are not the drug dealers, but the tens of millions of Americans who are worse off in one way or another as a consequence of the existence and failure of the drug-prohibition laws.

All public policies create beneficiaries and victims, both intended and unintended. When a public policy results in a disproportionate magnitude of unintended victims, there is good reason to reevaluate the assumptions and design of the policy. In the case of drug-prohibition policies, the intended beneficiaries are those individuals who would become drug abusers but for the existence and enforcement of the drug laws. The intended victims are those who traffic in illicit drugs and suffer the legal consequences. The unintended beneficiaries, conversely, are the drug producers and traffickers who profit handsomely from the illegality of the market, while avoiding arrest by the authorities and the violence perpetrated by other criminals. The unintended victims of drug prohibition policies are rarely recognized as such, however. Viewed narrowly, they are the 30 million Americans who use illegal drugs, thereby risking loss of their jobs, imprisonment, and the damage done to health by ingesting illegally produced drugs; viewed broadly, they are all Americans, who pay the substantial costs of our present ill-considered policies, both as taxpayers and as the potential victims of crime. These unintended victims are generally thought to be victimized by the unintended beneficiaries (i.e., the drug dealers), when in fact it is the drug-prohibition policies themselves that are primarily responsible for their plight.

If law-enforcement efforts could succeed in significantly reducing either the supply of illicit drugs or the demand for them, we would probably have little need to seek alternative drug-control policies. But since those efforts have repeatedly failed to make much of a difference and show little indication of working better in the future, at this point we must focus greater attention on their costs. Unlike the demand and supply of illicit drugs, which have remained relatively indifferent to legislative initiatives, the costs of drug-enforcement measures can be affected— quite dramatically—by legislative measures. What tougher criminal sanctions and more police have failed to accomplish, in terms of reducing drug-related violence, corruption, death, and social decay, may well be better accomplished by legislative repeal of the drug laws, and adoption of less punitive but more effective measures to prevent and treat substance abuse. . . .

PHYSICAL AND MORAL COSTS

Perhaps the most paradoxical consequence of the drug laws is the tremendous harm they cause to the millions of drug users who have not been deterred from using illicit drugs in the first place. Nothing resembling an underground Food and Drug Administration has arisen to impose quality control on the illegal-drug market and provide users with accurate information on the drugs they consume. Imagine that Americans could not tell whether a bottle of wine contained 6 percent, 30 percent, or 90 percent alcohol, or whether an aspirin tablet contained 5 or 500 grams of aspirin. Imagine, too, that no controls existed to prevent winemakers from diluting their product with methanol and other dangerous impurities, and that vineyards and tobacco fields were fertilized with harmful substances by ignorant growers and sprayed with poisonous herbicides by government agents. Fewer people would use such substances, but more of those who did would get sick. Some would die.

The above scenario describes, of course, the current state of the illicit drug market. Many marijuana smokers are worse off for having smoked cannabis that was grown with dangerous fertilizers, sprayed with the herbicide paraquat, or mixed with more dangerous substances. Consumers of heroin and the various synthetic substances sold on the street face even severer consequences, including fatal overdoses and poisonings from unexpectedly potent or impure drug supplies. More often than not, the quality of a drug addict's life depends greatly upon his or her access to reliable supplies. Drug-enforcement operations that succeed in temporarily disrupting supply networks are thus a double-edged sword: they encourage some addicts to seek admission into drug-treatment programs, but they oblige others to seek out new and hence less reliable suppliers; the result is that more, not fewer, drug-related emergencies and deaths occur. . . .

Most Americans perceive the drug problem as a moral issue and draw a moral distinction between use of the illicit drugs and use of alcohol and tobacco. Yet when one subjects this distinction to reasoned analysis, it quickly disintegrates. The most consistent moral perspective of those who favor drug laws is that of the Mormons and the Puritans, who regard as immoral any intake of substances to alter one's state of consciousness or otherwise cause pleasure: they forbid not only the illicit drugs and alcohol, but also tobacco, caffeine, and even chocolate. The vast majority of Americans are hardly so consistent with respect to the propriety of their pleasures. Yet once one acknowledges that there is nothing immoral about drinking alcohol or smoking tobacco for non-medicinal purposes, it becomes difficult to condemn the consumption of marijuana, cocaine, and other substances on moral grounds. The "moral" condemnation of some substances and not others proves to be little more than a prejudice in favor of some drugs and against others.

The same false distinction is drawn with respect to those who provide the psychoactive substances to users and abusers alike. If degrees of immorality were measured by the levels of harm caused by one's products, the "traffickers" in tobacco and alcohol would be vilified as the most evil of all substance purveyors. That they are perceived instead as respected members of our community, while providers of the no more dangerous illicit substances are punished with long prison sentences, says much about the prejudices of most Americans with respect to psychoactive substances, but little about the morality or immorality of their activities. . . .

Although a valid moral distinction cannot be drawn between the licit and the illicit psychoactive substances, one can point to a different kind of moral justification for the drug laws: they arguably reflect a paternalistic obligation to protect those in danger of succumbing to their own weaknesses. If drugs were legally available, most people would either abstain from using them or would use them responsibly and in moderation. A minority without self-restraint, however, would end up harming themselves if the substances were more readily available. Therefore, the majority has a moral obligation to deny itself legal access to certain substances because of the plight of the minority. This obligation is presumably greatest when children are included among the minority.

At least in principle, this argument seems to provide the strongest moral justification for the drug laws. But ultimately the moral quality of laws must be judged not by how those laws are intended to work in principle, but by how they function in practice. When laws intended to serve a moral end inflict great damage on innocent parties, we must rethink our moral position.

Because drug-law violations do not create victims with an interest in notifying the police, drug-enforcement agents rely heavily on undercover operations, electronic surveillance, and information provided by informants. These techniques are indispensable to effective law enforcement, but they are also among the least palatable investigative methods employed by the police. The same is true of drug testing: it may be useful and even necessary for determining liability in accidents, but it also threatens and undermines the right of privacy to which many Americans believe they are entitled. There are good reasons for requiring that such measures be used sparingly.

Equally disturbing are the increasingly vocal calls for people to inform not only on drug dealers but also on neighbors, friends, and even family members who use illicit drugs. Government calls on people not only to "just say no," but also to report those who have not heeded the message. Intolerance of illicit-drug use and users is heralded not only as an indispensable ingredient in the war against drugs, but also as a mark of good citizenship. Certainly every society requires citizens to assist in the enforcement of criminal laws. But societies—particularly democratic and pluralistic ones—also rely strongly on an ethic of tolerance toward those who are different but do no harm to others. Overzealous enforcement of the drug laws risks undermining that ethic, and encouraging the creation of a society of informants.

This results in an immorality that is far more dangerous in its own way than that associated with the use of illicit drugs.

THE BENEFITS OF LEGALIZATION

Repealing the drug-prohibition laws promises tremendous advantages. Between reduced government expenditures on enforcing drug laws and new tax revenue from legal drug production and sales, public treasuries would enjoy a net benefit of at least ten billion dollars a year, and possibly much more. The quality of urban life would rise significantly. Homicide rates would decline. So would robbery and burglary rates. Organized criminal groups, particularly the newer ones that have yet to diversify out of drugs, would be dealt a devastating setback. The police, prosecutors, and courts would focus their resources on combatting the types of crimes that people cannot walk away from. More ghetto residents would turn their backs on criminal careers and seek out legitimate opportunities instead. And the health and quality of life of many drug users—and even drug abusers—would improve significantly.

All the benefits of legalization would be for naught, however, if millions more Americans were to become drug abusers. Our experience with alcohol and tobacco provides ample warnings. Today, alcohol is consumed by 140 million Americans and tobacco by 50 million. All of the health costs associated with abuse of the illicit drugs pale in comparison with those resulting from tobacco and alcohol abuse. In 1986, for example, alcohol was identified as a contributing factor in 10 percent of work-related injuries, 40 percent of suicide attempts, and about 40 percent of the approximately 46,000 annual traffic deaths in 1983. An estimated eighteen million Americans are reported to be either alcoholics or alcohol abusers. The total cost of alcohol abuse to American society is estimated at over 100 billion dollars annually. Alcohol has been identified as the direct cause of 80,000 to 100,000 deaths annually, and as a contributing factor in an additional 100,000 deaths. The health costs of tobacco use are of similar magnitude. In the United States alone, an estimated 320,000 people die prematurely each year as a consequence of their consumption of tobacco. By comparison, the National Council on Alcoholism reported that only 3,562 people were known to have died in 1985 from use of all illegal drugs combined. Even if we assume that thousands more deaths were related in one way or another to illicit drug abuse but not reported as such, we are still left with the conclusion that all of the health costs of marijuana, cocaine, and heroin combined amount to only a small fraction of those caused by tobacco and alcohol.

Most Americans are just beginning to recognize the extensive costs of alcohol and tobacco abuse. At the same time, they seem to believe that there is something fundamentally different about alcohol and tobacco that supports the legal distinction between those two substances, on the one hand, and the illicit ones, on the other. The most common distinction is based on the assumption that the illicit drugs are more dangerous than the licit ones. Cocaine, heroin, the various hallucinogens, and (to a lesser extent) marijuana are widely perceived as, in the words of the President's Commission on Organized Crime, "inherently destructive to mind and body." They are also believed to be more addictive and more likely to cause dangerous and violent behavior than alcohol and tobacco. All use of illicit drugs is therefore thought to be abusive; in other words, the distinction between use and abuse of psychoactive substances that most people recognize with respect to alcohol is not acknowledged with respect to the illicit substances.

Most Americans make the fallacious assumption that the government would not criminalize certain psychoactive substances if they were not in fact dangerous. They then jump to the conclusion that any use of those substances is a form of abuse. The government, in its effort to discourage people from using illicit drugs, has encouraged and perpetuated these misconceptions—not only in its rhetoric but also in its purportedly educational materials. Only by reading between the lines can one discern the fact that the vast majority of Americans who have used illicit drugs have done so in moderation, that relatively few have suffered negative short-term consequences, and that few are likely to suffer long-term harm. . . .

There is no question that legalization is a risky policy, since it may lead to an increase in the number of people who abuse drugs. But that is a risk—not a certainty. At the same time, current drug-control policies are failing, and new proposals promise only to be more costly and more repressive. We know that repealing the drug-prohibition laws would eliminate or greatly reduce many of the ills that people commonly identify as part and parcel of the "drug problem." Yet legalization is repeatedly and vociferously dismissed, without any attempt to evaluate it openly and objectively. The past twenty years have demonstrated that a drug policy shaped by exaggerated rhetoric designed to arouse fear has only led to our current disaster. Unless we are willing to honestly evaluate our options, including various legalization strategies, we will run a still greater risk: we may never find the best solution for our drug problems.

QUESTIONS

1 Which approach to legalization is morally preferable—Nadelmann's harm-reduction strategy or Szasz's more sweeping approach?
2 Does moral consistency require that we either (a) legally prohibit alcohol sale and use or (b) legalize the use of currently illicit drugs, such as marijuana and cocaine?

Against the Legalization of Drugs

James Q. Wilson

Wilson argues that crack-dependent people and heroin users cause all sorts of harm to others, such as producing crack-addicted babies and neglecting spouses and children. In his view, drug legalization would result in a sharp increase in

Reprinted with the permission of The American Enterprise Institute for Public Policy Research, Washington, D.C., from James Q. Wilson, *On Character* (1991), pp. 149–163.

drug use, a more widespread degradation of the human personality, and a greater rate of accidents and violence. Whereas Nadelmann stresses the benefits of legalization, Wilson stresses the benefits of the current system. Whereas Nadelmann sees our treatment of tobacco and alcohol, on the one hand, and currently illicit drugs, on the other, as morally inconsistent, Wilson advances reasons in support of this differential treatment.

In 1972 President Richard Nixon appointed me chairman of the National Advisory Council for Drug Abuse Prevention. Created by Congress, the council was charged with providing guidance on how best to coordinate the national war on drugs. (Yes, we called it a war then too.) In those days the drug we were chiefly concerned with was heroin. When I took office, heroin use had been increasing dramatically. Everybody was worried that this increase would continue. Such phrases as "heroin epidemic" were commonplace.

That same year the eminent economist Milton Friedman published an essay in *Newsweek* in which he called for legalizing heroin. His argument was on two grounds: as a matter of ethics the government has no right to tell people not to use heroin (or to drink or to commit suicide); as a matter of economics the prohibition of drug use imposes costs on society that far exceed the benefits. Others, such as the psychoanalyst Thomas Szasz, made the same argument. . . .

RELIVING THE PAST

Suppose we had taken Friedman's advice in 1972. What would have happened? We cannot be entirely certain, but at a minimum we would have placed the young heroin addicts (and, above all, the prospective addicts) in a different position from the one in which they actually found themselves. Heroin would have been legal. Its price would have been reduced by 95 percent (minus whatever we chose to recover in taxes). Now that it could have been sold by the same people who make aspirin, its quality would have been assured: no poisons, no adulterants. Sterile hypodermic needles would have been readily available at the neighborhood drugstore, probably at the same counter where the heroin was sold. No need to travel to big cities or unfamiliar neighborhoods—heroin could have been purchased anywhere, perhaps by mail order.

There would no longer have been any financial or medical reason to avoid heroin use. Anybody could have afforded it. We might have tried to prevent children from buying it, but as we have learned from our efforts to prevent minors from buying alcohol and tobacco, young people have a way of penetrating markets theoretically reserved for adults. Returning Vietnam veterans would have discovered that Omaha and Raleigh had been converted into the pharmaceutical equivalent of Saigon.

Under these circumstances can we doubt for a moment that heroin use would have grown exponentially? . . .

BACK TO THE FUTURE

Now cocaine, especially in its potent form, crack, is the focus of attention. Now as in 1972 the government is trying to reduce its use. Now as then some people are advocating legalization. Is there any more reason to yield to those arguments today than there was almost two decades ago?

I think not. If we had yielded in 1972, we almost certainly would have had today a permanent population of several million, not several hundred thousand, heroin addicts. If we yield now, we will have a far more serious problem with cocaine. . . .

Women are much more likely to use crack than heroin, and if they are pregnant, the effects on their babies are tragic. Douglas Besharov, who has been following the effects of drugs on infants for twenty years, writes that nothing he learned about heroin prepared him for the devastation of cocaine. Cocaine harms the fetus and can lead to physical deformities or neurological damage. Some crack babies have for all practical purposes suffered a disabling stroke while still in the womb. The long-term consequences of this brain damage are lowered cognitive ability and the onset of mood disorders. Besharov estimates that about 30,000 to 50,000 such babies are born every year, about 7,000 in New York City alone. There may be ways to treat such infants, but from everything we know, the treatment will be long, difficult, and expensive. Worse, the mothers who are most likely to produce crack babies are precisely the ones who, because of poverty or temperament, are least able and willing to obtain such treatment. In fact anecdotal evidence suggests that crack mothers are likely to abuse their infants.

The notion that abusing drugs such as cocaine is a victimless crime is not only absurd but dangerous. Even ignoring the fetal drug syndrome, crack-dependent people, like heroin addicts, are individuals who regularly victimize their children by neglect, their spouses by improvidence, their employers by lethargy, and their co-workers by carelessness. Society is not and could never be a collection of autonomous individuals. We all have a stake in ensuring that each of us displays a minimal level of dignity, responsibility, and empathy. We cannot of course coerce people into goodness, but we can and should insist that some standards must be met if society itself—on which the existence of the human personality depends—is to persist. Drawing the line that defines those standards is difficult and contentious, but if crack and heroin use does not fall below it, what does? . . .

BENEFITS OF ILLEGALITY

The advocates of legalization find nothing to be said in favor of the current system except, possibly, that it keeps the number of addicts smaller than it would otherwise be. In fact the benefits are more substantial than that.

First, treatment: all the talk about providing treatment on demand implies a demand for treatment. That is not quite right. Some drug-dependent people genuinely want treatment and will remain in it if offered; they should receive it. But far more want only short-term help after a bad crash; once stabilized and bathed, they are back on the street again, hustling. And even many of the addicts who enroll in a program and honestly want help drop out after a short while when they discover that help takes time and commitment. Drug-dependent people have short time horizons and a weak capacity for commitment. These two groups—those looking for a quick fix and those unable to stick with a long-term fix—are not easily helped. Even if we increase the number of treatment slots—as we should—we would have to do something to make treatment more effective.

One thing that can often make it more effective is compulsion. Douglas Anglin of UCLA, in common with many other researchers, has found that the longer one stays in a treatment program, the better the chances of a reduction in drug dependency. But he, again like most other researchers, has found that dropout rates are high. He has also found, however, that patients who enter treatment under legal compulsion stay in the program longer than those not subject to such pressure. His research on the California civil commitment program, for example, found that heroin users involved with its required drug-testing program had over the long term a lower rate of heroin use than similar addicts who were free of such constraints. If compulsion is a useful component of treatment for many addicts, it is not clear how compulsion could be achieved in a society in which purchasing, possessing, and using the drug were legal. It could be managed, I suppose, but I would not want to have to answer the challenge from the American Civil Liberties Union that it is wrong to compel a person to undergo treatment for consuming a legal commodity.

Next, education: we are now investing substantially in drug-education programs in the schools. Although we do not yet know for certain what will work, there are some promising leads. But I wonder how credible such programs would be if they were aimed at dissuading children from doing something perfectly legal. We could of course treat drug education like smoking education: inhaling crack and inhaling tobacco are both legal, but you should not do it because it is bad for you. That tobacco is bad for you is easily shown; the surgeon general has seen to that. But what do we say about crack? It is pleasurable, but devoting yourself to so much pleasure is not a good idea (though perfectly legal)? Unlike tobacco, cocaine will not give you cancer or emphysema, but it will lead you to neglect your duties to family, job, and neighborhood? Everybody is doing cocaine, but you should not?

Again it might be possible under a legalized regime to have effective drug-prevention programs, but their effectiveness would depend heavily on first having decided that cocaine use, like tobacco use, is purely a matter of practical consequences; no fundamental moral significance attaches to either. But if we believe—as I do—that dependency on certain mind-altering drugs is a moral issue and that their illegality rests in part on their immorality, then legalizing them undercuts, if it does not eliminate altogether, the moral message.

That message is at the root of the distinction we now make between nicotine and cocaine. Both are highly addictive; both have harmful physical effects. But we treat the two drugs differently, not simply because nicotine is so widely used as to be beyond the reach of effective prohibition but because its use does not destroy the user's essential humanity. Tobacco shortens one's life, cocaine debases it. Nicotine alters one's habits, cocaine alters one's soul. The heavy use of crack, unlike the heavy use of tobacco, corrodes those natural sentiments of sympathy and duty that constitute our human nature and make possible our social life. To say, as does Nadelmann, that distinguishing morally between tobacco and cocaine is "little more than a transient prejudice" is close to saying that morality itself is but a prejudice.

THE ALCOHOL PROBLEM

Now we have arrived where many arguments about legalizing drugs begin: is there any reason to treat heroin and cocaine differently from the way we treat alcohol?

There is no easy answer to that question because, as with so many human problems, one cannot decide simply on the basis either of moral principles or of individual consequences; one has to temper any policy by a common-sense judgment of what is possible. Alcohol, like heroin, cocaine, PCP, and marijuana, is a drug—that is, a mood-altering substance—and consumed to excess, it certainly has harmful consequences: auto accidents, barroom fights, bedroom shootings. It is also, for some people, addictive. We cannot confidently compare the addictive powers of these drugs, but the best evidence suggests that crack and heroin are much more addictive than alcohol.

Many people, Nadelmann included, argue that since the health and financial costs of alcohol abuse are so much higher than those of cocaine or heroin abuse, it is hypocritical folly to devote our efforts to preventing cocaine or drug use. But as Mark Kleiman of Harvard has pointed out, this comparison is quite misleading. What Nadelmann is doing is showing that a legalized drug (alcohol) produces greater social harm than illegal ones (cocaine and heroin). But of course. Suppose that in the 1920s we had made heroin and cocaine legal and alcohol illegal. Can anyone doubt that Nadelmann would now be writing that it is folly to continue our ban on alcohol because cocaine and heroin are so much more harmful?

And let there be no doubt about it—widespread heroin and cocaine use are associated with all manner of ills. Thomas Bewley found that the mortality rate of British heroin addicts in 1968 was twenty-eight times as high as the death rate of the same age group of nonaddicts. Even though in England at the time an addict could obtain free or low-cost heroin and clean needles from British clinics. Perform the following mental experiment: suppose we legalized heroin and cocaine in this country. In what proportion of auto fatalities would the state police report that the driver was nodding off on heroin or recklessly driving on a coke high? In what proportion of spouse assault and child abuse cases would the local police report that crack was involved? In what proportion of industrial accidents would safety investigators report that the forklift or drill-press operator was in a drug-induced stupor or frenzy? We do not know exactly what the proportion would be, but anyone who asserts that it would not be much higher than it is now would have to believe that these drugs have little appeal except when they are illegal. And that is nonsense.

An advocate of legalization might concede that social harm—perhaps harm equivalent to that already produced by alcohol—would follow from making cocaine and heroin generally available. But at least, he might add, we would have the problem out in the open, where it could be treated as a matter of public health. That is well and good if we knew how to treat—that is, cure—heroin and cocaine abuse. But we do not know how to do it for all the people who would need such help. We are having only limited success in coping with chronic alcoholics. Addictive behavior is immensely difficult to change, and the best methods for changing it—living in drug-free therapeutic communities, becoming faithful members of Alcoholics Anonymous or Narcotics Anonymous—require great personal commitment, a quality that is, alas, in short supply among the persons—young people, disadvantaged people—who are often most at risk for addiction.

Suppose that today we had not 15 million alcohol abusers but half a million. Suppose that we already knew what we have learned from our long experience with the widespread use of alcohol. Would we make whiskey legal? I do not know, but I suspect there would be a lively debate. The surgeon general would remind us of the risks alcohol poses to pregnant woman. The National Highway Traffic Safety Administration would point to the likelihood of more highway fatalities caused by drunk drivers. The Food and Drug Administration might find that there is a nontrivial increase in cancer associated with alcohol consumption. At the same time the police would report great difficulty in keeping illegal whiskey out of our cities, officers being corrupted by bootleggers, and alcohol addicts often resorting to crime to feed their habit. Libertarians for their part would argue that every citizen has a right to drink anything he wishes and that drinking is in any event a victimless crime.

However the debate might turn out, the central fact would be that the problem was still at that point a small one. The government cannot legislate away the addictive tendencies in all of us nor can it remove completely even the most dangerous addictive substances. But it can cope with harms when the harms are still manageable. . . .

IF I AM WRONG

No one can know what our society would be like if we changed the law to make access to cocaine, heroin, and PCP easier. I believe, for reasons given, that the result would be a sharp increase in use, a more widespread degradation of the human personality, and a greater rate of accidents and violence.

I may be wrong. If I am, then we will needlessly have incurred heavy costs in law enforcement and some forms of criminality. But if I am right, and the legalizers prevail anyway, then we will have consigned millions of people, hundreds of thousands of infants, and hundreds of neighborhoods to a life of oblivion and disease. To the lives and families destroyed by alcohol, we will have added countless more destroyed by cocaine, heroin, PCP, and whatever else a basement scientist can invent.

Human character is formed by society; indeed human character is inconceivable without society, and good character is less likely in a bad society. Will we, in the name of an abstract doctrine of radical individualism, and with the false comfort of suspect predictions, decide to take the chance that somehow individual decency can survive amid a more general level of degradation?

I think not. The American people are too wise for that, whatever the academic essayists and cocktail party pundits may say. But if Americans today are less wise than I suppose, then Americans at some future time will look back on us now and wonder, what kind of people were they that they could have done such a thing?

QUESTIONS

1 Are there good reasons to believe that legalizing currently illicit drugs will result in a serious increase in addiction?
2 Is Wilson correct in claiming that drugs such as cocaine and heroin are dehumanizing? What does it mean to be dehumanized?

Addiction and Drug Policy

Daniel Shapiro

Shapiro advances an argument to undercut the worry that legalizing cocaine and heroin would produce an explosion of addiction. He rejects what he calls the "standard view"—the view that these drugs are highly and inherently addictive due to the pharmacological effects they have on the brain. Shapiro proposes an alternative view of addiction, which focuses on the individual's mindset and social or cultural setting in explaining his or her use or abuse of drugs. Finally, Shapiro looks at cigarette smoking and examines the interaction among tobacco's pharmacological effects, the smoker's mindset, and the social setting.

Most people think that illegal drugs, such as cocaine and heroin, are highly addictive. Usually their addictiveness is explained by pharmacology: their chemical composition and its effects on the brain are such that, after a while, it's hard to stop using them. This view of drug addiction—I call it the standard view—underlies most opposition to legalizing cocaine and heroin. James Wilson's (1990) arguments are typical: legalization increases access, and increased access to addictive drugs increases addiction. The standard view also underlies the increasingly popular opinion, given a philosophical defense by Robert Goodin (1989), that cigarette smokers are addicts in the grip of a powerful drug.

However, the standard view is false: pharmacology, I shall argue, does not by itself do much to explain drug addiction. I will offer a different explanation of drug addiction and discuss its implications for the debate about drug legalization.

PROBLEMS WITH THE STANDARD VIEW

We label someone as a drug addict because of his behavior. A drug addict uses drugs repeatedly, compulsively, and wants to stop or cut back on his use but finds it's difficult to do so; at its worst, drug addiction dominates or crowds out other activities and concerns. The standard view attempts to explain this compulsive behavior by

This is a slightly revised version of the essay that appears in *Social Ethics,* 6th ed. Reprinted with permission of Daniel Shapiro from *Morality and Moral Controversies,* 7th ed. (Pearson Prentice-Hall, 2005), edited by John Arthur, pp. 515–521. The essay's addendum is omitted here.

the drug's effects on the brain. Repeated use of an addictive drug induces cravings and the user comes to need a substantial amount to get the effect she wants, i.e., develops tolerance. If the user tries to stop, she then suffers very disagreeable effects, called withdrawal symptoms. (For more detail on the standard view, see American Psychiatric Association 1994, 176–81.)

Cravings, tolerance, and withdrawal symptoms: do these explain drug addiction? A craving or strong desire to do something doesn't *make* one do something: one can act on a desire or ignore it *or* attempt to extinguish it. Tolerance explains why the user increases her intake to get the effect she wants, but that doesn't explain why she would find it difficult to *stop wanting* this effect. Thus, the key idea in the standard view is really withdrawal symptoms, because that is needed to explain the difficulty in extinguishing the desire to take the drug or to stop wanting the effects the drug produces. However, for this explanation to work, these symptoms have to be really bad, for if they aren't, why not just put up with them as a small price to pay for getting free of the drug? However, withdrawal symptoms aren't *that* bad. Heroin is considered terribly addictive, yet pharmacologists describe its withdrawal symptoms as like having a bad flu for about a week: typical withdrawal symptoms include fever, diarrhea, sneezing, muscle cramps, and vomiting (Kaplan 1983, 15, 19, 35). While a bad flu is quite unpleasant, it's not so bad that one has little choice but to take heroin rather than experience it. Indeed, most withdrawal symptoms for any drug cease within a few weeks, yet most heavy users who relapse do so after that period and few drug addicts report withdrawal symptoms as the reason for their relapse (Peele 1985, 19–20, 67; Schacter 1982, 436–44; Waldorf, Reinarman, and Murphy 1991, 241).

Thus, cravings, tolerance, and withdrawal symptoms cannot explain addiction. An additional problem for the standard view is that most drug users, whether they use legal or illegal drugs, do not become addicts, and few addicts remain so permanently. (Cigarette smokers are a partial exception, which I discuss later.) Anonymous surveys of drug users by the Substance Abuse and Mental Health Services Administration indicate that less than 10 percent of those who have tried powder cocaine use it monthly (National Household Survey of Drug Abuse 2001, tables H1 and H2). Furthermore, most monthly users are not addicts; a survey of young adults, for example (Johnston, O'Malley, and Bachman for the National Institute on Drug Abuse 1996, 84–5), found that less than 10 percent of monthly cocaine users used it daily. (Even a daily user need not be an addict; someone who drinks daily is not thereby an alcoholic.) The figures are not appreciably different for crack cocaine (Erickson, Smart, and Murray 1994, 167–74, 231–32, Morgan and Zimmer 1997, 142–44) and only slightly higher for heroin (Husak 1992, 125; Sullum 2003, 228). These surveys have been confirmed by longitudinal studies—studies of a set of users over time—which indicate that moderate and/or controlled use of these drugs is the norm, not the exception, and that even heavy users do not inevitably march to addiction, let alone remain permanent addicts (Waldorf, Reinarman, and Murphy 1991, Erickson, Smart, and Murray 1994; Zinberg 1984, 111–34, 152–71). The standard view has to explain the preeminence of controlled use by arguing that drug laws reduce access to illegal drugs. However, I argue below that even with easy access to drugs most people use them responsibly, and so something other than the law and pharmacology must explain patterns of drug use.

AN ALTERNATIVE VIEW

I will defend a view of addiction summed up by Norman Zinberg's book, *Drug, Set, and Setting* (1984). "Drug" means pharmacology; "set" means the individual's mindset, his personality, values, and expectations; and "setting" means the cultural or social surroundings of drug use. This should sound like common sense. Humans are interpretative animals, and so what results from drug use depends not just on the experience or effects produced by the drug but *also* on the interpretation of that experience or effects. And how one interprets or understands the experience depends on one's individuality and the cultural or social setting. I begin with setting. Hospital patients that get continuous and massive doses of narcotics rarely get addicted or crave the drugs after release from the hospital (Peele 1985, 17; Falk 1996, 9). The quantity and duration of their drug use pales in significance compared with the setting of their drug consumption: subsequent ill effects from the drug are rarely interpreted in terms of addiction. A study of Vietnam veterans, the largest study of untreated heroin users ever conducted, provides more dramatic evidence of the role of setting. Three-quarters of Vietnam vets who used heroin in Vietnam became addicted, but after coming home, only half of heroin users in Vietnam continued to use, and of those only 12 percent were addicts (Robins, Heltzer, Hesselbrock, and Wish 1980). Wilson also mentions this study and says that the change was because heroin is illegal in the U.S. (1990, 22), and while this undoubtedly played a role, so did the difference in social setting: Vietnam, with its absence of work and family, as well as loneliness and fear of death, helped to promote acceptance of heavy drug use.

Along the same lines, consider the effects of alcohol in different cultures. In Finland, for example, violence and alcohol are linked, for sometimes heavy drinkers end up in fights; in Greece, Italy, and other Mediterranean countries, however, where almost all drinking is moderate and controlled, there is no violence-alcohol link (Peele 1985, 25). Why the differences? Humans are social or cultural animals, not just products of their biochemistry, and this means, in part, that social norms or rules play a significant role in influencing behavior. In cultures where potentially intoxicating drugs such as alcohol are viewed as supplements or accompaniments to life, moderate and controlled use will be the norm—hence, even though Mediterranean cultures typically consume large amounts of alcohol, there is little alcoholism—while in cultures where alcohol is also viewed as a way of escaping one's problems, alcoholism will be more prevalent, which may explain the problem in Finland and some other Scandinavian cultures. In addition to cultural influences, most people learn to use alcohol responsibly by observing their parents. They see their parents drink at a ball game or to celebrate special occasions or with food at a meal, but rarely on an empty stomach; they learn it's wrong to be drunk at work, to drink and drive; they learn that uncontrolled behavior with alcohol is generally frowned upon; they absorb certain norms and values such as "know your limit," "don't drink alone," "don't drink in the morning," and so forth. They learn about rituals which reinforce moderation, such as the phrase "let's have a drink." These informal rules and rituals teach most people how to use alcohol responsibly (Zinberg 1987, 258–62).

While social controls are harder to develop with illicit drugs—accurate information is pretty scarce, and parents feel uncomfortable teaching their children about controlled use—even here sanctions and rituals promoting moderate use exist. For example, in a study of an eleven-year follow-up of an informal network of middle-class cocaine users largely connected through ties of friendship, most of whom were moderate users, the authors concluded that:

> Rather than cocaine overpowering user concerns with family, health, and career, we found that the high value most of our users placed upon family, health, and career achievement . . . mitigated against abuse and addiction. Such group norms and the informal social controls that seemed to stem from them (e.g., expressions of concern, warning about risks, the use of pejorative names like "coke hog," refusal to share with abusers) mediated the force of pharmacological, physiological, and psychological factors which can lead to addiction (Murphy 1989: 435).

Even many heavy cocaine users are able to prevent their use from becoming out of control (or out of control for significant periods of time) by regulating the time and circumstances of use (not using during work, never using too late at night, limiting use on weekdays), using with friends rather than alone, employing fixed rules (paying bills before spending money on cocaine), etc. (Waldorf, Reinarman, and Murphy 1991). Unsurprisingly, these studies of controlled cocaine use generally focus on middle-class users: their income and the psychological support of friends and family put them at less of a risk of ruining their lives by drug use than those with little income or hope (Peele 1991, 159–60).

I now examine the effects of set on drug use, that is, the effect of expectations, personality, and values. Expectations are important because drug use occurs in a pattern of ongoing activity, and one's interpretation of the drug's effects depends upon expectations of how those effects will fit into or alter those activities. Expectations explain the well-known placebo effect: if people consume something they mistakenly believe will stop or alleviate their pain, it often does. Along the same lines, in experiments with American college-age men, aggression and sexual arousal increased when these men were told they were drinking liquor, even though they were drinking 0 proof, while when drinking liquor and told they were not, they acted normally (Peele 1985, 17). The role of expectations also explains why many users of heroin, cocaine, and other psychoactive drugs do not like or even recognize the effects when they first take it and have to be taught to or learn how to appreciate the effects (Peele 1985, 13–14; Waldorf, Reinarman, and Murphy 1991, 264; Zinberg 1984, 117). The importance of expectations means that those users who view the drug as overpowering them will tend to find their lives dominated by the drug, while those who view it as an enhancement or a complement to certain experiences or activities will tend not to let drugs dominate or overpower their other interests (Peele 1991, 156–58, 169–70).

As for the individual's personality and values, the predictions of common sense are pretty much accurate. Psychologically healthy people are likely to engage in controlled, moderate drug use, or if they find themselves progressing to uncontrolled use, they tend to cut back. On other hand, drug addicts of all kinds tend to have more psychological problems before they started using illicit drugs (Peele 1991, 153–54, 157, Zinberg 1984, 74–76.) People who are motivated to control their own lives will tend to make drug use an accompaniment or an ingredient in their lives, not the dominant factor. Those who place a high value on responsibility, work, family, productivity, etc., will tend to fit drug use into their lives rather than letting it run their lives (Waldorf, Reinarman, and Murphy 1991, 267; Peele 1991, 160–66). That's why drug use of all kinds, licit or illicit, tends to taper off with age: keeping a job, raising a family, and so forth leave limited time or motivation for uncontrolled or near continuous drug use (Peele 1985, 15). And it's why it's not uncommon for addicts to explain their addiction by saying that they drifted into the addict's life; with little to compete with their drug use, or lacking motivation to substitute other activities or interests, drug use comes to dominate their lives (DeGrandpre and White 1996, 44–46). Those with richer lives, or who are motivated on an individual and/or cultural level to get richer lives, are less likely to succumb to addiction. To summarize: even with easy access to intoxicating drugs, most drug users don't become addicts, or if they do, don't remain addicts for that long, because most people have and are motivated to find better things to do with their lives. These better things result from their individual personality and values and their social or cultural setting.

CIGARETTE SMOKING AND THE ROLE OF PHARMACOLOGY

I've discussed how set and setting influence drug use, but where does pharmacology fit in? Its role is revealed by examining why it is much harder to stop smoking cigarettes—only half of smokers that try to stop smoking succeed in quitting—than to stop using other substances. (For more detail in what follows, see Shapiro 1994 and the references cited therein).

Smokers smoke to relax; to concentrate; to handle anxiety, stress, and difficult interpersonal situations; as a way of taking a break during the day; as a social lubricant; as a means of oral gratification—and this is a partial list. Since smoking is a means to or part of so many activities, situations, and moods, stopping smoking is a major life change and major life changes do not come easily. Part of the reason smoking is so integrated into people's lives is pharmacological. Nicotine's effects on the brain are mild and subtle: it doesn't disrupt your life. While addicts or heavy users of other drugs such as cocaine, heroin, or alcohol *also* use their drugs as a means to or part of a variety of activities, situations, and moods, most users of these drugs are not lifelong addicts or heavy users, because these drugs are not so mild and heavy use has a stronger tendency over time to disrupt people's lives.

The pharmacology of smoking, however, cannot be separated from its social setting. Smoking doesn't disrupt people's lives in part because it is legal. Even with increasing regulations, smokers still can smoke in a variety of situations (driving, walking on public streets, etc.), while one cannot use illegal drugs except in a furtive and secretive manner. Furthermore, the mild effects of nicotine are due to its mild potency—smokers can carefully control their nicotine intake, getting small doses throughout the day—and its mild potency is due partly to smoking being legal. Legal drugs tend to have milder potencies than illegal ones for two reasons. First, illegal markets create incentives for stronger potencies, as sellers will favor concentrated forms of a drug that can be easily concealed and give a big bang for the buck. Second, in legal markets different potencies of the same drug openly compete, and over time the weaker ones come to be preferred—consider the popularity of low tar/nicotine cigarettes and wine and beer over hard liquor.

Thus, pharmacology and setting interact: smoking is well integrated into people's lives because the nicotine in cigarettes has mild pharmacological effects and because smoking is legal, and nicotine has those mild effects in part because smoking is legal. Pharmacology also interacts with what I've been calling set. The harms of smoking are slow to occur, are cumulative, and largely affect one's health, not one's ability to perform normal activities (at least prior to getting seriously ill). Furthermore, to eliminate these harms requires complete smoking cessation; cutting back rarely suffices (even light smokers increase their chances of getting lung cancer, emphysema, and heart disease). Thus, quitting smoking requires strong motivation, since its bad effects are not immediate and it does not disrupt one's life. Add to this what I noted earlier, that stopping smoking means changing one's life, and it's unsurprising that many find it difficult to stop.

Thus, it is a mistake to argue, as Goodin did, that the difficulty in quitting is mainly explicable by the effects of nicotine. Smokers are addicted to smoking, an *activity,* and their being addicted to it is not reducible to their being addicted to a *drug.* If my explanation of the relative difficulty of quitting smoking is correct, then the standard view of an addictive drug is quite suspect. That view suggests that knowledge of a drug's pharmacology provides a basis for making reasonable predictions about a drug's addictiveness. However, understanding nicotine's effects upon the brain (which is what Goodin stressed in his explanation of smokers' addiction) does not tell us that it's hard to stop smoking; we only know that once we add information about set and setting. Generalizing from the case of smoking, all we can say is:

> The milder the effects upon the brain, the easier for adults to purchase, the more easily integrated into one's life, and the more the bad effects are cumulative, slow-acting and only reversible upon complete cessation, the more addictive the drug.

Besides being a mouthful, this understanding of drug addiction requires introducing the *interaction* of set and setting with pharmacology to explain the addictiveness potential of various drugs. It is simpler and less misleading to say that people tend to *addict themselves* to various substances (and activities), this tendency varying with various cultural and individual influences.

CONCLUSION

My argument undercuts the worry that legalizing cocaine and heroin will produce an explosion of addiction because people will have access to inherently and powerfully addictive drugs. The standard view that cocaine and heroin are inherently addictive is false, because no drug is *inherently* addictive. The desire of most people to lead responsible and productive lives in a social setting that rewards such desires is what controls and limits most drug use. Ironically, if cocaine and heroin in a legal market would be as disruptive as many drug prohibitionists fear, then that is an excellent reason why addiction would not explode under legalization—drug use that tends to thrive is drug use that is woven into, rather than disrupts, responsible people's lives. . . .

REFERENCES

American Psychiatric Association. 1994. *Diagnostic and Statistical Manual of Mental Disorders.* 4th ed. Washington, D.C.: American Psychiatric Association.

DeGrandpre, R., and E. White. 1996. "Drugs: In Care of the Self." *Common Knowledge* 3: 27–48.

Erickson. P., E. Edward, R. Smart, and G. Murray. 1994. *The Steel Drug: Crack and Cocaine in Perspective,* 2nd ed. New York: MacMillan.

Falk, J, 1996. "Environmental Factors in the Instigation and Maintenance of Drug Abuse." In W. Bickel and R. DeGrandpre, eds., *Drug Policy and Human Nature.* New York: Plenum Press.

Goodin, R. 1989. "The Ethics of Smoking." *Ethics* 99: 574–624.

Husak, D. 1992. *Drugs and Rights.* New York: Cambridge University Press.

Johnston. L. D., P. M. O'Malley, and J. G. Bachman. 1996. *Monitoring the Future Study, 1975–1994; National Survey Results on Drug Use.* Volume II: *College Students and Young Adults.* Rockville, Md.: National Institute on Drug Abuse.

Kaplan, J. 1983. *The Hardest Drug: Heroin and Public Policy.* Chicago: University of Chicago Press.

Morgan, J., and L. Zimmerman. 1997. "The Social Pharmacology of Smokeable Cocaine: Not All It's Cracked Up to Be." In C. Reinarman and H. Levine, eds., *Crack in America: Demon Drugs and Social Justice,* Berkeley: University of California Press.

Murphy, S., C. Reinarman, and D. Waldorf. 1989. "An 11 Year Follow-Up of a Network of Cocaine Users," *British Journal of Addiction* 84: 427–36.

Peele, S. 1985. *The Meaning of Addiction; Compulsive Experience and Its Interpretation.* Lexington, Mass.: D.C. Heath and Company.

Peele, S. 1991. *The Diseasing of America: Addiction Treatment Out of Control.* Boston: Houghton Mifflin Company.

Robins, L., J. Helzer. M. Hesselbrock, and E. Wish. 1980. "Vietnam Veterans Three Years After Vietnam: How Our Study Changed Our View of Heroin." In L. Brill and C. Winick, eds., *The Yearbook of Substance Use and Abuse.* Vol. 2. New York: Human Sciences Press.

Schacter, S. 1982. "Recidivism and Self-Cure of Smoking and Obesity." *American Psychologist* 37: 436–44.

Shapiro. D. 1994. "Smoking Tobacco: Irrationality, Addiction and Paternalism." *Public Affairs Quarterly* 8: 187–203.

Substance Abuse and Mental Health Services Administration. 2002. *Tables from the 2001 National Household Survey on Drug Abuse,* Department of Health and Human Services, available online at http://www.samhsa.gov/oas/NHSDA/2k1NHSDA/vol2/appendixh_l.htm.

Sullum. J. 2003. *Saying Yes: In Defense of Drug Use.* New York: Tarcher/Putnam.

Waldorf, D., C. Reinarman, and S. Murphy. 1991. *Cocaine Changes: The Experience of Using and Quitting.* Philadelphia: Temple University Press.

Wilson, J. 1990. "Against the Legalization of Drugs." *Commentary* 89: 21–28.

Zinberg, N. 1984. *Drug, Set, and Setting.* New Haven, Conn.: Yale University Press.

Zinberg, N. 1987. "The Use and Misuse of Intoxicants." In R. Hamowy, ed., *Dealing with Drugs.* Lexington, Mass.: D. C. Heath and Company.

QUESTIONS

1 Can Wilson's position on addiction be defended against Shapiro's critique of the standard view?

2 Taking into account the various arguments that can be made for and against drug legalization, what overall drug policy would you endorse?

SUGGESTED ADDITIONAL READINGS FOR CHAPTER 4

BELENKO, STEVEN R., ed: *Drugs and Drug Policy in America.* Westport, Conn.: Greenwood Press, 2000. This is an excellent documentary history of American drug policy. It combines explanatory commentary with a variety of original documents, including enacted laws and other government documents, court decisions, scholarly writings, and articles from the popular media.

BROCK, DAN: "The Use of Drugs for Pleasure." In Thomas H. Murray, Willard Gaylin, and Ruth Macklin, eds., *Feeling Good and Doing Better: Ethics and Nontherapeutic Drug Use.* Clifton. N J.: Humana Press, 1984, pp. 83–106. Brock argues in support of ethical hedonism, maintaining that the pleasure derived from drug use does not necessarily conflict with living the good life and may even be compatible with it.

DE MARNEFFE, PETER: "Do We Have a Right to Use Drugs?" *Public Affairs Quarterly.* vol. 10, July 1996, pp. 229–247. De Marneffe argues that there is no overriding moral reason why democratic governments should not enact and enforce some laws against drug sale and use.

DUKE, STEVEN B.: "Drug Prohibition: An Unnatural Disaster." *Connecticut Law Review,* vol. 27, Winter 1995, pp. 571–612. Duke argues that drug prohibition has far eclipsed alcohol prohibition as America's costliest and most catastrophic social program.

HUSAK, DOUGLAS N.: *Drugs and Rights.* New York: Cambridge University Press, 1992. Husak focuses on the moral rights of adult users of recreational drugs. Defending a moderate position on the issue, he develops criteria to be used in determining which drugs should be criminalized.

LOKEN, GREGORY A.: "The Importance of Being More Than Earnest: Why the Case for Drug Legalization Remains Unproven." *Connecticut Law Review,* vol. 27, Winter 1995, pp. 660–691. Loken rejects the view that drug prohibition is the cause of an increase in crime. He argues that the drug war has successfully reduced crime and that legalization would have disastrous consequences, especially for children.

MURRAY, THOMAS H.: "The Coercive Power of Drugs in Sports." *The Hastings Center Report,* vol. 13, August 1983, pp. 24–30. Murray argues against the use of drugs in sports. He offers arguments in support for sanctioning both competing athletes who take performance-enhancing drugs and their coaches.

ZIMMER, LYNN, and JOHN P. MORGAN: *Marijuana Myths, Marijuana Facts: A Review of the Scientific Evidence.* New York: The Lindesmith Center, 1997. Zimmer and Morgan review the scientific research on marijuana. They list numerous claims made about the harmful effects of marijuana, some of which are found in government documents as well as magazines and newspapers. They refute each claim, basing their refutations on relevant scientific research.

Capital Punishment Notes

The following are some court cases relevant to the issue of capital punishment:

Furman v. Georgia (1972): Capital punishment, as then administered, was determined by the Supreme Court to be cruel and unusual punishment. The Supreme Court did not deny the legality of capital punishment, just the way it was being determined. It found that prisoners were being found guilty by a "standardless discretion." In other words, the guilt or innocence was often decided in an arbitrary fashion and too many variations occured from place to place, state to state. This case began the process of establishing standards for capital punishment that could be considered acceptable under the Constitution.

Gregg v. Georgia (1976): The case of Tony Gregg on the count of two murders during the commission of a robbery was determined to follow the standards set for capital punishment. In other words, the Supreme Court determined it was not an issue under the Constitution.

Atkins v. Virginia (2002): This is the case where it was determined that the execution of the mentally retarded was unconstitutional because executing a mentally retarded person did not serve either the deterrent nor retributive purpose of capital punishment.

Roper v. Simmons (2005): This is the case that abolished capital punishment for juvenile offenders under the age of 18.

McClesky v. Kemp (1987): This case introduced statistical evidence showing clear bias along racial and economic lines. However, the Supreme Court concluded that such evidence plays no part in the constitutionality of capital punishment. It is an indication that justice needs to be better (more fairly) administered, but not that the law itself is wrong.

Some interesting background on the issue:

1 Since DNA testing, over 100 prisoners on death row have been found innocent of the crimes for which they were sentenced to death.

2 The United States, Saudi Arabia, China, and Iran are the four nations in the world that execute the most people each year.

3 Most industrialized nations have banned capital punishment as barbaric.

4 In the U.S. Constitution, the ban on "cruel and unusual punishment" comes from the 8th Amendment. The issue is whether capital punishment is cruel and unusual.

5 Statistically, studies have shown that there is no difference in the crime rate between states that have capital punishment and states that do not. In fact, the state with the lowest rate of murders is one that has banned capital punishment since 1870. In other words, it has not been shown that capital punishment creates a deterrent to murder.

6 Most murders are crimes of passion, and in that mental state, a person does not stop to consider the consequences.

7 In spite of the above, a clear bias against minorities and the poor and the fact that so many have been wrongfully found guilty and executed, over half of the American public finds capital punishment "appropriate and necessary."

The ethical issues of a death penalty revolve around the following two positions:

Retentionists: Retentionists favor the retention of a death penalty, arguing that it is need for the following reasons:

1 Justice and retribution
2 Social utility and deterrence
3 Argument that what people fear the most will be the greatest deterrent
4 Argument that it is better err on the side of safety (better to execute a few innocent people than let loose a killer)

Abolitionists: Abolitionists favor the elimination of the death penalty, arguing the following:

1 It is inhumane punishment
2 Retribution is barbaric
3 Justice does not require death
4 It is impossible to guarantee mistakes aren't made and death is irrevocable
5 There is a pattern of discrimination against the poor and minorities

Justices Stewart, Powell, and Stevens: In the "*Majority Opinion in Gregg v. Georgia*" case, Tony Gregg is charge with two counts of armed robbery and two counts of murder. He is found guilty and sentenced to death. The claim that the death penalty is unconstitutional reaches the Supreme Court. Justice Stewart, Powell, and Stevens uphold the constitutionality of the death penalty as applied in this case.

The majority opinion says the constitutionality of the death penalty must meet two standards to be cleared of any claim to be "cruel and unusual" punishment:

1 It must meet the "evolving standards of decency" in society.
2 It must accord with the "dignity of man."

In addition, it must not be seen as excessive. To be excessive means:

1 Unnecessary and/or wanton infliction of pain.
2 Grossly out of proportion to the severity of the crime.

Justices Stewart, Powell, and Stevens believe the death penalty meets the above criteria. They contend that it meets two goals:

1 Retribution and deterrence—it meets the "evolving standards of decency" and is in accord with the "dignity of man." The justices, in discussing the deterrent effect of the death penalty admit that is does not serve as a deterrent in crimes of passion, but it may very well serve as a deterrent in other situations.

2 Proportional to the crime—it is not an "unnecessary and/or wanton infliction of pain" nor is it out of proportion to the severity of the crime.

Justice Thurgood Marshall: Justice Marshall voices the dissenting opinion in *Gregg v. Georgia.* In this court case, Marshall argues that the death penalty is unconstitutional because (1) it is excessive, and (2) the American people, if fully informed (about how the death is performed), would consider it morally unacceptable.

Marshall argues that the death penalty is not necessary to promote the goal of deterrence or to further any legitimate notion of retribution. The notion that a murderer "deserves" death constitutes a denial of the wrongdoer's human dignity and worth.

Marshall disagrees with the majority of the justices on the Supreme Court (although, in later years some will change their mind and agree with Marshall). The majority argue that the instinct for retribution is a part of human nature and, if people believe that offenders do not get the penalty they deserve, that vigilante justice might prevail. Marshall does not agree.

Marshall concludes that the death penalty, although utilitarian, is not necessary. The same results could be achieved by other means.

Igor Primoratz: Primoratz asks, "Is this punishment ever proportionate retribution for the offense committed, and thus deserved, just, and justified?"

He answers that the value of human life exceeds the value of anything else because we are all made in the image of God. Therefore, taking a life is the worse crime that can be committed. The right to life is fundamental, but not absolute. A person only has the right to life so long as he acknowledges and respects the same rights for others. If a person violates the rights of others, he looses that same right for himself.

Primoratz believes that the fact that an occasional innocent person is wrongly convicted and put to death is not a valid argument against the death penalty. When a person is wrongly executed, it is a reflection of a bad court system, not a bad law.

Steven Nathanson: Nathanson argues against the concept of retribution. The concept of retribution, he explains, is based on the following concepts:

1 What a person deserves is related to what he does.

2 The punishment does not depend on any particular legal or political institution.

3 The punishment provides a measure of appropriate punishment as a guide for creating laws.

Nathanson mainly addresses this last point. He believes retentionist arguments are flawed because "equality retribution" is too specific to be generally applied and "proportional retribution" is not specific enough. He explains these two ways of accessing the legitimacy of the death penalty as follows:

1   Equality Retribution is based on "an eye for an eye." The problem is that this concept does not provide adequate criterion for determining appropriate levels of punishment in many cases. In other words, in order to be a guideline for punishment, it must apply (be a guideline) to all situations. "An eye for an eye" sounds good. It works for murder cases. If a life is taken then a life is the cost. But what happens when it is a case of arson? To claim an "eye for an eye" as punishment, do we could burn down the arsonist's home? What if he rents? And how do we punish prostitution? Refuse to pay?

Equality retribution works only in a very narrow, specific case—the case of murder—but is not general enough to apply to the concept of just punishment as a whole.

2   Proportional Retribution is based on the idea that the worst punishment be reserved for the worst crime. The problem with this concept is that in matching the severity of the crime with the severity of the punishment, there is nothing that says the death penalty need be a part of the list. It merely says: worst crime—worst punishment. Perhaps a fine is the worst punishment or exile or life in prison.

Proportional retribution works as a general principle, but fails to support specifics, or that executions need to be designated as a punishment.

Louis P. Pojman: Pojman points out that sociological/psychological studies (such as that done by Ehrlich) are unable to show any conclusive evidence for or against the effectiveness of the death penalty. He argues that other reasons, such as the Best Bet argument or the Commonsense argument, work better to support and justify the death penalty.

The **Best Bet Argument** (proposed by Ernest van den Haag) is the idea that it is better to risk the unjust loss of life of a few (the innocent who are wrongly convicted), than to risk the life of the many innocents who might be murdered if a truly guilty person were released back into society (rather than executed).

The **Commonsense Argument** is the idea that what people fear most will provide the greatest deterrent. Since people fear death over almost anything else, a death penalty should provide the greatest deterrent to crime.

Based on the above, Pojman concludes that we should support some uses of the death penalty, especially in the case of first degree murder, murder of a police officer, murder of a political leader, etc.

Jeffrey Reiman: Reiman argues against the Best Bet and Commonsense arguments. Please do not become confused when reading Reiman's article. He does not define the best-bet and commonsense arguments the same way as Pojman, so just read the reasons they don't work, and don't worry over much about the exact definition. Reiman points out that there is little evidence to show that having a death penalty impacts the crime rate.

1 Reiman points out that what research we do have suggest that there is no difference in the impact on crime between areas that have a death penalty and areas that do not have a death penalty. In fact, the areas of the world where the death penalty is used the most, tend to also be the areas where there are the highest rates of murder. This is not to suggest that there is a causal link between capital punishment and crime rates, but it does suggest that the death penalty does not create a deterrent to crime.

2 Reiman also points out that every year crimes are committed that lead to a criminal's death during the commission of the crime. Yet, this does not stop people from committing the crimes and gambling with their lives. If the knowledge that the commission of a crime might lead to an immediate risk of death does not deter a person, then why would the prospect of being executed be a deterrent. After all, to be executed required being caught, tried, going through all sorts of appeals. Even if convicted, a criminal may spend many years before actually being executed.

Reiman concludes his article with the suggestion that abolishing the death penalty would serve to teach a lesson far more valuable that having a death penalty. If we abolished capital punishment, we would be sending out a message about the sanctity of life and the wrongfulness of taking a life (even under the law).

David Dolinko: Dolinko points out the problems with our justice system, particularly when a wrong verdict may mean taking a life. We know that punishments are arbitrary. What results in a ten year sentence in one court may only earn a three year sentence is another. We know that there is a racial bias in the court system. We know that there is a problem with the poor being able to obtain good legal representation. Dolinko believes the arbitrary and discriminatory nature of our legal system makes capital punishment very problematic.

CHAPTER 5

The Death Penalty

Strong convictions are firmly entrenched on both sides of the death penalty controversy. From one side, we hear in forceful tones that "murderers deserve to die." We are also told that no lesser punishment than the death penalty will suffice to deter potential murderers. From the other side of the controversy, in tones of equal conviction, we are told that the death penalty is a cruel and barbarous practice, effectively serving no purpose that could not be equally well served by a more humane punishment. "How long," it is asked, "must we indulge this uncivilized and pointless lust for revenge?" In the face of such strongly held but opposed views, each of us is invited to confront an important ethical issue: the morality of the death penalty. Before approaching the death penalty in its ethical dimensions, however, it will be helpful to briefly discuss its constitutional dimensions. Many of the considerations raised in discussions of the constitutionality of the death penalty parallel those raised in discussions of its morality.

THE CONSTITUTIONALITY OF THE DEATH PENALTY

The Eighth Amendment to the Constitution of the United States explicitly prohibits the infliction of *cruel and unusual* punishment. If the death penalty is a cruel and unusual punishment, it is unconstitutional. But is it cruel and unusual? In a landmark case, *Furman v. Georgia* (1972), the United States Supreme Court ruled that the death penalty was unconstitutional *as then administered*. The Court did not rule, however, that the death penalty is unconstitutional *by its very nature*. Indeed, subsequent developments in the Court have led to the conclusion that the death penalty is constitutionally permissible—as long as it is administered in accordance with certain procedural requirements.

The decision reached in *Furman* was by a mere five-to-four majority. Moreover, there was a basic divergence of viewpoint among those who voted with the majority. Both Justice Marshall and Justice Brennan argued straightforwardly that the death penalty is a cruel and unusual punishment *by its very nature*. From this perspective, it would not matter how much the procedures of its administration might be modified. It would still remain a cruel and unusual punishment. Among the reasons advanced to support this contention, two are especially noteworthy: (1) The death penalty is excessive in the sense of being unnecessary; lesser penalties are capable of serving the desired legislative purpose. (2) The death penalty is abhorrent to currently existing moral values.

The other three justices (Douglas, White, and Stewart) who voted with the majority did not commit themselves to the position that the death penalty is unconstitutional *by its very nature*. Leaving this underlying issue unresolved, they simply advanced the more guarded contention that the death penalty was unconstitutional *as then administered*. In their view, the death penalty was unconstitutional primarily because it was being administered in an arbitrary and capricious manner. The essence of their argument can be reconstructed in the following way. The death penalty is typically imposed at the discretion of a jury (or sometimes a judge). The absence of explicit standards to govern the decision between life and death allows a wide range of unchecked prejudice to operate freely under the heading of *discretion*. For example, discretion seems to have rendered blacks more prone than whites to the death penalty. Such standardless discretion violates not only the Eighth Amendment but also the Fourteenth Amendment, which guarantees "due process of law."

As matters developed in the wake of *Furman,* it was the Court's objection to *standardless discretion* that provided an opening for the many individual states still eager to retain the death penalty as a viable component of their legal systems. These states were faced with the challenge of devising procedures for imposing the death penalty that would not be open to the charge of standardless discretion. Two such approaches gained prominence. (1) Some states (e.g., North Carolina) moved to dissolve the objection of standardless discretion by simply making the death penalty *mandatory* for certain crimes. (2) Other states (e.g., Georgia) took an equally obvious approach, attempting to establish standards that would provide guidance for the jury (or the judge) in deciding between life and death.

Subsequent developments have led to the conclusion that the second approach is constitutionally acceptable, whereas the first is not. In *Woodson v. North Carolina* (1976), the Court ruled (although by a mere five-to-four majority) that mandatory death sentences are unconstitutional. In *Gregg v. Georgia* (1976), however, the Court ruled (with only Justice Marshall and Justice Brennan dissenting) that the death penalty is not unconstitutional when imposed at the discretion of a jury for the *crime of murder,*[1] as long as appropriate safeguards are provided against any arbitrary or capricious imposition. Most important, there must be explicit standards established for the guidance of jury deliberations. The attitude of the Court in this

[1]In *Gregg,* the Supreme Court considered only the constitutionality of imposing the death penalty for the *crime of murder*. In *Coker v. Georgia* (1977), the Court subsequently considered the constitutionality of imposing the death penalty for the *crime of rape*. Holding death to be a "grossly disproportionate" punishment for the crime of rape, the Court declared such an employment of the death penalty unconstitutional. Although the Court has never retreated from its holding in *Gregg* that the death penalty is a constitutionally permissible form of punishment for the crime of murder, it has on occasion provided further clarification about procedural requirements for the imposition of the death penalty and has recently placed some notable restrictions on the scope of those who may be executed. In *Atkins v. Virginia* (2002), the Court ruled that the execution of a mentally retarded criminal is unconstitutional. In *Roper v. Simmons* (2005), the Court ruled that it is unconstitutional to execute killers who committed their crimes when they were younger than eighteen.

regard is made clear by Justices Stewart, Powell, and Stevens in their opinion in *Gregg,* which appears in this chapter. Also appearing in this chapter is the dissenting opinion of Justice Marshall.

THE ETHICAL ISSUE

In any discussion of the morality of the death penalty, it is important to remember that the death penalty is a kind of punishment. Indeed, it is normally thought to be the most serious kind of punishment; hence it is called *capital* punishment. Most philosophers agree that punishment in general (as contrasted with capital punishment in particular) is a morally justified social practice. For one thing, however uneasy we might feel about inflicting harm on another person, it is hard to visualize a complex society managing to survive without an established legal system of punishment. However, to say that most philosophers agree that punishment is a morally justified social practice is not to say that there are no dissenters from this view. Some argue that it is possible to structure society in ways that would not necessitate commitment to a legal system of punishment as we know it. One suggested possibility is that undesirable social behavior could be adequately kept in check by therapeutic treatment rather than by traditional kinds of punishment. Such a system would seem to have the advantage of being more humane, but surely it is implausible to believe that present therapeutic techniques are anywhere near adequate to the task. Perhaps future advances in the behavioral sciences will render such an alternative more viable. If so, it may one day be plausible to argue that the whole practice of (nontherapeutic) punishment must be rejected on moral grounds. Still, for now, there is widespread agreement on the moral defensibility of punishment as an overall social practice. What stands out as an open and hotly debated ethical issue is whether or not the death penalty, as a distinctive kind of punishment, should continue to play a role in our legal system of punishment.

Those in favor of retaining the death penalty are commonly called *retentionists.* Retentionists differ among themselves regarding the kinds of cases in which they find it appropriate to employ the death penalty. They also differ among themselves regarding the supporting arguments they find acceptable. But anyone who supports the retention of the death penalty—for employment in whatever kinds of cases and for whatever reasons—is by definition a retentionist. Those in favor of abolishing the death penalty are commonly called *abolitionists.* Abolitionists, by definition, refuse to support any employment of the death penalty. Like the retentionists, however, they differ among themselves concerning the supporting arguments they find acceptable.

There is one extreme, and not widely embraced, abolitionist line of thought. It is based on the belief that the sanctity of human life demands absolute nonviolence. On this view, killing of any kind, for whatever reason, is always and everywhere morally wrong. No one has the right to take a human life—not in self-defense, not in war, not in any circumstance. Thus, since the death penalty obviously involves a kind of killing, it is a morally unacceptable form of punishment and must be abolished. This general view, which is associated with the Quakers and other pacifists, has struck most moral philosophers as implausible. Can we really think that killing, when it is the only course that will save oneself from an unprovoked violent assault, is morally wrong? Can we really think that it would be morally wrong to kill a terrorist if that were the *only* possible way of stopping him or her from exploding a bomb in the midst of a kindergarten class? The defender of absolute nonviolence is sometimes inclined to argue at this point that violence will only breed violence. There may indeed be much truth in this claim. Still, most people do not believe that such a claim provides adequate support for the contention that *all* killing is morally wrong, and, if some killing is morally acceptable, perhaps the death penalty is as well. What arguments can be made on its behalf?

RETENTIONIST ARGUMENTS

Broadly speaking, arguments for the retention of the death penalty usually emphasize either (1) considerations of *justice* or (2) considerations of *social utility*. Those who emphasize considerations of justice typically develop their case along the following line: When the moral order is upset by the commission of an offense, it is only right that the disorder be rectified by punishment that is equal to or proportional to the offense. This view is reflected in remarks such as "The scales of justice demand retribution" and "The offender must pay for the crime." Along this line, the philosopher Immanuel Kant (1724–1804) is famous for his unequivocal defense of the *lex talionis*—the law (or principle) of retaliation, often expressed as "an eye for an eye." According to this principle, punishment is to be inflicted in a measure that will equalize the offense. And, when the offense is murder, *only* capital punishment is sufficient to equalize it.

In one of this chapter's readings, Igor Primoratz argues for retention of the death penalty on retributive grounds. Stephen Nathanson, an abolitionist, provides a contrasting point of view. Nathanson argues that no adequate retributive rationale can be provided for the death penalty.

Although the demand for retribution continues to play a prominent role in the overall case for the death penalty, many retentionists (and, obviously, abolitionists as well) have come to feel quite uneasy with the notion of imposing the death penalty "because the wrongdoer *deserves* it." Perhaps this uneasiness can be traced, at least in part, to our growing awareness of the way in which social conditions, such as ghetto living, seem to spawn criminal activity. If so, then it seems that we have arrived at a point of intersection with a venerable—and vexing—philosophical problem: the problem of "freedom and determinism." Pure retributive thinking seems to presuppose a radical sense of human freedom and its correlate: a radical sense of personal responsibility and accountability for one's actions. This is undoubtedly why retentionists who espouse a retributive rationale often insist that the death penalty does not constitute a denial of the wrongdoer's dignity and worth as a human being. On the contrary, they say, the death penalty reaffirms the dignity and worth of a convicted murderer—by holding the person strictly responsible for the crime that has been committed and giving the person what he or she deserves. Of course, if someone is uneasy with the radical sense of human freedom that seems to underlie pure retributive thinking, that person will surely be uneasy with the retributive rationale for retention of the death penalty. But we must also consider the utilitarian side of the retentionist coin.

Since considerations of social utility are commonly advanced in defense of the practice of punishment in general, it is not surprising to find that they are also commonly advanced in defense of retaining the death penalty. Utilitarianism, as a distinct school of moral philosophy, locates the primary justification of punishment in its social utility. Utilitarians recognize that punishment consists of the infliction of evil on another person, but they hold that such evil is far outweighed by the future benefits that will accrue to society. Imprisonment, for example, might lead to such socially desirable effects as (1) *rehabilitation* of the criminal, (2) *incapacitation,* whereby we achieve temporary or permanent protection from the imprisoned criminal, and (3) *deterrence* of other potential criminals. When utilitarian considerations are recruited in support of the retention of the *death* penalty, it is clear that rehabilitation of the criminal can play no part in the case. But retentionists do frequently promote considerations of incapacitation and deterrence.

Retentionists who appeal to considerations of incapacitation typically argue that the death penalty is the only effective way to protect society from a certain subset of convicted murderers—namely, those who are at once *violence-prone and irreformable.* (Notice that an important difficulty here would be specifying effective criteria for the identification of those already convicted murderers who are truly violence-prone and irreformable.) Life imprisonment, it is said, cannot assure society of the needed protection, because even if "life imprisonment" were really life imprisonment—that is, even if a sentence of life imprisonment excluded the possibility of parole—violence-prone and irreformable inmates would still pose an imminent threat to prison guards and fellow inmates. Furthermore, escape is always possible. Thus, the death penalty is the only truly effective way of achieving societal protection against the continuing threat posed by some convicted murderers.

According to many retentionists, however, the fundamental justification for retaining the death penalty lies in the fact that the death penalty is a *uniquely effective deterrent.* But is this central factual claim true? Is the death penalty really a more substantial deterrent than life imprisonment or even long-term imprisonment? At this point, a natural move is to look to the findings of the social sciences, but many scholars familiar with the social science literature on this issue would say that the available evidence is conflicting and ultimately inconclusive. If it is true that empirical studies have failed to resolve the central factual question, what else can be said about the deterrence rationale for the death penalty?

Many retentionists, willing to acknowledge that scientific findings are inconclusive, argue that we must simply rely on common sense. Since people typically fear death much more than they fear life imprisonment, it just stands to reason, they say, that the death penalty is superior to life imprisonment as a deterrent. Although the threat of life imprisonment or even long-term imprisonment may well be sufficient to deter many would-be murderers, the threat of execution would deter an even greater number. Thus, the death penalty ought to be retained in our system of criminal justice because common sense testifies to the fact that it is a more substantial deterrent than life imprisonment.

The commonsense argument for the death penalty as a uniquely effective deterrent might be countered with the following claim: it does not follow from the mere fact that one punishment is more severe than another that the former will be a more substantial deterrent than the latter. Indeed, it might be the case that anyone *capable of being deterred* from murder by the threat of the death penalty would be equally well deterred by the threat of life imprisonment. Jeffrey Reiman makes this counterargument, among others, as he takes issue in this chapter with the commonsense argument for the death penalty as a uniquely effective deterrent. Providing a contrasting view, Louis P. Pojman argues in this chapter that commonsense or anecdotal evidence is sufficient to establish the conclusion that the death penalty is a uniquely effective deterrent.

There is one other important argument made by retentionists dedicated to the deterrence rationale. This argument, often referred to as the *best bet argument,* has been most prominently advanced by Ernest van den Haag, a well-known retentionist who has also recurrently advanced the commonsense argument. The best bet argument takes uncertainty—our uncertainty whether or not the death penalty is a uniquely effective deterrent—as its point of departure. If we retain the death penalty, the argument goes, we run the risk of needlessly eradicating the lives of convicted murderers; perhaps the death penalty is *not* a uniquely effective deterrent. On the other hand, if we abolish the death penalty, we run the risk of innocent people becoming future murder victims; perhaps the death penalty is a uniquely effective deterrent. Faced with such uncertainty, the argument concludes, it is our moral obligation to retain the death penalty. Whichever way we go, there is a risk to be run, but it is better from a moral point of view to risk the lives of the guilty than to risk the lives of the innocent. "I believe we have no right to risk additional future victims of murder for the sake of sparing convicted murderers."[2]

Pojman makes clear in this chapter that he endorses the best bet argument, but a critic might respond as follows. In claiming that retention risks the lives of the guilty, whereas abolition risks the lives of the innocent, the best bet argument overlooks the possibility that retention of the death penalty has what is sometimes called "a counter-deterrent effect." The idea here is that state-sponsored killing in the form of execution has a brutalizing effect on society, that it actually weakens inhibitions on the part of the populace against killing. Thus, in the long run, there might well be more murders in a retentionist society than there would be in an abolitionist society. So it is not correct to say that retention of the death penalty risks only guilty lives; relative to the possibility that the death penalty has a counter-deterrent effect, retention also places innocent lives at risk. Reiman argues along very similar lines in this chapter, although he develops his argument in terms of "a deterrent effect from not executing" rather than "a counter-deterrent effect" of executing.

THE CASE FOR ABOLITION

What can be said of the abolitionist case against the death penalty? Most abolitionists do not care to argue the extreme position, already discussed, of absolute nonviolence, yet they typically do want to commit themselves seriously to the "sanctity of human life." They emphasize the inherent worth and dignity of each individual and insist that the taking of a human life, although perhaps sometimes

[2]Ernest van den Haag, "On Deterrence and the Death Penalty," *Ethics,* vol. 78, July 1968, p. 287.

morally permissible, is a very serious matter and not to be permitted in the absence of weighty overriding reasons. At face value, they argue, the death penalty is cruel and inhumane; since retentionists have failed to advance substantial reasons in its defense, it must be judged a morally unacceptable practice. Against retentionist arguments based on retribution as a demand of justice, abolitionists often argue that the "demand of justice" is nothing but a mask for a barbarous vengeance. At a more fundamental level, they simply argue that justice does not require the death penalty for the crime of murder. Against retentionist arguments based on considerations of social utility, abolitionists simply argue that other, more humane punishments will serve equally well. We do not need the death penalty to incapacitate convicted murderers because life imprisonment without the possibility of parole can provide us with a sufficient measure of societal protection. Also, since there is no reason to believe that the death penalty is a uniquely effective deterrent, retention cannot be justified on the basis of considerations of deterrence.

In addition to advancing arguments that directly counter retentionist claims, abolitionists often incorporate two further arguments into their overall case against the death penalty. The first of these arguments can be stated as follows: It is impossible to guarantee that mistakes will not be made in the administration of punishment, but this factor is especially important in the case of the death penalty, because only *capital* punishment is irrevocable. That is, only the death penalty eradicates the possibility of compensating an innocent person who has been wrongly punished. A second abolitionist argument focuses attention on patterns of discrimination in the administration of the death penalty. In our society, according to one version of the argument, blacks are more likely to receive the death penalty than whites, and the poor and uneducated are more likely to receive the death penalty than the affluent and educated. A retentionist counter to each of these abolitionist arguments is provided in this chapter by Primoratz.

According to a more recent construction of the racial bias problem, it is the *race of the victim,* rather than the *race of the killer,* that is the operative racial factor—and a very significant one—in the administration of the death penalty. "Other things being equal, the studies show, killers of white people are more likely to receive death sentences than killers of blacks."[3] Although the moral implications of this finding may be arguable, many contemporary abolitionists insist that racial disparities in the administration of the death penalty, at least in combination with other perceived procedural irregularities, provide a compelling moral objection to retention of the death penalty.

In this chapter's final reading, David Dolinko offers an analysis of three procedural arguments against the death penalty. In addition to considering the *mistake* argument and the *discrimination* argument, he also offers some commentary on the *arbitrariness* argument. In Dolinko's view, the mistake argument is the most powerful procedural argument against the death penalty. Indeed, an abolitionist interested in pressing the mistake argument might make reference to some notable factual findings reported in September 2004 by the Death Penalty Information Center. A total of 116 death-row inmates in the United States have been exonerated

[3]Erik Eckholm, "Studies Find Death Penalty Tied to Race of the Victims," *New York Times,* February 24, 1995, p. B1.

since 1973, and forty-nine of these exonerations have taken place in the 1997–2004 period, DNA evidence playing an important role in several of these more recent exonerations.[4] In January 2003, Illinois Governor George Ryan—citing seventeen cases in which Illinois death-row inmates had been exonerated and calling attention to multiple procedural problems plaguing that state's capital punishment system— commuted the death sentences of all Illinois death-row inmates.

Thomas A. Mappes

[4]"Innocence and the Crisis in the American Death Penalty," September 2004. This report is available on the DPIC website (www.deathpenaltyinfo.org).

Opinion in *Gregg v. Georgia*

Justices Potter Stewart, Lewis F. Powell, Jr., and John Paul Stevens

The state of Georgia reacted to the United States Supreme Court's decision in *Furman v. Georgia* (1972) by drafting a death penalty statute calculated to avoid the Court's objection to standardless discretion. Georgia's approach, in contrast to the approach of those states that made the death penalty mandatory for certain crimes, embodied an effort to specify standards that would guide a jury (or a judge) in deciding between the death penalty and life imprisonment. In this case, with only Justice Marshall and Justice Brennan dissenting, the Court upheld the constitutionality of imposing the death penalty for the crime of murder under the law of Georgia.

Justices Stewart, Powell, and Stevens initially consider the contention that the death penalty for the crime of murder is, under all circumstances, cruel and unusual punishment, thus unconstitutional. On their analysis, a punishment is cruel and unusual if it fails to accord with "evolving standards of decency." Moreover, even if a punishment does accord with contemporary values, it must still be judged cruel and unusual if it fails to accord with the "dignity of man," the "basic concept underlying the Eighth Amendment." They take this second stipulation to rule out "excessive" punishment, identified as (1) that which involves the unnecessary and wanton infliction of pain or (2) that which is grossly out of proportion to the severity of the crime. In light of these considerations, Justices Stewart, Powell, and Stevens argue that the imposition of the death penalty for the crime of murder does not invariably violate the Constitution. They contend that legislative developments since *Furman* have made clear that the death penalty is acceptable to contemporary society. Moreover, they contend, the death penalty is not invariably excessive: (1) It may properly be considered necessary to achieve two principal social purposes—retribution and deterrence. (2) When the death penalty is imposed for the crime of murder, it may properly be considered not disproportionate to the severity of the crime.

United States Supreme Court. 428 U.S. 153 (1976).

Turning their attention to the death sentence imposed under the law of Georgia in this case, Justices Stewart, Powell, and Stevens maintain that a carefully drafted statute, ensuring "that the sentencing authority is given adequate information and guidance," makes it possible to avoid imposing the death penalty in an arbitrary or capricious manner. The revised Georgia statutory system under which Gregg was sentenced to death, they conclude, does not violate the Constitution.

The issue in this case is whether the imposition of the sentence of death for the crime of murder under the law of Georgia violates the Eighth and Fourteenth Amendments.

I

The petitioner, Troy Gregg, was charged with committing armed robbery and murder. In accordance with Georgia procedure in capital cases, the trial was in two stages, a guilt stage and a sentencing stage. . . .

. . . The jury found the petitioner guilty of two counts of armed robbery and two counts of murder.

At the penalty stage, which took place before the same jury, . . . the trial judge instructed the jury that it could recommend either a death sentence or a life prison sentence on each count. . . . The jury returned verdicts of death on each count.

The Supreme Court of Georgia affirmed the convictions and the imposition of the death sentences for murder. . . . The death sentences imposed for armed robbery, however, were vacated on the grounds that the death penalty had rarely been imposed in Georgia for that offense. . . .

II

. . . The Georgia statute, as amended after our decision in *Furman v. Georgia* (1972), retains the death penalty for six categories of crime: murder, kidnaping for ransom or where the victim is harmed, armed robbery, rape, treason, and aircraft hijacking. . . .

III

We address initially the basic contention that the punishment of death for the crime of murder is, under all circumstances, "cruel and unusual" in violation of the Eighth and Fourteenth Amendments of the Constitution. In Part IV of this opinion, we will consider the sentence of death imposed under the Georgia statutes at issue in this case.

The Court on a number of occasions has both assumed and asserted the constitutionality of capital punishment. In several cases that assumption provided a necessary foundation for the decision, as the Court was asked to decide whether a particular method of carrying out a capital sentence would be allowed to stand under the Eighth Amendment. But until *Furman v. Georgia* (1972), the Court never confronted squarely the fundamental claim that the punishment of death always, regardless of the enormity of the offense or the procedure followed in imposing the sentence, is cruel and unusual punishment in violation of the Constitution. Although this issue was presented and addressed in *Furman,* it was not resolved by the Court. Four Justices would have held that capital punishment is not unconstitutional *per se;* two justices would have reached the opposite conclusion; and three Justices, while agreeing that the statutes then before the Court were invalid as applied, left open the question whether such punishment may ever be imposed. We now hold that the punishment of death does not invariably violate the Constitution.

A

The history of the prohibition of "cruel and unusual" punishment already has been reviewed at length. The phrase first appeared in the English Bill of Rights of 1689, which was drafted by Parliament at the accession of William and Mary. The English version appears to have been directed against punishments unauthorized by statute and beyond the jurisdiction of the sentencing court, as well as those disproportionate to the offense involved. The American draftsmen, who adopted the English phrasing in drafting the Eighth Amendment, were primarily concerned, however, with proscribing "tortures" and other "barbarous" methods of punishment.

In the earliest cases raising Eighth Amendment claims, the Court focused on particular methods of execution to determine whether they were too cruel to pass constitutional muster. The constitutionality of the sentence of death itself was not at issue, and the criterion used to evaluate the mode of execution was its similarity to "torture" and other "barbarous" methods. . . .

But the Court has not confined the prohibition embodied in the Eighth Amendment to "barbarous" methods that were generally outlawed in the 18th century. Instead, the Amendment has been interpreted in a flexible and dynamic manner. The Court early recognized that a "principle to be vital must be capable of wider application than the mischief which gave it birth." Thus the Clause forbidding "cruel and unusual" punishments "is not fastened to the obsolete but may acquire meaning as public opinion becomes enlightened by a humane justice." . . .

It is clear from the foregoing precedents that the Eighth Amendment has not been regarded as a static concept. As Mr. Chief Justice Warren said, in an oftquoted phrase, "[t]he Amendment must draw its meaning from the evolving standards of decency that mark the progress of a maturing society." Thus, an assessment of contemporary values concerning the infliction of a challenged sanction is relevant to the application of the Eighth Amendment. As we develop below more fully, this assessment does not call for a subjective judgment. It requires, rather, that we look to objective indicia that reflect the public attitude toward a given sanction.

But our cases also make clear that public perceptions of standards of decency with respect to criminal sanctions are not conclusive. A penalty also must accord with "the dignity of man," which is the "basic concept underlying the Eighth Amendment." This means, at least, that the punishment not be "excessive." When a form of punishment in the abstract (in this case, whether capital punishment may ever be imposed as a sanction for murder) rather than in the particular (the propriety of death as a penalty to be applied to a specific defendant for a specific crime) is under consideration, the inquiry into "excessiveness" has two aspects. First, the punishment must not involve the unnecessary and wanton infliction of pain. Second, the punishment must not be grossly out of proportion to the severity of the crime.

B

Of course, the requirements of the Eighth Amendment must be applied with an awareness of the limited role to be played by the courts. This does not mean that judges have no role to play, for the Eighth Amendment is a restraint upon the exercise of legislative power. . . .

But, while we have an obligation to insure that constitutional bounds are not overreached, we may not act as judges as we might as legislators. . . .

Therefore, in assessing a punishment selected by a democratically elected legislature against the constitutional measure, we presume its validity. We may not require the legislature to select the least severe penalty possible so long as the penalty selected is not cruelly inhumane or disproportionate to the crime involved. And a heavy burden rests on those who would attack the judgment of the representatives of the people.

This is true in part because the constitutional test is intertwined with an assessment of contemporary standards and the legislative judgment weighs heavily in ascertaining such standards. "[I]n a democratic society legislatures, not courts, are constituted to respond to the will and consequently the moral values of the people."

The deference we owe to the decisions of the state legislatures under our federal system is enhanced where the specification of punishments is concerned, for "these are peculiarly questions of legislative policy." Caution is necessary lest this Court become, "under the aegis of the Cruel and Unusual Punishment Clause, the ultimate arbiter of the standards of criminal responsibility . . . throughout the country." A decision that a given punishment is impermissible under the Eighth Amendment cannot be reversed short of a constitutional amendment. The ability of the people to express their preference through the normal democratic processes, as well as through ballot referenda, is shut off. Revisions cannot be made in the light of further experience.

C

In the discussion to this point we have sought to identify the principles and considerations that guide a court in addressing an Eighth Amendment claim. We now consider specifically whether the sentence of death for the crime of murder is a *per se* violation of the Eighth and Fourteenth Amendments to the Constitution. We note first that history and precedent strongly support a negative answer to this question.

The imposition of the death penalty for the crime of murder has a long history of acceptance both in the United States and in England. . . .

It is apparent from the text of the Constitution itself that the existence of capital punishment was accepted by the Framers. At the time the Eighth Amendment was ratified, capital punishment was a common sanction in every State. Indeed, the First Congress of the United States enacted legislation providing death as the penalty for specified crimes. . . .

For nearly two centuries, this Court, repeatedly and often expressly, has recognized that capital punishment is not invalid *per se*. . . .

Four years ago, the petitioners in *Furman* and its companion cases predicated their argument primarily upon the asserted proposition that standards of decency had evolved to the point where capital punishment no longer could be tolerated. The petitioners in those cases said, in effect, that the evolutionary process had come to an end, and that standards of decency required that the Eighth Amendment be construed finally as prohibiting capital punishment for any crime regardless of its depravity and impact on society. This view was accepted by two Justices. Three other Justices were unwilling to go so far; focusing on the procedures by which convicted defendants were selected for the death penalty rather than on the actual punishment inflicted, they joined in the conclusion that the statutes before the Court were constitutionally invalid.

The petitioners in the capital cases before the Court today renew the "standards of decency" argument, but developments during the four years since *Furman* have undercut substantially the assumptions upon which their argument rested. Despite the continuing debate, dating back to the 19th century, over the morality and utility of capital punishment, it is now evident that a large proportion of American society continues to regard it as an appropriate and necessary criminal sanction.

The most marked indication of society's endorsement of the death penalty for murder is the legislative response to *Furman*. The legislatures of at least 35 States have enacted new statutes that provide for the death penalty for at least some crimes that result in the death of another person. And the Congress of the United States, in 1974, enacted a statute providing the death penalty for aircraft piracy that results in death. These recently adopted statutes have attempted to address the concerns expressed by the Court in *Furman* primarily (i) by specifying the factors to be weighed and the procedures to be followed in deciding when to impose a capital sentence, or (ii) by making the death penalty mandatory for specified crimes. But all of the post-*Furman* statutes make clear that capital punishment itself has not been rejected by the elected representatives of the people. . . .

The jury also is a significant and reliable objective index of contemporary values because it is so directly involved. The Court has said that "one of the most important functions any jury can perform in making . . . a selection [between life imprisonment and death for a defendant convicted in a capital case] is to maintain a link between contemporary community values and the penal system." It may be true that evolving standards have influenced juries in recent decades to be more discriminating in imposing the sentence of death. But the relative infrequency of jury verdicts imposing the death sentence does not indicate rejection of capital punishment *per se*. Rather, the reluctance of juries in many cases to impose the sentence may well reflect the humane feeling that this most irrevocable of sanctions should be reserved for a small number of extreme cases. Indeed, the actions of juries in many States since *Furman* are fully compatible with the legislative judgments, reflected in the new statutes, as to the continued utility and necessity of capital punishment in appropriate cases. At the close of 1974 at least 254 persons had been sentenced to death since *Furman,* and by the end of March 1976, more than 460 persons were subject to death sentences.

As we have seen, however, the Eighth Amendment demands more than that a challenged punishment be acceptable to contemporary society. The Court also must ask whether it comports with the basic concept of human dignity at the core of the Amendment. Although we cannot "invalidate a category of penalties because we deem less severe penalties adequate to serve the ends of penology," the sanction imposed cannot be so totally without penological justification that it results in the gratuitous infliction of suffering.

The death penalty is said to serve two principal social purposes: retribution and deterrence of capital crimes by prospective offenders.[1]

In part, capital punishment is an expression of society's moral outrage at particularly offensive conduct. This function may be unappealing to many, but it is essential in an ordered society that asks its citizens to rely on legal processes rather than self-help to vindicate their wrongs.

> The instinct of retribution is part of the nature of man, and channeling that instinct in the administration of criminal justice serves an important purpose in promoting the stability of a society governed by law. When people begin to believe that organized society is unwilling or unable to impose upon criminal offenders the punishment they "deserve," then there are sown the seeds of anarchy—of self-help, vigilante justice, and lynch law. *Furman v. Georgia* (Stewart, J., concurring).

"Retribution is no longer the dominant objective of the criminal law," but neither is it a forbidden objective nor one inconsistent with our respect for the dignity of men. Indeed, the decision that capital punishment may be the appropriate sanction in extreme cases is an expression of the community's belief that certain crimes are themselves so grievous an affront to humanity that the only adequate response may be the penalty of death.

Statistical attempts to evaluate the worth of the death penalty as a deterrent to crimes by potential offenders have occasioned a great deal of debate. The results simply have been inconclusive. . . .

Although some of the studies suggest that the death penalty may not function as a significantly greater deterrent than lesser penalties, there is no convincing empirical evidence either supporting or refuting this view. We may nevertheless assume safely that there are murderers, such as those who act in passion, for whom the threat of death has little or no deterrent effect. But for many others, the death penalty undoubtedly is a significant deterrent. There are carefully contemplated murders, such as murder for hire, where the possible penalty of death may well enter into the cold calculus that precedes the decision to act. And there are some categories of murder, such as murder by a life prisoner, where other sanctions may not be adequate.

The value of capital punishment as a deterrent of crime is a complex factual issue the resolution of which properly rests with the legislatures, which can evaluate the results of statistical studies in terms of their own local conditions and with a flexibility of approach that is not available to the courts. Indeed, many of the post-*Furman* statutes reflect just such a responsible effort to define those crimes and those criminals for which capital punishment is most probably an effective deterrent.

In sum, we cannot say that the judgment of the Georgia Legislature that capital punishment may be necessary in some cases is clearly wrong. Considerations of federalism, as well as respect for the ability of a legislature to evaluate, in terms of its particular State, the moral consensus concerning the death penalty and its social utility as a sanction, require us to conclude, in the absence of more convincing evidence, that the infliction of death as a punishment for murder is not without justification and thus is not unconstitutionally severe.

Finally, we must consider whether the punishment of death is disproportionate in relation to the crime for which it is imposed. There is no question that death as a punishment is unique in its severity and irrevocability. When a defendant's life is at stake, the Court has been particularly sensitive to insure that every safeguard is observed. But we are concerned here only with the imposition of capital punishment for the crime of murder, and when a life has been taken deliberately by the offender,[2] we cannot say that the punishment is invariably disproportionate to the crime. It is an extreme sanction, suitable to the most extreme of crimes.

We hold that the death penalty is not a form of punishment that may never be imposed, regardless of the circumstances of the offense, regardless of the character of the offender, and regardless of the procedure followed in reaching the decision to impose it.

IV

We now consider whether Georgia may impose the death penalty on the petitioner in this case.

A

While *Furman* did not hold that the infliction of the death penalty *per se* violates the Constitution's ban on cruel and unusual punishments, it did recognize that the penalty of death is different in kind from any other punishment imposed under our system of criminal justice. Because of the uniqueness of the death penalty, *Furman* held that it could not be imposed under sentencing procedures that created a substantial risk that it would be inflicted in an arbitrary and capricious manner. . . .

Furman mandates that where discretion is afforded a sentencing body on a matter so grave as the determination of whether a human life should be taken or spared, that discretion must be suitably directed and limited so as to minimize the risk of wholly arbitrary and capricious action.

It is certainly not a novel proposition that discretion in the area of sentencing be exercised in an informed manner. We have long recognized that "[f]or the determination of sentences, justice generally requires . . . that there be taken into account the circumstances of the offense together with the character and propensities of the offender." . . .

Jury sentencing has been considered desirable in capital cases in order "to maintain a link between contemporary community values and the penal system—a link without which the determination of punishment could hardly reflect 'the evolving standards of decency that mark the progress of a maturing society.'" But it creates special problems. Much of the information that is relevant to the sentencing decision may have no relevance to the question of guilt, or may even be extremely prejudicial to a fair determination of that question. This problem, however, is scarcely insurmountable. Those who have studied the question suggest that a bifurcated procedure—one in which the question of sentence is not considered until the determination of guilt has been made—is the best answer. . . . When a human life is at stake and when the jury must have information prejudicial to the question of guilt but relevant to the question of penalty in order to impose a rational sentence, a bifurcated system is more likely to ensure elimination of the constitutional deficiencies identified in *Furman.*

But the provision of relevant information under fair procedural rules is not alone sufficient to guarantee that the information will be properly used in the imposition of punishment, especially if sentencing is performed by a jury. Since the members of a jury will have had little, if any, previous experience in sentencing, they are unlikely to be skilled in dealing with the information they are given. To the extent that this problem is inherent in jury sentencing, it may not be totally correctable. It seems clear, however, that the problem will be alleviated if the jury is given guidance regarding the factors about the crime and the defendant that the State, representing organized society, deems particularly relevant to the sentencing decision. . . .

While some have suggested that standards to guide a capital jury's sentencing deliberations are impossible to formulate, the fact is that such standards have been developed. When the drafters of the Model Penal Code faced this problem, they concluded "that it is within the realm of possibility to point to the main circumstances of aggravation and of mitigation that should be weighed *and weighed against each other* when they are presented in a concrete case.[3] While such standards are by necessity somewhat general, they do provide guidance to the sentencing authority and thereby reduce the likelihood that it will impose a sentence that fairly can be called capricious or arbitrary. Where the sentencing authority is required to specify the factors it relied upon in reaching its decision, the further safeguard of meaningful appellate review is available to ensure that death sentences are not imposed capriciously or in a freakish manner.

In summary, the concerns expressed in *Furman* that the penalty of death not be imposed in an arbitrary or capricious manner can be met by a carefully drafted statute that ensures that the sentencing authority is given adequate information and guidance. As a general proposition these concerns are best met by a system that provides for a bifurcated proceeding at which the sentencing authority is apprised of the information relevant to the imposition of sentence and provided with standards to guide its use of the information.

We do not intend to suggest that only the above-described procedures would be permissible under *Furman* or that any sentencing system constructed along these general lines would inevitably satisfy the concerns of *Furman,* for each distinct system must be examined on an individual basis. Rather, we have embarked upon this general exposition to make clear that it is possible to construct capital-sentencing systems capable of meeting *Furman*'s constitutional concerns.

B

We now turn to consideration of the constitutionality of Georgia's capital-sentencing procedures. In the wake of *Furman,* Georgia amended its capital punishment statute, but chose not to narrow the scope of its murder provisions. Thus, now as before *Furman,* in Georgia "[a] person commits murder when he unlawfully and with malice aforethought, either express or implied, causes the death of another human being." All persons convicted of murder "shall be punished by death or by imprisonment for life."

Georgia did act, however, to narrow the class of murderers subject to capital punishment by specifying 10 statutory aggravating circumstances, one of which must be found by the jury to exist beyond a reasonable doubt before a death sentence can ever be imposed. In addition, the jury is authorized to consider any other appropriate aggravating or mitigating circumstances. The jury is not required to find any mitigating circumstance in order to make a recommendation of mercy that is binding on the trial court, but it must find a *statutory* aggravating circumstance before recommending a sentence of death.

These procedures require the jury to consider the circumstances of the crime and the criminal before it recommends sentence. No longer can a Georgia jury do as Furman's jury did: reach a finding of the defendant's guilt and then, without guidance or direction, decide whether he should live or die. Instead, the jury's attention is directed to the specific circumstances of the crime: Was it committed in the course of another capital felony? Was it committed for money? Was it committed upon a peace officer or judicial officer? Was it committed in a particularly heinous way or in a manner that endangered the lives of many persons? In addition, the jury's attention is focused on the characteristics of the person who committed the crime: Does he have a record of prior convictions for capital offenses? Are there any special facts about this defendant that mitigate against imposing capital punishment (*e.g.,* his youth, the extent of his cooperation with the police, his emotional state at the time of the crime). As a result, while some jury discretion still exists, "the discretion to be exercised is controlled by clear and objective standards so as to produce non-discriminatory application."

As an important additional safeguard against arbitrariness and caprice, the Georgia statutory scheme provides for automatic appeal of all death sentences to the State's Supreme Court. That court is required by statute to review each sentence of death and determine whether it was imposed under the influence of passion or prejudice, whether the evidence supports the jury's finding of a statutory aggravating circumstance, and whether the sentence is disproportionate compared to those sentences imposed in similar cases.

In short, Georgia's new sentencing procedures require as a prerequisite to the imposition of the death penalty specific jury findings as to the circumstances of the crime or the character of the defendant. Moreover, to guard further against a situation comparable to that presented in *Furman,* the Supreme Court of Georgia compares each death sentence with the sentences imposed on similarly situated defendants to ensure that the sentence of death in a particular case is not disproportionate. On their face these procedures seem to satisfy the concerns of *Furman.* No longer should there be "no meaningful basis for distinguishing the few cases in which [the death penalty] is imposed from the many cases in which it is not." . . .

V

The basic concern of *Furman* centered on those defendants who were being condemned to death capriciously and arbitrarily. Under the procedures before the Court in that case, sentencing authorities were not directed to give attention to the nature or circumstances of the crime committed or to the character or record of the defendant. Left unguided, juries imposed the death sentence in a way that could only be called freakish. The new Georgia sentencing procedures, by contrast, focus the jury's attention on the particularized nature of the crime and the particularized characteristics of the individual defendant. While the jury is permitted to consider any aggravating or mitigating circumstances, it must find and identify at least one statutory aggravating factor before it may impose a penalty of death. In this way the jury's discretion is channeled. No longer can a jury wantonly and freakishly impose the death sentence; it is always circumscribed by the legislative guidelines. In addition, the review function of the Supreme Court of Georgia affords additional assurance that the concerns that prompted our decision in *Furman* are not present to any significant degree in the Georgia procedure applied here.

For the reasons expressed in this opinion, we hold that the statutory system under which Gregg was sentenced to death does not violate the Constitution. Accordingly, the judgment of the Georgia Supreme Court is affirmed.

NOTES

1 Another purpose that has been discussed is the incapacitation of dangerous criminals and the consequent prevention of crimes that they may otherwise commit in the future.
2 We do not address here the question whether the taking of the criminal's life is a proportionate sanction where no victim has been deprived of life—for example, when capital punishment is imposed for rape, kidnaping, or armed robbery that does not result in the death of any human being.
3 The Model Penal Code proposes the following standards:
   "(3) Aggravating Circumstances.
   "(a) The murder was committed by a convict under sentence of imprisonment.
   "(b) The defendant was previously convicted of another murder or of a felony involving the use or threat of violence to the person.
   "(c) At the time the murder was committed the defendant also committed another murder.
   "(d) The defendant knowingly created a great risk of death to many persons.
   "(e) The murder was committed while the defendant was engaged or was an accomplice in the commission of, or an attempt to commit, or flight after committing or attempting to commit robbery, rape or deviate sexual intercourse by force or threat of force, arson, burglary or kidnaping.
   "(f) The murder was committed for the purpose of avoiding or preventing a lawful arrest or effecting an escape from lawful custody.
   "(g) The murder was committed for pecuniary gain.
   "(h) The murder was especially heinous, atrocious or cruel, manifesting exceptional depravity.
   "(4) Mitigating Circumstances.
   "(a) The defendant has no significant history of prior criminal activity.
   "(b) The murder was committed while the defendant was under the influence of extreme mental or emotional disturbance.

"(c) The victim was a participant in the defendant's homicidal conduct or consented to the homicidal act.
"(d) The murder was committed under circumstances which the defendant believed to provide a moral justification or extenuation for his conduct.
"(e) The defendant was an accomplice in a murder committed by another person and his participation in the homicidal act was relatively minor.
"(f) The defendant acted under duress or under the domination of another person.
"(g) At the time of the murder, the capacity of the defendant to appreciate the criminality [wrongfulness] of his conduct or to conform his conduct to the requirements of law was impaired as a result of mental disease or defect or intoxication.
"(h) The youth of the defendant at the time of the crime." ALI Model Penal Code § 210.6 (Proposed Official Draft 1962).

QUESTIONS

1 With regard to the imposition of the death penalty for the crime of murder, Justices Stewart, Powell, and Stevens write, "We cannot say that the punishment is invariably disproportionate to the crime." The Georgia statute under which Gregg was sentenced, however, retained the death penalty not only for the crime of murder but also for "kidnaping for ransom or where the victim is harmed, armed robbery, rape, treason, and aircraft hijacking." In your view, is the death penalty a disproportionate punishment for such crimes?
2 In note 3, we find a set of proposed model standards for the guidance of a jury in deciding whether a murderer warrants the death penalty or a lesser penalty—typically, life imprisonment. Is the proposed set of aggravating circumstances (those whose presence should incline a jury toward the death penalty) defensible and complete? Is the proposed set of mitigating circumstances (those whose presence should incline a jury away from the death penalty) defensible and complete?

Dissenting Opinion in *Gregg v. Georgia*

Justice Thurgood Marshall

Justice Marshall reaffirms the conclusion he had reached in *Furman v. Georgia* (1972): The death penalty is unconstitutional for two individually sufficient reasons. (1) It is excessive. (2) The American people, if fully informed, would consider it morally unacceptable. He insists that his conclusion in *Furman* has not been undercut by subsequent developments. Despite the fact that legislative activity since *Furman* would seem to indicate that the American people do not consider the death penalty morally unacceptable, Justice Marshall continues to maintain that the citizenry, *if fully informed,* would consider it morally unacceptable. At any rate, he maintains, the death penalty is unconstitutional

United States Supreme Court. 428 U.S. 153 (1976).

because it is excessive—that is, unnecessary to accomplish a legitimate legislative purpose. Neither deterrence nor retribution, the principal purposes asserted by Justices Stewart, Powell, and Stevens, can sustain the death penalty as nonexcessive in Justice Marshall's view. Since the available evidence does not show the death penalty to be a more effective deterrent than life imprisonment, he contends, the death penalty is not necessary to promote the goal of deterrence. Moreover, the death penalty is unnecessary to "further any legitimate notion of retribution." According to Justice Marshall, the notion that a murderer "deserves" death constitutes a denial of the wrongdoer's dignity and worth and, thus, is fundamentally at odds with the Eighth Amendment.

In *Furman v. Georgia* (1972) (concurring opinion), I set forth at some length my views on the basic issue presented to the Court in [this case]. The death penalty, I concluded, is a cruel and unusual punishment prohibited by the Eighth and Fourteenth Amendments. That continues to be my view.

I have no intention of retracing the "long and tedious journey" that led to my conclusion in *Furman*. My sole purposes here are to consider the suggestion that my conclusion in *Furman* has been undercut by developments since then, and briefly to evaluate the basis for my Brethren's holding that the extinction of life is a permissible form of punishment under the Cruel and Unusual Punishments Clause.

In *Furman* I concluded that the death penalty is constitutionally invalid for two reasons. First, the death penalty is excessive. And second, the American people, fully informed as to the purposes of the death penalty and its liabilities, would in my view reject it as morally unacceptable.

Since the decision in *Furman*, the legislatures of 35 States have enacted new statutes authorizing the imposition of the death sentence for certain crimes, and Congress has enacted a law providing the death penalty for air piracy resulting in death. I would be less than candid if I did not acknowledge that these developments have a significant bearing on a realistic assessment of the moral acceptability of the death penalty to the American people. But if the constitutionality of the death penalty turns, as I have urged, on the opinion of an *informed* citizenry, then even the enactment of new death statutes cannot be viewed as conclusive. In *Furman*, I observed that the American people are largely unaware of the information critical to a judgment on the morality of the death penalty, and concluded that if they were better informed they would consider it shocking, unjust, and unacceptable. A recent study, conducted after the enactment of the post-*Furman* statutes, has confirmed that the American people know little about the death penalty, and that the opinions of an informed public would differ significantly from those of a public unaware of the consequences and effects of the death penalty.

Even assuming, however, that the post-*Furman* enactment of statutes authorizing the death penalty renders the prediction of the views of an informed citizenry an uncertain basis for a constitutional decision, the enactment of those statutes has no bearing whatsoever on the conclusion that the death penalty is unconstitutional because it is excessive. An excessive penalty is invalid under the Cruel and Unusual Punishments Clause "even though popular sentiment may favor" it. The inquiry here, then, is simply whether the death penalty is necessary to accomplish the legitimate legislative purposes in punishment, or whether a less severe penalty—life imprisonment—would do as well.

The two purposes that sustain the death penalty as nonexcessive in the Court's view are general deterrence and retribution. In *Furman,* I canvassed the relevant data on the deterrent effect of capital punishment. The state of knowledge at that point, after literally centuries of debate, was summarized as follows by a United Nations Committee:

> It is generally agreed between the retentionists and abolitionists, whatever their opinions about the validity of comparative studies of deterrence, that the data which now exist show no correlation between the existence of capital punishment and lower rates of capital crime.

The available evidence, I concluded in *Furman,* was convincing that "capital punishment is not necessary as a deterrent to crime in our society." . . .

. . . The evidence I reviewed in *Furman* remains convincing, in my view, that "capital punishment is not necessary as a deterrent to crime in our society." The justification for the death penalty must be found elsewhere.

The other principal purpose said to be served by the death penalty is retribution. The notion that retribution can serve as a moral justification for the sanction of death finds credence in the opinion of my Brothers STEWART, POWELL, and STEVENS. . . . It is this notion that I find to be the most disturbing aspect of today's unfortunate [decision].

The concept of retribution is a multifaceted one, and any discussion of its role in the criminal law must be undertaken with caution. On one level, it can be said that the notion of retribution or reprobation is the basis of our insistence that only those who have broken the law be punished, and in this sense the notion is quite obviously central to a just system of criminal sanctions. But our recognition that retribution plays a crucial role in determining who may be punished by no means requires approval of retribution as a general justification for punishment. It is the question whether retribution can provide a moral justification for punishment—in particular, capital punishment—that we must consider.

My Brothers STEWART, POWELL, and STEVENS offer the following explanation of the retributive justification for capital punishment:

> The instinct for retribution is part of the nature of man, and channeling that instinct in the administration of criminal justice serves an important purpose in promoting the stability of a society governed by law. When people begin to believe that organized society is unwilling or unable to impose upon criminal offenders the punishment they "deserve," then there are sown the seeds of anarchy—of self-help, vigilante justice, and lynch law.

This statement is wholly inadequate to justify the death penalty. As my Brother BRENNAN stated in *Furman,* "[t]here is no evidence whatever that utilization of imprisonment rather than death encourages private blood feuds and other disorders." It simply defies belief to suggest that the death penalty is necessary to prevent the American people from taking the law into their own hands.

In a related vein, it may be suggested that the expression of moral outrage through the imposition of the death penalty serves to reinforce basic moral values—that it marks some crimes as particularly offensive and therefore to be avoided. The argument is akin to a deterrence argument, but differs in that it contemplates the individual's shrinking from antisocial conduct, not because he fears punishment, but because he has been told in the strongest possible way that the conduct is wrong. This contention, like the previous one, provides no support for the death penalty. It is inconceivable that any individual concerned about conforming his conduct to what society says is "right" would fail to realize that murder is "wrong" if the penalty were simply life imprisonment.

The foregoing contentions—that society's expression of moral outrage through the imposition of the death penalty pre-empts the citizenry from taking the law into its own hands and reinforces moral values—are not retributive in the purest sense. They are essentially utilitarian in that they portray the death penalty as valuable because of its beneficial results. These justifications for the death penalty are inadequate because the penalty is, quite clearly I think, not necessary to the accomplishment of those results.

There remains for consideration, however, what might be termed the purely retributive justification for the death penalty—that the death penalty is appropriate, not because of its beneficial effect on society, but because the taking of the murderer's life is itself morally good. Some of the language of the opinion of my Brothers STEWART, POWELL, and STEVENS . . . appears positively to embrace this notion of retribution for its own sake as a justification for capital punishment. They state:

> [T]he decision that capital punishment may be the appropriate sanction in extreme cases is an expression of the community's belief that certain crimes are themselves so grievous an affront to humanity that the only adequate response may be the penalty of death.

They then quote with approval from Lord Justice Denning's remarks before the British Royal Commission on Capital Punishment:

> The truth is that some crimes are so outrageous that society insists on adequate punishment, because the wrong-doer deserves it, irrespective of whether it is a deterrent or not.

Of course, it may be that these statements are intended as no more than observations as to the popular demands that it is thought must be responded to in order to prevent anarchy. But the implication of the statements appears to me to be quite different—namely, that society's judgment that the murderer "deserves" death must be respected not simply because the preservation of order requires it, but because it is appropriate that society make the judgment and carry it out. It is this latter notion, in particular, that I consider to be fundamentally at odds with the Eighth Amendment. The mere fact that the community demands the murderer's life in return for the evil he has done cannot sustain the death penalty, for as JUSTICES STEWART, POWELL, and STEVENS remind us, "the Eighth Amendment demands more than that a challenged punishment be acceptable to contemporary society." To be sustained under the Eighth Amendment, the death penalty must "compor[t] with the basic concept of human dignity at the core of the Amendment;" the objective in imposing it must be "[consistent] with our respect for the dignity of [other] men." Under these standards, the taking of life "because the wrongdoer deserves it" surely must fail, for such a punishment has as its very basis the total denial of the wrongdoer's dignity and worth.

The death penalty, unnecessary to promote the goal of deterrence or to further any legitimate notion of retribution, is an excessive penalty forbidden by the Eighth and Fourteenth Amendments. I respectfully dissent from the Court's judgment upholding the [sentence] of death imposed upon the [petitioner in this case].

QUESTIONS

1 Is Justice Marshall correct in claiming that the American people, *if fully informed* about the death penalty, would consider it morally unacceptable?
2 Is the death penalty, as Justice Marshall claims, "unnecessary to promote the goal of deterrence or to further any legitimate notion of retribution"?

A Life for a Life

Igor Primoratz

Primoratz endorses a retributive rationale for the retention of the death penalty and defends this rationale against commonly made abolitionist arguments. He rejects the idea that the death penalty violates a murderer's right to life and insists that there is no contradiction involved in a system of criminal law that prohibits murder and yet allows the state to administer the death penalty. He also defends the retributive rationale against arguments claiming to show that the death penalty is in reality a disproportionate penalty for the crime of murder. Finally, Primoratz argues that neither the possibility of executing an innocent person nor the discriminatory application of the death penalty can provide a credible basis for abolition.

. . . According to the retributive theory, consequences of punishment, however important from the practical point of view, are irrelevant when it comes to its justification; *the* moral consideration is its justice. Punishment is morally justified insofar as it is meted out as retribution for the offense committed. When someone has committed an offense, he deserves to be punished: it is just, and consequently justified, that he be punished. The offense is the sole ground of the state's right and duty to punish. It is also the measure of legitimate punishment: the two ought to be proportionate. So the issue of capital punishment within the retributive approach comes down to the question, Is this punishment ever proportionate retribution for the offense committed, and thus deserved, just, and justified?

The classic representatives of retributivism believed that it was, and that it was the only proportionate and hence appropriate punishment, if the offense was *murder*— that is, criminal homicide perpetrated voluntarily and intentionally or in wanton

From Igor Primoratz, *Justifying Legal Punishment* (1989), pp. 158–159, 161–166. Reprinted with the permission of Humanities Press International, Atlantic Highlands, NJ.

disregard of human life. In other cases, the demand for proportionality between offense and punishment can be satisfied by fines or prison terms;[1] the crime of murder, however, is an exception in this respect, and calls for the literal interpretation of the *lex talionis*. The uniqueness of this crime has to do with the uniqueness of the value which has been deliberately or recklessly destroyed. We come across this idea as early as the original formulation of the retributive view—the biblical teaching on punishment: "You shall accept no ransom for the life of a murderer who is guilty of death; but he shall be put to death."[2] The rationale of this command—one that clearly distinguishes the biblical conception of the criminal law from contemporaneous criminal law systems in the Middle East—is that man was not only created *by* God, like every other creature, but also, alone among all the creatures, *in the image of God:*

> That man was made in the image of God . . . is expressive of the peculiar and supreme worth of man. Of all creatures, Genesis 1 relates, he alone possesses this attribute, bringing him into closer relation to God than all the rest and conferring upon him the highest value. . . . This view of the uniqueness and supremacy of human life. . . places life beyond the reach of other values. The idea that life may be measured in terms of money or other property. . . is excluded. Compensation of any kind is ruled out. The guilt of the murderer is infinite because the murdered life is invaluable; the kinsmen of the slain man are not competent to say when he has been paid for. An absolute wrong has been committed, a sin against God which is not subject to human discussion. . . . Because human life is invaluable, to take it entails the death penalty.[3]

This view that the value of human life is not commensurable with other values, and that consequently there is only one truly equivalent punishment for murder, namely death, does not necessarily presuppose a theistic outlook. It can be claimed that, simply because we have to be alive if we are to experience and realize any other value at all, there is nothing equivalent to the murderous destruction of a human life except the destruction of the life of the murderer. Any other retribution, no matter how severe, would still be less than what is proportionate, deserved, and just. As long as the murderer is alive, no matter how bad the conditions of his life may be, there are always at least *some* values he can experience and realize. This provides a plausible interpretation of what the classical representatives of retributivism as a philosophical theory of punishment, such as Kant and Hegel, had to say on the subject.[4]

It seems to me that this is essentially correct. With respect to the larger question of the justification of punishment in general, it is the retributive theory that gives the right answer. Accordingly, capital punishment ought to be retained where it obtains, and reintroduced in those jurisdictions that have abolished it, although we have no reason to believe that, as a means of deterrence, it is any better than a very long prison term. It ought to be retained, or reintroduced, for one simple reason: that justice be done in cases of murder, that murderers be punished according to their deserts.

There are a number of arguments that have been advanced against this rationale of capital punishment. . . .

[One] abolitionist argument . . . simply says that capital punishment is illegitimate because it violates the right to life, which is a fundamental, absolute, sacred right belonging to each and every human being, and therefore ought to be respected even in a murderer.[5]

If any rights are fundamental, the right to life is certainly one of them; but to claim that it is absolute, inviolable under any circumstances and for any reason, is a different matter. If an abolitionist wants to argue his case by asserting an absolute right to life, she will also have to deny moral legitimacy to taking human life in war, revolution, and self-defense. This kind of pacifism is a consistent but farfetched and hence implausible position.

I do not believe that the right to life (nor, for that matter, any other right) is absolute. I have no general theory of rights to fall back upon here; instead, let me pose a question. Would we take seriously the claim to an absolute, sacred, inviolable right to life—coming from the mouth of a *confessed murderer*? I submit that we would not, for the obvious reason that it is being put forward by the person who confessedly denied another human being this very right. But if the murderer cannot plausibly claim such a right for himself, neither can *anyone else* do that in his behalf. This suggests that there is an element of reciprocity in our general rights, such as the right to life or property. I can convincingly claim these rights only so long as I acknowledge and respect the same rights of others. If I violate the rights of others, I thereby lose the same rights. If I am a murderer, I have no *right* to live.

Some opponents of capital punishment claim that a criminal law system which includes this punishment is contradictory, in that it prohibits murder and at the same time provides for its perpetration: "It is one and the same legal regulation which prohibits the individual from murdering, while allowing the state to murder. . . . This is obviously a terrible irony, an abnormal and immoral logic, against which everything in us revolts."[6]

This seems to be one of the more popular arguments against the death penalty, but it is not a good one. If it were valid, it would prove too much. Exactly the same might be claimed of other kinds of punishment: of prison terms, that they are "contradictory" to the legal protection of liberty; of fines, that they are "contradictory" to the legal protection of property. Fortunately enough, it is not valid, for it begs the question at issue. In order to be able to talk of the state as "murdering" the person it executes, and to claim that there is "an abnormal and immoral logic" at work here, which thrives on a "contradiction," one has to use the word "murder" in the very same sense—that is, in the usual sense, which implies the idea of the *wrongful* taking the life of another—both when speaking of what the murderer has done to the victim and of what the state is doing to him by way of punishment. But this is precisely the question at issue: whether capital punishment *is* "murder," whether it is wrongful or morally justified and right.

The next two arguments attack the retributive rationale of capital punishment by questioning the claim that it is only this punishment that satisfies the demand for proportion between offense and punishment in the case of murder. The first points out that any two human lives are different in many important respects, such as age, health, physical and mental capability, so that it does not make much sense to consider them equally valuable. What if the murdered person was very old, practically at the very end of her natural life, while the murderer is young, with most of his life still ahead of him, for instance? Or if the victim was gravely and incurably ill, and thus doomed to live her life in suffering and hopelessness, without being able to experience almost anything that makes a human life worth living, while the murderer is in every respect capable of experiencing and enjoying things life has to offer? Or the other way round? Would not the death penalty in such cases amount either to taking a more valuable life as a punishment for destroying a less valuable one, or *vice versa*? Would it not be either too much, or too little, and in both cases disproportionate, and thus unjust and wrong, from the standpoint of the retributive theory itself?[7]

Any plausibility this argument might appear to have is the result of a conflation of differences between, and value of, human lives. No doubt, any two human lives are *different* in innumerable ways, but this does not entail that they are not *equally valuable*. I have no worked-out general theory of equality to refer to here, but I do not think that one is necessary in order to do away with this argument. The modern humanistic and democratic tradition in ethical, social, and political thought is based on the idea that all human beings are equal. This finds its legal expression in the principle of equality of people under the law. If we are not willing to give up this principle, we have to stick to the assumption that, all differences notwithstanding, any two human lives, *qua* human lives, are equally valuable. If, on the other hand, we allow that, on the basis of such criteria as age, health, or mental or physical ability, it can be claimed that the life of one person is more or less valuable than the life of another, and we admit such claims in the sphere of law, including criminal law, we shall thereby give up the principle of equality of people under the law. In all consistency, we shall not be able to demand that property, physical and personal integrity, and all other rights and interests of individuals be given equal consideration in courts of law either—that is, we shall have to accept systematic discrimination between individuals on the basis of the same criteria across the whole field. I do not think anyone would seriously contemplate an overhaul of the whole legal system along these lines.

The second argument having to do with the issue of proportionality between murder and capital punishment draws our attention to the fact that the law normally provides for a certain period of time to elapse between the passing of a death sentence and its execution. It is a period of several weeks or months; in some cases it extends to years. This period is bound to be one of constant mental anguish for the condemned. And thus, all things considered, what is inflicted on him is disproportionately hard and hence unjust. It would be proportionate and just only in the case of "a criminal who had warned his victim of the date at which he would inflict a horrible death on him and who, from that moment onward, had confined him at his mercy for months."[8]

The first thing to note about this argument is that it does not support a full-fledged abolitionist stand; if it were valid, it would not show that capital punishment is *never* proportionate and just, but only that it is *very rarely* so. Consequently, the conclusion would not be that it ought to be abolished outright, but only that it ought to be restricted to those cases that would satisfy the condition cited above. Such cases do happen, although, to be sure, not very often; the murder of Aldo Moro, for instance, was of this kind. But this is not the main point. The main point is that the argument actually does not hit at capital punishment itself, although it is presented with that aim in view. It hits at something else: a particular way of carrying out this punishment, which is widely adopted in our time. Some hundred years ago and more, in the Wild West, they frequently hanged the man convicted to die almost immediately after pronouncing the sentence. I am not arguing here that we should follow this example today; I mention this piece of historical fact only in order to show that the interval between sentencing someone to death and carrying out the sentence is not a *part* of capital punishment itself. However unpalatable we might find those Wild West hangings, whatever objections we might want to voice against the speed with which they followed the sentencing, surely we shall not deny them the *description* of "executions." So the implication of the argument is not that we ought to do away with capital punishment altogether, nor that we ought to restrict it to those cases of murder where the murderer had warned the victim weeks or months in advance of what he was going to do to her, but that we ought to reexamine the procedure of carrying out this kind of punishment. We ought to weigh the reasons for having this interval between the sentencing and executing against the moral and human significance of the repercussions such an interval inevitably carries with it.

These reasons, in part, have to do with the possibility of miscarriages of justice and the need to rectify them. Thus we come to the argument against capital punishment which, historically, has been the most effective of all: many advances of the abolitionist movement have been connected with discoveries of cases of judicial errors. Judges and jurors are only human, and consequently some of their beliefs and decisions are bound to be mistaken. Some of their mistakes can be corrected upon discovery; but precisely those with most disastrous repercussions— those which result in innocent people being executed—can never be rectified. In all other cases of mistaken sentencing we can revoke the punishment, either completely or in part, or at least extend compensation. In addition, by exonerating the accused we give moral satisfaction. None of this is possible after an innocent person has been executed; capital punishment is essentially different from all other penalties by being completely irrevocable and irreparable.[9] Therefore, it ought to be abolished.

A part of my reply to this argument goes along the same lines as what I had to say on the previous one. It is not so far-reaching as abolitionists assume; for it would be quite implausible, even fanciful, to claim that there have *never* been cases of murder which left no room whatever for reasonable doubt as to the guilt and full responsibility of the accused. Such cases may not be more frequent than those others, but they do happen. Why not retain the death penalty at least for them?

Actually, this argument, just as the preceding one, does not speak out against capital punishment itself, but against the existing procedures for trying capital cases. Miscarriages of justice result in innocent people being sentenced to death and executed, even in the criminal law systems in which greatest care is taken to ensure that it never comes to that. But this does not stem from the intrinsic nature of the institution of capital punishment; it results from deficiencies, limitations, and imperfections of the criminal law procedures in which this punishment is meted out. Errors of justice do not demonstrate the need to do away with capital punishment; they simply make it incumbent on us to do everything possible to improve even further procedures of meting it out.

To be sure, this conclusion will not find favor with a diehard abolitionist. "I shall ask for the abolition of Capital Punishment until I have the infallibility of human judgement demonstrated to me," that is, as long as there is even the slightest possibility that innocent people may be executed because of judicial errors, Lafayette said in his day.[10] Many an opponent of this kind of punishment will say the same today. The demand to do away with capital punishment altogether, so as to eliminate even the smallest chance of that ever happening—the chance which, admittedly, would remain even after everything humanly possible has been done to perfect the procedure, although then it would be very slight indeed—is actually a demand to give a privileged position to murderers as against all other offenders, big and small. For if we acted on this demand, we would bring about a situation in which proportionate penalties would be meted out for all offenses, *except* for murder. Murderers would not be receiving the only punishment truly proportionate to their crimes, the punishment of death, but some other, lighter, and thus disproportionate penalty. All other offenders would be punished according to their deserts; only murderers would be receiving less than *they* deserve. In all other cases justice would be done in full; only in cases of the gravest of offenses, the crime of murder, justice would not be carried out in full measure. It is a great and tragic miscarriage of justice when an innocent person is mistakenly sentenced to death and executed, but systematically giving murderers advantage over all other offenders would also be a grave injustice. Is the fact that, as long as capital punishment is retained, there is a possibility that over a number of years, or even decades, an injustice of the first kind may be committed, unintentionally and unconsciously, reason enough to abolish it altogether, and thus end up with a system of punishments in which injustices of the second kind are perpetrated daily, consciously, and inevitably?[11]

There is still another abolitionist argument that actually does not hit out against capital punishment itself, but against something else. Figures are sometimes quoted which show that this punishment is much more often meted out to the uneducated and poor than to the educated, rich, and influential people; in the United States, much more often to blacks than to whites. These figures are adduced as a proof of the inherent injustice of this kind of punishment. On account of them, it is claimed that capital punishment is not a way of doing justice by meting out deserved punishment to murderers, but rather a means of social discrimination and perpetuation of social injustice.

I shall not question these findings, which are quite convincing, and anyway, there is no need to do that in order to defend the institution of capital punishment. For there seems to be a certain amount of discrimination and injustice not only in sentencing people to death and executing them, but also in meting out other penalties. The social structure of the death rows in American prisons, for instance, does not seem to be basically different from the general social structure of American penitentiaries. If this argument were valid, it would call not only for abolition of the penalty of death, but for doing away with other penalties as well. But it is not valid; as Burton Leiser has pointed out,

> . . . this is not an argument, either against the death penalty or against any other form of punishment. It is an argument against the unjust and inequitable distribution of penalties.

If the trials of wealthy men are less likely to result in convictions than those of poor men, then something must be done to reform the procedure in criminal courts. If those who have money and standing in the community are less likely to be charged with serious offenses than their less affluent fellow citizens, then there should be a major overhaul of the entire system of criminal justice. . . . But the maldistribution of penalties is no argument against any particular form of penalty.[12]

NOTES

1 Cf. I. Primoratz, *Justifying Legal Punishment* (Atlantic Highlands, N.J.: Humanities Press, 1989), pp. 85–94.
2 Numbers 35.31 (R.S.V.).
3 M. Greenberg, "Some Postulates of Biblical Criminal Law," in J. Goldin (ed.), *The Jewish Expression* (New York: Bantam, 1970), pp. 25–26. (Post-biblical Jewish law evolved toward the virtual abolition of the death penalty, but that is of no concern here.)
4 "There is no *parallel* between death and even the most miserable life, so that there is no equality of crime and retribution [in the case of murder] unless the perpetrator is judicially put to death" (I. Kant, "The Metaphysics of Morals," *Kant's Political Writings,* ed. H. Reiss, trans. H. B. Nisbet [Cambridge: Cambridge University Press, 1970], p. 156). "Since life is the full compass of a man's existence, the punishment [for murder] cannot simply consist in a 'value', for none is great enough, but can consist only in taking away a second life" (G. W. F. Hegel, *Philosophy of Right,* trans. T. M. Knox [Oxford: Oxford University Press, 1965], p. 247).
5 For an example of this view, see L. N. Tolstoy, *Smertnaya kazn i hristianstvo* (Berlin: I. P. Ladizhnikov, n.d.), pp. 40–41.
6 S. V. Vulović, *Problem smrtne kazne* (Belgrade: Geca Kon, 1925), pp. 23–24.
7 Cf. W. Blackstone, *Commentaries on the Laws of England,* 4th ed., ed. J. DeWitt Andrews (Chicago: Callaghan & Co., 1899), p. 1224.
8 A. Camus, "Reflections on the Guillotine," *Resistance, Rebellion and Death,* trans. J. O'Brien (London: Hamish Hamilton, 1961), p. 143.
9 For an interesting critical discussion of this point, see M. Davis, "Is the Death Penalty Irrevocable?" *Social Theory and Practice* 10 (1984).
10 Quoted in E. R. Calvert, *Capital Punishment in the Twentieth Century* (London: G. P. Putnam's Sons, 1927), p. 132.
11 For a criticism of this argument, see L. Sebba, "On Capital Punishment—a Comment," *Israel Law Review* 17 (1982), pp. 392–395.
12 B. M. Leiser, *Liberty, Justice and Morals: Contemporary Value Conflicts* (New York: Macmillan, 1973), p. 225.

QUESTIONS

1 Would you endorse a retributive rationale for the retention of the death penalty? If so, would you say that *all* murderers deserve to die or just *some*? If just some deserve to die, which ones?
2 If blacks are more likely to receive the death penalty than whites, if the poor and uneducated are more likely to receive the death penalty than the affluent and educated, does it follow that we should abolish the death penalty?

An Eye for an Eye?

Stephen Nathanson

Nathanson, an abolitionist, distinguishes between *equality* retributivism and *proportional* retributivism and argues that neither of these retributive approaches can provide a justification for the death penalty. In his view: (1) Equality retributivism—committed to the principle that punishment should be equal to the crime ("an eye for an eye")—fails because it does not provide a systematically satisfactory criterion for determining appropriate punishment. (2) Proportional retributivism—committed to the principle that punishment should be proportional to the crime—fails because it does not require that murderers be executed. Nathanson also argues that a societal decision to abolish the death penalty would convey two important symbolic messages. First, we would thereby express our respect for the dignity of all human beings, even those guilty of murder. Second, in restraining the expression of our anger against murderers, we would reinforce the conviction that only defensive violence is justifiable.

Suppose we . . . try to determine what people deserve from a strictly moral point of view. How shall we proceed?

The most usual suggestion is that we look at a person's actions because what someone deserves would appear to depend on what he or she does. A person's actions, it seems, provide not only a basis for a moral appraisal of the person but also a guide to how he should be treated. According to the *lex talionis* or principle of "an eye for an eye," we ought to treat people as they have treated others. What people deserve as recipients of rewards or punishments is determined by what they do as agents.

This is a powerful and attractive view, one that appears to be backed not only by moral common sense but also by tradition and philosophical thought. The most famous statement of philosophical support for this view comes from Immanuel Kant, who linked it directly with an argument for the death penalty. Discussing the problem of punishment, Kant writes,

> What kind and what degree of punishment does legal justice adopt as its principle and standard? None other than the principle of equality . . . the principle of not treating one side more favorably than the other. Accordingly, any undeserved evil that you inflict on someone else among the people is one that you do to yourself. If you vilify, you vilify yourself; if you steal from him, you steal from yourself; if you kill him, you kill yourself. Only the law of retribution (*jus talionis*) can determine exactly the kind and degree of punishment.[1]

Kant's view is attractive for a number of reasons. First, it accords with our belief that what a person deserves is related to what he does. Second, it appeals to a moral standard and does not seem to rely on any particular legal or political institutions.

Reprinted with permission of Rowman & Littlefield, Publishers, from Stephen Nathanson, *An Eye for an Eye?* (1987), pp. 72–77, 138–140, 145.

Third, it seems to provide a measure of appropriate punishment that can be used as a guide to creating laws and instituting punishments. It tells us that the punishment is to be identical with the crime. Whatever the criminal did to the victim is to be done in turn to the criminal.

In spite of the attractions of Kant's view, it is deeply flawed. When we see why, it will be clear that the whole "eye for an eye" perspective must be rejected.

PROBLEMS WITH THE EQUAL PUNISHMENT PRINCIPLE

. . . [Kant's view] does not provide an adequate criterion for determining appropriate levels of punishment.

. . . We can see this, first, by noting that for certain crimes, Kant's view recommends punishments that are not morally acceptable. Applied strictly, it would require that we rape rapists, torture torturers, and burn arsonists whose acts have led to deaths. In general, where a particular crime involves barbaric and inhuman treatment, Kant's principle tells us to act barbarically and inhumanly in return. So, in some cases, the principle generates unacceptable answers to the question of what constitutes appropriate punishment.

This is not its only defect. In many other cases, the principle tells us nothing at all about how to punish. While Kant thought it obvious how to apply his principle in the case of murder, his principle cannot serve as a general rule because it does not tell us how to punish many crimes. Using the Kantian version or the more common "eye for an eye" standard, what would we decide to do to embezzlers, spies, drunken drivers, airline hijackers, drug users, prostitutes, air polluters, or persons who practice medicine without a license? If one reflects on this question, it becomes clear that there is simply no answer to it. We could not in fact design a system of punishment simply on the basis of the "eye for an eye" principle.

In order to justify using the "eye for an eye" principle to answer our question about murder and the death penalty, we would first have to show that it worked for a whole range of cases, giving acceptable answers to questions about amounts of punishment. Then, having established it as a satisfactory general principle, we could apply it to the case of murder. It turns out, however, that when we try to apply the principle generally, we find that it either gives wrong answers or no answers at all. Indeed, I suspect that the principle of "an eye for an eye" is no longer even a principle. Instead, it is simply a metaphorical disguise for expressing belief in the death penalty. People who cite it do not take it seriously. They do not believe in a kidnapping for a kidnapping, a theft for a theft, and so on. Perhaps "an eye for an eye" once was a genuine principle, but now it is merely a slogan. Therefore, it gives us no guidance in deciding whether murderers deserve to die.

In reply to these objections, one might defend the principle by saying that it does not require that punishments be strictly identical with crimes. Rather, it requires only that a punishment produce an amount of suffering in the criminal which is equal to the amount suffered by the victim. Thus, we don't have to hijack airplanes belonging to airline hijackers, spy on spies, etc. We simply have to reproduce in them the harm done to others.

Unfortunately, this reply really does not solve the problem. It provides no answer to the first objection, since it would still require us to behave barbarically in our treatment of those who are guilty of barbaric crimes. Even if we do not reproduce their actions exactly, any action which caused equal suffering would itself be barbaric. Second, in trying to produce equal amounts of suffering, we run into many problems. Just how much suffering is produced by an airline hijacker or a spy? And how do we apply this principle to prostitutes or drug users, who may not produce any suffering at all? We have rough ideas about how serious various crimes are, but this may not correlate with any clear sense of just how much harm is done.

Furthermore, the same problem arises in determining how much suffering a particular punishment would produce for a particular criminal. People vary in their tolerance of pain and in the amount of unhappiness that a fine or a jail sentence would cause them. Recluses will be less disturbed by banishment than extroverts. Nature lovers will suffer more in prison than people who are indifferent to natural beauty. A literal application of the principle would require that we tailor punishments to individual sensitivities, yet this is at best impractical. To a large extent, the legal system must work with standardized and rather crude estimates of the negative impact that punishments have on people.

The move from calling for a punishment that is identical to the crime to favoring one that is equal in the harm done is no help to us or to the defense of the principle. "An eye for an eye" tells us neither what people deserve nor how we should treat them when they have done wrong.

PROPORTIONAL RETRIBUTIVISM

The view we have been considering can be called "equality retributivism," since it proposes that we repay criminals with punishments equal to their crimes. In the light of problems like those I have cited, some people have proposed a variation on this view, calling not for equal punishments but rather for punishments which are *proportional* to the crime. In defending such a view as a guide for setting criminal punishments, Andrew von Hirsch writes:

> If one asks how severely a wrongdoer deserves to be punished, a familiar principle comes to mind: Severity of punishment should be commensurate with the seriousness of the wrong. Only grave wrongs merit severe penalties; minor misdeeds deserve lenient punishments. Disproportionate penalties are undeserved—severe sanctions for minor wrongs or vice versa. This principle has variously been called a principle of "proportionality" or "just deserts"; we prefer to call it commensurate deserts.[2]

Like Kant, von Hirsch makes the punishment which a person deserves depend on that person's actions, but he departs from Kant in substituting proportionality for equality as the criterion for setting the amount of punishment.

In implementing a punishment system based on the proportionality view, one would first make a list of crimes, ranking them in order of seriousness. At one end would be quite trivial offenses like parking meter violations, while very serious crimes such as murder would occupy the other. In between, other crimes would be ranked according to their relative gravity. Then a corresponding scale of punishments would be constructed, and the two would be correlated. Punishments would be proportionate to crimes so long as we could say that the more serious the crime was, the higher on the punishment scale was the punishment administered.

This system does not have the defects of equality retributivism. It does not require that we treat those guilty of barbaric crimes barbarically. This is because we can set the upper limit of the punishment scale so as to exclude truly barbaric punishments. Second, unlike the equality principle, the proportionality view is genuinely general, providing a way of handling all crimes. Finally, it does justice to our ordinary belief that certain punishments are unjust because they are too severe or too lenient for the crime committed.

The proportionality principle does, I think, play a legitimate role in our thinking about punishments. Nonetheless, it is no help to death penalty advocates, because it does not require that murderers be executed. All that it requires is that if murder is the most serious crime, then murder should be punished by the most severe punishment on the scale. The principle does not tell us what this punishment should be, however, and it is quite compatible with the view that the most severe punishment should be a long prison term.

This failure of the theory to provide a basis for supporting the death penalty reveals an important gap in proportional retributivism. It shows that while the theory is general in scope, it does not yield any *specific* recommendations regarding punishment. It tells us, for example, that armed robbery should be punished more severely than embezzling and less severely than murder, but it does not tell us how much to punish any of these. This weakness is, in effect, conceded by von Hirsch, who admits that if we want to implement the "commensurate deserts" principle, we must supplement it with information about what level of punishment is needed to deter crimes.[3] In a later discussion of how to "anchor" the punishment system, he deals with this problem in more depth, but the factors he cites as relevant to making specific judgments (such as available prison space) have nothing to do with what people deserve. He also seems to suggest that a range of punishments may be appropriate for a particular crime. This runs counter to the death penalty supporter's sense that death alone is appropriate for some murderers.[4]

Neither of these retributive views, then, provides support for the death penalty. The equality principle fails because it is not in general true that the appropriate punishment for a crime is to do to the criminal what he has done to others. In some cases this is immoral, while in others it is impossible. The proportionality principle may be correct, but by itself it cannot determine specific punishments for specific crimes. Because of its flexibility and open-endedness, it is compatible with a great range of different punishments for murder.[5] . . .

THE SYMBOLISM OF ABOLISHING THE DEATH PENALTY

What is the symbolic message that we would convey by deciding to renounce the death penalty and to abolish its use?

I think that there are two primary messages. The first is the most frequently emphasized and is usually expressed in terms of the sanctity of human life, although I think we could better express it in terms of respect for human dignity.

One way we express our respect for the dignity of human beings is by abstaining from depriving them of their lives, even if they have done terrible deeds. In defense of human well-being, we may punish people for their crimes, but we ought not to deprive them of everything, which is what the death penalty does.

If we take the life of a criminal, we convey the idea that by his deeds he has made himself worthless and totally without human value. I do not believe that we are in a position to affirm that of anyone. We may hate such a person and feel the deepest anger against him, but when he no longer poses a threat to anyone, we ought not to take his life.

But, one might ask, hasn't the murderer forfeited whatever rights he might have had to our respect? Hasn't he, by his deeds, given up any rights that he had to decent treatment? Aren't we morally free to kill him if we wish?

These questions express important doubts about the obligation to accord any respect to those who have acted so deplorably, but I do not think that they prove that any such forfeiture has occurred. Certainly, when people murder or commit other crimes, they do forfeit some of the rights that are possessed by the law-abiding. They lose a certain right to be left alone. It becomes permissible to bring them to trial and, if they are convicted, to impose an appropriate—even a dreadful—punishment on them.

Nonetheless, they do not forfeit all their rights. It does not follow from the vileness of their actions that we can do anything whatsoever to them. This is part of the moral meaning of the constitutional ban on cruel and unusual punishments. No matter how terrible a person's deeds, we may not punish him in a cruel and unusual way. We may not torture him, for example. His right not to be tortured has not been forfeited. Why do these limits hold? Because this person remains a human being, and we think that there is something in him that we must continue to respect in spite of his terrible acts.

One way of seeing why those who murder still deserve some consideration and respect is by reflecting again on the idea of what it is to *deserve* something. In most contexts, we think that what people deserve depends on what they have done, intended, or tried to do. It depends on features that are qualities of individuals. The best person for the job deserves to be hired. The person who worked especially hard deserves our gratitude. We can call the concept that applies in these cases *personal* desert.

There is another kind of desert, however, that belongs to people by virtue of their humanity itself and does not depend on their individual efforts or achievements. I will call this impersonal kind of desert *human* desert. We appeal to this concept when we think that everyone deserves a certain level of treatment no matter what their individual qualities are. When the signers of the Declaration of Independence affirmed that people had inalienable rights to "life, liberty, and the pursuit of happiness," they were appealing to such an idea. These rights do not have to be earned by people. They are possessed "naturally," and everyone is bound to respect them.

According to the view that I am defending, people do not lose all of their rights when they commit terrible crimes. They still deserve some level of decent treatment simply because they remain living, functioning human beings. This level of moral desert need not be earned, and it cannot be forfeited. This view may sound controversial, but in fact everyone who believes that cruel and unusual punishment should be forbidden implicitly agrees with it. That is, they agree that even after someone has committed a terrible crime, we do not have the right to do anything whatsoever to him.

What I am suggesting is that by renouncing the use of death as a punishment, we express and reaffirm our belief in the inalienable, unforfeitable core of human dignity.

Why is this a worthwhile message to convey? It is worth conveying because this belief is both important and precarious. Throughout history, people have found innumerable reasons to degrade the humanity of one another. They have found qualities in others that they hated or feared, and even when they were not threatened by these people, they have sought to harm them, deprive them of their liberty, or take their lives from them. They have often felt that they had good reasons to do these things, and they have invoked divine commands, racial purity, and state security to support their deeds.

These actions and attitudes are not relics of the past. They remain an awful feature of the contemporary world. By renouncing the death penalty, we show our determination to accord at least minimal respect even to those whom we believe to be personally vile or morally vicious. This is, perhaps, why we speak of the *sanctity* of human life rather than its value or worth. That which is sacred remains, in some sense, untouchable, and its value is not dependent on its worth or usefulness to us. Kant expressed this ideal of respect in the famous second version of the Categorical Imperative: "So act as to treat humanity, whether in thine own person or in that of any other, in every case as an end withal, never as a means only." . . .

[THE SECOND SYMBOLIC MESSAGE]

. . . When the state has a murderer in its power and could execute him but does not, this conveys the idea that even though this person has done wrong and even though we may be angry, outraged, and indignant with him, we will nonetheless control ourselves in a way that he did not. We will not kill him, even though we could do so and even though we are angry and indignant. We will exercise restraint, sanctioning killing only when it serves a protective function.

Why should we do this? Partly out of a respect for human dignity. But also because we want the state to set an example of proper behavior. We do not want to encourage people to resort to violence to settle conflicts when there are other ways available. We want to avoid the cycle of violence that can come from retaliation and counter-retaliation. Violence is a contagion that arouses hatred and anger, and if unchecked, it simply leads to still more violence. The state can convey the message that the contagion must be stopped, and the most effective principle for stopping it is the idea that only defensive violence is justifiable. Since the death penalty is not an instance of defensive violence, it ought to be renounced.

We show our respect for life best by restraining ourselves and allowing murderers to live, rather than by following a policy of a life for a life. Respect for life and restraint of violence are aspects of the same ideal. The renunciation of the death penalty would symbolize our support of that ideal.

NOTES

1 Kant, *Metaphysical Elements of Justice,* translated by John Ladd (Indianapolis: Bobbs-Merrill, 1965), 101.
2 *Doing Justice* (New York: Hill & Wang, 1976), 66; reprinted in *Sentencing,* edited by H. Gross and A. von Hirsch (Oxford University Press, 1981), 243. For a more recent discussion and further defense by von Hirsch, see his *Past or Future Crimes* (New Brunswick, N.J.: Rutgers University Press, 1985).
3 Von Hirsch, *Doing Justice,* 93–94. My criticisms of proportional retributivism are not novel. For helpful discussions of the view, see Hugo Bedau, "Concessions to Retribution in Punishment," in *Justice and Punishment,* edited by J. Cederblom and W. Blizek (Cambridge, Mass.: Ballinger, 1977), and M. Golding, *Philosophy of Law* (Englewood Cliffs, N.J.: Prentice Hall, 1975), 98–99.
4 See von Hirsch, *Past or Future Crimes,* ch. 8.
5 For more positive assessments of these theories, see Jeffrey Reiman, "Justice, Civilization, and the Death Penalty," *Philosophy and Public Affairs* 14 (1985): 115–48; and Michael Davis, "How to Make the Punishment Fit the Crime," *Ethics* 93 (1983).

QUESTIONS

1 To what extent, if at all, should the principle of "an eye for an eye" be incorporated into our system of criminal justice?
2 Can a retributive rationale for retention of the death penalty be defended against the objections presented by Nathanson?
3 Does Nathanson's appeal to "the symbolism of abolishing the death penalty" provide a compelling argument for abolition? Could a retentionist develop a compelling argument based on the symbolism of *retaining* the death penalty?

Deterrence and the Death Penalty

Louis P. Pojman

Pojman acknowledges that there is no conclusive statistical evidence supporting the claim that the death penalty is a uniquely effective deterrent. Nevertheless, he espouses the deterrence rationale for retention of the death penalty, and he does so on the basis of (1) the so-called best bet argument and (2) commonsense or anecdotal evidence. The best bet argument, predicated on our uncertainty concerning the deterrent effect of the death penalty (i.e., whether or not it is a uniquely effective deterrent), leads to the conclusion that we must retain the death penalty because running the risk of needlessly eradicating the lives of convicted murderers is morally better than running the risk of innocent people becoming future murder victims. In discussing the commonsense case for the death penalty

Reprinted with permission of Rowman & Littlefield Publishers from Louis P. Pojman and Jeffrey Reiman, *The Death Penalty: For and Against* (1998), pp. 37–41, 43, 44–49, 51.

as a uniquely effective deterrent, Pojman argues in particular that, since the death penalty is the most feared (humane) punishment, it follows that the death penalty is a superior deterrent.

The utilitarian argument for capital punishment is that it deters would-be offenders from committing first-degree murder. Thorstein Sellin's study of comparing states with and without capital punishment concludes that the death penalty is not a better deterrent of homicides than imprisonment.[1] On the other hand, Isaac Ehrlich's study, the most thorough study to date, takes into account the problems of complex sociological data in terms of race, heredity, regional lines, standards of housing, education, opportunities, cultural patterns, intelligence, and so forth, and concludes that the death penalty does deter. His simultaneous equation regression model suggests that over the period 1933–1969 "an additional execution per year . . . may have resulted on the average in 7 or 8 fewer murders."[2] It should be noted that Ehrlich began his study as an abolitionist, but his data forced him to change his position. However, Ehrlich's study has been criticized, largely for technical reasons, so that his conclusion that we have significant statistical evidence that the death penalty deters better than prison sentences is not conclusive.[3] The problems seem to be that there are simply too many variables to control in comparing demographic patterns (culture, heredity, poverty, education, religion, and general environmental factors) and that the death penalty isn't carried out frequently enough to have the effect that it might have under circumstances of greater use. . . . A consensus is wanting, so that at present we must conclude that we lack strong statistical evidence that capital punishment deters. But this should not be construed as evidence against the deterrence thesis. There is no such evidence for nondeterrence either. The statistics available are simply inconclusive either way.

Precisely on the basis of this inconclusivity with regard to the evidence, some abolitionists . . . argue that deterrence cannot be the moral basis for capital punishment. . . . I think [they are] wrong about this. There is some nonstatistical evidence based on common sense that gives credence to the hypothesis that the threat of the death penalty deters and that it does so better than long prison sentences. I will discuss the commonsense case below, but first I want to present an argument for the deterrent effect of capital punishment that is agnostic as to whether the death penalty deters better than lesser punishments.

Ernest van den Haag has set forth what he calls the Best Bet Argument.[4] He argues that even though we don't know for certain whether the death penalty deters or prevents other murders, we should bet that it does. Indeed, due to our ignorance, any social policy we take is a gamble. Not to choose capital punishment for first-degree murder is as much a bet that capital punishment doesn't deter as choosing the policy is a bet that it does. There is a significant difference in the betting, however, in that to bet against capital punishment is to bet against the innocent and for the murderer, while to bet for it is to bet against the murderer and for the innocent. . . .

Suppose that we choose a policy of capital punishment for capital crimes. In this case we are betting that the death of some murderers will be more than compensated for by the lives of some innocents not being murdered (either by these murderers or others who would have murdered). If we're right, we have saved the lives of the innocent. If we're wrong, unfortunately, we've sacrificed the lives of some murderers. But say we choose not to have a social policy of capital punishment. If capital punishment doesn't work as a deterrent, we've come out ahead, but if it does work, then we've missed an opportunity to save innocent lives. If we value the saving of innocent lives more highly than the loss of the guilty, then to bet on a policy of capital punishment turns out to be rational. . . .

. . . As van den Haag writes, "Though we have no proof of the positive deterrence of the penalty, we also have no proof of zero or negative effectiveness. I believe we have no right to risk additional future victims of murder for the sake of sparing convicted murderers; on the contrary, our moral obligation is to risk the possible ineffectiveness of executions."[5] . . .

. . . [I]f you had to choose between saving an innocent person and saving one who had just committed cold-blooded murder, which would you choose? We generally judge that conscientiously moral people are more worthy than viciously immoral ones, that the innocent are more worthy of aid than those who are guilty of squandering aid. Van den Haag's argument only formalizes these comparisons and applies them to the practice of capital punishment. Some humans are worth more than others, and some have forfeited their right not to be killed, whereas most people have not. Our practices should take this into account. . . .

[It is not true] that we have no evidence at all about the deterrent effect of capital punishment. . . . We have evidence, though not statistical proof, based on commonsense experience, which makes the case for deterrence even stronger than the Best Bet Argument. I now turn to the Argument from Anecdotal Evidence, a commonsense argument.

THE ARGUMENT FROM ANECDOTAL EVIDENCE

Abolitionists like Stephen Nathanson argue that because the statistical evidence in favor of the deterrent effect of capital punishment is indecisive, we have no basis for concluding that it is a better deterrent than long prison sentences.[6] If I understand these opponents, their argument presents us with an exclusive disjunct: Either we must have conclusive statistical evidence (i.e., a proof) for the deterrent effect of the death penalty, or we have no grounds for supposing that the death penalty deters. Many people accept this argument. Just this morning a colleague said to me, "There is no statistical evidence that the death penalty deters," as if to dismiss the argument from deterrence altogether. This is premature judgment, for the argument commits the fallacy of supposing that only two opposites are possible. There is a middle position that holds that while we cannot prove conclusively that the death penalty deters, the weight of evidence supports its deterrence. Furthermore, I think there are too many variables to hold constant for us to prove via statistics the deterrence hypothesis, and even if the requisite statistics were available, we could question whether they were cases of mere correlation versus causation. On the other hand, commonsense or anecdotal evidence may provide insight into the psychology of human motivation, providing evidence that fear of the death penalty deters some types of would-be criminals from committing murder. Granted, people are sometimes deceived about their motivation. But usually they are not deceived, and, as a rule, we should presume they know their motives until we have evidence to the contrary. The general commonsense argument goes like this:

1 What people (including potential criminals) fear more will have a greater deterrent effect on them.
2 People (including potential criminals) fear death more than they do any other humane punishment.
3 The death penalty is a humane punishment.
4 Therefore, people (including criminals) will be deterred more by the death penalty than by any other humane punishment.

Since the purpose of this argument is to show that the death penalty very likely deters more than long-term prison sentences, I am assuming it is *humane,* that is, acceptable to the moral sensitivities of the majority in our society. Torture might deter even more, but it is not considered humane. . . .

Common sense informs us that most people would prefer to remain out of jail, that the threat of public humiliation is enough to deter some people, that a sentence of twenty years will deter most people more than a sentence of two years, that a life sentence will deter most would-be criminals more than a sentence of twenty years. I think that we have commonsense evidence that the death penalty is a better deterrent than prison sentences. For one thing, as Richard Herrnstein and James Q. Wilson have argued in *Crime and Human Nature,* a great deal of crime is committed on a cost-benefit schema, wherein the criminal engages in some form of risk assessment as to his or her chances of getting caught and punished in some manner. If he or she estimates the punishment mild, the crime becomes inversely attractive, and vice versa. The fact that those who are condemned to death do everything in their power to get their sentences postponed or reduced to long-term prison sentences, in a way lifers do not, shows that they fear death more than life in prison.

The point is this: Imprisonment constitutes one evil, the loss of freedom, but the death penalty imposes a more severe loss, that of life itself. If you lock me up, I may work for a parole or pardon, I may learn to live stoically with diminished freedom, and I can plan for the day when my freedom has been restored. But if I believe that my crime may lead to death, or loss of freedom followed by death, then I have more to fear than mere imprisonment. I am faced with a great evil plus an even greater evil. I fear death more than imprisonment because it alone takes from me all future possibility. . . .

Some of the commonsense evidence is anecdotal as the following quotation shows. British member of Parliament Arthur Lewis explains how he was converted from an abolitionist to a supporter of the death penalty:

> One reason that has stuck in my mind, and which has proved [deterrence] to me beyond question, is that there was once a professional burglar in [my] constituency who consistently boasted of the fact that he had spent about one-third of his life in prison. . . . He said to me "I am a professional burglar. Before we go out on a job we plan it down to every detail. Before we go into the boozer to have a drink we say 'Don't forget, no shooters'—shooters being guns." He adds "We did our job and didn't have shooters because at that time there was capital punishment. Our wives, girlfriends and our

mums said, 'Whatever you do, do not carry a shooter because if you are caught you might be topped [executed].' If you do away with capital punishment they will all be carrying shooters."[7]

It is difficult to know how widespread this reasoning is. My own experience corroborates this testimony. Growing up in the infamous Cicero, Illinois, home of Al Capone and the Mafia, I had friends who went into crime, mainly burglary and larceny. It was common knowledge that one stopped short of killing in the act of robbery. A prison sentence could be dealt with—especially with a good lawyer—but being convicted of murder, which at that time included a reasonable chance of being electrocuted, was an altogether different matter. No doubt exists in my mind that the threat of the electric chair saved the lives of some of those who were robbed in my town. No doubt some crimes are committed in the heat of passion or by the temporally (or permanently) insane, but some are committed through a process of risk assessment. Burglars, kidnappers, traitors and vindictive people will sometimes be restrained by the threat of death. We simply don't know how much capital punishment deters, but this sort of commonsense, anecdotal evidence must be taken into account in assessing the institution of capital punishment.

John Stuart Mill admitted that capital punishment does not inspire terror in hardened criminals, but it may well make an impression on prospective murderers. "As for what is called the failure of the death punishment, who is able to judge of that? We partly know who those are whom it has not deterred; but who is there who knows whom it has deterred, or how many human beings it has saved who would have lived to be murderers if that awful association had not been thrown round the idea of murder from their earliest infancy."[8] Mill's points are well taken: (1) Not everyone will be deterred by the death penalty, but some will; (2) The potential criminal need not consciously calculate a cost-benefit analysis regarding his crime to be deterred by the threat. The idea of the threat may have become a subconscious datum "from their earliest infancy." The repeated announcement and regular exercise of capital punishment may have deep causal influence. . . .

It seems likely that the death penalty does not deter as much as it could due to its inconsistent and rare use. . . . If potential murderers perceived the death penalty as a highly probable outcome of murder, would they not be more reluctant to kill? . . .

If the Best Bet Argument is sound, or if the death penalty does deter would-be murderers, as common sense suggests, then we should support some uses of the death penalty. It should be used for those who commit first-degree murder, for whom no mitigating factors are present, and especially for those who murder police officers, prison guards, and political leaders. Many states rightly favor it for those who murder while committing another crime, e.g., burglary or rape. It should also be used for treason and terrorist bombings.

NOTES

1 Thorstein Sellin, *The Death Penalty* (1959) reprinted in *The Death Penalty in America,* ed. Hugo Bedau (Anchor Books, 1967).
2 Isaac Ehrlich, "The Deterrent Effect of Capital Punishment: A Question of Life and Death," *American Economic Review* 65 (June 1975): 397–417.

3 See for example David Baldus and James Cole, "A Comparison of the Work of Thorstein Sellin and Isaac Ehrlich on the Deterrent Effect of Capital Punishment," *Yale Law Journal* 85 (1975).
4 Ernest van den Haag, "On Deterrence and the Death Penalty," *Ethics* 78 (July 1968).
5 Ibid.
6 Stephen Nathanson, *An Eye for an Eye?* (Lanham, Md.: Rowman & Littlefield, 1987). Chap. 2.
7 British *Parliamentary Debates,* fifth series, vol. 23, issue 1243, House of Commons, 11 May 1982. Quoted in Tom Sorell, *Moral Theory and Capital Punishment* (Oxford: Blackwell, 1987), 36.
8 *Parliamentary Debates,* third series, April 21, 1868. Reprinted in Peter Singer, ed., *Applied Ethics* (Oxford University Press, 1986), 97–104.

QUESTIONS

1 Is commonsense or anecdotal evidence sufficient to establish the conclusion that the death penalty is a uniquely effective deterrent?
2 Is the life of a convicted murderer worth as much as the life of a potential murder victim?
3 Would you endorse either of the following claims? (a) We should abolish the death penalty unless retentionists can prove that it is a uniquely effective deterrent. (b) We should retain the death penalty unless abolitionists can prove that it is not a uniquely effective deterrent.

Common Sense, the Deterrent Effect of the Death Penalty, and the Best Bet Argument

Jeffrey Reiman

Reiman directly counters the commonsense argument for the death penalty as a uniquely effective deterrent, and he also takes issue with the best bet argument. He initially considers the commonsense argument in a version put forth by Ernest van den Haag and presents three counterarguments. In developing his third counterargument, Reiman relies on the claim that abolition of the death penalty would have a civilizing impact on society, and thus he speaks of "a deterrent effect from *not executing.*" Subsequently, in formulating a reply to the views of Pojman in the previous selection, Reiman deepens his critique of the commonsense argument by focusing attention on what he calls "the continuously rising disinclination premise." (This part of Reiman's overall critique is best understood in conjunction with the first of his three initial counterarguments.) Reiman concludes by advancing two counterarguments against the best bet argument.

Reprinted with permission of Rowman & Littlefield Publishers from Louis P. Pojman and Jeffrey Reiman, *The Death Penalty: For and Against* (1998), pp. 102–107, 156–161.

Conceding that it has not been proven that the death penalty deters more murders than life imprisonment, Ernest van den Haag has argued that neither has it been proven that the death penalty does not deter more murders.[1] Thus, his argument goes, we must follow common sense, which teaches that the higher the cost of something, the fewer the people who will choose it. Therefore, at least some potential murderers who would not be deterred by life imprisonment will be deterred by the death penalty. Van den Haag continues:

> [O]ur experience shows that the greater the threatened penalty, the more it deters. . . .
>
> Life in prison is still life, however unpleasant. In contrast, the death penalty does not just threaten to make life unpleasant—it threatens to take life altogether. This difference is perceived by those affected. We find that when they have the choice between life in prison and execution, 99% of all prisoners under sentence of death prefer life in prison. . . .
>
> From this unquestioned fact a reasonable conclusion can be drawn in favor of the superior deterrent effect of the death penalty. Those who have the choice in practice . . . fear death more than they fear life in prison. . . . If they do, it follows that the threat of the death penalty, all other things equal, is likely to deter more than the threat of life in prison. One is most deterred by what one fears most. From which it follows that whatever statistics fail, or do not fail, to show, the death penalty is likely to be more deterrent than any other.[2]

Those of us who recognize how commonsensical it was, and still is, to believe that the sun moves around the earth will be less willing than van den Haag to follow common sense here, especially when it comes to doing something awful to our fellows. Moreover, there are good reasons for doubting common sense on this matter. Here are three.

1. From the fact that one penalty is more feared than another, it does not follow that the more feared penalty will deter more than the less feared, unless we know that the less feared penalty is not fearful enough to deter everyone who can be deterred—and this is just what we don't know with regard to the death penalty. This point is crucial because it shows that *the commonsense argument includes a premise that cannot be based on common sense,* namely, that the deterrence impact of a penalty rises without limit in proportion to the fearfulness of the penalty. All that common sense could possibly indicate is that deterrence impact increases with fearfulness of penalty *within a certain normally experienced range.* Since few of us ever face a choice between risking death and risking lifetime confinement, common sense has no resources for determining whether this difference in fearfulness is still within the range that increases deterrence. To figure that out, we will have to turn to social science—as a matter of common sense! And when we do, we find that most of the research we have on the comparative deterrent impact of execution versus life imprisonment suggests that there is no difference in deterrent impact between the death penalty and life imprisonment.

Since it seems to me that whoever would be deterred by a given likelihood of death would be deterred by an *equal* likelihood of life behind bars, I suspect that the commonsense argument only seems plausible because we evaluate it while unconsciously assuming that potential criminals will face larger likelihoods of death sentences than of life sentences. If the likelihoods were equal, it seems to me that where life imprisonment were improbable enough to make it too distant a possibility to worry much about, a similar low probability of death would have the same effect. After all, we are undeterred by small likelihoods of death every time we walk the streets. And if life imprisonment were sufficiently probable to pose a real deterrent threat, it would pose as much of a deterrent threat as death. And then it seems that any lengthy prison sentence—say, twenty years—dependably imposed and not softened by parole, would do the same.

2. In light of the fact that the number of privately owned guns in America is substantially larger than the number of households in America, as well as the fact that about twelve hundred suspected felons are killed or wounded by the police in the line of duty every year, it must be granted that anyone contemplating committing a crime already faces a substantial risk of ending up dead as a result. It's hard to see why anyone *who is not already deterred by this* would be deterred by the addition of the more distant risk of death after apprehension, conviction, and appeal.

3. Van den Haag has maintained that deterrence works not only by means of cost-benefit calculations made by potential criminals, but also by the lesson about the wrongfulness of murder that is slowly learned in a society that subjects murderers to the ultimate punishment.[3] If, however, I am correct in claiming that the refusal to execute even those who deserve it has a civilizing effect, then the refusal to execute also teaches a lesson about the wrongfulness of murder. My claim here is admittedly speculative, but no more so than van den Haag's to the contrary. And my view has the added virtue of accounting for the failure of research to show an increased deterrent effect from executions, *without having to deny the plausibility of van den Haag's commonsense argument that at least some additional potential murderers will be deterred by the prospect of the death penalty*. If there is a deterrent effect from *not executing,* then it is understandable that while executions will deter some murderers, this effect will be balanced out by the weakening of the deterrent effect of not executing, such that no net reduction in murders will result.[4] This, by the way, also disposes of van den Haag's argument that, in the absence of knowledge one way or the other on the deterrent effect of executions, we should execute murderers rather than risk the lives of innocent people whose murders might have been deterred if we had executed. If there is a deterrent effect of not executing, it follows that we risk innocent lives either way. And if this is so, it seems that the only reasonable course of action is to refrain from imposing what we know is a horrible fate.

I conclude then that we have no good reason to think that we need the death penalty to protect innocent people from murder. Life in prison (or, at least, a lengthy prison term without parole) dependably meted out, will do as well. . . .

REPLY TO LOUIS P. POJMAN

. . . Pojman, contending that the research has not proven that the death penalty does not deter more than life imprisonment, seeks to bolster his case by putting forth the so-called best bet argument, which he takes to be agnostic on the issue of whether the death penalty is a superior deterrent to imprisonment, and he follows this argument with the commonsense argument, which purports to prove that, whatever the research shows, the death penalty is a greater deterrent after all. Since I think that the best bet argument is not really agnostic, but in fact gets some of its force from the commonsense argument, I take up the commonsense argument first.

We have already seen the commonsense argument formulated by Ernest van den Haag. . . . Pojman follows suit. The argument starts from the premise that "what people (including potential criminals) fear more will have a greater deterrent effect on them," and it goes on to say that, since people fear death more than life in prison, they "will be deterred more by the death penalty" than by other available punishments, such as life in prison. I [contend] . . . that the first premise here is a nonstarter. As David Conway pointed out, the fact that one penalty is feared more than another does not imply that the more feared penalty deters more than the less feared, since the less feared penalty may already deter me as much as I can be deterred. Says Conway,

> given the choice, I would strongly prefer one thousand years in hell to eternity there. Nonetheless, if one thousand years in hell were the penalty for some action, it would be quite sufficient to deter me from performing that action. The additional years would do nothing to discourage me further. Similarly, the prospect of the death penalty, while worse, may not have any greater deterrent effect than does that of life imprisonment.[5]

Since this argument was made more than twenty years ago and still has not deterred van den Haag . . . and now Pojman from using the commonsense argument, I am convinced that more must be said to show just how devastating the implications of this point are for any version of the commonsense argument. Conway's argument shows that the commonsense argument contains a questionable premise, namely, the idea that *people's disinclination to act in some way rises continuously and without limit as the fearsomeness of the penalty for that act rises.* Without this premise, the commonsense argument fails. If people's disinclination doesn't keep rising but instead tops out at some point, it is no longer possible to infer from the greater fearfulness of the death penalty its greater deterrent impact since people's disinclination may have topped out at life imprisonment. What is really devastating about Conway's point is that the continuously rising disinclination premise is part of a technical theory, and no part of common sense. Those who put forth the commonsense argument are really putting forth a theory that isn't commonsensical at all, and they're calling it common sense!

What theory is this that underlies the idea that disinclination continuously correlates with fearfulness? It is some version of psychological hedonism of the sort that one finds in textbooks of neoclassical economic theory, in which people are thought to seek continuously to maximize their net satisfaction. What we have here, then, is not the behavior of commonsense folks. It's the behavior of idealized rational consumers! The giveaway is Pojman's claim that criminals do cost-benefit analyses before deciding to break the law. Beware of equivocation here. I don't doubt that would-be criminals consider costs and benefits of potential crimes in a rough manner. I will shortly suggest a "model" of how they do so. What is highly implausible, however, is that criminals do cost-benefit analyses in the technical sense of that term, such that every increment of cost and every increment of benefit are taken into account. This is what we have to think at least a significant number of criminals are doing in order to ignore the social science findings and insist, as Pojman (and van den Haag . . .) do, that an increase in penalty from life in prison to execution will figure in the motivation of potential murderers enough to deter additional murders. And that is simply implausible. . . .

. . . Rather than finely calibrating their reactions to increasingly negative outcomes, commonsense people seem to batch negative outcomes into qualitative groupings, such as "worth a great effort to avoid," "worth a substantial effort to avoid," and "worth only a minor effort to avoid." So being killed painfully or painlessly, being locked in prison for your whole life or for much of your life, being paralyzed, being blinded, and losing both arms or both legs are all, irrespective of their relative differences in awfulness, worth a great effort to avoid. Breaking a bone, losing a finger, getting a serious (but not permanently damaging) beating, and being injured seriously (but not gravely and permanently) in a car accident are worth a substantial effort to avoid. And getting a splinter, stubbing a toe, and falling in the street, as well as worse but very unlikely things, such as getting hit by lightning, killed in a train derailment, or contracting a rare and terrible disease, are worth only a minor effort to avoid.

I do not insist on the details of this description. I say only that it is something like what commonsensically rational people do in the face of statistically possible negative outcomes, and there's nothing irrational about it, unless one is already assuming a theory of rationality, such as that used in economics. Then, when you think of potential criminals, it's only commonsensical to suppose that they do the same, treating any serious criminal penalty as "worth a great effort to avoid." I contend that the so-called cost-benefit analyses that Pojman thinks some criminals engage in amount to no finer calculation than this. And this is not only closer to the actual way in which commonsense folks treat risks, it also fits perfectly with the majority of social science studies on the death penalty, which show that the difference between life in prison and death does not alter people's inclination or disinclination to commit murder—just as if would-be murderers had batched these two penalties under one rubric and acted accordingly. I conclude that the commonsense argument for the death penalty is an impostor. It is a theory of rational behavior and not even a very plausible one. The commonsense argument fails for lack of common sense. . . .

I turn now to the best bet argument. The best bet argument holds that, because execution *might* deter murderers, it is better to execute murderers than not to. Executing murderers may deter someone from killing an innocent person, and if not, all we have lost is one dead murderer. Not executing may have no impact on future criminals, but if there are any who would have been deterred by execution, then we have failed to stop the killing of an innocent person. Since it seems worse to fail to stop the killing of the innocent than to kill a murderer without a deterrent gain, our best bet is to execute murderers.

I put off dealing with the best bet argument until now because that argument looks very weak without the commonsense argument accompanying it. For unless there is some reason to expect the death penalty to be a superior deterrent to life in prison, the best bet argument calls for the merest toying with human beings, which seems offensive even when the human beings are murderers. It is one thing to kill murderers when there is reason to think it will protect innocents, but to kill them because of the bare possibility that this might happen seems like exactly the kind of disrespectful treatment of the murderer that Kant condemned. So, without either a showing from social science or from common sense that the death penalty is likely to save lives, I think the best bet argument fails.

Some people may resist this conclusion, holding that, since murderers are of less worth than innocent people . . . , the bare possibility that executing a murderer might save an innocent is enough to justify the death penalty as our best bet. There is, I think, a further argument against this approach that I think refutes it finally. Recall that [earlier] I argued that, by refraining from executing murderers, the state will contribute to the general repugnance of murder, and I speculated that *this will lead to fewer murders over time*. Moreover, there is a line of social science research defending the so-called brutalization hypothesis, which purports to show that murders increase in the period following executions and that these are real increases (not just changes in timing). If either or both of these claims are plausible, then the outcomes facing us in the best bet argument are dramatically changed. Now, in addition to no evidence that the death penalty deters more murders, there is the additional possibility that the death penalty increases the number of murders. Then, there is no reason to bet on executions over life imprisonment in the name of future innocent victims. Executions may protect them or jeopardize them. With that, the best bet argument evaporates.

NOTES

1 Ernest van den Haag and John P. Conrad, *The Death Penalty: A Debate* (New York: Plenum, 1983), 65.
2 Ibid., 68–69.
3 Ibid., 63.
4 A related claim has been made by those who defend the so-called brutalization hypothesis by presenting evidence to show that murders increase following an execution. See, for example, William J. Bowers and Glenn L. Pierce, "Deterrence or Brutalization: What Is the Effect of Executions?" *Crime and Delinquency* 26, no. 4 (October 1980): 453–84. Bowers and Pierce conclude that each execution gives rise to two additional homicides in the month following and that these are real additions, not just a change in timing of the homicides (481). My claim, it should be noted, is not identical to this, since, as I indicate in the text, what I call "the deterrent effect of not executing" is not something whose impact is to be seen immediately following executions, but an effect that occurs over the long haul; further, my claim is compatible with finding no net increase in murders due to executions. Nonetheless, should the brutalization hypothesis be borne out by further studies, it would certainly lend support to the notion that there is a deterrent effect of not executing.
5 David A. Conway, "Capital Punishment and Deterrence: Some Considerations in Dialogue Form," *Philosophy and Public Affairs* 3, no. 4 (Summer 1974), 433.

QUESTIONS

1 Can the commonsense argument for the death penalty as a uniquely effective deterrent be defended against the counterarguments advanced by Reiman?

2 Is it plausible to believe that abolition of the death penalty would produce "a deterrent effect from not executing"?

3 If we are unsure whether or not the death penalty is a uniquely effective deterrent, does our uncertainty favor retention, abolition, or neither?

Procedural Arguments Against the Death Penalty

David Dolinko

Dolinko identifies three procedural arguments employed by abolitionists against the death penalty: (1) the arbitrariness argument, (2) the discrimination argument, and (3) the mistake argument. In his critical examination of these three arguments, he sometimes incorporates a discussion of both retentionist counterarguments and abolitionist responses to these counterarguments. Dolinko's analysis ultimately suggests that the mistake argument is the most powerful procedural argument against the death penalty.

. . . Abolitionists . . . rely . . . on a number of *procedural* arguments—claims that one or another serious flaw infects the methods used to select those killers who will actually be executed. (The following discussion of procedural arguments is a condensed version of that in Dolinko, 1986.)

Procedural arguments can be dismissed by insisting that capital punishment systems need not exhibit the particular features of the American system. But speculation about hypothetical utopian systems does little to blunt the critique of what is, after all, almost the only functioning death penalty in a modern industrialized democracy. (Japan, where capital punishment is shrouded in remarkable secrecy, is believed to have executed about 35 people during the 1990s.)

One procedural argument is that capital punishment is inflicted "arbitrarily"— without any rational, principled distinction between the murderers who are executed and the far larger number who receive prison sentences. (In the United States in recent years, only some 6.25–12.5 percent of persons convicted of potentially capital murder have actually received death sentences; see figures in Bedau, 1997: 31–2.) The most explicit, detailed version of this argument contends that most of the crucial steps in a homicide prosecution that results in execution are taken "under no standards at all or under pseudo-standards without discoverable meaning" (Black, 1981: 29). No articulated standard, for example, controls a prosecutor's discretionary decision to bring capital charges in the first place or to reject a plea to a lesser offense. And the concept of "premeditation," frequently a prerequisite for a capital murder conviction, is an example of a "pseudo-standard" in those (many) states where juries are told that "premeditation" can occur in a single instant and need occur no more than a moment before the killing.

Another procedural argument, which many people find more troubling, is that capital punishment is inflicted in a racially discriminatory manner. This claim is supported by many empirical studies which show that killers of whites are more likely to be sentenced to death than killers of blacks. A 1990 review of then-existing research by the US government's General Accounting Office reported that "In 82 percent of the studies, race of victim was found to influence the likelihood of being charged with capital murder or receiving the death penalty," a finding "remarkably consistent across data sets, states, data collection methods, and analytic techniques" (Bedau, 1997: 271). Controlling for a variety of legitimate, relevant non-racial variables reduced but did not eliminate the evidence of race-of-victim bias.

The most prominent retentionist academic, Ernest Van Den Haag, has dismissed both of these arguments by insisting that the justice of executing any individual killer depends wholly on whether execution is what that individual deserves, and is unaffected by whether others who deserve death are more leniently treated either "arbitrarily" or for racially biased reasons (Van Den Haag, 1982). That response is question-begging with regard to the arbitrariness argument, whose crucial claim is the lack of any rational method for determining which killers "deserve" death. Moreover, it assumes an idiosyncratic, narrow view of justice as having no *comparative* dimension. Yet justice has been equated with "treating like cases alike" as persistently as with "giving each his due"—indeed, both characterizations stem from the same passage in Aristotle. Besides, if we do take a wholly non-comparative view of justice, we are given no convincing reason to believe justice, so conceived, must always be preferred to equality—Van Den Haag's premise for inferring that undeserved leniency to some murderers cannot impugn the propriety of executing those who receive their "just deserts."

Whatever the weaknesses of Van Den Haag's position, however, the arbitrariness and discrimination arguments do invite serious objections. The empirical basis for the arbitrariness argument is questionable. Proponents tend to focus wholly on whether capital decision-makers are bound by *explicit* rules that effectively con-strain their discretion. Yet decisions not subject to explicit rules may none the less be made in a consistent, rationally explicable manner—and standards vague and indeterminate in theory may in practice receive a narrow and principled interpreta-tion. Indeed, some empirical studies of capital sentencing suggest that a small num-ber of factors will predict the sentences in capital cases rather accurately, so that these sentences are much less "arbitrary" than abolitionists assume.

The empirical evidence of race-of-victim discrimination, while not wholly conclusive, is powerful, and certainly far stronger than the evidence of "arbitrari-ness." Yet this evidence is open to conflicting interpretations. For example, polls reveal more hostility to capital punishment among blacks than whites, which might translate into less community support for pressing capital charges in cases with black victims. Then, too, the great majority of murders are intra-racial—meaning black victims tend to die at the hands of black killers—so prosecutors trying to avoid an appearance of bias against black defendants might end up appearing to discount the lives of black victims.

Regardless of the plausibility of explaining away the race-of-victim effect in these or similar ways, the discrimination argument shares one big defect with the arbitrariness argument. Neither depends on any special feature of death as a punishment—each, if valid, indicts the criminal justice system regardless of what penalty is reserved for the very worst crimes. Suppose, for example, that the criminal justice system is as riddled with standardless discretion as proponents of the arbitrariness argument allege. Then *whatever* penalty is employed against those convicted of "the worst crimes" would be imposed in a manner too shockingly capricious and irrational to be morally legitimate. One killer might receive life without parole, another life *with* parole, a third a five-year sentence, while a fourth goes free altogether—all as the upshot of decisions made "under no standards at all or under pseudo-standards without discoverable meaning." Now assume that killers of whites are more likely to receive death sentences than killers of blacks because prejudiced prosecutors, judges, and juries value white lives more highly than black lives. Abolishing capital punishment would not affect those prejudices, so killers of whites would then receive the most severe *non*-capital punishment disproportionately often compared to killers of blacks. What both arguments suggest, then, is not that capital punishment should be abolished but that the mechanism for picking out "the worst criminals" and inflicting on them whatever is our most severe penalty needs thoroughgoing reform if it is to be morally acceptable.

Of course, death is not merely the most severe punishment in the contemporary repertoire, it is qualitatively different from even the lengthiest prison sentence in taking *everything* from the criminal and in doing so *irrevocably*. But the arbitrariness and discrimination arguments do not trade on those features of capital punishment. In particular, their force does not stem from a fear that we might discover we have executed someone either "arbitrarily" or for discriminatory reasons and be unable to revoke the punishment and make amends. They are *systemic* arguments—that no principled criteria distinguish *the class* of murderers who get executed; that killers of whites *as a class* are more harshly treated—not claims that in particular, identifiable cases we may discover arbitrariness or discrimination.

A third procedural argument, however, appeals squarely to the unique irrevocability of capital punishment. This is the claim that the unavoidable imperfections of all human fact-finding and decision procedures make mistakes in capital sentencing inevitable. Every now and then—perhaps extremely rarely, but *sometimes*—innocent people will be convicted of capital crimes, sentenced to death, and in at least some instances will actually end up being executed. (Talk of "innocent people" here is an oversimplification because there are other capital sentencing "mistakes," like finding a killing premeditated when it was actually impulsive, convicting of murder a defendant who actually killed in legitimate self-defense, or erroneously rejecting a valid insanity defense.) This argument does derive its force from the chilling prospect of learning that a person has been erroneously executed and being unable to call off the punishment or compensate the hideously mistreated innocent. It has been an increasingly influential argument with Americans in recent years in the wake of several widely reported instances of death row prisoners winning release after new evidence established their innocence. Most notably, the governor of Illinois ordered a moratorium on executions in that state in January 2000 after the exoneration of the thirteenth death-row prisoner found to have been wrongly convicted there since 1977.

Retentionists have two responses to the mistake argument. The first is that abolitionists grossly exaggerate the likelihood of executing innocent persons. Actually, retentionists assert, the multiple layers of review and due process protections built into the American capital-punishment system make it extraordinarily unlikely that a genuinely innocent person will ever be executed. When abolitionists note that more than ninety prisoners have been released from American death rows since 1973 when evidence of their wrongful convictions emerged, retentionists counter that this merely reinforces their claim that the system works to ferret out erroneous capital convictions before mistaken executions ever occur.

Second, retentionists argue that the risk of mistake is only one moral consideration relevant to whether execution is morally permissible, and can be outweighed or overridden by competing moral considerations (just as we regard the use of automobiles as morally legitimate despite knowing their use will cause the deaths of faultless individuals). In particular, it could be permissible to run the risk of someday executing an innocent person so long as capital punishment provides sufficiently large countervailing benefits either by way of increased deterrence—yielding a net *saving* of innocent lives—or by "doing justice," giving the worst killers their retributivist just deserts.

Abolitionists challenge both of these responses to the mistake argument. They insist that execution of the innocent is not so remote a possibility, claiming that at least twenty-four such miscarriages occurred in the 1900s (Radelet et al., 1992). The protections and reviews supposedly built into the system, they argue, are frequently more apparent than real, given the often abysmally poor legal representation of indigent capital defendants at trial and the formidable legal barriers to meaningful post-conviction review, especially review of the substantive correctness of the outcome as opposed to whether procedural errors were committed. Tellingly, actual instances of overturned capital convictions often arise from the almost fortuitous intervention of media figures, college students, and other actors wholly outside the formal criminal justice system.

As for the benefits of capital punishment outweighing the risk of mistake, recall first that there is little evidence of death's superior deterrent efficacy. And "doing justice" can provide a retributive "benefit" sufficient to justify risking execution of the innocent only if we agree both that some murderers deserve death as their punishment, and that it would therefore be *unjust* to give them a lesser penalty. . . .

REFERENCES

Bedau, H. A. (ed.) (1997) *The Death Penalty in America: Current Controversies.* New York and Oxford: Oxford University Press.

Black, C. (1981) *Capital Punishment: The Inevitability of Caprice and Mistake,* 2nd edn. New York: W. W. Norton.

Dolinko, D. (1986) How to criticize the death penalty. *Journal of Criminal Law and Criminology,* 77: 546–601.

Radelet, M. L., Bedau, H. A., and Putnam, C. E. (1992) *In Spite of Innocence: Erroneous Convictions in Capital Cases.* Boston: Northeastern University Press.

Van Den Haag, E. (1982) In defense of the death penalty: a practical and moral analysis. In H. A. Bedau (ed.), *The Death Penalty in America,* 3rd edn. Oxford: Oxford University Press.

QUESTIONS

1 If it is true that the race of the victim is a significant factor in the imposition of the death penalty, does it follow that the death penalty should be abolished?

2 Is the mistake argument in itself sufficient to make the case for abolition?

3 Are procedural arguments against the death penalty collectively sufficient to make the case for abolition?

SUGGESTED ADDITIONAL READINGS FOR CHAPTER 5

BAIRD, ROBERT M., and STUART E. ROSENBAUM, eds.: *Punishment and the Death Penalty: The Current Debate.* Amherst, N.Y.: Prometheus, 1995. Part One of this anthology provides a set of articles on the justification of punishment. Part Two provides a wide range of articles on the death penalty.

BEDAU, HUGO ADAM: "Capital Punishment." In Hugh LaFollette, ed., *The Oxford Handbook of Practical Ethics.* Oxford: Oxford University Press, 2003, pp. 705–733. Bedau, a prominent abolitionist, offers commentary on numerous retentionist and abolitionist arguments, concluding his discussion with a consideration of "the best argument for abolition."

BERNS, WALTER: *For Capital Punishment.* New York: Basic, 1979. In this book, which provides a wide-ranging discussion of issues relevant to the death penalty controversy, Berns insists that capital punishment can be defended effectively on retributive grounds.

BLACK, CHARLES L., JR.: *Capital Punishment: The Inevitability of Caprice and Mistake,* 2d ed. New York: Norton, 1981. Black argues for abolition on the grounds that it is virtually impossible to eliminate arbitrariness and mistake from the numerous decisions that lead to the imposition of the death penalty.

DAVIS, MICHAEL: "Death, Deterrence, and the Method of Common Sense." *Social Theory and Practice,* vol. 7, Summer 1981, pp. 146–177. Davis argues that common sense is sufficient to establish the claim that death is the most effective deterrent. For other reasons, however, he is unwilling to endorse retention of the death penalty.

NATHANSON, STEPHEN: *An Eye for an Eye? The Immorality of Punishing by Death,* 2d ed. Lanham, Md.: Rowman & Littlefield, 2001. Nathanson touches on all aspects of the death penalty controversy and constructs an overall case for abolition.

POJMAN, LOUIS P., and JEFFREY REIMAN: *The Death Penalty: For and Against.* Lanham, Md.: Rowman & Littlefield, 1998. Each author first contributes a long essay, Pojman arguing for retention of the death penalty and Reiman arguing for abolition. Then each author provides a shorter essay in reply to the views of the other.

REIMAN, JEFFREY H.: "Justice, Civilization, and the Death Penalty: Answering van den Haag." *Philosophy and Public Affairs,* vol. 14, Spring 1985, pp. 115–148. Reiman argues that "abolition of the death penalty is part of the civilizing mission of modern states." In his view, although it is just to execute murderers, it is not unjust to forgo execution and punish murderers with long-term imprisonment. Counterarguments by Ernest van den Haag can be found in the same issue—"Refuting Reiman and Nathanson" (pp. 165–176).

RYAN, GEORGE: "'I Must Act'." In Hugo Adam Bedau and Paul G. Cassell, eds., *Debating the Death Penalty*. New York: Oxford University Press, 2004, pp. 218–234. This is the text of the January 11, 2003, speech in which the Illinois governor, arguing that "the Illinois capital punishment system is broken," announces that he is commuting the death sentences of all Illinois death-row inmates.

SORELL, TOM: "Aggravated Murder and Capital Punishment." *Journal of Applied Philosophy,* vol. 10, 1993, pp. 201–213. Sorell appeals to both John Stuart Mill and Immanuel Kant in constructing a "hybrid argument," which "provides at least the basis for a sound defense of execution for the most serious murders."

VAN DEN HAAG, ERNEST, and JOHN P. CONRAD: *The Death Penalty: A Debate.* New York: Plenum, 1983. Van den Haag (a retentionist) and Conrad (an abolitionist) touch on all aspects of the death penalty controversy as they develop their respective cases and critically respond to each other's arguments.

Unit Four

Euthanasia and Physician-Assisted Suicide Notes

Euthanasia falls into five definitions:

1 Passive voluntary euthanasia—The patient is rational and alert and asks that treatment be discontinued. This form of euthanasia is legal everywhere, because forcing treatment on a patient constitutes battery. Unless a patient has the right to say "no" to a treatment, than saying "yes" has little meaning.

2 Passive non-voluntary euthanasia—The patient is in a coma and the medical team withdraws extraordinary care. Please note that this is "non-voluntary" rather than "involuntary." Non-voluntary means the patient could not participate in the decision and has not left a living will to indicate his or her wishes. This is probably one of the most common forms of euthanasia, when the family is asked to make the decision of continuing or withdrawing treatment that may be deemed of little or no use.

3 Physician-assisted suicide—The patient is rational and alert and asks the doctor to give him a lethal dose of medication by prescription so that he may commit suicide. Currently, there are three states where this form of euthanasia is legal: Oregon, Washington and Montana. See below for further details.

4 Active voluntary euthanasia—The patient is rational and alert and asks to be given a lethal injection by the physician. This form of euthanasia is not legal in the U.S., but is legal in some European nations, Holland being the best known. See below for further details.

5 Active non-voluntary euthanasia—The patient is no longer able to communicate (perhaps is in a coma) and there is no living will. The family requests that a lethal injection be administered. This is the most controversial of all forms of euthanasia, and is the one argued to most likely lead to cases of abuse.

Other definitions that may prove helpful:

1 Living Will—A Living Will is a written document that you fill out to indicate what you would like to be done in case you are severely injured or terminally ill and you are unable to speak. You can indicate whether, if there is no hope of recovering any quality of life (and you can explain what you mean by this), that treatment not be started or may be discontinued if already started.

2 Durable Power of Attorney (also known as a Medical Power of Attorney)—A durable power of attorney is a legal document that requires the signatures of two witnesses and a witnessed by someone with Notary power. It gives the power to

265

make medical decisions concerning your welfare to another person—but only if you cannot speak for yourself. It is important to distinguish this type of power of attorney from the type of power of attorney that allows someone else to sign your name in legal transactions, such as selling a house or purchasing a car. The Durable or Medical power of attorney is strictly for medical decisions.

3 DNR—most people have heard of this term. It stands for Do Not Resuscitate. DNR orders may be a part of the Living Will. For example, if you are dying and unconscious and suffer a heart attack, then there should be no heroic efforts to save you. You want comfort care, but no attempts to save your life (or prolong your death—depending on how one looks at it).

To compare the active forms of euthanasia used in the three states where it is legal in the U.S. compared to that of Holland, see below:

Oregon, Washington and Montana	Holland
Physician-Assisted euthanasia (suicide)	**Active Voluntary Euthanasia**
Must be patient initiated	Must be patient initiated
Must be confirmed by second opinion	Must be confirmed by second opinion
Must have a life expectancy of less less than 6 months	Must have "unrelieved suffering"
Must be by prescription	May be done by physician by injection

You may notice that the first two guidelines are identical. It is when we get down to the last two that the differences become apparent. In the readings, you will find that authors talk about "killing" or "allowing to die." The term, "killing," is applied to forms of active euthanasia. The argument is that an action is being done to bring about the death of the patient. The term, "allowing to die," is used in forms of passive euthanasia. The argument is that by removing treatment there is no intent to cause a death. If the patient were healthy, removing treatment, such as a breathing tube, would not cause death. Therefore, it is the underlying illness that is causing the death, not the removal of treatment. See both Rachels' and Callahan's articles for opposite views on the use of these terms.

James Rachels: Rachels argues that "killing" vs. "allowing to die" are meaningless terms. In both cases, the patient dies, but in killing (active voluntary euthanasia) the patient has control and sometimes death is the more humane option. He uses the case of a Down's Syndrome child to illustrate the meaninglessness of "killing" vs. "allowing to die." He makes the same point with the story of Smith and Jones. His contention is that intent cannot be proved. It may be useful to try and prove intent in a legal case, but in terms of ethics there may be no difference. He divides his argument into four segments.

Daniel Callahan: Callahan defends his support of the traditional AMA position on euthanasia (that passive forms are acceptable, but active forms are not) with three arguments divided into "metaphysics," "morality," and "medical." If we combine the arguments, they all come together in the following chart:

Killing	Allowing to die
Is the direct action of another	Results from impersonal forces
Is caused by human action	Is caused by non-human events
Someone can be held responsible	No human agent can be held responsible
The death is intended	The death is not intended

What Callahan is arguing is that in when a death is a result of "killing," it is significantly different from a merely a death as a result of "allowing to die." In the case of killing, there is human interference and cause, and, therefore, the person involved may be held responsible and accountable. In the case of "allowing to die," the cause of death is natural, and, therefore, no one is responsible.

Daniel Brock: The main thing to look for in Brock's article is the argument he makes for allowing voluntary forms of euthanasia, including physician-assisted. He maintains that the confidence in physicians would be increased rather than decreased—as long as it is at the request of a competent patient and under the right circumstances.

Stephen G. Potts: Potts is not against the right to die or the right to suicide. What he objects to is the institutionalization (legalization) of the right to *assistance* in suicide. He believes that if we permit assistance in suicide, then we will end up with doctors who have a duty to assist. He says this starts a slippery slope, and the worst case scenario would be one where the voluntary nature of euthanasia might be compromised and the right to die would become the duty to die.

David Watts and Timothy Howell: Watts and Howell argue that assisted-suicide is substantially different from voluntary active euthanasia. However, they also divide assisted-suicide into three categories. They approve only of the forms of suicide that provide information or the means to commit suicide. They do not approve of any direct assistance.

Chief Justice William H. Rehnquist: Rehnquist gives the majority opinion in *Washington v. Glucksberg*, the case that considered the constitutionality of *assisted-*suicide. When the 9th District Court heard this case, it agreed that the ban on assisted-suicide was unconstitutional. The Supreme Court reversed this decision. The Supreme Court began by reviewing the history of suicide and the laws concerning suicide. The Court acknowledged that people have the right to commit suicide (this right was established in the *Cruzon* case, where the right was set to refuse nutrition and hydration), but concludes that this is substantially different from a right to have assistance in suicide. However, Rehnquist points out that the Constitution is silent on this point and, therefore, it is something that must be determined by individual states. It is this case that gives final authority to the state of Oregon to become the first U.S. state to allow a form of physician-assisted suicide. The next state is Washington, and then Wyoming. It is now up to each state as to whether or not physician-assistance in suicide is made legal or not.

Justice Sandra Day O'Connor: O'Connor is also responding to the *Washington v. Glucksberg* case. She agrees with the ban on assisted-suicide (although, as we have seen, this is not a constitutional issue and is to be decided state by state), in the Glucksberg case. She justifies her position by saying that terminal illnesses are difficult to predict and the request for assistance in dying might not be truly voluntary. In other words, she gives the same criticism that will be the main criticism leveled against the guidelines for physician-assisted suicide in Oregon and other states. The guidelines say that the patient must be terminally ill and projected to die within six months. The problem is that errors can be made in whether an illness is terminal and projecting the time of death is a very inexact science. However, O'Connor does argue that if the patient is in pain, then relief should be given—even if such relief might actually hasten or inadvertently cause the death of the patient.

Franklin G. Miller and Diane E. Meier: Miller and Meier argue that we do not need to legalized physician-assisted suicide or any other form of active euthanasia because a patient already has the right to commit suicide through dehydration and starvation (established by the *Cruzon* case). The reason the issue of terminal dehydration and starvation ever came up is because, in the *Cruzon* case, the patient was unable to take the cap off a bottle of pills, or follow any active form of suicide. For the hospital to send her home to die would have been inhumane. She needed care, but wanted to be allowed to die. The court decided that if she refused nutrition or hydration, she had a right to do so, that she could not be forced to be fed, but that she still had the right to comfort care. Miller and Meier are suggesting that this precedent is sufficient for patients who wish to end their life. Their justification is that dying of starvation isn't such a bad thing.

Obviously, they have not seen people or animals that are dying of starvation. It is a horrible death.

CHAPTER 6

Euthanasia and Physician-Assisted Suicide

The mercy killing of patients by physicians, whether called "active euthanasia" (as it is here) or simply "euthanasia," is a topic of long-standing controversy. Can active euthanasia—especially in response to the request of a competent patient—be morally justified? Should it be legalized? Parallel questions can be raised about physician-assisted suicide, a closely related topic that has also generated intense discussion. This chapter is designed to deal with ethical and social-policy questions about active euthanasia and physician-assisted suicide.

EUTHANASIA: SOME IMPORTANT DISTINCTIONS

There is both a narrow and a broad sense of *euthanasia,* and the difference between the two is best understood by reference to the categories of killing and allowing to die, although the distinction between killing and allowing to die is itself a controversial one. Understood in the narrow sense, the category of euthanasia is limited to mercy *killing.* Thus, if a physician believes a terminally ill patient is better off dead and for that reason (mercifully) administers a lethal dose of a drug to the patient, this act is a paradigm of euthanasia. On the other hand, if a physician *allows a patient to die* (e.g., by withholding or withdrawing a respirator), this does not count as euthanasia. Although the narrow sense of *euthanasia* is becoming increasingly common, many writers still use the word in the broad sense. Understood in the broad sense, the category of euthanasia encompasses both killing and allowing to die (on grounds of mercy). Of course, the underlying assumption in conceptualizing the withholding or withdrawing of treatment under the heading of euthanasia is that the physician withholds or withdraws life-sustaining treatment (mercifully) for the precise purpose of bringing about the patient's death. Those who employ the broad sense of *euthanasia* typically distinguish between *active* euthanasia (i.e., killing) and *passive* euthanasia (i.e., allowing to die).

One other distinction is of central importance in discussions of euthanasia. *Voluntary* euthanasia proceeds in response to the (informed) request of a competent patient. *Nonvoluntary* euthanasia involves an individual who is incompetent to give consent. The possibility of nonvoluntary euthanasia might arise with regard to adults who have for any number of reasons (e.g., Alzheimer's disease) lost their decision-making capacity, and it might arise with regard to newborn infants, children, and severely retarded adults. Both voluntary and nonvoluntary euthanasia may be further distinguished from *involuntary* euthanasia, which entails acting against the will or, at any rate, without the permission of a competent person. It is important to note, however, that some writers use the phrase *involuntary euthanasia* in referring to what has been identified here as *nonvoluntary euthanasia*.

If the voluntary/nonvoluntary distinction is combined with the active/passive distinction, four types of euthanasia can be distinguished: (1) voluntary active euthanasia, (2) nonvoluntary active euthanasia, (3) voluntary passive euthanasia, and (4) nonvoluntary passive euthanasia. Contemporary debate, however, focuses on the moral legitimacy of active euthanasia, especially voluntary active euthanasia. There is far less controversy about the moral legitimacy of passive euthanasia, whether voluntary or nonvoluntary. At any rate, the idea that it can be morally appropriate to withhold or withdraw life-sustaining treatment is firmly established, at least in the United States. This is not to say, of course, that there are no issues related to the specific conditions that must be satisfied in order for the withholding or withdrawing of life-sustaining treatment to be morally appropriate. In particular, there are areas of controversy related to withholding or withdrawing life-sustaining treatment from incompetent patients in various categories (e.g., severely impaired newborn infants).

ADVANCE DIRECTIVES

Depending on a patient's particular circumstances, life-sustaining treatment can take a variety of forms—for example, mechanical respiration, cardiopulmonary resuscitation, kidney dialysis, surgery, antibiotics, and artificial nutrition and hydration. The ordinary presumption is that a competent adult has both a moral and a legal right to refuse any medical treatment, including life-sustaining treatment. However, the rigors of incurable illness and the dying process frequently deprive previously competent patients of their decision-making capacity. How can a person best ensure that his or her personal wishes with regard to life-sustaining treatment (in various possible circumstances) will be honored even if decision-making capacity is lost? Although communication of one's attitudes and preferences to one's physician, family, and friends surely provides some measure of protection, it is frequently asserted that the most effective protection comes through the formation of *advance directives*.

There are two basic types of advance directives, and each has legal status in almost all, if not all, of the states. In executing an *instructional* directive, a person specifies instructions about his or her care in the event that decision-making capacity is lost. Such a directive, especially when it deals specifically with a person's wishes regarding life-sustaining treatment in various possible circumstances, is commonly called a *living will*. In executing a *proxy* directive, a person specifies a substitute decision maker to make health-care decisions for him or her in the event that decision-making capacity is lost. The legal mechanism for executing a proxy directive is often called a *durable power of attorney for health care*. Since purging ambiguities from even the most explicit written directives is difficult, as is foreseeing all the contingencies that might give rise to a need for treatment decisions, many commentators recommend the execution of a durable power of attorney for health care even if a person has already executed a living will.

THE MORALITY OF ACTIVE EUTHANASIA

James Rachels argues in this chapter for the moral legitimacy of active euthanasia. One of his central claims is that there is no morally significant distinction between killing and allowing to die. Daniel Callahan, by way of contrast, defends the coherence and moral importance of the distinction between killing and allowing to die. Callahan is opposed to active euthanasia and argues that killing patients is incompatible with the role of the physician in society. In his view, the power of the physician must be used "only to cure or comfort, never to kill." Dan W. Brock, in turn, rejects the idea that active euthanasia is incompatible with the fundamental professional commitments of a physician. Furthermore, in stating a case for the moral legitimacy of voluntary active euthanasia, Brock appeals to the centrality of two fundamental values—individual autonomy (self-determination) and individual well-being.

Those, like Rachels, who argue for the moral legitimacy of active euthanasia usually emphasize considerations of humaneness. When the intent of argument (as in the case of Brock) is to provide a defense of *voluntary* active euthanasia, the humanitarian appeal is typically conjoined with an appeal to the primacy of individual autonomy. Thus, the overall case for the moral legitimacy of voluntary active euthanasia incorporates two basic arguments: (1) It is cruel and inhumane to refuse the plea of a terminally ill person for his or her life to be mercifully ended in order to avoid future suffering and/or indignity. (2) Individual choice should be respected to the extent that it does not result in harm to others. Since no one is harmed—at least in typical cases—by terminally ill patients' undergoing active euthanasia, a decision to have one's life ended in this fashion should be respected.

Those who argue against the moral legitimacy of active euthanasia typically rest their case on one or all of the following claims: (1) Killing an innocent person is intrinsically wrong. (2) Killing is incompatible with the professional responsibilities of the physician. (3) Any systematic acceptance of active euthanasia would lead to detrimental social consequences (e.g., via a lessening of respect for human life). This third line of argument is the one that is typically most emphasized in discussions concerning the legalization of active euthanasia.

PHYSICIAN-ASSISTED SUICIDE

Any discussion of physician-assisted suicide is likely to bring to mind questions about the morality and rationality of suicide itself—questions that cannot be fully addressed in this chapter.[1] Suicide, according to a more or less standard definition, is the intentional termination of one's own life. Under what conditions, if any, is suicide morally acceptable? Classical literature on the morality of suicide provides a number of sources who issue a strong moral condemnation of suicide. The traditional arguments against suicide include religiously based arguments as well as arguments that are philosophical in character. Saint Thomas Aquinas (1225–1274), for example, argues that suicide is to be condemned not only because it violates our duty to God but also because it violates the natural law, and, moreover, because it injures the community. A contrasting point of view has a more contemporary ring but is not without support in the classical literature: Suicide is morally acceptable to the extent that it does no substantial damage to the interests of other individuals.

Closely associated with the issue of the morality of suicide is the issue of the rationality of suicide. Clearly, many suicides are irrational, the product of disordered thinking. But it is sometimes asserted that a suicidal intention is necessarily irrational and thus a symptom of mental illness and incompetence. In other words, it is impossible for a *competent* adult to have a suicidal intention. Although this point seems to be built into some psychiatric theories, many philosophers—and, today, many psychiatrists as well—consider it an implausible contention. Consider, in particular, the case of a terminally ill patient experiencing intense suffering with no realistic prospect of relief. If it is correct to say that such a person is better off dead, then it is hard to deny that suicide could be a rational choice. Of course, none of this is meant to deny the distorting effects that depression can exercise over human judgment.

Arguments for and against the moral legitimacy of physician-assisted suicide largely parallel the standard arguments for and against the moral legitimacy of voluntary active euthanasia, and one might wonder if there is a morally significant difference between these two practices. Physician-assisted suicide typically involves a physician in one or both of the following roles: (1) providing *information* to a patient about how to commit suicide in an effective manner and (2) providing the *means* necessary for an effective suicide (most commonly, by writing a prescription for a lethal amount of medication). Other modes of physician assistance in suicide might include providing moral support for the patient's decision, "supervising" the actual suicide, and helping the patient carry out the necessary physical actions. For example, a very frail patient might need a certain amount of physical assistance just to take pills.

In both physician-assisted suicide and voluntary active euthanasia, a physician plays an active role in bringing about the death of a patient. However, at face value, there is a difference between the two: In voluntary active euthanasia it is the physician

---

[1]For one avenue into the philosophical literature on suicide, see M. Pabst Battin and David J. Mayo, eds., *Suicide: The Philosophical Issues* (New York: St. Martin's Press, 1980). This valuable collection of articles includes material on the concept of suicide, the morality of suicide, and the rationality of suicide.

who ultimately kills the patient, whereas in physician-assisted suicide it is the patient who ultimately kills himself or herself, albeit with the assistance of the physician. It is a controversial issue whether this difference in terms of ultimate causal agency can serve as a basis for the claim that there is a morally significant difference between physician-assisted suicide and voluntary active euthanasia.

An important development in the public debate over physician-assisted suicide took place in 1997, when the United States Supreme Court unanimously upheld the constitutionality of state statutes prohibiting physician assistance in suicide. In *Washington v. Glucksberg,* the Court rejected the claim that the Due Process Clause of the Fourteenth Amendment encompasses a fundamental right to physician-assisted suicide. In the companion case *Vacco v. Quill,* the Court rejected the claim that the Equal Protection Clause of the Fourteenth Amendment is violated by a state prohibiting physician-assisted suicide while at the same time permitting the withdrawal of life-sustaining treatment. In resolving this second case, the Court explicitly committed itself to the legitimacy and importance of drawing a distinction between assisting suicide and withdrawing life-sustaining treatment.

Each of the physician-assisted suicide cases was decided by a nine-to-zero vote, but the Court is not nearly so unified on the construction of the underlying issues as these unanimous votes might suggest. The Court's underlying fragmentation of viewpoint is reflected in a host of concurring opinions generated by the cases. Chief Justice William H. Rehnquist wrote the "Opinion of the Court" in each of the cases, but only four other justices actually concurred in these opinions, and one of these four, Justice Sandra Day O'Connor, also crafted a concurring opinion. The opinion of Chief Justice Rehnquist in *Washington v. Glucksberg* is reprinted in this chapter, as is the concurring opinion of Justice O'Connor.

ACTIVE EUTHANASIA, PHYSICIAN-ASSISTED SUICIDE, AND SOCIAL POLICY

Should active euthanasia be legalized? If so, in what form or forms and with what safeguards? Although active euthanasia is presently illegal in all fifty states and the District of Columbia, proposals for its legalization have been recurrently advanced. Most commonly, these proposals call for the legalization of *voluntary* active euthanasia.

There are some who consider active euthanasia in any form intrinsically immoral (sometimes on overtly religious grounds) and, for this reason, oppose the legalization of voluntary active euthanasia. Others are opposed to legalization because of their conviction that physicians in particular should not kill. Still others, such as Stephen G. Potts in this chapter, do not necessarily object to individual acts of voluntary active euthanasia but still stand opposed to any social policy that would permit its practice. The concern here is with the adverse social consequences of legalization. In this vein, it is alleged that vulnerable persons would be subject to abuse, that a disincentive for the availability of supportive services for the dying would be created, and that public trust and confidence in physicians would be undermined. Another consequentialist concern is embodied in a frequently made "slippery slope" argument: The legalization of voluntary active euthanasia would lead us down a slippery slope to the legalization of nonvoluntary (and perhaps involuntary) euthanasia. Those who support the legalization of voluntary active euthanasia recognize that some unfortunate consequences may result from legalization. However, they typically seek to establish that potential dangers are either overstated or can be minimized with appropriate safeguards.

Although arguments advanced against the legalization of physician-assisted suicide largely parallel those advanced against the legalization of voluntary active euthanasia, it is frequently argued that there is far less risk of abuse involved in the legalization of physician-assisted suicide. This point of view is embraced by David T. Watts and Timothy Howell in one of this chapter's readings. These two physicians recommend the legalization of physician-assisted suicide, although they do not favor allowing a physician to "supervise" or directly aid a patient in committing suicide. They would restrict physicians to providing information about suicide and writing prescriptions for a lethal amount of medication. According to another point of view, since terminally ill patients are already free to refuse nutrition and hydration, and thereby bring about death, there is no compelling need to legalize physician-assisted suicide (or voluntary active euthanasia).[2] Franklin G. Miller and Diane E. Meier give voice to this point of view in an article included in this chapter.

The Oregon Model

One concrete model for the legalization of physician-assisted suicide has emerged in Oregon. In November 1994, voters in Oregon approved by a margin of 51 to 49 percent a ballot initiative known as the Oregon Death with Dignity Act. This law survived constitutional challenges and ultimately went into effect on October 27, 1997; it also survived a second referendum in November 1997 in which Oregon voters opposed repeal by a margin of 60 to 40 percent. The law permits Oregon physicians to prescribe lethal drugs for Oregon adult residents who are terminally ill and who want to end their own lives. In order for a patient to be eligible for such assistance, the attending physician must determine that the patient has a terminal disease—a diagnosis entailing that the patient is expected to die within six months—and a consulting physician must confirm this diagnosis. The following requirements are also stipulated. (1) The patient must make an initial oral request, reiterate the oral request after fifteen days have passed, and also submit a written request, supported by two witnesses. (2) Before writing the prescription, the attending physician must wait at least fifteen days after the patient's initial request and at least forty-eight hours after the written request. (3) The attending physician must fully inform the patient about the diagnosis, prognosis, and feasible alternatives— including comfort care, hospice care, and pain control. (4) Both the attending physician and the consulting physician must certify that the patient is "capable" (i.e., has decision-making capacity), is acting voluntarily, and has made an informed

---

[2]A related argument identifies the availability of *terminal sedation* as a reason why it is not necessary to legalize physician-assisted suicide. The idea of terminal sedation naturally arises in those (presumably) few cases in which the severe pain or suffering of a terminally ill patient is resistant to established palliative techniques and cannot be alleviated except by *sedation into unconsciousness* until death occurs.

choice. (5) If either physician believes that the patient's judgment might be impaired (e.g., by depression), the patient must be referred for counseling. The Oregon law allows the attending physician and others to be present when the patient takes the lethal dose.

The Oregon Department of Human Services is charged with the responsibility of reporting annually on the practice of physician-assisted suicide in Oregon.[3] In 2004, thirty-seven patients in Oregon used physician-assisted suicide to end their lives, accounting for about one of every 800 Oregon deaths that year. In the seven-year period subsequent to legalization, 1998–2004, a total of 208 Oregonians used physician-assisted suicide to end their lives. With the United States Supreme Court ruling in *Gonzales v. Oregon* (2006), the practice of physician-assisted suicide in Oregon survived another legal challenge. The Bush administration had contended that physicians in Oregon who prescribe lethal drugs for the purpose of assisting suicide are in violation of the Controlled Substances Act, but the Court rejected this claim and upheld the Oregon law.

Consider, for a moment, some of the issues that might arise in specifying appropriate limits for the practice of physician-assisted suicide and/or voluntary active euthanasia. Would we want to restrict availability to patients who are terminally ill (according to some definition), to patients who are experiencing unbearable suffering (according to some definition), or to patients who are *both* terminally ill and experiencing unbearable suffering?[4] And if voluntary active euthanasia is at issue, would we want to insist that a patient be competent at the time he or she undergoes active euthanasia, or would we also want to allow for the possibility of active euthanasia in accordance with an advance directive?

Voluntary active euthanasia is a well-established practice in the Netherlands. One of the interesting aspects of the Dutch system is its requirement that active euthanasia be available only if the patient is experiencing unbearable suffering (with no prospect of improvement), but there is no requirement that the patient be terminally ill. Another interesting feature of the Dutch system is its explicit acceptance of an advance-directive principle. That is, active euthanasia may be provided for patients who have become incompetent but who had clearly expressed their request for active euthanasia in a written declaration while competent.

The Dutch Model

Both voluntary active euthanasia (VAE) and physician-assisted suicide (PAS) have been openly available to patients in the Netherlands for many years. For example, a government-sponsored study reported that in 1990 there were 2,300 cases of VAE and 400 cases of PAS, accounting for about 3 percent of overall mortality that year. And yet, until more recently, these practices were not strictly legal. Rather, the

[3]These annual reports are available on the Oregon Department of Human Services home page (www.dhs.state.or.us/publichealth/chs/pas/pas.cfm).
[4]For an argument to restrict availability (at least at the present time) to those who are terminally ill, see Martin Gunderson and David J. Mayo, "Restricting Physician-Assisted Death to the Terminally Ill," *Hastings Center Report*, vol. 30, November-December 2000, pp. 17–23.

operational understanding was that Dutch physicians would be immune from prosecution as long as they adhered to a set of guidelines worked out by agreement of the medical and legal communities. In 2002, however, the year in which the Dutch Termination of Life on Request and Assisted Suicide Act (TLRASA) went into effect, VAE and PAS were formally legalized in the Netherlands.

The TLRASA stipulates that any physician who properly conforms to "due care criteria" in the provision of VAE/PAS and promptly reports to a regional review committee any case in which VAE or PAS has been provided will be immune from prosecution. Further, in order to comply with the due care criteria, the TLRASA specifies that the physician must:

(a) be satisfied that the patient has made a voluntary and carefully considered request;
(b) be satisfied that the patient's suffering was unbearable, and that there was no prospect of improvement;
(c) have informed the patient about his situation and his prospects;
(d) have come to the conclusion, together with the patient, that there is no reasonable alternative in light of the patient's situation;
(e) have consulted at least one other, independent physician, who must have seen the patient and given a written opinion on the due care criteria referred to in (a) to (d) above; and (f) have terminated the patient's life or provided assistance with suicide with due medical care and attention.

A regional review committee is charged with the responsibility of reviewing each reported case of VAE/PAS in order to determine if physician actions have properly conformed to the due care criteria.

The TLRASA explicitly allows for the possibility of active euthanasia in accordance with an advance-directive principle. That is, in essence, active euthanasia may be provided for a presently incompetent patient who, while competent, made a written declaration requesting that his or her life be terminated under specified circumstances. The TLRASA further allows for the possibility of VAE/PAS in the case of a minor who is at least twelve years old and "is deemed to be capable of making a reasonable appraisal of his own interests." Requests from sixteen- and seventeen-year-olds can be complied with but only on the condition of *consultation* with parents (or guardian), although parental/guardian approval is not required. Requests from twelve- to fifteen-year-olds can also be complied with but only on the condition of parental/guardian *consent*.

Several questions naturally arise. Does the Dutch system provide a morally sound framework for the practice of active euthanasia and physician-assisted suicide? In particular, are the TLRASA provisions related to minors morally sound? Does the Dutch system incorporate adequate safeguards against abuse? Should active euthanasia be legalized in the United States along the lines of the Dutch model? As would be expected, opponents of legalization in the United States typically advance numerous criticisms of the Dutch system, but even many proponents of legalization in the United States are somewhat wary of the Dutch model, believing that it does not incorporate adequate safeguards against abuse—or, at any rate, that it would not provide adequate safeguards within the framework of American society.

Thomas A. Mappes

Active and Passive Euthanasia

James Rachels

In this classic article, Rachels identifies the "conventional doctrine" on the morality
of euthanasia as the doctrine that allows passive euthanasia but does not allow
active euthanasia. He then argues that the conventional doctrine may be challenged
for four reasons. First, active euthanasia is in many cases more humane than
passive euthanasia. Second, the conventional doctrine leads to decisions concerning
life and death on irrelevant grounds. Third, the doctrine rests on a distinction
between killing and letting die that itself has no moral importance. Fourth, the most
common argument in favor of the doctrine is invalid.

The distinction between active and passive euthanasia is thought to be crucial for
medical ethics. The idea is that it is permissible, at least in some cases, to withhold
treatment and allow a patient to die, but it is never permissible to take any direct
action designed to kill the patient. This doctrine seems to be accepted by most doctors, and it is endorsed in a statement adopted by the House of Delegates of the
American Medical Association on December 4, 1973:

> The intentional termination of the life of one human being by another—mercy killing—
> is contrary to that for which the medical profession stands and is contrary to the policy
> of the American Medical Association.
>
> The cessation of the employment of extraordinary means to prolong the life of the
> body when there is irrefutable evidence that biological death is imminent is the decision
> of the patient and/or his immediate family. The advice and judgment of the physician
> should be freely available to the patient and/or his immediate family.

However, a strong case can be made against this doctrine. In what follows, I will
set out some of the relevant arguments, and urge doctors to reconsider their views
on this matter.

To begin with a familiar type of situation, a patient who is dying of incurable
cancer of the throat is in terrible pain, which can no longer be satisfactorily alleviated. He is certain to die within a few days, even if present treatment is continued,
but he does not want to go on living for those days since the pain is unbearable. So
he asks the doctor for an end to it, and his family joins in the request.

Suppose the doctor agrees to withhold treatment, as the conventional doctrine
says he may. The justification for his doing so is that the patient is in terrible agony,
and since he is going to die anyway, it would be wrong to prolong his suffering
needlessly. But now notice this. If one simply withholds treatment, it may take the
patient longer to die, and so he may suffer more than he would if more direct action
were taken and a lethal injection given. This fact provides strong reason for thinking that, once the initial decision not to prolong his agony has been made, active
euthanasia is actually preferable to passive euthanasia, rather than the reverse. To

Reprinted with permission from *The New England Journal of Medicine,* vol. 292, no. 2 (January 9,
1975), pp. 78–80.

say otherwise is to endorse the option that leads to more suffering rather than less, and is contrary to the humanitarian impulse that prompts the decision not to prolong his life in the first place.

Part of my point is that the process of being "allowed to die" can be relatively slow and painful, whereas being given a lethal injection is relatively quick and painless. Let me give a different sort of example. In the United States about one in 600 babies is born with Down's syndrome. Most of these babies are otherwise healthy—that is, with only the usual pediatric care, they will proceed to an otherwise normal infancy. Some, however, are born with congenital defects such as intestinal obstructions that require operations if they are to live. Sometimes, the parents and the doctor will decide not to operate, and let the infant die. Anthony Shaw describes what happens then:

> . . . When surgery is denied [the doctor] must try to keep the infant from suffering while natural forces sap the baby's life away. As a surgeon whose natural inclination is to use the scalpel to fight off death, standing by and watching a salvageable baby die is the most emotionally exhausting experience I know. It is easy at a conference, in a theoretical discussion, to decide that such infants should be allowed to die. It is altogether different to stand by in the nursery and watch as dehydration and infection wither a tiny being over hours and days. This is a terrible ordeal for me and the hospital staff—much more so than for the parents who never set foot in the nursery.[1]

I can understand why some people are opposed to all euthanasia, and insist that such infants must be allowed to live. I think I can also understand why other people favor destroying these babies quickly and painlessly. But why should anyone favor letting "dehydration and infection wither a tiny being over hours and days"? The doctrine that says that a baby may be allowed to dehydrate and wither, but may not be given an injection that would end its life without suffering, seems so patently cruel as to require no further refutation. The strong language is not intended to offend, but only to put the point in the clearest possible way.

My second argument is that the conventional doctrine leads to decisions concerning life and death made on irrelevant grounds.

Consider again the case of the infants with Down's syndrome who need operations for congenital defects unrelated to the syndrome to live. Sometimes, there is no operation, and the baby dies, but when there is no such defect, the baby lives on. Now, an operation such as that to remove an intestinal obstruction is not prohibitively difficult. The reason why such operations are not performed in these cases is, clearly, that the child has Down's syndrome and the parents and doctor judge that because of that fact it is better for the child to die.

But notice that this situation is absurd, no matter what view one takes of the lives and potentials of such babies. If the life of such an infant is worth preserving, what does it matter if it needs a simple operation? Or, if one thinks it better that such a baby should not live on, what difference does it make that it happens to have an unobstructed intestinal tract? In either case, the matter of life and death is being decided on irrelevant grounds. It is the Down's syndrome, and not the intestines, that is the issue. The matter should be decided, if at all, on that basis, and not be allowed to depend on the essentially irrelevant question of whether the intestinal tract is blocked.

What makes this situation possible, of course, is the idea that when there is an intestinal blockage, one can "let the baby die," but when there is no such defect there is nothing that can be done, for one must not "kill" it. The fact that this idea leads to such results as deciding life or death on irrelevant grounds is another good reason why the doctrine should be rejected.

One reason why so many people think that there is an important moral difference between active and passive euthanasia is that they think killing someone is morally worse than letting someone die. But is it? Is killing, in itself, worse than letting die? To investigate this issue, two cases may be considered that are exactly alike except that one involves killing whereas the other involves letting someone die. Then, it can be asked whether this difference makes any difference to the moral assessments. It is important that the cases be exactly alike, except for this one difference, since otherwise one cannot be confident that it is this difference and not some other that accounts for any variation in the assessments of the two cases. So, let us consider this pair of cases:

In the first, Smith stands to gain a large inheritance if anything should happen to his six-year-old cousin. One evening while the child is taking his bath, Smith sneaks into the bathroom and drowns the child, and then arranges things so that it will look like an accident.

In the second, Jones also stands to gain if anything should happen to his six-year-old cousin. Like Smith, Jones sneaks in planning to drown the child in his bath. However, just as he enters the bathroom Jones sees the child slip and hit his head, and fall face down in the water. Jones is delighted; he stands by, ready to push the child's head back under if it is necessary, but it is not necessary. With only a little thrashing about the child drowns all by himself, "accidentally," as Jones watches and does nothing.

Now Smith killed the child, whereas Jones "merely" let the child die. That is the only difference between them. Did either man behave better, from a moral point of view? If the difference between killing and letting die were in itself a morally important matter, one should say that Jones's behavior was less reprehensible than Smith's. But does one really want to say that? I think not. In the first place, both men acted from the same motive, personal gain, and both had exactly the same end in view when they acted. It may be inferred from Smith's conduct that he is a bad man, although that judgment may be withdrawn or modified if certain further facts are learned about him— for example, that he is mentally deranged. But would not the very same thing be inferred about Jones from his conduct? And would not the same further considerations also be relevant to any modification of this judgment? Moreover, suppose Jones pleaded, in his own defense, "After all, I didn't do anything except just stand there and watch the child drown. I didn't kill him; I only let him die." Again, if letting die were in itself less bad than killing, this defense should have at least some weight. But it does not. Such a "defense" can only be regarded as a grotesque perversion of moral reasoning. Morally speaking, it is no defense at all.

Now, it may be pointed out, quite properly, that the cases of euthanasia with which doctors are concerned are not like this at all. They do not involve personal gain or the destruction of normally healthy children. Doctors are concerned only with cases in which the patient's life is of no further use to him, or in which the patient's life has become or will soon become a terrible burden. However, the point is the same in these cases: the bare difference between killing and letting die does not, in itself, make a moral difference. If a doctor lets a patient die, for humane reasons, he is in the same moral position as if he had given the patient a lethal injection for humane reasons. If his decision was wrong—if, for example, the patient's illness was in fact curable—the decision would be equally regrettable no matter which method was used to carry it out. And if the doctor's decision was the right one, the method used is not in itself important.

The AMA policy statement isolates the crucial issue very well; the crucial issue is "the intentional termination of the life of one human being by another." But after identifying this issue, and forbidding "mercy killing," the statement goes on to deny that the cessation of treatment is the intentional termination of a life. This is where the mistake comes in, for what is the cessation of treatment, in these circumstances, if it is not "the intentional termination of the life of one human being by another?" Of course, it is exactly that, and if it were not, there would be no point to it.

Many people will find this judgment hard to accept. One reason, I think, is that it is very easy to conflate the question of whether killing is, in itself, worse than letting die, with the very different question of whether most actual cases of killing are more reprehensible than most actual cases of letting die. Most actual cases of killing are clearly terrible (think, for example, of all the murders reported in the newspapers), and one hears of such cases every day. On the other hand, one hardly ever hears of a case of letting die, except for the actions of doctors who are motivated by humanitarian reasons. So one learns to think of killing in a much worse light than of letting die. But this does not mean that there is something about killing that makes it in itself worse than letting die, for it is not the bare difference between killing and letting die that makes the difference in these cases. Rather, the other factors—the murderer's motive of personal gain, for example, contrasted with the doctor's humanitarian motivation—account for different reactions to the different cases.

I have argued that killing is not in itself any worse than letting die; if my contention is right, it follows that active euthanasia is not any worse than passive euthanasia. What arguments can be given on the other side? The most common, I believe, is the following:

"The important difference between active and passive euthanasia is that, in passive euthanasia, the doctor does not do anything to bring about the patient's death. The doctor does nothing, and the patient dies of whatever ills already afflict him. In active euthanasia, however, the doctor does something to bring about the patient's death: he kills him. The doctor who gives the patient with cancer a lethal injection has himself caused his patient's death; whereas if he merely ceases treatment, the cancer is the cause of the death."

A number of points need to be made here. The first is that it is not exactly correct to say that in passive euthanasia the doctor does nothing, for he does do one thing that is very important: he lets the patient die. "Letting someone die" is certainly different, in some respects, from other types of action—mainly in that it is a kind of action that one may perform by way of not performing certain other actions.

For example, one may let a patient die by way of not giving medication, just as one may insult someone by way of not shaking his hand. But for any purpose of moral assessment, it is a type of action nonetheless. The decision to let a patient die is subject to moral appraisal in the same way that a decision to kill him would be subject to moral appraisal: it may be assessed as wise or unwise, compassionate or sadistic, right or wrong. If a doctor deliberately let a patient die who was suffering from a routinely curable illness, the doctor would certainly be to blame for what he had done, just as he would be to blame if he had needlessly killed the patient. Charges against him would then be appropriate. If so, it would be no defense at all for him to insist that he didn't "do anything." He would have done something very serious indeed, for he let his patient die.

Fixing the cause of death may be very important from a legal point of view, for it may determine whether criminal charges are brought against the doctor. But I do not think that this notion can be used to show a moral difference between active and passive euthanasia. The reason why it is considered bad to be the cause of someone's death is that death is regarded as a great evil—and so it is. However, if it has been decided that euthanasia—even passive euthanasia—is desirable in a given case, it has also been decided that in this instance death is no greater an evil than the patient's continued existence. And if this is true, the usual reason for not wanting to be the cause of someone's death simply does not apply.

Finally, doctors may think that all of this is only of academic interest—the sort of thing that philosophers may worry about but that has no practical bearing on their own work. After all, doctors must be concerned about the legal consequences of what they do, and active euthanasia is clearly forbidden by the law. But even so, doctors should also be concerned with the fact that the law is forcing upon them a moral doctrine that may well be indefensible, and has a considerable effect on their practices. Of course, most doctors are not now in the position of being coerced in this matter, for they do not regard themselves as merely going along with what the law requires. Rather, in statements such as the AMA policy statement that I have quoted, they are endorsing this doctrine as a central point of medical ethics. In that statement, active euthanasia is condemned not merely as illegal but as "contrary to that for which the medical profession stands," whereas passive euthanasia is approved. However, the preceding considerations suggest that there is really no moral difference between the two, considered in themselves (there may be important moral differences in some cases in their *consequences,* but, as I pointed out, these differences may make active euthanasia, and not passive euthanasia, the morally preferable option). So, whereas doctors may have to discriminate between active and passive euthanasia to satisfy the law, they should not do any more than that. In particular, they should not give the distinction any added authority and weight by writing it into official statements of medical ethics.

NOTE

1 A. Shaw: "Doctor, Do We Have a Choice?" *The New York Times Magazine,* Jan. 30, 1972, p. 54.

QUESTIONS

1 Can the conventional doctrine on active and passive euthanasia be defended against Rachels's arguments?
2 Rachels seems to argue for the moral legitimacy of active euthanasia in general, not the moral legitimacy of *voluntary* active euthanasia in particular. Is nonvoluntary active euthanasia ever morally justified?
3 Can you imagine medical circumstances in which you would be better off dead? If so, would you welcome the possibility of active euthanasia, or only passive euthanasia? Do your religious beliefs play any role in your thinking on this issue?

Killing and Allowing to Die

Daniel Callahan

Callahan maintains that there is a valid distinction between killing and allowing to die, and he defends the distinction by reference to three overlapping perspectives—metaphysical, moral, and medical. In terms of a metaphysical perspective, Callahan emphasizes that the external world is distinct from the self and has its own causal dynamism. In terms of a moral perspective, he emphasizes the difference between *physical causality* and *moral culpability*. In conjunction with a medical perspective, he insists that killing patients is incompatible with the role of the physician in society.

. . . No valid distinction, many now argue, can be made between killing and allowing to die, or between an act of commission and one of omission. The standard distinction being challenged rests on the commonplace observation that lives can come to an end as the result of: (a) the direct action of another who becomes the cause of death (as in shooting a person), and (b) the result of impersonal forces where no human agent has acted (death by lightning, or by disease). The purpose of the distinction has been to separate those deaths caused by human action, and those caused by nonhuman events. It is, as a distinction, meant to say something about human beings and their relationship to the world. It is a way of articulating the difference between those actions for which human beings can be held rightly responsible, or blamed, and those of which they are innocent. At issue is the difference between physical causality, the realm of impersonal events, and moral culpability, the realm of human responsibility.

The challenges encompass two points. The first is that people can become equally dead by our omissions as well as our commissions. We can refrain from

Reprinted with permission of the author and the publisher from *Hastings Center Report*, vol. 19 (January/February 1989), Special Supplement, pp. 5–6. © The Hastings Center.

saving them when it is possible to do so, and they will be just as dead as if we shot them. It is our decision itself that is the reason for their death, not necessarily how we effectuate that decision. That fact establishes the basis of the second point: if we *intend* their death, it can be brought about as well by omitted acts as by those we commit. The crucial moral point is not how they die, but our intention about their death. We can, then, be responsible for the death of another by intending that they die and accomplish that end by standing aside and allowing them to die.

Despite these criticisms—resting upon ambiguities that can readily be acknowledged—the distinction between killing and allowing to die remains, I contend, perfectly valid. It not only has a logical validity but, no less importantly, a social validity whose place must be central in moral judgments. As a way of putting the distinction into perspective, I want to suggest that it is best understood as expressing three different, though overlapping, perspectives on nature and human action. I will call them the metaphysical, the moral, and the medical perspectives.

Metaphysical   The first and most fundamental premise of the distinction between killing and allowing to die is that there is a sharp difference between the self and the external world. Unlike the childish fantasy that the world is nothing more than a projection of the self, or the neurotic person's fear that he or she is responsible for everything that goes wrong, the distinction is meant to uphold a simple notion: there is a world external to the self that has its own, and independent, causal dynamism. The mistake behind a conflation of killing and allowing to die is to assume that the self has become master of everything within and outside of the self. It is as if the conceit that modern man might ultimately control nature has been internalized: that, if the self might be able to influence nature by its actions, then the self and nature must be one.

Of course that is a fantasy. The fact that we can intervene in nature, and cure or control many diseases, does not erase the difference between the self and the external world. It is as "out there" as ever, even if more under our sway. That sway, however great, is always limited. We can cure disease, but not always the chronic illness that comes with the cure. We can forestall death with modern medicine, but death always wins in the long run because of the innate limitations of the body, inherently and stubbornly beyond final human control. And we can distinguish between a diseased body and an aging body, but in the end if we wait long enough they always become one and the same body. To attempt to deny the distinction between killing and allowing to die is, then, mistakenly to impute more power to human action than it actually has and to accept the conceit that nature has now fallen wholly within the realm of human control. Not so.

Moral   At the center of the distinction between killing and allowing to die is the difference between physical causality and moral culpability. To bring the life of another to an end by an injection kills the other directly; our action is the physical cause of the death. To allow someone to die from a disease we cannot cure (and that we did not cause) is to permit the disease to act as the cause of death. The notion of physical causality in both cases rests on the difference between human agency and the action of external nature. The ambiguity arises precisely because we can be morally culpable for killing someone (if we have no moral right to do so, as we would in self-defense) and no less culpable for allowing someone to die (if we have both the possibility and the obligation of keeping that person alive). Thus there are cases where, morally speaking, it makes no difference whether we killed or allowed to die; we are equally responsible. In those instances, the lines of physical causality and moral culpability happen to cross. Yet the fact that they can cross in some cases in no way shows that they are always, or even usually, one and the same. We can normally find the difference in all but the most obscure cases. We should not, then, use the ambiguity of such cases to do away altogether with the distinction between killing and allowing to die. The ambiguity may obscure, but does not erase, the line between the two.

There is one group of ambiguous cases that is especially troublesome. Even if we grant the ordinary validity between killing and allowing to die, what about those cases that combine (a) an illness that renders a patient unable to carry out an ordinary biological function (to breathe or eat on his own, for example), and (b) our turning off a respirator or removing an artificial feeding tube? On the level of physical causality, have we killed the patient or allowed him to die? In one sense, it is our action that shortens his life, and yet in another sense his underlying disease brings his life to an end. I believe it reasonable to say that, since his life was being sustained by artificial means (respirator or feeding tube) made necessary because of the fact that he had an incapacitating disease, his disease is the ultimate reality behind his death. But for its reality, there would be no need for artificial sustenance in the first place and no moral issue at all. To lose sight of the paramount reality of the disease is to lose sight of the difference between our selves and the outer world.

I quickly add, and underscore, a moral point: the person who, without good moral reason, turns off a respirator or pulls a feeding tube, can be morally culpable; that the patient has been allowed to die of his underlying condition does not morally excuse him. The moral question is whether we are obliged to continue treating a life that is being artifically sustained. To cease treatment may or may not be morally acceptable; but it should be understood, in either case, that the physical cause of death was the underlying disease.

Medical   An important social purpose of the distinction between killing and allowing to die has been that of protecting the historical role of the physician as one who tries to cure or comfort patients rather than to kill patients. Physicians have been given special knowledge about the body, knowledge that can be used to kill or to cure. They are also given great privileges in making use of that knowledge. It is thus all the more important that physicians' social role and power be, and be seen to be, a limited power. It may be used only to cure or comfort, never to kill. They have not been given, nor should they be given, the power to use their knowledge and skills to bring life to an end. It would open the way for powerful misuse and, no less importantly, represent an intrinsic violation of what it has meant to be a physician.

Yet if it is possible for physicians to misuse their knowledge and power to kill people directly, are they thereby required to use that same knowledge always to keep people alive, always to resist a disease that can itself kill the patient? The traditional answer has been: not necessarily. For the physician's ultimate obligation is to the welfare of the patient, and excessive treatment can be as detrimental to that welfare as inadequate treatment. Put another way, the obligation to resist the lethal power of disease is limited—it ceases when the patient is unwilling to have it resisted, or where the resistance no longer serves the patient's welfare. Behind this moral premise is the recognition that disease (of some kind) ultimately triumphs and that death is both inevitable sooner or later and not, in any case, always the greatest human evil. To demand of the physician that he always struggle against disease, as if it was in his power always to conquer it, would be to fall into the same metaphysical trap mentioned above: that of assuming that no distinction can be drawn between natural and human agency.

A final word. I suggested [in an earlier discussion] that the most potent motive for active euthanasia and assisted suicide stems from a dread of the power of medicine. That power then seems to take on a drive of its own regardless of the welfare or wishes of patients. No one can easily say no—not physicians, not patients, not families. My guess is that happens because too many have already come to believe that it is their choice, and their choice alone, which brings about death; and they do not want to exercise that kind of authority. The solution is not to erase the distinction between killing and allowing to die, but to underscore its validity and importance. We can bring disease as a cause of death back into the care of the dying.

QUESTIONS

1 Is there a valid distinction between killing and allowing to die?

2 Do you agree with Callahan that the power of the physician must be used "only to cure or comfort, never to kill"?

Voluntary Active Euthanasia

Dan W. Brock

In this excerpt from a much longer article, Brock argues that two fundamental ethical values support the ethical permissibility of voluntary active euthanasia. These values are individual self-determination (autonomy) and individual well-being, the same two values that support the consensus view that patients have a right to make decisions about life-sustaining treatment. Brock also argues that allowing physicians to perform euthanasia is not incompatible with the "moral center" of medicine.

Reprinted with permission of the author and the publisher from *Hastings Center Report*, vol. 22 (March/April 1992), pp. 11, 16. © The Hastings Center.

. . . The central ethical argument for [voluntary active] euthanasia is familiar. It is that the very same two fundamental ethical values supporting the consensus on patient's rights to decide about life-sustaining treatment also support the ethical permissibility of euthanasia. These values are individual self-determination or autonomy and individual well-being. By self-determination as it bears on euthanasia, I mean people's interest in making important decisions about their lives for themselves according to their own values or conceptions of a good life, and in being left free to act on those decisions. Self-determination is valuable because it permits people to form and live in accordance with their own conception of a good life, at least within the bounds of justice and consistent with others doing so as well. In exercising self-determination people take responsibility for their lives and for the kinds of persons they become. A central aspect of human dignity lies in people's capacity to direct their lives in this way. The value of exercising self-determination presupposes some minimum of decision-making capacities or competence, which thus limits the scope of euthanasia supported by self-determination; it cannot justifiably be administered, for example, in cases of serious dementia or treatable clinical depression.

Does the value of individual self-determination extend to the time and manner of one's death? Most people are very concerned about the nature of the last stage of their lives. This reflects not just a fear of experiencing substantial suffering when dying, but also a desire to retain dignity and control during this last period of life. Death is today increasingly preceded by a long period of significant physical and mental decline, due in part to the technological interventions of modern medicine. Many people adjust to these disabilities and find meaning and value in new activities and ways. Others find the impairments and burdens in the last stage of their lives at some point sufficiently great to make life no longer worth living. For many patients near death, maintaining the quality of one's life, avoiding great suffering, maintaining one's dignity, and insuring that others remember us as we wish them to become of paramount importance and outweigh merely extending one's life. But there is no single, objectively correct answer for everyone as to when, if at all, one's life becomes all things considered a burden and unwanted. If self-determination is a fundamental value, then the great variability among people on this question makes it especially important that individuals control the manner, circumstances, and timing of their dying and death.

The other main value that supports euthanasia is individual well-being. It might seem that individual well-being conflicts with a person's self-determination when the person requests euthanasia. Life itself is commonly taken to be a central good for persons, often valued for its own sake, as well as necessary for pursuit of all other goods within a life. But when a competent patient decides to forgo all further life-sustaining treatment then the patient, either explicitly or implicitly, commonly decides that the best life possible for him or her with treatment is of sufficiently poor quality that it is worse than no further life at all. Life is no longer considered a benefit by the patient, but has now become a burden. The same judgment underlies a request for euthanasia: continued life is seen by the patient as no longer a benefit, but now a burden. Especially in the often severely compromised and debilitated states of many critically ill or dying patients, there is no objective standard, but only the competent patient's judgment of whether continued life is no longer a benefit.

Of course, sometimes there are conditions, such as clinical depression, that call into question whether the patient has made a competent choice, either to forgo life-sustaining treatment or to seek euthanasia, and then the patient's choice need not be evidence that continued life is no longer a benefit for him or her. Just as with decisions about treatment, a determination of incompetence can warrant not honoring the patient's choice; in the case of treatment, we then transfer decisional authority to a surrogate, though in the case of voluntary active euthanasia a determination that the patient is incompetent means that choice is not possible.

The value or right of self-determination does not entitle patients to compel physicians to act contrary to their own moral or professional values. Physicians are moral and professional agents whose own self-determination or integrity should be respected as well. If performing euthanasia became legally permissible, but conflicted with a particular physician's reasonable understanding of his or her moral or professional responsibilities, the care of a patient who requested euthanasia should be transferred to another. . . .

. . . Permitting physicians to perform euthanasia, it is said, would be incompatible with their fundamental moral and professional commitment as healers to care for patients and to protect life. Moreover, if euthanasia by physicians became common, patients would come to fear that a medication was intended not to treat or care, but instead to kill, and would thus lose trust in their physicians. This position was forcefully stated in a paper by Willard Gaylin and his colleagues:

> The very soul of medicine is on trial. . . . This issue touches medicine at its moral center; if this moral center collapses, if physicians become killers or are even licensed to kill, the profession—and, therewith, each physician—will never again be worthy of trust and respect as healer and comforter and protector of life in all its frailty.

These authors go on to make clear that, while they oppose permitting anyone to perform euthanasia, their special concern is with physicians doing so:

> We call on fellow physicians to say that they will not deliberately kill. We must also say to each of our fellow physicians that we will not tolerate killing of patients and that we shall take disciplinary action against doctors who kill. And we must say to the broader community that if it insists on tolerating or legalizing active euthanasia, it will have to find nonphysicians to do its killing.[1]

If permitting physicians to kill would undermine the very "moral center" of medicine, then almost certainly physicians should not be permitted to perform euthanasia. But how persuasive is this claim? Patients should not fear, as a consequence of permitting *voluntary* active euthanasia, that their physicians will substitute a lethal injection for what patients want and believe is part of their care. If active euthanasia is restricted to cases in which it is truly voluntary, then no patient should fear getting it unless she or he has voluntarily requested it. (The fear that we might in time also come to accept nonvoluntary, or even involuntary, active euthanasia is a slippery slope worry I address [in a later section].) Patients' trust of their physicians could be increased, not eroded, by knowledge that physicians will provide aid in dying when patients seek it.

Might Gaylin and his colleagues nevertheless be correct in their claim that the moral center of medicine would collapse if physicians were to become killers? This question raises what at the deepest level should be the guiding aims of medicine, a question that obviously cannot be fully explored here. But I do want to say enough to indicate the direction that I believe an appropriate response to this challenge should take. In spelling out above what I called the positive argument for voluntary active euthanasia, I suggested that two principal values—respecting patients' self-determination and promoting their well-being—underlie the consensus that competent patients, or the surrogates of incompetent patients, are entitled to refuse any life-sustaining treatment and to choose from among available alternative treatments. It is the commitment to these two values in guiding physicians' actions as healers, comforters, and protectors of their patients' lives that should be at the "moral center" of medicine, and these two values support physicians' administering euthanasia when their patients make competent requests for it.

What should not be at that moral center is a commitment to preserving patients' lives as such, without regard to whether those patients want their lives preserved or judge their preservation a benefit to them. . . .

REFERENCE

1 Willard Gaylin, Leon R. Kass, Edmund D. Pellegrino, and Mark Siegler, "Doctors Must Not Kill," *JAMA* 259 (1988): 2139–40.

QUESTIONS

1 Are considerations of self-determination and individual well-being sufficient to establish the moral legitimacy of voluntary active euthanasia?
2 Is the provision of voluntary active euthanasia by physicians "incompatible with their fundamental moral and professional commitment as healers"? If voluntary active euthanasia were legalized, would patients lose trust in physicians?

Objections to the Institutionalisation of Euthanasia

Stephen G. Potts

Potts argues against any scheme that would institutionalize—that is, legalize—(voluntary active) euthanasia. He identifies and briefly discusses a wide range of risks posed by legalization, and he insists that the burden of proof falls on the proponents of legalization. Potts endorses the "right to die" but insists that this right does not entail the right to receive assistance in suicide or the right to be killed.

Reprinted with permission of the publisher from Stephen G. Potts, "Looking for the Exit Door: Killing and Caring in Modern Medicine," *Houston Law Review,* vol. 25 (1988), pp. 504–509, 510–511.

[I am opposed] to any attempt to institutionalise euthanasia . . . because the risks of such institutionalisation are so grave as to outweigh the very real suffering of those who might benefit from it.

RISKS OF INSTITUTIONALISATION

Among the potential effects of a legalised practice of euthanasia are the following:

1   Reduced Pressure to Improve Curative or Symptomatic Treatment   If euthanasia had been legal forty years ago, it is quite possible that there would be no hospice movement today. The improvement in terminal care is a direct result of attempts made to minimise suffering. If that suffering had been extinguished by extinguishing the patients who bore it, then we may never have known the advances in the control of pain, nausea, breathlessness and other terminal symptoms that the last twenty years have seen.

Some diseases that were terminal a few decades ago are now routinely cured by newly developed treatments. Earlier acceptance of euthanasia might well have undercut the urgency of the research efforts which led to the discovery of those treatments. If we accept euthanasia now, we may well delay by decades the discovery of effective treatments for those diseases that are now terminal.

2   Abandonment of Hope   Every doctor can tell stories of patients expected to die within days who surprise everyone with their extraordinary recoveries. Every doctor has experienced the wonderful embarrassment of being proven wrong in their pessimistic prognosis. To make euthanasia a legitimate option as soon as the prognosis is pessimistic enough is to reduce the probability of such extraordinary recoveries from low to zero.

3   Increased Fear of Hospitals and Doctors   Despite all the efforts at health education, it seems there will always be a transference of the patient's fear of illness from the illness to the doctors and hospitals who treat it. This fear is still very real and leads to large numbers of late presentations of illnesses that might have been cured if only the patients had sought help earlier. To institutionalise euthanasia, however carefully, would undoubtedly magnify all the latent fear of doctors and hospitals harbored by the public. The inevitable result would be a rise in late presentations and, therefore, preventable deaths.

4   Difficulties of Oversight and Regulation   [Proposals to legalise euthanasia typically] list sets of precautions designed to prevent abuses. They acknowledge that such abuses are a possibility. I am far from convinced that the precautions are sufficient to prevent either those abuses that have been foreseen or those that may arise after passage of the law. The history of legal "loopholes" is not a cheering one: Abuses might arise when the patient is wealthy and an inheritance is at stake, when the doctor has made mistakes in diagnosis and treatment and hopes to avoid detection, when insurance coverage for treatment costs is about to expire, and in a host of other circumstances.

5   Pressure on the Patient   [Proposals to legalise euthanasia typically] seek to limit the influence of the patient's family on the decision, again acknowledging the risks posed by such influence. Families have all kinds of subtle ways, conscious and unconscious, of putting pressure on a patient to request euthanasia and relieve them of the financial and social burden of care. Many patients already feel guilty for imposing burdens on those who care for them, even when the families are happy to bear that burden. To provide an avenue for the discharge of that guilt in a request for euthanasia is to risk putting to death a great many patients who do not wish to die.

6   Conflict with Aims of Medicine   The pro-euthanasia movement cheerfully hands the dirty work of the actual killing to the doctors who, by and large, neither seek nor welcome the responsibility. There is little examination of the psychological stresses imposed on those whose training and professional outlook are geared to the saving of lives by asking them to start taking lives on a regular basis. Euthanasia advocates seem very confident that doctors can be relied on to make the enormous efforts sometimes necessary to save some lives, while at the same time assenting to requests to take other lives. Such confidence reflects, perhaps, a high opinion of doctors' psychic robustness, but it is a confidence seriously undermined by the shocking rates of depression, suicide, alcoholism, drug addiction, and marital discord consistently recorded among this group.

7   Dangers of Societal Acceptance   It must never be forgotten that doctors, nurses, and hospital administrators have personal lives, homes, and families, or that they are something more than just doctors, nurses, or hospital administrators. They are *citizens* and a significant part of the society around them. I am very worried about what the institutionalisation of euthanasia will do to society, in general, and, particularly, how much it will further erode our attachment to the sixth commandment. ["Thou shalt not kill."] How will we regard murderers? What will we say to the terrorist who justifies killing as a means to his political end when we ourselves justify killing as a means to a humanitarian end? I do not know and I daresay the euthanasia advocates do not either, but I worry about it and they appear not to. They need to justify their complacency.

8   The Slippery Slope   How long after acceptance of voluntary euthanasia will we hear the calls for nonvoluntary euthanasia? There are thousands of comatose or demented patients sustained by little more than good nursing care. They are an enormous financial and social burden. How soon will the advocates of euthanasia be arguing that we should "assist them in dying"—for, after all, they won't mind, will they?

How soon after *that* will we hear the calls for involuntary euthanasia, the disposal of the burdensome, the unproductive, the polluters of the gene pool? We must never forget the way the Nazi euthanasia programme made this progression in a few short years. "Oh, but they were barbarians," you say, and so they were, but not at the outset.

If developments in terminal care can be represented by a progression from the CURE mode of medical care to the CARE mode, enacting voluntary euthanasia legislation would permit a further progression to the KILL mode. The slippery slope argument represents the fear that, if this step is taken, then it will be difficult to avoid a further progression to the CULL mode, as illustrated:

CURE   The central aim of medicine
CARE   The central aim of terminal care once patients are beyond cure
KILL   The aim of the proponents of euthanasia for those patients beyond cure and not helped by care
CULL   The feared result of weakening the prohibition on euthanasia

I do not know how easy these moves will be to resist once voluntary euthanasia is accepted, but I have seen little evidence that the modern euthanasia advocates care about resisting them or even worry that they might be possible.

9   Costs and Benefits   Perhaps the most disturbing risk of all is posed by the growing concern over medical costs. Euthanasia is, after all, a very cheap service. The cost of a dose of barbiturates and curare and the few hours in a hospital bed that it takes them to act is minute compared to the massive bills incurred by many patients in the last weeks and months of their lives. Already in Britain, there is a serious underprovision of expensive therapies like renal dialysis and intensive care, with the result that many otherwise preventable deaths occur. Legalising euthanasia would save substantial financial resources which could be diverted to more "useful" treatments. These economic concerns already exert pressure to accept euthanasia, and, if accepted, they will inevitably tend to enlarge the category of patients for whom euthanasia is permitted.

Each of these objections could, and should, be expanded and pressed harder. I do not propose to do so now, for it is sufficient for my purposes to list them as *risks,* not inevitabilities. Several elements go into our judgment of the severity of a risk: the *probability* that the harm in question will arise (the odds), the *severity* of the harm in question (the stakes), and the ease with which the harm in question can be corrected (the *reversibility*). The institutionalisation of euthanasia is such a radical departure from anything that has gone before in Western society that we simply cannot judge the probability of any or all of the listed consequences. Nor can we rule any of them out. There must, however, be agreement that the severity of each of the harms listed is enough to give serious cause for concern, and the severity of all the harms together is enough to horrify. Furthermore, many of the potential harms seem likely to prove very difficult, if not impossible, to reverse by reinstituting a ban on euthanasia.

WEIGHING THE RISKS

For all these reasons, the burden of proof *must* lie with those who would have us gamble by legalising euthanasia. They should demonstrate beyond reasonable doubt that the dangers listed will not arise, just as chemical companies proposing to introduce a new drug are required to demonstrate that it is safe as well as beneficial.

Thus far, the proponents of euthanasia have relied exclusively on the compassion they arouse with tales of torment mercifully cut short by death, and have made little or no attempt to shoulder the burden of proving that legalising euthanasia is safe. Until they make such an attempt and carry it off successfully, their proposed legislation must be rejected outright.

THE RIGHT TO DIE AND THE DUTY TO KILL

The nature of my arguments should have made it clear by now that I object, not so much to individual acts of euthanasia, but to institutionalising it as a practice. All the pro-euthanasia arguments turn on the individual case of the patient in pain, suffering at the center of an intolerable existence. They exert powerful calls on our compassion, and appeal to our pity; therefore, we assent too readily when it is claimed that such patients have a *"right to die"* as an escape from torment. So long as the right to die means no more than the right to refuse life-prolonging treatment and the right to rational suicide, I agree. The advocates of euthanasia want to go much further than this though. They want to extend the right to die to encompass the right to receive assistance in suicide and, beyond that, the right to be killed. Here, the focus shifts from the patient to the agent, and from the killed to the killer; but, the argument begins to break down because our compassion does not extend this far.

If it is true that there is a right to be assisted in suicide or a right to be killed, then it follows that someone, somewhere, has a *duty* to provide the assistance or to do the killing. When we look at the proposed legislation, it is very clear upon whom the advocates of euthanasia would place this duty: the doctor. It would be the doctor's job to provide the pills and the doctor's job to give the lethal injection. The regulation of euthanasia is meant to prevent anyone, other than the doctor, from doing it. Such regulation would ensure that the doctor does it with the proper precautions and consultations, and would give the doctor security from legal sanctions for doing it. The emotive appeal of euthanasia is undeniably powerful, but it lasts only so long as we can avoid thinking about who has to do the killing, and where, and when, and how. Proposals to institutionalise euthanasia force us to think hard about these things, and the chill that their contemplation generates is deep enough to freeze any proponent's ardor. . . .

[One final objection to the institutionalisation of euthanasia] relates to another set out above (#5. Pressure on the patient). The objection turns on the concern that many requests for euthanasia will not be truly voluntary because of pressure on the patient or the patient's fear of becoming a burden. There is a significant risk that legalising voluntary euthanasia out of respect for the *right* to die will generate many requests for euthanasia out of a perceived *duty* to die. . . .

QUESTIONS

1 Does Potts provide a compelling case against the legalization of voluntary active euthanasia?
2 Should voluntary active euthanasia be legalized? If so, what procedures and safeguards should be introduced to govern the practice?

Assisted Suicide Is Not Voluntary Active Euthanasia

David T. Watts and Timothy Howell

Watts and Howell argue that it is important to distinguish between voluntary active euthanasia and physician-assisted suicide and to distinguish among three types of assisted suicide: (1) providing information, (2) providing the means (typically, by writing a prescription for a lethal amount of medication), and (3) supervising or directly aiding. Although they believe that the legalization of voluntary active euthanasia would have severe adverse consequences, and thus endorse many of the standard arguments against voluntary active euthanasia, they find the same arguments to be substantially weaker when directed against assisted suicide. In their view, physician-assisted suicide should be legalized. However, they argue that physicians should be limited to indirect participation in a patient's suicide—that is, the provision of information or means; physicians should not be permitted to supervise or directly aid a patient in committing suicide.

. . . [Ongoing] developments highlight some of the confusion emerging from dis-cussions of voluntary active euthanasia (V.A.E.) and assisted suicide. A significant source of confusion has been the tendency to join these concepts or even to con-sider them synonymous. For example, the AGS Position Statement on V.A.E. and a recent article by Teno and Lynn in the *Journal of the American Geriatrics Society* both reject easing restrictions on V.A.E. and assisted suicide while making argu-ments *only* against euthanasia.[1,2] The National Hospice Organization also opposes euthanasia and assisted suicide, but it, too, appears to blur the distinction between them in stating that "euthanasia encompasses . . . in some settings, physician-assisted suicide."[3] Others appear to use the terms euthanasia and assisted suicide synonymously in arguing against both.

In contrast, the AMA Ethics and Health Policy Counsel argues against physi-cian-assisted suicide and distinguishes this from euthanasia.[4] The AMA Council on Ethical and Judicial Affairs also acknowledges there is "an ethically relevant dis-tinction between euthanasia and assisted suicide that makes assisted suicide a more attractive option." Yet it then goes on to assert that "the ethical concerns about physician-assisted suicide are similar to those of euthanasia since both are essen-tially interventions intended to cause death."[5]

In order to weigh and appreciate the merits of the different arguments for and against V.A.E. and physician-assisted suicide, it is critical that appropriate dis-tinctions be made. For example, we believe the arguments made in the references cited above and by others[6,7] against euthanasia are telling. However, we find that these same arguments are substantially weaker when used against assisted suicide. And while we agree with the AMA Council on Ethical and Judicial Affairs that

Reprinted with permission of Blackwell Publishing Ltd. from *Journal of the American Geriatrics Society,* vol. 40 (October 1992), pp. 1043–1046.

an ethically relevant distinction exists between euthanasia and assisted suicide, we think it is important to distinguish further between different forms of assisted suicide. Only by doing so can we begin to sort out some of the apparent confusion in attitudes toward these issues. We caution our readers that the literature on this topic, while growing, remains preliminary, with little empirical research yet completed. Our arguments, however, are philosophical in nature and do not ultimately stand or fall on empirical data.

DEFINITIONS

Voluntary active euthanasia: Administration of medications or other interventions intended to cause death at a patient's request.

   Assisted suicide: Provision of information, means, or direct assistance by which a patient may take his or her own life. Assisted suicide involves several possible levels of assistance: *providing information,* for example, may mean providing toxicological information or describing techniques by which someone may commit suicide; *providing the means* can involve written prescriptions for lethal amounts of medication; *supervising or directly aiding* includes inserting an intravenous line and instructing on starting a lethal infusion.

   These levels of assistance have very different implications. Providing only information or means allows individuals to retain the greatest degree of control in choosing the time and mode of their deaths. Physician participation is only indirect. This type of limited assistance is exemplified by the widely reported case of Dr. Timothy Quill, who prescribed a lethal quantity of barbiturates at the request of one of his patients who had leukemia.[8] By contrast, supervising or directly aiding is the type of physician involvement characterizing the case of Dr. Jack Kevorkian and Janet Adkins. Adkins was a 54-year-old woman with a diagnosis of Alzheimer-type dementia who sought Kevorkian's assistance in ending her life. Dr. Kevorkian inserted an intravenous catheter and instructed Mrs. Adkins on activating a lethal infusion of potassium following barbiturate sedation, a process personally monitored by Kevorkian. This form of assisted suicide carries significant potential for physician influence or control of the process, and from it there is only a relatively short step to physician initiation (i.e., active euthanasia). We therefore reject physician-supervised suicide for the arguments commonly made against V.A.E., namely, that legalization would have serious adverse consequences, including potential abuse of vulnerable persons, mistrust of physicians, and diminished availability of supportive services for the dying.[2,3,5–7] We find each of these arguments, however, insufficient when applied to more limited forms of physician-assisted suicide (i.e., providing information or means).

WILL ASSISTED SUICIDE LEAD TO ABUSE OF VULNERABLE PERSONS?

A major concern is that some patients will request euthanasia or assisted suicide out of convenience to others.[2,4] It is certainly possible that a patient's desire to avoid being a burden could lead to such a request. With euthanasia, there is danger that a patient's request might find too ready acceptance. With assisted suicide, however, the ultimate decision, and the ultimate action, are the patient's, not the physician's. This places an important check and balance on physician initiation or patient acquiescence in euthanasia. As the AMA Council on Ethical and Judicial Affairs acknowledges, a greater level of patient autonomy is afforded by physician-assisted suicide than by euthanasia.[5]

Culturally or socially mediated requests for assisted suicide would remain a significant concern. Patients might also request aid in suicide out of fear, pain, ambivalence, or depression. The requirement that patients commit the ultimate act themselves cannot alone provide a sufficient safeguard. It would be incumbent on physicians to determine, insofar as possible, that requests for assisted suicide were not unduly influenced and that reversible conditions were optimally treated. As to how physicians might respond to such requests, data from the Netherlands indicate that about 75% of euthanasia requests in that country are refused.[9] It is our impression that most requests for assisted suicide, therefore, appear to represent opportunities for improved symptom control. We believe most serious requests would likely come from patients experiencing distressing symptoms of terminal illness.[10] By opening the door for counseling or treatment of reversible conditions, requests for assisted suicide might actually lead to averting some suicides which would have otherwise occurred.

Another concern regarding euthanasia is that it could come to be accepted without valid consent and that such a practice would more likely affect the frail and impoverished. The Remmelink Commission's investigation of euthanasia in the Netherlands appeared to justify such concerns in estimating that Dutch physicians may have performed 1,000 acts of involuntary euthanasia involving incompetent individuals.[11] But while euthanasia opens up the possibility of invalid consent, with assisted suicide consent is integral to the process. Because the choice of action clearly rests with the individual, there is substantially less likelihood for the abuse of assisted suicide as a societal vehicle for cost containment. And there is little basis for assuming that requests for assisted suicide would come primarily from frail and impoverished persons. Prolonged debilitation inherent in many illnesses is familiar to an increasing number of patients, family members, and health professionals. Such illnesses represent a greater financial threat to the middle- and upper-middle class, since the poor and disenfranchised have less to spend down to indigency. Thus, we suspect requests for assisted suicide might actually be more common from the educated, affluent, and outspoken.

Patients diagnosed with terminal or debilitating conditions are often vulnerable. We agree that such patients might request assisted suicide out of fear of pain, suffering, or isolation, and that too ready acceptance of such requests could be disastrous. Yet, we believe that patients' interests can be safeguarded by requirements for persistent, competent requests as well as thorough assessments for conditions, such as clinical depression, which could be reversed, treated, or ameliorated. Foley recently outlined an approach to the suicidal cancer patient.[12] We share her view that many such patients' requests to terminate life are altered by the availability of expert, continuing hospice services. We concur with Foley and others in calling for the wider availability of such services,[1,2] so that requests for assisted suicide arising from pain, depression, or other distressing symptoms can be reduced to a minimum.

WOULD ASSISTED SUICIDE UNDERMINE TRUST BETWEEN PATIENTS AND PHYSICIANS?

The cardinal distinction between V.A.E. and assisted suicide is that V.A.E. is killing by physicians, while suicide is self-killing. Prohibiting both euthanasia and physician-supervised suicide (i.e., with direct physician involvement) should diminish worries that patients might have about physicians wrongly administering lethal medicine. At present, physician-patient trust is compromised by widespread concern that physicians try too hard to keep dying patients alive. The very strength of the physician-patient relationship has been cited as a justification for physician involvement in assisted suicide.[13]

A number of ethicists have expressed concern that both euthanasia and assisted suicide, if legalized, would have a negative impact on the way society perceives the role of physicians.[2,4,6,7] Limited forms of assisted suicide, however, have been viewed more positively.[14] Public and professional attitudes appear to be evolving on this issue. A 1990 Gallup poll found that 66% of respondents believed someone in great pain, with "no hope of improvement," had the moral right to commit suicide; in 1975 the figure was 41%.[15] A panel of distinguished physicians has stated that it is not immoral for a physician to assist in the rational suicide of a terminally ill person.[16] The recent publication of a book on techniques of committing or assisting suicide evoked wide interest and significant support for the right of people to take control of their dying.[17] For a significant segment of society, physician involvement in assisted suicide may be welcomed, not feared. Furthermore, while relatively few might be likely to seek assistance with suicide if stricken with a debilitating illness, a substantial number might take solace knowing they could request such assistance.

There is another argument raised against V.A.E. that we believe also falters when used to object to assisted suicide. It has been maintained that prohibiting euthanasia forces physicians to focus on the humane care of dying patients, including meticulous attention to their symptoms.[2,10] This argument implies that physicians find it easier to relieve the suffering of dying patients by ending their lives rather than attempting the difficult task of palliating their symptoms. But for some patients, the suffering may not be amenable to even the most expert palliation. Even in such instances, some argue that limited forms of assisted suicide should be prohibited on the grounds that not to forbid them would open the door for more generalized, less stringent applications of assisted suicide.

To us, this "slippery slope" argument seems to imply that the moral integrity of the medical profession must be maintained, even if at the cost of prolonged, unnecessary suffering by at least some dying patients. We believe such a posture is itself inhumane and not acceptable. It contradicts a fundamental principle that is an essential ingredient of physician-patient trust: that patient comfort should be a primary goal of the physician in the face of incurable illness. Furthermore, by allowing limited physician involvement in assisted suicide, physicians can respect both the principle of caring that guides them and the patients for whom caring alone is insufficient. We concede that there is another alternative: terminally ill patients who cannot avoid pain while awake may be given continuous anesthetic levels of medication.[2] But this is exactly the sort of dying process we believe many in our society want to avoid.

WILL ASSISTED SUICIDE AND EUTHANASIA WEAKEN SOCIETAL RESOLVE TO INCREASE RESOURCES ALLOCATED TO CARE OF THE DYING?

This argument assumes that V.A.E. and assisted suicide would both be widely practiced, and that their very availability would decrease tangible concern for those not choosing euthanasia or suicide. However, euthanasia is rarely requested even by terminal cancer patients.[2] In the Netherlands, euthanasia accounts for less than 2% of all deaths.[9] These data suggest that even if assisted suicide were available to those with intractable pain or distressing terminal conditions, it would likely be an option chosen by relatively few. With assisted suicide limited to relatively few cases, this argument collapses. For with only a few requesting assisted suicide, the vast number of patients with debilitating illnesses would be undiminished, and their numbers should remain sufficient to motivate societal concern for their needs. Furthermore, to withhold assisted suicide from the few making serious, valid requests would be to subordinate needlessly the interests of these few to those of the many. Compounding their tragedy would be the fact that these individuals could not even benefit from any increase in therapeutic resources prompted by their suffering, insofar as their conditions are, by definition, not able to be ameliorated.

CONCLUSION

We have argued that assisted suicide and voluntary active euthanasia are different and that each has differing implications for medical practice and society. Further discussion should consider the merits and disadvantages of each, a process enhanced by contrasting them. We have further argued that different forms of assisted suicide can be distinguished both clinically and philosophically. Although some may argue that all forms of assisted suicide are fundamentally the same, we believe the differences can be contrasted as starkly as a written prescription and a suicide machine.

We do not advocate ready acceptance of requests for suicide, nor do we wish to romanticize the concept of rational suicide.[18] In some situations, however, where severe debilitating illness cannot be reversed, suicide may represent a rational choice. If this is the case, then physician assistance could make the process more humane. Along with other geriatricians, we often face dilemmas involving the management of chronic illnesses in late life. We believe we can best serve our patients, and preserve their trust, by respecting their desire for autonomy, dignity, and quality, not only of life, but of dying.

REFERENCES

1 AGS Public Policy Committee. Voluntary active euthanasia. J Am Geriatr Soc 1991;39:826.
2 Teno J, Lynn J. Voluntary active euthanasia: The individual case and public policy. J Am Geriatr Soc 1991;39:827–830.
3 National Hospice Organization. Statement of the National Hospice Organization Opposing the Legalization of Euthanasia and Assisted Suicide. Arlington, VA: National Hospice Organization, 1991.

4 Orentlicher D. Physician participation in assisted suicide. JAMA 1989;262:1844–1845.
5 AMA. Report of the Council on Ethical and Judicial Affairs: Decisions Near the End of Life. Chicago, IL: American Medical Association, 1991.
6 Singer PA. Should doctors kill patients? Can Med Assoc J 1988;138:1000–1001.
7 Singer PA, Siegler M. Euthanasia—a critique. N Engl J Med 1990;322:1881–1883.
8 Quill TE. Death and dignity: A case of individualized decision making. N Engl J Med 1991;324:691–694.
9 Van der Maas PJ, Van Delden JJM, Pijnenborg L, Looman CWN. Euthanasia and other medical decisions concerning the end of life. Lancet 1991;338:669–674.
10 Palmore EB. Arguments for assisted suicide (letter). Gerontologist 1991;31:854.
11 Karel R. Undertreatment of pain, depression needs to be addressed before euthanasia made legal in U.S. Psychiatric News, December 20, 1991, pp. 5, 13, 23.
12 Foley KM. The relationship of pain and symptom management to patient requests for physician-assisted suicide. J Pain Symptom Manag 1991;6:289–297.
13 Jecker NS. Giving death a hand. When the dying and the doctor stand in a special relationship. J Am Geriatr Soc 1991;39:831–835.
14 American College of Physicians. ACP to DA, Grand Jury: Dr. Quill acted "humanely." ACP Observer, September, 1991, p. 5.
15 Ames K, Wilson L, Sawhill R et al. Last rights. Newsweek August 26, 1991, pp. 40–41.
16 Wanzer SH, Federman DD, Adelstein SJ et al. The physician's responsibility toward hopelessly ill patients: A second look. N Engl J Med 1989;320:844–849.
17 Humphry D. Final Exit: The Practicalities of Self-Deliverance and Assisted Suicide for the Dying. Eugene, OR: The Hemlock Society (distributed by Carol Publishing, Secaucus, NJ), 1991.
18 Conwell Y, Caine ED. Rational suicide and the right to die: Reality and myth. N Engl J Med 1991;325:1100–1103.

QUESTIONS

1 Would the social consequences of legalizing physician-assisted suicide be less problematic than the social consequences of legalizing voluntary active euthanasia?

2 Should physician-assisted suicide be legalized? If so, should physicians be permitted to supervise or directly aid a patient in committing suicide, or should they be limited to providing information and means?

Opinion of the Court in *Washington v. Glucksberg*

Chief Justice William H. Rehnquist

At issue in this case is the constitutionality of Washington State's ban on assisted suicide—in particular, whether it violates the Due Process Clause of the Fourteenth Amendment. Although the Supreme Court unanimously upholds

United States Supreme Court. 521 U.S. 702 (1997).

Washington's assisted-suicide ban, the fact that this case has produced five separate concurring opinions indicates that the Court remains fragmented on the most appropriate way of constructing the underlying issues. Chief Justice Rehnquist, in this opinion joined by four other justices, rejects the contention (asserted by the Ninth Circuit Court of Appeals) that a competent, terminally ill adult can claim a constitutionally protected right to physician assistance in suicide. On his analysis, no such liberty interest is protected by the Due Process Clause of the Fourteenth Amendment; thus, no basis exists for a fundamental-right claim. It follows, he argues, that the constitutionality of Washington's assisted-suicide ban can be established merely by showing that the ban is rationally related to legitimate government interests. In order to display how this requirement is clearly met, the Chief Justice identifies and discusses the relevant state interests.

The question presented in this case is whether Washington's prohibition against "caus[ing]" or "aid[ing]" a suicide offends the Fourteenth Amendment to the United States Constitution. We hold that it does not.

It has always been a crime to assist a suicide in the State of Washington. In 1854, Washington's first Territorial Legislature outlawed "assisting another in the commission of self-murder." Today, Washington law provides: "A person is guilty of promoting a suicide attempt when he knowingly causes or aids another person to attempt suicide." Wash. Rev. Code 9A.36.060(1) (1994). "Promoting a suicide attempt" is a felony, punishable by up to five years' imprisonment and up to a $10,000 fine. At the same time, Washington's Natural Death Act, enacted in 1979, states that the "withholding or withdrawal of life-sustaining treatment" at a patient's direction "shall not, for any purpose, constitute a suicide."

Petitioners in this case are the State of Washington and its Attorney General. Respondents Harold Glucksberg, M.D., Abigail Halperin, M.D., Thomas A. Preston, M.D., and Peter Shalit, M.D., are physicians who practice in Washington. These doctors occasionally treat terminally ill, suffering patients, and declare that they would assist these patients in ending their lives if not for Washington's assisted-suicide ban. In January 1994, respondents, along with three gravely ill, pseudonymous plaintiffs who have since died and Compassion in Dying, a non-profit organization that counsels people considering physician-assisted suicide, sued in the United States District Court, seeking a declaration that Wash. Rev. Code 9A.36.060(1) (1994) is, on its face, unconstitutional. *Compassion in Dying v. Washington* (WD Wash. 1994).

The plaintiffs asserted "the existence of a liberty interest protected by the Fourteenth Amendment which extends to a personal choice by a mentally competent, terminally ill adult to commit physician-assisted suicide." Relying primarily on *Planned Parenthood v. Casey* (1992) and *Cruzan v. Director, Missouri Dept. of Health* (1990), the District Court agreed and concluded that Washington's assisted-suicide ban is unconstitutional because it "places an undue burden on the exercise of [that] constitutionally protected liberty interest." The District Court also decided that the Washington statute violated the Equal Protection Clause's requirement that "'all persons similarly situated . . . be treated alike.'"

A panel of the Court of Appeals for the Ninth Circuit reversed, emphasizing that "[i]n the two hundred and five years of our existence no constitutional right to aid in killing oneself has ever been asserted and upheld by a court of final jurisdiction." *Compassion in Dying v. Washington* (1995). The Ninth Circuit reheard the case en banc, reversed the panel's decision, and affirmed the District Court. *Compassion in Dying v. Washington* (1996). Like the District Court, the en banc Court of Appeals emphasized our *Casey* and *Cruzan* decisions. The court also discussed what is described as "historical" and "current societal attitudes" toward suicide and assisted suicide, and concluded that "the Constitution encompasses a due process liberty interest in controlling the time and manner of one's death—that there is, in short, a constitutionally-recognized 'right to die.'" After "[w]eighing and then balancing" this interest against Washington's various interests, the court held that the State's assisted-suicide ban was unconstitutional "as applied to terminally ill competent adults who wish to hasten their deaths with medication prescribed by their physicians." The court did not reach the District Court's equal-protection holding. We granted certiorari and now reverse.

I

We begin, as we do in all due-process cases, by examining our Nation's history, legal traditions, and practices. In almost every State—indeed, in almost every western democracy—it is a crime to assist a suicide. The States' assisted-suicide bans are not innovations. Rather, they are longstanding expressions of the States' commitment to the protection and preservation of all human life. Indeed, opposition to and condemnation of suicide—and, therefore, of assisting suicide—are consistent and enduring themes of our philosophical, legal, and cultural heritages.

More specifically, for over 700 years, the Anglo-American common-law tradition has punished or otherwise disapproved of both suicide and assisting suicide. . . .

For the most part, the early American colonies adopted the common-law approach. . . . [For example,] Virginia . . . required ignominious burial for suicides, and their estates were forfeit to the crown.

Over time, however, the American colonies abolished these harsh common-law penalties. . . . [H]owever, . . . the movement away from the common law's harsh sanctions did not represent an acceptance of suicide; rather, . . . this change reflected the growing consensus that it was unfair to punish the suicide's family for his wrongdoing. . . . [C]ourts continued to condemn [suicide] as a grave public wrong.

That suicide remained a grievous, though non-felonious, wrong is confirmed by the fact that colonial and early state legislatures and courts did not retreat from prohibiting assisting suicide. . . . And the prohibitions against assisting suicide never contained exceptions for those who were near death. . . .

The earliest American statute explicitly to outlaw assisting suicide was enacted in New York in 1828. . . . By the time the Fourteenth Amendment was ratified, it was a crime in most States to assist a suicide. . . .

Though deeply rooted, the States' assisted-suicide bans have in recent years been reexamined and, generally, reaffirmed. Because of advances in medicine and technology, Americans today are increasingly likely to die in institutions, from chronic illnesses. Public concern and democratic action are therefore sharply focused on how best to protect dignity and independence at the end of life, with the result that there have been many significant changes in state laws and in the attitudes these laws reflect. Many States, for example, now permit "living wills," surrogate health-care decisionmaking, and the withdrawal or refusal of life-sustaining medical treatment. At the same time, however, voters and legislators continue for the most part to reaffirm their States' prohibitions on assisting suicide. . . .

. . . Against this backdrop of history, tradition, and practice, we now turn to respondents' constitutional claim.

II

The Due Process Clause guarantees more than fair process, and the "liberty" it protects includes more than the absence of physical restraint. The Clause also provides heightened protection against government interference with certain fundamental rights and liberty interests. In a long line of cases, we have held that, in addition to the specific freedoms protected by the Bill of Rights, the "liberty" specially protected by the Due Process Clause includes the rights to marry, to have children, to direct the education and upbringing of one's children, to marital privacy, to use contraception, to bodily integrity, and to abortion. We have also assumed, and strongly suggested, that the Due Process Clause protects the traditional right to refuse unwanted lifesaving medical treatment.

But we "ha[ve] always been reluctant to expand the concept of substantive due process because guideposts for responsible decisionmaking in this unchartered area are scarce and open-ended." By extending constitutional protection to an asserted right or liberty interest, we, to a great extent, place the matter outside the arena of public debate and legislative action. We must therefore "exercise the utmost care whenever we are asked to break new ground in this field," lest the liberty protected by the Due Process Clause be subtly transformed into the policy preferences of the members of this Court.

Our established method of substantive-due-process analysis has two primary features: First, we have regularly observed that the Due Process Clause specially protects those fundamental rights and liberties which are, objectively, "deeply rooted in this Nation's history and tradition" and "implicit in the concept of ordered liberty," such that "neither liberty nor justice would exist if they were sacrificed." Second, we have required in substantive-due-process cases a "careful description" of the asserted fundamental liberty interest. Our Nation's history, legal traditions, and practices thus provide the crucial "guideposts for responsible decisionmaking" that direct and restrain our exposition of the Due Process Clause. As we stated recently . . . , the Fourteenth Amendment "forbids the government to infringe . . . 'fundamental' liberty interests *at all,* no matter what process is provided, unless the infringement is narrowly tailored to serve a compelling state interest." . . .

Turning to the claim at issue here, the Court of Appeals stated that "[p]roperly analyzed, the first issue to be resolved is whether there is a liberty interest in determining the time and manner of one's death," or, in other words, "[i]s there a right to die?" Similarly, respondents assert a "liberty to choose how to die" and a right to "control of one's final days," and describe the asserted liberty as "the right to choose a humane, dignified death" and "the liberty to shape death." As noted above, we have a tradition of carefully formulating the interest at stake in substantive-due-process cases. For example, although *Cruzan* is often described as a "right to die" case, we were, in fact, more precise: we assumed that the Constitution granted competent persons a "constitutionally protected right to refuse lifesaving hydration and nutrition." The Washington statute at issue in this case prohibits "aid[ing] another person to attempt suicide," Wash. Rev. Code §9A.36.060(1) (1994), and, thus, the question before us is whether the "liberty" specially protected by the Due Process Clause includes a right to commit suicide which itself includes a right to assistance in doing so.

We now inquire whether this asserted right has any place in our Nation's traditions. Here, as discussed above, we are confronted with a consistent and almost universal tradition that has long rejected the asserted right, and continues explicitly to reject it today, even for terminally ill, mentally competent adults. To hold for respondents, we would have to reverse centuries of legal doctrine and practice, and strike down the considered policy choice of almost every State.

Respondents contend, however, that the liberty interest they assert *is* consistent with this Court's substantive-due-process line of cases, if not with this Nation's history and practice. Pointing to *Casey* and *Cruzan,* respondents read our jurisprudence in this area as reflecting a general tradition of "self-sovereignty" and as teaching that the "liberty" protected by the Due Process Clause includes "basic and intimate exercises of personal autonomy." According to respondents, our liberty jurisprudence, and the broad, individualistic principles it reflects, protects the "liberty of competent, terminally ill adults to make end-of-life decisions free of undue government interference." The question presented in this case, however, is whether the protections of the Due Process Clause include a right to commit suicide with another's assistance. With this "careful description" of respondents' claim in mind, we turn to *Casey* and *Cruzan.*

In *Cruzan,* we considered whether Nancy Beth Cruzan, who had been severely injured in an automobile accident and was in a persistive vegetative state, "ha[d] a right under the United States Constitution which would require the hospital to withdraw life-sustaining treatment" at her parents' request. We began with the observation that "[a]t common law, even the touching of one person by another without consent and without legal justification was a battery." We then discussed the related rule that "informed consent is generally required for medical treatment." After reviewing a long line of relevant state cases, we concluded that "the common-law doctrine of informed consent is viewed as generally encompassing the right of a competent individual to refuse medical treatment." Next, we reviewed our own cases on the subject, and stated that "[t]he principle that a competent person has a constitutionally protected liberty interest in refusing unwanted medical treatment may be inferred from our prior decisions." Therefore, "for purposes of [that] case, we assume[d] that the United States Constitution would grant a competent person a constitutionally protected right to refuse lifesaving hydration and nutrition." We concluded that, notwithstanding this right, the Constitution permitted Missouri to require clear and convincing evidence of an incompetent patient's wishes concerning the withdrawal of life-sustaining treatment.

Respondents contend that in *Cruzan* we "acknowledged that competent, dying persons have the right to direct the removal of life-sustaining medical treatment and thus hasten death," and that "the constitutional principle behind recognizing the patient's liberty to direct the withdrawal of artificial life support applies at least as strongly to the choice to hasten impending death by consuming lethal medication." Similarly, the Court of Appeals concluded that "*Cruzan,* by recognizing a liberty interest that includes the refusal of artificial provision of life-sustaining food and water, necessarily recognize[d] a liberty interest in hastening one's own death."

The right assumed in *Cruzan,* however, was not simply deduced from abstract concepts of personal autonomy. Given the common-law rule that forced medication was a battery, and the long legal tradition protecting the decision to refuse unwanted medical treatment, our assumption was entirely consistent with this Nation's history and constitutional traditions. The decisions to commit suicide with the assistance of another may be just as personal and profound as the decision to refuse unwanted medical treatment, but it has never enjoyed similar legal protection. Indeed, the two acts are widely and reasonably regarded as quite distinct. See *Quill v. Vacco* (1997). In *Cruzan* itself, we recognized that most States outlawed assisted suicide—and even more do today—and we certainly gave no intimation that the right to refuse unwanted medical treatment could be somehow transmuted into a right to assistance in committing suicide.

Respondents also rely on *Casey.* There, the Court's opinion concluded that "the essential holding of *Roe v. Wade* should be retained and once again reaffirmed." We held, first, that a woman has a right, before her fetus is viable, to an abortion "without undue interference from the State"; second, that States may restrict post-viability abortions, so long as exceptions are made to protect a woman's life and health; and third, that the State has legitimate interests throughout a pregnancy in protecting the health of the woman and the life of the unborn child. In reaching this conclusion, the opinion discussed in some detail this Court's substantive-due-process tradition of interpreting the Due Process Clause to protect certain fundamental rights and "personal decisions relating to marriage, procreation, contraception, family relationships, child rearing, and education," and noted that many of those rights and liberties "involv[e] the most intimate and personal choices a person may make in a lifetime."

The Court of Appeals, like the District Court, found *Casey* "'highly instructive'" and "'almost prescriptive'" for determining "'what liberty interest may inhere in a terminally ill person's choice to commit suicide'":

> Like the decision of whether or not to have an abortion, the decision how and when to die is one of "the most intimate and personal choices a person may make in a lifetime," a choice "central to personal dignity and autonomy."

. . . That many of the rights and liberties protected by the Due Process Clause sound in personal autonomy does not warrant the sweeping conclusion that any and all important, intimate, and personal decisions are so protected, and *Casey* did not suggest otherwise.

The history of the law's treatment of assisted suicide in this country has been and continues to be one of the rejection of nearly all efforts to permit it. That being the case, our decisions lead us to conclude that the asserted "right" to assistance in committing suicide is not a fundamental liberty interest protected by the Due Process Clause. The Constitution also requires, however, that Washington's assisted-suicide ban be rationally related to legitimate government interests. This requirement is unquestionably met here. As the court below recognized, Washington's assisted-suicide ban implicates a number of state interests.

First, Washington has an "unqualified interest in the preservation of human life." The State's prohibition on assisted suicide, like all homicide laws, both reflects and advances its commitment to this interest. This interest is symbolic and aspirational as well as practical:

> While suicide is no longer prohibited or penalized, the ban against assisted suicide and euthanasia shores up the notion of limits in human relationships. It reflects the gravity with which we view the decision to take one's own life or the life of another, and our reluctance to encourage or promote these decisions. New York State Task Force on Life and the Law, When Death Is Sought: Assisted Suicide and Euthanasia in the Medical Context 131–132 (May 1994) (hereinafter New York Task Force).

Respondents admit that "[t]he State has a real interest in preserving the lives of those who can still contribute to society and enjoy life." The Court of Appeals also recognized Washington's interest in protecting life, but held that the "weight" of this interest depends on the "medical condition and the wishes of the person whose life is at stake." Washington, however, has rejected this sliding-scale approach and, through its assisted-suicide ban, insists that all persons' lives, from beginning to end, regardless of physical or mental condition, are under the full protection of the law. As we have previously affirmed, the States "may properly decline to make judgments about the 'quality' of life that a particular individual may enjoy." This remains true, as *Cruzan* makes clear, even for those who are near death.

Relatedly, all admit that suicide is a serious public-health problem, especially among persons in otherwise vulnerable groups. The State has an interest in preventing suicide, and in studying, identifying, and treating its causes.

Those who attempt suicide—terminally ill or not—often suffer from depression or other mental disorders. See New York Task Force 13–22, 126–128 (more than 95% of those who commit suicide had a major psychiatric illness at the time of death; among the terminally ill, uncontrolled pain is a "risk factor" because it contributes to depression). Research indicates . . . that many people who request physician-assisted suicide withdraw that request if their depression and pain are treated. The New York Task Force, however, expressed its concern that, because depression is difficult to diagnose, physicians and medical professionals often fail to respond adequately to seriously ill patients' needs. Thus, legal physician-assisted suicide could make it more difficult for the State to protect depressed or mentally ill persons, or those who are suffering from untreated pain, from suicidal impulses.

The State also has an interest in protecting the integrity and ethics of the medical profession. In contrast to the Court of Appeals' conclusion that "the integrity of the medical profession would [not] be threatened in any way by [physician-assisted suicide]," the American Medical Association, like many other medical and physicians' groups, has concluded that "[p]hysician-assisted suicide is fundamentally incompatible with the physician's role as healer." American Medical Association, Code of Ethics §2.211 (1994). And physician-assisted suicide could, it is argued, undermine the trust that is essential to the doctor-patient relationship by blurring the time-honored line between healing and harming.

Next, the State has an interest in protecting vulnerable groups—including the poor, the elderly, and disabled persons—from abuse, neglect, and mistakes. The Court of Appeals dismissed the State's concern that disadvantaged persons might be pressured into physician-assisted suicide as "ludicrous on its face." We have recognized, however, the real risk of subtle coercion and undue influence in end-of-life situations. Similarly, the New York Task Force warned that "[l]egalizing physician-assisted suicide would pose profound risks to many individuals who are ill and vulnerable. . . . The risk of harm is greatest for the many individuals in our society whose autonomy and well-being are already compromised by poverty, lack of access to good medical care, advanced age, or membership in a stigmatized social group." New York Task Force 120. If physician-assisted suicide were permitted, many might resort to it to spare their families the substantial financial burden of end-of-life health-care costs.

The State's interest here goes beyond protecting the vulnerable from coercion; it extends to protecting disabled and terminally ill people from prejudice, negative and inaccurate stereotypes, and "societal indifference." The State's assisted-suicide ban reflects and reinforces its policy that the lives of terminally ill, disabled, and elderly people must be no less valued than the lives of the young and healthy, and that a seriously disabled person's suicidal impulses should be interpreted and treated the same way as anyone else's.

Finally, the State may fear that permitting assisted suicide will start it down the path to voluntary and perhaps even involuntary euthanasia. The Court of Appeals struck down Washington's assisted-suicide ban only "as applied to competent, terminally ill adults who wish to hasten their deaths by obtaining medication prescribed by their doctors." Washington insists, however, that the impact of the court's decision will not and cannot be so limited. If suicide is protected as a matter of constitutional right, it is argued, "every man and woman in the United States must enjoy it." The Court of Appeals' decision, and its expansive reasoning, provide ample support for the State's concerns. The court noted, for example, that the "decision of a duly appointed surrogate decision maker is for all legal purposes the decision of the patient himself," that "in some instances, the patient may be unable to self-administer the drugs and . . . administration by the physician . . . may be the only way the patient may be able to receive them," and that not only physicians, but also family members and loved ones, will inevitably participate in assisting suicide. Thus, it turns out that what is couched as a limited right to "physician-assisted suicide" is likely, in effect, a much broader license, which could prove extremely difficult to police and contain. Washington's ban on assisting suicide prevents such erosion. . . .

We need not weigh exactly the relative strengths of these various interests. They are unquestionably important and legitimate, and Washington's ban on assisted suicide is at least reasonably related to their promotion and protection. We therefore hold that Wash. Rev. Code §9A36.060(1) (1994) does not violate the Fourteenth Amendment, either on its face or "as applied to competent, terminally ill adults who wish to hasten their deaths by obtaining medication prescribed by their doctors."

Throughout the Nation, Americans are engaged in an earnest and profound debate about the morality, legality, and practicality of physician-assisted suicide. Our holding permits this debate to continue, as it should in a democratic society. The decision of the en banc Court of Appeals is reversed. . . .

QUESTIONS

1 How important is a terminally ill person's interest in controlling the time and manner of death?
2 Chief Justice Rehnquist points out that the Court's holding in this case permits the debate over physician-assisted suicide to continue. Would you endorse legalization of physician-assisted suicide in your state?

Concurring Opinion in *Washington v. Glucksberg* and *Vacco v. Quill*

Justice Sandra Day O'Connor

In this concurring opinion, Justice O'Connor emphasizes that, in both Washington and New York (the setting of *Vacco*), there are presently no legal barriers to terminally ill patients' obtaining adequate pain-relieving medication, "even to the point of causing unconsciousness and hastening death." If terminally ill patients did not, in fact, have access to such palliative care, she seems to suggest, there might be grounds for a different conclusion regarding physician-assisted suicide.

Death will be different for each of us. For many, the last days will be spent in physical pain and perhaps the despair that accompanies physical deterioration and a loss of control of basic bodily and mental functions. Some will seek medication to alleviate that pain and other symptoms.

The Court frames the issue in *Washington v. Glucksberg* as whether the Due Process Clause of the Constitution protects a "right to commit suicide which itself includes a right to assistance in doing so," and concludes that our Nation's

United States Supreme Court, 521 U.S. 702 (1997).

history, legal traditions, and practices do not support the existence of such a right. I join the Court's opinions because I agree that there is no generalized right to "commit suicide." But respondents urge us to address the narrower question whether a mentally competent person who is experiencing great suffering has a constitutionally cognizable interest in controlling the circumstances of his or her imminent death. I see no need to reach that question in the context of the facial challenges to the New York and Washington laws at issue here. ("The Washington statute at issue in this case prohibits 'aid[ing] another person to attempt suicide,' . . . and, thus, the question before us is whether the 'liberty' specially protected by the Due Process Clause includes a right to commit suicide which itself includes a right to assistance in doing so"). The parties and *amici* agree that in these States a patient who is suffering from a terminal illness and who is experiencing great pain has no legal barriers to obtaining medication, from qualified physicians, to alleviate that suffering, even to the point of causing unconsciousness and hastening death. In this light, even assuming that we would recognize such an interest, I agree that the State's interests in protecting those who are not truly competent or facing imminent death, or those whose decisions to hasten death would not truly be voluntary, are sufficiently weighty to justify a prohibition against physician-assisted suicide.

Every one of us at some point may be affected by our own or a family member's terminal illness. There is no reason to think the democratic process will not strike the proper balance between the interests of terminally ill, mentally competent individuals who would seek to end their suffering and the State's interests in protecting those who might seek to end life mistakenly or under pressure. As the Court recognizes, States are presently undertaking extensive and serious evaluation of physician-assisted suicide and other related issues. In such circumstances, "the . . . challenging task of crafting appropriate procedures for safeguarding . . . liberty interests is entrusted to the 'laboratory' of the States . . . in the first instance."

In sum, there is no need to address the question whether suffering patients have a constitutionally cognizable interest in obtaining relief from the suffering that they may experience in the last days of their lives. There is no dispute that dying patients in Washington and New York can obtain palliative care, even when doing so would hasten their deaths. The difficulty in defining terminal illness and the risk that a dying patient's request for assistance in ending his or her life might not be truly voluntary justifies the prohibitions on assisted suicide we uphold here.

QUESTIONS

1 If there are no *legal* barriers to terminally ill patients' obtaining adequate palliative care, does it follow that patients actually have access to such care?

2 To the extent that terminally ill patients actually have access to adequate palliative care, "even to the point of causing unconsciousness and hastening death," is there a compelling need to legalize physician-assisted suicide?

Voluntary Death: A Comparison of Terminal Dehydration and Physician-Assisted Suicide

Franklin G. Miller and Diane E. Meier

Miller and Meier argue that terminal dehydration should be more explicitly recognized as an alternative to physician-assisted suicide. Because competent patients who have terminal or incurable illnesses are already free to forgo nutrition and hydration, and thus bring about their deaths by terminal dehydration, the authors suggest that there may be no compelling need to legalize physician-assisted suicide. They point out various advantages that terminal dehydration has over physician-assisted suicide, arguing in particular that there is a stronger moral basis for voluntary death by terminal dehydration than by physician-assisted suicide. Miller and Meier briefly discuss concerns about the humaneness of terminal dehydration and also briefly discuss issues associated with the integration of terminal dehydration into clinical practice.

The deeply divisive question of whether to legalize physician-assisted suicide has become a pressing matter of public policy at a time of radical change in the U.S. health care system. Managed care has expanded rapidly and now serves as the form of health care coverage for more than half of Americans with health insurance. Although this organizational change seems to have reduced the growth of health care expenditures, approximately 40 million Americans (15% of the population) continue to lack health insurance. That a legal option of physician-assisted suicide could become a "quick fix" for dying patients is a serious risk in view of the built-in incentives of managed care plans to limit treatment, coupled with the documented deficiencies of physicians in providing adequate pain relief and diagnosing and treating depression in terminally ill patients.

Given the potential for abuse if physician-assisted suicide were to be legalized in a climate of overarching cost containment in health care, careful consideration of alternative ways for patients to retain some control over the timing and circumstances of death seems warranted. The debate over legalizing physician-assisted suicide has failed to give due attention to terminal dehydration as an alternative. With terminal dehydration, competent patients who have terminal or incurable illness seek voluntary death by forgoing artificial nutrition and hydration or by ceasing to eat and drink. Terminal dehydration, accompanied by standard measures of palliative care, offers patients a way to escape agonizing, incurable conditions that they consider to be worse than death, without requiring transformation of the law and medical ethics.

In this article, we analyze clinical, ethical, and policy issues relating to terminal dehydration as an alternative to physician-assisted suicide, building on the foundation

Reprinted with permission of the publisher from *Annals of Internal Medicine*, vol. 128, no. 7 (April 1, 1998), pp. 559–562. Many references omitted.

laid in 1993 by Bernat and colleagues (1) in their seminal article on patient refusal of hydration and nutrition. This topic warrants revisiting in light of the Oregon referendums to legalize physician-assisted suicide and recent federal court decisions on this issue. A balanced assessment of physician-assisted suicide and terminal dehydration is important because each method has substantial advantages and disadvantages.

MERITS OF TERMINAL DEHYDRATION

Evidence indicates that death by terminal dehydration is not painful and that attendant physical discomfort can be adequately alleviated. Pain and suffering caused by the underlying disease can be treated by standard palliative measures, including administration of sedation to the level of unconsciousness as a last resort.

A stronger moral basis exists for voluntary death by terminal dehydration than by physician-assisted suicide. The right to forgo food and water, whether by mouth or by artificial means, derives from the fundamental right of competent patients to refuse medical treatment and to be free of unwanted bodily intrusion. Physicians are morally obligated to honor a competent patient's refusal of food and water, but they are not morally obligated to comply with a competent patient's request for lethal medication. Although physician-assisted suicide may be justifiable as a last resort in extraordinary cases, a patient's right to assisted suicide does not carry the same moral force as a patient's right to forgo treatment. This difference can be seen by considering the significance of thwarting these two paths to voluntary death. Force-feeding a competent patient who clearly refuses food and water violates autonomy, liberty, and dignity. In contrast, refusal of a carefully considered request for physician-assisted suicide interferes with a patient's self-determination but does not amount to a personal assault. Moreover, the patient whose request for physician-assisted suicide is denied remains free to exercise the right to voluntary death by forgoing food and water.

Self-Determination

Terminal dehydration offers a method of voluntary death that is entirely under the control of competent patients; it is not necessary for the physician to intervene by prescribing or administering lethal medication. Death by terminal dehydration demands a resolute determination to resist food and water. Because it typically takes several days to a few weeks for death to occur by this means, the patient who seeks death by terminal dehydration retains an opportunity to change his or her mind. In contrast, the patient who ingests a lethal dose of medication quickly loses consciousness and rapidly progresses to death. This difference in time to death means that terminal dehydration, unlike physician-assisted suicide, cannot be accomplished impulsively.

Physician-assisted suicide, because it involves prescribing lethal medication, could subject patients to greater external influence in favor of death than that associated with terminal dehydration. Owing to the cultural authority of medicine, a prescription of lethal medication may carry social legitimization for some patients and signify that it is medically appropriate for the patient to hasten death. Terminal dehydration lacks this legitimization. The physician may accept the patient's decision to die by terminal dehydration, but no affirmative act by the physician is required.

Access

In 1996, the U.S. Court of Appeals for the Second Circuit held that prohibiting physician-assisted suicide violates "equal protection." It argued that it is unfair to permit competent, dying patients to die by forgoing life-sustaining treatment but prohibit physician-assisted suicide for equally competent, dying patients who are not able to hasten death by stopping a treatment (2). The option of terminal dehydration, which the court did not consider, undercuts this argument: It is available to all suffering patients who are able to make decisions, including patients who are not receiving life-sustaining treatment. Accordingly, terminal dehydration is more widely available than physician-assisted suicide, which is limited to patients who can ingest lethal medication. Even a patient with a condition as debilitating as the "locked-in syndrome" can seek death by terminal dehydration. The setting, however, may influence the availability of terminal dehydration because caregivers in some nursing homes and hospitals may be reluctant to comply with a patient's refusal of food and water.

Professional Integrity

Several noted physician-ethicists have argued that physician-assisted suicide is always wrong because it violates the healing vocation of medicine (3, 4). Although this absolute claim is open to challenge, the prescription or administration of lethal medication by physicians poses a serious threat to their professional integrity. A request for physician-assisted suicide by a competent, dying patient who is suffering intolerably places the physician in a moral conflict between the duty to relieve suffering and the duty not to kill or to help kill. With terminal dehydration, the physician is not responsible for providing the means of death and therefore is not subjected to such a conflict. Terminal dehydration remains morally challenging, however, in view of professional commitments to preserve life and to help terminally ill patients cope until death arrives naturally. Physicians retain the right to advocate in favor of the patient's continued life as long as they refrain from coercion.

Social Implications

No controversial change in the law or public policy is required to permit patients to die by terminal dehydration. Because the legitimacy of terminal dehydration derives from the patient's legal and moral right to refuse medical treatment, wider understanding and use of this option is apt to be less socially divisive than legalization of physician-assisted suicide. Terminal dehydration can be used openly by patients, which is a distinct advantage as long as physician-assisted suicide remains illegal.

The reluctance of many physicians to confront death and to undertake the demanding work of palliative care, coupled with incentives that operate within managed care, creates the potential for physician-assisted suicide to become a "quick fix." Physician-assisted suicide offers a swift exit, putting an end to the patient's suffering and the need for costly continued care. The determination and patience required to die by terminal dehydration, compared with the relative ease of ingesting lethal medication, make terminal dehydration much less likely to become routine for terminally ill patients.

IS TERMINAL DEHYDRATION HUMANE?

Many of the features that make terminal dehydration potentially superior to physician-assisted suicide derive from the relatively long interval between the patient's decision to die by forgoing nutrition and hydration and the occurrence of death. However, this factor also accounts for some of the major difficulties of this method. Terminal dehydration can be made painless but not swift. Although death by terminal dehydration normally takes several days to occur, some case reports indicate a period of 3 to 4 weeks from when the process is started to when the patient dies. The time required for death by terminal dehydration is likely to make this method seem less humane than physician-assisted suicide. Indeed, it may seem repugnant that a competent, informed patient who resolutely seeks voluntary death must stop eating and drinking and wait for an undetermined period for death to arrive. The vigil of family members awaiting their loved one's death may be burdensome and stressful. Moreover, minimal drinking in response to thirst or the urging of concerned relatives may further prolong the process of dying. Those who die by terminal dehydration typically lapse into unconsciousness before death, which may seem intolerable to some patients and their family members.

The difference between the lengths of time it takes to die of terminal dehydration and of physician-assisted suicide should be assessed in light of regulations likely to govern any legalized access to physician-assisted suicide. The Oregon Death with Dignity Act mandates a 2-week waiting period after a request for physician-assisted suicide. A waiting period of similar length is described in a model statute for legalizing physician-assisted suicide (5). Most patients who seek death by terminal dehydration would achieve their goal within 2 weeks.

Does terminal dehydration require more determination and fortitude than can be reasonably expected? Patients seeking death may be reluctant to accept terminal dehydration out of fear that their physicians and family members will not provide the support and care required to make this a tolerable option. Patients who choose this means of voluntary death remain vulnerable to persuasive pressure from family members or physicians to change their mind. They may succumb to such pressures either because life has again begun to seem worthwhile or because emotional and physical fatigue limits their ability to persist, forcing them to endure an unwanted existence.

Physician-assisted suicide also has deficiencies as a humane means of voluntary death. The patient may botch the suicide attempt and possibly be left in a condition worse than that resulting from the terminal illness. Family or friends have felt compelled in some cases to place a plastic bag over the head of a person attempting physician-assisted suicide to complete the deed. Those who assist in a loved one's death by giving them pills or applying a plastic bag may suffer debilitating guilt and a prolonged and complicated bereavement.

Some patients who seek death may feel that terminal dehydration is, at best, less desirable than physician-assisted suicide. They may choose terminal dehydration only because legal or ethical concerns prevent their physicians from complying with a request for lethal medication. However, anecdotal evidence suggests that terminal dehydration can provide a peaceful and dignified process of dying.

INTEGRATING TERMINAL DEHYDRATION INTO CLINICAL PRACTICE

Like patients who request physician-assisted suicide, patients who seek death by terminal dehydration may be depressed or may be motivated by concerns about being a burden to others. Clinicians involved in the care of patients who decide to forgo food and water must be sure that the patient is able to make decisions and that the patient's decision is informed and voluntary. Moreover, support from a physician may help counteract the patient's fear of being a burden. Because some data show an association between depression and a desire to hasten death, physicians are justified in encouraging a trial of antidepressant therapy, counseling, or both before supporting a patient's decision to die by terminal dehydration. To obviate undue influence from the physician, the initiative to explore the option of terminal dehydration should come from the patient.

Clinicians should continue to provide palliative care to patients who seek voluntary death by terminal dehydration, even if they view the patient's decision as problematic or unwarranted. Competent patients have the right to forgo food and water. Although physicians may legitimately deny a patient's request for assisted suicide, they have the responsibility to provide palliative care to patients who have resolutely chosen voluntary death. Just as a physician must continue to provide palliative care for a competent patient who refuses to have surgery and is dying of sepsis from a gangrenous extremity, palliation remains a physician's obligation for a patient who chooses to die by terminal dehydration. Patients who voluntarily choose this option after being informed about their alternatives should be assured that they will not be abandoned and that every effort will be made to promote comfort until death arrives. This commitment to provide palliative care also helps alleviate the distress of family members.

RESPONSE TO EXTRAORDINARY CASES

No adult of sound mind should be forced to endure an existence that he or she rationally considers to be intolerable. Accordingly, the physician has a moral obligation not to foreclose the option of voluntary death. We acknowledge that, in rare cases, physician-assisted suicide offers a superior alternative to terminal dehydration. Nonetheless, the existence of a small number of compelling cases does not, by itself, warrant a change in policy in favor of legalizing physician-assisted suicide. We do not view legalization of physician-assisted death as a matter of individual rights. The debate should focus on whether legalization of physician-assisted suicide will enable our society to provide better care for dying and incurably ill patients, without causing intolerable abuses. The already-available option of terminal dehydration deserves careful consideration as an alternative to physician-assisted suicide.

REFERENCES

1 Bernat JL, Gert B, Mogielnicki RP. Patient refusal of hydration and nutrition: an alternative to physician-assisted suicide or voluntary active euthanasia. Arch Intern Med. 1993;153:2723–8.
2 *Quill v. Vacco,* 80 F. 3d 716 (2d Cir. 1996).
3 Kass LR. Neither for love nor money: why doctors must not kill. Public Interest. 1989;94:25–46.
4 Pellegrino ED. Doctors must not kill. J Clin Ethics. 1992;3:95–102.
5 Baron CH, Bergstresser C, Brock DW, Cole GF, Dorfman NS, Johnson JA, et al. A model state act to authorize and regulate physician-assisted suicide. Harvard Journal of Legislation. 1996;33:1–34.

QUESTIONS

1 Does the availability of terminal dehydration provide the basis of a compelling argument against the legalization of physician-assisted suicide?
2 If you were terminally ill and enduring significant pain and/or indignity, would you welcome the possibility of physician-assisted suicide? Would terminal dehydration serve your purposes just as well?

SUGGESTED ADDITIONAL READINGS FOR CHAPTER 6

BATTIN, MARGARET P., ROSAMOND RHODES, and ANITA SILVERS, eds.: *Physician-Assisted Suicide: Expanding the Debate.* New York: Routledge, 1998. The essays in Part Two of this extensive collection debate the projected impact of physician-assisted suicide on vulnerable patients. Part Three considers physician-assisted suicide in reference to the practice of medicine. Part Four provides contrasting viewpoints on the issue of legalization, and Part Five presents religious perspectives.
GOMEZ, CARLOS F.: *Regulating Death: Euthanasia and the Case of The Netherlands.* New York: Free Press, 1991. Gomez describes and criticizes the practices of (active) euthanasia in the Netherlands. He argues that the Dutch system is plagued with inadequate controls
Hastings Center Report, vol. 22, March–April 1992. This issue provides a collection of articles on (active) euthanasia and physician-assisted suicide. In particular, Dan W. Brock offers an extensive defense of voluntary active euthanasia, which Daniel Callahan opposes in "When Self-Determination Runs Amok."
LEGEMAATE, JOHAN: "The Dutch Euthanasia Act and Related Issues." *Journal of Law and Medicine,* vol. 11, February 2004, pp. 312–323. Legemaate provides a discussion of the 2002 Dutch Termination of Life on Request and Assisted Suicide Act. He sets this legislation in historical context and considers international reactions to it. The full text of the act itself is included as an appendix to the article.

MILLER, FRANKLIN G., et al.: "Regulating Physician-Assisted Death." *New England Journal of Medicine,* vol. 331, July 14, 1994, pp. 119–123. A group of six authors, well known in bioethics, argues for the legalization of "physician-assisted death"—that is, both physician-assisted suicide and voluntary active euthanasia—in accordance with a detailed proposal for regulation of the practice.

THE NEW YORK STATE TASK FORCE ON LIFE AND THE LAW: *When Death Is Sought: Assisted Suicide and Euthanasia in the Medical Context.* Albany: Health Education Services, 1994. Providing an extensive analysis of clinical, legal, and ethical considerations, the task force unanimously recommends that the laws prohibiting assisted suicide and (active) euthanasia in New York not be changed.

PELLEGRINO, EDMUND D.: "Doctors Must Not Kill." *The Journal of Clinical Ethics,* vol. 3, Summer 1992, pp. 95–102. Pellegrino contends that (1) the moral arguments in favor of (active) euthanasia are flawed, (2) killing by physicians would seriously distort the healing relationship, and (3) the social consequences of allowing such killing would be very detrimental.

QUILL, TIMOTHY E., and MARGARET P. BATTIN, eds.: *Physician-Assisted Dying: The Case for Palliative Care and Patient Choice.* Baltimore: Johns Hopkins University Press, 2004. The collection of essays in this book has been assembled to present an overall case for the legalization of physician-assisted death.

QUILL, TIMOTHY E., BERNARD LO, and DAN W. BROCK: "Palliative Options of Last Resort: A Comparison of Voluntarily Stopping Eating and Drinking, Terminal Sedation, Physician-Assisted Suicide, and Voluntary Active Euthanasia." *JAMA,* vol. 278, December 17, 1997, pp. 2099–2104. The authors compare and contrast the four identified practices, presenting both a clinical and an ethical analysis. They also provide a brief discussion of appropriate safeguards for hastening death by any of the methods under discussion.

STEINBOCK, BONNIE, and ALASTAIR NORCROSS, eds.: *Killing and Letting Die,* 2d ed. New York: Fordham University Press, 1994. This anthology provides a wealth of material on the distinction between killing and letting die.

Terrorism, Human Rights, and Civil Liberties Notes

This chapter brings up some interesting discussions on the definition of terrorism. Here are some of the definitions under consideration:

Patriot Act: Instituted after 9/11, this act does away with the Constitutional rights of an individual if that individual is suspected of an association with terrorism.

Collateral Damage or Principle of Double Effect: This is the concept that some unintended deaths may occur (and are justified) if they are the result of being close to an intended target. The term is usually applied to civilian deaths that occur when a military target is the intended goal. The civilian deaths are justified because they are not intentionally targeted. They are "collateral damage."

Just War: The idea of a Just War is that war is justified because two principles are met, the Principle of Proportionality and the Principle of Discrimination. *The Principle of Proportionality* is that the level of force must be proportional to the good intended by the war. *The Principle of Discrimination* is that the force used respects the difference between combatants and non-combatants. The original concept of a "just war" is explained by **St. Thomas Aquinas** in response the Catholic Church's question about under what conditions may a war be waged.

Violence: Your authors will have differing definitions of violence, but it is usually the use of physical and/or psychological harm done by force or **coercion**.

Innocents or Non-Combatants: The concept of an innocent person is, perhaps, the most controversial of the definitions. Outside of infants and small children, are "innocents" people who are not directly involved in combat, or are they people who are involved in some support level of combat but not armed, or are they only people who have no military involvement? On the other hand, is there anyone who is truly an "innocent"? Some authors would say that anyone who elected officials who go to war are no longer neutral, and therefore, not "innocent."

Terrorism: Again, this is a controversial term and often depends on which side of a dispute is speaking. Generally, terrorism, is any action that involves the use of violence or threat of violence to further personal or political agendas. The FBI defines terrorism as "the unlawful use of force or violence against persons or property to intimidate or coerce a government, the civil population, or any segment thereof, in furtherance of political or social objectives." The problem is who defines "lawful" from "unlawful" and what constitutes violence. Is violence only physical violence or does it also include threats of harm? Does the harm or threat of harm have to be sudden and physical, or can it also include slow forms of harm and be psychological in nature? Are "political agendas" ever separate from personal agendas? If an individual, unconnected to any political group, blows up a school, is this an act of terrorism? Is domestic violence an act of terrorism if it is persistent? If the definition of terrorism depends on it being "unlawful" then is an act instigated by a government automatically "lawful" and, therefore, not an act of terrorism? Some authors will define the dropping of the atomic bomb on the civilian population of Hiroshima and Nagasaki as acts of terrorism.

Stephen Nathanson: Nathanson says we need a definition of "terrorism" that is (1) neutral with respect to who commits the action and is (2) consistent and even-handed in it applications of moral criteria. In other words, we need a definition of terrorism that is not politically biased.

He begins by looking at the most common inclusions in definitions of terrorism. They usually include the following:

1 Terrorism involves acts of serious, deliberate violence or destruction.

2 Terrorism is generally committed by groups as part of a campaign to promote a political or social agenda.

3 Generally targets a limited numbers of people, but aims to influence larger groups and/or leaders who make decisions for the group.

4 They (terrorists) usually kill or injure innocent people or pose a serious threat of such harm to them.

The problem, for Nathanson, is that some have used the above definition but made exceptions when they feel is to be politically convenient. For example, some have argued that the U.S. bombing of German cities in WWII or the bombing of Hiroshima and Nagasaki were cases of "extreme emergency" that warranted the destruction of civilian targets as a measure of last resort. Nathanson argues that we can't have it both ways: we can't argue for terrorism as defined above, deliberately targeting "innocent" people (civilian populations) and, at the same time, argue against terrorism went it is directed towards us. Either it is alright to intentionally bomb civilians or it isn't. Our bombing of civilian targets, such as Hiroshima, is considered a case of terrorism by many.

Nathanson believes there can be no exceptions. Any bombing of cities and the concept of "collateral damage" is morally wrong. Instead, he proposes that we add a "bend over backwards" guide to avoid any action that might be seen as terrorist in nature. Even in war, we should:

1 target our attacks narrowly on military resources,

2 avoid targets where civilian deaths are likely,

3 avoid the use of indiscriminate weapons (such as cluster bombs),

4 and if the choice is between damage to civilian lives or damage to military personnel, the priority should be to save civilian lives.

According to Nathanson, including the "bend over backwards" criteria will eliminate the problem of allowing exceptions and fulfill his goals of making the definition of terrorism: (1) neutral with respect to who commits the action and a (2)
consistent and even-handed application of moral criteria.

Alison Jaggar: Jaggar believes any definition of terrorism must be consistent and
non-arbitrary, precise, and impartial. She points out that Webster's Dictionary
defines terrorism as the "use of terror and violence to intimidate and subjugate,
especially as a political weapon or policy."

She argues that the above definition (as well as most other definitions of terrorism) does not meet the criteria of being "non-arbitrary, precise, and impartial" for
the following reasons:

1 The problem with the term "politically motivated" is that the "use of terror
and violence to intimidate and subjugate" on a political level excludes the fact that
it may be personal. Jaggar argues that gang or domestic violence may also be
considered "terrorism."

2 The distinction between personal and political is not always clear. The goal
may be political, but it could also be for personal gain of power.

3 Goals may not always be unjust. For example, terrorist tactics may be used to
free a population from tyranny (a good goal and not to "subjugate"), but still be
terrorist in nature.

4 The definition of terrorism usually assumes that the action is directed against
"innocent" victims, but the victims of terrorism may be primary or secondary. In
other words, it may be the person who is directly harmed, but the person may also
be harmed in indirect ways. For example, destruction of the infrastructure that supports a society is also a terrorist act because it may leave the population with no
resources to live.

5 Terrorism is usually not considered to be part of a government's policy, but
terrorism is not confined to sub-groups. Terrorism can also be a weapon used by
official governments, such as gender apartheid in Afghanistan and Saudi Arabia,
Latin American death squads, the Serbian policy of rape, or the U.S. bombing of
Japan and its support of the "Contras" in Nicaragua.

6 When terrorism is defined as something that subjugates or intimidates, these
are very subjective terms. What intimidates one person may be totally ignored by
another. A more precise definition would be that the action is terrorist in nature if
it creates fear that is long-lasting enough to influence future behavior.

Jaggar believes that terrorism is usually morally wrong because it (1) is engaged
in coercion and intimidation and (2) it harms or threatens harm to those who have
not harmed or threatened others and do not deserve harm.

However, Jaggar believes that in some extreme circumstances terrorism may be
justified (see #3 above). She says that to justify terrorism all the following need to
be in place:

1 It must be for a just cause (to secure people's basic rights).
2 It must represent competent authority and the majority.
3 It must have the right intention (the same criteria present that would justify a war).

4 It must be proportional (it must achieve more overall good than harm).

5 It must only be used as a last resort. All other means, including war, must be unavailable.

6 There must be a reasonable hope of success—more than required to justify a war.

7 The aim must be peace.

Jaggar proposes the following definition for terrorism:

"Terrorism is the use of extreme threats or violence designed to intimidate or subjugate governments, groups, or individuals. It is a tactic of coercion intended to promote further ends that in themselves may be good, bad, or indifferent. Terrorism may be practiced by governments or international bodies or forces, substate groups or even individuals. Its threats or violence are aimed directly or immediately at the bodies or belongings of innocent civilians but these are typically terrorists' secondary targets; the primary targets of terrorists are the governments, groups or individuals that they wish to intimidate."

David Luban: Luban points out that there are two models of how to treat people accused of crimes. There is the "war model" and the "Justice model." The "war model" is meant to address the treatment of soldier during war. The "Justice model" is meant to address how to treat civilians in a civilian setting. The problem, according to Luban, is that, with the Patriot Act, the U.S. government has combined the two models in a way to eliminate the protections granted to each. Luban calls this combination a "hybrid model."

1 The War Model of action allows for the use of lethal force on enemy troops regardless of their degree of involvement. The Justice Model does not permit the use of force (harm/killing) against criminals (until proven guilty with a trial by jury). The Patriot Act uses the War Model to allow the use of force, but against civilians suspected of associating with anything having to do with terrorism.

2 The problem is that no proof is required of the person's involvement. The War Model does not require proof. The Legal Model requires proof that someone is involved in a criminal activity before they can be arrested and held. The Patriot Act uses the War Model on civilians. There is no need of proof of involvement in any illegal activity. It is enough that the government suspects someone might be involved or know someone who might be involved to warrant that person being arrested and held.

3 In the War Model, the military can attack without concern if the people under attack deserve such treatment or not. The Legal Model requires there be a good cause in order to prosecute an individual. The Patriot Act uses the War Model against civilians, not requiring that there be any cause for prosecution.

4 Under the War Model, "collateral damage" is allowed. In other words, if a few innocent people are killed in the process of war against military targets, that is seen as regrettable, but ethical. The Legal Model does not permit harming, jailing, or killing of the innocent. The Patriot Act uses the War Model against civilians. If an innocent person is held, tortured, possibly killed and then found innocent, that is regrettable, but considered allowable.

5 Under the Geneva Convention, in war, combatants are protected from injury or retribution for their role in war. They may "not be threatened, insulted, or exposed to unpleasant or disadvantageous treatment of any kind." At the end of the war, the combatants must be repatriated. The Patriot Act does not follow the Geneva Convention because, it claims, the Convention is designed for the War Model. Instead, the Patriot Act uses a hybrid model, eliminating the rights expected under both the War Model and the Legal Model. There is nothing that says a person must ever be released, even if found innocent.

6 The result is that, under the Patriot Act, there are no rights. Capture is based on what someone might do rather than what someone has done (Legal Model). There are no rights to a hearing. No attorney is required to represent or counsel a prisoner. No charges are needed in order to arrest someone. The prisoner may be tortured. The person may end up dying (even though this is not the goal or intended, it is allowable under "collateral damage"). The person under arrest looses both the rights expected under the War Model and the Legal Model.

Luban points out that the "war on terror" model of the Patriot Act and the U.S. government has become the model of politics, both domestically and internationally (it is used by other governments besides our own). It means the end of human rights because this hybrid model isn't something that will go away soon. As long as terrorism exists, and it is here to stay, and we are willing to give up our rights to fight terrorism, we will lose the very rights that are the basis of our wars in the Middle East.

Justice Hugo Black: On December 7, 1941, Pearl Harbor was bombed by the Japanese. On May 8, 1942, all persons of Japanese ancestry (2/3 of them American citizens), living on the West Coast of the United States, were forced to leave their homes and businesses and were sent to internment camps in California. 120,000 Japanese and Japanese-Americans were involved. There was no distinction made between newborn infants and adults or the elderly and disabled. All were imprisoned and their property and businesses lost. They were left to their own devices to provide education for the children in the camp and the living conditions were miserable.

Fred Korematsu, a U.S. citizen, refused to report to the internment camp. He was able to get a lawyer and appealed his case up to the U.S. Supreme Court. Justice Black represented the majority, which upheld the order.

After the war, this act of placing American citizens in internment camps was seen as morally wrong and compensation was given to the survivors. However, the loss of two years of their lives, their businesses, careers, etc. could never really be replaced. Today, no one would dispute that this act had a racial basis and was one of the low points in the history of the U.S. To put this in perspective, no Americans of German or Italian descent were ever sent to internment camps on the East Coast. In Hawaii, Japanese Americans fought as regular American citizens and won many medals of valor fighting as members of the United States military.

The majority in the Court justified their position by saying that it was impossible to tell "good" Japanese from "bad" Japanese because all Japanese looked alike, and the internment camps were just one of those hardships of war. They insisted that this was not a case of racial prejudice.

Justice Frank Murphy: There were several justices who disagreed with the majority opinion in this case. Justice Murphy argued that the depravation of Constitutional rights must be reasonably related to immediate and imminent danger. This argument is called the "reasonability test."

Justice Murphy argued that the Korematsu case did not meet the "reasonability test." There was no attempt by the U.S. military or government to assess any danger (disloyalty) on an individual basis. There were no distinctions made between loyal or disloyal Japanese-Americans. The internment was made on the erroneous assumptions of racial guilt. There was no evidence of disloyalty. Not one person of Japanese ancestry was ever accused or convicted of espionage or sabotage after Pearl Harbor while they were still free. The internment included infants and children, women, the elderly, the infirm, with no consideration. Justice Murphy and the dissenting justices concluded that there must be the same guaranteed rights for all American citizens regardless of ancestry.

Jeremy Waldron: Waldron calls for caution in giving up civil liberties for security. He points out that:

1 It is "magical thinking...that the risk from that power [of the government] goes down as the risk from terrorism goes up." In other words, giving the government power is a risky proposition and, once the government gains power, it seldom gives it up after the emergency is over. These sentiments are echoed in the next two points made by Waldron.

2 We should look at whether giving up liberties to our government will actually be an effective means of fighting terrorism.

3 The government (any government) is always ready to take away liberties and the treat from the government itself (to the American people) "goes up as the power accorded to the state increases."

4 He also cautions that the liberties we are ready to give up, thinking that the repressive measures will only be used against terrorists, can and will end up being used against us. The problem is in thinking that the power granted the government won't be abused. Currently, under the Patriot Act, ordinary citizens can be held without hearings or any legal recourse on suspicion alone. People can just "disappear" and the government does not have to account for what happens to them.

CHAPTER 7

Terrorism, Human Rights, and Civil Liberties

Although terrorism is not a new phenomenon, the September 11, 2001, attacks on the World Trade Center in New York and on the Pentagon in Washington brought terrorism home to Americans and exposed a vulnerability to new kinds of terrorist acts that had not been recognized before. The ensuing war on terrorism, proclaimed by President George W. Bush in response to these attacks, has resulted in wars in Afghanistan and Iraq and the internment of terrorist suspects at Guantánamo Bay. It has also had domestic consequences including the passage of the Patriot Act, which has given rise to a concern about possible infringements on civil liberties.

The conceptual and moral issues raised by terrorism and by the war on terrorism are complex. This chapter deals with only a few of these issues. What is terrorism? Are terrorist acts ever morally justified? Can we draw a morally principled distinction between terrorist acts and acts of war if both result in harm to individuals whom we might describe as civilians, noncombatants, or innocents? How do we reconcile the need to maintain national security, on the one hand, with the need to respect human rights and guarantee civil liberties on the other?

DEFINITIONS OF TERRORISM

How should we understand the word *terrorism*? Answers to this question are crucially intertwined with answers to questions related to the moral issues raised by terrorist acts and responses to them. Yet no definition of *terrorism* is universally accepted. Various U.S. government documents, for example, adopt different definitions. The United States State Department, in its *Patterns of Global Terrorism,* uses the following definition: "'terrorism' means premeditated, politically motivated violence perpetrated against noncombatant targets by subnational groups or clandestine agents, usually intended to influence an audience."[1] The FBI, using a definition from the Code of Federal Regulations,[2] states that terrorism is "the unlawful use of force and violence against persons or property to intimidate or coerce a government, the civilian population, or any segment thereof, in furtherance of political or social objectives."[3] Other government documents work with other definitions.

Among philosophers, disagreement is also widespread. The following two examples illustrate one of these points of disagreement. The definition of *terrorism* advanced by Stephen Nathanson in a reading in this chapter includes as a central element the killing or injuring of innocent people or the threat of such harms to them. By contrast, Virginia Held maintains that the targeting of "innocents," as in Nathanson's definition, or "noncombatants" as in the State Department's definition, is not an essential characteristic of terrorist acts. Held defines *terrorism* as "political violence that usually involves sudden attacks to spread fear to a wider group than those attacked, often doing so by targeting civilians."[4] In keeping with government definitions, such as those given above, as well as many philosophical ones not included here, it is conceptually impossible for states to perpetrate terrorist acts. In contrast, according to both Nathanson's and Held's definitions, it is conceptually possible for states as well as nonstate entities to be perpetrators of terrorism.

Discussions concerning the defining features of terrorism center on the attribution of the following characteristics to terrorist acts:

1 They involve the use of violence or the threat of violence.
2 They are politically motivated.
3 They are perpetrated by subnational groups or individuals.
4 They target innocents.

The first two features are usually accepted as stating essential characteristics of terrorism, although Alison M. Jaggar, in a reading in this chapter, rejects political motivation as an essential part of the definition of terrorism. But these two features are surely not sufficient to constitute terrorism. In respect to the violence requirement, think of someone angrily punching another person or someone tackling a man wielding a semiautomatic weapon in order to prevent harm to passersby. Although these are violent acts, it would be inappropriate to call them acts of terrorism. Thus terrorist acts can be seen as falling into a subcategory of violent acts, but we need other criteria to determine which acts qualify as terrorist.

The second feature, political motivation, does provide a plausible criterion for distinguishing terrorist acts from others involving violence. Politically motivated violence has been seen as a feature of terrorist acts ever since the word was first used in France to describe the reign of terror during the French Revolution. However, wars are also waged for political reasons. If there are important reasons for keeping terrorism and war in separate categories, then we need to find a criterion

[1]*Patterns of Global Terrorism,* May 2002 (http://www.state.gov).
[2]28 Code of Federal Regulations, Section 0.85.
[3]http://www.fbi.gov/publications/terror/terror2000_2001.pdf.
[4]Virginia Held, "Legitimate Authority in Non-State Groups Using Violence," *Journal of Social Philosophy,* vol. 36, no. 2, 2005:178.

that applies to the former but not the latter. Acceptance of the third feature would make that possible. If we limit the category of perpetrators of terrorism to subnationals or individuals, we shut out the possibility that states could be perpetrators of terrorism. But unless the distinction is rationally grounded, it seems arbitrary. Examples of state actions some label as terrorist abound in the literature. Think, for example, of the Russian destruction of Grozny during the Chechen war. It is not surprising, then, that there is so much disagreement about the third feature.

In contrast, it is easy to see why most framers of definitions of terrorism consider the fourth feature to be an essential element in terrorist acts. First, many acts commonly considered terrorist do target innocents. Second, the harming of innocents is sufficient to establish a presumption that these acts are morally wrong, giving us at the very least a prima facie moral basis for our condemnations of terrorism. Yet this criterion raises important questions. Who are the innocents? Infants and young children? Certainly. But what about voters who support a government that is performing acts of violence to which the terrorists may be reacting? What about civilian populations in wartime whose efforts on the home front make the continuation of wartime violence possible? In light of such difficulties, writers sometimes talk of *noncombatants* rather than *innocents*. Yet, this too raises difficulties. On this description, members of the military in wartime would be legitimate targets of violence while civilian officeholders who issue orders to military personnel would not. One suggested approach, discussed by Jaggar in this chapter, is to amend the fourth feature as follows: Terrorist acts target innocent civilians. Of course, on this view, there is still a problem of determining just who is and who is not an innocent civilian. After the bombing of the World Trade Center, defenders of the bombing claimed that the civilians who were killed and injured in that attack were not innocents because they were engaged in the kind of global business practices that were inimical to the terrorists. But even if that claim were true, it would not apply to others who were killed in the attack, such as restaurant employees.

Several writers have maintained that the fourth criterion, even as amended, is too restrictive. One reason given for that criticism is that in our ordinary ascriptions, we often describe as terrorist not only actions that primarily target innocent civilians but also actions whose primary targets have been members of the military. The attack on the *USS Cole* is one example; the September 11, 2001, attack on the Pentagon is another. One attempt to take account of this reasoning is seen in Held's definition above, which states that terrorist acts *often* target civilians.

CAN TERRORISM EVER BE MORALLY JUSTIFIED?

Many people believe that terrorism is always morally wrong. For them, the word *terrorism* functions like the word *murder*—just as any act of murder is wrong by definition, so, too, is any act of terrorism. On this approach, the possibility of justified terrorism is nonexistent. But on a wider understanding of terrorism, such as Held's above or Jaggar's in this chapter, the question is an intelligible one.

Attempts to provide a principled basis for either condemning all terrorist actions or leaving open the possibility that some terrorist acts may be morally justified frequently focus on the differences and similarities between war and terrorism. Those who use this approach often place their reasoning within the context of *just war theory,* which falls into two parts. The first part presents principles that are to be used to determine whether the war itself is just (*jus ad bellum* or "right to go to war"). The second presents principles to be used to determine whether the actions performed in the conduct of the war are just (*jus in bello* or "right conduct in war").

Just war theorists have given different accounts of the conditions that must hold before a nation has a right to go to war. The following statement is one way of capturing their central concerns. One nation (A) is justified in engaging in war with another nation (B) if and only if:

• A is attacked by B, or is attempting to help another nation C that has been attacked by B, or A or C are about to be attacked by B (*the just cause requirement*).

• The individuals in A who declare war on B are those members of A who have the legitimate authority to do so (*the legitimate authority requirement*).

• A's intentions in waging war are limited to repelling B's attack and establishing a fair peace (*the good intentions requirement*).

• A has a reasonable hope of successfully achieving the good it intends (*the reasonable hope of success requirement*).

• The good A can reasonably hope to achieve is proportional to the evils that can reasonably be expected to result from waging war (*the proportionality of just cause to means requirement*).

• A has exhausted all peaceful alternatives, and fighting the war is the last resort (*the last resort requirement*).

• A does not use or anticipate using immoral means in waging war (*the moral means requirement*).

In just war doctrine, two principles are central in determining what types of action are morally permissible in warfare:

1 *The principle of proportionality*—The level of force employed must be proportional to the good that the action is intended to achieve.

2 *The principle of discrimination*—Force should be used in a way that respects the difference between combatants and noncombatants.

The principle of discrimination is usually understood as prohibiting the direct intentional killing of *noncombatants*. In the conduct of wars, however, civilian deaths are sometimes unavoidable. Those who argue that some civilian deaths can be morally justified often invoke the *doctrine of double effect*. On this doctrine, civilian casualties are justifiable if their deaths, although foreseen, are not intended. (Some of the problems with the doctrine of double effect are discussed by Nathanson in this chapter.)

Moral evaluations of terrorism usually focus on the principle of discrimination. If the intentional infliction of harm on innocent civilians is an essential characteristic of terrorism, then, in the views of many, terrorism, which violates that principle, can never be morally justified. However, countless acts of war have targeted civilians. Think of the atomic bombing of Hiroshima or the bombing of Dresden in World War II. Such examples pose problems for those who would condemn all terrorism while refusing to condemn similar wartime actions. Stephen Nathanson, in this chapter, addresses the moral issues raised by this apparent discrepancy.

He suggests principles that could be used to distinguish between those wartime acts that are legitimate even when they harm innocent civilians, on the one hand, and illegitimate wartime acts and all terrorist acts, on the other. By contrast, Alison Jaggar, in this chapter, suggests that the principles used to determine whether a war is just (*jus ad bellum*) can also be used in judging the actions of terrorists, leaving open the possibility that some of the latter might be justified.

Most moral evaluations of terrorism focus on terrorist attacks and do not consider the reasons why terrorists employ such tactics. As we saw above, in evaluating wars as just or unjust, we ask not only if the means used in conducting the war were morally legitimate but also whether going to war was just in the first place. One of Jaggar's principles for evaluating terrorism is a version of the principle of last resort: Terrorist tactics must be a last resort. All other means of remedying the perceived injustice, including conventional warfare, must be unavailable or have failed.

In applying the principle of last resort, we would have to look at several factors. We would need to understand the causes that led to terrorism in order to determine if the cause is just. We would also have to look at what steps the group took to achieve its ends by other means. In doing this, we would need to determine what possibilities for peaceful resolution were available to it. This would require examining not only the acts of the terrorists but also those of the governments against which the terrorism is aimed. If actions by those governments were such as to make any peaceful resolutions impossible, then it seems as if the latter would bear some responsibility for the ensuing terrorism. Take, for example, the terrorism in South Africa that was directed against the policy of apartheid. If the government blocked every other avenue for achieving the end of apartheid, which involved gross violations of human rights, and left the groups fighting against it no other recourse, then the antiapartheid terrorist activities might be in keeping with the principle of last resort. Of course, there are other principles that would have to be satisfied as well.

SECURITY, HUMAN RIGHTS, AND CIVIL LIBERTIES

Time and again throughout its history, when the security of the United States has been seriously threatened, measures have been adopted that involved serious infringements on civil liberties and yet were upheld by the courts. In hindsight, government officials and others have often acknowledged that the infringements were unjust and that they played no essential role in achieving victory. A paradigm example of such misguided measures was the internment of Japanese and Japanese-Americans during World War II. Several challenges to the constitutionality of the infringements on the liberties and rights of Japanese and Japanese-Americans culminated in United States Supreme Court cases. In one such case, *Korematsu v. United States* (1944), the Court ruled against the challenger, Fred T. Korematsu, despite a great deal of disagreement among the justices. Excerpts from both the majority opinion written by Justice Black and a dissenting opinion written by Justice Murphy are reprinted in this chapter. Although in this and other cases, the Court upheld the constitutionality of the actions taken against Japanese-Americans, later presidents and a government-appointed commission appointed by Congress to investigate the treatment of Japanese-Americans during World War II acknowledged their wrongness. In 1988, President Reagan declared the Japanese internment a grave injustice. Korematsu himself was awarded the Presidential Medal of Freedom.

Once again, the United States is under serious threat of harm as illustrated by the attacks on September 11, 2001, as well as other terrorist threats. And once again infringements on civil liberties and violations of human rights are often held to be justified in the name of national security. Some of these measures are reflected in the U.S. treatment of prisoners held at Guantánamo Bay. Labeled as unlawful combatants, the detainees are said not to be entitled to the protections extended to prisoners of war by the Geneva Convention. At the same time, they are not considered to be criminals entitled to the legal protections built into the criminal justice system. In a reading in this chapter, David Luban discusses the moral issues raised by such imprisonments and argues that as long as it continues, "the war on terrorism" means the end of human rights for those "near enough to be touched by the fire of battle."

On the domestic front, various executive orders as well as the U.S.A. Patriot Act[5] are seen by many as a serious threat to civil liberties. Geoffrey R. Stone identifies the following as among the more questionable restrictions on freedom:

> . . . indefinite detention, with no access to judicial review, of more than a thousand noncitizens who were lawfully in the United States and had not been charged with any crime; blanket secrecy concerning the identity of these detainees; refusal to permit many of these detainees to communicate with an attorney; an unprecedented assertion of authority to eavesdrop on constitutionally protected attorney-client communications; secret deportation proceedings; the incarceration for more than two years of an American citizen, arrested on American soil, incommunicado, with no access to a lawyer, solely on the basis of an executive determination that he was an "enemy combatant"; significant new limitations on the scope of the Freedom of Information Act; expanded authority to conduct undercover infiltration and surveillance of political and religious groups; increased power to wiretap, engage in electronic eavesdropping, and covertly review Internet and e-mail communications; new power to secretly review banking, brokerage, and other financial records; and expanded authority to conduct clandestine physical searches.[6]

No one would deny that terrorism is currently a serious threat to the security of the United States and other countries throughout the world. Nor would anyone deny that governments have a responsibility to protect their people against such threats. But, as in other critical times, there is a risk that rights and civil liberties may be infringed upon unnecessarily in the interest of national security. Those who defend the most recent infringements on liberty frequently assert that there is a need to strike an appropriate balance between security and freedom. In one of this chapter's readings, Jeremy Waldron examines this assertion.

Jane S. Zembaty

[5]The U.S.A. Patriot Act (Uniting and Strengthening America by Providing Appropriate Tools Required to Intercept and Obstruct Terrorism) was enacted by Congress in 2001 and renewed, with some modifications, in 2006.

[6]Geoffrey R. Stone, *Perilous Times: Free Speech in Wartime* (New York: Norton, 2004), p. 552. Stone gives extensive documentation for these statements in endnotes on p. 689.

Can Terrorism Be Morally Justified?

Stephen Nathanson

In Nathanson's view, from a moral perspective, the central feature of terrorist acts is that they kill or injure innocent people or threaten them with serious harms. Since some violent acts committed in warfare also share this feature, Nathanson focuses on whether there can be a morally significant difference between acts of war and acts committed by terrorists. He examines, criticizes, and rejects several arguments that others have advanced to distinguish between legitimate acts of warfare and terrorist acts. In conclusion, Nathanson offers his "bend over backwards" rule as a principled basis for condemning terrorist acts, on the one hand, and for justifying legitimate acts of warfare, on the other. He also uses the rule to distinguish between morally unacceptable acts of warfare and legitimate ones.

Can terrorism be morally justified?

Even asking this question can seem like an insult—both to victims of terrorist actions and to moral common sense. One wants to say: if the murder of innocent people by terrorists is not clearly wrong, what is?

But the question is more complicated than it looks. We can see this by broadening our focus and considering some of the other beliefs held by people who condemn terrorism. Very few of us accept the pacifist view that all violence is wrong. Most of us believe that some acts of killing and injuring people are morally justified. Indeed, most of us think that war is sometimes justified, even though it involves organized, large-scale killing, injuring, and destruction and even though innocent civilians are usually among the victims of war. So, most of us believe that even the killing of innocent people is sometimes morally justified. It is this fact that makes the condemnation of terrorism morally problematic. We pick out terrorism for special condemnation because its victims are civilian, noncombatants rather than military or governmental officials, but we also believe that such killings are sometimes morally permissible. Seen in this broader context, judgments about terrorism often seem hypocritical.

Seen in a broader context, moral judgments of terrorism often seem hypocritical. They often presuppose self-serving definitions of "terrorism" that allow people to avoid labeling actions that they approve as instances of terrorism, even though these actions are indistinguishable from other acts that are branded with this negative label. On other occasions, moral judgments of terrorism rest on biased, uneven applications of moral principles to the actions of friends and foes. Principles that are cited to condemn the actions of foes are ignored when similar actions are committed by friends.

Reprinted with permission of the author from *Morality in Practice*, 7th ed. (Wadsworth, 2004), edited by James P. Sterba, pp. 602–610.

We need to ask then: Can people who believe that war is sometimes morally permissible consistently condemn terrorist violence? Or are such condemnations necessarily hypocritical and self-serving?

If we are to avoid hypocrisy, then we need both (a) a definition of terrorism that is neutral with respect to who commits the actions, and (b) moral judgments of terrorism that derive from the consistent, even-handed applications of moral criteria.

This paper aims to achieve both of these things. First, I begin with a definition of terrorism and then discuss why terrorism is always wrong. In addition, I want to show that the condemnation of terrorism does not come without other costs. A consistent approach to terrorism requires us to revise some common judgments about historical events and forces us to reconsider actions in which civilians are killed as "collateral damage" (i.e., side effects) of military attacks.

My aim, then, is to criticize both terrorist actions and a cluster of widespread moral views about violence and war. This cluster includes the following beliefs:

1 Terrorism is always immoral.
2 The allied bombing of cities in World War II was morally justified because of the importance of defeating Nazi Germany and Japan.
3 It is morally permissible to kill civilians in war if these killings are not intended.

The trouble with this cluster is that the first belief expresses an absolute prohibition of acts that kill innocent people while the last two are rather permissive. If we are to avoid inconsistency and hypocrisy, we must revise our views either (a) by accepting that terrorism is sometimes morally permissible, or (b) by judging that city bombings and many collateral damage killings are morally wrong. I will defend the second of these options.

DEFINING TERRORISM

I offer the following definition of terrorism to launch my discussion of the moral issues.[1] Terrorist acts have the following features:

1 They are acts of serious, deliberate violence or destruction.
2 They are generally committed by groups as part of a campaign to promote a political or social agenda.
3 They generally target limited numbers of people but aim to influence a larger group and/or the leaders who make decisions for the group.
4 They either kill or injure innocent people or pose a serious threat of such harms to them.

This definition helps in a number of ways. First, it helps us to distinguish acts of terrorism from other acts of violence. Nonviolent acts are not terrorist acts; nor are violent actions that are unrelated to a political or social agenda. Ironically, some terrible kinds of actions are not terrorist because they are too destructive. As condition 3 tells us, terrorism generally targets limited numbers of people in order to influence a larger group. Acts of genocide that aim to destroy a whole group are not acts of terrorism, but the reason why makes them only worse, not better.

Second, the definition helps us to identify the moral crux of the problem with terrorism. Condition 1 is not the problem because most of us believe that some acts of violence are morally justified. Condition 2 can't be the problem because anyone who believes in just causes of war must accept that some causes are so important that violence may be a legitimate way to promote them. Condition 3 is frequently met by permissible actions, as when we punish some criminals to deter other people from committing crimes. Condition 4 seems closer to what is essentially wrong with terrorism. If terrorism is always immoral, it is because it kills and injures innocent people.

As I have already noted, however, morally conscientious people sometimes want to justify acts that kill innocent people. If a blanket condemnation of terrorism is to be sustained, then we must either condemn all killings of innocent people, or we must find morally relevant differences between the killing of innocents by terrorists and the killing of innocents by others whose actions we find morally acceptable.

TERRORISM AND CITY BOMBING: THE SAME OR DIFFERENT?

Many people who condemn terrorism believe that city bombing in the war against Nazism was justified, even though the World War II bombing campaigns intentionally targeted cities and their inhabitants. This view is defended by some philosophical theorists, including Michael Walzer, in his book *Just and Unjust Wars* and G. Wallace in "Terrorism and the Argument from Analogy."[2] By considering these theorists, we can see if there are relevant differences that allow us to say that terrorism is always wrong but that the World War II bombings were morally justified.

One of the central aims of Michael Walzer's *Just and Unjust Wars* is to defend what he calls the "war convention," the principles that prohibit attacks on civilians in wartime. Walzer strongly affirms the principle of noncombatant immunity, calling it a "fundamental principle [that] underlies and shapes the judgments we make of wartime conduct." He writes:

> A legitimate act of war is one that does not violate the rights of the people against whom it is directed. . . . [N]o one can be threatened with war or warred against, unless through some act of his own he has surrendered or lost his rights.[3]

Unlike members of the military, civilians have not surrendered their rights in any way, and therefore, Walzer says, they may not be attacked.

Given Walzer's strong support for noncombatant immunity and his definition of terrorism as the "method of random murder of innocent people," it is no surprise that he condemns terrorism.[4] At one point, after describing a terrorist attack on an Algerian milk bar frequented by teenagers, he writes:

> Certainly, there are historical moments when armed struggle is necessary for the sake of human freedom. But if dignity and self-respect are to be the outcomes of that struggle, it cannot consist of terrorist attacks against children.[5]

Here and elsewhere, Walzer denounces terrorism because it targets innocent people.

Nonetheless, he claims that the aerial attacks on civilians by the British early in World War II were justified. In order to show why, he develops the concept of a "supreme emergency." Nazi Germany, he tells us, was no ordinary enemy; it was an "ultimate threat to everything decent in our lives."[6] Moreover, in 1940, the Nazi threat to Britain was imminent. German armies dominated Europe and sought to control the seas. Britain feared an imminent invasion by a country that threatened the basic values of civilization.

According to Walzer, the combination of the enormity and the imminence of the threat posed by Nazi Germany produced a supreme emergency, a situation in which the rules prohibiting attacks on civilians no longer held. If killing innocents was the only way to ward off this dreadful threat, then it was permissible. Since air attacks on German cities were the only means Britain had for inflicting harm on Germany, it was morally permissible for them to launch these attacks.

Walzer does not approve all of the city bombing that occurred in World War II. The emergency lasted, he thinks, only through 1942. After that, the threat diminished, and the constraints of the war convention should once again have been honored. In fact, the bombing of cities continued throughout the war, climaxing in massive attacks that killed hundreds of thousands of civilians: the bombing of Dresden, the fire bombings of Japanese cities by the United States, and the atomic bombings of Hiroshima and Nagasaki. According to Walzer, none of these later attacks were justified because the supreme emergency had passed.[7]

While Walzer's discussion begins with the special threat posed by Nazism, he believes that supreme emergencies can exist in more ordinary situations. In the end, he supports the view that if a single nation is faced by "a threat of enslavement or extermination[,]" then its "soldiers and statesmen [may] override the rights of innocent people for the sake of their own political community. . . ."[8] While he expresses this view with "hesitation and worry," he nevertheless broadens the reach of the concept of "supreme emergency" to include circumstances that arise in many wars.

The problem for Walzer is that his acceptance of the broad "supreme emergency" exception threatens to completely undermine the principle of noncombatant immunity that lies at the heart of his own view of the ethics of warfare. How can the principle of noncombatant immunity be fundamental if it can be overridden in some cases? Moreover, his condemnation of terrorism is weakened because it seems to be possible that people might resort to terrorism in cases that qualify as supreme emergencies, as when their own people are threatened by extermination or enslavement. Walzer's defense of the bombing of cities, then, seems to be inconsistent with his sweeping denunciation of terrorism.

WALLACE'S ARGUMENT FROM ANALOGY

While Walzer does not directly address the tension between the two parts of his view, G. Wallace explicitly tries to defend the view that terrorism is wrong and that the bombing of cities was justified. According to Wallace, the bombing campaign was justified because it satisfied all four of the following criteria:[9]

1 It was a measure of last resort.
2 It was an act of collective self-defense.
3 It was a reply in kind against a genocidal, racist aggressor.
4 It had some chance of success.

He then asks whether acts of terrorism might be justified by appeal to these very same criteria.

Wallace's answer is that terrorism cannot meet these criteria. Or, more specifically, he says that while any one of the criteria might be met by a terrorist act, all four of them cannot be satisfied. Why not? The problem is not with criteria 2 and 3; a community might well be oppressed by a brutal regime and might well be acting in its own defense. In these respects, its situation would be like that of Britain in 1940.

But, Wallace claims, conditions 1 and 4 cannot both be satisfied in this case. If the community has a good chance of success through the use of terrorism (thus satisfying condition 4), then other means of opposition might work as well, and terrorism will fail to be a last resort. Hence it will not meet condition 1. At the same time, if terrorist tactics are a last resort because all other means of opposition will fail, then the terrorist tactics are also likely to fail, in which case condition 4 is not met.

What Wallace has tried to show is that there are morally relevant differences between terrorism and the city bombings by Britain. Even if some of the criteria for justified attacks on civilians can be met by would-be terrorists, all of them cannot be. He concludes that "[E]ven if we allow that conditions (1) and (4) can be met separately, their joint satisfaction is impossible."[10]

Unfortunately, this comforting conclusion—that the British city bombing was justified but that terrorism cannot be—is extremely implausible. Both terrorism and city bombing involve the intentional killing of innocent human beings in order to promote an important political goal. Wallace acknowledges this but claims that the set of circumstances that justified city bombing could not possibly occur again so as to justify terrorism.

There is no basis for this claim, however. Wallace accepts that the right circumstances occurred in the past, and so he should acknowledge that it is at least possible for them to occur in the future. His conclusion ought to be that if city bombing was justifiable, then terrorism is in principle justifiable as well. For these reasons, I believe that Wallace, like Walzer, is logically committed to acknowledging the possibility of morally justified terrorism.

This is not a problem simply for these two authors. Since the historical memory of city bombing in the United States and Britain sees these as justifiable means of war, the dilemma facing these authors faces our own society. We condemn terrorists for intentionally killing innocent people while we think it was right to use tactics in our own wars that did the same. Either we must accept the view that terrorism can sometimes be justified, or we must come to see our own bombings of cities as violations of the prohibitions on killing civilians in wartime.[11]

TERRORISM, COLLATERAL DAMAGE, AND THE PRINCIPLE OF DOUBLE EFFECT

Many of us believe that wars are sometimes justified, but we also know that even if civilians are not intentionally killed, the deaths of civilians is a common feature of warfare. Indeed, during the twentieth century, civilian deaths became a larger and larger proportion of the total deaths caused by war. A person who believes that wars may be justified but that terrorism cannot be must explain how this can be.

One common approach focuses on the difference between intentionally killing civilians, as terrorists do, and unintentionally killing civilians, as sometimes happens in what we regard as legitimate acts of war. According to this approach, terrorism is wrong because it is intentional while so-called "collateral damage" killings and injuries are morally permissible because they are not intended.

This type of view is developed by Igor Primoratz in "The Morality of Terrorism."[12] Primoratz attempts to show why terrorism is morally wrong and how it differs from other acts of wartime killing that are morally permissible.

First, he makes it clear that, by definition, terrorism always involves the intentional killing of innocent people. He then offers a number of arguments to show why such killings are wrong. The first two have to do with the idea that persons are moral agents who are due a high level of respect and concern. He writes:

> [E]very human being is an individual, a person separate from other persons, with a unique, irreproducible thread of life and a value that is not commensurable with anything else.[13]

Given the incommensurable value of individual persons, it is wrong to try to calculate the worth of some hoped-for goal by comparison with the lives and deaths of individual people. This kind of calculation violates the ideal of giving individual lives our utmost respect and concern. Terrorists ignore this central moral ideal. They treat innocent people as political pawns, ignoring their individual worth and seeing their deaths simply as means toward achieving their goals.

In addition, Primoratz argues, terrorists ignore the moral relevance of guilt and innocence in their treatment of individuals. They attack people who have no responsibility for the alleged evils that the terrorists oppose and thus violate the principle that people should be treated in accord with what they deserve.

Terrorists, Primoratz tells us, also forsake the ideal of moral dialogue amongst equals. They not only decide who will live and who will die, but they feel no burden to justify their actions in ways that the victims might understand and accept. People who take moral ideals seriously engage in open discussion in order to justify their actions. They engage others in moral debate. Ideally, according to Primoratz, a moral person who harms others should try to act on reasons that are so compelling that they could be acknowledged by the victims. Terrorist acts cannot be justified to their victims, and terrorists are not even interested in trying to do so.[14]

Though these ideas are sketched out rather than fully developed, Primoratz successfully expresses some important moral values. Drawing on these values, he concludes that terrorism is incompatible with "some of the most basic moral beliefs many of us hold."[15]

Primoratz vs. Trotsky

Having tried to show why terrorism is wrong, Primoratz considers an objection put forward by Leon Trotsky, who defended terrorism as a revolutionary tactic. Trotsky claims that people who approve traditional war but condemn revolutionary violence are in a weak position because the differences between these are morally arbitrary. If wars that kill innocent people can be justified, Trotsky claims, then so can revolutions that kill innocent people.

Primoratz replies by arguing that there is an important moral difference between terrorism and some acts of war that kill innocent people. While he acknowledges that the "suffering of civilians . . . is surely inevitable not only in modern, but in almost all wars," Primoratz stresses that the moral evaluation of acts of killing requires that we "attend not only to the suffering inflicted, but also to the way it is inflicted."[16] By this, he means that we need, among other things, to see what the person who did the act intended.

To illustrate his point, he contrasts two cases of artillery attacks on a village. In the first case, the artillery attack is launched with the explicit goal of killing the civilian inhabitants of the village. The civilians are the target of the attack. This attack is the equivalent of terrorism since both intentionally target innocent people, and just like terrorism, it is immoral.

In a second case, the artillery attack is aimed at "soldiers stationed in the village." While the soldiers know that innocent people will be killed, that is not their aim.

> Had it been possible to attack the enemy unit without endangering the civilians in any way, they would certainly have done so. This was not possible, so they attacked although they knew that the attack would cause civilian casualties too; but they did their best to reduce those inevitable, but undesired consequences as much as possible.[17]

In this second case, the civilian deaths and injuries are collateral damage produced by an attack on a legitimate military target. That is the key difference between terrorism and legitimate acts of war. Terrorism is intentionally directed at civilians, while legitimate acts of war do not aim to kill or injure civilians, even when this is their effect.

Primoratz concludes that Trotsky and other defenders of terrorism are wrong when they equate war and terrorism. No doubt, the intentional killing of civilians does occur in war, and when it does, Primoratz would condemn it for the same reason he condemns terrorism. But if soldiers avoid the intentional killing of civilians, then their actions can be morally justified, even when civilians die as a result of what they do. As long as soldiers and revolutionaries avoid the intentional killing of innocent people, they will not be guilty of terrorist acts.

Problems with Primoratz's View

Primoratz's view has several attractive features. Nonetheless, it has serious weaknesses.

In stressing the role of intentions, Primoratz appeals to the same ideas expressed by what is called the "principle of double effect." According to this principle, we should evaluate actions by their intended goals rather than their actual consequences. An act that produces collateral damage deaths is an unintentional killing and hence is not wrong in the way that the same act would be if the civilians' deaths were intended.

While the principle of double effect is plausible in some cases, it is actually severely defective. To see this, suppose that the September 11 attackers had only intended to destroy the Pentagon and the World Trade Center and had no desire to kill anyone. Suppose that they knew, however, that thousands would die in the attack on the buildings. And suppose, following the attack, they said "We are not murderers. We did not mean to kill these people."

What would be our reaction? I very much doubt that we would think them less culpable. They could not successfully justify or excuse their actions by saying that although they foresaw the deaths of many people, these deaths were not part of their aim. We would certainly reject this defense. But if we would reject the appeal to double effect in this case, then we should do so in others.

In Primoratz's example, the artillery gunners attack the village with full knowledge of the high probability of civilian deaths. The artillery gunners know they will kill innocent people, perhaps even in large numbers, and they go ahead with the attack anyway. If it would not be enough for my imagined September 11 attackers to say that they did not intend to kill people, then it is not enough for Primoratz's imagined soldiers to say that they did not mean to kill the villagers when they knew full well that this would result from their actions.

If we accept Primoratz's defense of collateral damage killings, his argument against terrorism is in danger of collapsing because terrorists can use Primoratz's language to show that their actions, too, may be justifiable. If Primoratz succeeds in justifying the collateral damage killings and if the distinction between these killings and terrorism cannot rest solely on whether the killings are intentional, then the criteria that he uses may justify at least some terrorist acts. Like the soldiers in his example, the terrorists may believe that the need for a particular attack is "so strong and urgent that it prevailed over the prohibition of killing or maiming a comparatively small number of civilians." Consistency would require Primoratz to agree that the terrorist act was justified in this case.

Recall, too, Primoratz's claim that actions need to be capable of being justified to the victims themselves. Would the victims of the artillery attack accept the claim that the military urgency justified the "killing or maiming a comparatively small number of civilians?"[18] Why should they accept the sacrifice of their own lives on the basis of this reasoning?

In the end, then, Primoratz does not succeed in showing why terrorism is immoral while collateral damage killing can be morally justified. Like Wallace and Walzer, he has trouble squaring the principles that he uses to condemn terrorism with his own approval of attacks that produce foreseeable collateral damage deaths.

The problem revealed here is not merely a problem for a particular author. The view that collateral damage killings are permissible because they are unintended is a very widespread view. It is the view that United States officials appealed to when our bombings in Afghanistan produced thousands of civilian casualties.[19] Our government asserted that we did not intend these deaths to occur, that we were aiming at legitimate targets, and that the civilian deaths were merely collateral damage. Similar excuses are offered when civilians are killed by cluster bombs and land mines, weapons whose delayed detonations injure and kill people indiscriminately, often long after a particular attack is over.[20]

There are many cases in which people are morally responsible for harms that they do not intend to bring about, but if these harms can be foreseen, their claims that they "did not mean to do it" are not taken seriously. We use labels like "reckless disregard" for human life or "gross negligence" to signify that wrongs have been done, even though they were not deliberate. When such actions lead to serious injury and death, we condemn such actions from a moral point of view, just as we condemn terrorism. The principle of double effect does not show that these condemnations are mistaken. If we want to differentiate collateral damage killings from terrorism so as to be consistent in our moral judgments, we will need something better than the principle of double effect and the distinction between intended and unintended effects.

A SKETCH OF A DEFENSE

I want to conclude by sketching a better rationale for the view that terrorist attacks on civilians are always wrong but that some attacks that cause civilian deaths and injuries as unintended consequences are morally justified.

I have argued that a central problem with standard defenses of collateral damage killings is that they lean too heavily on the distinction between what is intended and what is foreseen. This distinction, when used with the doctrine of double effect, is too slippery and too permissive. As I noted above, it might provide an excuse for the September 11 attacks if (contrary to fact) the attackers were only targeting the World Trade Center *building* and the Pentagon *building* and did not actually aim to kill innocent civilians.

Michael Walzer makes a similar criticism of the double effect principle. "Simply not to intend the death of civilians is too easy," he writes. "What we look for in such cases is some sign of a positive commitment to save civilian lives."[21] Walzer calls his revised version the principle of "double intention." It requires military planners and soldiers to take positive steps to avoid or minimize these evils, even if these precautions increase the danger to military forces.

Walzer's rule is a step in the right direction, but we need to emphasize that the positive steps must be significant. They cannot be *pro forma* or minimal efforts. In order to show a proper respect for the victims of these attacks, serious efforts must be made to avoid death and injury to them. I suggest the following set of requirements for just, discriminate fighting, offering them as a sketch rather than a full account. The specifics might have to be amended, but the key point is that serious efforts must be made to avoid harm to civilians. Not intending harm is not enough. In addition, military planners must really exert themselves. They must, as we say, *bend over backwards* to avoid harm to civilians. For example, they must:

1 Target attacks as narrowly as possible on military resources;
2 Avoid targets where civilian deaths are extremely likely;
3 Avoid the use of inherently indiscriminate weapons (such as land mines and cluster bombs) and inherently indiscriminate strategies (such as high-altitude bombing of areas containing both civilian enclaves and military targets); and
4 Accept that when there are choices between damage to civilian lives and damage to military personnel, priority should be given to saving civilian lives.

If a group has a just cause for being at war and adheres to principles like these, then it could be said to be acknowledging the humanity and value of those who are harmed by its actions. While its attacks might expose innocent people to danger, its adherence to these principles would show that it was not indifferent to their well-being. In this way, it would show that its actions lack the features that make terrorism morally objectionable.

Why is this? Because the group is combining its legitimate effort to defend itself or others with serious efforts to avoid civilian casualties. The spirit of their effort is captured in the phrase I have already used: "bending over backwards." The "bend over backwards" ideal is superior to the principle of double effect in many ways. First, it goes beyond the weak rule of merely requiring that one not intend to kill civilians. Second, while the double effect rule's distinction between intended and unintended results permits all sorts of fudges and verbal tricks, the "bend over backwards" rule can be applied in a more objective and realistic way. It would be less likely to approve sham compliance than is the doctrine of double effect.

The "bend over backwards" rule might even satisfy Primoratz's requirement that acts of violence be justifiable to their victims. Of course, no actual victim is likely to look favorably on attacks by others that will result in the victim's death or serious injury. But suppose we could present the following situation to people who might be victims of an attack (a condition that most of us inhabit) and have them consider it from something like Rawls's veil of ignorance. We would ask them to consider the following situation:

- Group A is facing an attack by group B; if successful, the attack will lead to death or the severest oppression of group A.
- The only way that group A can defend itself is by using means that will cause death and injury to innocent members of group B.
- You are a member of one of the groups, but you do not know which one.

Would you approve of means of self-defense that will kill and injure innocent members of B in order to defend group A?

In this situation, people would not know whether they would be victims or beneficiaries of whatever policy is adopted. In this circumstance, I believe that they would reject a rule permitting either intentional or indiscriminate attacks on civilians. Thus, they would reject terrorism as a legitimate tactic, just as they would reject indiscriminate attacks that kill and injure civilians.

At the same time, I believe that they would approve a rule that combined a right of countries to defend themselves against aggression with the restrictions on means of fighting contained in the "bend over backwards" rule. This would have the following benefits. If one were a member of a group that had been attacked, one's group would have a right of self-defense. At the same time, if one were an innocent citizen in the aggressor country, the defenders would be required to take serious steps to avoid injury or death to you and other civilians.

If people generally could accept such a rule, then actions that adhere to that rule would be justifiable to potential victims as well as potential attackers. This would include actions that cause civilian casualties but that adhere to the "bend over backwards" principle.

I believe that this sort of approach achieves what nonpacifist critics of terrorism want to achieve. It provides a principled basis for condemning terrorism, no matter who it is carried out by, and a principled justification of warfare that is genuinely defensive. Moreover, the perspective is unified in a desirable way. Terrorist actions cannot be morally justified because the *intentional* targeting of civilians is the most obvious kind of violation of the "bend over backwards" rule.

At the same time that these principles allow for the condemnation of terrorism, they are immune to charges of hypocrisy because they provide a basis for criticizing not only terrorist acts but also the acts of any group that violates the "bend over backwards" rule, either by attacking civilians directly or by failing to take steps to avoid civilian deaths.

CONCLUSION

Can terrorism be morally justified? Of course not. But if condemnations of terrorism are to have moral credibility, they must rest on principles that constrain our own actions and determine our judgments of what we ourselves do and have done. To have moral credibility, opponents of terrorism must stand by the principles underlying their condemnations, apply their principles in an evenhanded way, and bend over backwards to avoid unintended harms to civilians. Only in this way can we begin inching back to a world in which those at war honor the moral rules that prohibit the taking of innocent human lives. As long as condemnations of terrorism are tainted by hypocrisy, moral judgments will only serve to inflame people's hostilities rather than reminding them to limit and avoid serious harms to one another.

NOTES

1 For development and defense of this definition, see my "Prerequisites for Morally Credible Condemnations of Terrorism," in William Crotty, ed., *The Politics of Terrorism: Consequences for an Open Society* (Boston: Northeastern University Press, 2003).

2 Michael Walzer. *Just and Unjust Wars* (New York: Basic Books, 1977); Gerry Wallace, "Terrorism and the Argument from Analogy," *Journal of Moral and Social Studies,* vol. 6 (1991), 149–160.

3 Walzer, 135.

4 Walzer, 197.

5 Walzer, 205.

6 Walzer, 253.

7 Kenneth Brown, "'Supreme Emergency': A Critique of Michael Walzer's Moral Justification for Allied Obliteration Bombing in World War II," *Manchester College Bulletin of the Peace Studies Institute,* 1983 (13, nos. 1–2), 6–15.

8 Walzer, 254.

9 Wallace, 155.

10 Wallace, 155–156.

11 See Rawls on city bombing and the atomic bombings in *The Law of Peoples* and *Collected Papers.*

12 Igor Primoratz, "The Morality of Terrorism?" *Journal of Applied Philosophy,* vol. 14 (1997), 222. Primoratz defends his definition of terrorism in "What Is Terrorism?" *Journal of Applied Philosophy,* vol. 7 (1990), 129–138. These subjects are also helpfully discussed in Haig Khatchadourian, "Terrorism and Morality," *Journal of Applied Philosophy,* vol. 5 (1988), 131–145.

13 Primoratz, 224.
14 For a similar idea, see Thomas Nagel, *Equality and Partiality* (New York: Oxford, 1991), 23. "[W]e are looking for principles to deal with conflict that can at some level be endorsed by everyone. . . ."
15 Primoratz, "The Morality of Terrorism," 225.
16 Primoratz, 227.
17 Primoratz, 227.
18 Primoratz, 228.
19 Marc Herold, an economist at the University of New Hampshire, studied foreign press reports and has concluded that over 3,500 Afghan civilians were killed in the first 2 months of U.S. attacks in Afghanistan (http://pubpages.unh.edu/~mwherold and http://www.media-alliance.org/article.php?story=20031108153733172). The *Boston Globe* estimated 1,000 civilian deaths, but their estimate is based on investigations at 14 sites, which they admit "represent only a small fraction of the total sites targeted by the 18,000 bombs, missiles, and ordnance fired by U.S. forces since October. . . ." See John Donnelly and Anthony Shadid, "Civilian toll in US raids put at 1,000," *Boston Globe*, Feb. 17, 2002, 1. For further information on attacks on civilian targets, see John Donnelly, "U.S. targeting of vehicles is detailed," *Boston Globe*, Feb. 19, 2002, 1.
20 According to Human Rights Watch, cluster bombs "have proven to be a serious and long-lasting threat to civilians, soldiers, peacekeepers, and even clearance experts." Human Rights Watch, "Cluster Bombs in Afghanistan," www.hrw.org/backgrounder/arms/cluster-bck1031.htm.
21 Walzer, 155–156.

QUESTIONS

1 Is Nathanson correct in holding that being part of a campaign to promote a political or social agenda is one of the defining features of terrorism?
2 Do you agree with Nathanson that it is possible to draw a principled distinction between (a) terrorist actions and (b) some acts of warfare that result in harm to innocent people?

What Is Terrorism, Why Is It Wrong, and Could It Ever Be Morally Permissible?

Alison M. Jaggar

Jaggar offers several criteria to be used in evaluating answers to questions about the meaning of terrorism and applies them when developing her account. Jaggar's definition of terrorism is very broad. It allows for the possibility of state terrorism. It also allows attacks on nonhuman targets—such as infrastructure,

Reprinted with permission of the publisher from *Journal of Social Philosophy*, vol. 36, no. 2 (Summer 2005), pp. 202, 205–209, 211–217. © 2005 Blackwell Publishing Inc.

businesses, or buildings of religious, political, or other symbolic significance—to count as instances of terrorism. On Jaggar's definition, it is conceptually possible for some acts of terrorism to be morally justified. However, in explaining why terrorism is morally reprehensible, Jaggar makes it clear that the burden of proof of justifying some specific act of terrorism is a heavy one. Jaggar concludes by suggesting conditions, grounded in just war theory, for determining whether an act of terrorism is morally justified.

In the liberal democracies of North America and the European Union, terrorism is almost universally condemned. Moreover, few wish to question the "moral clarity" that denies any "moral equivalence" between terrorists and those who fight them (Held 2004, 59–60). However, the seeming consensus on the moral reprehensibility of terrorism is undermined by substantial disagreement about just what terrorism is. The United Nations has long been unable to agree on workable criteria for terrorism— though it may now be moving to a new consensus—and even the various agencies of the U.S. government disagree with each other. The primary purpose of this paper is to propose an account of terrorism capable of facilitating a more productive moral debate. I conclude by opening—though certainly not closing—the question of when, if ever, terrorism might be morally permissible. . . .

WHAT IS TERRORISM?

. . . I should like to propose an . . . account of terrorism. In undertaking this task, I assume that a good account meets the following desiderata:

1 Conservatism. First, a good account disturbs existing usage as little as possible. Proposals to modify common interpretations of a term must be given a plausible and appropriate rationale.

2 Consistency and non-arbitrariness. One appropriate rationale for modifying existing usage is an argument that such a change will improve consistency. Proposals for expanding or limiting the ways in which a term is used often point to continuities or discontinuities between the proposed usage and the term's central and generally accepted meanings.

3 Precision. Another appropriate rationale for modifying a term's interpretation is an argument that such a modification would improve precision, helping differentiate among phenomena that may otherwise be confused. For instance, a good account of terrorism should facilitate understanding terrorism's relation to such phenomena as war, guerrilla war, crime, revenge, hostage taking, and so on. Although precision is desirable, definitions should not be sharpened to the point where they remove genuine uncertainties by *fiat*. Concepts are always somewhat fuzzy, especially morally laden concepts, and dispute over borderline cases can never be excluded completely.

4 Impartiality. Finally, any term that has a moral dimension should be interpreted in such a way as to resist moral arbitrariness and bias. A good account should be impartial in the sense of not begging disputed moral and political questions, leaving these open to be debated on their merits.

Webster's Dictionary defines "terrorism" as the use of terror and violence to intimidate and subjugate, especially as a political weapon or policy, and as the intimidation and subjugation so produced. This definition leaves open several disputed questions about terrorism, which I will discuss in turn, drawing on the desiderata identified above. The account that I end up proposing is more inclusive than that implied by much recent usage but I suggest that it is more consistent, precise and impartial.

The Purposes or Goals of Terrorism

It is generally agreed that the immediate purpose of terrorism is to create a climate of terror. Thus, acts of terror are often marked by a concern for symbolic and dramatic effect; tumbrils rolling toward the guillotine were a powerful spectacle. As the nineteenth century anarchists put it, terrorism is "propaganda by the deed."

Can anything be said about terrorism's longer-range goals? Webster's definition seems to require that terrorism be ideologically or politically motivated, a suggestion that accords with the original Jacobin case and with much common usage, including my own in earlier work (Jaggar 2003). Defining terrorism as politically motivated meets the desideratum of conservatism, but I now suggest that this requirement be dropped because retaining it violates the remaining desiderata. First, it is empirically arbitrary to deny that the deliberate creation of terror for reasons that are unprincipled or personally motivated is indeed terrorism; if gang violence or even domestic violence is otherwise indistinguishable from politically motivated violence, acknowledging either as terrorist consistently extends the term. Second, insisting that terrorism be politically motivated is incompatible with the desideratum of precision, because the distinction between personal and political is often unclear, both in principle and in practice. In principle, theorists such as feminists contest the distinction, speaking of the politics of personal life and arguing that domestic violence is sometimes a form of terrorism (Card 2003); in practice, personal and political motivations are often intertwined, as in the case of a strongman who seizes state power in order to enrich himself from the sale of its resources. Thus, requiring that terrorism be politically or ideologically motivated will frequently result in indeterminacy concerning whether or not specific threats or intimidation are terrorist. Third and finally, it is morally arbitrary to withhold the usually pejorative term "terrorism" from any violence intended to create a climate of terror.

Because terrorists employ means that are widely perceived as evil or crazy, their long-range goals are often dismissed as evil or crazy but ends can be distinguished conceptually from means; *ius ad bellum* is distinct from *ius in bello*. Although non-ideological forms of terrorism leave little space for raising questions of moral justification, the use of terrorism to promote political or ideological ends raises significant moral questions. If a definition of "terrorism" is to be impartial, it must separate the moral assessment of terrorists' ends from the moral assessment of the means they choose to promote them. Therefore, I propose an account of "terrorism" that leaves open the possibility that its goals may be political or personal, just or unjust, noble or base.

The Objects or Targets of Terrorism

Terrorism uses extreme fear to subjugate and intimidate. Carl Wellman notes that the direct target of terrorist violence or threats is usually its secondary rather than its primary target; the primary target is usually a wider population that the terrorists wish to intimidate (Wellman 1979).

Little philosophical discussion has occurred concerning the identity of terrorism's primary (though indirect) targets. If terrorism is understood as motivated exclusively [by] ideological or political goals, the primary targets of terrorism presumably must be those whom the terrorists can influence politically. However a more inclusive account, which allows for the possibility that terrorism might not be ideologically motivated, sets no *a priori* limit on the individuals or groups that might be terrorism's indirect (though primary) targets. They might be governments, populations, political factions, demographic groups (racial, caste, ethnic, religious, gender, sexual), gangs, families, or even individuals.

The identity of terrorism's direct (though secondary) targets has been discussed more explicitly and most accounts of terrorism stipulate that its direct targets be civilian. This is true of the definition accepted by the State Department of the United States and of the definition emerging in international law, though a few philosophers disagree.[1] I propose that the targets of terrorism be identified not as civilians *simpliciter* but instead as civilians who are innocent by Jeffrie Murphy's helpful definition of innocence in war. In Murphy's view, innocence in war does not mean overall legal or moral innocence; rather it means being a non-combatant. Murphy argues that combatants include all those engaged in the attempt to destroy you, whatever their place in the chain of command or responsibility; thus, they include not only frontline military personnel but also the civilians who issue orders to those personnel. This account assumes a context of war between states but it is also adaptable to situations of popular uprising against unpopular or colonial governments. Murphy recognizes that his account of combatant status does not eliminate borderline cases, such as workers in factories that make products both for daily life and for war, but he asserts that these are cases of genuine uncertainty, not to be resolved by definitional *fiat*.[2] His definition leaves open the possibility that armed adult settlers who colonize a territory already inhabited by others perhaps should be counted as combatants rather than innocent civilians.

In contemporary usage, terrorism includes attacks not only on human but also on non-human targets, such as infrastructure, businesses, homes, and buildings of religious, political, or other symbolic significance. Direct threats to such targets are often effective in causing terror; indeed, people's lives become impossible if enough of their infrastructure is damaged. For this reason, intentionally destroying water supplies and power sources or harming the natural environment, through means such as defoliation or uranium poisoning, is terrorist if those primarily affected are innocent civilians.

The Agents of Terrorism

The most significant shift in the usage of "terrorism" over the past two centuries has been the move away from recognizing states as possible agents of terrorism.

However, if our account of terrorism is not only to be compatible with the original usage but also to be consistent, precise, and impartial, the possibility of state terrorism should be acknowledged.

Outside the United States, most people are well aware that governments or states may create terror in many ways. Sometimes governments terrorize segments of their own populations by means of discriminatory law enforcement and even legislation; examples include officially sanctioned violence against Jews and gypsies and the regimes of racist apartheid in South Africa and gender apartheid in Afghanistan or Saudi Arabia. Sometimes governments terrorize their own populations covertly rather than overtly, using unofficial militias to assassinate political opponents or labor leaders. In the 1970s and 1980s, extra-judicial death squads linked with governments were common in several Latin American countries. Governments may also use terrorist tactics to intimidate foreign rather than local populations. In wartime, states may use terrorism against enemy populations; for instance, they may initiate campaigns of looting and rape or they may use weapons that predictably incur large civilian casualties. They may even order direct attacks on civilian targets; the United States bombing of Japan at the end of World War II was described routinely at the time as terror bombing. Finally, covert state terrorism, like overt terrorism, sometimes extends beyond a country's own borders. In the 1980s, the U.S. government supported the so-called "contras" (counter-revolutionaries) in Nicaragua, who sought to undermine the Sandinista government by attacking infrastructure such as farms and clinics.

Denying the possibility of state terrorism is not only incompatible with the original usage of the term; it is also inconsistent, arbitrary, and biased. State terrorism has always caused far more harm than non-state terrorism, since the resources available to states are typically far more powerful and destructive than those available to private individuals or small groups, and it should remain central in our understanding terrorism. Recognizing the possibility of state terrorism reduces the bias against the weak implicit in accounts that deny this possibility, while still leaving completely open the question of whether terrorism might ever be morally justified.

The Methods of Terrorism

Since terrorism intends to intimidate or subjugate, it is natural to question how it is distinguished from other forms of threat or coercion. Because terror is an extreme state of fear, induced by threats perceived as especially horrifying, minor threats or damage do not ordinarily count as terrorist. However, since different things horrify different people, terrorism cannot be identified by reference to any particular method of intimidation. Cruelty to animals, especially pets, might be enough to induce terror in some people; others may be terrified by the prospect of social humiliation. Terrorist practices are distinguished from more ordinary threats not because they involve any particular methods of producing fear, but instead because they are intended to create a state of fear that is acute and long-lasting enough to influence future behavior. This is why terrorist attacks are often spectacular and directed toward symbolic targets. Typically, they are not "one-off" threats or atrocities but instead parts of wider campaigns of intimidation or "reigns" of terror, intersecting with other forms of struggle and negotiation (Tilly 2004, 10).

Proposed Account of Terrorism

The preceding discussion suggests the following account of terrorism:

> Terrorism is the use of extreme threats or violence designed to intimidate or subjugate governments, groups, or individuals. It is a tactic of coercion intended to promote further ends that in themselves may be good, bad or indifferent. Terrorism may be practiced by governments or international bodies or forces, sub-state groups or even individuals. Its threats or violence are aimed directly or immediately at the bodies or belongings of innocent civilians but these are typically terrorists' secondary targets; the primary targets of terrorists are the governments, groups or individuals that they wish to intimidate.

This account is quite inclusive, categorizing as terrorist several classes of action excluded by other recent accounts, but it is also precise because it distinguishes terrorism conceptually from a number of other phenomena with which it is often conflated. . . .

SOME ADVANTAGES OF THE PROPOSED ACCOUNT OF TERRORISM

. . . Although the public image of terrorism has changed over two centuries, its moral connotations have not improved. Unlike war, which is generally regarded as sometimes justifiable and even glorious, terrorism is widely thought to be inexcusably wrong and it has been integrated into the lexicon of war in a way that aligns it with the negative side of many dichotomies that characterize this lexicon. The terrorist is contrasted with the true warrior, he fights for some ideology rather than to defend his country, his cause is illegitimate rather than legitimate, he is uncivilized rather than civilized, undisciplined rather than disciplined, a bandit, barbarian, or savage. Whereas the soldier is brave, the terrorist is cowardly; he uses means that are treacherous and dishonorable rather than open and honorable; he is not above resorting to weapons of mass destruction. He is not a warrior but a murderer. Because of its negative moral associations, terrorism is much more likely to be attributed to "them" rather than to "us." As Held puts it, what "they" do is terrorism and what "we" do is not (Held 2004, 65). If "we" do anything that looks at all like terrorism, we call ourselves "freedom fighters" or "martyrs," or "law enforcers."

Although I dispute many of the dichotomies that characterize the contemporary vocabulary of war and although I do not believe that it is always "they" rather than "we" who are terrorist, I share the view that terrorism is bad and my account illuminates why it is so morally repugnant.

First, terrorism is morally repugnant because terrorists engage in coercion and intimidation, which are regarded ordinarily as morally wrong. Moreover, terrorists seek to produce not mere anxiety or apprehension but rather widespread, acute and long-lasting fear and to do this they use threats or violence that are especially horrifying.

Second, terrorism is morally repugnant because terrorists harm or threaten those who have not harmed them and do not threaten them, people who can in no way be said to deserve the harm.

By clarifying these elements, the proposed definition explains the widespread belief that terrorism is morally wrong and shows why the burden of justifying it is heavy.

Although my proposed account does not present terrorism as morally neutral and indeed clarifies why it is morally reprehensible, it is nonetheless impartial in that it does not close disputed questions arbitrarily or by *fiat*. Instead, it offers criteria to address such questions. Thus, by leaving open the question of who may be agents of terrorism, excluding none by stipulation, it counters the moral bias of recent usage, which tends to obscure and so justify terrorist intimidation by official forces. . . . The account's willingness to recognize state terrorism also expands the universe of moral discourse by making it possible to look beyond specific incidents or practices, such as disappearances or torture, and enabling us to question whether social institutions might be systematically terrorist. It allows us to question whether trade sanctions or embargos against economically weak countries might sometimes be terrorist (Gordon 2002) and to envision the possibility that not only specific practices of law enforcement might be terrorist but also whole systems of legislation, such as those that mandate race or gender apartheid.

Finally, the account proposed does not constrain moral discourse by stipulating that terrorism can never be morally justified; instead, it allows important moral questions to remain open, while showing how difficult they are to answer.

IS TERRORISM EVER MORALLY PERMISSIBLE?

. . . Terrorism is certainly heinous but that something is heinous does not entail that it is prohibited in all circumstances; it merely entails that anyone wishing to argue its moral permissibility bears a heavy burden of proof. As the proposed definition brings out, terrorism involves threats and violence against innocent civilians, who are used as means to the ends of others. However, most people who believe that war is sometimes justified also believe that it is occasionally morally justified to threaten and knowingly harm innocent civilians and to use some people as means to others' ends; such thinking is inherent in the doctrine of double effect, for instance, as well as in the expression "necessary evil." In his doctrine of a "Supreme Emergency," Michael Walzer argues that very extreme circumstances may occasionally justify the use of horrifying means to achieve ends that have great moral significance (Walzer 1977).

Although war is bad, it is often justified by appeal to various just war principles. However these principles specifically prohibit terrorism because this deliberately targets or fails adequately to protect innocent civilians, and so violates non-combatant immunity or protection, one of the two fundamental criteria regulating the just use of force, *ius in bello*. Nevertheless, it is not inconceivable that very extreme circumstances might justify violating such immunity; for instance, R. M. Hare contends that at least some of the terrorism practiced by the European Resistance during World War II might have been morally justified (Hare 1979).

I cannot explore such questions here but I would like to end with a suggestion that may serve as a starting point for a more careful and comprehensive discussion. The suggestion is that the traditional *ius ad bellum* criteria defining the right to resort to force also suggest several necessary, and perhaps jointly sufficient, conditions for justifying terrorism. For instance:

1 Just cause. For terrorism to be morally permissible, a necessary though certainly not sufficient condition is that it must be intended to secure people's most basic rights.

2 Competent authority. Early versions of just war theory limited permissible uses of force to those authorized by public authorities, a statist bias that made it impossible to justify uprisings against those authorities. Current international law recognizes rebel movements as having "belligerent status" if they control their territory but even this might-makes-right criterion may be too stringent since many rebel movements, especially in their early stages, are too weak to control the territory in which they operate, at least by day (Lackey 1989, 29–31). The question of when terrorists may legitimately claim to represent some oppressed population is difficult to answer, both in principle and in practice, although some indication may be provided by the extent of popular protest or rejoicing over terrorist acts.

3 Right intention. For their conduct to have a chance of being justified, terrorists must be convinced that all of the conditions necessary to justifying a war must be met. If terrorists are able to choose whether or not to participate in terrorist activity while military personnel are conscripted, then their subjective beliefs are even more important to assessing the conduct of terrorists than to assessing the conduct of official military personnel.

4 Proportionality. The use of force is justified in traditional just war theory only if the overall good it achieves is greater than the harm it causes. Since terrorism is even more atrocious than war, for reasons given above, the cause of the terrorist must be overwhelming in its righteousness. Only massive and systematic violations of human rights, not small injustices, could ever begin to justify the adoption of terrorist tactics and use of these tactics must be kept to a minimum, in terms of both quantity and quality.

5 Last resort. Terrorist tactics must be a last resort. All other means of remedying the perceived injustice, including conventional warfare, must be unavailable or have failed.

6 Reasonable hope of success. Those waging a just war must have a reasonable hope of success in achieving their ends. Because terrorism is so reprehensible, it seems plausible to insist that terrorism can be justified only when the hope of success is much more certain than required to justify war.

7 The aim of peace. Like a just war, any justified terrorism should aim at a just peace.

Whether these (or any other) conditions for justifying terrorism are ever met in practice will always be a matter of dispute. However, dramatically accelerating political and economic inequality, on both a national and international level, is likely to encourage increasing numbers of people to believe more frequently that they are met. For instance, as Held notes, the growing asymmetry of warfare makes it increasingly difficult for forces on the weaker side to attack the actual combatants of powerful countries. (Held 2004, 61). Similarly, as poverty deepens and ever larger populations are politically marginalized in countries run by authoritarian and well-armed governments, increasing numbers of marginalized and impoverished people are likely to regard their cause as just and terrorism as their only option.

Finally, when anti-government terrorism occurs, we may ask whether it is ever morally justified for powerful governments to strike back with terrorist tactics. French argues that it may sometimes be morally justified for the weaker party in an asymmetric conflict to abandon conventional *ius in bello* restrictions on the conduct of warfare but that this party then cannot complain if the stronger side also abandons those restrictions. She contends, in other words, that both sides must be constrained by the same rules (French 2003). I agree that the conduct of all parties in any conflict should be constrained by the same moral principles but I do not think that these principles necessarily require that all sides face identical moral constraints on their conduct. A powerful government cannot justify its use of terrorism simply by noting that its weaker opponents employ this strategy. In order to justify its use of terrorism, the powerful government would have to show, among other things, that no other means of continuing the conflict were available to it and, in an asymmetrical conflict, it is much more likely that the weaker than the stronger side will be able to make this argument convincingly. Finally, the use of terrorism by a powerful government would undermine that government's claim to legitimacy because "official disregard" for human rights is more egregious than private violations of rights (Pogge 2002, chap. 2).

NOTES

1 Walzer (2002) contends that the targets of terrorism are civilian but Virginia Held refuses to limit "terrorism" to attacks on civilian targets, because she argues that this limitation is inconsistent with existing usage, which typically describes isolated attacks on military targets as terrorist. In addition, she contends that this limitation would put the burden of being a "legitimate target" exclusively on the ordinary soldiers and sailors who are the lowest levels of the military hierarchy (Held 2004, 63–66).

2 Murphy also suggests the moral principle that individuals should be assumed "noncombatant until proven otherwise" (Murphy 1985, 66).

REFERENCES

Card, Claudia. 2003. "Making War on Terrorism in Response to 9/11." In *Terrorism and International Justice,* ed. James P. Sterba. Oxford and New York: Oxford University Press.

French, Shannon E. 2003. "Murderers, Not Warriors: The Moral Distinction between Terrorists and Legitimate Fighters in Asymmetric Conflicts." In *Terrorism and International Justice,* ed. James P. Sterba. Oxford and New York: Oxford University Press.

Gordon, Joy. 2002. "Cool War. Economic Sanctions as a Weapon of Mass Destruction." In *Harper's Magazine* (November). Retrieved from http://harpers.org/CoolWar.html.

Hare, R. M. 1979. "On Terrorism." *Journal of Value Inquiry* 13: 240–49.

Held, Virginia. 2004. "Terrorism and War." *The Journal of Ethics* 8: 59–75.

Jaggar, Alison M. 2003. "Responding to the Evil of Terrorism." *Hypatia* 18:1 (Winter): 175–82.
Lackey, Douglas P. 1989. *The Ethics of War and Peace.* Englewood Cliffs, NJ: Prentice Hall.
Murphy, Jeffrie. 1985, "The Killing of the Innocent." In *The Ethics of War and Nuclear Deterrence,* ed. James P. Sterba. Belmont, CA: Wadsworth, 61–67.
Pogge, Thomas. 2002. *World Poverty and Human Rights.* Cambridge, UK: Polity Press; Malden, MA: Blackwell Publishers. Inc.
Tilly, Charles. 2004. "Terror, Terrorism, Terrorists." *Sociological Theory* 22:1 (March): 5–13.
Walzer, Michael. 1977. *Just and Unjust Wars: A Moral Argument with Historical Illustrations.* New York: Basic Books.
———. 2002. "Five Questions about Terrorism." *Dissent* 49: 5–10.
Wellman, Carl. 1979. "On Terrorism Itself." *Journal of Value Inquiry,* 13: 250–58.

QUESTIONS

1 Jaggar offers a very broad definition of terrorism. In her view, for example, even domestic violence could be construed as terrorism. Do you agree with her definition?
2 Do you agree with the criteria Jaggar offers for determining if an act of terrorism is morally justified? Why or why not?

The War on Terrorism and the End of Human Rights

David Luban

Luban distinguishes between two models of state action—the war model and the criminal law model—and explains the protections built into both. He argues that in its war on terrorism, the U.S. government has blurred the distinction between these models and adopted a hybrid war-law model in its treatment of terrorist suspects, thereby denying them the protections of both models. Luban then considers the arguments for and against the hybrid approach. Considering the ways in which the hybrid model depresses human rights from their peacetime standard to the war level, he expresses concern about the extent to which the war on terrorism means the end of human rights.

In the immediate aftermath of September 11, President Bush stated that the perpetrators of the deed would be brought to justice. Soon afterwards, the President announced that the United States would engage in a war on terrorism. The first of these statements adopts the familiar language of criminal law and criminal justice. It treats the September 11 attacks as horrific crimes—mass murders—and the

Reprinted with permission of Rowman & Littlefield Publishers from Verna V. Gehring, ed., *War After September 11* (2003), pp. 51–60.

government's mission as apprehending and punishing the surviving planners and conspirators for their roles in the crimes. The War on Terrorism is a different proposition, however, and a different model of governmental action—not law but war. Most obviously, it dramatically broadens the scope of action, because now terrorists who knew nothing about September 11 have been earmarked as enemies. But that is only the beginning.

THE HYBRID WAR-LAW APPROACH

The model of war offers much freer rein than that of law, and therein lies its appeal in the wake of 9/11. First, in war but not in law it is permissible to use lethal force on enemy troops regardless of their degree of personal involvement with the adversary. The conscripted cook is as legitimate a target as the enemy general. Second, in war but not in law "collateral damage," that is, foreseen but unintended killing of non-combatants, is permissible. (Police cannot blow up an apartment building full of people because a murderer is inside, but an air force can bomb the building if it contains a military target.) Third, the requirements of evidence and proof are drastically weaker in war than in criminal justice. Soldiers do not need proof beyond a reasonable doubt, or even proof by a preponderance of evidence, that someone is an enemy soldier before firing on him or capturing and imprisoning him. They don't need proof at all, merely plausible intelligence. Thus, the U.S. military remains regretful but unapologetic about its January 2002 attack on the Afghani town of Uruzgan, in which 21 innocent civilians were killed, based on faulty intelligence that they were al Qaeda fighters. Fourth, in war one can attack an enemy without concern over whether he has done anything. Legitimate targets are those who in the course of combat *might* harm us, not those who *have* harmed us. No doubt there are other significant differences as well. But the basic point should be clear: given Washington's mandate to eliminate the danger of future 9/11s, so far as humanly possible, the model of war offers important advantages over the model of law.

There are disadvantages as well. Most obviously, in war but not in law, fighting back is a *legitimate* response of the enemy. Second, when nations fight a war, other nations may opt for neutrality. Third, because fighting back is legitimate, in war the enemy soldier deserves special regard once he is rendered harmless through injury or surrender. It is impermissible to punish him for his role in fighting the war. Nor can he be harshly interrogated after he is captured. The Third Geneva Convention provides: "Prisoners of war who refuse to answer [questions] may not be threatened, insulted, or exposed to unpleasant or disadvantageous treatment of any kind." And, when the war concludes, the enemy soldier must be repatriated.

Here, however, Washington has different ideas, designed to eliminate these tactical disadvantages in the traditional war model. Washington regards international terrorism not only as a military adversary, but also as a criminal activity and criminal conspiracy. In the law model, criminals don't get to shoot back, and their acts of violence subject them to legitimate punishment. That is what we see in Washington's prosecution of the War on Terrorism. Captured terrorists may be tried before military or civilian tribunals, and shooting back at Americans, including

American troops, is a federal crime (for a statute under which John Walker Lindh was indicted criminalizes anyone regardless of nationality, who "outside the United States attempts to kill, or engages in a conspiracy to kill, a national of the United States" or "engages in physical violence with intent to cause serious bodily injury to a national of the United States; or with the result that serious bodily injury is caused to a national of the United States"). Furthermore, the U.S. may rightly demand that other countries not be neutral about murder and terrorism. Unlike the war model, a nation may insist that those who are not with us in fighting murder and terror are against us, because by not joining our operations they are providing a safe haven for terrorists or their bank accounts. By selectively combining elements of the war model and elements of the law model, Washington is able to maximize its own ability to mobilize lethal force against terrorists while eliminating most traditional rights of a military adversary, as well as the rights of innocent bystanders caught in the crossfire.

A LIMBO OF RIGHTLESSNESS

The legal status of al Qaeda suspects imprisoned at the Guantanamo Bay Naval Base in Cuba is emblematic of this hybrid war-law approach to the threat of terrorism. In line with the war model, they lack the usual rights of criminal suspects—the presumption of innocence, the right to a hearing to determine guilt, the opportunity to prove that the authorities have grabbed the wrong man. But, in line with the law model, they are considered *unlawful* combatants. Because they are not uniformed forces, they lack the rights of prisoners of war and are liable to criminal punishment. Initially, the American government declared that the Guantanamo Bay prisoners have no rights under the Geneva Conventions. In the face of international protests, Washington quickly backpedaled and announced that the Guantanamo Bay prisoners would indeed be treated as decently as POWs—but it also made clear that the prisoners have no right to such treatment. Neither criminal suspects nor POWs, neither fish nor fowl, they inhabit a limbo of rightlessness. Secretary of Defense Rumsfeld's assertion that the U.S. may continue to detain them even if they are acquitted by a military tribunal dramatizes the point.

To understand how extraordinary their status is, consider an analogy. Suppose that Washington declares a War on Organized Crime. Troops are dispatched to Sicily and a number of Mafiosi are seized, brought to Guantanamo Bay, and imprisoned without a hearing for the indefinite future, maybe the rest of their lives. They are accused of no crimes, because their capture is based not on what they have done but on what they might do. After all, to become "made" they took oaths of obedience to the bad guys. Seizing them accords with the war model: they are enemy foot soldiers. But they are foot soldiers out of uniform; they lack a "fixed distinctive emblem," in the words of The Hague Convention. That makes them unlawful combatants, so they lack the rights of POWs. They may object that it is only a unilateral declaration by the American President that has turned them into combatants in the first place—he called it a war, they didn't—and that, since they do not regard themselves as literal foot soldiers it never occurred to them to wear a fixed distinctive emblem. They have a point. It seems too easy for the President to divest anyone in the world of rights and liberty simply by announcing that the U.S. is at war with them and then declaring them unlawful combatants if they resist. But, in the hybrid war-law model, they protest in vain.

Consider another example. In January 2002, U.S. forces in Bosnia seized five Algerians and a Yemeni suspected of al Qaeda connections and took them to Guantanamo Bay. The six had been jailed in Bosnia, but a Bosnian court released them for lack of evidence, and the Bosnian Human Rights Chamber issued an injunction that four of them be allowed to remain in the country pending further legal proceedings. The Human Rights Chamber, ironically, was created under U.S. auspices in the Dayton peace accords, and it was designed specifically to protect against treatment like this. Ruth Wedgwood, a well-known international law scholar at Yale and a member of the Council on Foreign Relations, defended the Bosnian seizure in war-model terms. "I think we would simply argue this was a matter of self-defense. One of the fundamental rules of military law is that you have a right ultimately to act in self-defense. And if these folks were actively plotting to blow up the U.S. embassy, they should be considered combatants and captured as combatants in a war." Notice that Professor Wedgwood argues in terms of what the men seized in Bosnia were *planning to do,* not what they *did*; notice as well that the decision of the Bosnian court that there was insufficient evidence does not matter. These are characteristics of the war model.

More recently, two American citizens alleged to be al Qaeda operatives (Jose Padilla, a.k.a. Abdullah al Muhajir, and Yasser Esam Hamdi) have been held in American military prisons, with no crimes charged, no opportunity to consult counsel, and no hearing. The President described Padilla as "a bad man" who aimed to build a nuclear "dirty" bomb and use it against America; and the Justice Department has classified both men as "enemy combatants" who may be held indefinitely. Yet, as military law expert Gary Solis points out, "Until now, as used by the attorney general, the term 'enemy combatant' appeared nowhere in U.S. criminal law, international law or in the law of war." The phrase comes from the 1942 Supreme Court case *Ex parte Quirin,* but all the Court says there is that "an enemy combatant who without uniform comes secretly through the lines for the purpose of waging war by destruction of life or property" would "not . . . be entitled to the status of prisoner of war, but . . . [they would] be offenders against the law of war subject to trial and punishment by military tribunals." For the Court, in other words, the status of a person as a non-uniformed enemy combatant makes him a criminal rather than a warrior, and determines *where* he is tried (in a military, rather than a civilian, tribunal) but not *whether* he is tried. Far from authorizing open-ended confinement, *Ex parte Quirin* presupposes that criminals are entitled to hearings: without a hearing how can suspects prove that the government made a mistake? *Quirin* embeds the concept of "enemy combatant" firmly in the law model. In the war model, by contrast, POWs may be detained without a hearing until hostilities are over. But POWs were captured in uniform, and only their undoubted identity as enemy soldiers justifies such open-ended custody. Apparently, Hamdi and Padilla will get the worst of both models—open-ended custody with no trial, like POWs, but no certainty beyond the U.S. government's say-so that they really are "bad men." This is the hybrid war-law model. It combines the *Quirin* category of "enemy combatant without uniform," used in the law model to justify a military trial, with the war model's practice of indefinite confinement with no trial at all.

THE CASE FOR THE HYBRID APPROACH

Is there any justification for the hybrid war-law model, which so drastically diminishes the rights of the enemy? An argument can be offered along the following lines. In ordinary cases of war among states, enemy soldiers may well be morally and politically innocent. Many of them are conscripts, and those who aren't do not necessarily endorse the state policies they are fighting to defend. But enemy soldiers in the War on Terrorism are, by definition, those who have embarked on a path of terrorism. They are neither morally nor politically innocent. Their sworn aim— "Death to America!"—is to create more 9/11s. In this respect, they are much more akin to criminal conspirators than to conscript soldiers. Terrorists will fight as soldiers when they must, and metamorphose into mass murderers when they can.

Furthermore, suicide terrorists pose a special, unique danger. Ordinary criminals do not target innocent bystanders. They may be willing to kill them if necessary, but bystanders enjoy at least some measure of security because they are not primary targets. Not so with terrorists, who aim to kill as many innocent people as possible. Likewise, innocent bystanders are protected from ordinary criminals by whatever deterrent force the threat of punishment and the risk of getting killed in the act of committing a crime offer. For a suicide bomber, neither of these threats is a deterrent at all—after all, for the suicide bomber one of the hallmarks of a *successful* operation is that he winds up dead at day's end. Given the unique and heightened danger that suicide terrorists pose, a stronger response that grants potential terrorists fewer rights may be justified. Add to this the danger that terrorists may come to possess weapons of mass destruction, including nuclear devices in suitcases. Under circumstances of such dire menace, it is appropriate to treat terrorists as though they embody the most dangerous aspects of both warriors and criminals. That is the basis of the hybrid war-law model.

THE CASE AGAINST EXPEDIENCY

The argument against the hybrid war-law model is equally clear. The U.S. has simply chosen the bits of the law model and the bits of the war model that are most convenient for American interests, and ignored the rest. The model abolishes the rights of potential enemies (and their innocent shields) by fiat—not for reasons of moral or legal principle, but solely because the U.S. does not want them to have rights. The more rights they have, the more risk they pose. But Americans' urgent desire to minimize our risks doesn't make other people's rights disappear. Calling our policy a War on Terrorism obscures this point.

The theoretical basis of the objection is that the law model and the war model each comes as a package, with a kind of intellectual integrity. The law model grows out of relationships within states, while the war model arises from relationships between states. The law model imputes a ground-level community of values to those subject to the law—paradigmatically, citizens of a state, but also visitors and foreigners who choose to engage in conduct that affects a state. Only because law imputes shared basic values to the community can a state condemn the conduct of criminals and inflict punishment on them. Criminals deserve condemnation and punishment because their conduct violates norms that we are entitled to count on their sharing. But, for the same reason—the imputed community of values—those subject to the law ordinarily enjoy a presumption of innocence and an expectation of safety. The government cannot simply grab them and confine them without making sure they have broken the law, nor can it condemn them without due process for ensuring that it has the right person, nor can it knowingly place bystanders in mortal peril in the course of fighting crime. They are our fellows, and the community should protect them just as it protects us. The same imputed community of values that justifies condemnation and punishment creates rights to due care and due process.

War is different. War is the ultimate acknowledgment that human beings do not live in a single community with shared norms. If their norms conflict enough, communities pose a physical danger to each other, and nothing can safeguard a community against its enemies except force of arms. That makes enemy soldiers legitimate targets; but it makes our soldiers legitimate targets as well, and, once the enemy no longer poses a danger, he should be immune from punishment, because if he has fought cleanly he has violated no norms that we are entitled to presume he honors. Our norms are, after all, *our* norms, not his.

Because the law model and war model come as conceptual packages, it is unprincipled to wrench them apart and recombine them simply because it is in America's interest to do so. To declare that Americans can fight enemies with the latitude of warriors, but if the enemies fight back they are not warriors but criminals, amounts to a kind of heads-I-win-tails-you-lose international morality in which whatever it takes to reduce American risk, no matter what the cost to others, turns out to be justified. This, in brief, is the criticism of the hybrid war-law model.

To be sure, the law model could be made to incorporate the war model merely by rewriting a handful of statutes. Congress could enact laws permitting imprisonment or execution of persons who pose a significant threat of terrorism whether or not they have already done anything wrong. The standard of evidence could be set low and the requirement of a hearing eliminated. Finally, Congress could authorize the use of lethal force against terrorists regardless of the danger to innocent bystanders, and it could immunize officials from lawsuits or prosecution by victims of collateral damage. Such statutes would violate the Constitution, but the Constitution could be amended to incorporate anti-terrorist exceptions to the Fourth, Fifth, and Sixth Amendments. In the end, we would have a system of law that includes all the essential features of the war model.

It would, however, be a system that imprisons people for their intentions rather than their actions, and that offers the innocent few protections against mistaken detention or inadvertent death through collateral damage. Gone are the principles that people should never be punished for their thoughts, only for their deeds, and that innocent people must be protected rather than injured by their own government. In that sense, at any rate, repackaging war as law seems merely cosmetic, because it replaces the ideal of law as a protector of rights with the more problematic goal of protecting some innocent people by sacrificing others. The hypothetical legislation incorporates war into law only by making law as partisan and ruthless as war. It no longer resembles law as Americans generally understand it.

THE THREAT TO INTERNATIONAL HUMAN RIGHTS

In the War on Terrorism, what becomes of international human rights? It seems beyond dispute that the war model poses a threat to international human rights, because honoring human rights is neither practically possible nor theoretically required during war. Combatants are legitimate targets; non-combatants maimed by accident or mistake are regarded as collateral damage rather than victims of atrocities; cases of mistaken identity get killed or confined without a hearing because combat conditions preclude due process. To be sure, the laws of war specify minimum human rights, but these are far less robust than rights in peacetime—and the hybrid war-law model reduces this schedule of rights even further by classifying the enemy as unlawful combatants.

One striking example of the erosion of human rights is tolerance of torture. It should be recalled that a 1995 al Qaeda plot to bomb eleven U.S. airliners was thwarted by information tortured out of a Pakistani suspect by the Philippine police—an eerie real-life version of the familiar philosophical thought-experiment. The *Washington Post* reports that since September 11 the U.S. has engaged in the summary transfer of dozens of terrorism suspects to countries where they will be interrogated under torture. But it isn't just the United States that has proven willing to tolerate torture for security reasons. Last December, the Swedish government snatched a suspected Islamic extremist to whom it had previously granted political asylum, and the same day had him transferred to Egypt, where Amnesty International reports that he has been tortured to the point where he walks only with difficulty. Sweden is not, to say the least, a traditionally hard-line nation on human rights issues. None of this international transportation is lawful—indeed, it violates international treaty obligations under the Convention against Torture that in the U.S. have constitutional status as "supreme Law of the Land"—but that may not matter under the war model, in which even constitutional rights may be abrogated.

It is natural to suggest that this suspension of human rights is an exceptional emergency measure to deal with an unprecedented threat. This raises the question of how long human rights will remain suspended. When will the war be over?

Here, the chief problem is that the War on Terrorism is not like any other kind of war. The enemy, Terrorism, is not a territorial state or nation or government. There is no opposite number to negotiate with. There is no one on the other side to call a truce or declare a ceasefire, no one among the enemy authorized to surrender. In traditional wars among states, the war aim is, as Clausewitz argued, to impose one state's political will on another's. The *aim* of the war is not to kill the enemy—killing the enemy is the *means* used to achieve the real end, which is to force capitulation. In the War on Terrorism, no capitulation is possible. That means that the real aim of the war is, quite simply, to kill or capture all of the terrorists—to keep on killing and killing, capturing and capturing, until they are all gone.

Of course, no one expects that terrorism will ever disappear completely. Everyone understands that new anti-American extremists, new terrorists, will always arise and always be available for recruitment and deployment. Everyone understands that even if al Qaeda is destroyed or decapitated, other groups, with other leaders, will arise in its place. It follows, then, that the War on Terrorism will be a war that can only be abandoned, never concluded. The War has no natural resting point, no moment of victory or finality. It requires a mission of killing and capturing, in territories all over the globe, that will go on in perpetuity. It follows as well that the suspension of human rights implicit in the hybrid war-law model is not temporary but permanent.

Perhaps with this fear in mind, Congressional authorization of President Bush's military campaign limits its scope to those responsible for September 11 and their sponsors. But the War on Terrorism has taken on a life of its own that makes the Congressional authorization little more than a technicality. Because of the threat of nuclear terror, the American leadership actively debates a war on Iraq regardless of whether Iraq was implicated in September 11; and the President's yoking of Iraq, Iran, and North Korea into a single axis of evil because they back terror suggests that the War on Terrorism might eventually encompass all these nations. If the U.S. ever unearths tangible evidence that any of these countries is harboring or abetting terrorists with weapons of mass destruction, there can be little doubt that Congress will support military action. So too, Russia invokes the American War on Terrorism to justify its attacks on Chechen rebels, China uses it to deflect criticisms of its campaign against Uighur separatists, and Israeli Prime Minister Sharon explicitly links military actions against Palestinian insurgents to the American War on Terrorism. No doubt there is political opportunism at work in some or all of these efforts to piggy-back onto America's campaign, but the opportunity would not exist if "War on Terrorism" were merely the code-name of a discrete, neatly-boxed American operation. Instead, the War on Terrorism has become a model of politics, a world-view with its own distinctive premises and consequences. As I have argued, it includes a new model of state action, the hybrid war-law model, which depresses human rights from their peace-time standard to the war-time standard, and indeed even further. So long as it continues, the War on Terrorism means the end of human rights, at least for those near enough to be touched by the fire of battle.

QUESTIONS

1 Is the hybrid approach a morally acceptable way of dealing with terrorist suspects? Why or why not?

2 Do you agree with Luban that the continuation of the "War on Terrorism" means the end of human rights for "those near enough to be touched by the fire of battle?"

Majority Opinion in *Korematsu v. United States*
Justice Hugo Lafayette Black

On December 7, 1941, the Japanese bombed Pearl Harbor. On February 19, 1942, in the interest of preventing acts of espionage and sabotage, President Franklin D. Roosevelt signed Executive Order 9066, which authorized certain military commanders to prescribe military areas and define their extent. On February 20, 1942, Lieutenant General DeWitt was made military commander of the Western Defense Command, covering the westernmost states of the United States, about one-fourth of the total area of the nation. On March 21, 1942, Congress passed an act making it a misdemeanor to enter, remain in, leave, or commit any act in any military area or military zone prescribed by any military commander contrary to the restrictions issued by the military. Subsequently, General DeWitt instituted a curfew for certain areas under his command that required all persons of Japanese ancestry to remain in their residences between 8 P.M. and 6 A.M. The curfew order was challenged by Gordon Hirabayashi in *Hirabayashi v. United States* (1943). The United States Supreme Court upheld Hirabayashi's conviction for violating the curfew.

In May 1942, General DeWitt issued Civilian Exclusion Order No. 34, which provided that after noon, May 8, 1942, all persons of Japanese ancestry, both alien and nonalien, were to be excluded from an area that included the county of Alameda. Residents of Japanese ancestry like Fred T. Korematsu, were required to go to an assembly center. Of the 120,000 individuals of Japanese descent forced to leave their homes and subsequently sent to internment camps, two-thirds were American citizens.

Fred T. Korematsu was a native-born citizen of the United States. He was convicted of refusing to report to the authorities for eventual internment. Korematsu appealed to the United States Supreme Court. The Court refused to overturn the military judgment although there were very strong disagreements among the justices, three of whom wrote dissenting opinions. Justice Black delivered the opinion of the Court.

Justice Black avers that the principles used in the Court's reasoning in *Hirabayashi* also apply in *Korematsu*. In *Hirabayashi,* the curfew was seen as a legitimate exercise of the government's power to act in ways necessary to prevent espionage and sabotage in an area threatened by Japanese attack. Similarly, Black upholds the military judgment that the exclusion order was a military necessity because of the threat of harm posed by disloyal Japanese and Japanese-Americans and the impossibility of immediately segregating those who were loyal from those who were not.

It should be noted, to begin with, that all legal restrictions which curtail the civil rights of a single racial group are immediately suspect. That is not to say that all such restrictions are unconstitutional. It is to say that courts must subject them to the most rigid scrutiny. Pressing public necessity may sometimes justify the existence of such restrictions; racial antagonism never can.

United States Supreme Court. 323 U.S. 214 (1944).

In the instant case prosecution of the petitioner was begun by information charging violation of an Act of Congress, of March 21,1942, 56 Stat. 173, which provides that

> . . . whoever shall enter, remain in, leave, or commit any act in any military area or military zone prescribed, under the authority of an Executive order of the President, by the Secretary of War, or by any military commander designated by the Secretary of War, contrary to the restrictions applicable to any such area or zone or contrary to the order of the Secretary of War or any such military commander, shall, if it appears that he knew or should have known of the existence and extent of the restrictions or order and that his act was in violation thereof, be guilty of a misdemeanor and upon conviction shall be liable to a fine of not to exceed $5,000 or to imprisonment for not more than one year, or both, for each offense.

Exclusion Order No. 34, which the petitioner knowingly and admittedly violated, was one of a number of military orders and proclamations, all of which were substantially based upon Executive Order No. 9066, 7 Fed. Reg. 1407. That order, issued after we were at war with Japan, declared that "the successful prosecution of the war requires every possible protection against espionage and against sabotage to national-defense material, national-defense premises, and national-defense utilities. . . ."

One of the series of orders and proclamations, a curfew order, which like the exclusion order here was promulgated pursuant to Executive Order 9066, subjected all persons of Japanese ancestry in prescribed West Coast military areas to remain in their residences from 8 P.M. to 6 A.M. As is the case with the exclusion order here, that prior curfew order was designed as a "protection against espionage and against sabotage." In *Hirabayashi* v. *United States,* we sustained a conviction obtained for violation of the curfew order. The *Hirabayashi* conviction and this one thus rest on the same 1942 Congressional Act and the same basic executive and military orders, all of which orders were aimed at the twin dangers of espionage and sabotage.

The 1942 Act was attacked in the *Hirabayashi* case as an unconstitutional delegation of power; it was contended that the curfew order and other orders on which it rested were beyond the war powers of the Congress, the military authorities and of the President, as Commander in Chief of the Army; and finally that to apply the curfew order against none but citizens of Japanese ancestry amounted to a constitutionally prohibited discrimination solely on account of race. To these questions, we gave the serious consideration which their importance justified. We upheld the curfew order as an exercise of the power of the government to take steps necessary to prevent espionage and sabotage in an area threatened by Japanese attack.

In the light of the principles we announced in the *Hirabayashi* case, we are unable to conclude that it was beyond the war power of Congress and the Executive to exclude those of Japanese ancestry from the West Coast war area at the time they did. True, exclusion from the area in which one's home is located is a far greater deprivation than constant confinement to the home from 8 P.M. to 6 A.M. Nothing short of apprehension by the proper military authorities of the gravest imminent danger to the public safety can constitutionally justify either. But exclusion from a threatened area, no less than curfew, has a definite and close relationship to the prevention of espionage and sabotage. The military authorities, charged with the primary responsibility of defending our shores, concluded that curfew provided inadequate protection and ordered exclusion. They did so, as pointed out in our *Hirabayashi* opinion, in accordance with Congressional authority to the military to say who should, and who should not, remain in the threatened areas.

In this case the petitioner challenges the assumptions upon which we rested our conclusions in the *Hirabayashi* case. He also urges that by May 1942, when Order No. 34 was promulgated, all danger of Japanese invasion of the West Coast had disappeared. After careful consideration of these contentions we are compelled to reject them.

Here, as in the *Hirabayashi* case, ". . . we cannot reject as unfounded the judgment of the military authorities and of Congress that there were disloyal members of that population, whose number and strength could not be precisely and quickly ascertained. We cannot say that the war-making branches of the Government did not have ground for believing that in a critical hour such persons could not readily be isolated and separately dealt with, and constituted a menace to the national defense and safety, which demanded that prompt and adequate measures be taken to guard against it."

Like curfew, exclusion of those of Japanese origin was deemed necessary because of the presence of an unascertained number of disloyal members of the group, most of whom we have no doubt were loyal to this country. It was because we could not reject the finding of the military authorities that it was impossible to bring about an immediate segregation of the disloyal from the loyal that we sustained the validity of the curfew order as applying to the whole group. In the instant case, temporary exclusion of the entire group was rested by the military on the same ground. The judgment that exclusion of the whole group was for the same reason a military imperative answers the contention that the exclusion was in the nature of group punishment based on antagonism to those of Japanese origin. That there were members of the group who retained loyalties to Japan has been confirmed by investigations made subsequent to the exclusion. Approximately five thousand American citizens of Japanese ancestry refused to swear unqualified allegiance to the United States and to renounce allegiance to the Japanese Emperor, and several thousand evacuees requested repatriation to Japan.

We uphold the exclusion order as of the time it was made and when the petitioner violated it. Cf. *Chastleton Corporation v. Sinclair, Block v. Hirsh.* In doing so, we are not unmindful of the hardships imposed by it upon a large group of American citizens. Cf. *Ex parte Kawato.* But hardships are part of war, and war is an aggregation of hardships. All citizens alike, both in and out of uniform, feel the impact of war in greater or lesser measure. Citizenship has its responsibilities as well as its privileges, and in time of war the burden is always heavier. Compulsory exclusion of large groups of citizens from their homes, except under circumstances of direst emergency and peril, is inconsistent with our basic governmental institutions. But when under conditions of modern warfare our shores are threatened by hostile forces, the power to protect must be commensurate with the threatened danger. . . .

It is said that we are dealing here with the case of imprisonment of a citizen in a concentration camp solely because of his ancestry, without evidence or inquiry concerning his loyalty and good disposition towards the United States. Our task would be simple, our duty clear, were this a case involving the imprisonment of a loyal citizen in a concentration camp because of racial prejudice. Regardless of the true nature of the assembly and relocation centers—and we deem it unjustifiable to call them concentration camps with all the ugly connotations that term implies—we are dealing specifically with nothing but an exclusion order. To cast this case into outlines of racial prejudice, without reference to the real military dangers which were presented, merely confuses the issue. Korematsu was not excluded from the Military Area because of hostility to him or his race. He *was* excluded because we are at war with the Japanese Empire, because the properly constituted military authorities feared an invasion of our West Coast and felt constrained to take proper security measures, because they decided that the military urgency of the situation demanded that all citizens of Japanese ancestry be segregated from the West Coast temporarily, and finally, because Congress, reposing its confidence in this time of war in our military leaders—as inevitably it must—determined that they should have the power to do just this. There was evidence of disloyalty on the part of some, the military authorities considered that the need for action was great, and time was short. We cannot—by availing ourselves of the calm perspective of hindsight—now say that at that time these actions were unjustified.

Affirmed.

QUESTIONS

1 In the past, in times of crisis, the United States has adopted measures—later recognized as morally wrong—that curtailed civil liberties in the interest of security. Does the current American response to terrorism involve a morally unacceptable curtailment of liberties? Why or why not?

2 Japanese-Americans who were interned during World War II have received some compensation from the government. Should individuals who were interned at Guantanamo Bay for a long period of time and later released with no charges made against them be compensated?

Dissenting Opinion in *Korematsu v. United States*

Justice Frank Murphy

Justice Murphy maintains that before individuals can be validly deprived of any of their constitutional rights on a plea of military necessity, the deprivation must be reasonably related to a public danger that is so immediate, imminent, and impending that it precludes any delays caused by the intervention of ordinary constitutional processes to alleviate the danger. In his view, Exclusion Order No. 34, which bans all

United States Supreme Court. 323 U.S. 214 (1944).

persons of Japanese ancestry from restricted areas of the Pacific Coast, does not meet the reasonability test. The order cannot be reasonable because it rests on false cultural and social assumptions regarding all Japanese and Japanese-Americans. Murphy notes that no attempts were made to treat persons of Japanese ancestry on an individual basis to differentiate those who were loyal to the United States from those who were not. He rejects what he sees as the legalization of racism.

This exclusion of "all persons of Japanese ancestry, both alien and non-alien," from the Pacific Coast area on a plea of military necessity in the absence of martial law ought not to be approved. Such exclusion goes over "the very brink of constitutional power" and falls into the ugly abyss of racism.

In dealing with matters relating to the prosecution and progress of a war, we must accord great respect and consideration to the judgments of the military authorities who are on the scene and who have full knowledge of the military facts. The scope of their discretion must, as a matter of necessity and common sense, be wide. And their judgments ought not to be overruled lightly by those whose training and duties ill-equip them to deal intelligently with matters so vital to the physical security of the nation.

At the same time, however, it is essential that there be definite limits to military discretion, especially where martial law has not been declared. Individuals must not be left impoverished of their constitutional rights on a plea of military necessity that has neither substance nor support. Thus, like other claims conflicting with the asserted constitutional rights of the individual, the military claim must subject itself to the judicial process of having its reasonableness determined and its conflicts with other interests reconciled. "What are the allowable limits of military discretion, and whether or not they have been overstepped in a particular case, are judicial questions." *Sterling v. Constantin.*

The judicial test of whether the Government, on a plea of military necessity, can validly deprive an individual of any of his constitutional rights is whether the deprivation is reasonably related to a public danger that is so "immediate, imminent, and impending" as not to admit of delay and not to permit the intervention of ordinary constitutional processes to alleviate the danger. *United States v. Russell, Mitchell v. Harmony, Raymond v. Thomas.* Civilian Exclusion Order No. 34, banishing from a prescribed area of the Pacific Coast "all persons of Japanese ancestry, both alien and non-alien," clearly does not meet that test. Being an obvious racial discrimination, the order deprives all those within its scope of the equal protection of the laws as guaranteed by the Fifth Amendment. It further deprives these individuals of their constitutional rights to live and work where they will, to establish a home where they choose and to move about freely. In excommunicating them without benefit of hearings, this order also deprives them of all their constitutional rights to procedural due process. Yet no reasonable relation to an "immediate, imminent, and impending" public danger is evident to support this racial restriction which is one of the most sweeping and complete deprivations of constitutional rights in the history of this nation in the absence of martial law.

It must be conceded that the military and naval situation in the spring of 1942 was such as to generate a very real fear of invasion of the Pacific Coast, accompanied by fears of sabotage and espionage in that area. The military command was therefore justified in adopting all reasonable means necessary to combat these dangers. In adjudging the military action taken in light of the then apparent dangers, we must not erect too high or too meticulous standards; it is necessary only that the action have some reasonable relation to the removal of the dangers of invasion, sabotage and espionage. But the exclusion, either temporarily or permanently, of all persons with Japanese blood in their veins has no such reasonable relation. And that relation is lacking because the exclusion order necessarily must rely for its reasonableness upon the assumption that *all* persons of Japanese ancestry may have a dangerous tendency to commit sabotage and espionage and to aid our Japanese enemy in other ways. It is difficult to believe that reason, logic or experience could be marshalled in support of such an assumption.

That this forced exclusion was the result in good measure of this erroneous assumption of racial guilt rather than bona fide military necessity is evidenced by the Commanding General's Final Report on the evacuation from the Pacific Coast area.[1] In it he refers to all individuals of Japanese descent as "subversive," as belonging to "an enemy race" whose "racial strains are undiluted," and as constituting "over 112,000 potential enemies . . . at large today" along the Pacific Coast. In support of this blanket condemnation of all persons of Japanese descent, however, no reliable evidence is cited to show that such individuals were generally disloyal, or had generally so conducted themselves in this area as to constitute a special menace to defense installations or war industries, or had otherwise by their behavior furnished reasonable ground for their exclusion as a group.

Justification for the exclusion is sought, instead, mainly upon questionable racial and sociological grounds not ordinarily within the realm of expert military judgment, supplemented by certain semi-military conclusions drawn from an unwarranted use of circumstantial evidence. Individuals of Japanese ancestry are condemned because they are said to be "a large, unassimilated, tightly knit racial group, bound to an enemy nation by strong ties of race, culture, custom and religion." They are claimed to be given to "emperor worshipping ceremonies" and to "dual citizenship." Japanese language schools and allegedly pro-Japanese organizations are cited as evidence of possible group disloyalty, together with facts as to certain persons being educated and residing at length in Japan. It is intimated that many of these individuals deliberately resided "adjacent to strategic points," thus enabling them "to carry into execution a tremendous program of sabotage on a mass scale should any considerable number of them have been inclined to do so." The need for protective custody is also asserted. The report refers without identity to "numerous incidents of violence" as well as to other admittedly unverified or cumulative incidents. From this, plus certain other events not shown to have been connected with the Japanese Americans, it is concluded that the "situation was fraught with danger to the Japanese population itself" and that the general public "was ready to take matters into its own hands." Finally, it is intimated, though not directly charged or proved, that persons of Japanese ancestry were responsible for three minor isolated shellings and bombings of the Pacific Coast area, as well as for unidentified radio transmissions and night signalling.

The main reasons relied upon by those responsible for the forced evacuation, therefore, do not prove a reasonable relation between the group characteristics of

Japanese Americans and the dangers of invasion, sabotage and espionage. The reasons appear, instead, to be largely an accumulation of much of the misinformation, half-truths and insinuations that for years have been directed against Japanese Americans by people with racial and economic prejudices—the same people who have been among the foremost advocates of the evacuation. A military judgment based upon such racial and sociological considerations is not entitled to the great weight ordinarily given the judgments based upon strictly military considerations. Especially is this so when every charge relative to race, religion, culture, geographical location, and legal and economic status has been substantially discredited by independent studies made by experts in these matters.

The military necessity which is essential to the validity of the evacuation order thus resolves itself into a few intimations that certain individuals actively aided the enemy, from which it is inferred that the entire group of Japanese Americans could not be trusted to be or remain loyal to the United States. No one denies, of course, that there were some disloyal persons of Japanese descent on the Pacific Coast who did all in their power to aid their ancestral land. Similar disloyal activities have been engaged in by many persons of German, Italian and even more pioneer stock in our country. But to infer that examples of individual disloyalty prove group disloyalty and justify discriminatory action against the entire group is to deny that under our system of law individual guilt is the sole basis for deprivation of rights. Moreover, this inference, which is at the very heart of the evacuation orders, has been used in support of the abhorrent and despicable treatment of minority groups by the dictatorial tyrannies which this nation is now pledged to destroy. To give constitutional sanction to that inference in this case, however well-intentioned may have been the military command on the Pacific Coast, is to adopt one of the cruelest of the rationales used by our enemies to destroy the dignity of the individual and to encourage and open the door to discriminatory actions against other minority groups in the passions of tomorrow.

No adequate reason is given for the failure to treat these Japanese Americans on an individual basis by holding investigations and hearings to separate the loyal from the disloyal, as was done in the case of persons of German and Italian ancestry. See House Report No. 2124 (77th Cong., 2d Sess.) 247–52. It is asserted merely that the loyalties of this group "were unknown and time was of the essence." Yet nearly four months elapsed after Pearl Harbor before the first exclusion order was issued; nearly eight months went by until the last order was issued; and the last of these "subversive" persons was not actually removed until almost eleven months had elapsed. Leisure and deliberation seem to have been more of the essence than speed. And the fact that conditions were not such as to warrant a declaration of martial law adds strength to the belief that the factors of time and military necessity were not as urgent as they have been represented to be.

Moreover, there was no adequate proof that the Federal Bureau of Investigation and the military and naval intelligence services did not have the espionage and sabotage situation well in hand during this long period. Nor is there any denial of the fact that not one person of Japanese ancestry was accused or convicted of espionage or sabotage after Pearl Harbor while they were still free, a fact which is some evidence of the loyalty of the vast majority of these individuals and of the effectiveness of the established methods of combatting these evils. It seems incredible that under these circumstances it would have been impossible to hold loyalty hearings for the mere 112,000 persons involved—or at least for the 70,000 American citizens—especially when a large part of this number represented children and elderly men and women. Any inconvenience that may have accompanied an attempt to conform to procedural due process cannot be said to justify violations of constitutional rights of individuals.

I dissent, therefore, from this legalization of racism. Racial discrimination in any form and in any degree has no justifiable part whatever in our democratic way of life. It is unattractive in any setting but it is utterly revolting among a free people who have embraced the principles set forth in the Constitution of the United States. All residents of this nation are kin in some way by blood or culture to a foreign land. Yet they are primarily and necessarily a part of the new and distinct civilization of the United States. They must accordingly be treated at all times as the heirs of the American experiment and as entitled to all the rights and freedoms guaranteed by the Constitution.

NOTE

1 Final Report, Japanese Evacuation from the West Coast, 1942, by Lt. Gen. J. L. DeWitt. This report is dated June 5, 1943, but was not made public until January, 1944. [All subsequent references in Justice Murphy's opinion to claims regarding racial and cultural characterizations of Japanese people are from this report.]

QUESTIONS

1 Is Murphy's reasonability test defensible?
2 To what extent are civil liberties presently being infringed upon in the interest of combating terrorism? Could these infringements pass Justice Murphy's reasonability test?

Security and Liberty: The Image of Balance

Jeremy Waldron

Waldron examines the following proposition: "a change in the scale and nature of the harms that threaten us explains and justifies a change in our scheme of civil liberties; and that process is best understood in terms of 'striking a new balance between liberty and security.'" His examination falls into three parts. First, he looks at what it would mean to take the idea of striking a new balance more or less

Reprinted with permission of the publisher from *The Journal of Political Philosophy*, vol. 11, no. 2 (2003), pp. 191–195, 200–208, 210. © 2003 Blackwell Publishing Ltd.

literally. Second, he looks at the issues raised by the distribution of the proposed changes in liberty and security, which limit the liberties of some minorities more than those of other members of society. Finally, he discusses the unintended effects of giving the government powers that had previously been denied to it.

I.

There seems to be general acceptance in the wake of the terrorist attacks of September 11, 2001 that some adjustment in our scheme of civil liberties is inevitable. This is partly the product of political defeatism: the state is always looking to limit liberty, and a terrorist emergency provides a fine opportunity. People become more than usually deferential to the demands of their rulers in these circumstances and more than usually fearful that if they criticize the proposed adjustments they will be reproached for being insufficiently patriotic. There is also little likelihood that reductions in civil liberties will be opposed by the courts. Even in countries like the United States with strong judicial review, the courts have proved reluctant to oppose reductions in civil liberties in times of war or war-like emergency. . . .

Political realism aside, there is also a sense that some curtailment of liberty might be *appropriate* in the wake of the terrorist attacks, and that it might be *unreasonable* to insist on the same restrictions on state action after September 11 as we insisted on before September 11.

A common suggestion invites us to think about this in terms of the idea of *balance*. According to this suggestion, it is *always* necessary—even in normal circumstances—to balance liberty against security. We always have to strike a balance between the individual's liberty to do as he pleases and society's need for protection against the harm that may accrue from some of the things it might please an individual to do. The former surely, cannot be comprehensive even under the most favorable circumstances—nobody argues for anarchy—and the latter has to be given some weight in determining how much liberty people should have. So there is always a balance to be struck. And—the suggestion continues—that balance is bound to change (and it is appropriate that it should change) as the threat to security becomes graver or more imminent. One newspaper columnist, Nicholas Kristoff, put it this way:

> [T]errorist incidents in the 1970s (such as at the Munich Olympics) had maximum death tolls of about a dozen; attacks in the 1980s and 1990s raised the scale (as in the Air India and Pan Am 103 bombings) to the hundreds; 9/11 lifted the toll into the thousands; and terrorists are now nosing around weapons of mass destruction that could kill hundreds of thousands. As risks change, we who care about civil liberties need to realign balances between security and freedom. It is a wrenching, odious task, but we liberals need to learn from 9/11 just as much as the FBI does.[1]

This is the proposition I want to examine: a change in the scale and nature of the harms that threaten us explains and justifies a change in our scheme of civil liberties; and that process is best understood in terms of "striking a new balance between liberty and security."

II.

The idea of striking a new balance can be interpreted more or less literally. We know the language of balance is used in morality and politics when there are things to be said on both sides of an issue, values that pull us in opposite directions. But what does it mean to say that we confront this array of values or reasons by *balancing* the competing considerations? And what are we implying when we say the balance has shifted? Is it just a matter of our having thought of a new reason, or of new facts having given rise to new reasons, which weigh more on one side than the other? That we can make sense of: there is now (say, since September 11, 2001) something new to be said on one side of a familiar debate and nothing new to be said on the other. But "balance" also has connotations of quantity and precision, as when we use it to describe the reconciliation of a set of accounts or the relative weight of two quantities of metal. Where is the warrant for our reliance on this quantitative imagery when we say that the new consideration not only adds something to the debate but "outweighs" all considerations on the other side?

Here is one possibility. We know that liberty is in some respects a matter of more or less. For example: I can range more or less widely without restrictions on my travel; or I may be permitted to come closer to or be kept back from important public sites or important public officials. So we may be able to make at least ordinal comparisons between different quantities of liberty L_x and L_y (for example, between one person's liberty and another's, or between my liberty one day and my liberty the following day). And security may be conceived quantitatively, too, in terms of the extent of risk (R) faced by a person (where R equals the magnitude of a possible harm times the probability of its occurrence): we might say that a person is less secure the greater R is with regard to that person. With this primitive apparatus, we might then be able to express the idea of the security cost to a person A of another person B having a certain amount of liberty. The security cost to A of B's having a higher amount of liberty L_y rather than a lower amount L_x is the difference between two risks, the higher risk (let us call it R_n) to A from B's having the greater liberty (L_y) and the lower risk (R_m) to A of B's having the lesser liberty (L_x).

Now, if we assume (for the sake of argument) that the balance between security and liberty was exactly right on September 10, 2001, then maybe what happened the following day was that we became aware (or it became the case) that the risks of ceding a given amount of liberty were greater than we thought. Even on September 10, we knew that any amount of liberty carried with it a certain risk of harm. But we were prepared to accept a certain risk—say, R_n rather than a lower risk R_m—because any attempt to secure R_m would mean giving up something we valued at least as much as that extra security, namely, a certain degree of liberty: on September 10, we thought that to secure R_m we would have to diminish individual liberty from L_y to L_x; and we were not prepared to do that. However even on September 10 we were not prepared to cede a greater degree of liberty than L_y— say L_z—because we knew that that would carry a risk of harm greater than R_n. And we were not prepared to accept a greater risk than R_n. However, it now turns out (in light of the events of September 11) that the cost of L_y (which we *were* prepared to concede) is much greater than we thought—say, R_o rather than R_n. Since we were prepared on September 10 to give up any degree of liberty that would pose a risk greater than R_n, consistency indicates that now we are going to have to settle for an amount of liberty much less than L_y—say, L_x—on September 12. That I think is what the case for "striking a new balance" is supposed to amount to. We have an idea of the maximum risk we are prepared to bear as a result of people's liberty, and we adjust their liberties downwards when it appears that the risk associated with a given quantum of liberty is greater than we thought (or greater than it used to be).

Of course it is possible that we could make the adjustment in the other direction. Instead of beginning with an idea of the maximum risk, R_n, we were prepared to bear as a result of people's liberty, we might begin with an idea of the minimum liberty, L_y, we were prepared to accept. The recalculation after September 11 would then require us not to accept less liberty but to brave a higher risk for the sake of the liberty we cherish. The appropriate changes in public policy, then, would be calls to greater courage, rather than diminutions of liberty. Most probably we work at the matter from both ends, and perhaps this is where talk of "balance" really comes into its own. Our liberties are not untouched. There has been a downward adjustment, to help address some of the graver risks. But even with the adjustments in civil liberties that have been put in place (and are likely to be put in place) since September 11, no one feels as secure as before: so everyone has to be a little braver for the sake of the modicum of liberty that is left.

III.

Readers may think all this is over-fussy. Surely everyone knows what we mean when we talk about the balance between liberty and security, and surely it is obvious that some adjustment has to be made after it becomes evident that terrorists can take advantage of our traditional liberties to commit murder on such a scale. Does it really need to be spelled out with this sort of algebra? Well, I think we *do* need to subject the balancing rhetoric to careful analytic scrutiny, and this for [at least two reasons]: . . .

(i) *Difficulties with distribution.* Though we may talk of balancing our liberties against our security, we need to pay some attention to the fact that the real diminution in liberty may affect some people more than others. So, as well as the objection to consequentialism, justice requires that we pay special attention to the distributive character of the changes that are proposed and to the possibility that the change involves, in effect, a proposal to trade off the liberties of a few against the security of the majority.

(ii) *Unintended effects.* When liberty is conceived as *negative* liberty, a reduction in liberty is achieved by enhancing the power of the state. This is done so that the enhanced power can be used to combat terrorism. But it would be naive to assume that this is the only thing that that enhanced power can be used for. We need to consider the possibility that diminishing liberty might also diminish security against the state, even as it enhances security against terrorism. . . .

I will discuss [each of] these concerns . . . in more detail in Sections IV . . . [and V] of this article, and I will try to show how they might apply to various issues of civil liberty.

As we pursue that discussion, we will need to bear in mind that the class of civil liberties at stake here is not necessarily a homogenous class of rights, principles, or guarantees. The term "civil liberties" represents a variety of concerns about the impact of governmental powers upon individual freedom. Because the issue of a change in the "balance" between civil liberties and security plays out slightly differently for different kinds of concern, let me briefly set out some distinctions.

(a) In its most straightforward meaning, "civil liberties" refers to certain freedoms understood as actions that individuals might wish to perform, which (it is thought) the state should not restrict. Free speech, religious freedom, freedom of travel fall into this category.

(b) We also use the phrase "civil liberties" to refer to more diffuse concerns about government power, which are not necessarily driven by any sense of a privileged type of action which individuals should be left free to perform. For example, the government's ability to listen in on telephone conversations is a civil liberties concern, even though the "liberty" in question—sometimes referred to as "privacy"—does not amount to very much more than the condition of not being subjected to this scrutiny.

(c) Sometimes "civil liberties" refers to procedural rights and powers which we think individuals should have when the state detains them or brings charges against them or plans to punish them. These are rights like the right not to be detained without trial, the right to a fair trial process, the right to counsel, etc.

This short list is by no means complete. A comprehensive account would also say something about (d) the rights associated with democracy and civic participation. Fortunately these rights have not been an issue in the current crisis. So for the rest of the article, I will focus mainly on (a), (b), and (c) and consider how the concerns I have outlined . . . apply to them.

IV.

My [first] point is this: in order to evaluate the balancing argument, we have to ask tough questions about the *distribution* of the various changes envisaged in liberty and security. It is tempting to read the argument set out in Section II in terms of a diminution in liberty for everyone—everyone's liberty is reduced from L_y to L_x—in order to secure the same amount of security for everyone. But often it does not work out that way.

The perpetrators of the September 11 attacks were foreigners, members of a foreign organization, and the U.S. government has taken that as grounds for drawing some quite sharp distinctions in its subsequent legislation between the protections accorded to the civil liberties of Americans and the protections accorded to others who are legally in the United States. Section 214 of the USA Patriot Act, for example, alters existing legislation concerning wire-tapping so that "investigation of a United States person is not conducted solely upon the basis of activities protected by the first amendment to the Constitution." (The class of "United States persons" includes American citizens and legally admitted permanent residents; but it does not include non-resident aliens legally present in the United States.) More importantly perhaps, the perpetrators of the September 11 attacks were not just non-residents but also members of a fairly visible ethnic group: and their actions mean that everyone (whether a United States person or not) who looks or dresses or speaks in any way like them is likely to face much greater levels of suspicion. Most of the changes in civil liberties are aimed specifically at suspected perpetrators or accomplices or persons who might be thought to have information about past or future terrorist actions, and most Americans assume that persons in these categories will look quite different from themselves.

True—as a legalistic matter, the changes in civil liberties may be formulated innocuously enough—"Anyone who is officially suspected of doing A or knowing B will have his or her liberty reduced from L_y to L_x,"—and the "anyone" term seems universalizable. However, we must avoid a certain childish formalism in making the claim that civil liberties are diminished equally for everyone. As Ronald Dworkin points out,

> None of the administration's decisions and proposals will affect more than a tiny number of American citizens: almost none of us will be indefinitely detained for minor violations or offenses, or have our houses searched without our knowledge, or find ourselves brought before military tribunals on grave charges carrying the death penalty. Most of us pay almost nothing in personal freedom when such measures are used against those the President suspects of terrorism.[2]

So perhaps the balance we ought to be discussing is not so much a balance between one thing we all like (liberty) and another thing we all like (security). It is more like the balance that is sometimes referred to when we say we should balance the interests of a dissident individual or minority against the interests of the community as a whole.

Ronald Dworkin has argued in a number of places that there is some confusion in the idea of a balance of interests between the individual and the community: "The interests of each individual are already balanced into the interests of the community as a whole, and the idea of a further balance, between their separate interests and the results of the first balance, is itself therefore mysterious."[3] But confusion is not the problem; the problem is moral, not logical. There are in fact two ways of parsing the idea of a balance between the interests of an individual and the interests of the community in the present context, neither of them reassuring.

First, talk of balancing the interests of the individual against the interests of the community may be a way of indicating that "the individual" in question is not really thought of as a member of the community at all: he is an alien, a foreigner, and so his interests have *not* already been counted in "the interests of the community." Alternatively, if we say that his interests *are* already counted in the interests of the community—for example, because he too is more secure from being blown up, as a result of what we do to the liberties of suspicious characters (like him)—we may mean to indicate that a balance must be struck between (i) what *justice* requires in the way of respect for his interests and (ii) what would best promote the aggregate interests—his included—calculated in a way that is indifferent to justice.

This second account is quite complicated, so let me explain it a little further. We know that "the interest of the community" is often calculated in a way that sidelines issues of justice and distribution: utilitarians do this all the time. To take a very crude example: suppose that a choice between two policies (I and II) offers the following pay-offs to three individuals:

	I	II
A	20	30
B	20	10
C	20	30

Plainly policy II best promotes the interests of the community (comprising A, B, and C) in an aggregate sense: the total pay-off is higher and so is the average. But someone who believes this may also acknowledge that the outcome of policy I is more fair; and let us assume for the sake argument that they are right. Now, since fairness is concerned particularly with what happens to individuals (rather than to arithmetical totals), and since A and C are both better off as individuals under the less fair policy, a concern about fairness and about the issue of sacrificing fairness to aggregate utility is likely to focus particularly on B. It would not be surprising if this concern were *abbreviated* as a concern about the balance between B's interests and the aggregate interests of the community, even though B's interests are actually counted in the aggregate interests of the community. Another way of putting it would be to say that the real issue is the relation between a concern for justice, on the one hand, and the prospect of gains (to some or to the aggregate) from ignoring justice, on the other.

Talk of "balance" here is quite insidious. Although it all sounds very moderate, the implication is that we should have *some* concern for justice but not too much: a proper sense of balance requires us to give up on justice when the costs of pursuing it (to those who would benefit from injustice) become too high. Now A and C might not think this in the choice between policy I and policy II above: there the cost to them of justice is not very great. But if we imagine that a new set of policy choices presents itself (say, on September 11), which greatly increases what A and C have to lose from sticking with justice—

	III	IV
A	10	30
B	10	5
C	10	30

—then we might be tempted to talk about "adjusting the balance" between justice and utility. After all, it is one thing to require A and C each to give up ten units of goodies for the sake of justice in the choice between I and II; it is quite another thing—and the afficionado of balance may say it is quite unreasonable—to expect them to give up twice that in the choice between III and IV.

I have put this provocatively—with what I hope is an ill-concealed sneer of outrage at the idea of "striking a new balance" between the demands of justice on the one hand, and what most members of a society could get for themselves if they were allowed to arrange their society unjustly on the other. But mainly what I am trying to establish is the need for care with the idea of balancing. If security-gains for most people are being balanced against liberty-losses for a few, then we need to pay attention to the few/most dimension of the balance, not just the liberty/security dimension. Given that the few/most dimension presents an issue of justice, it is by no means clear—I think it is clearly false—that simply adding something to the "most" side of the balance is sufficient by itself to justify taking something away from the "few".

Someone may respond by observing that the "few" in our present case are terrorists or persons suspected of participation or complicity in terrorism. No one believes that criminals should have the same rights as the rest of us, and even those who are suspected but not convicted of criminal activity have lesser rights even in ordinary times: they may be held pending trial, or required to surrender their passports, etc. The point may be accepted, but the issue is whether we should now make some additional downward adjustments to the scheme that already puts criminal suspects in a special position of more restricted liberty. The civil liberties in category (c) define the procedures and protections that are offered to those suspected of ordinary crimes, from the trivial to the heinous. Is there a good reason for changing these, in the light of the events of September 11?

Ronald Dworkin observes a temptation to think that the extraordinary gravity of the crimes that were committed on September 11 (or that terrorists are presently conspiring to commit) is itself a reason for diminishing the protections afforded to those who are charged with such offenses. But, as he said, that makes no sense: "If they are innocent, the injustice of convicting and punishing them is at least as great as the injustice in convicting some other innocent person for a less serious crime."[4] The "civil liberties" in category (c) are oriented in large part towards preventing such injustice, and the case for respecting them increases rather than diminishes the greater the crime that the suspect stands accused of. (This is because category (c) liberties are designed to protect people against condemnation and punishment, and both will be greater the more serious the charge.)

Can it not also be said, though, that the greater the crime the greater the dangers of a wrongful acquittal? It is not true in all cases, but it may be true with terrorists. Michael Dorf put the point this way:

> The traditional way we balance these things is with the maxim, "It's better that 10 guilty men go free than one innocent man be in jail." I think people are a little nervous about applying that maxim where the 10 guilty men who are going to go free could have biological weapons.[5]

The implicit suggestion that the 1:10 ratio needs to be adjusted in light of the greater damage that the ten may do sounds reasonable enough. But we must not give the impression that it is only a matter of striking a different balance between this one (innocent) suspect and these ten (guilty) ones. That is not who the balance is between. We are not balancing the rights of the innocent against the rights of the guilty. We are balancing the interests in life or liberty of the one innocent man against the security interests of those of the rest of us (nonsuspects) that will be served if the ten guilty men are convicted by the procedures that lead to the wrongful conviction of the innocent.

The innocent man is being put to death or imprisoned, and his reputation drastically and wrongly besmirched, so that *we* may be safer. It may not be done intentionally, but the gist of the proposal is that it is something we are entitled to be reckless about. There was a way of taking care that it should not happen (or that it should happen less often)—that is what the civil liberties safeguards represent—but for our own benefit we have decided to take less care.

James Fitzjames Stephen remarked, in connection with this business of trading off a certain number of guilty acquittals against innocent convictions that "[e]verything depends on what the guilty men have been doing, and something depends on the way in which the innocent man came to be suspected."[6] The first point is like Dorf's. But Stephen's second point is relevant too. If the innocent persons who are sacrificed to security in this way are sacrificed because it was in the circumstances perfectly reasonable to suspect them of terrorist offenses (though, as it turned out, mistaken)—that is one thing. But if they were suspected in the first place because of appearance, ethnicity, or religion, and if the changes in the scheme of civil liberties facilitated suspicion on just that basis, and removed some of the safeguards that would prevent or mitigate that sort of suspicion—then, that is quite another thing. The injustice associated with the reckless conviction of one innocent man for the sake of the greater good becomes particularly acute—and the "balancing" talk that underwrites it becomes particularly objectionable—when it is associated with ethnic or religious prejudice. At that stage, our worrying has to go beyond the issue of individual costs and benefits and look to the moral corruption of the system as a whole.

[V.]

A [second] reason for taking care with balancing arguments is that one of the terms—"liberty"—is a relational term, so that it has ramifications for both sides of the balance.

When liberty is understood (as it usually is) in a negative sense, it is something that cannot be reduced without increasing something else, namely the powers and means and mechanisms that obstruct or punish the ability of individuals to do what they want. Reducing liberty may prevent an action taking place which would otherwise pose a risk of harm. But it necessarily also increases the power of the state, and there is a corresponding risk that this enhanced power may also be used to cause harm.

It is important not to lose sight of this possibility. The protection of civil liberties is not just a matter of (a) cherishing certain freedoms that we particularly value. It is also a matter of suspicion of power, an apprehension that power given to the state is seldom ever used only for the purposes for which it is given, but is always and endemically liable to abuse. Category (b) of our civil liberties concerns picks this up precisely. Whether there is a freedom at stake or not, there are certain powers which we have traditionally thought it better that the state should not have.

Another way of putting this is to say that a commitment to civil liberties is born in part of a "liberalism of fear" (to use Judith Shklar's phrase),[7] that is, an apprehension about what may be done to us using the overwhelming means of force available to the state. True, the events of September 11 have heightened our fear of the worst that can be done to us by individuals and groups other than the state. And an increase in the power of the state may be necessary to prevent or diminish the prospect of that horror. *But the existence of a threat from terrorist attack does not diminish the threat that liberals have traditionally apprehended from the state.* The former complements the latter; it does not diminish it, and it may enhance it. In this regard Shklar notes that the liberalism of fear owes a lot to the political philosophy of John Locke.[8] It will not do, said Locke, in justifying strong unconstrained government, to point to the perils that it might protect us from: "This is to think, that Men are so foolish, that they take care to avoid what Mischiefs may be done them by *Pole-Cats,* or *Foxes,* but are content, nay think it Safety, to be devoured by *Lions.*"[9] We have to worry that the very means given to the government to combat our enemies will be used by the government against *its* enemies—and although these those two classes "enemies of the people" and "enemies of the state" overlap, they are not necessarily co-extensive.

Nowhere is this point clearer than in our apprehensions about the use of torture. We all hope and pray that our government will not have resort to this expedient, although there have been suggestions from hitherto respectable civil libertarians that it should do so. There are official assurances that its use is out of the question, though that has to be balanced against the depressing precedent of two of our closest allies in the war against terrorism—the United Kingdom and Israel—having resorted in recent memory to methods very close to torture in dealing with their own terrorist emergencies. And even if we could rely on the official assurances that torture will not be used—and to do so we would want governments that have been rather less mendacious than ours have been about their support for such practices by other regimes in the past—it is worth pondering why this expedient is unthinkable and what that should tell us about other areas where we are less reluctant to sacrifice civil liberties.

On the face of it, the prohibition against torture should be exactly the sort of thing that gives way in the present atmosphere of adjusting the balance between liberty and security. What we are desperate for in the war against terrorism is information—who is planning what—and torture is supposed to be an effective way of securing information. Philosophy classes studying consequentialism thrive on hypotheticals involving scenarios of grotesque disproportion between the pain that a torturer might inflict on an informant and the pain that might be averted by timely use of the information extracted from him: a little bit of pain from the electrodes for him versus five hundred thousand people saved from nuclear incineration. But now the hypotheticals are beginning to look a little less fantastic. Alan Dershowitz asks: what if on September 11 law enforcement officials had "arrested terrorists boarding one of the planes and learned that other planes, then airborne, were heading towards unknown occupied buildings"? Would they not have been justified in torturing the terrorists in their custody—just enough to get the information that would allow the target buildings to be evacuated?[10] How could anyone object to the use of torture if it were dedicated specifically to saving thousands of lives in a case like this?

The answer comes from Henry Shue: "I can see no way to deny the permissibility of torture in a case *just like this.*"[11] But few cases are *just like this:* few have the certainty of Dershowitz's law school classroom formulation or the clean precision of the philosopher's hypothetical. Think of the background conditions that need to be assumed:

> The torture will not be conducted in the basement of a small-town jail in the provinces by local thugs popping pills; the prime minister and chief justice are being informed; and a priest and doctor are present. The victim will not be raped or forced to eat excrement and will not collapse with a heart attack or become deranged before talking; while avoiding irreparable damage, the antiseptic pain will carefully be increased only up to the point at which the necessary information is divulged, and the doctor will then immediately administer an antibiotic and a tranquillizer. . . . Most important, such incidents do not continue to happen. There are not so many people with grievances against this government that torture is becoming necessary more often, and in the smaller cities, and for slightly lesser threats, and with a little less care, and so on.[12]

There is, as Shue notes, "considerable evidence of all torture's metastatic tendency."[13] In the last hundred years or so, it has shown itself not to be the sort of thing that can be kept under rational control. On the contrary—from a point near the beginning of the twentieth century in which it was thought it might disappear altogether, torture has returned and now flourishes on a colossal scale. What Judith Shklar calls the liberalism of fear is a response to this actuality—to the prospect that if we allow ourselves to be seduced into "adjusting the balance" in this regard, there is no telling what we will let ourselves in for.[14]

As I said, so long as there is no serious proposal to use it, the argument about torture is important mainly as an illustration of a more general misgiving, about the dangers of metastasis in regard to other powers which had previously been withheld from government now being fearfully assigned to it. One troubling example is the power of detention without trial. It seems now that the United States has a policy of detaining even its own nationals indefinitely as "enemy combatants," not in order to charge them with anything but to find out what they know.[15] It is not hard to think of scenarios where detention without trial is justified. But it is hard to think of methods of ensuring that this power is not abused, that it does not get out of hand, and that detention does not turn into "disappearance." Once again, one's confidence would be greater if we were dealing with governments that had resolutely opposed all such abuses by their allies and client-states in the past. But we know, on the contrary, that in the recent past the United States, for example, has been complicit in abuses of the detention power in Latin America and elsewhere. There is a sort of magical thinking that we are supposed to forget all about such abuses when we evaluate what is being presently proposed from a civil liberties perspective: it is as though we are supposed to think that now, for the first time, remarkably, we have a government that *can* be trusted to tell the truth about its intentions. (Another, sadder way of putting this is to say that there are costs to the sort of mendacity that in the past U.S. government officials have routinely indulged in: such mendacity leaves no basis for trust when, later, trust may be desperately needed.)

Against all this, some will say that the threat from a more powerful state as a result of a reduction in civil liberties is nothing but an hysterical hypothesis, whereas the threat from terrorism is *real*. In response we can say two things. First, no one but a fool thinks that the threat from the state is zero. Of course opinions about the magnitude of that threat may vary. But there is no reason to suppose that the introduction of a heightened threat from terrorism makes it *less* likely than it was (say on September 10) that the state will act oppressively. So unless we assume that the motivation to do so has somehow magically evaporated, we must assume that the net threat from the state goes up as the power accorded to the state increases. Secondly, even though the terrorist threat is very real, the hypothesis that an increase in governmental power will diminish it is in many ways no less fanciful than the hypothesis that the government will abuse the extra power given to it. We must not confuse the means with the end. An enhanced ability to combat terrorism is not the same as an actual diminution in terrorist threat. . . .

[VI.]

This article does not embrace any particular policy or proposal. It is intended mainly as a call for care and caution. We should be cautious about giving up our civil liberties. We should be even more careful about giving up our commitment to the civil liberties of a minority, so that we can enjoy *our* liberties in greater security. We should be worried about the enhanced power of the state (and we should reject as magical thinking the idea that the risk from that power goes down as the risk from terrorism goes up). And finally, if we do remain receptive to the need to compromise civil liberty, we must insist that those who talk the balancing-talk step up to the plate with some actual predictions about effectiveness. We should not give up our liberties, or anyone else's liberties, for the sake of purely symbolic gains in the war against terrorism.

NOTES

1 Nicholas Kristoff, "Liberal reality check: we must look anew at freedom vs. security," *Pittsburgh Post-Gazette* June 3, 2002, p. A9.
2 See Dworkin, "The threat to patriotism." See also Dworkin's more general discussion of the proposition that "[i]t is never true, at any time, that all members of a society are equally likely to be accused of any particular crime," in his essay "Principle, policy, procedure," in *A Matter of Principle* (Cambridge, Mass.: Harvard University Press, 1985), p. 87.
3 Dworkin, "Principle, policy, procedure," p. 73.
4 Dworkin, "The threat to patriotism."
5 As quoted in Pam Belluck, "Hue and murmur over curbed rights," *New York Times,* Nov. 17, 2001, at B8.
6 James Fitzjames Stephen, *A History of the Criminal Law of England*, Vol. I, p. 438, quoted by Richard H. Menard, "Ten reasonable men," *American Criminal Law Review,* 38 (2001), 179 at p. 199.
7 See Judith Shklar, "The liberalism of fear," *Liberalism and the Moral Life,* ed. Nancy L. Rosenblum (Cambridge, Mass.: Harvard University Press, 1989), esp. pp. 26 ff.
8 Ibid., p. 30.
9 John Locke, *Two Treatises of Government* ed. Peter Laslett (Cambridge: Cambridge University Press, 1988), II, section 93.

10 Alan Dershowitz, *Shouting Fire: Civil Liberties in a Turbulent Age* (New York: Little, Brown, 2002), p. 477.
11 Henry Shue, "Torture," *Philosophy and Public Affairs,* 7 (1978), 124, at p. 141.
12 Ibid., p. 142.
13 Ibid., p. 143.
14 The formulations in this paragraph are adapted from Shklar; "Liberalism of fear," p. 27.
15 I infer this from the recent case of Jose Padilla, held for having talked about the possibility of detonating a radiological bomb in Washington D.C. See Benjamin Weiser with Dana Canedy, "Traces of terror: the bomb plot," *New York Times,* June 12, 2002, p. A24.

QUESTIONS

1 If laws passed in the interest of security do, in effect, trade off the liberties of a few to safeguard the security of the majority, are such laws morally justifiable? Why or why not?
2 Which civil liberties, if any, should we be willing to give up in the interests of security? What risks would we run if those liberties were curtailed?

SUGGESTED ADDITIONAL READINGS FOR CHAPTER 7

COADY, C. A. J.: "Terrorism and Innocence." *The Journal of Ethics,* vol. 8, March 2004, pp. 37–58. Beginning with a discussion of different definitions of terrorism, Coady advances his own tactical definition. He then focuses on explicating the concept of innocents in definitions of terrorism, unpacking it in terms of noncombatants.
CORLETT, J. ANGELO: *Terrorism: A Philosophical Analysis.* Dordrecht: Kluwer Academic Publishers, 2003. Corlett's analysis covers terrorism and related concepts such as the obligation to obey the law, pacifism, civil disobedience, nonviolent direct action, political violence, revolution, and assassination.
CROTTY, WILLIAM, ed.: *The Politics of Terror: The U.S. Response to 9/11.* Boston: Northeastern University Press, 2003. The primary question addressed in this anthology is, Following 9/11, how can the U.S. strike a balance between national security and civil liberties? The book is divided into four major sections: moral dilemmas, the public response, civil liberties, and institutions and public policy.
DARMER, KATHERINE B., ROBERT M. BAIRD, and STUART E. ROSENBAUM, eds.: *Civil Liberties vs. National Security in a Post-9/11 World.* Amherst, N.Y.: Prometheus Books, 2004. This informative book is divided into six sections: the history of civil liberty issues in wartime, domestic surveillance and the U.S.A. Patriot Act, racial profiling, the use of torture in confessions, the designation of "enemy combatants," plus some recent developments such as the Abu Ghraib prison scandal.
HELD, VIRGINIA: "Terrorism and War." *The Journal of Ethics,* vol. 8, March 2004, pp. 59–75. Held compares terrorism to small wars and argues that just as some wars are less unjustifiable than others, so, too with terrorism. She maintains that we need to make comparable judgments, morally evaluating not simply the actions of terrorists who are seeking change but also the violent actions adopted by governments in order to prevent the changes.
KATCHADOURIAN, HAIG: *Terrorism and Morality.* New York: Peter Lang, 1998. After defining terrorism, Katchadourian argues that all forms of terrorism, even those designed to bring about a moral good, are always wrong because they deprive those who are terrorized of their basic humanity.

STERBA, JAMES P.: *Terrorism and International Justice,* New York: Oxford University Press, 2003. Although some of the articles in this anthology are written by members of other professions, the majority of the writers are philosophers. The articles explore answers to questions such as the following: Is terrorism always wrong, or are there morally justified acts of terrorism? Is war a morally defensible response to the terrorism of 9/11? Do failures of international justice motivate acts of terrorism?

STONE, GEOFFREY R.: *Perilous Times: Free Speech in Wartime.* New York: Norton, 2004. In his exploration of civil liberties in wartime, Stone provides an in-depth constitutional analysis as well as an account of the historical events that gave rise to attempts to curtail free speech. This excellent and informative book begins with the Sedition Act of 1798 and ends with the war on terrorism.

WALZER, MICHAEL: *Just and Unjust Wars: A Moral Argument with Historical Illustrations.* New York: Basic Books, 1977. After developing and defending just war theory, Walzer applies it to various wars including World War II and the war in Vietnam.

Unit Five

Animals Notes

The shared vocabulary for the last two chapters appears below:

Anthropocentric Position: Only humans have inherent worth and rights.

Sentientist Position: All sentient life has inherent worth. All sentient life has inherent rights, appropriate to its kind. (Sentient: capacity for pleasure and pain)

Biocentric Position: All life has inherent worth, whether sentient or not. This includes biotic communities. Also known as a "life-centered" position

Biotic Community: Any ecosystem that has a balanced flora and fauna which permits it to be self-sufficient.

Flora: plant life

Fauna: animal life

***Prima facie* Obligations**: Prima (first) facie (face). Those obligations that are primary obligations.

Human: biological, genetic-based definition of species.

Personhood: those qualities considered sufficient for assuming that there is a mind capable of making independent choices. Personhood is the basis for an assumption of inherent rights. Characteristics may include such things as ability to communicate, to make analytical judgments, to have the capacity for pleasure and pain (both physical and mental), to distinguish self as well as self as part of a group, and to distinguish degrees of difference in others.

Peter Singer: Singer writes about speciesism in his book, *Animal Liberation*. Speciesism is like racism or sexism. It implies a bias in favor of one's own speciesism. Singer's argument defines rights according to sentience, similar to Rollin (next chapter on "Environment"). However, Singer goes much further than Rollin as far as what sort of rights animals might have. One of the reasons Singer is such a controversial figure is that he believes that the degree of interest or rights of a sentient creature depends on the degree to which that "creature" has an investment in the world—the more awareness of a future, family, and life, the stronger the rights of that individual. In other words, if we have to choose whether to use a five year old dog in a research experiment or a newborn human, Singer would say that the dog has a stronger right not to be used than the infant. He explains this by saying animals should have "equal consideration." When he describes "equal consideration" for animals and humans, he means we should only use animals in medical experiments if we are equally willing to use a brain-damaged or newborn human for the same experiment. He does not mean that animals have equal rights as humans.

When he talks about "liberation" for animals, he means that there are rights appropriate to particular animals. For example, a gazelle is an animal that is built to run and jump. To place it in a small cage would be a violation of it needs. On the other hand, placing it in a large enclosure where it can pursue the needs of that species to achieve pleasure/happiness would be acceptable. Singer believes that to be ethical, we need to be consistent with our theories. If we base our own human rights on a theory of sentience (because we can feel pain we have a right to avoid it and because we have the capacity for happiness we have a right to the conditions that allow us to pursue it), and other life forms share that same capacity, then they must also be accorded the same privilege of avoidance and pursuit.

Tom Reagan: Reagan believes animals have inherent value. If you look at the definition of "human" in the vocabulary above, you will see that the definition is based on biology. It is "personhood" that gives us our political rights, but just being human also gives us "inherent" rights. In other words, just being human accords us the right to respect and the right not to be harmed (remember the Tuskegee case?). It does not matter if we are mentally competent, rich, famous, powerful or not. We still must be treated with respect and dignity. Even when we die, our bodies must be treated with respect and dignity. This is because we have inherent value. We must never be treated as a means to an end (remember Kant?). We have value apart from any usefulness we may have to another.

Reagan believes animals have this same inherent value. Just as we should not take advantage of someone's helplessness to use that person in an experiment, we should not use an animal in an experiment because it, too, has inherent value.

Reagan argues for the total abolition of the use of animals in science, commercial animal agriculture, and commercial/sport hunting and trapping. He advocates this ban because he points out the right to avoid suffering is not enough protection for animals. Avoiding suffering on the basis that an animal is sentient would still allow an animal to be killed—so long as it is done humanely without pain or suffering.

R.G. Frey: Frey argues that both Singer and Reagan miss the point. Their arguments are about moral theory: rights, killing, and suffering. Instead of arguing about whether or not we are violating their moral rights or making them suffer, Frey suggests the default position should be that we do not eat animals—period. To Frey, it is odd to justify killing animals as long as we don't make them suffer. Think about this argument in other contexts: would it be alright to kill a human as long as we didn't make them suffer?

Frey believes that the decision not to kill animals involves a whole way of life—a decision on how we will live in the world. It means living a life where we see ourselves as a part of the other living things in the world, rather than separate and apart from them. It is an attempt "to live in harmony" with the world.

Carl Cohen: Cohen argues for the use of animals in medical research because animals do not have rights. According to Cohen, to have rights, one must be a "moral agent." For Cohen, a "moral agent" is someone who can claim rights (in a court of law). Animals cannot claim rights. Therefore, they have none.

Cohen addresses the three major recommendations for the use of animals in research. The recommendations most often heard are that we should (1) reduce the number of animals used in research, (2) replace (substitute) animals whenever possible with alternatives, and (3) be more consistent (share knowledge rather than having the experiments duplicated at many laboratories).

Cohen totally disagrees with the three usual recommendations above. He believes the more animals should be used in research, that there is no substitute for the use of animals, and that the more separate experiments are going on, the more likely we will come up with solutions.

Mary Ann Warren: Warren supports partial animal rights. Warren uses the example of liberty to illustrate her position. She points out that an animal placed in a habitat with plenty of room and with good food and the company of other animals, could live a contented life. A human placed in a similar situation (plenty of room and good conditions, but confined to that area), might still feel unhappy because of the lack of liberty to choose. Warren's conclusion is that, while both humans and animals have similar rights, they may not have them to the same degree. She also discusses the problem of communication. Warren does not believe that it matters whether animals have the autonomy to be moral agents or not. She points out that animals may suffer even worse than humans because they can't distract themselves from painful procedures the way humans can and they don't understand what is happening.

CHAPTER 8

Animals

Human beings are responsible for a great deal of animal suffering. We use animals in experiments, raise and slaughter animals for food, and hunt and kill animals, sometimes merely for sport. Our treatment of animals raises numerous moral questions, some of which are discussed in this chapter.

SPECIESISM AND THE MORAL STATUS OF ANIMALS

In a now well-known book, *Animal Liberation,* Peter Singer, a utilitarian, forcefully calls attention to the suffering that human beings routinely inflict on nonhuman animals. (Utilitarianism holds that an action or practice is morally correct only if it is likely to produce the greatest balance of good over evil, everyone considered.) In order to satisfy human desires for meat, we raise animals in such a way that their short lives are dominated by pain and suffering. In order to obtain information, purportedly for the benefit of humans, we devise experimental projects that involve the infliction of intense pain on animals. Our experimentation on animals and our meat-eating habits are paradigm examples, for Singer, of morally unacceptable practices in regard to animals. Because Singer finds human beings so willing to subordinate important animal interests (e.g., an interest in avoiding suffering) to much less important human interests, he charges the human community with *speciesism.* In an excerpt from *Animal Liberation* reprinted in this chapter, Singer defines speciesism as a "prejudice or attitude of bias toward the interests of members of one's own species and against those of members of other species." Singer uses the term *speciesism* in order to emphasize the similarities between sexist and racist practices, on the one hand, and our treatment of animals, on the other. In Singer's view, it is just as wrong to discriminate against animals because of their species as it is to discriminate against women because of their sex and blacks because of their race.

Singer's arguments, in effect, attribute moral status to animals. An entity has moral status if it is due moral consideration in its own right and not simply because of its relations to other beings. Some philosophers have argued that animals have no moral status. In their view, any obligations we have regarding animals are based on the interests or rights of human beings. If we have an obligation not to mistreat dogs, for example, it may be because the mistreatment of dogs causes suffering to human beings, many of whom sympathetically identify with the suffering of animals. Singer, in contrast, appeals directly to animal interests in condemning much of our current use of animals. He holds, in effect, that sentience is the relevant criterion in determining whether an entity has moral status. Sentience can be described as the capacity to have conscious experiences, such as pleasure and pain. *All* sentient beings, Singer maintains, have interests, including an interest in avoiding pain and suffering. A fundamental principle of morality—*the principle of equal consideration of interests*—requires us to give equal consideration to the interests of all beings affected by our decisions. Animals, like human beings, are sentient beings with an interest in avoiding pain and suffering. Hence, we violate a fundamental principle of morality when we make decisions about the use of animals in experiments if we consider only human interests and fail to give equal consideration to the interests that animals have in avoiding suffering.

Whereas Singer focuses on animal *interests* as he advances a utilitarian line of reasoning, Tom Regan in this chapter focuses on animal *rights* as he advances his attack on speciesism. On Regan's analysis, animals, like humans, are bearers of rights because animals, like humans, have inherent value. To have inherent value, Regan maintains, an entity must be a conscious creature whose welfare is valuable or important to it, so that its having value is not dependent on its usefulness to others. Since animals are creatures of this sort, they have rights, which must be respected. Regan rejects the view that animals, while having some inherent value, have less inherent value than human beings. In his view, all entities that have inherent value have it equally and have an equal right to be treated with respect. Any attempt to specify a difference (e.g., rationality) between human beings and animals, which would purport to justify the attribution of lesser inherent value to the latter, would require us to attribute a lesser degree of inherent value to some "nonparadigm" human beings (e.g., the severely brain-damaged) if we were to be consistent in our moral reasoning. The same problem is faced, Regan maintains, by those who attempt to specify a criterion that rights holders must possess (e.g., the capacity for autonomy) that would exclude animals from the class of entities having rights.

Regan's claim that animals have rights is attacked by Carl Cohen in this chapter. Cohen's position rests on his conception of rights as claims or potential claims within a community of moral agents. Moral agency presupposes a capacity for free moral judgment and for exercising and responding to moral claims. To be a moral agent, one must have a capacity to understand the rules of duty that govern all members of the human community and to act in accordance with these rules. Only human beings have the relevant capacities. Hence, for Cohen, only human beings have moral rights. Cohen rejects Regan's contention that any criterion that might be used to exclude all animals from the class of entities having rights would also require us to exclude nonparadigm humans. In Cohen's view, although animals cannot have rights because they lack the relevant capacities, nonparadigm humans who also lack the relevant capacities (e.g., the severely mentally retarded) do have rights. In his view, such nonparadigmatic humans are still the bearers of rights because they belong to a species whose members are normally capable of moral agency. Cohen does not deny that animals have some sort of moral status. He grants that we do have some obligations to animals, including an obligation not to cause them needless suffering. In contrast to Singer, however, Cohen maintains that it is wrong to give animal and human interests equal consideration. Whatever moral status animals have because of their sentience, it is significantly less than that of human beings.

The question of possible differences in the moral status of human beings and animals is addressed by Mary Anne Warren in this chapter's final reading. A distinction between full moral status and partial moral status is useful here. Entities have full moral status if they have the same rights as paradigmatic (i.e., normal adult) human beings. They have partial moral status if their rights are lesser in some sense than those of paradigmatic humans. In comparing and contrasting human and animal rights, Warren effectively ascribes partial moral status to animals. According to her analysis, animal and human rights differ in respect to both their content and their strength (i.e., in the strength of the reasons required to override them). Warren holds that sentience is the basis for at least some rights. Thus, she rejects Cohen's conception of rights. Warren argues, however, that moral agency (moral autonomy), as well as other differences between humans and animals, may be a basis for attributing stronger rights to human beings than to animals. In respect to nonparadigmatic humans, Warren advances reasons to support her claim that we can consistently grant them the same rights as those of paradigmatic humans while attributing only lesser rights to animals.

VEGETARIANISM

Is the human interest in eating meat sufficiently important to justify our practice of raising and slaughtering animals? Intertwined with this question is the issue of a vegetarian diet. Advocates of vegetarianism offer diverse arguments to support their position. Some advocate a vegetarian diet simply because they believe it to be superior in terms of health benefits. If a vegetarian diet does offer special health advantages (a controversial claim), then each individual, as a matter of personal prudence, would be well advised to adopt it. Apart from this *prudential argument,* many vegetarians advance *moral arguments* in defense of their diet. One common moral argument, closely related to the considerations developed in Chapter 2, is based on the fact that hunger, malnutrition, and starvation seriously threaten many people in our world. It is morally indefensible, the argument goes, to waste desperately needed protein by feeding our grain to animals, which we then eat. Eight pounds of protein in the form of grain are necessary, on the average, to produce one pound of protein in the form of meat. Since this process is so inefficient, we are morally obliged to adopt a vegetarian diet so that our protein resources in the form of grain can be shared with those who desperately need help. Though this particular moral argument is not without force, it would not seem to establish a need for a completely vegetarian diet. It may well be that world hunger could effectively be alleviated if people in affluent countries were simply to consume *less meat.*

Probably the most important moral arguments advanced in defense of a vegetarian diet are those that take account of the impact of meat production on the animals themselves. Two lines of argument in this category can be distinguished: (1) Although it is not necessarily wrong to kill animals for food (assuming the killing is relatively painless), it is morally indefensible to subject them to the cruelty of "factory farming." Since the meat available in our society is produced in just this way, we are morally obliged not to eat it. R. G. Frey, in a reading in this chapter, labels this *the argument from pain and suffering*. (2) It is morally wrong to kill animals for food, however painless the killing; animals, like human beings, have a right to life. Regan's approach in this chapter exemplifies this second line of reasoning, which Frey labels *the argument from moral rights*. A different approach to vegetarianism, also discussed by Frey, is related to material in Chapter 9. According to this approach, what is required is a fundamental shift in our attitudes toward animals and the rest of the natural world, such that any eating of animal flesh is morally unacceptable, regardless of how animals are raised or killed.

ANIMAL EXPERIMENTATION

The use of animals in scientific experimentation intended to benefit human beings raises its own set of troubling questions. Is there any need to use animals in experimentation intended to benefit human beings? If there is a genuine need, can this provide a moral justification for the resulting pain, or even death, of animals? It is possible to distinguish four major lines of reasoning on the morality of animal experimentation: (1) Animal experimentation is never justified because using animals in this way is inconsistent with treating them with the respect due to entities having inherent worth. Entities of this sort cannot be used merely as things for others' benefit. Just as the use of human beings in experiments without their informed consent violates their right to be treated with the respect due those with inherent value, so, too, does the use of animals in experiments conducted in order to benefit humans. This first line of reasoning is in keeping with Regan's position. (2) Animal experimentation is justified only in those cases where we would be willing to conduct the same experiments on brain-damaged human subjects. This is Singer's claim. The underlying reasoning here can be expressed as follows: There may be relevant differences between "normal, adult" humans and animals that would justify our using the latter but not the former in some experiments—those that might be essential to save human lives or prevent great suffering. However, animals and certain nonparadigm humans do not differ in relevant respects. Hence, we are justified in using the former in experiments only where we are justified in using the latter. (3) Given sufficiently important human interests, the presumption against using animals as experimental subjects may be overridden. Although animals, because of their sentience, have rights, which must be taken into account, serious human interests can override them. The rights of nonparadigm humans cannot be overridden on the same grounds, however, since their rights are grounded not only in sentience but in other considerations. Warren's article exemplifies this third line of argument. (4) Animal experimentation for the benefit of humans is justifiable simply by appeal to human rights and interests. However, although animals do not have rights, not every experiment using animals is morally acceptable. If the same results could be achieved by using alternative methods (e.g., computer simulation), for example, then it would be morally wrong to conduct an experiment that inflicts needless suffering on animals. Cohen accepts this fourth position. He states, however, that it would be a mistake to think that alternative techniques could shortly replace most of the present experimentation using live animals as subjects.

Jane S. Zembaty

All Animals Are Equal

Peter Singer

Singer rejects speciesism, which he defines as a prejudice or an attitude of bias in favor of the interests of members of one's own species and against those of members of other species. In his view, speciesism is analogous to racism and sexism. Just as we have a moral obligation to give equal consideration to the interests of all human beings, regardless of sex or skin color, so, too, we have a moral obligation to give equal consideration to the interests of animals. Insofar as animals, like humans, have the capacity to suffer, they have an interest in not suffering. Not to take that interest into account is speciesist and immoral. Singer attacks our current practice of using animals in experiments that frequently inflict tremendous suffering, often for very trivial reasons. As a guiding principle for determining when an experiment using animals might be morally justifiable, Singer suggests that an experiment is justifiable only if it is so important that the use of brain-damaged humans would also be justifiable.

"Animal Liberation" may sound more like a parody of other liberation movements than a serious objective. The idea of "The Rights of Animals" actually was once used to parody the case for women's rights. When Mary Wollstonecraft, a forerunner of today's feminists, published her *Vindication of the Rights of Woman* in 1792, her views were widely regarded as absurd, and before long an anonymous publication appeared entitled *A Vindication of the Rights of Brutes*. The author of this satirical work (now known to have been Thomas Taylor, a distinguished Cambridge philosopher) tried to refute Mary Wollstonecraft's arguments by showing that they could be carried one stage further. If the argument for equality was sound when applied to women, why should it not be applied to dogs, cats, and horses? The reasoning seemed to hold for these "brutes" too; yet to hold that brutes had rights was manifestly absurd. Therefore the reasoning by which this conclusion had been reached must be unsound, and if unsound when applied to brutes, it must also be unsound when applied to women, since the very same arguments had been used in each case.

Reprinted with permission of the author from *Animal Liberation*, New York Review, second edition (1990), pp. 1–9, 36–37, 40, 81–83, 85–86.

In order to explain the basis of the case for the equality of animals, it will be helpful to start with an examination of the case for the equality of women. Let us assume that we wish to defend the case for women's rights against the attack by Thomas Taylor. How should we reply?

One way in which we might reply is by saying that the case for equality between men and women cannot validly be extended to nonhuman animals. Women have a right to vote, for instance, because they are just as capable of making rational decisions about the future as men are; dogs, on the other hand, are incapable of understanding the significance of voting, so they cannot have the right to vote. There are many other obvious ways in which men and women resemble each other closely, while humans and animals differ greatly. So, it might be said, men and women are similar beings and should have similar rights, while humans and nonhumans are different and should not have equal rights.

The reasoning behind this reply to Taylor's analogy is correct up to a point, but it does not go far enough. There are obviously important differences between humans and other animals, and these differences must give rise to some differences in the rights that each have. Recognizing this evident fact, however, is no barrier to the case for extending the basic principle of equality to nonhuman animals. The differences that exist between men and women are equally undeniable, and the supporters of Women's Liberation are aware that these differences may give rise to different rights. Many feminists hold that women have the right to an abortion on request. It does not follow that since these same feminists are campaigning for equality between men and women they must support the right of men to have abortions too. Since a man cannot have an abortion, it is meaningless to talk of his right to have one. Since dogs can't vote, it is meaningless to talk of their right to vote. There is no reason why either Women's Liberation or Animal Liberation should get involved in such nonsense. The extension of the basic principle of equality from one group to another does not imply that we must treat both groups in exactly the same way, or grant exactly the same rights to both groups. Whether we should do so will depend on the nature of the members of the two groups. The basic principle of equality does not require equal or identical *treatment;* it requires equal consideration. Equal consideration for different beings may lead to different treatment and different rights.

So there is a different way of replying to Taylor's attempt to parody the case for women's rights, a way that does not deny the obvious differences between human beings and nonhumans but goes more deeply into the question of equality and concludes by finding nothing absurd in the idea that the basic principle of equality applies to so-called brutes. At this point such a conclusion may appear odd; but if we examine more deeply the basis on which our opposition to discrimination on grounds of race or sex ultimately rests, we will see that we would be on shaky ground if we were to demand equality for blacks, women, and other groups of oppressed humans while denying equal consideration to nonhumans. To make this clear we need to see, first, exactly why racism and sexism are wrong. When we say that all human beings, whatever their race, creed, or sex, are equal, what is it that we are asserting? Those who wish to defend hierarchical, inegalitarian societies have often pointed out that by whatever test we choose it simply is not true that all

humans are equal. Like it or not we must face the fact that humans come in different shapes and sizes; they come with different moral capacities, different intellectual
abilities, different amounts of benevolent feeling and sensitivity to the needs of others, different abilities to communicate effectively, and different capacities to experience pleasure and pain. In short, if the demand for equality were based on the actual
equality of all human beings, we would have to stop demanding equality.

Still, one might cling to the view that the demand for equality among human
beings is based on the actual equality of the different races and sexes. Although, it
may be said, humans differ as individuals, there are no differences between the races
and sexes as such. From the mere fact that a person is black or a woman we cannot
infer anything about that person's intellectual or moral capacities. This, it may be
said, is why racism and sexism are wrong. The white racist claims that whites are
superior to blacks, but this is false; although there are differences among individuals, some blacks are superior to some whites in all of the capacities and abilities that
could conceivably be relevant. The opponent of sexism would say the same: a person's sex is no guide to his or her abilities, and this is why it is unjustifiable to discriminate on the basis of sex.

The existence of individual variations that cut across the lines of race or sex, however, provides us with no defense at all against a more sophisticated opponent of
equality, one who proposes that, say, the interests of all those with IQ scores below
100 be given less consideration than the interests of those with ratings over 100.
Perhaps those scoring below the mark would, in this society, be made the slaves of
those scoring higher. Would a hierarchical society of this sort really be so much better than one based on race or sex? I think not. But if we tie the moral principle of
equality to the factual equality of the different races or sexes, taken as a whole, our
opposition to racism and sexism does not provide us with any basis for objecting to
this kind of inegalitarianism.

There is a second important reason why we ought not to base our opposition to
racism and sexism on any kind of factual equality, even the limited kind that asserts
that variations in capacities and abilities are spread evenly among the different
races and between the sexes: we can have no absolute guarantee that these capacities and abilities really are distributed evenly, without regard to race or sex, among
human beings. So far as actual abilities are concerned there do seem to be certain
measurable differences both among races and between sexes. These differences do
not, of course, appear in every case, but only when averages are taken. More important still, we do not yet know how many of these differences are really due to the
different genetic endowments of the different races and sexes, and how many are
due to poor schools, poor housing, and other factors that are the result of past and
continuing discrimination. Perhaps all of the important differences will eventually
prove to be environmental rather than genetic. Anyone opposed to racism and sexism will certainly hope that this will be so, for it will make the task of ending discrimination a lot easier; nevertheless, it would be dangerous to rest the case against
racism and sexism on the belief that all significant differences are environmental in
origin. The opponent of, say, racism who takes this line will be unable to avoid
conceding that if differences in ability did after all prove to have some genetic connection with race, racism would in some way be defensible.

Fortunately there is no need to pin the case for equality to one particular outcome of a scientific investigation. The appropriate response to those who claim to have found evidence of genetically based differences in ability among the races or between the sexes is not to stick to the belief that the genetic explanation must be wrong, whatever evidence to the contrary may turn up; instead we should make it quite clear that the claim to equality does not depend on intelligence, moral capacity, physical strength, or similar matters of fact. Equality is a moral idea, not an assertion of fact. There is no logically compelling reason for assuming that a factual difference in ability between two people justifies any difference in the amount of consideration we give to their needs and interests. *The principle of the equality of human beings is not a description of an alleged actual equality among humans: it is a prescription of how we should treat human beings.*

Jeremy Bentham, the founder of the reforming utilitarian school of moral philosophy, incorporated the essential basis of moral equality into his system of ethics by means of the formula: "Each to count for one and none for more than one." In other words, the interests of every being affected by an action are to be taken into account and given the same weight as the like interests of any other being. A later utilitarian, Henry Sidgwick, put the point in this way: "The good of any one individual is of no more importance, from the point of view (if I may say so) of the Universe, than the good of any other." More recently the leading figures in contemporary moral philosophy have shown a great deal of agreement in specifying as a fundamental presupposition of their moral theories some similar requirement that works to give everyone's interests equal consideration—although these writers generally cannot agree on how this requirement is best formulated.[1]

It is an implication of this principle of equality that our concern for others and our readiness to consider their interests ought not to depend on what they are like or on what abilities they may possess. Precisely what our concern or consideration requires us to do may vary according to the characteristics of those affected by what we do: concern for the well-being of children growing up in America would require that we teach them to read; concern for the well-being of pigs may require no more than that we leave them with other pigs in a place where there is adequate food and room to run freely. But the basic element—the taking into account of the interests of the being, whatever those interests may be—must, according to the principle of equality, be extended to all beings, black or white, masculine or feminine, human or nonhuman.

Thomas Jefferson, who was responsible for writing the principle of the equality of men into the American Declaration of Independence, saw this point. It led him to oppose slavery even though he was unable to free himself fully from his slaveholding background. He wrote in a letter to the author of a book that emphasized the notable intellectual achievements of Negroes in order to refute the then common view that they had limited intellectual capacities:

> Be assured that no person living wishes more sincerely than I do, to see a complete refutation of the doubts I myself have entertained and expressed on the grade of understanding allotted to them by nature, and to find that they are on a par with ourselves . . . but whatever be their degree of talent it is no measure of their rights. Because Sir Isaac Newton was superior to others in understanding, he was not therefore lord of the property or persons of others.[2]

Similarly, when in the 1850s the call for women's rights was raised in the United States, a remarkable black feminist named Sojourner Truth made the same point in more robust terms at a feminist convention:

> They talk about this thing in the head; what do they call it? ["Intellect," whispered someone nearby.] That's it. What's that got to do with women's rights or Negroes' rights? If my cup won't hold but a pint and yours holds a quart, wouldn't you be mean not to let me have my little half-measure full?[3]

It is on this basis that the case against racism and the case against sexism must both ultimately rest; and it is in accordance with this principle that the attitude that we may call "speciesism," by analogy with racism, must also be condemned. Speciesism—the word is not an attractive one, but I can think of no better term—is a prejudice or attitude of bias in favor of the interests of members of one's own species and against those of members of other species. It should be obvious that the fundamental objections to racism and sexism made by Thomas Jefferson and Sojourner Truth apply equally to speciesism. If possessing a higher degree of intelligence does not entitle one human to use another for his or her own ends, how can it entitle humans to exploit nonhumans for the same purpose?[4]

Many philosophers and other writers have proposed the principle of equal consideration of interests, in some form or other, as a basic moral principle; but not many of them have recognized that this principle applies to members of other species as well as to our own. Jeremy Bentham was one of the few who did realize this. In a forward-looking passage written at a time when black slaves had been freed by the French but in the British dominions were still being treated in the way we now treat animals, Bentham wrote:

> The day *may* come when the rest of the animal creation may acquire those rights which never could have been withholden from them but by the hand of tyranny. The French have already discovered that the blackness of the skin is no reason why a human being should be abandoned without redress to the caprice of a tormentor. It may one day come to be recognized that the number of the legs, the villosity of the skin, or the termination of the *os sacrum* are reasons equally insufficient for abandoning a sensitive being to the same fate. What else is it that should trace the insuperable line? Is it the faculty of reason, or perhaps the faculty of discourse? But a full-grown horse or dog is beyond comparison a more rational, as well as a more conversable animal, than an infant of a day or a week or even a month, old. But suppose they were otherwise, what would it avail? The question is not, Can they *reason*? nor Can they *talk*? but, Can they *suffer*?[5]

In this passage Bentham points to the capacity for suffering as the vital characteristic that gives a being the right to equal consideration. The capacity for suffering—or more strictly, for suffering and/or enjoyment or happiness—is not just another characteristic like the capacity for language or higher mathematics. Bentham is not saying that those who try to mark "the insuperable line" that determines whether the interests of a being should be considered happen to have chosen the wrong characteristic. By saying that we must consider the interests of all beings with the capacity for suffering or enjoyment Bentham does not arbitrarily exclude from consideration any interests at all—as those who draw the line with reference to the possession of reason or language do. The capacity for suffering and enjoyment is *a prerequisite for having interests at all,* a condition that must be satisfied before we can speak of interests in a meaningful way. It would be nonsense to say that it was not in the interests of a stone to be kicked along the road by a schoolboy. A stone does not have interests because it cannot suffer. Nothing that we can do to it could possibly make any difference to its welfare. The capacity for suffering and enjoyment is, however, not only necessary, but also sufficient for us to say that a being has interests—at an absolute minimum, an interest in not suffering. A mouse, for example, does have an interest in not being kicked along the road, because it will suffer if it is.

Although Bentham speaks of "rights" in the passage I have quoted, the argument is really about equality rather than about rights. Indeed, in a different passage, Bentham famously described "natural rights" as "nonsense" and "natural and imprescriptible rights" as "nonsense upon stilts." He talked of moral rights as a shorthand way of referring to protections that people and animals morally ought to have; but the real weight of the moral argument does not rest on the assertion of the existence of the right, for this in turn has to be justified on the basis of the possibilities for suffering and happiness. In this way we can argue for equality for animals without getting embroiled in philosophical controversies about the ultimate nature of rights.

In misguided attempts to refute the arguments of this book, some philosophers have gone to much trouble developing arguments to show that animals do not have rights.[6] They have claimed that to have rights a being must be autonomous, or must be a member of a community, or must have the ability to respect the rights of others, or must possess a sense of justice. These claims are irrelevant to the case for Animal Liberation. The language of rights is a convenient political shorthand. It is even more valuable in the era of thirty-second TV news clips than it was in Bentham's day; but in the argument for a radical change in our attitude to animals, it is in no way necessary.

If a being suffers there can be no moral justification for refusing to take that suffering into consideration. No matter what the nature of the being, the principle of equality requires that its suffering be counted equally with the like suffering—insofar as rough comparisons can be made—of any other being. If a being is not capable of suffering, or of experiencing enjoyment or happiness, there is nothing to be taken into account. So the limit of sentience (using the term as a convenient if not strictly accurate shorthand for the capacity to suffer and/or experience enjoyment) is the only defensible boundary of concern for the interests of others. To mark this boundary by some other characteristic like intelligence or rationality would be to mark it in an arbitrary manner. Why not choose some other characteristic, like skin color?

Racists violate the principle of equality by giving greater weight to the interests of members of their own race when there is a clash between their interests and the interests of those of another race. Sexists violate the principle of equality by favoring the interests of their own sex. Similarly, speciesists allow the interests of their own species to override the greater interests of members of other species. The pattern is identical in each case.

ANIMALS AND RESEARCH

Most human beings are speciesists. . . . Ordinary human beings—not a few exceptionally cruel or heartless humans, but the overwhelming majority of humans—take an active part in, acquiesce in, and allow their taxes to pay for practices that require the sacrifice of the most important interests of members of other species in order to promote the most trivial interests of our own species. . . .

The practice of experimenting on nonhuman animals as it exists today throughout the world reveals the consequences of speciesism. Many experiments inflict severe pain without the remotest prospect of significant benefits for human beings or any other animals. Such experiments are not isolated instances, but part of a major industry. In Britain, where experimenters are required to report the number of "scientific procedures" performed on animals, official government figures show that 3.5 million scientific procedures were performed on animals in 1988.[7] In the United States there are no figures of comparable accuracy. Under the Animal Welfare Act, the U.S. secretary of agriculture publishes a report listing the number of animals used by facilities registered with it, but this is incomplete in many ways. It does not include rats, mice, birds, reptiles, frogs, or domestic farm animals used for experimental purposes; it does not include animals used in secondary schools; and it does not include experiments performed by facilities that do not transport animals interstate or receive grants or contracts from the federal government.

In 1986 the U.S. Congress Office of Technology Assessment (OTA) published a report entitled "Alternatives to Animal Use in Research, Testing and Education." The OTA researchers attempted to determine the number of animals used in experimentation in the U.S. and reported that "estimates of the animals used in the United States each year range from 10 million to upwards of 100 million." They concluded that the estimates were unreliable but their best guess was "at least 17 million to 22 million."[8]

This is an extremely conservative estimate. In testimony before Congress in 1966, the Laboratory Animal Breeders Association estimated that the number of mice, rats, guinea pigs, hamsters, and rabbits used for experimental purposes in 1965 was around 60 million.[9] In 1984 Dr. Andrew Rowan of Tufts University School of Veterinary Medicine estimated that approximately 71 million animals are used each year. In 1985 Rowan revised his estimates to distinguish between the number of animals produced, acquired, and actually used. This yielded an estimate of between 25 and 35 million animals used in experiments each year.[10] (This figure omits animals who die in shipping or are killed before the experiment begins.) A stock market analysis of just one major supplier of animals to laboratories, the Charles River Breeding Laboratory, stated that this company alone produced 22 million laboratory animals annually.[11]

The 1988 report issued by the Department of Agriculture listed 140,471 dogs, 42,271 cats, 51,641 primates, 431,457 guinea pigs, 331,945 hamsters, 459,254 rabbits, and 178,249 "wild animals": a total of 1,635,288 used in experimentation.

Remember that this report does not bother to count rats and mice, and covers at most an estimated 10 percent of the total number of animals used. Of the nearly 1.6 million animals reported by the Department of Agriculture to have been used for experimental purposes, over 90,000 are reported to have experienced "unrelieved pain or distress." Again, this is probably at most 10 percent of the total number of animals suffering unrelieved pain and distress—and if experimenters are less concerned about causing unrelieved pain to rats and mice than they are to dogs, cats, and primates, it could be an even smaller proportion.

Other developed nations all use large numbers of animals. In Japan, for example, a very incomplete survey published in 1988 produced a total in excess of eight million.[12] . . .

Among the tens of millions of experiments performed, only a few can possibly be regarded as contributing to important medical research. Huge numbers of animals are used in university departments such as forestry and psychology; many more are used for commercial purposes, to test new cosmetics, shampoos, food coloring agents, and other inessential items. All this can happen only because of our prejudice against taking seriously the suffering of a being who is not a member of our own species. Typically, defenders of experiments on animals do not deny that animals suffer. They cannot deny the animals' suffering, because they need to stress the similarities between humans and other animals in order to claim that their experiments may have some relevance for human purposes. The experimenter who forces rats to choose between starvation and electric shock to see if they develop ulcers (which they do) does so because the rat has a nervous system very similar to a human being's, and presumably feels an electric shock in a similar way.

There has been opposition to experimenting on animals for a long time. This opposition has made little headway because experimenters, backed by commercial firms that profit by supplying laboratory animals and equipment, have been able to convince legislators and the public that opposition comes from uninformed fanatics who consider the interests of animals more important than the interests of human beings. But to be opposed to what is going on now it is not necessary to insist that all animal experiments stop immediately. All we need to say is that experiments serving no direct and urgent purpose should stop immediately, and in the remaining fields of research, we should whenever possible, seek to replace experiments that involve animals with alternative methods that do not. . . .

When are experiments on animals justifiable? Upon learning of the nature of many of the experiments carried out, some people react by saying that all experiments on animals should be prohibited immediately. But if we make our demands as absolute as this, the experimenters have a ready reply: Would we be prepared to let thousands of humans die if they could be saved by a single experiment on a single animal?

This question is, of course, purely hypothetical. There has never been and never could be a single experiment that saved thousands of lives. The way to reply to this hypothetical question is to pose another: Would the experimenters be prepared to carry out their experiment on a human orphan under six months old if that were the only way to save thousands of lives?

If the experimenters would not be prepared to use a human infant then their readiness to use nonhuman animals reveals an unjustifiable form of discrimination on the basis of species, since adult apes, monkeys, dogs, cats, rats, and other animals are more aware of what is happening to them, more self-directing, and, so far as we can tell, at least as sensitive to pain as a human infant. (I have specified that the human infant be an orphan, to avoid the complications of the feelings of parents. Specifying the case in this way is, if anything, overgenerous to those defending the use of nonhuman animals in experiments, since mammals intended for experimental use are usually separated from their mothers at an early age, when the separation causes distress for both mother and young.)

So far as we know, human infants possess no morally relevant characteristic to a higher degree than adult nonhuman animals, unless we are to count the infants' potential as a characteristic that makes it wrong to experiment on them. Whether this characteristic should count is controversial—if we count it, we shall have to condemn abortion along with experiments on infants, since the potential of the infant and the fetus is the same. To avoid the complexities of this issue, however, we can alter our original question a little and assume that the infant is one with irreversible brain damage so severe as to rule out any mental development beyond the level of a six-month-old infant. There are, unfortunately, many such human beings, locked away in special wards throughout the country, some of them long since abandoned by their parents and other relatives, and, sadly, sometimes unloved by anyone else. Despite their mental deficiencies, the anatomy and physiology of these infants are in nearly all respects identical with those of normal humans. If, therefore, we were to force-feed them with large quantities of floor polish or drip concentrated solutions of cosmetics into their eyes [as has been done in experiments using animals], we would have a much more reliable indication of the safety of these products for humans than we now get by attempting to extrapolate the results of tests on a variety of other species. . . .

So whenever experimenters claim that their experiments are important enough to justify the use of animals, we should ask them whether they would be prepared to use a brain-damaged human being at a similar mental level to the animals they are planning to use. I cannot imagine that anyone would seriously propose carrying out the experiments described in this chapter on brain-damaged human beings. Occasionally it has become known that medical experiments have been performed on human beings without their consent; one case did concern institutionalized intellectually disabled children, who were given hepatitis. When such harmful experiments on human beings become known, they usually lead to an outcry against the experimenters, and rightly so. They are, very often, a further example of the arrogance of the research worker who justifies everything on the grounds of increasing knowledge. But if the experimenter claims that the experiment is important enough to justify inflicting suffering on animals, why is it not important enough to justify inflicting suffering on humans at the same mental level? What difference is there between the two? Only that one is a member of our species and the other is not? But to appeal to that difference is to reveal a bias no more defensible than racism or any other form of arbitrary discrimination. . . .

We have still not answered the question of when an experiment might be justifiable. It will not do to say "Never!" Putting morality in such black-and-white terms is appealing, because it eliminates the need to think about particular cases; but in extreme circumstances, such absolutist answers always break down. Torturing a human being is almost always wrong, but it is not absolutely wrong. If torture were the only way in which we could discover the location of a nuclear bomb hidden in a New York City basement and timed to go off within the hour, then torture would be justifiable. Similarly, if a single experiment could cure a disease like leukemia, that experiment would be justifiable. But in actual life the benefits are always more remote, and more often than not they are nonexistent. So how do we decide when an experiment is justifiable?

We have seen that experimenters reveal a bias in favor of their own species whenever they carry out experiments on nonhumans for purposes that they would not think justified them in using human beings, even brain-damaged ones. This principle gives us a guide toward an answer to our question. Since a speciesist bias, like a racist bias, is unjustifiable, an experiment cannot be justifiable unless the experiment is so important that the use of a brain-damaged human would also be justifiable.

This is not an absolutist principle. I do not believe that it could never be justifiable to experiment on a brain-damaged human. If it really were possible to save several lives by an experiment that would take just one life, and there were no other way those lives could be saved, it would be right to do the experiment. But this would be an extremely rare case. Admittedly, as with any dividing line, there would be a gray area where it was difficult to decide if an experiment could be justified. But we need not get distracted by such considerations now. . . . We are in the midst of an emergency in which appalling suffering is being inflicted on millions of animals for purposes that on any impartial view are obviously inadequate to justify the suffering. When we have ceased to carry out all those experiments, then there will be time enough to discuss what to do about the remaining ones which are claimed to be essential to save lives or prevent greater suffering. . . .

NOTES

1 For Bentham's moral philosophy, see his *Introduction to the Principles of Morals and Legislation,* and for Sidgwick's see *The Methods of Ethics,* 1907 (the passage is quoted from the seventh edition; reprint, London: Macmillan, 1963), p. 382. As examples of leading contemporary moral philosophers who incorporate a requirement of equal consideration of interests, see R. M. Hare, *Freedom and Reason* (New York: Oxford University Press, 1963), and John Rawls, *A Theory of Justice* (Cambridge: Harvard University Press, Belknap Press, 1972). For a brief account of the essential agreement on this issue between these and other positions, see R. M. Hare, "Rules of War and Moral Reasoning," *Philosophy and Public Affairs* 1 (2) (1972).
2 Letter to Henry Gregoire, February 25, 1809.
3 Reminiscences by Francis D. Gage, from Susan B. Anthony, *The History of Woman Suffrage,* vol. 1; the passage is to be found in the extract in Leslie Tanner, ed., *Voices from Women's Liberation* (New York: Signet, 1970).

4 I owe the term "speciesism" to Richard Ryder. It has become accepted in general use since the first edition of this book, and now appears in *The Oxford English Dictionary*, second edition (Oxford: Clarendon Press, 1989).

5 *Introduction to the Principles of Morals and Legislation*, chapter 17.

6 See M. Levin, "Animal Rights Evaluated," *Humanist* 37:14–15 (July/August 1977); M. A. Fox, "Animal Liberation: A Critique," *Ethics* 88: 134–138 (1978); C. Perry and G. E. Jones, "On Animal Rights," *International Journal of Applied Philosophy* 1: 39–57 (1982).

7 *Statistics of Scientific Procedures on Living Animals, Great Britain, 1988*, Command Paper 743 (London: Her Majesty's Stationery Office, 1989).

8 U.S. Congress Office of Technology Assessment, *Alternatives to Animal Use in Research, Testing and Education* (Washington, D.C.: Government Printing Office, 1986), p. 64.

9 Hearings before the Subcommittee on Livestock and Feed Grains of the Committee on Agriculture, U.S. House of Representatives, 1966, p. 63.

10 See A. Rowan, *Of Mice, Models and Men* (Albany: State University of New York Press, 1984), p. 71; his later revision is in a personal communication to the Office of Technology Assessment; see *Alternatives to Animal Use in Research, Testing and Education*, p. 56.

11 OTA, *Alternatives to Animal Use in Research, Testing and Education*, p. 56.

12 *Experimental Animals* 37: 105 (1988).

QUESTIONS

1 Is speciesism analogous to sexism and racism? Why or why not?

2 Has Singer advanced convincing reasons in support of the claim that an experiment using animals cannot be justifiable unless the experiment is so important that the use of a brain-damaged human would also be justifiable?

The Case for Animal Rights

Tom Regan

Like Singer, Regan attacks speciesism. In his view, animals, like humans, have rights, which are violated when they are not treated with the respect due to beings who have inherent value. Regan maintains not only that animals, like humans, have inherent value but also that all beings that have inherent value have it equally. In his view, any attempt to specify a characteristic, such as intelligence, as a basis for attributing a lesser degree of inherent value to animals must be rejected, since consistency in our moral reasoning would require us to attribute a lesser degree of inherent value to some human beings. Regan concludes by calling for the abolition of all scientific experiments using animals and the dissolution of all commercial animal agriculture.

Reprinted with permission of Basil Blackwell, Inc. from *In Defense of Animals* (1985), edited by Peter Singer, pp. 13–15, 21–25.

I regard myself as an advocate of animal rights—as a part of the animal rights movement. That movement, as I conceive it, is committed to a number of goals, including:

- the total abolition of the use of animals in science;
- the total dissolution of commercial animal agriculture;
- the total elimination of commercial and sport hunting and trapping.

There are, I know, people who profess to believe in animal rights but do not avow these goals. Factory farming, they say, is wrong—it violates animals' rights—but traditional animal agriculture is all right. Toxicity tests of cosmetics on animals violate their rights, but important medical research—cancer research, for example—does not. The clubbing of baby seals is abhorrent, but not the harvesting of adult seals. I used to think I understood this reasoning. Not any more. You don't change unjust institutions by tidying them up.

What's wrong—fundamentally wrong—with the way animals are treated isn't the details that vary from case to case. It's the whole system. The forlornness of the veal calf is pathetic, heart wrenching; the pulsing pain of the chimp with electrodes planted deep in her brain is repulsive; the slow, tortuous death of the racoon caught in the leg-hold trap is agonizing. But what is wrong isn't the pain, isn't the suffering, isn't the deprivation. These compound what's wrong. Sometimes—often—they make it much, much worse. But they are not the fundamental wrong.

The fundamental wrong is the system that allows us to view animals as *our resources,* here for *us*—to be eaten, or surgically manipulated, or exploited for sport or money. Once we accept this view of animals—as our resources—the rest is as predictable as it is regrettable. Why worry about their loneliness, their pain, their death? Since animals exist for us, to benefit us in one way or another, what harms them really doesn't matter—or matters only if it starts to bother us, makes us feel a trifle uneasy when we eat our veal escalope, for example. So, yes, let us get veal calves out of solitary confinement, give them more space, a little straw, a few companions. But let us keep our veal escalope.

But a little straw, more space and a few companions won't eliminate—won't even touch—the basic wrong that attaches to our viewing and treating these animals as our resources. A veal calf killed to be eaten after living in close confinement is viewed and treated in this way: but so, too, is another who is raised (as they say) 'more humanely'. To right the wrong of our treatment of farm animals requires more than making rearing methods 'more humane'; it requires the total dissolution of commercial animal agriculture.

How we do this, whether we do it or, as in the case of animals in science, whether and how we abolish their use—these are to a large extent political questions. People must change their beliefs before they change their habits. Enough people, especially those elected to public office, must believe in change—must want it—before we will have laws that protect the rights of animals. This process of change is very complicated, very demanding, very exhausting, calling for the efforts of many hands in education, publicity, political organization and activity, down to the licking of envelopes and stamps. As a trained and practising philosopher, the sort of contribution I can make is limited but, I like to think, important. The currency of philosophy is ideas—their meaning and rational foundation—not the nuts and bolts of the legislative process, say, or the mechanics of community organization. That's what I have been exploring over the past ten years or so in my essays and talks and, most recently, in my book, *The Case for Animal Rights*. I believe the major conclusions I reach in the book are true because they are supported by the weight of the best arguments. I believe the idea of animal rights has reason, not just emotion, on its side.

In the space I have at my disposal here I can only sketch, in the barest outline, some of the main features of the book. Its main themes—and we should not be surprised by this—involve asking and answering deep, foundational moral questions about what morality is, how it should be understood and what is the best moral theory, all considered. I hope I can convey something of the shape I think this theory takes. . . .

What to do? Where to begin? . . . Suppose we consider that you and I, for example, do have value as individuals—what we'll call *inherent value*. To say we have such value is to say that we are something more than, something different from, mere receptacles. Moreover, to ensure that we do not pave the way for such injustices as slavery or sexual discrimination, we must believe that all who have inherent value have it equally, regardless of their sex, race, religion, birthplace and so on. Similarly to be discarded as irrelevant are one's talents or skills, intelligence and wealth, personality or pathology, whether one is loved and admired or despised and loathed. The genius and the retarded child, the prince and the pauper, the brain surgeon and the fruit vendor, Mother Teresa and the most unscrupulous used-car salesman—all have inherent value, all possess it equally, and all have an equal right to be treated with respect, to be treated in ways that do not reduce them to the status of things, as if they existed as resources for others. My value as an individual is independent of my usefulness to you. Yours is not dependent on your usefulness to me. For either of us to treat the other in ways that fail to show respect for the other's independent value is to act immorally, to violate the individual's rights.

Some of the rational virtues of this view—what I call the rights view—should be evident. . . . For example, the rights view *in principle* denies the moral tolerability of any and all forms of racial, sexual or social discrimination; and . . . this view *in principle* denies that we can justify good results by using evil means that violate an individual's rights—denies, for example, that it could be moral to kill my Aunt Bea to harvest beneficial consequences for others. That would be to sanction the disrespectful treatment of the individual in the name of the social good, something the rights view will not—categorically will not—ever allow.

The rights view, I believe, is rationally the most satisfactory moral theory. It surpasses all other theories in the degree to which it illuminates and explains the foundation of our duties to one another—the domain of human morality. On this score it has the best reasons, the best arguments, on its side. Of course, if it were possible to show that only human beings are included within its scope, then a person like myself, who believes in animal rights, would be obliged to look elsewhere.

But attempts to limit its scope to humans only can be shown to be rationally defective. Animals, it is true, lack many of the abilities humans possess. They can't read, do higher mathematics, build a bookcase or make *baba ghanoush*.

Neither can many human beings, however, and yet we don't (and shouldn't) say that they (these humans) therefore have less inherent value, less of a right to be treated with respect, than do others. It is the *similarities* between those human beings who most clearly, most non-controversially have such value (the people reading this, for example), not our differences, that matter most. And the really crucial, the basic similarity is simply this: we are each of us the experiencing subject of a life, a conscious creature having an individual welfare that has importance to us whatever our usefulness to others. We want and prefer things, believe and feel things, recall and expect things. And all these dimensions of our life, including our pleasure and pain, our enjoyment and suffering, our satisfaction and frustration, our continued existence or our untimely death—all make a difference to the quality of our life as lived, as experienced, by us as individuals. As the same is true of those animals that concern us (the ones that are eaten and trapped, for example), they too must be viewed as the experiencing subjects of a life, with inherent value of their own.

Some there are who resist the idea that animals have inherent value. 'Only humans have such value,' they profess. How might this narrow view be defended? Shall we say that only humans have the requisite intelligence, or autonomy, or reason? But there are many, many humans who fail to meet these standards and yet are reasonably viewed as having value above and beyond their usefulness to others. Shall we claim that only humans belong to the right species, the species *Homo sapiens*? But this is blatant speciesism. Will it be said, then, that all—and only—humans have immortal souls? Then our opponents have their work cut out for them. I am myself not ill-disposed to the proposition that there are immortal souls. Personally, I profoundly hope I have one. But I would not want to rest my position on a controversial ethical issue on the even more controversial question about who or what has an immortal soul. That is to dig one's hole deeper, not to climb out. Rationally, it is better to resolve moral issues without making more controversial assumptions than are needed. The question of who has inherent value is such a question, one that is resolved more rationally without the introduction of the idea of immortal souls than by its use.

Well, perhaps some will say that animals have some inherent value, only less than we have. Once again, however, attempts to defend this view can be shown to lack rational justification. What could be the basis of our having more inherent value than animals? Their lack of reason, or autonomy, or intellect? Only if we are willing to make the same judgement in the case of humans who are similarly deficient. But it is not true that such humans—the retarded child, for example, or the mentally deranged—have less inherent value than you or I. Neither, then, can we rationally sustain the view that animals like them in being the experiencing subjects of a life have less inherent value. *All* who have inherent value have it *equally,* whether they be human animals or not.

Inherent value, then, belongs equally to those who are the experiencing subjects of a life. Whether it belongs to others—to rocks and rivers, trees and glaciers, for example—we do not know and may never know. But neither do we need to know, if we are to make the case for animal rights. We do not need to know, for example, how many people are eligible to vote in the next presidential election before we can know whether I am. Similarly, we do not need to know how many individuals have inherent value before we can know that some do. When it comes to the case for animal rights, then, what we need to know is whether the animals that, in our culture, are routinely eaten, hunted and used in our laboratories, for example, are like us in being subjects of a life. And we do know this. We do know that many—literally, billions and billions—of these animals are the subjects of a life in the sense explained and so have inherent value if we do. And since, in order to arrive at the best theory of our duties to one another, we must recognize our equal inherent value as individuals, reason—not sentiment, not emotion—reason compels us to recognize the equal inherent value of these animals and, with this, their equal right to be treated with respect.

That, *very* roughly, is the shape and feel of the case for animal rights. Most of the details of the supporting argument are missing. They are to be found in the book to which I alluded earlier. Here, the details go begging, and I must, in closing, limit myself to [one] final point. . . .

Having set out the broad outlines of the rights view, I can now say why its implications for farming and science, among other fields, are both clear and uncompromising. In the case of the use of animals in science, the rights view is categorically abolitionist. Lab animals are not our tasters; we are not their kings. Because these animals are treated routinely, systematically as if their value were reducible to their usefulness to others, they are routinely, systematically treated with a lack of respect, and thus are their rights routinely, systematically violated. This is just as true when they are used in trivial, duplicative, unnecessary or unwise research as it is when they are used in studies that hold out real promise of human benefits. We can't justify harming or killing a human being (my Aunt Bea, for example) just for these sorts of reason. Neither can we do so even in the case of so lowly a creature as a laboratory rat. It is not just refinement or reduction that is called for, not just larger, cleaner cages, not just more generous use of anaesthetic or the elimination of multiple surgery, not just tidying up the system. It is complete replacement. The best we can do when it comes to using animals in science is—not to use them. That is where our duty lies, according to the rights view.

As for commercial animal agriculture, the rights view takes a similar abolitionist position. The fundamental moral wrong here is not that animals are kept in stressful close confinement or in isolation, or that their pain and suffering, their needs and preferences are ignored or discounted. All these *are* wrong, of course, but they are not the fundamental wrong. They are symptoms and effects of the deeper, systematic wrong that allows these animals to be viewed and treated as lacking independent value, as resources for us—as, indeed, a renewable resource. Giving farm animals more space, more natural environments, more companions does not right the fundamental wrong, any more than giving lab animals more anaesthesia or bigger, cleaner cages would right the fundamental wrong in their case. Nothing less than the total dissolution of commercial animal agriculture will do this, just as, for similar reasons I won't develop at length here, morality requires nothing less than the total elimination of hunting and trapping for commercial and sporting ends. The rights view's implications, then, as I have said, are clear and uncompromising. . . .

QUESTIONS

1 Do all sentient beings have the same inherent value? Why or why not?
2 Is it always wrong to use animals in experiments intended to benefit human beings?

Moral Vegetarianism and the Argument from Pain and Suffering

R. G. Frey

Frey identifies three arguments advanced by proponents of moral vegetarianism: the argument from moral rights, the argument from killing, and the argument from pain and suffering. Frey argues that Singer and others who advance these kinds of arguments are committed only to conditional vegetarianism. That is, they are committed to the view that the wrongness of using animals for food is conditional on whether our treatment of animals in converting them into food violates their moral right to life and/or freedom from unnecessary suffering. The argument from pain and suffering, in particular, would have no force if animal raising and slaughtering practices were changed so as to eliminate both. In contrast, according to unconditional vegetarianism, it is always wrong to eat animals, irrespective of how they are raised or killed. This type of vegetarianism is rooted in a way of life—one that involves an attempt to live in harmony with everything else in the world, encroaching as little as possible on other creatures and things.

By moral vegetarianism, then, I have in mind those cases for vegetarianism which locate the moral basis for boycotting meat in our treatment of animals in rearing and converting them into food.

Modern proponents of vegetarianism on this basis have relied principally upon three arguments to show that eating meat is wrong.

The Argument from Moral Rights   This is the view that our present treatment of animals in converting them into food violates their moral right to life and/or freedom from unnecessary suffering. It is wrong to eat meat, then, because animals' moral rights have been violated in the course of their reaching our tables.

The Argument from Killing   This is the view that it is wrong to kill animals or to kill them for food, except, if at all, under conditions which few of us can pretend to be in.[1] It is wrong to eat meat because animals have undergone the irretrievable wrong of being killed, in the course of becoming food for human consumption.

Reprinted with permission of Blackwell Publishers from R. G. Frey, *Rights, Killing, and Suffering* (1983), pp. 21–23, 27, 30–35.

The Argument from Pain and Suffering This is the view . . . that it is wrong
to eat meat, because factory-farmed (and perhaps even some traditionally-farmed)
animals have suffered a good deal and, thus, been wrongly treated, in the course of
being turned into food. . . .

THE ARGUMENT FROM PAIN AND SUFFERING

This argument, championed by Peter Singer in *Animal Liberation*[2] and *Practical
Ethics,*[3] by Stephen Clark in *The Moral Status of Animals,*[4] and by many others,
moves either directly or indirectly to moral vegetarianism from the pain and suffering which animals undergo in being bred, raised, and slaughtered for food. . . .

The argument from pain and suffering, of course, has a past; its use by Singer
and others is but the most recent among several. The significance it has come to
have, especially under the stimulus of *Animal Liberation,* stems from its application to intensive methods of food production, to factory or commercial farming.
What Singer, amongst others, has done is to give the argument new and important
life, by describing how some aspects of intensive farming involve animal suffering
and then using the argument to combat these farming practices.

I do not believe it betrays undue sensitivity to find certain practices employed
on factory farms profoundly disturbing. To put no finer point on the matter, there
are practices afoot on them, pre-eminently in the cases of laying hens and veal
calves, of which we cannot be proud. Even if such practices are necessary to sustain the level of profits by which farmers, their families, the meat industry as a
whole, and, through it, a very great many others prosper, we still do well not to be
proud of having to resort to them. Some might suggest that the great pleasure
human beings receive from consuming veal more than outweighs the suffering (no
grain, no straw-bedding, no exercise, perpetual confinement in tiny slatted stalls,
little muscle-growth, induced iron-deficiency and anemia, almost no daylight,
tethered to prevent seeking iron and exercise)[5] which these calves undergo in
reaching the table. Even so, treatment such as this is not the sort of thing in which,
morally, we take pride; and if it is something required in order to sustain a level or
style of life to which we have become accustomed, we still do well to be disturbed
that this is so.

As information about the treatment of, for example, veal calves has been more
widely disseminated, more people have come to see this treatment as wrong. But
this is by no means the end or even the essence of the matter for Singer; for it is
central to his position—in fact, it seems the main feature of his position—that
moral vegetarianism is *the means by which each of us* can move directly to eliminate the pains of food animals. Once we come to see our treatment of veal calves
as wrong, vegetarianism is seen by Singer as the means by which each of us can do
something about this treatment. This emerges very clearly from the central argument of *Animal Liberation.*

Animals can suffer, and since they can suffer, they have interests. In view of this
fact, the moral principle of the equal consideration of interests applies to them, and
this means that we are not morally justified in setting aside, ignoring, or otherwise

devaluing their interests. This, however, is precisely what some factory farming practices, with their accompaniment of animal suffering, appear to involve, and the immorality which this represents is, if anything, accentuated by the fact that we do not need meat in order to survive and to lead healthy lives.

We can, on the other hand, do something about this situation: by boycotting meat, we can draw down market forces upon the head of the factory farmer and so reduce or eliminate the suffering of food animals. When demand slackens, prices fall; when prices fall, profits diminish; and when profits diminish, the factory farmer has less capital to re-invest in food stock. (The same is true for farmers who employ traditional methods of farming.) By becoming a vegetarian, then, each of us hits directly and immediately at factory farming; for in giving up meat, we reduce the number of food animals bred and raised for market and thereby total animal suffering. Accordingly, a genuine concern for the interests of animals and so with a diminution in their suffering requires that we cease rearing animals for food and cease eating them.

The picture one carries away from Singer's book, then, is that becoming a moral vegetarian is the means by which each of us can reduce animal suffering and so help in the effort to right a wrong. Once we have identified certain farming practices as wrong, we can use vegetarianism as the tool, as the direct and immediate means for eliminating or mitigating those practices. What is more, this means is relatively painless on us, given that there are wholesome and nutritious alternatives to meat readily available. . . .

TWO CONCEPTIONS OF THE STATUS OF VEGETARIANISM

There is a curious feature of the arguments from moral rights, killing, and pain and suffering that I am sure many readers have noticed. It consists in the fact that, even if we were to regard the arguments as completely successful, they would by no means bar or eliminate all meat-eating. In this can be found the basis for distinguishing two very different conceptions of the status of vegetarianism.

Partial and Absolute Exclusions

When I first arrived at Oxford from Virginia, I became friendly with a mathematician from Calcutta. He was a vegetarian and abstained from all meat. Meals in college were very unpleasant for him, since they invariably featured meat dishes, and what vegetables there were were unappetizing, always the same, and—the great English gastronomic failure—overcooked. He regarded eating meat as an abomination; there were no circumstances—apart, perhaps from direst necessity, and even this was uncertain—in which he would allow it to be right. Eating meat was simply excluded from consideration, and there was an end to it.

The arguments from moral rights, killing, and pain and suffering do not have the same absolutely dismissive effect. The reason is that the objections which they severally pose are not actually to eating animals but to the treatment animals receive in the course of being converted into food. The result is obvious: to animals which have not undergone the treatment in question, the arguments do not apply. Thus, since the argument from moral rights makes the wrongness of violating animals' moral rights crucial, it places no objection in the way of eating meat from animals whose rights have not been violated. Someone who is a vegetarian solely on the basis of this argument, then, has no reason *per se* to abstain from such meat, any more than someone who is a vegetarian on the basis of the argument from pain and suffering has any reason *per se* to abstain from eating the flesh of animals who have not been cruelly treated in being turned into food. This does not mean, of course, that these individuals will eat the meat in question, only that they must have one more shot in their lockers, if they are going to abstain on principle from this meat as well.

To my Indian friend, this situation would appear very strange indeed. For here are purported vegetarians who, *prima facie,* have no reason not to eat this meat. *He* does not eat meat at all; eating meat is quite excluded from consideration, whether the animal has had its rights violated or been killed or been made to suffer, or whether it has simply fallen from the heavens at one's feet or miraculously appeared in one's cooking pot. To him, it would be exceedingly peculiar to think that his vegetarianism required him to look carefully into the question of whether this chicken has had its rights violated, or had dropped dead from heart seizure, or had not suffered at some point in the past, as if one as opposed to some other answer would make it right for him to eat meat. The plain fact is that, so far as *his* vegetarianism is concerned, such questions are beside the point. Conversely, to the proponents of the three arguments, these questions are very much to the point, and their vegetarianism is conditioned by the responses given in their respective cases.

To this Indian, then, proponents of the three arguments appear more exercised by rights, killing, and suffering than by eating animals. What the arguments make out to be morally wrong is not actually eating animals but violating their alleged moral rights or killing them or making them suffer. Do none of these things, and the wrongness of eating meat vanishes. Here, then, are vegetarians of whom vegetarianism is only demanded if animals are treated one way rather than another. In the case of the argument from pain and suffering, this result gives rise to a view which *prima facie* seems very strange. For there seems something odd indeed about a view which says in effect that when animals are (treated in such a way as to be) miserable they may not be eaten but when they are (treated in such a way as to be) happy and content they may be eaten. One's natural inclination would be to say the opposite, that when animals are contented, their lives are a benefit to them and that then, if ever, vegetarianism is demanded of us. . . .

Conditional and Unconditional Conceptions

If we think of the position of this Indian mathematician as unconditional vegetarianism and that of the proponents of the three arguments as conditional vegetarianism, then how might we characterize the essential difference between these two conceptions of vegetarianism?

In his paper 'Utilitarianism and vegetarianism',[6] Peter Singer objects to Cora Diamond's claim[7] that his position yields the curious result that it is perfectly permissible to eat animals which are accident victims:

> Why is this curious? It is only curious on the assumption that vegetarians must think it *always* wrong to eat meat. No doubt some vegetarians are moral absolutists, just as there are absolute pacifists, absolute anti-abortionists and absolute truth-tellers who would never tell a lie. I reject all these forms of moral absolutism.[8]

Doubtless Singer would regard unconditional vegetarians as absolutists, and doubtless there is a significant difference between my Indian friend and Singer on this score. But the suggestion of the above passage—that some people think it always wrong to eat meat, whereas others, including Singer, think it only sometimes wrong— is not quite explicit as to the full difference between them.

If we think in terms of a distinction between unconditional and conditional vegetarianism, then the point I was making earlier can be put this way: when conditions of food animal treatment are one way rather than another, conditional vegetarianism ceases to have a ground, the result of which is, in the circumstances, to remove from conditional vegetarians their reason for abstaining from meat. When conditions are one way rather than another, vegetarianism is pointless; for the whole point of conditional vegetarianism is to improve the conditions in which animals are bred, raised, and slaughtered for food, and if conditions are already of the appropriate sort, then there is no point in adopting vegetarianism as the tactic by which to make them of that sort. Here, it seems to me, is encapsulated the essence of conditional vegetarianism: it is a tactic by means of which one hopes to improve the treatment of food animals. This is especially clear in the case of Singer, who . . . regards vegetarianism based upon the argument from pain and suffering as the means by which to combat the pains of factory-farmed animals.

At the core of conditional vegetarianism, then, is a conception of vegetarianism as a tactic for combating the treatment or pains of food animals. But tactics are appropriate to circumstances, and a change in circumstances can, as we have seen, render one's tactics pointless. In the case of a conditional vegetarian, to persist in abstaining from meat, even when circumstances are of the desired sort, becomes a needless gesture.

Accordingly, to say merely that what separates my Indian friend from Singer is a form of absolutism, to say merely that conditional vegetarianism is limited (or applies only in respect of some animals) whereas unconditional vegetarianism is unlimited, leaves out any mention of the tactical conception of vegetarianism, which essentially defines the conditional position. This omission is of the utmost importance; for no one even remotely in sympathy with the views of my Indian friend could accept such a conception of vegetarianism. To this Indian, vegetarianism is something quite different: it represents a decision about how he will live in the world, a decision tantamount in part to the adoption of a way of life, for a world which contains a multiplicity of creatures and things, each as much a part of the whole as he is. It represents an attempt to live in harmony with the creatures and things he finds around him and to encroach on them as little as they on the whole encroach on him. It represents an effort to see himself as part of the world, and not a world—and law—unto himself. So far as I can see, nothing could be further from a tactical conception of vegetarianism than this conception of how we shall live in a world where we are but part of the whole, of which conception of vegetarianism is a constituent.

(Someone armed with such a conception of vegetarianism is very likely to find Singer's emphasis upon pain rather puzzling. For though my Indian friend is not indifferent to the pains of animals, it is not by virtue of the fact that they can feel pain that he thinks they warrant and obtain his respect. If asked whether it was because animals can feel pain that he tries to live in harmony with them, as one part of nature with another, he would, I think, view both the question and the questioner with deep puzzlement, not least because many portions of the whole of which he sees himself as a part *cannot* feel pain. In time, I believe he would come to think that only someone with a particular theory would seize upon pain in this way and elevate it or its avoidance to supreme importance in ethics.)

I myself am as much opposed to moral absolutisms as is Singer and, I suspect, for many of the same reasons. I have used the example of this Indian mathematician simply in order to bring out the tactical conception of vegetarianism, which lies at the heart of conditional vegetarianism, especially that of Singer.

Counter-Argument and Competing Tactics

Apart from the fact that, as we have seen, some vegetarians reject the tactical conception of vegetarianism, this conception is exposed to counter-arguments of a specific type. If we stick with Singer as our example, then these counter-arguments stem directly from the literature on utilitarianism.

The specific type of counter-argument is this: if vegetarianism is a tactic for combating the pains of food animals, then this tactic ceases to have any point whatever, if we develop ways of breeding, raising, and slaughtering animals painlessly. In this eventuality, we could eat all the meat we liked, and Singer would have no ground for complaint.

It will be claimed, however, that there is no meat available from animals which have not, in particular, been reared by painful methods. To this, there are three responses.

First, it is factually false; there are millions upon millions of animals presently being farmed but not factory-farmed. It is both tempting to argue and not obviously wrong to suggest that because traditional farming methods are held, even by vegetarians, to be vastly less painful than intensive ones, the argument from pain and suffering does not provide a reason for abstaining from the flesh of traditionally-farmed animals. . . .

Second, not all intensively farmed animals suffer to anything like the degree of veal calves, or have the same methods of production used upon them. To give but a single example, in the United States, dairy cows are commercially farmed, and when their days as milk-producers come to an end, they are sent to slaughter. However, their lives are by no means as miserable as those of veal calves.

Third, if we focus solely upon factory-farmed animals, then we can see clearly to what the tactical conception of vegetarianism finally exposes Singer. For just as not eating meat is a tactic for dealing with the pains of food animals, so, too, is the package involving, among other things, maintaining and expanding traditional farming techniques, progressivly eliminating painful practices in intensive farming, and funding research into and developing pain-killing drugs. As tactics, both are on all fours; one is not *per se* more morally correct than the other. Moreover, the latter tactic has two further attractions: first, it enables us not only to deal with animal pain but also to retain our present, meat-based diet intact, and second, it enables us to meet the claim that the heavy demand for meat today can only be satisfied by intensive methods of production.

In this way, vegetarianism, Singer's tactic, is confronted with competition. That is, we are confronted with different tactics for combating the pains of food animals, and the central issue between them becomes simply the degree of effectiveness in achieving this end. The determination of which of two tactics is more effective in lessening animal pain is not a piece of theory but a matter of fact. If technological developments succeed in the encompassing way the one tactic envisages, then it may well be, on grounds of effectiveness, the preferred one, as new and better pain-killers, administered painlessly, reach more and more animals. This very real possibility cannot be eliminated *a priori* through any theoretical considerations. This is especially true for utilitarians such as Singer, for whom it must always remain a contingent affair whether the implementation of one policy has consequences which, in comparison with those of the implementation of another, make it the preferred or right policy. Effectiveness, then, is everything, and vegetarianism must confront and defeat (or at least not be defeated by) one after another competitor on this score; it by no means is *obviously* the most effective tactic for reducing the pains of food animals, so that all potential competitors can be ignored *ab initio*. . . .

To my Indian friend, of course, all this squabbling over effectiveness is beside the point; for whether it is Singer or his opponent who has the more effective means for coming to grips with animal pain, eating meat remains an abomination, and that is that.

NOTES

1 I have in mind conditions of necessity, where the killing and eating of animals is necessary for our survival.
2 Peter Singer, *Animal Liberation,* London, Jonathan Cape, 1976.
3 Peter Singer, *Practical Ethics,* Cambridge, Cambridge University Press, 1980.
4 Stephen Clark, *The Moral Status of Animals,* Oxford, Clarendon Press, 1977.
5 Slaughter normally occurs anywhere from 12 to 15 weeks of this treatment.
6 Peter Singer, 'Utilitarianism and vegetarianism,' *Philosophy and Public Affairs,* vol. 9, 1980, pp. 325–37.
7 Cora Diamond, 'Eating meat and eating people,' *Philosophy,* vol. 53, 1978, pp. 465–79.
8 Singer, 'Utilitarianism and vegetarianism,' pp. 327–28; italics in original.

QUESTIONS

1 Is Frey correct in his claim that Singer is committed only to conditional vegetarianism?
2 Would Regan agree with Frey's understanding of the argument from moral rights?
3 Are we morally obliged to become vegetarians?

The Case for the Use of Animals in Biomedical Research

Carl Cohen

Cohen, identifying himself as a speciesist, attacks both Singer and Regan and defends the use of animals in biomedical research. Against Regan, Cohen argues that animals have no rights, since they lack the capacities for free moral judgment and for exercising or responding to moral claims. Against Singer, he maintains that speciesism is not analogous to racism and sexism and that not all sentient beings have equal moral standing. Furthermore, Cohen argues, we have an obligation to enlarge the use of animals in research in the interest of protecting potential human subjects. In his view, although we do have obligations to animals, they have no rights against us on which research can infringe.

Using animals as research subjects in medical investigations is widely condemned on two grounds: first, because it wrongly violates the *rights* of animals,[1] and second, because it wrongly imposes on sentient creatures much avoidable *suffering*.[2] Neither of these arguments is sound. The first relies on a mistaken understanding of rights; the second relies on a mistaken calculation of consequences. Both deserve definitive dismissal.

WHY ANIMALS HAVE NO RIGHTS

A right, properly understood, is a claim, or potential claim, that one party may exercise against another. The target against whom such a claim may be registered can be a single person, a group, a community, or (perhaps) all humankind. The content of rights claims also varies greatly: repayment of loans, nondiscrimination by employers, noninterference by the state, and so on. To comprehend any genuine right fully, therefore, we must know *who* holds the right, *against whom* it is held, and *to what* it is a right.

Alternative sources of rights add complexity. Some rights are grounded in constitution and law (e.g., the right of an accused to trial by jury); some rights are moral but give no legal claims (e.g., my right to your keeping the promise you gave me); and some rights (e.g., against theft or assault) are rooted both in morals and in law.

The differing targets, contents, and sources of rights, and their inevitable conflict, together weave a tangled web. Notwithstanding all such complications, this much is clear about rights in general: they are in every case claims, or potential claims, within a community of moral agents. Rights arise, and can be intelligibly defended, only among beings who actually do, or can, make moral claims against one another. Whatever else rights may be, therefore, they are necessarily human; their possessors are persons, human beings.

Reprinted with permission from *The New England Journal of Medicine,* vol. 315 (October 2, 1986), pp. 865–870.

The attributes of human beings from which this moral capability arises have been described variously by philosophers, both ancient and modern: the inner consciousness of a free will (Saint Augustine[3]); the grasp, by human reason, of the binding character of moral law (Saint Thomas[4]); the self-conscious participation of human beings in an objective ethical order (Hegel[5]); human membership in an organic moral community (Bradley[6]); the development of the human self through the consciousness of other moral selves (Mead[7]); and the underivative, intuitive cognition of the rightness of an action (Prichard[8]). Most influential has been Immanuel Kant's emphasis on the universal human possession of a uniquely moral will and the autonomy its use entails.[9] Humans confront choices that are purely moral; humans—but certainly not dogs or mice—lay down moral laws, for others and for themselves. Human beings are self-legislative, morally *auto-nomous*.

Animals (that is, nonhuman animals, the ordinary sense of that word) lack this capacity for free moral judgment. They are not beings of a kind capable of exercising or responding to moral claims. Animals therefore have no rights, and they can have none. This is the core of the argument about the alleged rights of animals. The holders of rights must have the capacity to comprehend rules of duty, governing all including themselves. In applying such rules, the holders of rights must recognize possible conflicts between what is in their own interest and what is just. Only in a community of beings capable of self-restricting moral judgments can the concept of a right be correctly invoked.

Humans have such moral capacities. They are in this sense self-legislative, are members of communities governed by moral rules, and do possess rights. Animals do not have such moral capacities. They are not morally self-legislative, cannot possibly be members of a truly moral community, and therefore cannot possess rights. In conducting research on animal subjects, therefore, we do not violate their rights, because they have none to violate.

To animate life, even in its simplest forms, we give a certain natural reverence. But the possession of rights presupposes a moral status not attained by the vast majority of living things. We must not infer, therefore, that a live being has, simply in being alive, a "right" to its life. The assertion that all animals, only because they are alive and have interests, also possess the "right to life"[10] is an abuse of that phrase, and wholly without warrant.

It does not follow from this, however, that we are morally free to do anything we please to animals. Certainly not. In our dealings with animals, as in our dealings with other human beings, we have obligations that do not arise from claims against us based on rights. Rights entail obligations, but many of the things one ought to do are in no way tied to another's entitlement. Rights and obligations are not reciprocals of one another, and it is a serious mistake to suppose that they are.

Illustrations are helpful. Obligations may arise from internal commitments made: physicians have obligations to their patients not grounded merely in their patients' rights. Teachers have such obligations to their students, shepherds to their dogs, and cowboys to their horses. Obligations may arise from differences of status: adults owe special care when playing with young children, and children owe special care when playing with young pets. Obligations may arise from special relationships: the payment of my son's college tuition is something to

which he may have no right, although it may be my obligation to bear the burden if I reasonably can; my dog has no right to daily exercise and veterinary
care, but I do have the obligation to provide these things for her. Obligations
may arise from particular acts or circumstances: one may be obliged to another
for a special kindness done, or obliged to put an animal out of its misery in view
of its condition—although neither the human benefactor nor the dying animal
may have had a claim of right.

Plainly, the grounds of our obligations to humans and to animals are manifold
and cannot be formulated simply. Some hold that there is a general obligation to do
no gratuitous harm to sentient creatures (the principle of nonmaleficence); some
hold that there is a general obligation to do good to sentient creatures when that is
reasonably within one's power (the principle of beneficence). In our dealings with
animals, few will deny that we are at least obliged to act humanely—that is, to treat
them with the decency and concern that we owe, as sensitive human beings, to other
sentient creatures. To treat animals humanely, however, is not to treat them as humans
or as the holders of rights.

A common objection, which deserves a response, may be paraphrased as follows:

> If having rights requires being able to make moral claims, to grasp and apply moral laws,
> then many humans—the brain-damaged, the comatose, the senile—who plainly lack those
> capacities must be without rights. But that is absurd. This proves [the critic concludes] that
> rights do not depend on the presence of moral capacities.[1,10]

This objection fails; it mistakenly treats an essential feature of humanity as
though it were a screen for sorting humans. The capacity for moral judgment that
distinguishes humans from animals is not a test to be administered to human beings
one by one. Persons who are unable, because of some disability, to perform the full
moral functions natural to human beings are certainly not for that reason ejected
from the moral community. The issue is one of kind. Humans are of such a kind
that they may be the subject of experiments only with their voluntary consent. The
choices they make freely must be respected. Animals are of such a kind that it is
impossible for them, in principle, to give or withhold voluntary consent or to make
a moral choice. What humans retain when disabled, animals have never had.

A second objection, also often made, may be paraphrased as follows:

> Capacities will not succeed in distinguishing humans from the other animals. Animals also
> reason; animals also communicate with one another; animals also care passionately for their
> young; animals also exhibit desires and preferences.[11,12] Features of moral relevance—
> rationality, interdependence, and love—are not exhibited uniquely by human beings.
> Therefore [this critic concludes], there can be no solid moral distinction between humans
> and other animals.[10]

This criticism misses the central point. It is not the ability to communicate or to
reason, or dependence on one another, or care for the young, or the exhibition of
preference, or any such behavior that marks the critical divide. Analogies between
human families and those of monkeys, or between human communities and those
of wolves, and the like, are entirely beside the point. Patterns of conduct are not at
issue. Animals do indeed exhibit remarkable behavior at times. Conditioning, fear,

instinct, and intelligence all contribute to species survival. Membership in a community of moral agents nevertheless remains impossible for them. Actors subject to moral judgment must be capable of grasping the generality of an ethical premise in a practical syllogism. Humans act immorally often enough, but only they—never wolves or monkeys—can discern, by applying some moral rule to the facts of a case, that a given act ought or ought not to be performed. The moral restraints imposed by humans on themselves are thus highly abstract and are often in conflict with the self-interest of the agent. Communal behavior among animals, even when most intelligent and most endearing, does not approach autonomous morality in this fundamental sense.

Genuinely moral acts have an internal as well as an external dimension. Thus, in law, an act can be criminal only when the guilty deed, the *actus reus*, is done with a guilty mind, *mens rea*. No animal can ever commit a crime; bringing animals to criminal trial is the mark of primitive ignorance. The claims of moral right are similarly inapplicable to them. Does a lion have a right to eat a baby zebra? Does a baby zebra have a right not to be eaten? Such questions, mistakenly invoking the concept of right where it does not belong, do not make good sense. Those who condemn biomedical research because it violates "animal rights" commit the same blunder.

IN DEFENSE OF "SPECIESISM"

Abandoning reliance on animal rights, some critics resort instead to animal sentience—their feelings of pain and distress. We ought to desist from the imposition of pain insofar as we can. Since all or nearly all experimentation on animals does impose pain and could be readily forgone, say these critics, it should be stopped. The ends sought may be worthy, but those ends do not justify imposing agonies on humans, and by animals the agonies are felt no less. The laboratory use of animals (these critics conclude) must therefore be ended—or at least very sharply curtailed.

Argument of this variety is essentially utilitarian, often expressly so[13]; it is based on the calculation of the net product, in pains and pleasures, resulting from experiments on animals. Jeremy Bentham, comparing horses and dogs with other sentient creatures, is thus commonly quoted: "The question is not, Can they reason? nor Can they talk? but, Can they suffer?"[14]

Animals certainly can suffer and surely ought not to be made to suffer needlessly. But in inferring, from these uncontroversial premises, that biomedical research causing animal distress is largely (or wholly) wrong, the critic commits two serious errors.

The first error is the assumption, often explicitly defended, that all sentient animals have equal moral standing. Between a dog and a human being, according to this view, there is no moral difference; hence the pains suffered by dogs must be weighed no differently from the pains suffered by humans. To deny such equality, according to this critic, is to give unjust preference to one species over another; it is "speciesism." The most influential statement of this moral equality of species was made by Peter Singer:

The racist violates the principle of equality by giving greater weight to the interests of members of his own race when there is a clash between their interests and the interests of those of another race. The sexist violates the principle of equality by favoring the interests of his own sex. Similarly the speciesist allows the interests of his own species to override the greater interests of members of other species. The pattern is identical in each case.[2]

This argument is worse than unsound; it is atrocious. It draws an offensive moral conclusion from a deliberately devised verbal parallelism that is utterly specious. Racism has no rational ground whatever. Differing degrees of respect or concern for humans for no other reason than that they are members of different races is an injustice totally without foundation in the nature of the races themselves. Racists, even if acting on the basis of mistaken factual beliefs, do grave moral wrong precisely because there is no morally relevant distinction among the races. The supposition of such differences has led to outright horror. The same is true of the sexes, neither sex being entitled by right to greater respect or concern than the other. No dispute here.

Between species of animate life, however—between (for example) humans on the one hand and cats or rats on the other—the morally relevant differences are enormous, and almost universally appreciated. Humans engage in moral reflection; humans are morally autonomous; humans are members of moral communities, recognizing just claims against their own interest. Human beings do have rights; theirs is a moral status very different from that of cats or rats.

I am a speciesist. Speciesism is not merely plausible; it is essential for right conduct, because those who will not make the morally relevant distinctions among species are almost certain, in consequence, to misapprehend their true obligations. The analogy between speciesism and racism is insidious. Every sensitive moral judgment requires that the differing natures of the beings to whom obligations are owed be considered. If all forms of animate life—or vertebrate animal life?—must be treated equally, and if therefore in evaluating a research program the pains of a rodent count equally with the pains of a human, we are forced to conclude (1) that neither humans nor rodents possess rights, or (2) that rodents possess all the rights that humans possess. Both alternatives are absurd. Yet one or the other must be swallowed if the moral equality of all species is to be defended.

Humans owe to other humans a degree of moral regard that cannot be owed to animals. Some humans take on the obligation to support and heal others, both humans and animals, as a principal duty in their lives; the fulfillment of that duty may require the sacrifice of many animals. If biomedical investigators abandon the effective pursuit of their professional objectives because they are convinced that they may not do to animals what the service of humans requires, they will fail, objectively, to do their duty. Refusing to recognize the moral differences among species is a sure path to calamity. (The largest animal rights group in the country is People for the Ethical Treatment of Animals; its codirector, Ingrid Newkirk, calls research using animal subjects "fascism" and "supremacism." "Animal liberationists do not separate out the *human* animal," she says, "so there is no rational basis for saying that a human being has special rights. A rat is a pig is a dog is a boy. They're all mammals."[15])

Those who claim to base their objection to the use of animals in biomedical research on their reckoning of the net pleasures and pains produced make a second error, equally grave. Even if it were true—as it is surely not—that the pains of all animate beings must be counted equally, a cogent utilitarian calculation requires that we weigh all the consequences of the use, and of the nonuse, of animals in laboratory research. Critics relying (however mistakenly) on animal rights may claim to ignore the beneficial results of such research, rights being trump cards to which interest and advantage must give way. But an argument that is explicitly framed in terms of interest and benefit for all over the long run must attend also to the disadvantageous consequences of not using animals in research, and to all the achievements attained and attainable only through their use. The sum of the benefits of their use is utterly beyond quantification. The elimination of horrible disease, the increase of longevity, the avoidance of great pain, the saving of lives, and the improvement of the quality of lives (for humans and for animals) achieved through research using animals is so incalculably great that the argument of these critics, systematically pursued, establishes not their conclusion but its reverse: to refrain from using animals in biomedical research is, on utilitarian grounds, morally wrong.

When balancing the pleasures and pains resulting from the use of animals in research, we must not fail to place on the scales the terrible pains that would have resulted, would be suffered now, and would long continue had animals not been used. Every disease eliminated, every vaccine developed, every method of pain relief devised, every surgical procedure invented, every prosthetic device implanted—indeed, virtually every modern medical therapy is due, in part or in whole, to experimentation using animals. Nor may we ignore, in the balancing process, the predictable gains in human (and animal) well-being that are probably achievable in the future but that will not be achieved if the decision is made now to desist from such research or to curtail it.

Medical investigators are seldom insensitive to the distress their work may cause animal subjects. Opponents of research using animals are frequently insensitive to the cruelty of the results of the restrictions they would impose.[2] Untold numbers of human beings—real persons, although not now identifiable—would suffer grievously as the consequence of this well-meaning but shortsighted tenderness. If the morally relevant differences between humans and animals are borne in mind, and if all relevant considerations are weighed, the calculation of long-term consequences must give overwhelming support for biomedical research using animals.

CONCLUDING REMARKS

Substitution

The humane treatment of animals requires that we desist from experimenting on them if we can accomplish the same result using alternative methods—in vitro experimentation, computer simulation, or others. Critics of some experiments using animals rightly make this point.

It would be a serious error to suppose, however, that alternative techniques could soon be used in most research now using live animal subjects. No other methods now on the horizon—or perhaps ever to be available—can fully replace the testing of a drug, a procedure, or a vaccine, in live organisms. The flood of new medical possibilities being opened by the successes of recombinant DNA technology will turn to a trickle if testing on live animals is forbidden. When initial trials entail great risks, there may be no forward movement whatever without the use of live animal subjects. In seeking knowledge that may prove critical in later clinical applications, the unavailability of animals for inquiry may spell complete stymie. In the United States, federal regulations require the testing of new drugs and other products on animals, for efficacy and safety, before human beings are exposed to them.[16,17] We would not want it otherwise.

Every advance in medicine—every new drug, new operation, new therapy of any kind—must sooner or later be tried on a living being for the first time. That trial, controlled or uncontrolled, will be an experiment. The subject of that experiment, if it is not an animal, will be a human being. Prohibiting the use of live animals in biomedical research, therefore, or sharply restricting it, must result either in the blockage of much valuable research or in the replacement of animal subjects with human subjects. These are the consequences—unacceptable to most reasonable persons—of not using animals in research.

Reduction

Should we not at least reduce the use of animals in biomedical research? No, we should increase it, to avoid when feasible the use of humans as experimental subjects. Medical investigations putting human subjects at some risk are numerous and greatly varied. The risks run in such experiments are usually unavoidable, and (thanks to earlier experiments on animals) most such risks are minimal or moderate. But some experimental risks are substantial.

When an experimental protocol that entails substantial risk to humans comes before an institutional review board, what response is appropriate? The investigation, we may suppose, is promising and deserves support, so long as its human subjects are protected against unnecessary dangers. May not the investigators be fairly asked, Have you done all that you can to eliminate risk to humans by the extensive testing of that drug, that procedure, or that device on animals? To achieve maximal safety for humans we are right to require thorough experimentation on animal subjects before humans are involved.

Opportunities to increase human safety in this way are commonly missed; trials in which risks may be shifted from humans to animals are often not devised, sometimes not even considered. Why? For the investigator, the use of animals as subjects is often more expensive, in money and time, than the use of human subjects. Access to suitable human subjects is often quick and convenient, whereas access to appropriate animal subjects may be awkward, costly, and burdened with red tape. Physician-investigators have often had more experience working with human beings and know precisely where the needed pool of subjects is to be found and how they may be enlisted. Animals, and the procedures for their use, are often less familiar to these investigators. Moreover, the use of animals in place of humans is now more likely to be the target of zealous protests from without. The upshot is that humans are sometimes subjected to risks that animals could have borne, and should have borne, in their place. To maximize the protection of human subjects, I conclude, the wide and imaginative use of live animal subjects should be encouraged rather than discouraged. This enlargement in the use of animals is our obligation.

Consistency

Finally, inconsistency between the profession and the practice of many who oppose research using animals deserves comment. This frankly ad hominem observation aims chiefly to show that a coherent position rejecting the use of animals in medical research imposes costs so high as to be intolerable even to the critics themselves.

One cannot coherently object to the killing of animals in biomedical investigations while continuing to eat them. Anesthetics and thoughtful animal husbandry render the level of actual animal distress in the laboratory generally lower than that in the abattoir. So long as death and discomfort do not substantially differ in the two contexts, the consistent objector must not only refrain from all eating of animals but also protest as vehemently against others eating them as against others experimenting on them. No less vigorously must the critic object to the wearing of animal hides in coats and shoes, to employment in any industrial enterprise that uses animal parts, and to any commercial development that will cause death or distress to animals.

Killing animals to meet human needs for food, clothing, and shelter is judged entirely reasonable by most persons. The ubiquity of these uses and the virtual universality of moral support for them confront the opponent of research using animals with an inescapable difficulty. How can the many common uses of animals be judged morally worthy, while their use in scientific investigation is judged unworthy?

The number of animals used in research is but the tiniest fraction of the total used to satisfy assorted human appetites. That these appetites, often base and satisfiable in other ways, morally justify the far larger consumption of animals, whereas the quest for improved human health and understanding cannot justify the far smaller, is wholly implausible. Aside from the numbers of animals involved, the distinction in terms of worthiness of use, drawn with regard to any single animal, is not defensible. A given sheep is surely not more justifiably used to put lamb chops on the supermarket counter than to serve in testing a new contraceptive or a new prosthetic device. The needless killing of animals is wrong; if the common killing of them for our food or convenience is right, the less common but more humane uses of animals in the service of medical science are certainly not less right.

Scrupulous vegetarianism, in matters of food, clothing, shelter, commerce, and recreation, and in all other spheres, is the only fully coherent position the critic may adopt. At great human cost, the lives of fish and crustaceans must also be protected, with equal vigor, if speciesism has been forsworn. A very few consistent critics adopt this position. It is the reductio ad absurdum of the rejection of moral distinctions between animals and human beings.

Opposition to the use of animals in research is based on arguments of two different kinds—those relying on the alleged rights of animals and those relying on the consequences for animals. I have argued that arguments of both kinds must fail. We surely do have obligations to animals, but they have, and can have, no rights against us on which research can infringe. In calculating the consequences of animal research, we must weigh all the long-term benefits of the results achieved—to animals and to humans—and in that calculation we must not assume the moral equality of all animate species.

NOTES

1 Regan T. The case for animal rights. Berkeley, Calif.: University of California Press, 1983.
2 Singer P. Animal liberation. New York: Avon Books, 1977.
3 St. Augustine. Confessions. Book Seven. 397 A.D. New York: Pocketbooks, 1957:104–26.
4 St. Thomas Aquinas. Summa theologica. 1273 A.D. Philosophic texts. New York: Oxford University Press, 1960:353–66.
5 Hegel GWF. Philosophy of right. 1821. London: Oxford University Press, 1952:105–10.
6 Bradley FH. Why should I be moral? 1876. In: Melden AI, ed. Ethical theories. New York: Prentice-Hall, 1950:345–59.
7 Mead GH. The genesis of the self and social control. 1925. In: Reck AJ, ed. Selected writings. Indianapolis: Bobbs-Merrill, 1964:264–93.
8 Prichard HA. Does moral philosophy rest on a mistake? 1912. In: Cellars W, Hospers J, eds. Readings in ethical theory. New York: Appleton-Century-Crofts, 1952:149–63.
9 Kant I. Fundamental principles of the metaphysic of morals. 1785. New York: Liberal Arts Press, 1949.
10 Rollin BE. Animal rights and human morality. New York: Prometheus Books, 1981.
11 Hoff C. Immoral and moral uses of animals. N Engl J Med 1980; 302:115–8.
12 Jamieson D. Killing persons and other beings. In: Miller HB, Williams WH, eds. Ethics and animals. Clifton, N.J.: Humana Press, 1983:135–46.
13 Singer P. Ten years of animal liberation. New York Review of Books. 1985; 31:46–52.
14 Bentham J. Introduction to the principles of morals and legislation. London: Athlone Press, 1970.
15 McCabe K. Who will live, who will die? Washingtonian Magazine. August 1986:115.
16 U.S. Code of Federal Regulations, Title 21, Sect. 505(i). Food, drug, and cosmetic regulations.
17 U.S. Code of Federal Regulations, Title 16, Sect. 1500.40–2. Consumer product regulations.

QUESTIONS

1 Is speciesism a morally defensible position?
2 Do animals have rights?

Human and Animal Rights Compared

Mary Anne Warren

Along with Singer and Regan, Warren ascribes moral status to animals. In her view, animals, as sentient beings, do have rights. Her major concern, however, is with bringing out the *differences* between the rights of animals and those of human beings and with providing a justification for those differences. On

Reprinted with permission of the author from *Environmental Philosophy: A Collection of Readings* (Penn State University Press, 1983), edited by Robert Elliot and Arran Gare, pp. 112, 115–123.

Warren's account, the rights of animals and humans differ in respect to both their content and their *strength*—that is, in the strength of the reasons that are necessary to override them. Two reasons support the view that these differences are not arbitrary: (1) Human desires and interests are more extensive than those of animals, calling for differences in both the extent and strength of human rights. (2) The human capacity for moral autonomy, although not a necessary condition for having rights, can provide a reason for according somewhat stronger rights to human beings than to animals. Warren concludes by discussing the case of nonparadigm humans, who may not have a capacity for moral autonomy yet, unlike animals, have the *same* basic moral rights as paradigm humans, according to her analysis. She does not assert that animals and nonparadigm humans differ in their intrinsic value. Rather, both have intrinsic value and possess certain rights by virtue of their sentience. However, Warren argues, there are additional reasons, such as the value that nonparadigm humans have for paradigm humans, for ascribing stronger rights to nonparadigm humans than to animals.

None of the animal liberationists have thus far provided a clear explanation of how and why the moral status of (most) animals differs from that of (most) human beings; and this is a point which must be clarified if their position is to be made fully persuasive. That there is such a difference seems to follow from some very strong moral intuitions which most of us share. A man who shoots squirrels for sport may or may not be acting reprehensibly; but it is difficult to believe that his actions should be placed in *exactly* the same moral category as those of a man who shoots women, or black children, for sport. So too it is doubtful that the Japanese fishermen who slaughtered dolphins because the latter were thought to be depleting the local fish populations were acting quite *as* wrongly as if they had slaughtered an equal number of their human neighbours for the same reason. . . . There are two dimensions in which we may find differences between the rights of human beings and those of animals. The first involves the *content* of those rights, while the second involves their strength; that is, the strength of the reasons which are required to override them.

Consider, for instance, the right to liberty. The *human* right to liberty precludes imprisonment without due process of law, even if the prison is spacious and the conditions of confinement cause no obvious physical suffering. But it is not so obviously wrong to imprison animals, especially when the area to which they are confined provides a fair approximation of the conditions of their natural habitat, and a reasonable opportunity to pursue the satisfactions natural to their kind. Such conditions, which often result in an increased lifespan, and which may exist in wildlife sanctuaries or even well-designed zoos, need not frustrate the needs or interests of animals in any significant way, and thus do not clearly violate their rights. Similarly treated human beings, on the other hand (e.g., native peoples confined to prison-like reservations), do tend to suffer from their loss of freedom. Human dignity and the fulfillment of the sorts of plans, hopes and desires which appear (thus far) to be uniquely human, require a more extensive freedom of movement than is the case with at least many nonhuman animals. Furthermore, there are aspects of human freedom, such as freedom of thought, freedom of speech and freedom of political association, which simply do not apply in the case of animals.

Thus, it seems that the human right to freedom is more extensive; that is, it precludes a wider range of specific ways of treating human beings than does the corresponding right on the part of animals. The argument cuts both ways, of course. *Some* animals, for example, great whales and migratory birds, may require at least as much physical freedom as do human beings if they are to pursue the satisfactions natural to their kind, and this fact provides a moral argument against keeping such creatures imprisoned. And even chickens may suffer from the extreme and unnatural confinement to which they are subjected on modern "factory farms." Yet it seems unnecessary to claim for *most* animals a right to a freedom quite as broad as that which we claim for ourselves.

Similar points may be made with respect to the right to life. Animals, it may be argued, lack the cognitive equipment to value their lives in the way that human beings do. Ruth Cigman argues that animals have *no* right to life because death is no misfortune for them.[1] In her view, the death of an animal is not a misfortune, because animals have no desires which are *categorical;* that is which do not "merely presuppose being alive (like the desire to eat when one is hungry), but rather answer the question whether one wants to remain alive."[2] In other words, animals appear to lack the sorts of long-range hopes, plans, ambitions and the like, which give human beings such a powerful interest in continued life. Animals, it seems, take life as it comes and do not specifically desire that it go on. True, squirrels store nuts for the winter and deer run from wolves; but these may be seen as instinctive or conditioned responses to present circumstances, rather than evidence that they value life as such.

These reflections probably help to explain why the death of a sparrow seems less tragic than that of a human being. Human lives, one might say, have greater intrinsic value, because they are worth more *to their possessors.* But this does not demonstrate that no nonhuman animal has *any* right to life. Premature death may be a less *severe* misfortune for sentient nonhuman animals than for human beings, but it is a misfortune nevertheless. In the first place, it is a misfortune in that it deprives them of whatever pleasures the future might have held for them, regardless of whether or not they ever *consciously anticipated* those pleasures. The fact that they are not here afterwards, to *experience* their loss, no more shows that they have not lost anything than it does in the case of humans. In the second place, it is (possibly) a misfortune in that it frustrates whatever future-oriented desires animals *may* have, unbeknownst to us. Even now, in an age in which apes have been taught to use simplified human languages and attempts have been made to communicate with dolphins and whales, we still know very little about the operation of nonhuman minds. We know much too little to assume that nonhuman animals never consciously pursue relatively distant future goals. To the extent that they do, the question of whether such desires provide them with *reasons for living* or merely *presuppose* continued life, has no satisfactory answer, since they cannot contemplate these alternatives—or, if they can, we have no way of knowing what their conclusions are. All we know is that the more intelligent and psychologically complex an animal is, the more *likely* it is that it possesses specifically future-oriented desires, which would be frustrated even by *painless* death.

For these reasons, it is premature to conclude from the apparent intellectual inferiority of nonhuman animals that they have no right to life. A more plausible conclusion is that animals do have a right to life but that it is generally somewhat weaker than that of human beings. It is, perhaps, weak enough to enable us to justify killing animals when we have no other ways of achieving such vital goals as feeding or clothing ourselves, or obtaining knowledge which is necessary to save human lives. Weakening their right to life in this way does not render meaningless the assertion that they have such a right. For the point remains that *some* serious justification for the killing of sentient nonhuman animals is always necessary; they may not be killed merely to provide amusement or minor gains in convenience.

If animals' rights to liberty and life are somewhat weaker than those of human beings, may we say the same about their right to *happiness;* that is, their right not to be made to suffer needlessly or to be deprived of the pleasures natural to their kind? If so, it is not immediately clear why. There is little reason to suppose that pain or suffering are any less unpleasant for the higher animals (at least) than they are for us. Our large brains *may* cause us to experience pain more intensely than do most animals, and *probably* cause us to suffer more from the anticipation or remembrance of pain. These facts might tend to suggest that pain is, on the whole, a worse experience for us than for them. But it may also be argued that pain may be *worse* in some respects for nonhuman animals, who are presumably less able to distract themselves from it by thinking of something else, or to comfort themselves with the knowledge that it is temporary. Brigid Brophy points out that "pain is likely to fill the sheep's whole capacity for experience in a way it seldom does in us, whose intellect and imagination can create breaks for us in the immediacy of our sensations."[3]

The net result of such contrasting considerations is that we cannot possibly claim to know whether pain is, on the whole, worse for us than for animals, or whether their pleasures are any more or any less intense than ours. Thus, while we may justify assigning them a somewhat weaker right to life or liberty, on the grounds that they desire these goods less intensely than we do, we cannot discount their rights to freedom from needlessly inflicted pain or unnatural frustration on the same basis. There may, however, be *other* reasons for regarding all of the moral rights of animals as somewhat less stringent than the corresponding human rights.

A number of philosophers who deny that animals have moral rights point to the fact that nonhuman animals evidently lack the capacity for moral autonomy. Moral autonomy is the ability to act as a moral agent; that is, to act on the basis of an understanding of, and adherence to, moral rules or principles. H.J. McCloskey, for example, holds that "it is the capacity for moral autonomy . . . that is basic to the possibility of possessing a right."[4] McCloskey argues that it is inappropriate to ascribe moral rights to any entity which is not a moral agent, or *potentially* a moral agent, because a right is essentially an entitlement granted to a moral agent, licensing him or her to *act* in certain ways and to *demand* that other moral agents refrain from interference. For this reason, he says, "Where there is no possibility of [morally autonomous] action, potentially or actually . . . and where the being is not a member of a kind which is normally capable of [such] action, we withhold talk of rights."[5]

If moral autonomy—or being *potentially* autonomous, or a member of a kind which is *normally* capable of autonomy—is a necessary condition for having moral rights, then probably no nonhuman animal can qualify. For moral autonomy requires such probably uniquely human traits as "the capacity to be critically self-aware, manipulate concepts, use a sophisticated language, reflect, plan, deliberate, choose, and accept responsibility for acting."[6]

But why, we must ask, should the capacity for autonomy be regarded as a pre-condition for possessing moral rights? Autonomy is clearly crucial for the *exercise* of many human moral or legal rights, such as the right to vote or to run for public office. It is less clearly relevant, however, to the more basic human rights, such as the right to life or to freedom from unnecessary suffering. The fact that animals, like many human beings, cannot *demand* their moral rights (at least not in the words of any conventional human language) seems irrelevant. For, as Joel Feinberg points out, the interests of non-morally autonomous human beings may be defended by others, for example, in legal proceedings; and it is not clear why the interests of ani-mals might not be represented in a similar fashion.[7]

It is implausible, therefore, to conclude that because animals lack moral auton-omy they should be accorded *no moral rights whatsoever*. Nevertheless, it may be argued that the moral autonomy of (most) human beings provides a second reason, in addition to their more extensive interests and desires, for according somewhat *stronger* moral rights to human beings. The fundamental insight behind contractu-alist theories of morality is that, for morally autonomous beings such as ourselves, there is enormous mutual advantage in the adoption of a moral system designed to protect each of us from the harms that might otherwise be visited upon us by oth-ers. Each of us ought to accept and promote such a system because, to the extent that others also accept it, we will all be safer from attack by our fellows, more likely to receive assistance when we need it, and freer to engage in individual as well as cooperative endeavours of all kinds.

Thus, it is the possibility of *reciprocity* which motivates moral agents to extend *full and equal* moral rights, in the first instance, only to other moral agents. I respect your rights to life, liberty and the pursuit of happiness in part because you are a sen-tient being, whose interests have intrinsic moral significance. But I respect them as *fully equal to my own* because I hope and expect that you will do the same for me. Animals, insofar as they lack the degree of rationality necessary for moral auton-omy, cannot agree to respect our interests as equal in moral importance to their own, and neither do they expect or demand such respect from us. Of course, domes-tic animals may expect to be fed, etc. But they do not, and cannot, expect to be treated as moral equals, for they do not understand that moral concept or what it implies. Consequently, it is neither pragmatically feasible nor morally obligatory to extend to them the same *full and equal* rights which we extend to human beings.

Is this a speciesist conclusion? Defenders of a more extreme animal-rights posi-tion may point out that this argument, from the lack of moral autonomy, has exactly the same form as that which has been used for thousands of years to rationalize denying equal moral rights to women and members of "inferior" races. Aristotle, for example, argued that women and slaves are naturally subordinate beings, because they lack the capacity for moral autonomy and self-direction,[8] and con-temporary versions of this argument, used to support racist or sexist conclusions, are easy to find. Are we simply repeating Aristotle's mistake, in a different context?

The reply to this objection is very simple: animals, unlike women and slaves, really *are* incapable of moral autonomy, at least to the best of our knowledge. Aristotle certainly *ought* to have known that women and slaves are capable of morally autonomous action; their capacity to use moral language alone ought to have alerted him to this likelihood. If comparable evidence exists that (some) nonhuman animals are moral agents we have not yet found it. The fact that some apes (and, possibly, some cetaceans) are capable of learning radically simplified human languages, the terms of which refer primarily to objects and events in their immediate environment, in no way demonstrates that they can understand abstract moral concepts, rules or principles, or use this understanding to regulate their own behaviour.

On the other hand, this argument implies that if we *do* discover that certain non-human animals are capable of moral autonomy (which is certainly not impossible), then we ought to extend full and equal moral rights to those animals. Furthermore, if we someday encounter extraterrestrial beings, or build robots, androids or super-computers which function as self-aware moral agents, then we must extend full and equal moral rights to these as well. Being a member of the human species is not a necessary condition for the possession of full "human" rights. Whether it is nevertheless a *sufficient* condition is the question to which we now turn.

THE MORAL RIGHTS OF NONPARADIGM HUMANS

If we are justified in ascribing somewhat different, and also somewhat stronger, moral rights to human beings than to sentient but non-morally autonomous animals, then what are we to say of the rights of human beings who happen not to be capable of moral autonomy, perhaps not even potentially? Both Singer and Regan have argued that if any of the superior intellectual capacities of normal and mature human beings are used to support a distinction between the moral status of *typical,* or paradigm, human beings, and that of animals, then consistency will require us to place certain "nonparadigm" humans, such as infants, small children and the severely retarded or incurably brain damaged, in the same inferior moral category.[9] Such a result is, of course, highly counterintuitive.

Fortunately, no such conclusion follows from the autonomy argument. There are many reasons for extending strong moral rights to nonparadigm humans; reasons which do not apply to most nonhuman animals. Infants and small children are granted strong moral rights in part because of their *potential* autonomy. But *potential* autonomy, as I have argued elsewhere,[10] is not in itself a sufficient reason for the ascription of full moral rights; if it were, then not only human foetuses (from conception onwards) but even ununited human sperm-egg pairs would have to be regarded as entities with a right to life the equivalent of our own—thus making not only abortion, but any intentional failure to procreate, the moral equivalent of murder. Those who do not find this extreme conclusion acceptable must appeal to reasons other than the *potential* moral autonomy of infants and small children to explain the strength of the latter's moral rights.

One reason for assigning strong moral rights to infants and children is that they possess not just *potential* but *partial* autonomy, and it is not clear how much of it they have at any given moment. The fact that, unlike baby chimpanzees, they are already learning the things which will enable them to *become* morally autonomous, makes it likely that their minds have more subtleties than their speech (or the lack of it) proclaims. Another reason is simply that most of us tend to place a very high value on the lives and well-being of infants. Perhaps we are to some degree "programmed" by nature to love and protect them; perhaps our reasons are somewhat egocentric; or perhaps we value them for their potential. Whatever the explanation, the fact that we do feel this way about them is in itself a valid reason for extending to them stronger moral and legal protections than we extend to nonhuman animals, even those which may have just as well or better-developed psychological capacities. A third, and perhaps the most important, reason is that if we did *not* extend strong moral rights to infants, far too few of them would ever *become* responsible, morally autonomous adults; too many would be treated "like animals" (i.e., in ways that it is generally wrong to treat even animals), and would consequently become socially crippled, antisocial or just very unhappy people. If any part of our moral code is to remain intact, it seems that infants and small children *must* be protected and cared for.

Analogous arguments explain why strong moral rights should also be accorded to other nonparadigm humans. The severely retarded or incurably senile, for instance, may have no potential for moral autonomy, but there are apt to be friends, relatives or other people who care what happens to them. Like children, such individuals may have more mental capacities than are readily apparent. Like children, they are more apt to achieve, or return to moral autonomy if they are valued and well cared for. Furthermore, any one of us may someday become mentally incapacitated to one degree or another, and we would all have reason to be anxious about our own futures if such incapacitation were made the basis for denying strong moral rights.

There are, then, sound reasons for assigning strong moral rights even to human beings who lack the mental capacities which justify the general distinction between human and animal rights. Their rights are based not only on the value which they themselves place upon their lives and well-being, but also on the value which other human beings place upon them.

But is this a valid basis for the assignment of moral rights? . . . Regan argues that we cannot justify the ascription of stronger rights to nonparadigm humans than to nonhuman animals in the way suggested, because "what underlies the ascription of rights to any given X is that X has value independently of anyone's valuing X."[11] After all, we do not speak of expensive paintings or gemstones as having rights, although many people value them and have good reasons for wanting them protected.

There is, however, a crucial difference between a rare painting and a severely retarded or senile human being; the latter not only has (or may have) value for other human beings but *also* has his or her own needs and interests. It may be this which leads us to say that such individuals have intrinsic value. The sentience of nonparadigm humans, like that of sentient nonhuman animals, gives them a place in the sphere of rights holders. So long as the moral rights of all sentient beings are given due recognition, there should be no objection to providing some of them with *additional* protections, on the basis of our interests as well as their own. Some philosophers speak of such additional protections, which are accorded to X on the basis of interests other than X's own, as *conferred* rights, in contrast to *natural* rights, which are entirely based upon the properties of X itself. But such "conferred" rights are not necessarily any weaker or less binding upon moral agents than are "natural" rights. Infants, and most other nonparadigm humans have the *same* basic moral rights that the rest of us do, even though the reasons for ascribing those rights are somewhat different in the two cases. . . .

NOTES

1 Ruth Cigman, "Death, Misfortune, and Species Inequality," *Philosophy and Public Affairs* 10, no. 1 (Winter 1981): p. 48.
2 Ibid., pp. 57–58. The concept of a categorical desire is introduced by Bernard Williams, "The Makropoulous Case," in his *Problems of the Self* (Cambridge: Cambridge University Press), 1973.
3 Brigid Brophy, "In Pursuit of a Fantasy," in *Animals, Men and Morals,* ed. Stanley and Rosalind Godlovitch (New York: Taplinger Publishing Co., 1972), p. 129.
4 H. J. McCloskey, "Moral Rights and Animals," *Inquiry* 22, nos. 1–2 (1979): 31.
5 Ibid., p. 29.
6 Michael Fox, "Animal Liberation: A Critique," *Ethics* 88, no. 2 (January 1978): 111.
7 Joel Feinberg, "The Rights of Animals and Unborn Generations," in *Philosophy and Environmental Crisis,* ed. William T. Blackstone (Athens, Ga.: University of Georgia Press), 1974, pp. 46–47.
8 Aristotle, *Politics* I. 1254, 1260, and 1264.
9 Peter Singer, *Animal Liberation: A New Ethics for Our Treatment of Animals* (New York: Avon, 1975), pp. 75–76; Tom Regan, "One Argument Concerning Animal Rights," *Inquiry* 22, nos. 1–2 (1979): 189–217.
10 Mary Anne Warren, "Do Potential People Have Moral Rights?" *Canadian Journal of Philosophy* 7, no. 2 (June 1977): 275–89.
11 Regan, "One Argument Concerning Animal Rights," p. 189.

QUESTIONS

1 Is Warren correct in making the following claim? If we someday encounter extraterrestrial beings, or build robots, androids, or supercomputers which function as self-aware moral agents, then we must extend full and equal moral rights to these.
2 What human needs, if any, are sufficiently important to warrant the infliction of pain and suffering on animals?

SUGGESTED ADDITIONAL READINGS FOR CHAPTER 8

ARMSTRONG, SUSAN J, and RICHARD G. BOTZLER, eds.: *The Animal Ethics Reader.* New York: Routledge, 2003. This ten-chapter anthology includes chapters on theories of animal ethics, animal capacities, primates and cetaceans, the use of animals for food, and animal experimentation.
DeGRAZIA, DAVID: *Animal Rights: A Very Short Introduction.* New York: Oxford University Press, 2002. DeGrazia engages the issue of the moral status of animals, arguing that sentient animals are entitled to equal consideration. He also discusses the mental lives of animals and the various ways in which animals can be harmed Finally, he

considers the ethics of meat-eating, the ethics of keeping pets and zoo animals, and the ethics of animal research.

————: "The Ethics of Animal Research: What Are the Prospects for Agreement?" *Cambridge Quarterly of Healthcare Ethics,* vol. 8, Winter 1999, pp. 23–34. DeGrazia provides some background on the ethical and political debate over animal research and identifies significant points of potential agreement between the perspectives of biomedicine and animal advocates.

DOMBROWSKI, DANIEL A.: *The Philosophy of Vegetarianism.* Amherst: University of Massachusetts Press, 1984. This book provides an interesting historical background for contemporary philosophical discussions of vegetarianism. Its critical examination focuses primarily on ancient Greek sources, from the early poetic tradition of Hesiod and Homer down to the neoplatonists in the Christian era.

FOX, MICHAEL ALLEN: *Deep Vegetarianism.* Philadelphia: Temple University Press, 1999. Fox argues that an in-depth examination of the vegetarian outlook raises a broad spectrum of philosophical issues connected with the moral, social, and political spheres of our lives. Surveying and analyzing a variety of significant arguments for vegetarianism, he maintains that the spectrum of arguments should urge us toward a vegetarian commitment in both theory and practice.

FREY, R. G.: *Interests and Rights: The Case Against Animals.* Oxford: Clarendon, 1980. In Frey's view, animals do not have interests, and thus they do not have moral rights. Accordingly, he contends, arguments for vegetarianism that are based on the claim that animals have moral rights are unsound.

GEORGE, KATHRYN PAXTON: "Ethical Vegetarianism Is Unfair to Women and Children." In James P. Sterba, ed., *Earth Ethics,* 2d ed. Upper Saddle River, N.J.: Prentice-Hall, 2000. The author criticizes both Peter Singer's and Tom Regan's arguments for vegetarianism. In her view, the moral ideal presented in these arguments does not apply to the majority of people—women, children, and the elderly as well as many people in non-Western countries. Thus, it relegates members of these groups to a moral underclass of beings who, because of their physiological natures or cultures, are not capable of being fully moral.

REGAN, TOM: *The Case for Animal Rights.* Berkeley: University of California Press, 1983. Regan argues that animals have a basic moral right to respectful treatment. He derives the following conclusions: (1) Vegetarianism is obligatory; (2) hunting and trapping are wrong; (3) the use of animals in science is impermissible.

————, and PETER SINGER, eds.: *Animal Rights and Human Obligations,* 2d ed. Englewood Cliffs, N.J.: Prentice-Hall, 1989. This very useful anthology begins with a section on animals in the history of Western thought. Some of the other sections are "Animal Rights," "Killing and the Value of Life," "The Treatment of Farm Animals," and "The Treatment of Animals in Science."

ROLLIN, BERNARD E.: *The Unheeded Cry: Animal Consciousness, Animal Pain and Science.* Oxford: Oxford University Press, 1989. Rollin provides a study of American and European attitudes toward animal consciousness and their relation to scientific experimentation using animals, beginning with George Romanes in the nineteenth century. Also included is an extensive bibliography beginning with citations from 1879.

SINGER, PETER: *Animal Liberation,* 2d ed. New York: New York Review, 1990. Singer advances a vigorous critique of our present attitudes toward animals and our dealings with them. He also provides a wealth of relevant factual material.

The Environment Notes

William F. Baxter: Baxter talks about "**spheres of freedom**." What he means is that any culture has limited resources. If we use our resources to solve one problem, then those same resources may not be available to solve another, perhaps, equally important problem. Therefore, we have to compromise between issues such as clean air and the economic impact on jobs and profits that industries would bear in order to achieve clean air. He also questions how we define things. What do we mean by "clean" air? Do we mean air that is clean enough to support life, or air that is 100% pure? There will always be some compromises.

Baxter asks us to consider whether it is practical to consider animals and their needs. For example, if the air and water are clean enough for humans, then they are also clean enough for animals. In other words, if it benefits humans, it will also benefit animals and the environment. His argument is a classic example of an andropocentric position.

Jan Narveson: Narveson believes the way to keep our neighbors from harming us is through the courts—by suing them if they do things we dislike. If they pollute the air we need to breathe, then we should sue them. She justifies this position by arguing that not all people are bothered by the same things. She believes taking a person or a company to court would only happen if the claimant was really upset about the pollution or danger being caused. She does not believe governments should make laws that apply to all situations, since some people might not be bothered by it. In fact, government should not interfere at all.

Narveson also challenges our belief that pollution is dangerous. For example, she says claims that link smoking to cancer are just statistical. In other words, more people who smoke get cancer, but this doesn't tell us about individual risk. Therefore, people should be left to make their own decision about smoking. People who believe second-hand smoke is dangerous, can then sue the people who smoke, if they do it in the same building as the non-smokers. But, if the people in the building don't mind, then smokers would be free to smoke in the building.

She believes recycling is a waste of money. Companies would only have to clean up their pollution if enough people had enough money to bring the company to court and win a suite against them. There should be no government regulations.

You might want to consider Narveson's article in light of the oil spill in the gulf.... Can you imagine BP waiting for the years it would take to get through the court system to pay for any clean-up? What would Louisiana and the other gulf coast states look like if there were no regulations and no responsibility expected from the drilling companies?

Tony Smith: Smith makes the following arguments:

1 As long as there is a profit to be made while harming the environment, there will be little incentive to not to do harm.

2 If an area is destroyed by a company, the company will simply move to another area.

3 If we rely on liability laws, as suggested by Narveson, how many people could afford to the legal expenses.

4 Liability laws work best when there are direct causal links and provable chains of events. Things are not so simple. Some harm may be caused by multiple companies or multiple events. Separating them out may not be possible.

5 No court counts the detrimental effects that may be imposed on future generations. Courts only deal with the present.

6 Leaving the market place to decide what is a fair trade-off means leaving the decision in the hands of the people who are most likely to profit from abusing the system. And is profit really a fair trade if it costs human life? (There was a car company, years ago, that estimated that the cost of paying out for the loss of life caused by their cars still left them with a hefty profit margin. As a result, they simply put that in their annual budget and continued to sell the defective car. It wasn't until there was a public outcry and enough bad publicity that they stopped the car's manufacture.)

7 Non-corporate structures just do not have the money to purchase and set aside land for protection.

8 People have a right to a livable environment.

Peter Wenz: Wenz points out that garbage usually ends up being disposed of in the places where people have the least voice, the least power, to prevent it. He argues this happens, disproportionally, in black communities. He brings in a "doctrine of double effect." This is the argument that people "of color" are disproportionately burdened because they are poor. This makes the underlying reason one of poverty rather than race. Wenz says this is just not correct, and it is an important distinction because if the problem is due to racism, then there are legal remedies (racism is illegal), but if the problem is due to poverty, then there is no law that sets a precedence for protecting people just because they are poor.
Wenz argues that a disproportionate impact on the poor is a violation of "distributive justice," but that applies to philosophy, not law. Meanwhile, toxic waste and other LULUs (Locally Undesirable Land Uses) lower property value and create health hazards. People who can afford it, simply move to other locations, leaving behind those who do not have the resources. Wenz suggests that the communities that generate the most waste, should be the ones to also bear the greatest burden of its disposal.

Aldo Leopold: Leopold's article is an early example of environmental awareness and a call to preserve the land. His article is a classic in biocentric ethics.

Leopold begins his article with the story of Odysseus returning from Troy. Odysseus returns to find out that some of his household has been disloyal and promptly has them hung. The point being made is that, in the past, not all humans had rights. As our ethics evolved, rights were extended to all humans. If we look at our understanding of rights today, we see that rights (such as not to be neglected or tortured) have been extended, at least to some degree, to animals. Leopold asks us to shift our evolutionary notion of rights over just a bit further, to include environments.

Leopold describes the importance of the land itself in his "biotic pyramid." The pyramid's base rests on the land, on the earth. From that base, a "fountain of energy," that sustains all plant and animal life goes up through smaller and smaller areas, and then returns through death and decay, back to the land, to be renewed and sustain new life. It is a continual process of regeneration.

Bernard E. Rollin: Rollin argues that "rights arise out of a common moral theory." He means that we justify our own human rights by the claim that we are sentient creatures. To be sentient means to have the capacity for pleasure and pain. Because we can feel pain, we have the right not to be subjected to pain without our consent (for example, as when we need medical treatment). Because we can feel pleasure and have an interest in our welfare, we have a right to those things. However, to be consistent, that also means that if a non-human also has the capacity for sentience then we must extend the same rights not to be harmed to that non-human. Being human is not what gives us our rights. It is the fact that we are sentient. Rollin argues that means we must give some rights to animals as well as humans. For example, we do not have the right to torture an animal any more than we have the right to torture a person. This echoes the argument by Singer in the "Animal" chapter.

However, Rollin admits that animals have limited rights. He is not suggesting we ask our dog to vote. He is saying that our dog has the right to be fed and housed because our dog can feel pain and pleasure, just like us. The point Rollin is making is that some living things, such as people and many animals, have rights because they have certain capacities, and that trees, plants, and environments do not have rights because environments are not sentient, and, therefore, do not have the same capacities. Unlike people and animals, trees have no interest in whether they exist or not. Rocks do not feel pleasure or pain. Rollin uses the term "prima facie priority" to explain that giving rights to sentient creatures is a priority over giving rights to non-sentient objects.

Bill Duvall and George Sessions: Duvall and Sessions write about deep ecology and establish a chart comparing it with a dominant worldview. Deep ecology is the same as a biocentric perspective. In a way, Duvall and Sessions create an updated version of Aldo Leopold's article.

Dominant Worldview	Deep Ecology
Dominance over Nature	Harmony with Nature
Natural environment as resource for humans	All nature has intrinsic worth
Material/economic growth for growing human population	Elegantly simple material needs serving a larger goal of self-realization
Belief in ample resource reserves	"Supplies" limited
High technological progress and solution	Appropriate technology (not dominated by science)
Consumerism	Doing with enough/recycling
National/centralized economy	Minority tradition/bioregion

Ramachandra Guha: Guha critiques the major environmental movements as following a pattern established in the United States. He points out that the culture and geography of most third world nations is very different from that of the U.S. In the U.S., we have separate areas for cities, farms, and wilderness. This works well for us. However, for most third world countries, the separation is not so distinct. A large portion of the population may depend on its living from the land. When areas of land are set aside as wilderness preserves (habitat for various animal species), it is at the expense of the human population being displaced. Guha suggests the American model is more harmful than helpful when transferred to other areas of the world.

CHAPTER 9

The Environment

Much of our traditional thinking about morality is *anthropocentric*—that is, it assumes that moral obligation is essentially a function of *human* interests. Increasingly, however, anthropocentric approaches to morality are being challenged. Many thinkers concerned with our moral obligations with respect to the environment, like many of those concerned with our obligations with respect to animals, question whether an anthropocentric ethic can provide an adequate basis for all our moral obligations, including environmental ones. This chapter focuses on our moral obligations with respect to the environment and the appropriate moral foundation for those obligations. It also deals with issues of justice associated with the location of polluting industries, garbage dumps, and hazardous waste sites.

THE BASIS FOR OUR MORAL OBLIGATIONS REGARDING THE ENVIRONMENT

We are becoming increasingly aware of the extent to which human activities pollute and destroy the natural environment. This is perhaps most dramatically exemplified by the growing international concern with global warming, much of which is now believed to be the result of human activities that have resulted in the buildup of greenhouse gases—chiefly carbon dioxide, methane, and nitrous oxide. While scientists cannot predict as yet just what the impact of global warming will be in the future, they identify the following as being at risk—our health, agriculture, water resources, forests, wildlife, and coastal areas.[1] Most reflective people would agree that much of the ongoing pollution produced by human activities and the resultant environmental destruction is morally wrong. Philosophers and other writers who are concerned with environmental issues disagree, however, about *why* it is morally wrong, for example, to pollute the environment, destroy wilderness areas, or contribute to the destruction of species. What is the basis of our moral obligations regarding the natural environment? Three fundamentally different approaches can be distinguished in reference to this question: (1) anthropocentric approaches, (2) sentientist approaches, and (3) biocentric, or ecocentric, approaches.

[1] The U.S. Environmental Protection Agency (http://www.epa.gov). This website provides useful information about global warming.

Anthropocentric Approaches

On the anthropocentric approach, our obligations regarding the environment are to be determined solely on the basis of human interests. It seems clear, for example, that we can appeal to human interests in order to ground a prima facie duty not to pollute the environment—that is, a duty not to pollute unless there are overriding moral considerations. Human welfare—in fact, human life—crucially depends on such necessities as breathable air, drinkable water, and eatable food. Thus, in the absence of overriding moral considerations, pollution is morally unacceptable precisely because it is damaging to the public welfare. On an alternative construal, still using an anthropocentric approach, the prima facie duty not to pollute may be understood as based on a basic human right: the right to a livable environment. Thus, we can assert, with some confidence, that there is a prima facie duty not to pollute. We are left, however, with the problem of weighing the collective human interest in a nonpolluted environment against competing human interests, often economic ones.

The following schematic example illustrates some of the complexities that confront us when environmental and economic interests clash. An industrial plant, representing a (small, large, massive) financial investment, producing a product that is (unessential, very desirable, essential) to society and providing a (small, large, enormous) number of jobs, pollutes the environment in a (minor, substantial, major) way. In which of these several cases is the continued operation of the plant morally unacceptable? Certainly the general public interest in the quality of the environment must be recognized. But what about the economic interests of the owners, employees, and potential customers? In sum, how is the collective human interest in a nonpolluted environment to be equitably weighed against competing economic interests?

At this point, some ethicists tend to appeal to the kind of cost-benefit analyses that characterize utilitarian thinking. William F. Baxter, who defends an anthropocentric ethical stance in this chapter, adopts this cost-benefit approach in arguing for "optimal pollution"—pollution whose harms are outweighed by various human interests, including economic and aesthetic ones. Others, such as Jan Narveson in this chapter, adopt a free market approach to pollution in keeping with the libertarian position advanced by John Hospers in Chapter 3 and discussed in the introduction to that chapter. The following ideas characterize free market environmentalism: All lands and areas of nature are owned by private persons; there are no public lands; all "environmental problems" are to be worked out by negotiation among the affected parties; there is no environmental legislation. In keeping with this view, Narveson argues that the best solution to environmental problems is a hands-off government policy that allows marketplace transactions to determine the extent and distribution of pollution. Narveson's position is critically evaluated in this chapter by Tony Smith, who rejects free market environmentalism. In another of this chapter's readings, Peter S. Wenz rejects both the cost-benefit analysis and free market approaches. In his view, neither position will result in a just distribution of the burdens associated with waste and pollution. Focusing on toxic wastes, Wenz argues that the poor, who are often members of minority groups, bear a disproportionate share of the hazards associated with toxic wastes. He proposes the adoption of policies that would require those who benefit the most from the activities resulting in such hazards to bear a proportionate share of the resulting burdens. Although Wenz is not an anthropocentrist, his reasoning in this chapter is limited to the effects of the hazards associated with toxic wastes on human beings.

An anthropocentric moral approach can be taken to other environmental issues as well. For example, it can be argued that the preservation of wilderness serves numerous human interests, and these interests can be viewed as the basis for an obligation to preserve wilderness areas. In this vein, it is pointed out that many people find communing with nature in wilderness areas to be an important source of aesthetic experience and spiritual renewal, that wilderness areas provide significant recreational opportunities for human beings, that the biodiversity stockpiled in wilderness areas can be of great human benefit in connection with the search for substances that have medicinal value, and so on.

Those who believe that an anthropocentric approach is capable of providing an adequate foundation for our obligations with regard to the environment usually insist on the importance of considering a wide range of human interests, not just economic ones, and they also usually insist on taking seriously the interests of future generations of human beings, not just those of presently existing human beings. Since human well-being is so intimately intertwined with the well-being of the environment, they point out, we must resist forces of environmental degradation; otherwise, sooner or later, the possibility of human beings' leading healthy and happy lives will be severely compromised.

Sentientist Approaches

On a sentientist approach, the interests of sentient beings determine our obligations regarding the environment. All sentient beings (not just human beings) are seen as having inherent (intrinsic) value and not merely instrumental value. As the distinction between inherent and instrumental value is usually drawn, some things are valuable as a *means* to some valued end; thus, their value is instrumental. Other things are valuable in themselves and, thus, are said to have inherent or intrinsic value. (Singer in Chapter 10 takes a sentientist approach insofar as he uses sentience as the criterion for determining what sorts of things are entitled to an equal consideration of their interests.) Since sentient beings include human beings, it can be argued on a sentientist approach, just as on an anthropocentric one, that, for example, mountains, forests, and snail darters should be preserved because of their aesthetic value to human beings. But, insofar, as nonhuman animals are also sentient beings, a sentientist would insist that animal interests must also be considered when determining our environmental obligations. Bernard E. Rollin's reasoning in this chapter illustrates sentientist thinking. Rollin maintains that we might have a moral obligation to preserve some natural habitat that is of no value to human beings if its destruction would harm some nonhuman animals.

Biocentric (Ecocentric) Approaches

In recent years, various writers have argued for an even more radical revision of traditional approaches to morality than that proposed by sentientists. In fact, sentientism is sometimes criticized as analogous to both racism and speciesism insofar as all three can be viewed as giving unjustified preference to one's own "kind." John Rodman, who coined the term *sentientism,* criticizes the sentientist approach as follows:

> The rest of nature is left in a state of thinghood, having no intrinsic worth, acquiring instrumental value only as resources for the well-being of an elite of sentient beings. Homocentrist rationalism has widened out into a kind of zoocentrist sentientism. . . . If it would seem arbitrary to a visitor from Mars to find one species claiming a monopoly of intrinsic value by virtue of its allegedly exclusive possession of reason, free will, soul, or some other occult quality, would it not seem almost as arbitrary to find that same species claiming a monopoly of intrinsic value for itself and those species most resembling it . . . by virtue of their common and allegedly exclusive possession of sentience?[2]

Aldo Leopold (1887–1948), whose famous essay "The Land Ethic" is partially reprinted in this chapter, argues for a more revolutionary environmental ethic. Insisting that moral consideration must be extended to all of nature, he writes:

> The land ethic simply enlarges the boundaries of the community to include soils, waters, plants, and animals, or collectively the land. . . . In short, a land ethic changes the role of *Homo sapiens* from conqueror of the land-community to plain member and citizen of it. It implies respect for his fellow-members, and also respect for the community as such. . . . A thing is right when it tends to preserve the integrity, stability, and beauty of the biotic community. It is wrong when it tends otherwise.[3]

Leopold's approach to our moral obligations with regard to the environment is sometimes said to involve a biotic view (*biotic* means "relating to life") and is, therefore, called *biocentric.* Proponents of a biocentric ethic consider all life to be inherently valuable, and they often understand "life" in such a broad sense that it includes even things that are not themselves living organisms, such as rivers, landscapes, ecosystems, and "the living earth." To the extent that biocentric approaches attach moral standing to ecosystems, they may also be labeled *ecocentric.*[4] (An *ecosystem* can be defined as a unit made up of a community of living things taken in conjunction with the nonliving factors of its environment.)

Leopold's land ethic provides one important articulation of a biocentric point of view. Another well-known expression of a biocentric point of view can be located in a school of thought known as *deep ecology.* Deep ecology is principally defined

---

[2]John Rodman, "The Liberation of Nature?" *Inquiry,* vol. 20, 1977, p. 91.

[3]Aldo Leopold, "The Land Ethic," in *A Sand County Almanac* (New York: Oxford University Press, 1966), pp. 210, 220, 240.

[4]Although the biocentric approaches explicitly discussed in this chapter are correctly labeled *ecocentric,* there is no necessary connection between biocentrism and ecocentrism. Indeed, one position in environmental ethics is called *biocentric individualism.* On this view, moral consideration is to be extended to all *individual* living things, but is not to be extended (at least not directly extended) to ecosystems or the biosphere as a whole. See, for example, Paul W. Taylor, *Respect for Nature: A Theory of Environmental Ethics* (Princeton, N.J.: Princeton University Press, 1986).

in reference to the writings of Arne Naess, Bill Devall, and George Sessions. Naess is a Norwegian philosopher, and the other two writers are Americans. In one of this chapter's readings, Devall and Sessions present the worldview of deep ecology in contrast to the "dominant worldview."

Proponents of deep ecology often contrast their approach with what they call *shallow ecology*, and they identify shallow ecology with anthropocentric approaches, which are committed to constructing an account of environmental obligations solely in reference to human interests and concerns. At any rate, deep ecology firmly rejects both anthropocentric and sentientist approaches to environmental obligations. It calls for a radical, fundamental revision in our attitude toward the natural world. Naess and Sessions write:

> The well-being and flourishing of human and nonhuman Life on Earth have value in them-selves (synonyms: intrinsic value, inherent value). These values are independent of the usefulness of the nonhuman world for human purposes. . . . Richness and diversity of life forms contribute to the realization of these values and are also values in themselves. . . . Humans have no right to reduce this richness and diversity except to satisfy *vital* needs.[5]

CRITICISMS OF BIOCENTRIC APPROACHES

Two articles in this chapter incorporate criticisms of biocentric approaches. Rollin argues that moral consideration is appropriately extended to individual animals but not to other natural entities. Thus, he claims that neither nonsentient natural objects (e.g., plants and rivers) nor "quasi-abstract entities, such as species and ecosys-tems" possess intrinsic value. In his view, an adequate environmental ethic can be based solely on the instrumental value that other natural entities have for sentient creatures. Thus, the paradoxes and difficulties that arise when intrinsic value is attributed to nonsentient natural objects and quasi-abstract entities can be avoided.

Ramachandra Guha argues in this chapter from a third-world perspective. He presents a wide-ranging critique of what he calls the *American* deep ecology move-ment. Guha rejects the anthropocentric-biocentric distinction, which he identifies as a central tenet of American deep ecology. He maintains that the distinction is of little use in helping us understand the dynamics of environmental degradation. Guha argues for what he considers a much more radical approach to environmen-tal issues—an approach that he sees as exemplified in countries such as Germany and India. This approach emphasizes the need to change the sociopolitical basis of the consumerism and militarism that, in his view, are responsible for so much envi-ronmental destruction. Thus, Guha's approach is "radical" in a different way than are biocentric approaches. Biocentric approaches are radical insofar as they call for a revolutionary revision of our fundamental moral categories. Guha's approach is politically radical, however, insofar as it calls for a rethinking of some of our fun-damental sociopolitical institutions.

Jane S. Zembaty

---

[5]These statements are part of a platform of the deep ecology movement originally formulated by Naess and Sessions in 1984. The platform as a whole is included—under the heading "Basic Principles of Deep Ecology"—in the selection by Devall and Sessions in this chapter.

People or Penguins: The Case
for Optimal Pollution

William F. Baxter

Baxter adopts an anthropocentric approach to environmental trade-offs. He states
four general goals, which, in his view, should serve as criteria for evaluating
solutions to environmental problems. Baxter defends his anthropocentric approach
and briefly discusses the kinds of trade-offs involved when interests in controlling
pollution must be weighed against competing interests, including economic ones.

I start with the modest proposition that, in dealing with pollution, or indeed with
any problem, it is helpful to know what one is attempting to accomplish. Agreement
on how and whether to pursue a particular objective, such as pollution control, is
not possible unless some more general objective has been identified and stated with
reasonable precision. We talk loosely of having clean air and clean water, of preserving our wilderness areas, and so forth. But none of these is a sufficiently general objective: each is more accurately viewed as a means rather than as an end.

With regard to clean air, for example, one may ask, "how clean?" and "what does
clean mean?" It is even reasonable to ask, "why have clean air?" Each of these
questions is an implicit demand that a more general community goal be stated—a
goal sufficiently general in its scope and enjoying sufficiently general assent among
the community of actors that such "why" questions no longer seem admissible with
respect to that goal.

If, for example, one states as a goal the proposition that "every person should be
free to do whatever he wishes in contexts where his actions do not interfere with
the interests of other human beings," the speaker is unlikely to be met with a
response of "why." The goal may be criticized as uncertain in its implications or
difficult to implement, but it is so basic a tenet of our civilization—it reflects a cultural value so broadly shared, at least in the abstract—that the question "why" is
seen as impertinent or imponderable or both.

I do not mean to suggest that everyone would agree with the "spheres of freedom"
objective just stated. Still less do I mean to suggest that a society could subscribe
to four or five such general objectives that would be adequate in their coverage to
serve as testing criteria by which all other disagreements might be measured. One
difficulty in the attempt to construct such a list is that each new goal added will conflict, in certain applications, with each prior goal listed; and thus each goal serves
as a limited qualification on prior goals.

Without any expectation of obtaining unanimous consent to them, let me set forth
four goals that I generally use as ultimate testing criteria in attempting to frame solutions to problems of human organization. My position regarding pollution stems
from these four criteria. If the criteria appeal to you and any part of what appears

Reprinted with permission of Columbia University Press from William F. Baxter, *People or Penguins:
The Case for Optimal Pollution* (1974), pp. 1–13.

hereafter does not, our disagreement will have a helpful focus: which of us is correct, analytically, in supposing that his position on pollution would better serve these general goals. If the criteria do not seem acceptable to you, then it is to be expected that our more particular judgments will differ, and the task will then be yours to identify the basic set of criteria upon which your particular judgments rest.

My criteria are as follows:

1 The spheres of freedom criterion stated above.

2 Waste is a bad thing. The dominant feature of human existence is scarcity—our available resources, our aggregate labors, and our skill in employing both have always been, and will continue for some time to be, inadequate to yield to every man all the tangible and intangible satisfactions he would like to have. Hence, none of those resources, or labors, or skills, should be wasted—that is, employed so as to yield less than they might yield in human satisfactions.

3 Every human being should be regarded as an end rather than as a means to be used for the betterment of another. Each should be afforded dignity and regarded as having an absolute claim to an evenhanded application of such rules as the community may adopt for its governance.

4 Both the incentive and the opportunity to improve his share of satisfactions should be preserved to every individual. Preservation of incentive is dictated by the "no-waste" criterion and enjoins against the continuous, totally egalitarian redistribution of satisfactions, or wealth; but subject to that constraint, everyone should receive, by continuous redistribution if necessary, some minimal share of aggregate wealth so as to avoid a level of privation from which the opportunity to improve his situation becomes illusory.

The relationship of these highly general goals to the more specific environmental issues at hand may not be readily apparent, and I am not yet ready to demonstrate their pervasive implications. But let me give one indication of their implications. Recently scientists have informed us that use of DDT in food production is causing damage to the penguin population. For the present purposes let us accept that assertion as an indisputable scientific fact. The scientific fact is often asserted as if the correct implication—that we must stop agricultural use of DDT—followed from the mere statement of the fact of penguin damage. But plainly it does not follow if my criteria are employed.

My criteria are oriented to people, not penguins. Damage to penguins, or sugar pines, or geological marvels is, without more, simply irrelevant. One must go further, by my criteria, and say: Penguins are important because people enjoy seeing them walk about rocks; and furthermore, the well-being of people would be less impaired by halting use of DDT than by giving up penguins. In short, my observations about environmental problems will be people-oriented, as are my criteria. I have no interest in preserving penguins for their own sake.

It may be said by way of objection to this position, that it is very selfish of people to act as if each person represented one unit of importance and nothing else was of any importance. It is undeniably selfish. Nevertheless I think it is the only tenable starting place for analysis for several reasons. First, no other position corresponds to the way most people really think and act—i.e., corresponds to reality.

Second, this attitude does not portend any massive destruction of nonhuman flora and fauna, for people depend on them in many obvious ways, and they will be preserved because and to the degree that humans do depend on them.

Third, what is good for humans is, in many respects, good for penguins and pine trees—clean air for example. So that humans are, in these respects, surrogates for plant and animal life.

Fourth, I do not know how we could administer any other system. Our decisions are either private or collective. Insofar as Mr. Jones is free to act privately, he may give such preferences as he wishes to other forms of life: he may feed birds in winter and do with less himself, and he may even decline to resist an advancing polar bear on the ground that the bear's appetite is more important than those portions of himself that the bear may choose to eat. In short my basic premise does not rule out private altruism to competing life-forms. It does rule out, however, Mr. Jones' inclination to feed Mr. Smith to the bear, however hungry the bear, however despicable Mr. Smith.

Insofar as we act collectively on the other hand, only humans can be afforded an opportunity to participate in the collective decisions. Penguins cannot vote now and are unlikely subjects for the franchise—pine trees more unlikely still. Again each individual is free to cast his vote so as to benefit sugar pines if that is his inclination. But many of the more extreme assertions that one hears from some conservationists amount to tacit assertions that they are specially appointed representatives of sugar pines, and hence that their preferences should be weighted more heavily than the preferences of other humans who do not enjoy equal rapport with "nature." The simplistic assertion that agricultural use of DDT must stop at once because it is harmful to penguins is of that type.

Fifth, if polar bears or pine trees or penguins, like men, are to be regarded as ends rather than means, if they are to count in our calculus of social organization, someone must tell me how much each one counts, and someone must tell me how these life-forms are to be permitted to express their preferences, for I do not know either answer. If the answer is that certain people are to hold their proxies, then I want to know how those proxy-holders are to be selected: self-appointment does not seem workable to me.

Sixth, and by way of summary of all the foregoing, let me point out that the set of environmental issues under discussion—although they raise very complex technical questions of how to achieve any objective—ultimately raise a normative question: what *ought* we to do? Questions of *ought* are unique to the human mind and world—they are meaningless as applied to a nonhuman situation.

I reject the proposition that we *ought* to respect the "balance of nature" or to "preserve the environment" unless the reason for doing so, express or implied, is the benefit of man.

I reject the idea that there is a "right" or "morally correct" state of nature to which we should return. The word "nature" has no normative connotation. Was it "right" or "wrong" for the earth's crust to heave in contortion and create mountains and seas? Was it "right" for the first amphibian to crawl up out of the primordial ooze? Was it "wrong" for plants to reproduce themselves and alter the atmospheric composition in favor of oxygen? For animals to alter the atmosphere in favor of carbon dioxide both by breathing oxygen and eating plants? No answers can be given to these questions because they are meaningless questions.

All this may seem obvious to the point of being tedious, but much of the present controversy over environment and pollution rests on tacit normative assumptions about just such nonnormative phenomena: that it is "wrong" to impair penguins with DDT, but not to slaughter cattle for prime rib roasts. That it is wrong to kill stands of sugar pines with industrial fumes, but not to cut sugar pines and build housing for the poor. Every man is entitled to his own preferred definition of Walden Pond, but there is no definition that has any moral superiority over another, except by reference to the selfish needs of the human race.

From the fact that there is no normative definition of the natural state, it follows that there is no normative definition of clean air or pure water—hence no definition of polluted air—or of pollution—except by reference to the needs of man. The "right" composition of the atmosphere is one which has some dust in it and some lead in it and some hydrogen sulfide in it—just those amounts that attend a sensibly organized society thoughtfully and knowledgeably pursuing the greatest possible satisfaction for its human members.

The first and most fundamental step toward solution of our environmental problems is a clear recognition that our objective is not pure air or water but rather some optimal state of pollution. That step immediately suggests the question: How do we define and attain the level of pollution that will yield the maximum possible amount of human satisfaction?

Low levels of pollution contribute to human satisfaction but so do food and shelter and education and music. To attain ever lower levels of pollution, we must pay the cost of having less of these other things. I contrast that view of the cost of pollution control with the more popular statement that pollution control will "cost" very large numbers of dollars. The popular statement is true in some senses, false in others; sorting out the true and false senses is of some importance. The first step in that sorting process is to achieve a clear understanding of the difference between dollars and resources. Resources are the wealth of our nation; dollars are merely claim checks upon those resources. Resources are of vital importance; dollars are comparatively trivial.

Four categories of resources are sufficient for our purposes: At any given time a nation, or a planet if you prefer, has a stock of labor, of technological skill, of capital goods, and of natural resources (such as mineral deposits, timber, water, land, etc.). These resources can be used in various combinations to yield goods and services of all kinds—in some limited quantity. The quantity will be larger if they are combined efficiently, smaller if combined inefficiently. But in either event the resource stock is limited, the goods and services that they can be made to yield are limited; even the most efficient use of them will yield less than our population, in the aggregate, would like to have.

If one considers building a new dam, it is appropriate to say that it will be costly in the sense that it will require x hours of labor, y tons of steel and concrete, and z amount of capital goods. If these resources are devoted to the dam, then they cannot be used to build hospitals, fishing rods, schools, or electric can openers. That is the meaningful sense in which the dam is costly.

Quite apart from the very important question of how wisely we can combine our resources to produce goods and services is the very different question of how they get distributed—who gets how many goods? Dollars constitute the claim checks which are distributed among people and which control their share of national output. Dollars are nearly valueless pieces of paper except to the extent that they do represent claim checks to some fraction of the output of goods and services. Viewed as claim checks, all the dollars outstanding during any period of time are worth, in the aggregate, the goods and services that are available to be claimed with them during that period—neither more nor less.

It is far easier to increase the supply of dollars than to increase the production of goods and services—printing dollars is easy. But printing more dollars doesn't help because each dollar then simply becomes a claim to fewer goods, i.e., becomes worth less.

The point is this: many people fall into error upon hearing the statement that the decision to build a dam, or to clean up a river, will cost $X million. It is regrettably easy to say: "It's only money. This is a wealthy country, and we have lots of money." But you cannot build a dam or clean a river with $X million—unless you also have a match, you can't even make a fire. One builds a dam or cleans a river by diverting labor and steel and trucks and factories from making one kind of goods to making another. The cost in dollars is merely a shorthand way of describing the extent of the diversion necessary. If we build a dam for $X million, then we must recognize that we will have $X million less housing and food and medical care and electric can openers as a result.

Similarly, the costs of controlling pollution are best expressed in terms of the other goods we will have to give up to do the job. This is not to say the job should not be done. Badly as we need more housing, more medical care, more can openers, and more symphony orchestras, we could do with somewhat less of them, in my judgment at least, in exchange for somewhat cleaner air and rivers. But that is the nature of the trade-off, and analysis of the problem is advanced if that unpleasant reality is kept in mind. Once the trade-off relationship is clearly perceived, it is possible to state in a very general way what the optimal level of pollution is. I would state it as follows:

People enjoy watching penguins. They enjoy relatively clean air and smog-free vistas. Their health is improved by relatively clean water and air. Each of these benefits is a type of good or service. As a society we would be well advised to give up one washing machine if the resources that would have gone into that washing machine can yield greater human satisfaction when diverted into pollution control. We should give up one hospital if the resources thereby freed would yield more human satisfaction when devoted to elimination of noise in our cities. And so on, trade-off by trade-off, we should divert our productive capacities from the production of existing goods and services to the production of a cleaner, quieter, more pastoral nation up to—and no further than—the point at which we value more highly the next washing machine or hospital that we would have to do without than we value the next unit of environmental improvement that the diverted resources would create.

Now this proposition seems to me unassailable but so general and abstract as to be unhelpful—at least unadministerable in the form stated. It assumes we can measure in some way the incremental units of human satisfaction yielded by very different types of goods. . . . But I insist that the proposition stated describes the result for which we should be striving—and again, that it is always useful to know what your target is even if your weapons are too crude to score a bull's eye.

QUESTIONS

1 Does the life of a penguin have value only if humans value it?
2 Is human benefit the only morally relevant criterion in determining our obligations in regard to the rest of the natural world?

For Free Market Environmentalism

Jan Narveson

Narveson argues that the rational way to solve environmental problems is to adopt a libertarian, free market approach. Rejecting all governmental attempts to control pollution, he maintains that such matters are best left to individuals who, acting in their own interests, will decide for themselves how much pollution they are willing to accept for what benefits.

In a free market, individuals own and may do what they want with things, without fear of interference by others. Free market society is *consensual* society: exchanges occur only when owners believe they would be better off from them, compared with any other use they could make of their resources. If everything were owned by individuals or voluntary groups such as companies, the only means of dealing with what are usually treated as political matters would be private means. Would that be a good thing? I think so, but discuss here only the environmental questions. The free market philosophy's proposed moral rule for everything is: "No force or fraud, except to protect or compensate victims of force or fraud." On environmental matters, then, it is: "Do not use force against persons's utilizations of the environment, except by way of this very rule." The agreement not to employ force against each other is a strategy for handling the major source of evil in human lives—other people's actions. Each refrains from worsening the situation of the other provided the other will return that favor.

This version of a "social contract" is, in my view, the best and perhaps the only rational solution. It is hard to see how the use of force against people who have followed the above rule could ever *help* matters. Forcing is inherently *antiproductive.* Freedom allows each to produce whatever they wish, given the available possibilities. Would-be aggressors can put their energy to better use. Confining us all to

Reprinted with permission from *The Ag Bioethics Forum,* vol. 6, no. 2 (November 1994), pp. 2–5.

activities agreed to by all affected persons is the better way; unlike any others, it is "win-win."

THE ENVIRONMENT

One's environment is the rest of the world outside of oneself—the nonhuman part, for present purposes. What do we do about nature? My answer is the classic one: anyone is free to take anything not already taken by anyone else. This is effected simply by commencing to use it—say, by working on it. This classic view is shared by ordinary people, but denied by many philosophers, who think that the environment is *everybody's,* and that central control over it is essential. Let's see why they're wrong.

Suppose we all have our plots, our houses, our businesses. Where do environmental problems come in? There are two popular ones: resource exhaustion and pollution. Putting resources into the hands of individual people wanting to do the best they can with them solves the first problem, insofar as it is one. . . . I'll address only the pollution question. Pollutions are side effects of otherwise voluntary interactions, on people who didn't ask for them and don't want them. Polluted air or water has stuff in it that the breather or drinker disvalues: it stinks or it makes him sick. Some impurities affect health, some affect taste; both are evils, of different kinds. And frequently there must be trade-offs: manure makes the crops grow better, but it stinks. Each individual farmer decides whether he'd rather have the crops than the smell. But suppose the manure makes the neighbors' air smell worse? What are the rights and wrongs of this? They own their lungs; you insert things they don't want into them, violating their property rights. In principle, then, the free market view says, they may sue. But will they in fact? That depends on two things: how much they dislike it; and how much benefit they get from it. (I omit litigation costs.) Lower food prices made possible by your greater production may provide all the compensation desired, until smellfree fertilizers come along.

Suppose that what the owner puts in his neighbor's lungs not only stinks but harms his health. Does this automatically make it unacceptable? No. It still depends on the same two things: how much it damages their health, and how much that amount of health is worth to them. Some people prefer a smoke-filled life to a long life—say, 70 years with smoke to 80 without. It's their choice. But if their smoke infects my lungs, that is not their choice—smoke is no pleasure to me. You should refrain from smoking in my presence whenever we both have the right to be in that place together, unless you make it worth my while. Which you might: the pleasure of your company may outweigh both the risk to my health and the aesthetic cost of your smoking. People differ, and it is impossible to get a uniform schedule of costs for all. So it is inherently wrong-headed to go about such problems in the usual way: to empower a public law-making body with the power to make laws requiring all to conform.

Further problems arise from today's techno-political climate. Have scientists "discovered" that a certain body of water is "contaminated with a deadly poison"? Sounds bad—until you realize that every body of water in the world contains plenty of deadly poisons, as does practically all the food you eat, especially if it is "naturally" grown. To the question, "Could it kill you?"—the answer is always, "Yes"—if you eat enough of it, combine it with the wrong things, and so on. Should we avoid carcinogens? If we did, we'd all starve. But most carcinogens give us cancer at the ripe old age of 120, which we don't reach anyway. Even if they give it to us at 80, that might still be a good risk, especially if one would die of something else at 79 anyway.

It would be nice if we could know that x will give you cancer at age y. But we don't. We know only that the incidence of such-and-such types of cancer in populations that frequently eat x is higher than in other populations that don't. If eating x gives the J's a longer life-expectancy than the K's, a higher incidence of cancer among J's may be due to that very fact, since cancer increases dramatically with age. That's why so many of us get it now: not because we produce carcinogenic food additives, but because before our time people didn't live long enough to develop most cancers. In the above example, the J's should do nothing—least of all, stop eating x! Especially if they smoke.

Most of the touted pollution risks of death are on the order of 0.00000005. Should we do anything about that? No. The probability of death from other causes is several hundred times that. Imagine a pack-a-day smoker taking great care not to eat some food whose probability of inducing cancer is about 1% that of the cigarettes he smokes. He's like the man about to be executed who refuses a last cigarette on the ground that smoking is bad for his health! Almost all "environmental legislation" is exactly like that.

Before any action is taken, risks must be *significant*. Would I be able to distinguish my risks given the proposed procedure from those I face without it? Once we get into significant levels, we may negotiate: continue the pollution, with continued or increased compensation? Or decrease pollution and pay the costs of the decrease? In principle this is a situation between you and me, which we can settle to mutual advantage. Thus the free-market, libertarian solution to such problems lies precisely in the fact that liberty is not, contrary to Tony Smith's claim, a "moral absolute." Just the opposite: that's the contemporary regulator's view of it, not ours.

Pollution problems exist, of course. But they are always confined to particular groups of people, and usually to relatively small groups. What matters, for any given person, is whether that person is affected, and how much, and whether there are benefits derived from the pollutions that he prefers to the costs of cleanup. In all the currently popular cases, the benefits win.

Consider garbage, which in almost all of North America is handled by public agencies, and the frequent subject of newspaper diatribes about how the planet will ere long succumb to garbage unless we do something, and so forth. On this basis, people are required to spend hours sorting their garbage into two or *n* distinct varieties, each handled separately, with compulsory recycling—at four times the cost of unsorted garbage, not counting time lost. There would be no talk of a general garbage problem if we allowed these things to be handled rationally, on the free market. There it would be a private business. Garbage companies would charge by the bag, giving people an incentive to minimize garbage production, would dump it on land somebody owns. If it's poor for other uses, using it for waste storage will look attractive, if the price is right. And neighbors of a land-fill would be compensated for any damage to their property caused by leakages and the like—which will induce the garbage dump owners to minimize such leakage.

Is garbage disposal a looming environmental disaster, as we are told? Not at all. The fact is that it is quite trivial on the global landscape. All of the garbage that will be produced in North America in the entire 21st century would fit in a square land-fill 9 miles on a side and 300 feet deep—1/40,000 of the land surface of the United States. Some "disaster"! And of course, within that century better technologies will emerge anyway. Extensive recycling now is a waste of time and money.

To which we should add that giving a lot of *power* to certain people to decide what should be done about the environment and then do it is not a good way to do anything: the assumption that somehow state officials—*especially* democratically elected ones—know what to do about such matters boggles the mind. . . . Note how Tony Smith is forced to suggest, lamely, that the effect of absurd regulations will be to motivate entrepreneurs to find better ways of doing these things.

Aristotle pointed out that people tend to take the best care of what they them-selves own. By contrast, they are not nearly as good at looking after other peo-ple's property—or, especially, other people's money. That, and only that, is the story of The Environment now, as always. In sum: what we should do now is extend the market principle much farther than we have, get government out of the act—and live better lives as a result. That is the rational way with environmental problems.

QUESTIONS

1 Does justice require the enactment and enforcement of laws that require companies and individuals to clean up the pollution resulting from their activities?
2 Suppose a community, town, or city agrees to allow some of its land to be used for the stor-age of toxic wastes in exchange for an increase of tax revenues or a necessary hospital. Is this a morally just transaction?

Against Free Market Environmentalism

Tony Smith

Smith critically evaluates four arguments advanced by free market environmentalists: (1) the tragedy of the commons argument; (2) the argument that, if private property owners cannot pass on the costs of pollution to others, they will be motivated to reduce pollution; (3) the argument that free markets are necessary, since market prices provide an objective measure of environmental values; and (4) the argument that the only appropriate role of the state in environmental matters is that of enforcing property rights.

Reprinted with permission from *The Ag Bioethics Forum,* vol. 6, no. 2 (November 1994), pp. 2, 5–7.

Free market environmentalists believe that the extension of private property rights and market transactions is sufficient to address environmental difficulties. They rest their case on four arguments. The first is the "tragedy of the commons" argument: whenever something is subject to collective use, individuals will tend to use it up as fast as possible. If we wish to see pieces of land, bodies of water, or plant and animal species used in a sustainable way, private property rights to these entities ought to be created, for owners tend to preserve their property.

Second, if polluters are able to externalize the costs of pollution onto others, they have no motivation to reduce or eliminate that pollution. But if property rights are extended and strictly enforced, owners will be able to sue polluters for damages to their property. When these suits are successful, the polluters are forced to internalize the costs of pollution, leading them to reduce those costs in the future.

Third, a trade-off must be made between the benefits of providing environmental amenities and the costs of doing so. Market prices provide an "objective measure" of environmental values, and so the proper trade-offs cannot be made unless markets are established. If farmers cannot prevent fishermen and women from using streams bordering their farms, for instance, they have no incentive to incur the expenses necessary to ensure that these streams are well stocked with fish. But if these same farmers were given private rights to these streams, they could exclude all fishermen and women not willing to pay them a fee. The possibility of collecting these fees creates a powerful incentive for them to ensure an adequate habitat for fish populations. Or consider the relationship between environmental groups and land developers. If the former do not have to bear any of the costs of foregone development, then they are likely to ignore these costs. In contrast, in a market setting environmental groups wishing to keep lands in a pristine condition must purchase those lands from their owners. In this manner they are forced to consider seriously the opportunity costs of keeping the land out of development.

Finally, free market environmentalists argue that the state has no role to play in environmental matters beyond that of enforcing property rights. State bureaucrats have particular interests of their own, and they are also susceptible to the influence of special interest groups. And they are not in a position to weigh accurately the costs and benefits of their policies. Is it any surprise that the government's record of environmental management has been deeply flawed?

Do these four arguments for free market environmentalism hold up? 1. There is no invisible hand operating in markets that ensures that environmentally sound practices will be employed just because property rights are in private hands, especially if the dominant form of property is investment capital. Investment today is more mobile than ever before. Capital accumulated in one region need not be reinvested in that same area; if returns are greater elsewhere there is a great likelihood that it will not be reinvested there. Self-interested economic agents will calculate the costs of environmentally benign practices against the costs they will incur if they do not institute those practices. If they estimate the former to exceed the latter, environmentally sound practices will likely not be employed. The owners of capital generally make investments in order to attain a return within a given unit of time. The key question for them is not "What will the physical condition of my holdings be at the end of this time period?" but instead "How much capital will I have accumulated by then?" If considerable amounts of capital can be accumulated at the cost of harming their hold-ings, this is of little concern as long as attractive investment opportunities are avail-able elsewhere. If considerable amounts of capital can be accumulated at the cost of harming the environment, the environment may well be harmed as long as the harm does not foreclose investment opportunities elsewhere.

2. Can we rely on liability laws and the court system to force polluters to inter-nalize the social costs of pollution? Suppose that a firm with a vast army of well paid corporate lawyers engages in polluting activities that inflict damages on a poor household. What are the chances that the household will be able to afford lawyers with the resources of the corporate lawyers? One would have to be quite naive to believe that in these circumstances the legal system can always be relied upon to ensure that the firms in question internalize the costs of their damaging practices.

Another problem is that liability laws work best in cases where tracing the causal chain of events is a relatively simple matter. Unfortunately the world in which we live is not always so simple. In many cases there are a variety of individual firms engaging in a multiplicity of practices that may—or may not—have had a causal role in bringing about an environmental harm. The greater the number of plausible causal stories, the more difficult it is legally to establish the liability of any particular individual or firm.

There is also the problem that unsound environmental practices can inflict harm on future generations. Future generations cannot sue in court today. *No* corporation takes into account costs for which it may be liable in two or three generations. And so even if the liability system were to work flawlessly, it would still fail to force polluters to internalize all of the costs of their polluting activities.

3. We now come to the third claim, the idea that market prices provide an "objective measure" of environmental matters. If environmental regulations save or extend human lives, how can that benefit be assigned a market price? The value of lives is often mea-sured as a function of the wage premium coal miners, police, and other workers receive in return for facing dangerous conditions. Is a life worth only the wages necessary to attract workers with few alternatives into dangerous conditions? Other methods of fix-ing the value of a human life in price terms are equally controversial. This means that cost/benefit analysis performed in market prices has an inherent bias. All of the costs of environmental safeguards can be easily put in price terms by corporations, but many of their most profound benefits are not easily measured in market prices.

Leaving environmental trade-offs up to the marketplace means leaving them up to those with the greatest market power. It is true that groups like the Nature Conservancy Fund have been able to purchase land in order to take it out of devel-opment; the major environmental groups in the U.S. together have $414,607,984 in funds that in principle could be used in this fashion. But the Irvine Company owns land in areas south of Los Angeles whose value has been estimated to be in excess of $10 billion. If all of the major environmental groups in the U.S. pooled their entire resources together in order to prevent the environmental problems besetting Los Angeles (traffic jams, smog, noise, soil erosion, water shortages, etc.) from spreading south, they would still be $9,585,392,016 short of being able to purchase the holdings of just a single landholder in Southern California. Only giant land developers have access to this sort of capital, developers who have all too often not made environmental issues a central concern.

4. Finally there is the question of the state. Free market environmentalists talk of the provision of "environmental amenities." This language is far too weak. Citizens have a right to a livable environment, and enforcing rights is part of the legitimate function of government. The thesis that responsibility for the environment should be left entirely in the hands of private economic agents is as ludicrous as the idea that rights to freedom of speech or freedom of religion should be left entirely to the market. This means that governmental policies regarding the environment are in principle legitimate, such as bans on chemicals that are toxic to humans or that destroy the ozone layer.

Also, whatever the fantasies of libertarians might be, the state plays a crucial role in the development of technology. Since World War II federal expenditures have financed between one-half and two-thirds of total R&D in the U.S., and over two-thirds of basic research. The aerospace, communications, and electronics industries have thrived as a direct result of these public subsidies. Breakthroughs in environmental technologies are no less crucial to the public good. Publicly funded R&D programs ought to be established to develop manufacturing processes that are non-toxic to workers and pollution-free, along with programs addressing solid waste disposal, alternative sources of energy, environmental clean-ups, etc. Regulations minimizing pollutants and cutting allowable emissions are also a crucial part of technology policy; such regulations guarantee a market for innovations that attain these ends, and thus act as a spur to innovative activity.

It is true enough that state officials have all too often been swayed by the influence of private interest groups when formulating environmental policies. But there are measures that could be taken to lessen the possibility of this occurring (restrictions on lobbying, elimination of PAC funding, public funding of campaigns, etc.). It would be far more preferable to explore this direction than to simply rule out any role for public authorities in environmental matters, as the defenders of free market environmentalism advocate.

QUESTIONS

1 Can Narveson's position be defended against Smith's critique?
2 If corporate activities will result in harmful long-term consequences that will have a negative impact on future generations, should those activities be prohibited by law?

Just Garbage

Peter S. Wenz

Wenz questions the justice of the current distribution of hazards associated with toxic wastes and other *locally undesirable land uses* (LULUs). His concern is especially with the disproportionate effects that such distribution has on the poor, many of

Reprinted with permission of Rowman & Littlefield Publishers from *Faces of Environmental Racism* (1995), edited by Laura Westra and Peter S. Wenz, pp. 57–62, 65–71.

whom are minorities. In criticizing what he calls "environmental racism," Wenz invokes a principle of distributive justice—the "Principle of Commensurate Burdens and Benefits." According to this principle, all other things being equal, those who derive benefits should receive commensurate burdens. In his view, policies based on either the free market approach or the cost-benefit analysis approach are unjust, since they violate this principle of justice. Wenz's solution is a system that would assign LULU points to communities in accordance with the principle. Wealthier communities, which benefit the most from the activities resulting in LULUs, would be required to earn more LULU points than poorer ones. In his view, this would result in a more just system of distribution. Furthermore, since points could not be traded or sold, those who are wealthy would not be able to buy their way out of exposure to toxic waste and other LULUs. One possible result of this could be a decrease in toxic hazards, as members of economically advantaged groups who have the power to bring about the necessary changes will be motivated to do so. In Wenz's view, the LULU point approach should be applied intranationally, within all countries, as well as internationally, among countries.

Environmental racism is evident in practices that expose racial minorities in the United States, and people of color around the world, to disproportionate shares of environmental hazards. These include toxic chemicals in factories, toxic herbicides and pesticides in agriculture, radiation from uranium mining, lead from paint on older buildings, toxic wastes illegally dumped, and toxic wastes legally stored. In this [reading,] which concentrates on issues of toxic waste, both illegally dumped and legally stored, I will examine the justness of current practices as well as the arguments commonly given in their defense. I will then propose an alternative practice that is consistent with prevailing principles of justice.

A DEFENSE OF CURRENT PRACTICES

Defenders often claim that because economic, not racial, considerations account for disproportionate impacts on nonwhites, current practices are neither racist nor morally objectionable. Their reasoning recalls the Doctrine of Double Effect. According to that doctrine, an effect whose production is usually blameworthy becomes blameless when it is incidental to, although predictably conjoined with, the production of another effect whose production is morally justified. The classic case concerns a pregnant woman with uterine cancer. A common, acceptable treatment for uterine cancer is hysterectomy. This will predictably end the pregnancy, as would an abortion. However, Roman Catholic scholars who usually consider abortion blameworthy consider it blameless in this context because it is merely incidental to hysterectomy, which is morally justified to treat uterine cancer. The hysterectomy would be performed in the absence of pregnancy, so the abortion effect is produced neither as an end-in-itself, nor as a means to reach the desired end, which is the cure of cancer.

Defenders of practices that disproportionately disadvantage nonwhites seem to claim, in keeping with the Doctrine of Double Effect, that racial effects are blameless because they are sought neither as ends-in-themselves nor as means to reach a desired goal. They are merely predictable side effects of economic and political practices that disproportionately expose poor people to toxic substances. The argument is that burial of toxic wastes, and other locally undesirable land uses (LULUs), lower property values. People who can afford to move elsewhere do so. They are replaced by buyers (or renters) who are predominately poor and cannot afford housing in more desirable areas. Law professor Vicki Been puts it this way: "As long as the market allows the existing distribution of wealth to allocate goods and services, it would be surprising indeed if, over the long run, LULUs did not impose a disproportionate burden upon the poor." People of color are disproportionately burdened due primarily to poverty, not racism.[1] This defense against charges of racism is important in the American context because racial discrimination is illegal in the United States in circumstances where economic discrimination is permitted. Thus, legal remedies to disproportionate exposure of nonwhites to toxic wastes are available if racism is the cause, but not if people of color are exposed merely because they are poor.

There is strong evidence against claims of racial neutrality. Professor Been acknowledges that even if there is no racism in the process of siting LULUs, racism plays at least some part in the disproportionate exposure of African Americans to them. She cites evidence that "racial discrimination in the sale and rental of housing relegates people of color (especially African Americans) to the least desirable neighborhoods, regardless of their income level."[2]

Without acknowledging for a moment, then, that racism plays no part in the disproportionate exposure of nonwhites to toxic waste, I will ignore this issue to display a weakness in the argument that justice is served when economic discrimination alone is influential. I claim that even if the only discrimination is economic, justice requires redress and significant alteration of current practices. Recourse to the Doctrine of Double Effect presupposes that the primary effect, with which a second effect is incidentally conjoined, is morally justifiable. In the classic case, abortion is justified only because hysterectomy is justified as treatment for uterine cancer. I argue that disproportionate impacts on poor people violate principles of distributive justice, and so are not morally justifiable in the first place. Thus, current practices disproportionately exposing nonwhites to toxic substances are not justifiable even if incidental to the exposure of poor people.

Alternate practices that comply with acceptable principles of distributive justice are suggested below. They would largely solve problems of environmental racism (disproportionate impacts on nonwhites) while ameliorating the injustice of disproportionately exposing poor people to toxic hazards. They would also discourage production of toxic substances, thereby reducing humanity's negative impact on the environment.

THE PRINCIPLE OF COMMENSURATE BURDENS AND BENEFITS

We usually assume that, other things being equal, those who derive benefits should sustain commensurate burdens. We typically associate the burden of work with the benefit of receiving money, and the burdens of monetary payment and tort liability with the benefits of ownership.

There are many exceptions. For example, people can inherit money without working, and be given ownership without purchase. Another exception, which dissociates the benefit of ownership from the burden of tort liability, is the use of tax money to protect the public from hazards associated with private property, as in Superfund legislation. Again, the benefit of money is dissociated from the burden of work when governments support people who are unemployed.

The fact that these exceptions require justification, however, indicates an abiding assumption that people who derive benefits should shoulder commensurate burdens. The ability to inherit without work is justified as a benefit owed to those who wish to bequeath their wealth (which someone in the line of inheritance is assumed to have shouldered burdens to acquire). The same reasoning applies to gifts.

Using tax money (public money) to protect the public from dangerous private property is justified as encouraging private industry and commerce, which are supposed to increase public wealth. The system also protects victims in case private owners become bankrupt as, for example, in Times Beach, Missouri, where the government bought homes made worthless due to dioxin pollution. The company responsible for the pollution was bankrupt.

Tax money is used to help people who are out of work to help them find a job, improve their credentials, or feed their children. This promotes economic growth and equal opportunity. These exceptions prove the rule by the fact that justification for any deviation from the commensuration of benefits and burdens is considered necessary.

Further indication of an abiding belief that benefits and burdens should be commensurate is grumbling that, for example, many professional athletes and corporate executives are overpaid. Although the athletes and executives shoulder the burden of work, the complaint is that their benefits are disproportionate to their burdens. People on welfare are sometimes criticized for receiving even modest amounts of taxpayer money without shouldering the burdens of work, hence recurrent calls for "welfare reform." Even though these calls are often justified as means to reducing government budget deficits, the moral issue is more basic than the economic. Welfare expenditures are minor compared to other programs, and alternatives that require poor people to work are often more expensive than welfare as we know it.

The principle of commensuration between benefits and burdens is not the only moral principle governing distributive justice, and may not be the most important, but it is basic. Practices can be justified by showing them to conform, all things considered, to this principle. Thus, there is no move to "reform" the receipt of moderate pay for ordinary work, because it exemplifies the principle. On the other hand, practices that do not conform are liable to attack and require alternate justification, as we have seen in the cases of inheritance, gifts, Superfund legislation, and welfare.

Applying the principle of commensuration between burdens and benefits to the issue at hand yields the following: In the absence of countervailing considerations, the burdens of ill health associated with toxic hazards should be related to benefits derived from processes and products that create these hazards.

TOXIC HAZARDS AND CONSUMERISM

In order to assess, in light of the principle of commensuration between benefits and burdens, the justice of current distributions of toxic hazards, the benefits of their generation must be considered. Toxic wastes result from many manufacturing processes, including those for a host of common items and materials, such as paint, solvents, plastics, and most petrochemical-based materials. These materials surround us in the paint on our homes, in our refrigerator containers, in our clothing, in our plumbing, in our garbage pails, and elsewhere.

Toxins are released into the environment in greater quantities now than ever before because we now have a consumer-oriented society where the acquisition, use, and disposal of individually owned items is greatly desired. We associate the numerical dollar value of the items at our disposal with our "standard of living," and assume that a higher standard is conducive to, if not identical with, a better life. So toxic wastes needing disposal are produced as by-products of the general pursuit of what our society defines as valuable, that is, the consumption of material goods.

Our economy requires increasing consumer demand to keep people working (to produce what is demanded). This is why there is concern each Christmas season, for example, that shoppers may not buy enough. If demand is insufficient, people may be put out of work. Demand must increase, not merely hold steady, because commercial competition improves labor efficiency in manufacture (and now in the service sector as well), so fewer workers can produce desired items. More items must be desired to forestall labor efficiency-induced unemployment, which is grave in a society where people depend primarily on wages to secure life's necessities.

Demand is kept high largely by convincing people that their lives require improvement, which consumer purchases will effect. When improvements are seen as needed, not merely desired, people purchase more readily. So our culture encourages economic expansion by blurring the distinction between wants and needs.

One way the distinction is blurred is through promotion of worry. If one feels insecure without the desired item or service, and so worries about life without it, then its provision is easily seen as a need. Commercials, and other shapers of social expectations, keep people worried by adjusting downward toward the trivial what people are expected to worry about. People worry about the provision of food, clothing, and housing without much inducement. When these basic needs are satisfied, however, attention shifts to indoor plumbing, for example, then to stylish indoor plumbing. The process continues with need for a second or third bathroom, a kitchen disposal, and a refrigerator attached to the plumbing so that ice is made automatically in the freezer, and cold water can be obtained without even opening the refrigerator door. The same kind of progression results in cars with CD players, cellular phones, and automatic readouts of average fuel consumption per mile.

Abraham Maslow was not accurately describing people in our society when he claimed that after physiological, safety, love, and (self-) esteem needs are met, people work toward self-actualization, becoming increasingly their own unique selves by fully developing their talents. Maslow's Hierarchy of Needs describes people in our society less than Wenz's Lowerarchy of Worry. When one source of worry is put to rest by an appropriate purchase, some matter less inherently or obviously worrisome takes its place as the focus of concern. Such worry-substitution must be amenable to indefinite repetition in order to motivate purchases needed to keep the economy growing without inherent limit. If commercial society is supported by consumer demand, it is worry all the way down. Toxic wastes are produced in this context.

People tend to worry about ill health and early death without much inducement. These concerns are heightened in a society dependent upon the production of worry, so expenditure on health care consumes an increasing percentage of the gross domestic product. As knowledge of health impairment due to toxic substances increases, people are decreasingly tolerant of risks associated with their proximity. Thus, the same mindset of worry that elicits production that generates toxic wastes, exacerbates reaction to their proximity. The result is a desire for their placement elsewhere, hence the NIMBY syndrome—Not In My Back Yard. On this account, NIMBYism is not aberrantly selfish behavior, but integral to the cultural value system required for great volumes of toxic waste to be generated in the first place.

Combined with the principle of Commensurate Burdens and Benefits, that value system indicates who should suffer the burden of proximity to toxic wastes. Other things being equal, those who benefit most from the production of waste should shoulder the greatest share of burdens associated with its disposal. In our society, consumption of goods is valued highly and constitutes the principal benefit associated with the generation of toxic wastes. Such consumption is generally correlated with income and wealth. So other things being equal, justice requires that people's proximity to toxic wastes be related positively to their income and wealth. This is exactly opposite to the predominant tendency in our society, where poor people are more proximate to toxic wastes dumped illegally and stored legally. . . .

FREE MARKET APPROACH

Toxic wastes, a burden, could be placed where residents accept them in return for monetary payment, a benefit. Since market transactions often satisfactorily [result in] commensurate burdens and benefits, this approach may seem to honor the principle of commensuration between burdens and benefits.

Unlike many market transactions, however, whole communities, acting as corporate bodies, would have to contract with those seeking to bury wastes. Otherwise, any single individual in the community could veto the transaction. . . . Communities could receive money to improve such public facilities as schools, parks, and hospitals, in addition to obtaining tax revenues and jobs that result ordinarily from business expansion.

The major problem with this free market approach is that it fails to accord equal consideration to everyone's interests. Where basic or vital goods and services are at issue, we usually think equal consideration of interests requires ameliorating inequalities of distribution that markets tend to produce. For example, one reason, although not the only reason, for public education is to provide every child with the basic intellectual tools necessary for success in our society. A purely free market approach, by contrast, would result in excellent education for children of wealthy parents and little or no education for children of the nation's poorest residents. Opportunities for children of poor parents would be so inferior that we would say the children's interests had not been given equal consideration.

The reasoning is similar where vital goods are concerned. The United States has the Medicaid program for poor people to supplement market transactions in health care precisely because equal consideration of interests requires that everyone be given access to health care. The 1994 health care debate in the United States was, ostensibly, about how to achieve universal coverage, not about whether or not justice required such coverage. With the exception of South Africa, every other industrialized country already has universal coverage for health care. Where vital needs are concerned, markets are supplemented or avoided in order to give equal consideration to everyone's interests.

Another example concerns military service in time of war. The United States employed conscription during the Civil War, both world wars, the Korean War, and the war in Vietnam. When the national interest requires placing many people in mortal danger, it is considered just that exposure be largely unrelated to income and market transactions.

The United States does not currently provide genuine equality in education or health care, nor did universal conscription (of males) put all men at equal risk in time of war. In all three areas, advantage accrues to those with greater income and wealth. (During the Civil War, paying for a substitute was legal in many cases.) Imperfection in practice, however, should not obscure general agreement in theory that justice requires equal consideration of interests, and that such equal consideration requires rejecting purely free market approaches where basic or vital needs are concerned.

Toxic substances affect basic and vital interests. Lead, arsenic, and cadmium in the vicinity of children's homes can result in mental retardation of the children. Navaho teens exposed to radiation from uranium mine tailings have seventeen times the national average of reproductive organ cancer. Environmental Protection Agency (EPA) officials estimate that toxic air pollution in areas of South Chicago increases cancer risks one hundred to one thousand times. Pollution from Otis Air Force base in Massachusetts is associated with alarming increases in cancer rates. Non-Hodgkin's Lymphoma is related to living near stone, clay, and glass industry facilities, and leukemia is related to living near chemical and petroleum plants. In general, cancer rates are higher in the United States near industries that use toxic substances and discard them nearby.

In sum, the placement of toxic wastes affects basic and vital interests just as do education, health care, and wartime military service. Exemption from market decisions is required to avoid unjust impositions on the poor, and to respect people's interests equally. A child dying of cancer receives little benefit from the community's new swimming pool.

COST-BENEFIT ANALYSIS (CBA)

CBA is an economist's version of utilitarianism, where the sum to be maximized is society's wealth, as measured in monetary units, instead of happiness or preference satisfaction. Society's wealth is computed by noting (and estimating where necessary) what people are willing to pay for goods and services. The more people are willing to pay for what exists in society, the better off society is, according to CBA.

CBA will characteristically require placement of toxic wastes near poor people. Such placement usually lowers land values (what people are willing to pay for property). Land that is already cheap, where poor people live, will not lose as much value as land that is currently expensive, where wealthier people live, so a smaller loss of social wealth attends placement of toxic wastes near poor people. This is just the opposite of what the Principle of Commensurate Burdens and Benefits requires.

The use of CBA also violates equal consideration of interests, operating much like free market approaches. Where a vital concern is at issue, equal consideration of interests requires that people be considered irrespective of income. The placement of toxic wastes affects vital interests. Yet CBA would have poor people exposed disproportionately to such wastes.

In sum, . . . free market distribution . . . and cost-benefit analysis are inadequate principles and methodologies to guide the just distribution of toxic wastes.

LULU POINTS

An approach that avoids these difficulties assigns points to different types of locally undesirable land uses (LULUs) and requires that all communities earn LULU points.[3] In keeping with the Principle of Commensurate Burdens and Benefits, wealthy communities would be required to earn more LULU points than poorer ones. Communities would be identified by currently existing political divisions, such as villages, towns, city wards, cities, and counties.

Toxic waste dumps are only one kind of LULU. Others include prisons, half-way houses, municipal waste sites, low-income housing, and power plants, whether nuclear or coal fired. A large deposit of extremely toxic waste, for example, may be assigned twenty points when properly buried but fifty points when illegally dumped. A much smaller deposit of properly buried toxic waste may be assigned only ten points, as may a coal-fired power plant. A nuclear power plant may be assigned twenty-five points, while municipal waste sites are only five points, and one hundred units of low-income housing are eight points.

These numbers are only speculations. Points would be assigned by considering probable effects of different LULUs on basic needs, and responses to questionnaires investigating people's levels of discomfort with LULUs of various sorts. Once numbers are assigned, the total number of LULU points to be distributed in a given time period could be calculated by considering planned development and needs for prisons, power plants, low-income housing, and so on. One could also calculate points for a community's already existing LULUs. Communities could then be required to host LULUs in proportion to their income or wealth, with new allocation of LULUs (and associated points) correcting for currently existing deviations from the rules of proportionality.

Wherever significant differences of wealth or income exist between two areas, these areas should be considered part of different communities if there is any political division between them. Thus, a county with rich and poor areas would not be considered a single community for purposes of locating LULUs. Instead, villages or towns may be so considered. A city with rich and poor areas may similarly be reduced to its wards. The purpose of segregating areas of different income or wealth from one another is to permit the imposition of greater LULU burdens on wealthier communities. When wealthy and poor areas are considered as one larger community, there is the danger that the community will earn its LULU points by placing hazardous waste near its poorer members. This possibility is reduced when only relatively wealthy people live in a smaller community that must earn LULU points.

PRACTICAL IMPLICATIONS

Political strategy is beyond the scope of this [essay,] so I will refrain from commenting on problems and prospects for securing passage and implementation of the foregoing proposal. I maintain that the proposal is just. In a society where injustice is common, it is no surprise that proposals for rectifications meet stiff resistance.

Were the LULU points proposal implemented, environmental racism would be reduced enormously. To the extent that poor people exposed to environmental hazards are members of racial minorities, relieving the poor of disproportionate exposure would also relieve people of color.

This is not to say that environmental racism would be ended completely. Implementation of the proposal requires judgment in particular cases. Until racism is itself ended, such judgment will predictably be exercised at times to the disadvantage of minority populations. However, because most people of color currently burdened by environmental racism are relatively poor, implementing the proposal would remove 80 to 90 percent of the effects of environmental racism. While efforts to end racism at all levels should continue, reducing the burdens of racism is generally advantageous to people of color. Such reductions are especially worthy when integral to policies that improve distributive justice generally.

Besides improving distributive justice and reducing the burdens of environmental racism, implementing the LULU points proposal would benefit life on earth generally by reducing the generation of toxic hazards. When people of wealth, who exercise control of manufacturing processes, marketing campaigns, and media coverage, are themselves threatened disproportionately by toxic hazards, the culture will evolve quickly to find their production largely unnecessary. It will be discovered, for example, that many plastic items can be made of wood, just as it was discovered in the late 1980s that the production of many ozone-destroying chemicals is unnecessary. Similarly, necessity being the mother of invention, it was discovered during World War II that many women could work in factories. When certain interests are threatened, the impossible does not even take longer.

The above approach to environmental injustice should, of course, be applied internationally and intranationally within all countries. The same considerations of justice condemn universally, all other things being equal, exposing poor people to vital dangers whose generation predominantly benefits the rich. This implies that rich countries should not ship their toxic wastes to poor countries. Since many poorer countries, such as those in Africa, are inhabited primarily by nonwhites, prohibiting shipments of toxic wastes to them would reduce significantly worldwide environmental racism. A prohibition on such shipments would also discourage production of dangerous wastes, as it would require people in rich countries to live with whatever dangers they create. If the principle of LULU points were applied in all countries, including poor ones, elites in those countries would lose interest in earning foreign currency credits through importation of waste, as they would be disproportionately exposed to imported toxins.

In sum, we could reduce environmental injustice considerably through a general program of distributive justice concerning environmental hazards. Pollution would not thereby be eliminated, since to live is to pollute. But such a program would motivate significant reduction in the generation of toxic wastes, and help the poor, especially people of color, as well as the environment.

NOTES

1 Vicki Been, "Market Forces, Not Racist Practices, May Affect the Siting of Locally Undesirable Land Uses," in *At Issue: Environmental Justice,* ed. by Jonathan Petrikin (San Diego, Calif.: Greenhaven Press, 1995), 41.
2 Been, 41.
3 The idea of LULU points comes to me from Frank J. Popper, "LULUs and Their Blockage," in *Confronting Regional Challenges: Approaches to LULUs, Growth, and Other Vexing Governance Problems,* ed. by Joseph DiMento and Le Roy Graymer (Los Angeles, Calif.: Lincoln Institute of Land Policy, 1991), 13–27, especially 24.

QUESTIONS

1 Does environmental racism, as Wenz describes it, exist in your community? Can you give specific examples to illustrate your position?
2 In a just society, what principles should guide policies dealing with the placement of locally undesirable land uses (LULUs)?

The Land Ethic

Aldo Leopold

Leopold articulates a biocentric point of view under the heading of a *land ethic.* His understanding of "land" is very broad, including "soils, waters, plants, and animals." He argues that we must stop thinking of land merely as property and start thinking of it as worthy of respect and moral consideration in its own right. In accordance with Leopold's land ethic, humankind is not the conqueror of the "land-community" but "plain member and citizen" of it; we must respect fellow members of the community and the community as a whole. Leopold explicitly argues against a system of environmental conservation based solely on economic considerations. He also illustrates some of the interconnected workings of the land-community by employing the image of a pyramid. Leopold's discussion culminates in his famous statement of a moral principle formulated in reference to the "integrity, stability, and beauty of the biotic community."

When god-like Odysseus returned from the wars in Troy, he hanged all on one rope a dozen slave-girls of his household whom he suspected of misbehavior during his absence.

This hanging involved no question of propriety. The girls were property. The disposal of property was then, as now, a matter of expediency, not of right and wrong.

Concepts of right and wrong were not lacking from Odysseus' Greece: witness the fidelity of his wife through the long years before at last his black-prowed galleys clove the wine-dark seas for home. The ethical structure of that day covered wives, but had not yet been extended to human chattels. During the three thousand years which have since elapsed, ethical criteria have been extended to many fields of conduct, with corresponding shrinkages in those judged by expediency only.

THE ETHICAL SEQUENCE

This extension of ethics, so far studied only by philosophers, is actually a process in ecological evolution. Its sequences may be described in ecological as well as in philosophical terms. An ethic, ecologically, is a limitation on freedom of action in the struggle for existence. An ethic, philosophically, is a differentiation of social from anti-social conduct. These are two definitions of one thing. The thing has its origin in the tendency of interdependent individuals or groups to evolve modes of co-operation. The ecologist calls these symbioses. Politics and economics are advanced symbioses in which the original free-for-all competition has been replaced, in part, by co-operative mechanisms with an ethical content.

The complexity of co-operative mechanisms has increased with population density, and with the efficiency of tools. It was simpler, for example, to define the anti-social uses of sticks and stones in the days of the mastodons than of bullets and billboards in the age of motors.

The first ethics dealt with the relation between individuals; the Mosaic Decalogue is an example. Later accretions dealt with the relation between the individual and society. The Golden Rule tries to integrate the individual to society; democracy to integrate social organization to the individual.

There is as yet no ethic dealing with man's relation to land and to the animals and plants which grow upon it. Land, like Odysseus' slave-girls, is still property. The land-relation is still strictly economic, entailing privileges but not obligations.

The extension of ethics to this third element in human environment is, if I read the evidence correctly, an evolutionary possibility and an ecological necessity. It is the third step in a sequence. The first two have already been taken. Individual thinkers since the days of Ezekiel and Isaiah have asserted that the despoliation of land is not only inexpedient but wrong. Society, however, has not yet affirmed their belief. I regard the present conservation movement as the embryo of such an affirmation.

An ethic may be regarded as a mode of guidance for meeting ecological situations so new or intricate, or involving such deferred reactions, that the path of social expediency is not discernible to the average individual. Animal instincts are modes of guidance for the individual in meeting such situations. Ethics are possibly a kind of community instinct in-the-making.

THE COMMUNITY CONCEPT

All ethics so far evolved rest upon a single premise: that the individual is a member of a community of interdependent parts. His instincts prompt him to compete for his place in that community, but his ethics prompt him also to co-operate (perhaps in order that there may be a place to compete for).

The land ethic simply enlarges the boundaries of the community to include soils, waters, plants, and animals, or collectively, the land.

This sounds simple: do we not already sing our love for and obligation to the land of the free and the home of the brave? Yes, but just what and whom do we love? Certainly not the soil, which we are sending helter-skelter downriver. Certainly not the waters, which we assume have no function except to turn turbines, float barges, and carry off sewage. Certainly not the plants, of which we exterminate whole communities without batting an eye. Certainly not the animals, of which we have already extirpated many of the largest and most beautiful species. A land ethic of course cannot prevent the alteration, management, and use of these 'resources,' but it does affirm their right to continued existence, and, at least in spots, their continued existence in a natural state.

In short, a land ethic changes the role of *Homo sapiens* from conqueror of the land-community to plain member and citizen of it. It implies respect for his fellow-members, and also respect for the community as such.

In human history, we have learned (I hope) that the conqueror role is eventually self-defeating. Why? Because it is implicit in such a role that the conqueror knows, *ex cathedra,* just what makes the community clock tick, and just what and who is valuable, and what and who is worthless, in community life. It always turns out that he knows neither, and this is why his conquests eventually defeat themselves.

In the biotic community, a parallel situation exists. Abraham knew exactly what the land was for: it was to drip milk and honey into Abraham's mouth. At the present moment, the assurance with which we regard this assumption is inverse to the degree of our education.

The ordinary citizen today assumes that science knows what makes the community clock tick; the scientist is equally sure that he does not. He knows that the biotic mechanism is so complex that its workings may never be fully understood. . . .

SUBSTITUTES FOR A LAND ETHIC

When the logic of history hungers for bread and we hand out a stone, we are at pains to explain how much the stone resembles bread. I now describe some of the stones which serve in lieu of a land ethic.

One basic weakness in a conservation system based wholly on economic motives is that most members of the land community have no economic value. Wildflowers and songbirds are examples. Of the 22,000 higher plants and animals native to Wisconsin, it is doubtful whether more than 5 per cent can be sold, fed, eaten, or otherwise put to economic use. Yet these creatures are members of the biotic community, and if (as I believe) its stability depends on its integrity, they are entitled to continuance.

When one of these non-economic categories is threatened, and if we happen to love it, we invent subterfuges to give it economic importance. At the beginning of the century songbirds were supposed to be disappearing. Ornithologists jumped to the rescue with some distinctly shaky evidence to the effect that insects would eat us up if birds failed to control them. The evidence had to be economic in order to be valid.

It is painful to read these circumlocutions today. We have no land ethic yet, but we have at least drawn nearer the point of admitting that birds should continue as a matter of biotic right, regardless of the presence or absence of economic advantage to us.

A parallel situation exists in respect of predatory mammals, raptorial birds, and fish-eating birds. Time was when biologists somewhat overworked the evidence that these creatures preserve the health of game by killing weaklings, or that they control rodents for the farmer, or that they prey only on 'worthless' species. Here again, the evidence had to be economic in order to be valid. It is only in recent years that we hear the more honest argument that predators are members of the community, and that no special interest has the right to exterminate them for the sake of a benefit, real or fancied, to itself. . . .

Some species of trees have been 'read out of the party' by economics-minded foresters because they grow too slowly, or have too low a sale value to pay as timber crops: white cedar, tamarack, cypress, beech, and hemlock are examples. In Europe, where forestry is ecologically more advanced, the non-commercial tree species are recognized as members of the native forest community, to be preserved as such, within reason. Moreover, some (like beech) have been found to have a valuable function in building up soil fertility. The interdependence of the forest and its constituent tree species, ground flora, and fauna is taken for granted.

Lack of economic value is sometimes a character not only of species or groups, but of entire biotic communities: marshes, bogs, dunes, and 'deserts' are examples. Our formula in such cases is to relegate their conservation to government as refuges, monuments, or parks. The difficulty is that these communities are usually interspersed with more valuable private lands; the government cannot possibly own or control such scattered parcels. The net effect is that we have relegated some of them to ultimate extinction over large areas. . . .

To sum up: a system of conservation based solely on economic self-interest is hopelessly lopsided. It tends to ignore, and thus eventually to eliminate, many elements in the land community that lack commercial value, but that are (as far as we know) essential to its healthy functioning. It assumes, falsely, I think, that the economic parts of the biotic clock will function without the uneconomic parts. . . .

THE LAND PYRAMID

An ethic to supplement and guide the economic relation to land presupposes the existence of some mental image of land as a biotic mechanism. We can be ethical only in relation to something we can see, feel, understand, love, or otherwise have faith in.

The image commonly employed in conservation education is 'the balance of nature.' For reasons too lengthy to detail here, this figure of speech fails to describe accurately what little we know about the land mechanism. A much truer image is the one employed in ecology: the biotic pyramid. I shall first sketch the pyramid as a symbol of land. . . .

Plants absorb energy from the sun. This energy flows through a circuit called the biota, which may be represented by a pyramid consisting of layers. The bottom layer is the soil. A plant layer rests on the soil, an insect layer on the plants, a bird and rodent layer on the insects, and so on up through various animal groups to the apex layer, which consists of the larger carnivores.

The species of a layer are alike not in where they came from, or in what they look like, but rather in what they eat. Each successive layer depends on those below it for food and often for other services, and each in turn furnishes food and services to those above. Proceeding upward, each successive layer decreases in numerical abundance. Thus, for every carnivore there are hundreds of his prey, thousands of their prey, millions of insects, uncountable plants. The pyramidal form of the system reflects this numerical progression from apex to base. Man shares an intermediate layer with the bears, raccoons, and squirrels which eat both meat and vegetables.

The lines of dependency for food and other services are called food chains. Thus soil-oak-deer-Indian is a chain that has now been largely converted to soil-corn-cow-farmer. Each species, including ourselves, is a link in many chains. The deer eats a hundred plants other than oak, and the cow a hundred plants other than corn. Both, then, are links in a hundred chains. The pyramid is a tangle of chains so complex as to seem disorderly, yet the stability of the system proves it to be a highly organized structure. Its functioning depends on the co-operation and competition of its diverse parts.

In the beginning, the pyramid of life was low and squat, the food chains short and simple. Evolution has added layer after layer, link after link. Man is one of thousands of accretions to the height and complexity of the pyramid. Science has given us many doubts, but it has given us at least one certainty: the trend of evolution is to elaborate and diversify the biota.

Land, then, is not merely soil; it is a fountain of energy flowing through a circuit of soils, plants, and animals. Food chains are the living channels which conduct energy upward; death and decay return it to the soil. The circuit is not closed; some energy is dissipated in decay, some is added by absorption from the air, some is stored in soils, peats, and long-lived forests; but it is a sustained circuit, like a slowly augmented revolving fund of life. There is always a net loss by downhill wash, but this is normally small and offset by the decay of rocks. It is deposited in the ocean and, in the course of geological time, raised to form new lands and new pyramids.

The velocity and character of the upward flow of energy depend on the complex structure of the plant and animal community, much as the upward flow of sap in a tree depends on its complex cellular organization. Without this complexity, normal circulation would presumably not occur. Structure means the characteristic numbers, as well as the characteristic kinds and functions, of the component species. This interdependence between the complex structure of the land and its smooth functioning as an energy unit is one of its basic attributes.

When a change occurs in one part of the circuit, many other parts must adjust themselves to it. Change does not necessarily obstruct or divert the flow of energy; evolution is a long series of self-induced changes, the net result of which has been to elaborate the flow mechanism and to lengthen the circuit. Evolutionary changes, however, are usually slow and local. Man's invention of tools has enabled him to make changes of unprecedented violence, rapidity, and scope. . . .

THE OUTLOOK

It is inconceivable to me that an ethical relation to land can exist without love, respect, and admiration for land, and a high regard for its value. By value, I of course mean something far broader than mere economic value; I mean value in the philosophical sense. . . .

The 'key-log' which must be moved to release the evolutionary process for an ethic is simply this: quit thinking about decent land-use as solely an economic problem. Examine each question in terms of what is ethically and esthetically right, as well as what is economically expedient. A thing is right when it tends to preserve the integrity, stability, and beauty of the biotic community. It is wrong when it tends otherwise.

It of course goes without saying that economic feasibility limits the tether of what can or cannot be done for land. It always has and it always will. The fallacy the economic determinists have tied around our collective neck, and which we now need to cast off, is the belief that economics determines *all* land-use. This is simply not true. An innumerable host of actions and attitudes, comprising perhaps the bulk of all land relations, is determined by the land-users' tastes and predilections, rather than by his purse. The bulk of all land relations hinges on investments of time, forethought, skill, and faith rather than on investments of cash. As a land-user thinketh, so is he.

I have purposely presented the land ethic as a product of social evolution because nothing so important as an ethic is ever 'written.' Only the most superficial student of history supposes that Moses 'wrote' the Decalogue; it evolved in the minds of a thinking community, and Moses wrote a tentative summary of it for a 'seminar.' I say tentative because evolution never stops.

The evolution of a land ethic is an intellectual as well as emotional process. Conservation is paved with good intentions which prove to be futile, or even dangerous, because they are devoid of critical understanding either of the land, or of economic land-use. I think it is a truism that as the ethical frontier advances from the individual to the community, its intellectual content increases.

The mechanism of operation is the same for any ethic: social approbation for right actions; social disapproval for wrong actions.

By and large, our present problem is one of attitudes and implements. We are remodeling the Alhambra with a steamshovel, and we are proud of our yardage. We shall hardly relinquish the shovel, which after all has many good points, but we are in need of gentler and more objective criteria for its successful use.

QUESTIONS

1 Do songbirds and wildflowers have a right to exist? Do cockroaches and weeds have a right to exist?

2 Leopold claims that "[a] thing is right when it tends to preserve the integrity, stability, and beauty of the biotic community" and "[i]t is wrong when it tends otherwise." What are the implications of this principle for our way of life?
3 To what extent would you endorse Leopold's land ethic?

Environmental Ethics

Bernard E. Rollin

In contrast to Baxter's anthropocentric approach and Leopold's biocentric approach, Rollin adopts a sentientist approach to environmental issues. He contends that because humans and other animals are sentient beings who can be harmed, they have intrinsic value and moral rights. Rivers, forests, species, and ecosystems, in contrast, have only instrumental value, since they are not sentient beings and thus cannot be harmed, except in a metaphorical sense. Nonetheless, Rollin maintains, once we recognize the intrinsic value of *all* sentient beings, we can develop a rich environmental ethic based on the interests of human beings and other animals.

The past two decades have witnessed a major revolutionary thrust in social moral awareness, one virtually unknown in mainstream Western ethical thinking, although not unrecognized in other cultural traditions; for example, the Navajo, whose descriptive language for nature and animals is suffused with ethical nuances; the Australian Aboriginal people; and the ancient Persians. This thrust is the recognition that nonhuman entities enjoy some moral status as objects of moral concern and deliberation. Although the investigation of the moral status of nonhuman entities has sometimes been subsumed under the global rubric of environmental ethics, such a blanket term does not do adequate justice to the substantial conceptual differences of its components.

THE MORAL STATUS OF NONHUMAN THINGS

As a bare minimum, environmental ethics comprises two fundamentally divergent concerns—namely, concern with individual nonhuman animals as direct objects of moral concern and concern with species, ecosystems, environments, wilderness areas, forests, the biosphere, and other nonsentient natural or even abstract objects as direct objects of moral concern. Usually, although with a number of major exceptions,[1] those who give primacy to animals have tended to deny the moral significance of environments and species as direct objects of moral concern, whereas

Reprinted with permission from *Problems of International Justice* (Westview, 1988), edited by Steven Luper-Foy, pp. 125–131.

those who give moral primacy to enviro-ecological concerns tend to deny or at least downplay the moral significance of individual animals.[2] Significant though these differences are, they should not cloud the dramatic nature of this common attempt to break out of a moral tradition that finds loci of value only in human beings and, derivatively, in human institutions.

Because of the revolutionary nature of these attempts, they also remain somewhat undeveloped and embryonic. . . .

The most plausible strategy in attempting to revise traditional moral theory and practice is to show that the seeds of the new moral notions or extensions of old moral notions are, in fact, already implicit in the old moral machinery developed to deal with other issues. Only when such avenues are exhausted will it make sense to recommend major rebuilding of the machinery, rather than putting it to new uses. The classic examples of such extensions are obviously found in the extension of the moral/legal machinery of Western democracies to cover traditionally disenfranchised groups such as women and minorities. The relatively smooth flow of such applications owes much of its smoothness to the plausibility of a simple argument of the form:

> Our extant moral principles ought to cover all humans.
> Women are humans.
> ∴ Our extant moral principles ought to cover women.

On the other hand, conceptually radical departures from tradition do not lend themselves to such simple rational reconstruction. Thus, for example, the principle of *favoring* members of traditionally disenfranchised groups at the expense of innocent members of nondisenfranchised groups for the sake of rectifying historically based injustice is viewed as much more morally problematic and ambivalent than simply according rights to these groups. Thus, it would be difficult to construct a simple syllogism in defense of this practice that would garner universal acquiescence with the ease of the one indicated previously.

Thus, one needs to distinguish between moral revolutionary thrusts that are ostensibly paradoxical to common sense and practice because they have been ignored in a wholesale fashion, yet are in fact logical extensions of common morality, and those revolutionary thrusts that are genuinely paradoxical to previous moral thinking and practice because they are not implicit therein. Being genuinely paradoxical does not invalidate a new moral thrust—it does, however, place upon its proponents a substantially greater burden of proof. Those philosophers, like myself, who have argued for a recognition of the moral status of individual animals and the rights and legal status that derive therefrom, have attempted to place ourselves in the first category. We recognize that a society that kills and eats billions of animals, kills millions more in research, and disposes of millions more for relatively frivolous reasons and that relies economically on animal exploitation as a mainstay of social wealth, considers talk of elevating the moral status of animals as impossible and paradoxical. But this does not mean that such an elevation does not follow unrecognized from moral principles we all hold. Indeed, the abolition of slavery or the liberation of women appeared similarly paradoxical and economically impossible, yet gradually both were perceived as morally necessary, in part because both were implicit, albeit unrecognized, in previously acknowledged assumptions.[3]

My own argument for elevating the status of animals has been a relatively straightforward deduction of unnoticed implications of traditional morality. I have tried to show that no morally relevant grounds for excluding animals from the full application of our moral machinery will stand up to rational scrutiny. Traditional claims that rely on notions such as animals have no souls, are inferior to humans in power or intelligence or evolutionary status, are not moral agents, are not rational, are not possessed of free will, are not capable of language, are not bound by social contract to humans, and so forth, do not serve as justifiable reasons for excluding animals and their interests from the moral arena.

By the same token, morally relevant similarities exist between us and them in the case of the "higher" animals. Animals can suffer, as Jeremy Bentham said; they have interests; what we do to them matters to them; they can feel pain, fear, anxiety, loneliness, pleasure, boredom, and so on. Indeed, the simplicity and power of the argument calling attention to such morally relevant similarities has led Cartesians from Descartes to modern physiologists with a vested interest against attributing moral status to animals to declare that animals are machines with no morally relevant modes of awareness, a point often addressed today against moral claims such as mine. In fact, such claims have become a mainstay of what I have elsewhere called the "common sense of science." Thus, one who argues for an augmented moral status for animals finds it necessary to establish philosophically and scientifically what common sense takes for granted—namely, that animals *are* conscious.[4] Most people whose common sense is intact are not Cartesians and can see that moral talk cannot be withheld from animals and our treatment of them.

In my own work, appealing again to common moral practice, I have stressed our society's quasi-moral, quasi-legal notion of rights as a reflection of our commitment to the moral primacy of the individual, rather than the state. Rights protect what are hypothesized as the fundamental interests of human beings from cavalier encroachment by the common good—such interests as speech, assembly, belief, property, privacy, freedom from torture, and so forth. But those animals who are conscious also have fundamental interests arising out of *their* biologically given natures (or *teloi*), the infringement upon which matters greatly to them, and the fulfillment of which is central to their lives. Hence, I deduce the notion of animal rights from our common moral theory and practice and attempt to show that conceptually, at least, it is a deduction from the moral framework of the status quo rather than a major revision therein. Moral concern for individual animals follows from the hitherto ignored presence of morally relevant characteristics, primarily sentience, in animals. As a result, I am comfortable in attributing what Immanuel Kant called "intrinsic value," not merely use value, to animals if we attribute it to people.[5]

The task is far more formidable for those who attempt to make nonsentient natural objects, such as rivers and mountains, or, worse, quasi-abstract entities, such as species and ecosystems, into direct objects of moral concern. Interestingly enough, in direct opposition to the case of animals, such moves appear prima facie plausible to common morality, which has long expressed concern for the value and preservation of some natural objects, while condoning wholesale exploitation of others. In the same way, common practice often showed extreme concern for certain favored kinds of animals, while systematically exploiting others. Thus, many people in the United States strongly oppose scientific research on dogs and cats, but are totally unconcerned about such use of rodents or swine. What is superficially plausible, however, quite unlike the case of animals, turns out to be deeply paradoxical given the machinery of traditional morality.

Many leading environmental ethicists have attempted to do for nonsentient natural objects and abstract objects the same sort of thing I have tried to do for animals—namely, attempted to elevate their status to direct objects of intrinsic value, ends in themselves, which are morally valuable not only because of their relations and utility to sentient beings, but in and of themselves.[6] To my knowledge, none of these theorists has attempted to claim, as I do for animals, that the locus of such value lies in the fact that what we do to these entities matters to them. No one has argued that we can harm rivers, species, or ecosystems in ways that matter to them.

Wherein, then, do these theorists locate the intrinsic value of these entities? This is not at all clear in the writings, but seems to come down to one of the following doubtful moves:

1 Going from the fact that environmental factors are absolutely essential to the well-being or survival of beings that are loci of intrinsic value to the conclusion that environmental factors therefore enjoy a similar or even higher moral status. Such a move is clearly fallacious. Just because I cannot survive without insulin, and I am an object of intrinsic value, it does not follow that insulin is, too. In fact, the insulin is a paradigmatic example of instrumental value.

2 Going from the fact that the environment "creates" all sentient creatures to the fact that its welfare is more important than theirs. This is really a variation on (1) and succumbs to the same sort of criticism, namely, that this reasoning represents a genetic fallacy. The cause of something valuable need not itself be valuable and certainly not necessarily more valuable than its effect—its value must be established independently of its result. The Holocaust may have caused the state of Israel; that does not make the Holocaust more valuable than the state of Israel.

3 Confusing aesthetic or instrumental value for sentient creatures, notably humans, with intrinsic value and underestimating aesthetic value as a category. We shall return to this shortly, for I suspect it is the root confusion in those attempting to give nonsentient nature intrinsic value.

4 Substituting rhetoric for logic at crucial points in the discussions and using a poetic rhetoric (descriptions of natural objects in terms such as "grandeur," "majesty," "novelty," "variety") as an unexplained basis for according them "intrinsic value."

5 Going from the metaphor that infringement on natural objects "matters" to them in the sense that disturbance evokes an adjustment by their self-regulating properties, to the erroneous conclusion that such self-regulation, being analogous to conscious coping in animals, entitles them to direct moral status.

In short, traditional morality and its theory do not offer a viable way to raise the moral status of nonsentient natural objects and abstract objects so that they are direct objects of moral concern on a par with or even higher than sentient creatures. Ordinary morality and moral concern take as their focus the effects of actions on beings who can be helped and harmed, in ways that matter to them, either directly or by implication. If it is immoral to wreck someone's property, it is because it is someone's; if it is immoral to promote the extinction of species, it is because such extinction causes aesthetic or practical harm to humans or to animals or because a species is, in the final analysis, a group of harmable individuals.

There is nothing, of course, to stop environmental ethicists from making a recommendation for a substantial revision of common and traditional morality. But such recommendations are likely to be dismissed or whittled away by a moral version of Occam's razor: Why grant animals rights and acknowledge in animals intrinsic value? Because they are conscious and what we do to them matters to them? Why grant rocks, or trees, or species, or ecosystems rights? Because these objects have great aesthetic value, or are essential to us, or are basic for survival? But these are paradigmatic examples of *instrumental* value. A conceptual confusion for a noble purpose is still a conceptual confusion.

There is nothing to be gained by attempting to elevate the moral status of non-sentient natural objects to that of sentient ones. One can develop a rich environmental ethic by locating the value of nonsentient natural objects in their relation to sentient ones. One can argue for the preservation of habitats because their destruction harms animals; one can argue for preserving ecosystems on the grounds of unforeseen pernicious consequences resulting from their destruction, a claim for which much empirical evidence exists. One can argue for the preservation of animal species as the sum of a group of individuals who would be harmed by its extinction. One can argue for preserving mountains, snail darters, streams, and cockroaches on aesthetic grounds. Too many philosophers forget the moral power of aesthetic claims and tend to see aesthetic reasons as a weak basis for preserving natural objects. Yet the moral imperative not to destroy unique aesthetic objects and even nonunique ones is an onerous one that is well ingrained into common practice— witness the worldwide establishment of national parks, preserves, forests, and wildlife areas.

Rather than attempting to transcend all views of natural objects as instrumental by grafting onto nature a mystical intrinsic value that can be buttressed only by poetic rhetoric, it would be far better to nurture public appreciation of subtle instrumental value, especially aesthetic value. People can learn to appreciate the unique beauty of a desert, or of a fragile ecosystem, or even of a noxious creature like a tick, when they understand the complexity and history therein and can read the story each life form contains. I am reminded of a colleague in parasitology who is loath to destroy worms he has studied upon completing his research because he has aesthetically learned to value their complexity of structure, function, and evolutionary history and role.

It is important to note that the attribution of value to nonsentient natural objects as a relational property arising out of their significance (recognized or not) for sentient beings does not denigrate the value of natural objects. Indeed, this attribution does not even imply that the interests or desires of individual sentient beings always trump concern for nonsentient ones. Our legal system has, for example, valuable and irreplaceable property laws that forbid owners of aesthetic objects, say a collection of Vincent Van Gogh paintings, to destroy them at will, say by adding them to one's funeral pyre. To be sure, this restriction on people's right to dispose of their own property arises out of a recognition of the value of these objects to other humans, but this is surely quite sensible. How else would one justify such a restriction? Nor, as we said earlier, need one limit the value of natural objects to their relationship to humans. Philosophically, one could, for example, sensibly (and commonsensically) argue for preservation of acreage from the golf-course developer because failure to do so would mean the destruction of thousands of sentient creatures' habitats—a major infringement of their interests—while building the golf course would fulfill the rarefied and inessential interests of a few.

Thus, in my view, one would accord moral concern to natural objects in a variety of ways, depending on the sort of object being considered. Moral status for individual animals would arise from their sentience. Moral status of species and their protection from humans would arise from the fact that a species is a collection of morally relevant individuals; moral status also would arise from the fact that humans have an aesthetic concern in not letting a unique and irreplaceable aesthetic object (or group of objects) disappear forever from our *Umwelt* (environment). Concern for wilderness areas, mountains, deserts, and so on would arise from their survival value for sentient animals as well as from their aesthetic value for humans. (Some writers have suggested that this aesthetic value is so great as to be essential to human mental/physical health, a point perfectly compatible with my position.[7])

Nothing in what I have said as yet tells us how to weigh conflicting interests, whether between humans and other sentient creatures or between human desires and environmental protection. How does one weigh the aesthetic concern of those who oppose blasting away part of a cliff against the pragmatic concern of those who wish to build on a cliffside? But the problem of weighing is equally thorny in traditional ethics—witness lifeboat questions or questions concerning the allocation of scarce medical resources. Nor does the intrinsic value approach help in adjudicating such issues. How does one weigh the alleged intrinsic value of a cliffside against the interests of the (intrinsic-value-bearing) homebuilders?

Furthermore, the intrinsic value view can lead to results that are repugnant to common sense and ordinary moral consciousness. Thus, for example, it follows from what has been suggested by one intrinsic value theorist that if a migratory herd of plentiful elk were passing through an area containing an endangered species of moss, it would be not only permissible but obligatory to kill the elk in order to protect the moss because in one case we would lose a species, in another "merely" individuals.[8] In my view, such a case has a less paradoxical resolution. Destruction of the moss does not matter to the moss, whereas elk presumably care about living or being injured. Therefore, one would give prima facie priority to the elk. This might presumably be trumped if, for example, the moss were a substratum from which was extracted an ingredient necessary to stop a raging, lethal epidemic in humans or animals. But such cases—and indeed most cases of conflicting interests—must be decided on the actual occasion. These cases are decided by a careful examination of the facts of the situation. Thus, our suggestion of a basis for environmental ethics does not qualitatively change the situation from that of current ethical deliberation, whereas granting intrinsic value to natural objects would leave us with a "whole new ball game"—and one where we do not know the rules.

In sum, then, the question of environmental ethics . . . must be analyzed into two discrete components. First are those questions that pertain to direct objects of moral concern—nonhuman animals whose sentience we have good reason to suspect—and that require the application of traditional moral notions to a hitherto ignored domain of moral objects. Second are those questions pertaining to natural objects or abstract natural objects. Although it is nonsensical to attribute intrinsic or direct moral value to these objects, they nonetheless must become (and are indeed becoming) central to our social moral deliberations. This centrality derives from our increasing recognition of the far-reaching and sometimes subtle instrumental value these objects have for humans and animals. Knowing that contamination of remote desert areas by pollutants can destroy unique panoplies of fragile beauty, or that dumping wastes into the ocean can destroy a potential source of antibiotics, or that building a pipeline can have undreamed-of harmful effects goes a long way toward making us think twice about these activities—a far longer way than endowing them with quasi-mystical rhetorical status subject to (and begging for) positivistic torpedoing. . . .

NOTES

1 See the chapters in Tom Regan, *All That Dwell Therein* (Berkeley: University of California Press, 1982).
2 See Aldo Leopold, *A Sand County Almanac* (Oxford: Oxford University Press, 1949); J. Baird Callicott, "Animal Liberation: A Triangular Affair," *Environmental Ethics* 2 (1980):311–338; Holmes Rolston III, *Philosophy Gone Wild* (Buffalo, N.Y.: Prometheus Books, 1986).
3 See the discussions of this point in Peter Singer, *Animal Liberation* (New York: New York Review of Books, 1975); and B. Rollin, *Animal Rights and Human Morality* (Buffalo, N.Y.: Prometheus Books, 1981).
4 See my "Animal Pain," in M. Fox and L. Mickley (eds.), *Advances in Animal Welfare Science 1985* (The Hague; Martinus Nijhoff, 1985); and my "Animal Consciousness and Scientific Change," *New Ideas in Psychology* 4, no. 2 (1986):141–152, as well as the replies to the latter by P. K. Feyerabend, H. Rachlin, and T. Leahey in the same issue, p. 153. See also my *The Unheeded Cry: Animal Consciousness, Animal Pain, and Science* (Oxford: Oxford University Press, 1989).
5 See my *Animal Rights*, Part I.
6 See the works mentioned in footnotes 1 and 2.
7 This point is made with great rhetorical force in Edward Abbey, *Desert Solitaire* (New York: Ballantine Books, 1971).
8 See Holmes Rolston, "Duties to Endangered Species," *Philosophy Gone Wild*.

QUESTIONS

1 Is Rollin correct in holding that only sentient beings have intrinsic value?
2 Do you agree that, once we recognize the subtle instrumental value of ecosystems, forests, and so on, we will have a very strong foundation for revising those human activities that damage or destroy nonsentient natural objects?

Deep Ecology

Bill Devall and George Sessions

Devall and Sessions present deep ecology as a systematic alternative to "the dominant worldview of technocratic-industrial societies." They identify *self-realization* and *biocentric equality* as the two basic norms or intuitions underlying deep ecology. The norm of self-realization challenges the ordinary (Western) understanding of the self and ultimately requires each of us to identify with the nonhuman world. The norm of biocentric equality attributes equal intrinsic worth to "all organisms and entities in the ecosphere." Devall and Sessions also identify a set of eight principles considered basic to deep ecology. A commentary is then provided to explain each of the eight principles.

The term *deep ecology* was coined by Arne Naess in his 1973 article, "The Shallow and the Deep, Long-Range Ecology Movements."[1] Naess was attempting to describe the deeper, more spiritual approach to Nature exemplified in the writings of Aldo Leopold and Rachel Carson. He thought that this deeper approach resulted from a more sensitive openness to ourselves and nonhuman life around us. The essence of deep ecology is to keep asking more searching questions about human life, society, and Nature as in the Western philosophical tradition of Socrates. As examples of this deep questioning, Naess points out "that we ask why and how, where others do not. For instance, ecology as a science does not ask what kind of a society would be the best for maintaining a particular ecosystem—that is considered a question for value theory, for politics, for ethics." Thus deep ecology goes beyond the so-called factual scientific level to the level of self and Earth wisdom.

Deep ecology goes beyond a limited piecemeal shallow approach to environmental problems and attempts to articulate a comprehensive religious and philosophical worldview. The foundations of deep ecology are the basic intuitions and experiencing of ourselves and Nature which comprise ecological consciousness. Certain outlooks on politics and public policy flow naturally from this consciousness. And in the context of this book, we discuss the minority tradition as the type of community most conducive both to cultivating ecological consciousness and to asking the basic questions of values and ethics addressed in these pages.

Many of these questions are perennial philosophical and religious questions faced by humans in all cultures over the ages. What does it mean to be a unique human individual? How can the individual self maintain and increase its uniqueness while also being an inseparable aspect of the whole system wherein there are no sharp breaks between self and the *other*? An ecological perspective, in this deeper sense, results in what Theodore Roszak calls "an awakening of wholes greater than the sum of their parts. In spirit, the discipline is contemplative and therapeutic."[2]

Reprinted with permission of the publisher from Bill Devall and George Sessions, *Deep Ecology: Living as if Nature Mattered* (Salt Lake City: Gibbs M. Smith, Inc., Peregrine Smith Books, 1985), pp. 65–73.

Ecological consciousness and deep ecology are in sharp contrast with the dominant worldview of technocratic-industrial societies which regards humans as isolated and fundamentally separate from the rest of Nature, as superior to, and in charge of, the rest of creation. But the view of humans as separate and superior to the rest of Nature is only part of larger cultural patterns. For thousands of years, Western culture has become increasingly obsessed with the idea of *dominance:* with dominance of humans over nonhuman Nature, masculine over the feminine, wealthy and powerful over the poor, with the dominance of the West over non-Western cultures. Deep ecological consciousness allows us to see through these erroneous and dangerous illusions.

For deep ecology, the study of our place in the Earth household includes the study of ourselves as part of the organic whole. Going beyond a narrowly materialist scientific understanding of reality, the spiritual and the material aspects of reality fuse together. While the leading intellectuals of the dominant worldview have tended to view religion as "just superstition," and have looked upon ancient spiritual practice and enlightenment, such as found in Zen Buddhism, as essentially subjective, the search for deep ecological consciousness is the search for a more objective consciousness and state of being through an active deep questioning and meditative process and way of life.

Many people have asked these deeper questions and cultivated ecological consciousness within the context of different spiritual traditions—Christianity, Taoism, Buddhism, and Native American rituals, for example. While differing greatly in other regards, many in these traditions agree with the basic principles of deep ecology.

Warwick Fox, an Australian philosopher, has succinctly expressed the central intuition of deep ecology: "It is the idea that we can make no firm ontological divide in the field of existence: That there is no bifurcation in reality between the human and the non-human realms . . . to the extent that we perceive boundaries, we fall short of deep ecological consciousness."[3]

From this most basic insight or characteristic of deep ecological consciousness, Arne Naess has developed two *ultimate norms* or intuitions which are themselves not derivable from other principles or intuitions. They are arrived at by the deep questioning process and reveal the importance of moving to the philosophical and religious level of wisdom. They cannot be validated, of course, by the methodology of modern science based on its usual mechanistic assumptions and its very narrow definition of data. These ultimate norms are *self-realization* and *biocentric equality*.

I SELF-REALIZATION

In keeping with the spiritual traditions of many of the world's religions, the deep ecology norm of self-realization goes beyond the modern Western *self* which is defined as an isolated ego striving primarily for hedonistic gratification or for a narrow sense of individual salvation in this life or the next. This socially programmed sense of the narrow self or social self dislocates us, and leaves us prey to whatever fad or fashion is prevalent in our society or social reference group. We are thus robbed of beginning the search for our unique spiritual/biological personhood. Spiritual growth, or unfolding, begins when we cease to understand or see ourselves as isolated and narrow competing egos and begin to identify with other humans from our family and friends to, eventually, our species. But the deep ecology sense of self requires a further maturity and growth, an identification which goes beyond humanity to include the nonhuman world. We must see beyond our narrow contemporary cultural assumptions and values, and the conventional wisdom of our time and place, and this is best achieved by the meditative deep questioning process. Only in this way can we hope to attain full mature personhood and uniqueness.

A nurturing nondominating society can help in the "real work" of becoming a whole person. The "real work" can be summarized symbolically as the realization of "self-in-Self" where "Self" stands for organic wholeness. This process of the full unfolding of the self can also be summarized by the phrase, "No one is saved until we are all saved," where the phrase "one" includes not only me, an individual human, but all humans, whales, grizzly bears, whole rain forest ecosystems, mountains and rivers, the tiniest microbes in the soil, and so on.

II   BIOCENTRIC EQUALITY

The intuition of biocentric equality is that all things in the biosphere have an equal right to live and blossom and to reach their own individual forms of unfolding and self-realization within the larger Self-realization. This basic intuition is that all organisms and entities in the ecosphere, as parts of the interrelated whole, are equal in intrinsic worth. Naess suggests that biocentric equality as an intuition is true in principle, although in the process of living, all species use each other as food, shelter, etc. Mutual predation is a biological fact of life, and many of the world's religions have struggled with the spiritual implications of this. Some animal liberationists who attempt to side-step this problem by advocating vegetarianism are forced to say that the entire plant kingdom including rain forests have no right to their own existence. This evasion flies in the face of the basic intuition of equality.[4] Aldo Leopold expressed this intuition when he said humans are "plain citizens" of the biotic community, not lord and master over all other species.

Biocentric equality is intimately related to the all-inclusive Self-realization in the sense that if we harm the rest of Nature then we are harming ourselves. There are no boundaries and everything is interrelated. But insofar as we perceive things as individual organisms or entities, the insight draws us to respect all human and nonhuman individuals in their own right as parts of the whole without feeling the need to set up hierarchies of species with humans at the top.

The practical implications of this intuition or norm suggest that we should live with minimum rather than maximum impact on other species and on the Earth in general. Thus we see another aspect of our guiding principle: "simple in means, rich in ends." . . .

A fuller discussion of the biocentric norm as it unfolds itself in practice begins with the realization that we, as individual humans, and as communities of humans, have vital needs which go beyond such basics as food, water, and shelter to include love, play, creative expression, intimate relationships with a particular landscape (or Nature taken in its entirety) as well as intimate relationships with other humans, and the vital need for spiritual growth, for becoming a mature human being.

Fig. 1

Dominant Worldview	Deep Ecology
Dominance over Nature	Harmony with Nature
Natural environment as resource for humans	All nature has intrinsic worth/biospecies equality
Material/economic growth for growing human population	Elegantly simple material needs (material goals serving the larger goal of self-realization)
Belief in ample resource reserves	Earth "supplies" limited
High technological progress and solutions	Appropriate technology; nondominating science
Consumerism	Doing with enough/recycling
National/centralized community	Minority tradition/bioregion

Our vital material needs are probably more simple than many realize. In technocratic-industrial societies there is overwhelming propaganda and advertising which encourages false needs and destructive desires designed to foster increased production and consumption of goods. Most of this actually diverts us from facing reality in an objective way and from beginning the "real work" of spiritual growth and maturity.

Many people who do not see themselves as supporters of deep ecology nevertheless recognize an overriding vital human need for a healthy and high-quality natural environment for humans, if not for all life, with minimum intrusion of toxic waste, nuclear radiation from human enterprises, minimum acid rain and smog, and enough free flowing wilderness so humans can get in touch with their sources, the natural rhythms and the flow of time and place.

Drawing from the minority tradition and from the wisdom of many who have offered the insight of interconnectedness, we recognize that deep ecologists can offer suggestions for gaining maturity and encouraging the processes of harmony with Nature, but that there is no grand solution which is guaranteed to save us from ourselves.

The ultimate norms of deep ecology suggest a view of the nature of reality and our place as an individual (many in the one) in the larger scheme of things. They cannot be fully grasped intellectually but are ultimately experiential. . . .

As a brief summary of our position thus far, Figure 1 summarizes the contrast between the dominant worldview and deep ecology.

III   BASIC PRINCIPLES OF DEEP ECOLOGY

In April 1984, during the advent of spring and John Muir's birthday, George Sessions and Arne Naess summarized fifteen years of thinking on the principles of deep ecology while camping in Death Valley, California. In this great and special place, they articulated these principles in a literal, somewhat neutral way, hoping that they would be understood and accepted by persons coming from different philosophical and religious positions.

Readers are encouraged to elaborate their own versions of deep ecology, clarify key concepts and think through the consequences of acting from these principles.

Basic Principles

1 The well-being and flourishing of human and nonhuman Life on Earth have value in themselves (synonyms: intrinsic value, inherent value). These values are independent of the usefulness of the nonhuman world for human purposes.

2 Richness and diversity of life forms contribute to the realization of these values and are also values in themselves.

3 Humans have no right to reduce this richness and diversity except to satisfy *vital* needs.

4 The flourishing of human life and cultures is compatible with a substantial decrease of the human population. The flourishing of nonhuman life requires such a decrease.

5 Present human interference with the nonhuman world is excessive, and the situation is rapidly worsening.

6 Policies must therefore be changed. These policies affect basic economic, technological, and ideological structures. The resulting state of affairs will be deeply different from the present.

7 The ideological change is mainly that of appreciating *life quality* (dwelling in situations of inherent value) rather than adhering to an increasingly higher standard of living. There will be a profound awareness of the difference between big and great.

8 Those who subscribe to the foregoing points have an obligation directly or indirectly to try to implement the necessary changes.

Naess and Sessions Provide Comments on the Basic Principles

RE (1)   This formulation refers to the biosphere, or more accurately, to the ecosphere as a whole. This includes individuals, species, populations, habitat, as well as human and nonhuman cultures. From our current knowledge of all-pervasive intimate relationships, this implies a fundamental deep concern and respect. Ecological processes of the planet should, on the whole, remain intact. "The world environment should remain 'natural'" (Gary Snyder).

The term "life" is used here in a more comprehensive nontechnical way to refer also to what biologists classify as "nonliving"; rivers (watersheds), landscapes, ecosystems. For supporters of deep ecology, slogans such as "Let the river live" illustrate this broader usage so common in most cultures.

Inherent value as used in (1) is common in deep ecology literature ("The presence of inherent value in a natural object is independent of any awareness, interest, or appreciation of it by a conscious being.").[5]

RE (2)   More technically, this is a formulation concerning diversity and complexity. From an ecological standpoint, complexity and symbiosis are conditions for maximizing diversity. So-called simple, lower, or primitive species of plants and animals contribute essentially to the richness and diversity of life. They have value in themselves and are not merely steps toward the so-called higher or rational life forms. The second principle presupposes that life itself, as a process over evolutionary time, implies an increase of diversity and richness. The refusal to acknowledge that some life forms have greater or lesser intrinsic value than others (see points 1 and 2) runs counter to the formulations of some ecological philosophers and New Age writers.

Complexity, as referred to here, is different from complication. Urban life may be more complicated than life in a natural setting without being more complex in the sense of multifaceted quality.

RE (3) The term "vital need" is left deliberately vague to allow for considerable latitude in judgment. Differences in climate and related factors, together with differences in the structures of societies as they now exist, need to be considered (for some Eskimos, snowmobiles are necessary today to satisfy vital needs).

People in the materially richest countries cannot be expected to reduce their excessive interference with the nonhuman world to a moderate level overnight. The stabilization and reduction of the human population will take time. Interim strategies need to be developed. But this in no way excuses the present complacency—the extreme seriousness of our current situation must first be realized. But the longer we wait the more drastic will be the measures needed. Until deep changes are made, substantial decreases in richness and diversity are liable to occur: the rate of extinction of species will be ten to one hundred times greater than [in] any other period of earth history.

RE (4) The United Nations Fund for Population Activities in their State of World Population Report (1984) said that high human population growth rates (over 2.0 percent annum) in many developing countries "were diminishing the quality of life for many millions of people." During the decade 1974–1984, the world population grew by nearly 800 million—more than the size of India. "And we will be adding about one Bangladesh (population 93 million) per annum between now and the year 2000."

The report noted that "The growth rate of the human population has declined for the first time in human history. But at the same time, the number of people being added to the human population is bigger than at any time in history because the population base is larger."

Most of the nations in the developing world (including India and China) have as their official government policy the goal of reducing the rate of human population increase, but there are debates over the types of measures to take (contraception, abortion, etc.) consistent with human rights and feasibility.

The report concludes that if all governments set specific population targets as public policy to help alleviate poverty and advance the quality of life, the current situation could be improved.

As many ecologists have pointed out, it is also absolutely crucial to curb population growth in the so-called developed (i.e., overdeveloped) industrial societies. Given the tremendous rate of consumption and waste production of individuals in these societies, they represent a much greater threat and impact on the biosphere per capita than individuals in Second and Third World countries.

RE (5) This formulation is mild. For a realistic assessment of the situation, see the unabbreviated version of the I.U.C.N.'s *World Conservation Strategy*. There are other works to be highly recommended, such as Gerald Barney's *Global 2000 Report to the President of the United States*.

The slogan of "noninterference" does not imply that humans should not modify some ecosystems as do other species. Humans have modified the earth and will probably continue to do so. At issue is the nature and extent of such interference.

The fight to preserve and extend areas of wilderness or near-wilderness should continue and should focus on the general ecological functions of these areas (one such function: large wilderness areas are required in the biosphere to allow for continued evolutionary speciation of animals and plants). Most present designated wilderness areas and game preserves are not large enough to allow for such speciation.

RE (6) Economic growth as conceived and implemented today by the industrial states is incompatible with (1)–(5). There is only a faint resemblance between ideal sustainable forms of economic growth and present policies of the industrial societies. And "sustainable" still means "sustainable in relation to humans."

Present ideology tends to value things because they are scarce and because they have a commodity value. There is prestige in vast consumption and waste (to mention only several relevant factors).

Whereas "self-determination," "local community," and "think globally, act locally," will remain key terms in the ecology of human societies, nevertheless the implementation of deep changes requires increasingly global action—action across borders.

Governments in Third World countries (with the exception of Costa Rica and a few others) are uninterested in deep ecological issues. When the governments of industrial societies try to promote ecological measures through Third World governments, practically nothing is accomplished (e.g., with problems of desertification). Given this situation, support for global action through nongovernmental international organizations becomes increasingly important. Many of these organizations are able to act globally "from grassroots to grassroots," thus avoiding negative governmental interference.

Cultural diversity today requires advanced technology, that is, techniques that advance the basic goals of each culture. So-called soft, intermediate, and alternative technologies are steps in this direction.

RE (7) Some economists criticize the term "quality of life" because it is supposed to be vague. But on closer inspection, what they consider to be vague is actually the nonquantitative nature of the term. One cannot quantify adequately what is important for the quality of life as discussed here, and there is no need to do so.

RE (8) There is ample room for different opinions about priorities: what should be done first, what next? What is most urgent? What is clearly necessary as opposed to what is highly desirable but not absolutely pressing?

NOTES

1 Arne Naess, "The Shallow and the Deep, Long-Range Ecology Movements: A Summary," *Inquiry* 16 (Oslo, 1973), pp. 95–100.
2 Theodore Roszak, *Where the Wasteland Ends* (New York: Anchor, 1972).
3 Warwick Fox, "Deep Ecology: A New Philosophy of Our Time?" *The Ecologist*, v. 14, 5–6, 1984, pp. 194–200. Arne Naess replies, "Intuition, Intrinsic Value and Deep Ecology," *The Ecologist*, v. 14, 5–6, 1984, pp. 201–204.
4 Tom Regan, *The Case for Animal Rights* (New York: Random House, 1983). For excellent critiques of the animal rights movement, see John Rodman, "The Liberation of Nature?" *Inquiry* 20 (Oslo, 1977). J. Baird Callicott, "Animal Liberation," *Environmental Ethics* 2, 4 (1980); see also John Rodman, "Four Forms of Ecological Consciousness Reconsidered" in T. Attig and D. Scherer, eds., *Ethics and the Environment* (Englewood Cliffs, N.J.: Prentice-Hall, 1983).
5 Tom Regan, "The Nature and Possibility of an Environmental Ethic," *Environmental Ethics* 3 (1981), pp. 19–34.

QUESTIONS

1 To what extent would you endorse the two basic norms of deep ecology?
2 To what extent would you endorse the eight basic principles of deep ecology?
3 Critics sometimes complain that deep ecology is an "antihuman" philosophy. Is there any substance to this charge?

Radical American Environmentalism and Wilderness Preservation: A Third World Critique

Ramachandra Guha

Guha advances a critique of the American deep ecology movement from a third-world perspective. He states and criticizes three of the central tenets he identifies with American deep ecology: (1) its distinction between anthropocentric and biocentric approaches to environmental issues, (2) its focus on wilderness preservation, and (3) its conviction that the American version of deep ecology represents the most radical trend in environmentalism. In respect to (1), Guha argues that this distinction is of little use in helping us understand the dynamics of environmental degradation. In respect to (2), he maintains that the implementation of the wilderness agenda is causing serious deprivation in third-world countries. In respect to (3), Guha points out that American deep ecologists fail to seriously question the ecological and sociopolitical basis of the consumer society,

Reprinted with permission of the author and the publisher from *Environmental Ethics*, vol. 11 (Spring 1989), pp. 71–76, 78–83.

even though its consumerism is responsible for so much environmental degradation. He gives examples from other cultures (Germany and India) to illustrate what he considers a far more radical environmentalism—one that emphasizes equity and the integration of ecological concerns with livelihood and work.

I INTRODUCTION

The respected radical journalist Kirkpatrick Sale recently celebrated "the passion of a new and growing movement that has become disenchanted with the environmental establishment and has in recent years mounted a serious and sweeping attack on it—style, substance, systems, sensibilities and all."[1] The vision of those whom Sale calls the "New Ecologists"—and what I refer to in this article as deep ecology—is a compelling one. Decrying the narrowly economic goals of mainstream environmentalism, this new movement aims at nothing less than a philosophical and cultural revolution in human attitudes toward nature. In contrast to the conventional lobbying efforts of environmental professionals based in Washington, it proposes a militant defence of "Mother Earth," an unflinching opposition to human attacks on undisturbed wilderness. With their goals ranging from the spiritual to the political, the adherents of deep ecology span a wide spectrum of the American environmental movement. As Sale correctly notes, this emerging strand has in a matter of a few years made its presence felt in a number of fields: from academic philosophy (as in the journal *Environmental Ethics*) to popular environmentalism (for example, the group Earth First!).

In this article I develop a critique of deep ecology from the perspective of a sympathetic outsider. . . . I speak admittedly as a partisan, but of the environmental movement in India, a country with an ecological diversity comparable to the U.S., but with a radically dissimilar cultural and social history.

My treatment of deep ecology is primarily historical and sociological, rather than philosophical, in nature. Specifically, I examine the cultural rootedness of a philosophy that likes to present itself in universalistic terms. I make two main arguments: first, that deep ecology is uniquely American, and despite superficial similarities in rhetorical style, the social and political goals of radical environmentalism in other cultural contexts (e.g., West Germany and India) are quite different; second, that the social consequences of putting deep ecology into practice on a worldwide basis (what its practitioners are aiming for) are very grave indeed.

II THE TENETS OF DEEP ECOLOGY

While I am aware that the term *deep ecology* was coined by the Norwegian philosopher Arne Naess, this article refers specifically to the American variant.[2] Adherents of the deep ecological perspective in this country, while arguing intensely among themselves over its political and philosophical implications, share some fundamental premises about human-nature interactions. As I see it, [the following are three of] the defining characteristics of deep ecology:

First, deep ecology argues, that the environmental movement must shift from an "anthropocentric" to a "biocentric" perspective. In many respects, an acceptance of the primacy of this distinction constitutes the litmus test of deep ecology. A considerable effort is expended by deep ecologists in showing that the dominant motif in Western philosophy has been anthropocentric—i.e., the belief that man and his works are the center of the universe—and conversely, in identifying those lonely thinkers (Leopold, Thoreau, Muir, Aldous Huxley, Santayana, etc.) who, in assigning man a more humble place in the natural order, anticipated deep ecological thinking. In the political realm, meanwhile, establishment environmentalism (shallow ecology) is chided for casting its arguments in human-centered terms. Preserving nature, the deep ecologists say, has an intrinsic worth quite apart from any benefits preservation may convey to future human generations. The anthropocentric-biocentric distinction is accepted as axiomatic by deep ecologists, it structures their discourse, and much of the present discussion remains mired within it.

The second characteristic of deep ecology is its focus on the preservation of unspoilt wilderness—and the restoration of degraded areas to a more pristine condition—to the relative (and sometimes absolute) neglect of other issues on the environmental agenda. I later identify the cultural roots and portentous consequences of this obsession with wilderness. For the moment, let me indicate three distinct sources from which it springs. Historically, it represents a playing out of the preservationist (read *radical*) and utilitarian (read *reformist*) dichotomy that has plagued American environmentalism since the turn of the century. Morally, it is an imperative that follows from the biocentric perspective; other species of plants and animals, and nature itself, have an intrinsic right to exist. And finally, the preservation of wilderness also turns on a scientific argument—viz., the value of biological diversity in stabilizing ecological regimes and in retaining a gene pool for future generations. Truly radical policy proposals have been put forward by deep ecologists on the basis of these arguments. The influential poet Gary Snyder, for example, would like to see a 90 percent reduction in human populations to allow a restoration of pristine environments, while others have argued forcefully that a large portion of the globe must be immediately cordoned off from human beings.[3] . . .

Third, deep ecologists, whatever their internal differences, share the belief that they are the "leading edge" of the environmental movement. As the polarity of the shallow/deep and anthropocentric/biocentric distinctions makes clear, they see themselves as the spiritual, philosophical, and political vanguard of American and world environmentalism.

III   TOWARD A CRITIQUE

Although I analyze each of these tenets independently, it is important to recognize, as deep ecologists are fond of remarking in reference to nature, the interconnectedness and unity of these individual themes.

1 Insofar as it has begun to act as a check on man's arrogance and ecological hubris, the transition from an anthropocentric (human-centered) to a biocentric (humans as only one element in the ecosystem) view in both religious and scientific traditions is only to be welcomed. What is unacceptable are the radical conclusions drawn by deep ecology, in particular, that intervention in nature should be guided primarily by the need to preserve biotic integrity rather than by the needs of humans. The latter for deep ecologists is anthropocentric, the former biocentric. This dichotomy is, however, of very little use in understanding the dynamics of environmental degradation. The two fundamental ecological problems facing the globe are (i) overconsumption by the industrialized world and by urban elites in the Third World and (ii) growing militarization, both in a short-term sense (i.e., ongoing regional wars) and in a long-term sense (i.e., the arms race and the prospect of nuclear annihilation). Neither of these problems has any tangible connection to the anthropocentric-biocentric distinction. Indeed, the agents of these processes would barely comprehend this philosophical dichotomy. The proximate causes of the ecologically wasteful characteristics of industrial society and of militarization are far more mundane: at an aggregate level, the dialectic of economic and political structures, and at a micro-level, the life style choices of individuals. These causes cannot be reduced, whatever the level of analysis, to a deeper anthropocentric attitude toward nature; on the contrary, by constituting a grave threat to human survival, the ecological degradation they cause does not even serve the best interests of human beings! If my identification of the major dangers to the integrity of the natural world is correct, invoking the bogy of anthropocentricism is at best irrelevant and at worst a dangerous obfuscation.

2 If the above dichotomy is irrelevant, the emphasis on wilderness is positively harmful when applied to the Third World. If in the U.S. the preservationist/utilitarian division is seen as mirroring the conflict between "people" and "interests," in countries such as India the situation is very nearly the reverse. Because India is a long settled and densely populated country in which agrarian populations have a finely balanced relationship with nature, the setting aside of wilderness areas has resulted in a direct transfer of resources from the poor to the rich. Thus, Project Tiger, a network of parks hailed by the international conservation community as an outstanding success, sharply posits the interests of the tiger against those of poor peasants living in and around the reserve. The designation of tiger reserves was made possible only by the physical displacement of existing villages and their inhabitants; their management requires the continuing exclusion of peasants and livestock. The initial impetus for setting up parks for the tiger and other large mammals such as the rhinoceros and elephant came from two social groups, first, a class of ex-hunters turned conservationists belonging mostly to the declining Indian feudal elite and second, representatives of international agencies, such as the World Wildlife Fund (WWF) and the International Union for the Conservation of Nature and Natural Resources (IUCN), seeking to transplant the American system of national parks onto Indian soil. In no case have the needs of the local population been taken into account, and as in many parts of Africa, the designated wildlands are managed primarily for the benefit of rich tourists. Until very recently, wildlands preservation has been identified with environmentalism by the state and the conservation elite; in consequence, environmental problems that impinge far more directly on the lives of the poor—e.g., fuel, fodder, water shortages, soil erosion, and air and water pollution—have not been adequately addressed.[4]

Deep ecology provides, perhaps unwittingly, a justification for the continuation of such narrow and inequitable conservation practices under a newly acquired radical guise. Increasingly, the international conservation elite is using the philosophical, moral, and scientific arguments used by deep ecologists in advancing their wilderness crusade. A striking but by no means atypical example is the recent plea by a prominent American biologist for the takeover of large portions of the globe by the author and his scientific colleagues. Writing in a prestigious scientific forum, the *Annual Review of Ecology and Systematics,* Daniel Janzen argues that only biologists have the competence to decide how the tropical landscape should be used. As "the representatives of the natural world," biologists are "in charge of the future of tropical ecology," and only they have the expertise and mandate to "determine whether the tropical agroscape is to be populated only by humans, their mutualists, commensals, and parasites, or whether it will also contain some islands of the greater nature—the nature that spawned humans, yet has been vanquished by them." Janzen exhorts his colleagues to advance their territorial claims on the tropical world more forcefully, warning that the very existence of these areas is at stake: "if biologists want a tropics in which to biologize, they are going to have to buy it with care, energy, effort, strategy, tactics, time, and cash."[5]

This frankly imperialist manifesto highlights the multiple dangers of the preoccupation with wilderness preservation that is characteristic of deep ecology. As I have suggested, it seriously compounds the neglect by the American movement of far more pressing environmental problems within the Third World. But perhaps more importantly, and in a more insidious fashion, it also provides an impetus to the imperialist yearning of Western biologists and their financial sponsors, organizations such as the WWF and IUCN. The wholesale transfer of a movement culturally rooted in American conservation history can only result in the social uprooting of human populations in other parts of the globe. . . .

How radical, finally, are the deep ecologists? Notwithstanding their self-image and strident rhetoric (in which the label "shallow ecology" has an opprobrium similar to that reserved for "social democratic" by Marxist-Leninists), even within the American context their radicalism is limited and it manifests itself quite differently elsewhere.

To my mind, deep ecology is best viewed as a radical trend within the wilderness preservation movement. Although advancing philosophical rather than aesthetic arguments and encouraging political militancy rather than negotiation, its practical emphasis—viz., preservation of unspoilt nature—is virtually identical. For the mainstream movement, the function of wilderness is to provide a temporary antidote to modern civilization. As a special institution within an industrialized society, the national park "provides an opportunity for respite, contrast, contemplation, and affirmation of values for those who live most of their lives in the workaday world."[6] Indeed, the rapid increase in visitations to the national parks in postwar America is a direct consequence of economic expansion. The emergence of a popular interest in wilderness sites, the historian Samuel Hays points out, was "not a throwback to the primitive, but an integral part of the modern standard of living as people sought to add new 'amenity' and 'aesthetic' goals and desires to their earlier preoccupation with necessities and conveniences."[7]

Here, the enjoyment of nature is an integral part of the consumer society. The private automobile (and the life style it has spawned) is in many respects the ultimate ecological villain, and an untouched wilderness the prototype of ecological harmony; yet, for most Americans it is perfectly consistent to drive a thousand miles to spend a holiday in a national park. They possess a vast, beautiful, and sparsely populated continent and are also able to draw upon the natural resources of large portions of the globe by virtue of their economic and political dominance. In consequence, America can simultaneously enjoy the material benefits of an expanding economy and the aesthetic benefits of unspoilt nature. The two poles of "wilderness" and "civilization" mutually coexist in an internally coherent whole, and philosophers of both poles are assigned a prominent place in this culture. Paradoxically as it may seem, it is no accident that Star Wars technology and deep ecology both find their fullest expression in that leading sector of Western civilization, California.

Deep ecology runs parallel to the consumer society without seriously questioning its ecological and socio-political basis. In its celebration of American wilderness, it also displays an uncomfortable convergence with the prevailing climate of nationalism in the American wilderness movement. For spokesmen such as the historian Roderick Nash, the national park system is America's distinctive cultural contribution to the world, reflective not merely of its economic but of its philosophical and ecological maturity as well. In what Walter Lippman called the American century, the "American invention of national parks" must be exported worldwide. Betraying an economic determinism that would make even a Marxist shudder, Nash believes that environmental preservation is a "full stomach" phenomenon that is confined to the rich, urban, and sophisticated. Nonetheless, he hopes that "the less developed nations may eventually evolve economically and intellectually to the point where nature preservation is more than a business."[8]

The error which Nash makes (and which deep ecology in some respects encourages) is to equate environmental protection with the protection of wilderness. This is a distinctively American notion, born out of a unique social and environmental history. The archetypal concerns of radical environmentalists in other cultural contexts are in fact quite different. The German Greens, for example, have elaborated a devastating critique of industrial society which turns on the acceptance of environmental limits to growth. Pointing to the intimate links between industrialization, militarization, and conquest, the Greens argue that economic growth in the West has historically rested on the economic and ecological exploitation of the Third World. Rudolf Bahro is characteristically blunt:

> The working class here [in the West] is the richest lower class in the world. And if I look at the problem from the point of view of the whole of humanity, not just from that of Europe, then I must say that the metropolitan working class is the worst exploiting class in history. . . . What made poverty bearable in eighteenth or nineteenth-century Europe was the prospect of escaping it through exploitation of the periphery. But this is no longer a possibility, and continued industrialism in the Third World will mean poverty for whole generations and hunger for millions.[9]

Here the roots of global ecological problems lie in the disproportionate share of resources consumed by the industrialized countries as a whole *and* the urban elite

within the Third World. Since it is impossible to reproduce an industrial monocul-
ture worldwide, the ecological movement in the West must begin by cleaning up its
own act. The Greens advocate the creation of a "no growth" economy, to be
achieved by scaling down current (and clearly unsustainable) consumption levels.
This radical shift in consumption and production patterns requires the creation of
alternate economic and political structures—smaller in scale and more amenable to
social participation—but it rests equally on a shift in cultural values. The expan-
sionist character of modern Western man will have to give way to an ethic of renunciation and self-limitation, in which spiritual and communal values play an
increasing role in sustaining social life. This revolution in cultural values, however,
has as its point of departure an understanding of environmental processes quite different from deep ecology.

Many elements of the Green program find a strong resonance in countries such
as India, where a history of Western colonialism and industrial development has
benefited only a tiny elite while exacting tremendous social and environmental
costs. The ecological battles presently being fought in India have as their epicenter
the conflict over nature between the subsistence and largely rural sector and the
vastly more powerful commercial-industrial sector. Perhaps the most celebrated of
these battles concerns the Chipko (Hug the Tree) movement, a peasant movement
against deforestation in the Himalayan foothills. Chipko is only one of several
movements that have sharply questioned the nonsustainable demand being placed
on the land and vegetative base by urban centers and industry. These include opposition to large dams by displaced peasants, the conflict between small artisan fishing and large-scale trawler fishing for export, the countrywide movements against
commercial forest operations, and opposition to industrial pollution among down-
stream agricultural and fishing communities.[10]

Two features distinguish these environmental movements from their Western
counterparts. First, for the sections of society most critically affected by environmental degradation—poor and landless peasants, women, and tribals—it is a question of sheer survival, not of enhancing the quality of life. Second, and as a
consequence, the environmental solutions they articulate deeply involve questions
of equity as well as economic and political redistribution. Highlighting these differences, a leading Indian environmentalist stresses that "environmental protection
per se is of least concern to most of these groups. Their main concern is about the
use of the environment and who should benefit from it."[11] They seek to wrest control of nature away from the state and the industrial sector and place it in the hands
of rural communities who live within that environment but are increasingly denied
access to it. These communities have far more basic needs, their demands on the
environment are far less intense, and they can draw upon a reservoir of cooperative
social institutions and local ecological knowledge in managing the "commons"—
forests, grasslands, and the waters—on a sustainable basis. If colonial and capitalist expansion has both accentuated social inequalities and signaled a precipitous fall
in ecological wisdom, an alternate ecology must rest on an alternate society and
polity as well.

This brief overview of German and Indian environmentalism has some major
implications for deep ecology. Both German and Indian environmental traditions

allow for a greater integration of ecological concerns with livelihood and work. They also place a greater emphasis on equity and social justice (both within individual countries and on a global scale) on the grounds that in the absence of social regeneration environmental regeneration has very little chance of succeeding. Finally, and perhaps most significantly, they have escaped the preoccupation with wilderness preservation so characteristic of American cultural and environmental history.

IV   A HOMILY

In 1958, the economist J. K. Galbraith referred to overconsumption as the unasked question of the American conservation movement. There is a marked selectivity, he wrote, "in the conservationist's approach to materials consumption. If we are concerned about our great appetite for materials, it is plausible to seek to increase the supply, to decrease waste, to make better use of the stocks available, and to develop substitutes. But what of the appetite itself? Surely this is the ultimate source of the problem. If it continues its geometric course, will it not one day have to be restrained? Yet in the literature of the resource problem this is the forbidden question. Over it hangs a nearly total silence."[12]

The consumer economy and society have expanded tremendously in the three decades since Galbraith penned these words; yet his criticisms are nearly as valid today. I have said "nearly," for there are some hopeful signs. Within the environmental movement several dispersed groups are working to develop ecologically benign technologies and to encourage less wasteful life styles. Moreover, outside the self-defined boundaries of American environmentalism, opposition to the permanent war economy is being carried on by a peace movement that has a distinguished history and impeccable moral and political credentials.

It is precisely these (to my mind, most hopeful) components of the American social scene that are missing from deep ecology. In their widely noticed book, Bill Devall and George Sessions make no mention of militarization or the movements for peace, while activists whose practical focus is on developing ecologically responsible life styles (e.g., Wendell Berry) are derided as "falling short of deep ecological awareness."[13] A truly radical ecology in the American context ought to work toward a synthesis of the appropriate technology, alternate life style, and peace movements. By making the (largely spurious) anthropocentric-biocentric distinction central to the debate, deep ecologists may have appropriated the moral high ground, but they are at the same time doing a serious disservice to American and global environmentalism.

NOTES

1 Kirkpatrick Sale, "The Forest for the Trees: Can Today's Environmentalists Tell the Difference," *Mother Jones* 11, no. 8 (November 1986): 26.
2 One of the major criticisms I make in this essay concerns deep ecology's lack of concern with inequalities *within* human society. In the article in which he coined the term *deep ecology,* Naess himself expresses concerns about inequalities between and within nations. However, his concern with social cleavages and their impact on resource utilization patterns

and ecological destruction is not very visible in the later writings of deep ecologists. See Arne Naess, "The Shallow and the Deep, Long-Range Ecology Movement: A Summary," *Inquiry* 16 (1973): 96 (I am grateful to Tom Birch for this reference).

3 Gary Snyder, quoted in Sale, "The Forest for the Trees," p. 32. See also Dave Foreman, "A Modest Proposal for a Wilderness System," *Whole Earth Review,* no. 53 (Winter 1986–87): 42–45.

4 See Centre for Science and Environment, *India: The State of the Environment 1982: A Citizen's Report* (New Delhi: Centre for Science and Environment, 1982); R. Sukumar, "Elephant-Man Conflict in Karnataka," in Cecil Saldanha, ed., *The State of Karnataka's Environment* (Bangalore: Centre for Taxonomic Studies, 1985). For Africa, see the brilliant analysis by Helge Kjekshus, *Ecology Control and Economic Development in East African History* (Berkeley: University of California Press, 1977).

5 Daniel Janzen, "The Future of Tropical Ecology," *Annual Review of Ecology and Systematics* 17 (1986): 305–6; emphasis added.

6 Joseph Sax, *Mountains Without Handrails: Reflections on the National Parks* (Ann Arbor: University of Michigan Press, 1980), p. 42. Cf. also Peter Schmitt, *Back to Nature: The Arcadian Myth in Urban America* (New York: Oxford University Press, 1969), and Alfred Runte, *National Parks: The American Experience* (Lincoln: University of Nebraska Press, 1979).

7 Samuel Hays, "From Conservation to Environment: Environmental Politics in the United States Since World War Two," *Environmental Review* 6 (1982): 21. See also the same author's book entitled *Beauty, Health and Permanence: Environmental Politics in the United States, 1955–85* (New York: Cambridge University Press, 1987).

8 Roderick Nash, *Wilderness and the American Mind,* 3rd ed. (New Haven: Yale University Press, 1982).

9 Rudolf Bahro, *From Red to Green* (London: Verso Books, 1984).

10 For an excellent review, see Anil Agarwal and Sunita Narain, eds., *India: The State of the Environment, 1984–85: A Citizens Report* (New Delhi: Centre for Science and Environment, 1985). Cf. also Ramachandra Guha, *The Unquiet Woods: Ecological Change and Peasant Resistance in the Indian Himalaya* (Berkeley: University of California Press, 1990).

11 Anil Agarwal, "Human-Nature Interactions in a Third World Country," *The Environmentalist* 6, no. 3 (1986): 167.

12 John Kenneth Galbraith, "How Much Should a Country Consume?" in Henry Jarrett, ed., *Perspectives on Conservation* (Baltimore: Johns Hopkins Press, 1958), pp. 91–92.

13 Devall and Sessions, *Deep Ecology,* p. 122. For Wendell Berry's own assessment of deep ecology, see his "Amplications: Preserving Wildness," *Wilderness* 50 (Spring 1987): 39–40, 50–54.

QUESTIONS

1 Is overconsumption by the industrialized world and by urban elites in the third world one of the most serious ecological problems we face today? If yes, what changes would you be willing to make in your life to help solve the problem?

2 Should the overcoming of inequalities in a society have priority over concerns such as the preservation of wilderness areas?

SUGGESTED ADDITIONAL READINGS FOR CHAPTER 9

ATTFIELD, ROBIN: *Environmental Ethics: An Overview for the Twenty-First Century.* Oxford: Polity Press, in association with Blackwell Publishing Ltd., 2003. Writing for both students and scholars, Attfield presents and critiques some of the central positions in environmental ethics. He then discusses such topics as sustainable development, the global community, and global citizenship.

BECKERMAN, WILFRED, and JOANNA PASEK, eds.: *Justice, Posterity, and the Environment.* Oxford: Oxford University Press, 2001. Beckerman and Pasek address questions raised by conflicts of interest—between different generations, between rich and poor nations, and between different groups within the same nation—when environmental policy decisions have to be made. Their focus is on the ethical aspects of environmental policy decision making rather than simply on the economic ones.

Environmental Ethics. This journal, identifying itself as "An Interdisciplinary Journal Dedicated to the Philosophical Aspects of Environmental Problems," began publication in 1979. It is an invaluable source of material relevant to the issues under discussion in this chapter.

Hypatia: A Journal of Feminist Philosophy, vol. 6, Spring 1991. Karen J. Warren was guest editor for this special issue, which provides a collection of philosophical articles on ecological feminism.

LIST, PETER C., ed.: *Radical Environmentalism: Philosophy and Tactics.* Belmont, Calif.: Wadsworth, 1993. This collection of readings deals first with so-called radical environmental philosophies (e.g., deep ecology and ecofeminism) and then deals with the activism and tactics of radical environmentalists.

SESSIONS, GEORGE, ed.: *Deep Ecology for the 21st Century.* Boston: Shambhala, 1995. This collection of thirty-nine articles provides a wide range of perspectives on deep ecology. The writings of Arne Naess are especially featured.

SHIVA, VANDANA: "Ecological Balance in an Era of Globalization." In Nicholas Low, ed., *Global Ethics and Environment.* London and New York: Routledge, 1999. Shiva argues that globalization and liberalized trade and investment have created growth by destroying the environment and local, sustainable livelihoods as pollution-intensive industries are relocated in third-world countries. The result is an unjust distribution of good and bad local environment as the environmental costs are exported to the third world while the wealthier countries reap the benefits of globalization.

STONE, CHRISTOPHER D.: *Earth and Other Ethics: The Case for Moral Pluralism.* New York: Harper & Row, 1987. Arguing for a need to rethink some of the most basic assumptions of ethics, Stone says that no one ethical framework can provide answers to all our ethical dilemmas, including those centered on the environment.

WENZ, PETER S.: *Environmental Ethics Today.* New York and Oxford: Oxford University Press, 2001. In this wide-ranging introduction to environmental ethics, Wenz integrates current facts, real controversies, and individual stories into his discussion of abstract philosophical concepts and positions in environmental ethics. Topics include economic globalization, biodiversity, genetic engineering, and pollution permits for corporations.